COVID-19 AND THE LAW

The COVID-19 pandemic has had an enduring effect across the entire spectrum of law and policy, in areas ranging from health equity and racial justice, to constitutional law, the law of prisons, federal benefit programs, election law, and much more. This collection provides a critical reflection on what changes the pandemic has already introduced and what its legacy may be. Chapters evaluate how healthcare and government institutions have succeeded and failed during this global "stress test," and explore how the United States and the world will move forward to ensure we are better prepared for future pandemics. This timely volume identifies the right questions to ask as we take stock of pandemic realities and provides guidance for the many stakeholders of COVID-19's legal legacy. This book is also available as Open Access on Cambridge Core.

I. Glenn Cohen is Deputy Dean and the James A. Attwood and Leslie Williams Professor of Law at Harvard Law School as well as Faculty Director of the Petrie-Flom Center for Health Law Policy, Biotechnology, and Bioethics at Harvard Law School. He is one of the world's leading experts on the intersection of bioethics and the law, as well as health law. He also teaches civil procedure.

Abbe R. Gluck is the Alfred M. Rankin Professor of Law and Faculty Director of the Solomon Center for Health Law and Policy at Yale Law School and Professor of Medicine at Yale School of Medicine. She is one of America's leading experts in health law, Congress, litigation, and federalism and has served in numerous senior government positions, including most recently as Special Counsel to the President and lead lawyer for the White House COVID-19 Response Team.

Katherine L. Kraschel is Assistant Professor of Law and Health Sciences at Northeastern University. At the time of writing and editing this volume, she was the Executive Director of the Solomon Center for Health Law and Policy at Yale Law School, where she also co-taught its Reproductive Rights and Justice Clinic. Her work focuses on the intersections of health, gender, and reproduction.

Carmel Shachar is Assistant Clinical Professor of Law and Faculty Director of the Health Law and Policy Clinic at Harvard Law School. At the time of writing and editing this volume, she was the Executive Director of the Petrie-Flom Center at Harvard Law School. Her work focuses on access to care and digital health. She is the co-editor of several other volumes, including *Transparency in Health and Health Care* and *Disability, Law, Health, and Bioethics*.

COVID-19 and the Law

DISRUPTION, IMPACT AND LEGACY

Edited by

I. GLENN COHEN
Harvard Law School

ABBE R. GLUCK
Yale Law School

KATHERINE L. KRASCHEL
Yale Law School

CARMEL SHACHAR
Harvard Law School

CAMBRIDGE
UNIVERSITY PRESS

Shaftesbury Road, Cambridge CB2 8EA, United Kingdom

One Liberty Plaza, 20th Floor, New York, NY 10006, USA

477 Williamstown Road, Port Melbourne, VIC 3207, Australia

314–321, 3rd Floor, Plot 3, Splendor Forum, Jasola District Centre, New Delhi – 110025, India

103 Penang Road, #05–06/07, Visioncrest Commercial, Singapore 238467

Cambridge University Press is part of Cambridge University Press & Assessment, a department of the University of Cambridge.

We share the University's mission to contribute to society through the pursuit of education, learning and research at the highest international levels of excellence.

www.cambridge.org
Information on this title: www.cambridge.org/9781009265706

DOI: 10.1017/9781009265690

First published 2024

A catalogue record for this publication is available from the British Library

A Cataloging-in-Publication data record for this book is available from the Library of Congress

ISBN 978-1-009-26570-6 Hardback
ISBN 978-1-009-26572-0 Paperback

Cambridge University Press & Assessment has no responsibility for the persistence or accuracy of URLs for external or third-party internet websites referred to in this publication and does not guarantee that any content on such websites is, or will remain, accurate or appropriate.

I. Glenn Cohen
To Lee Adam, wherever I may find him

Abbe R. Gluck
*To the thousands of public servants and health care professionals who
selflessly and fearlessly served the world during this unprecedented time*

Katherine L. Kraschel
To William, our greatest gift during the pandemic

Carmel Shachar
In honor of Dr. Emanuel Eylan, my Saba Monya, who fought against viruses

Contents

Figures

Tables

Contributors

Zoe M. Adams, Massachusetts General Hospital; Harvard Medical School

Joaquin Baca, American Medical Association

Hannah Batchelor, Yale School of Medicine

Asees Bhasin, BU Center for Antiracist Research

Sven J.R. Bostyn, University of Copenhagen

Andrea Louise Campbell, Massachusetts Institute of Technology

I. Glenn Cohen, Harvard Law School

William H. Coe, NYU Grossman School of Medicine

Saida I. Coreas, National Institutes of Health

Fernando De Maio, American Medical Association; DePaul University

Elizabeth A. Dietz, Arizona State University

Taleed El-Sabawi, Florida International University School of Law

Joanna N. Erdman, Schulich School of Law, Dalhousie University

Daniel Farber, School of Law, University of California, Berkeley

Joseph J. Fins, Weill Cornell Medical College

Mona Gandhi, Yale University School of Nursing

Abbe R. Gluck, Yale Law School

Joelle Grogan, King's College London

Andrew Hammond, Indiana University Maurer School of Law

Laura C. Hoffman, Cleveland-Marshall College of Law

Sharona Hoffman, Case Western Reserve University School of Law

Nicole Huberfeld, Boston University School of Law

Jacob Hutt, Yale Law School

Ayana Jordan, NYU Grossman School of Medicine

Josephine Johnston, The Hastings Center; University of Otago

Gali Katznelson, University of Toronto

Mia Keeys, American Medical Association

Ryan P. Knox, Harvard-MIT Center for Regulatory Science

Ariel Jurow Kleiman, Loyola Law School, Los Angeles

Nina A. Kohn, Syracuse University College of Law

Katherine L. Kraschel, Yale Law School

Matthew B. Lawrence, Emory University School of Law

Aletha Maybank, American Medical Association

Michelle M. Mello, Stanford Law School; Stanford University School of Medicine

Jaimie Meyer, Yale School of Medicine

Timo Minssen, University of Copenhagen

Kimberly Mutcherson, Rutgers Law School

Marcella Nunez-Smith, Yale Schools of Medicine, Public Health, and Management

Marisol Orihuela, Yale Law School

Lisa Larrimore Ouellette, Stanford Law School

Wendy E. Parmet, Northeastern University School of Public Policy and Urban Affairs

Jeremy Paul, Northeastern University School of Law

Eliseo J. Pérez-Stable, National Institutes of Health

Govind Persad, Sturm College of Law

W. Nicholson Price II, University of Michigan Law School

Judith Resnik, Yale Law School

Jessica L. Roberts, University of Houston Law Center

Erik J. Rodriquez, National Institutes of Health

Rachel E. Sachs, Washington University in St. Louis School of Law

William M. Sage, Texas A&M University Schools of Law, Medicine, and Government

Ida Santana, Behavioral Health Group

Richard S. Saver, University of North Carolina School of Law; University of North Carolina School of Medicine

Gabriel Scheffler, University of Miami School of Law

Scott J. Schweikart, American Medical Association

Carmel Shachar, Harvard Law School

Jacob S. Sherkow, University of Illinois College of Law

Michael S. Sinha, Harvard-MIT Center for Regulatory Science

Victoria L. Tiase, University of Utah School of Medicine

Katharine Van Tassel, Case Western Reserve University School of Law

Brian Vandenberg, American Medical Association

Lindsay F. Wiley, University of California, Los Angeles School of Law

Tess Wise, Wake Forest University

Janan Wyatt, Yale School of Medicine

Alicia Ely Yamin, Harvard Law School; Harvard TH Chan School of Public Health; Partners in Health

Ruqaiijah Yearby, Moritz College of Law, The Ohio State University; The Institute for Healing Justice & Equity

Rachel L. Zacharias, University of Pennsylvania Law School

Acknowledgments

A book like this is the result of the hard work of many. We thank our student line editors and research assistants, Justin Cole (lead line editor), Cat Gassiot, Nina Leviten, Daniel Nathan, Ennely Medina, Katharine Fang, and Samantha Stroman, for their meticulous work. We are grateful to Laura Chong and Chloe Reichel for their administrative support in organizing the virtual seminar series that helped showcase much of the work in this book. We are also grateful for Laura Chong's hard work shepherding all the many pieces of this manuscript – she has been the most critical piece of this puzzle. In addition, we are thankful to Eugene Rusyn, who was an invaluable member of the Yale team supporting the work of this project, and to Jessenia Khalyat and Lise Cavallaro for terrific additional administrative support.

This book was made possible in part by the generosity and support of the Oswald DeN. Cammann Fund, for conference sponsorship, and the Oscar M. Ruebhausen Fund at Yale Law School. We thankfully acknowledge the Petrie-Flom Center for Health Law Policy, Biotechnology, and Bioethics at Harvard Law School as well as the Solomon Center for Health Law and Policy at Yale Law School. Finally, of course, we thank the contributors for their thoughtful and important scholarly contributions.

Introduction

Katherine L. Kraschel, I. Glenn Cohen, Abbe R. Gluck, and Carmel Shachar

There is a discussion and a delicate balance about what's the overall impact of shutting every-thing down completely for an indefinite period of time. So, there's a compromise. If you knock down the economy completely and disrupt infrastructure, you may be causing health issues, unintended consequences, for people who need to be able to get to places and can't. You do the best you can.

> Dr. Anthony Fauci, Chief Medical Adviser to the President of the United States and Director of US National Institute of Allergy and Infectious Diseases

Normal led to this. Normal was a world ever more prone to a pandemic but ever less ready for one. To avert another catastrophe, the [United States] needs to grapple with all the ways normal failed us. It needs a full accounting of every recent misstep and foundational sin, every unattended weakness and unheeded warning, every festering wound and reopened scar.

> Ed Yong, Science Journalist, *Atlantic*

Our Constitution principally entrusts '[t]he safety and the health of the people' to the politi-cally ac-countable officials of the States 'to guard and protect.' Jacobson v. Massachusetts, 197 U. S. 11, 38 (1905). When those officials 'undertake[ ] to act in areas fraught with medical and scientific uncertainties,' their latitude 'must be especially broad.' Marshall v. United States, 414 U. S.417, 427 (1974). Where those broad limits are not exceeded, they should not be subject to second-guessing by an 'unelected federal judiciary,' which lacks the background, competence, and expertise to assess public health and is not accountable to the people.

> South Bay United Pentecostal Church v. Chief Justice Roberts, concurring

COVID[-19] is a funhouse mirror that is amplifying issues that have existed forever. People are not dying of COVID[-19]. They are dying of racism, of economic inequality and it is not going to stop with COVID[-19].

> Dr. Shreya Kangovi, Associate Professor of Medicine, Perelman School of Medicine at the University of Pennsylvania

* * *

In December 2019, a number of people experienced shortness of breath and fever in Wuhan, Hubei Province, China and would eventually be the first people identified to have the SARS-Cov-2 virus that causes Coronavirus Disease 2019 (COVID-19). By January 31, 2020, US Secretary of Health and Human Services Alex Azar and the World Health Organization (WHO) declared the SARS-Cov-2 virus a public health emergency, and by March 15, 2020, U.S. states and many countries started shutting down schools, workplaces, and restaurants to stop the spread of the virus and lethal disease. The COVID-19 pandemic was, and continues to be, a public health tragedy of unmatched proportions in our lifetime, causing more than one million deaths in the United States alone in the first two years, with that toll falling inequitably across populations. It has caused a massive disruption of daily life, the global economy, and every major institution, on a scale and at a pace not seen in generations. The pace with which COVID-19 spread and the stress it placed on institutions left no place to hide and exposed weaknesses, foundational inequalities, and opportunities for innovation and change.

As this volume goes to press in late Spring 2023, the COVID-19 national emergency has been formally ended but the effects of the pandemic are far from over. Even a book as comprehensive as this one is in a sense "a snapshot in time," rather than the final word on the changes sparked by the pandemic. As of the time of writing, new variants continue to surface as the virus evolves. The implications of COVID-19 survivorship remain uncertain and far reaching. But the story that has unfolded is also one of resilience, unprecedented collaboration and innovation, governance challenges, and cultural inflection points.

COVID-19 has touched all aspects of daily life and countless institutions from health care to politics, to prisons, to the economy. Underlying all of these, though, is the law. Our focus in this volume is on how law has mediated and been mediated by these institutions' interactions with COVID-19 over the last three years. It is not possible for one book to exhaustively tell COVID-19's story; indeed, it is probably not possible for a hundred books to do so. Our aim is instead to critically reflect on some of what COVID-19 revealed about our health care system, public health policy, governance, and law. The pandemic's disruptive pressures have exposed strengths and weakness of pre-pandemic systems and demanded changes. Those lessons will be a large part of COVID-19's legal legacy.

As editors, we had to make some difficult decisions in determining the right time at which to stop requesting authors of this volume to update their contributions in light of new developments. The result is a volume about a focused moment in time, attentive primarily to the initial responses to an unprecedented global health disaster. Our hope is to capture the issues that, in the short term, will inform the next wave of policy interventions, while also memorializing the lessons that will inform the years to come, years when – we hope – the realities and challenges of COVID-19 are no longer as vivid as a day-to-day matter.

This book is organized into six parts. It first provides a broad view on COVID-19's initial disruption and the kinds of challenges that would endure. Part I describes the systems in place at the outset of the pandemic and COVID-19's initial disruptions. Part II explores the severe disparities in health that existed before the pandemic but that the pandemic further exposed and exacerbated. Part III dissects responses by the government – executive, legislative, administrative, and judicial. Part IV describes the unprecedented innovation and speed with which novel treatments and therapies, including the vaccine, were created, and the infrastructure surrounding their authorizations and approvals, as well as advances in health care access and delivery. Part V considers global responses to the pandemic. Finally, Part VI takes a broader lens, analyzing the global response to COVID-19.

Understanding COVID-19's disruptive force requires examining the structures in place at the time COVID-19 hit. While almost all chapters in this volume in part provide such insights to explain their point of view, Part I, "The Health Care System that COVID-19 Encountered," centers it explicitly. This part sketches a picture of the health care delivery system, the cultural proclivity to consume and amplify misinformation, and the structures fueling health care disparities in the United States at the outset of the pandemic.

The part begins in New York, one of the first American cities to experience the pandemic. Dr. Joseph Fins, medical ethics chief at a major academic medical center, takes us back to spring 2020 and the first surge by providing a firsthand account of the tragic choices and lack of preparedness physicians faced during that time, even as they were being applauded as "heroes." He reminds us that the lessons learned in the earliest days must be remembered moving forward so that the system can be better prepared to make equitable decisions in the face of scarcity and to prevent the need for such impossible decisions again.

Richard Saver unpacks some of the challenges Dr. Fins discusses, pointing to the ethos of clinical medicine to prioritize individual patient needs over public health and how ill suited this paradigm is for an infectious disease pandemic. Acknowledging the legal challenges inherent in expanding physicians' health duties beyond the patient, he argues for better integration between clinical medicine and public health.

Next, Dr. William Sage and Victoria Tiase focus on the protection of health care workers, also using the first surge in New York City as their subject of study. They discuss the necessity for stronger protections, not just for the sake of the workforce but also to maintain quality care standards. They applaud the call to duty many health care workers answered but note that "in a sustained and serious pandemic, a heroism-based ethical paradigm for accepting personal risk is as misleading as the myth of professional perfection has been for avoiding medical errors." They propose a number of reforms to improve protections for health care workers, including more equitable sharing of staff and supplies across hospital systems, a transition from the current individualistic culture to a community-based model, and more practical and emotional support.

Wendy Parmet and Jeremy Paul tackle a different challenge that has influenced the trajectory of the pandemic – the "post-truth" perspective that, they argue, existed prior to the pandemic and has fueled misinformation about vaccines, treatments, and more. They provocatively explain how developments in health law and bioethics may have inadvertently contributed to building the path towards a post-truth world, with those fields' modern emphases on individual choice and the resulting devaluation of expertise.

Finally, Sadia Coreas, Erik Rodriquez, and Dr. Eliseo Pérez-Stable examine one of the most disturbing truths about the pandemic – its disproportionate impact on people of color. They outline the systemic and structural factors that have long driven health care disparities in the United States, demonstrate how these disparities have persisted through every surge of the pandemic, and demand our attention and care to address health disparities related to COVID-19 and beyond.

The authors in Part II, "COVID-19, Disparities, and Vulnerable Populations," delve deeper into the issues faced by communities particularly vulnerable to COVID-19's impact. This part begins with a prologue by Dr. Marcella Nunez-Smith, co-chair of the Biden-Harris Transition COVID-19 Advisory Board, chair of the Biden Administration's COVID-19 Health Equity Task Force, and a member of Connecticut Governor Ned Lamont's Reopen Connecticut Advisory Group, as well as chair of its Community Committee.

Dr. Nunez-Smith provides a frontline view of the challenges that confronted policymakers tackling COVID-19 inequities, as well as the breakthroughs that helped ameliorate them. Testing and tracing, along with securing accurate data on COVID-19's impact on different communities, were major early challenges. After vaccines became available, ensuring equitable access became the next priority – with administration officials launching collaborative programs and partnerships meant to foster trust among diverse communities. She argues that investing in community-led solutions for ensuring health equity and creating greater accountability around health equity outcomes are some of COVID-19's most important lessons for the future

Dr. Jaimie Meyer, Marisol Orihuela, and Judith Resnik analyze the vulnerabilities of people incarcerated during the pandemic. They reveal how the plight of people in detention during the early days of the pandemic – often without adequate dedensification, access to proper hygiene, or testing – may prove an inflection point in prison reform and the abolition movement. They argue that both the Eighth Amendment and constitutional doctrines have fallen short in protecting the health of incarcerated persons – even absent a global pandemic.

Next, Scott Schweikart, Fernando De Maio, Mia Keeys, Joaquin Baca, Brian Vandenberg, and Dr. Aletha Maybank argue that the role of structural racism in COVID-19's disproportionate impact on Black, Indigenous, and People of Color communities demands a reexamination of public health data systems. They argue that the United States is at a political pivot point, one which emerged from the Black Lives Matter movement and arguably swelled as a result of the inequities of the pandemic and the murder of George Floyd. Furthermore, they suggest that this pivot point could prompt progressive reforms in health care access, criminal justice reform, housing, civil rights enforcement, and more.

Govind Persad and Jessica Roberts turn their attention to older persons and persons with disabilities, and detail the mechanisms used to allocate and distribute scarce resources during the pandemic – especially critical care services and vaccines. Persad and Roberts identify several barriers to adopting allocation policies that do not discriminate against older persons and persons with disabilities: implicit bias among even the most well-intentioned health care providers; preexisting challenges with utilizing and accessing technology; and serious transportation barriers. They propose debiasing strategies to ameliorate these harms.

Finally, Nina Kohn considers another population in a congregate living setting on which COVID-19 has shone a bright light: people in long-term care facilities. Kohn describes how regulatory failures that preceded the pandemic – such as the failure to impose minimum staffing requirements and the underreporting of health and safety threats – as well as a slow public health response to COVID-19 led to a tremendous number of deaths in long-term care facilities. She argues for regulatory reforms, including aligning payment incentives with quality care metrics, tying public funding to staffing minimums, and requiring states to provide coverage for in-home care at the same level as institutional care.

Part III, "Government Response and Reaction to COVID-19" further considers the role and powers of government in such an unprecedented public health crisis. COVID-19 is one of the most significant governance challenges in modern history; not only has it elicited responses across all levels and branches of government, it has also impacted governance infrastructures themselves.

Nicole Huberfeld's chapter leads this part and depicts the interactions among federal, state, local, and tribal bodies that constitute the US health care governance architecture. Our national health care system is a federalist system built on structural redundancies. Each level of government has emergency powers, and each used theirs during the pandemic – at times to fill in for the lack of leadership by other levels, including by the President himself. Despite the security of overlap, Huberfeld worries that our federalist model remains a driver for inequality and ineffective emergency response.

The next two chapters of Part III take up issues of the government's preparedness for a pandemic and its ability to respond. Matthew Lawrence describes "upstream fiscal determinants" of health – structures within the federal government, including the budget process, that fuel underinvestment in public health. Ariel Jurow Kleiman, Gabriel Scheffler, and Andrew Hammond hone in on the federal government's expansion of existing social safety net programs during the pandemic, such as through greater appropriations for the Supplemental Nutrition Assistance Program and the provision of higher tax credits for individuals who enrolled in marketplace health insurance plans under the Affordable Care Act. They describe how the government should have done more to provide essential resources and propose additional automatic actions that will allow a better response to future crises and mitigate inequalities that were exacerbated during the pandemic.

Ruqaiijah Yearby discusses the role of regulations. She provides a health justice critique, analyzing how the failure of federal and state governments to provide paid sick leave for all workers and the Occupational Safety and Heath Administration's decision to issue advisories instead of workplace requirements to limit the spread of COVID-19 exacerbated pandemic health inequities. She also proposes a model to design emergency preparedness plans for the next emergency with greater voice from the workers themselves.

The judicial branch – the courts – also took center stage in the first few years as the United States reacted to the pandemic. Lindsay Wiley details the complexities of the legal challenges brought against government actions – such as gathering restrictions – in the name of public health. For more than a century, courts have relied on a Supreme Court precedent, *Jacobson v. Massachusetts*, in deferring to the scientific and expert judgment of government officials to exercise their public health authorities. Wiley details how the post-*Jacobson* development of individual rights doctrine creates a tension that requires courts today not to suspend judicial review in the face of a public health emergency but to incorporate *Jacobson*'s core principle into new doctrines that seek to reconcile individual rights and community protection.

Part IV, "Innovation During COVID-19," deepens our inquiry into debates about whether COVID-19 represented an exceptional concurrence of events that overwhelmed good regulatory structures or exposed structures that were already ailing.

The first chapter of this part offers an expert account of the innovation infrastructure in place at the time of the pandemic provided by Rachel Sachs, Lisa Larrimore Ouellette, W. Nicholson Price II, and Jacob Sherkow. They describe the unique pressure that COVID-19 testing placed on interagency coordination, the difficult balance of quickly getting critical therapies to market with the need to make decisions informed by reliable data, and the incentive structures and role of government funding in facilitating the "warp speed" of COVID-19 vaccine development. They suggest future policymaking be informed by the lessons learned from COVID-19 – so that it is both responsive to the next pandemic and addresses issues such as access to medicine generally.

Dr. Michael Sinha, Sven Bostyn, and Timo Minssen delve deeper into intellectual property rights for COVID-19 vaccines and treatments. They focus on exclusivity rights and, among other things, argue that "safeguards are needed to guarantee global access to sufficient vaccines at reasonable prices."

Katharine Van Tassel and Sharona Hoffman round out this part with a chapter on vaccine injury compensation. They detail the two existing mechanisms to remedy vaccine-related harms and describe how the system places disproportionate burdens on vulnerable populations. They conclude by making the case for amending the Public Readiness and Emergency Preparedness Act to shift vaccines approved under emergency use authorizations to the more generous and accessible compensation program available for other vaccines.

Part V, "Opening New Pathways for Health Care Delivery and Access," considers different types of innovation – in health care delivery and access. Ryan Knox, Laura Hoffman, Asees Bhasin, and Abbe Gluck tackle the way COVID-19 accelerated one of the most significant shifts in the practice of medicine: telemedicine. After providing a concise but comprehensive background on the regulatory and legal barriers telemedicine faced in the United States prior to the pandemic, they describe the massive shifts the pandemic wrought, largely via emergency actions at both the state and federal levels. The national updating of telemedicine in the pandemic, they argue, helps make the case for lasting regulatory reforms to maintain access to telemedicine, while revealing some of the challenges – including significant access barriers for certain populations – that the pandemic telehealth experience illustrated and which must be addressed.

Dr. Zoe Adams, Taleed El-Sabawi, Dr. William H. Coe, Hannah Batchelor, Janan Wyatt, Mona Gandhi, Dr. Ida Santana, and Dr. Ayana Jordan focus on methadone for opioid use disorder, explaining the regulatory barriers that have accompanied the use of methadone for this disorder for nearly fifty years, which require patients to receive treatment in person. They tell the story of how these requirements were relaxed during the pandemic to minimize COVID-19 exposure. They then present qualitative survey data to illustrate the benefits and minimal risk that accompany the less stringent requirements and make the case for lasting reforms.

The last two chapters of Part V address abortion access during the pandemic. First, Rachel Zacharias, Elizabeth Dietz, Kimberly Mutcherson and Josephine Johnston provide an account of restrictions placed on medication abortion via the Risk Evaluation Mitigation Strategies program of the Food and Drug Administration (FDA). In contrast to treatment for opioid use disorder, the in-person provision requirements for medication abortion were not relaxed until the Biden administration came into office. And their chapter details the litigation that ensued against the FDA policy prohibiting distribution of mifepristone, the drug used for medication abortion, in an attempt to facilitate access. The authors employ a reproductive justice framework to consider these issues and critique the emphasis on personal responsibility in the discourse around abortion by providing examples of the ways it entrenches racial disparities. As this book goes to print, a case is winding its way through the court system challenging both the FDA's 20-year-old approval of abortion medication as well as the Biden Administration's relaxing of the REMS. Joanna Erdman's chapter takes a socio-legal perspective on at-home abortion and points to the ways improved access during the pandemic was achieved within a system of clinical control of abortion and social norms of abortion law. Despite shifts within the clinically controlled system during the pandemic, she suggests that the normalization of abortion in the home may lead to radical changes in its practice in the long term.

Part VI, "Global Responses to COVID-19," takes a broader lens. The chapters in this part both compare COVID-19 responses across countries and consider what differing responses mean for a connected, global economy and information ecosystem. In their chapter, Tess Wise, Gali Katznelson, Carmel Shachar, and Andrea Louise Campbell complicate pre-COVID-19 public health preparedness evaluations by organizations such as the World Bank and the WHO. They offer an empirical analysis examining the effectiveness of early COVID-19 response, as measured by disease spread and mortality rate, and conclude that those countries identified as being best prepared for a public health crisis, based upon political, legal, social, cultural, economic, and organizational factors, did not outperform other countries in mitigating the spread of the virus and reducing the number of deaths. They urge a different global consensus on public health in which "the risks and costs associated with sickness are shared by the whole society, not only sick individuals, emphasizing that justice and efficiency must be linked together."

In their chapter, Joelle Grogan and Alicia Ely Yamin also consider various countries' COVID-19 responses and the risk of human rights violations that may accompany governmental responses during a public health crisis. Based upon findings from two multi-country convenings, they show that there are stronger correlations between social and political environments and human rights violations than between the formal legal regimes in which the social and political environments operate and human rights violations.

The third chapter in this part, written by Daniel Farber, situates the emergent crisis of COVID-19 alongside the longer-term crisis of climate change. He considers COVID-19's short-term and direct impact on climate change itself by discussing the reduction of carbon emissions that accompanied the earliest stages of the pandemic, while noting that the longer-term impacts are unknown. He also contemplates two less direct ways that COVID-19 may shape climate change – leveraging COVID-19 stimulus funding to support green energy investment and what COVID-19 teaches us about governance challenges, particularly government interventions that require lasting behavioral changes to address a global collective problem.

Glenn Cohen provides the final chapter in the book. It addresses vaccine tourism – "queue jumping" by traveling from a community where vaccination is not readily available to a destination state or country where it is. Cohen first describes ethical concerns with vaccine tourism: the discordance between those who are able to participate in vaccine tourism and those who we may agree should be first to access vaccination; the displacement of those in the community with the supply of vaccines; and the concern with disease infection and transmission in the process of accessing vaccination. He then argues for communitarian principles to guide defining the groups who have compelling moral claims to vaccines in order to address the health justice and equity issues posed by vaccine tourism.

Finally, Abbe Gluck and Jacob Hutt offer an epilogue detailing the trajectory of the massive array of litigation that stemmed from COVID-19. In areas from workers' rights to prison health and election law, the litigation shined a salutary bright light on challenges and inequities that preexisted the pandemic but that the pandemic made impossible to ignore. But beyond its effect on countless individual areas of law, Gluck and Hutt argue that the arc of the litigation reflected changes in governments' responses to the pandemic itself and also more seismic shifts in Supreme Court doctrine. Early cases focused on the tension between modern civil rights and long-standing precedents counseling judicial deference to state government policies, such as the early COVID-19 business closures, implemented to protect public health. Later cases were part of larger debates at the Supreme Court about interpreting old federal laws – such as the CDC's long-standing public health authorities – and curtailing deference to executive-branch actions, such as federal vaccination mandates, taken under those laws.

When essential workers were left to bear the risks of COVID-19 exposure so that we could "flatten the curve" and when "Zoom" entered our daily vernacular, very few could have fathomed the loss of life that has followed or predicted that we would still be fending off another surge in 2022 and waiting to see what the next variant may bring in 2023. Debate continues today about whether we are in a "new normal," if the pandemic has evolved into its endemic phase, and how the government ought to be providing support and resolving issues that have come to the fore with COVID-19's disruption.

Yet COVID-19's impact on health, institutions, governance, and law already offers much from which we can learn. COVID-19 has taught us the limits of the designs of health care delivery and governance and demanded action to respond to the inequities in the system. It has helped to identify areas of inspiring innovations in treatment and access. It has forced us to appreciate that viruses do not respect borders. While the federal public health emergency is sunsetting, the effects of the last few years continue to be felt. But this is as good a moment as any to critically reflect on its lessons thus far with the hope that they might help mold COVID-19's legacy for the intersection of law and health.

The Health Care System That COVID-19 Encountered

Introduction

Carmel Shachar

Think of a play before the actors take the stage, with all the props set up as needed for the action to come. In many ways, Part I of this volume is that stage for much of what is discussed later in the book. The chapters in this part all consider the state of the US health care system as the COVID-19 pandemic started in spring 2020. Which structural factors helped shape the pandemic? Who were uniquely vulnerable to this novel virus? Which policy and regulatory choices played a role in how we first experienced the pandemic?

Understanding the structural stage-setting is important because it can reveal important lessons for how to build pandemic resiliency, either to the current COVID-19 pandemic or to the next infectious disease epidemic. To stretch the metaphor of a stage, Part I seeks to determine if we have the right props for the actors to use or if we need to redo our stage in light of past performances.

The first three chapters of Part I focus on the experience of stakeholders in the health care system, particularly health care workers, as the pandemic begins. In Chapter 1, "COVID-19 and Clinical Ethics: Reflections on New York's 2020 Spring Surge," Dr. Joseph Fins provides a firsthand account of a physician's experience in New York City during the early days of the pandemic. He calls this contribution a "living history," reminding us not to forget the lessons of the early days by overfocusing on post hoc analysis. Dr. Fins reminds us of the 7:00 PM clapping for health care heroes and hospital systems overrun with patients, a medical setting forced to innovate and create pop-up intensive care units. Dr. Fins's chapter was deliberately placed first in this volume to encourage readers to recall their experiences in spring 2020. But Dr. Fins also reflects on steps we can take to improve our pandemic response.

In Chapter 2, "Patients First, Public Health Last," Richard Saver helps contextualize the ethical considerations and challenges that physicians faced during those first days. Saver argues that physicians have been taught to put their patients first, and that ends up deprioritizing public health needs. Our legal system and medical norms, he notes, further enforce patient primacy over the collective good. Physicians are taught that their strong ethical obligations are to the patients sitting in front of them and are then cautioned that they may face legal consequences if they fail to fulfill such obligations. The focus on patient primacy is particularly ill suited to an infectious disease pandemic, and Saver argues that we need to better reconcile clinical ethics, especially as practiced, with public health ethics and to reintegrate the private physician into the public health system. Saver's work helps give the reader context for many of the choices made by individual health care providers and organizations.

In Chapter 3, "Risk, Responsibility, Resilience, Respect: COVID-19 and the Protection of Health Care Workers," Dr. William Sage and Victoria Tiase also contribute a firsthand account of the COVID-19 experience for health care workers in New York City. They note that "[t]he COVID-19 pandemic has shown us that the health care system we thought we had is not the health care system we actually have." Dr. Sage and Tiase compellingly illustrate how the vulnerabilities of patients and providers during the COVID-19 pandemic were two sides of a single coin. Without stronger labor protections for health care workers, especially nurses working in hospitals, patients run the risk of receiving inadequate care or not receiving any care at all. This was particularly salient during the first stages of the COVID-19 pandemic and continues to be true in subsequent years. Dr. Sage and Tiase urge reforms to better engage and support the health care workforce.

In Chapter 4, "Post-Truth Won't Set Us Free: Health Law, Patient Autonomy, and the Rise of the Infodemic," Wendy Parmet and Jeremy Paul pull the focus away from health care workers and shift it to the patient side of the equation. They dissect the "post-truth" problem we face, with rampant misinformation with respect to COVID-19 clogging social media and other venues. They then place this "post-truth" problem in the context of informed consent. While informed consent is an important legal and bioethical development, overemphasizing individual choice can lead to the erosion of professional expertise. Parmet and Paul urge bioethicists and health law scholars to consider the role that these fields may have played in nurturing the seeds of "post-truth," opening the door to the rejection of vaccines and the embrace of ivermectin.

In Chapter 5, "Individual and Structural Factors that Fueled COVID-19 Disparities," Sadia Coreas, Erik Rodriquez, and Dr. Eliseo Pérez-Stable focus on unpacking the structural factors that led to a dramatic disproportionate burden of COVID-19 illness among people of color. These factors, such as crowded, urban housing and a reliance on public transportation, contributed to a heightened risk of infection among these communities. Similar factors, including greater prevalence of preexisting conditions such as hypertension and severe obesity, likewise contributed to worse outcomes among Black and Latino COVID-19 patients as compared to Whites. They end their chapter by reminding the reader that these structural factors persist, contributing further to significant health disparities, both related to COVID-19 and not.

So what is set on the stage as we begin our tragic play? As our first three chapters argue, there are many policy and regulatory choices that shaped the health care workforce's initial experience with COVID-19. Professional norms, ethical obligations, and legal responsibilities created devastating vulnerabilities that were exploited by the pandemic. Also on stage is a society-wide turn toward "post-truth" that made individuals vulnerable to misinformation regarding the pandemic. Lastly, we have on the stage health disparities fueled by the social determinants of health, making certain communities more vulnerable to the pandemic.

Collectively, we see a stage that is ill equipped for what lies ahead. All of this stage-setting is important for the reader to remember as they read on in the book and consider how we could better respond to COVID-19 or to the next pandemic.

1

COVID-19 and Clinical Ethics

Reflections on New York's 2020 Spring Surge

Joseph J. Fins[*]

I LIVING HISTORY

Kierkegaard famously said life is lived forwards and understood backwards.[1] What is true for life is also true for pandemics and it is tempting to look at the dawning days of COVID-19 through the prism of reflection. But to do so would be to lose the lived experience of those who had to make fraught choices during the initial surge of the pandemic. What happened during March and April of 2020 should not be obscured by a post hoc analysis informed by what we learned about the SARS-COV-2 virus or about ourselves since those early days. That early history, unsanitized as it was, is essential to framing subsequent discourse. As an academic physician charged with coordinating a clinical ethics service at a major academic medical center during the spring surge in New York City, I can attest that what happened during the spring of 2020 in the city bears remembrance, not only to honor those who served – and died – but, just as importantly, to inform clinical care and public policy. Those lessons were hard-won and it would be unfortunate to lose them through the gauzy haze of memory.

II HOMETOWN HEROES

A daily ritual evolved that spring when New Yorkers came to the street each night to cheer, and revere, their health care heroes.[2] At 7:00 PM, people would gather on their fire escapes and street corners to clap, clang cow bells, and otherwise cheer

---

[*] Dr. Fins acknowledges with gratitude the collaboration and insights of his colleagues in the Division of Medical Ethics at Weill Cornell Medical College and the Solomon Center for Health Law & Policy at Yale Law School. The views expressed herein are those of Dr. Fins and do not represent those of the New York State Task Force on Life and the Law or any other organization with which Dr. Fins may be affiliated.

[1] Soren Kierkegaard, The Soul of Kierkegaard: Selections from His Journals 89 (Alexander Dru ed., Dover Press 2003) (1843); Joseph J. Fins, My Time in Medicine, 60 *Persps. Biology & Med.* 19 (2017).
[2] Andy Newman, What NYC Sounds Like Every Night at 7, NY Times (Apr. 10, 2020), www.nytimes.com/interactive/2020/04/10/nyregion/nyc-7pm-cheer-thank-you-coronavirus.html.

for those toiling away in the hospitals. Nietzsche might have viewed it as the bread and circuses moment of the pandemic.[3] New Yorkers wanted to express their gratitude. But they also needed to do so. They were scared and frightened and viewing health care workers as heroic made them feel better, more secure. Having said this, not a single one of my colleagues felt we were deserving of the adulation. Clinical failure, with which we were unaccustomed, had become the norm in our intensive care units (ICUs), both the regular kind and the pop-up variety that took care of the overflow of patients. During the weeks of March 22 through April 4, the weekly percentage of hospitalized New York City patients who subsequently died peaked (mean = 36.4 percent; range = 33.5 to 38.2 percent).[4] With these numbers, we did not feel like heroes.

We did not feel deserving, but the public needed to believe in us and those we represented because they had to believe in something. Civil society was in a state of chaos. The stores were bare, the supply chain broken. People were suddenly dying. But all would be well because they put their faith in their superheroes, who would rise up, rescue, and save them. Except we could not back then, although we tried. And some died – trying.

It was a valiant effort. In addition to meeting a novel disease head on, which reduced the most skilled clinicians to novice practitioners, they were charged with making triage decisions because we did not have adequate supplies – of, for example, personal protective equipment (PPE), drugs, and ventilators – and operated without crisis standards of care, which New York State failed to invoke. This placed clinicians under untenable stress.

One needs a tragedy to have heroes, and the situation was tragic for those who were lost, their families and loved ones, as well as the clinicians who were placed in a position where they had to do more than act as professionals. Professionalism should have been enough of an expectation; heroism was a bridge too far.[5] It was one that ultimately collapsed, both in how society came to view the doctors and nurses who stepped up, and in the mental health sequelae of the pandemic, what Victor Dzau, the president of the National Academy of Medicine, has described as its own epidemic.[6]

So much of the tragedy we were grappling with in New York could have been avoided. Others have written about the Trump Administration's downsizing of pandemic surveillance as a national security issue and the pulling of observers from

---

[3]   Friedrich Nietzsche, *Twilight of the Idols and the Anti-Christ: Or How to Philosophize with a Hammer* 34 (Penguin Books 1990) (1889).

[4]   Corinne N. Thompson et al., COVID-19 Outbreak – New York City, February 29–June 1, 2020, 69 *Morbidity & Mortality Wkly. Rep.* 1725 (2020).

[5]   Joseph J. Fins, Distinguishing Professionalism and Heroism When Disaster Strikes: Reflections on 9/11, Ebola and Other Emergencies, 24 *Cambridge Q. Healthcare Ethics* 373 (2015).

[6]   Victor J. Dzau, Darrell Kirch, & Thomas Nasca, Preventing a Parallel Pandemic – A National Strategy to Protect Clinicians' Well-Being, 383 *New Eng. J. Med.* 513 (2020); Kimberly S. Resnick & Joseph J. Fins, Professionalism and Resilience After COVID-19, 45 *Acad. Psychiatry* 552 (2021).

Wuhan, China, the presumptive ground zero of the pandemic.[7] But on a much more local level, hospitals suffered from the failure of New York State to promulgate crisis standards of care in response to the pandemic. It became clear that this failure was an abdication of governmental responsibility and of the state's obligation to protect its citizenry.

III ANTECEDENTS AND THE SURGE

New York had a huge head start on disaster planning. As far back as 2007, the New York Task Force on Life and the Law, on which I serve, began deliberating the question of ventilator allocation in the context of an Avian flu pandemic.[8] Ultimately, the Task Force issued a final report in 2015 delineating a ventilator allocation guideline. It was one we never hoped we would use, and it was written with a hefty dose of denial,[9] but we did write it all the same.

At the heart of the plan was the Sequential Organ Failure Assessment (SOFA) score, a methodology originally designed to physiologically assess a patient's need for ventilatory support if ill from influenza and to predict their short-term survival from that infection by tracking the functional status of several organ systems.[10] The triage process would be put into place once public health authorities declared a public health emergency and invoked crisis standards of care.[11] In New York this would be declared by the governor. Crisis standards of care would replace the "usual" standard of care with one that was "sufficient" given the circumstances.[12] But these guidelines were never put in place and, as a result, in March 2020, individual hospitals had to make determinations about the allocation of scarce resources without government guidance.

[7] Beth Cameron, I Ran the White House Pandemic Office. Trump Closed It, Wash. Post (Mar. 13, 2020), www.washingtonpost.com/outlook/nsc-pandemic-office-trump-closed/2020/03/13/a70deo9c-6491-11ea-acca-80c22bbee96f_story.html; Marisa Taylor, Exclusive: U.S. Slashed CDC Staff Inside China Prior to Coronavirus Outbreak, *Reuters* (Mar. 25, 2020), www.reuters.com/article/us-health-coronavirus-china-cdc-exclusiv-idUSKBN21C3N5.

[8] Tia Powell, Kelly C. Chris, & Guthrie S. Birkhead, Allocation of Ventilators in a Public Health Disaster, 2 *Disaster Med. Pub. Health Prep.* 20 (2008).

[9] Joseph J. Fins, When Endemic Disparities Catch the Pandemic Flu: Echoes of Kubler-Ross and Rawls, Hastings Ctr. (Apr. 30, 2009), www.thehastingscenter.org/when-endemic-disparities-catch-the-pandemic-flu/.

[10] Reza Shahpori et al., Sequential Organ Failure Assessment in H1N1 Pandemic Planning, 39 *Critical Care Med.* 827 (2011); Joseph J. Fins, Disabusing the Disability Critique of the New York State Task Force Report on Ventilator Allocation, Hastings Ctr. (Apr. 1, 2020), www.thehastingscenter.org/disabusing-the-disability-critique-of-the-new-york-state-task-force-report-on-ventilator-allocation/.

[11] Institute of Medicine. Crisis Standards of Care: A Systems Framework for Catastrophic Disaster Response (Dan Hanfling, Bruce M. Altevogt, Kristin Viswanathan, & Lawrence O. Gostin eds.) (The National Academies Press, 2012).

[12] Katherine Fischkoff et al., Society of Critical Care Medicine Crisis Standard of Care Recommendations for Triaging Critical Resources During the COVID-19 Pandemic, Society of Critical Care Medicine (2020), www.sccm.org/COVID19RapidResources/Resources/Triaging-Critical-Resources.

This lack of government action compounded our worst fears about the depth of the pandemic. The most elite academic health care systems were overwhelmed by the flood of patients who were desperately ill and in need of intensive care. In those dark days, even the most skilled practitioner became a student. We all became novices, grappling with a new disease we did not understand. The practice of medicine, which is so dependent upon time, was for a spell, atemporal.[13] It is worth recalling that even the most basic temporal dimensions of the virus, such as its period of incubation, duration of quarantine, and time course of treatments, were unknown. Collectively we were at sea. Practicing medicine without a clock is much like sailing without a compass. We were lost and striving to find our way.

To add to these challenges was the urgent redeployment of clinicians to meet staffing needs. Under normal circumstances, ICUs are run by pulmonology and critical care medicine attendings, their fellows and residents on rotation. To respond to the pandemic, doctors all over the hospital were reassigned to unfamiliar venues. Hospitalists, who provide in-patient care on medical services, worked in the ICUs as pediatricians backfilled on the medical services.

Psychiatrists handled phone consults for the sick and worried, and wondered if they had COVID-19 and should be tested. It was unfamiliar terrain for even the most experienced of practitioners.

The need was staggering. At New York Presbyterian Weill Cornell Medical Center between March 16 and May 10, 2020, we had 1,550 COVID-19 admissions and we increased our ICU capacity from 100 to 230 beds. Our colleagues at New York Presbyterian Columbia University Medical Center had 2,000 COVID-19 admissions and went from 117 to 300 ICU beds during the same period.[14]

But these numbers do not adequately convey the tragedy of individual narratives. In my role chairing our hospital's ethics committee, I recall a case of a patient who was nearing death from respiratory failure.[15] Her closest relative, a sibling, was approached about consenting to a do-not-resuscitate (DNR) order given the likely futility of resuscitation should she have a cardiac arrest. The ethics consult service was called when the clinical team encountered resistance. When our service became involved and elucidated the facts of the case, we found the reason for the sibling's reluctance: another family member had passed away earlier in the day from COVID-19. It was just too much.

While this vignette was an outlier, it spoke to the burden of illness and tragedy experienced by clinical staff. Elsewhere, I analogized the onslaught of patients to a plane crash at LaGuardia Airport, except that the influx of patients continued for

---

[13] Joseph J. Fins, COVID-19 Through Time, 37 *Issues Sci. Tech.* 73 (2021).

[14] Barrie J. Huberman & Debjani Mukherjee et al., Phases of a Pandemic Surge: The Experience of an Ethics Service in New York City During COVID-19, 31 *J. Clinical Ethics* 219 (2020); Fins, supra note 13.

[15] Certain details of the case have been altered to protect patient confidentiality.

weeks on end.[16] Hospitals across the city had to deal with a scarcity of medical personnel and material, notably PPE and ventilators. People wore single-use/disposable N95 masks for weeks on end. A nurse at Mt. Sinai Hospital was seen in a *New York Post* photograph wearing a garbage bag for protection.[17] That was the practice in many institutions. Unprepared for the onslaught, we had to improvise.

These shortages were the product of a just-in-time approach in which the presumption is that when there is a surge in need, resources will be readily available from the supply chain. This is cost-effective during normal times and avoids having to expend resources on supplies that sit unused in inventory. Some of these items may have a time-limited shelf-life, so having excess inventory represents a potential fiscal loss. A just-in-time approach works when there are isolated pockets of need and resources can be obtained expeditiously. It fails miserably when there is a sustained and systemic stressor or when the supply chain breaks. In response to the inadequacies of a just-in-time supply chain, hospitals are migrating to a just-in-case approach, which stockpiles resources and enhances staff preparedness training and readiness.[18]

But that would be a lesson from the pandemic. During the spring of 2020, we had to innovate to survive. To that end, hospitals created new ICUs out of thin air. Elective surgeries were canceled. Operating rooms were redeployed to provide ICU care and ventilators were reconfigured to provide support to two patients at a time.[19] Pop-up ICUs were built in hospital lobbies and football fields.[20] Parks were converted to field hospitals as the *USS Comfort*,[21] the Navy's hospital ship, made port in New York Harbor.[22]

All of this was done to provide care to an explosive volume of patients who had a novel disease that we did not yet fully understand. In those early days, we had no effective therapies. We were treating patients empirically with pharmaceutical

[16] Joseph J. Fins, Resuscitating Patient Rights During the Pandemic: COVID-19 and the Risk of Resurgent Paternalism, 30 *Cambridge Q. Healthcare Ethics* 215 (2021).

[17] Ebony Bowden, Carl Campanile, & Bruce Golding, Worker at NYC Hospital Where Nurses Wear Trash Bags as Protection Dies from Coronavirus, NY Post (Mar. 25, 2020), https://nypost.com/2020/03/25/worker-at-nyc-hospital-where-nurses-wear-trash-bags-as-protection-dies-from-coronavirus/.

[18] Joshua Barochas, Celine Gounder, & Syra Madad, Just-In-Time Versus Just-In-Case Pandemic Preparedness, Health Aff. Blog (Feb. 12, 2021), www.healthaffairs.org/do/10.1377/hblog20210208.534836/full.

[19] Columbia Develops Ventilator-Sharing Protocol for COVID-19 Patients, Columbia Univ. Irving Med. Ctr. (Apr. 1, 2020), www.cuimc.columbia.edu/news/columbia-develops-ventilator-sharing-protocol-covid-19-patients.

[20] Steve Burns, Columbia Sports Complex Transformed into COVID-19 Field Hospital, WCBS News Radio 88 (Apr. 11, 2020), https://wcbs880.radio.com/articles/columbia-sports-complex-transformed-into-field-hospital. www.nytimes.com/2020/04/15/nyregion/coronavirus-central-park-hospital-tent.html.

[21] Sheri Fink, Treating Coronavirus in a Central Park 'Hot Zone,' NY Times (Apr. 15, 2020), www.nytimes.com/2020/04/15/nyregion/coronavirus-central-park-hospital-tent.html.

[22] Geoff Ziezulewicz, The U.S.N.S. Comfort Is Now Taking COVID-19 Patients. Here's What to Expect, NY Times Magazine (Apr. 8, 2020), www.nytimes.com/2020/04/08/magazine/hospital-ship-comfort-new-york-coronavirus.html.

agents that would not be found to be efficacious (hydroxychloroquine and convalescent serum). In the beginning, we eschewed high-dose steroids, which were later found to be effective and a true game changer with respect to mortality.[23] We were months away from monoclonal antibodies, much less the miraculous mRNA vaccines that would hold so much promise.[24]

At one point in our institution, we were down to three days of dialysis fluid because so many patients with COVID-19 developed renal failure when critically ill. This was wholly unexpected since COVID-19 was initially believed to be a *respiratory* disease. We soon learned that COVID-19 also caused vasculitis and renal failure. This epidemic of kidney disease within the broader pandemic quickly led to a shortage of available supplies of dialysate, a problem that first manifested itself institutionally when the Renal Service asked for an ethics consult. They wanted guidance about who should get dialyzed for kidney failure and the *quality* of that intervention given the short supplies.

This type of question was new for ethics consultation. Unlike a traditional Clinical Ethics Consultation, which centers around the care of individual patients, this question required us to think about groups of patients who would receive care on a particular unit or clinical service. Here, the group was comprised of all those patients who might need dialysis and make a claim on scarce resources. In this scenario, the choice was to use scarce resources selectively and fully dialyze those patients we thought most likely to survive. This would provide the usual standard of care to a select few. The alternative was performing sub-optimal dialysis for a larger number of patients in the hope of temporizing until more dialysate could be secured. We recommended the second course of action.

In our published analysis of ethics consultation performed during the spring surge,[25] the first papers published on ethics consultation during the pandemic in the United States, we dubbed this collective consult as a *Service Practice Communications/Intervention* (SPCI).[26] This was a second level of ethical analysis pertaining to *groups* of patients rather than individuals. As such, it was a new epistemic category of consultation prompted by the exigencies of the pandemic and the need to think in utilitarian terms rather than the deontological ones that inform care under normal circumstances. In addition to SPCIs, we also provided normative advice to the institution under the guise of what we described as an

[23] David A. Berlin, Roy M. Gulick, & Fernando J. Martinez, Severe COVID-19, 383 *New Eng. J. Med.* 2451 (2020).

[24] Fernando P. Polack et al., Safety and Efficacy of the BNT162b2 mRNA COVID-19 Vaccine, 383 *New Eng. J. Med.* 2603 (2020); Lindsey R. Baden et al., Efficacy and Safety of the mRNA-1273 SARS-CoV-2 Vaccine, 384 *New Eng. J. Med.* 403 (2021).

[25] See Nietzsche, supra note 3; Thompson et al., supra note 4; Sheri Fink, The Deadly Choices at Memorial, NY Times (Aug. 25, 2009), www.nytimes.com/2009/08/30/magazine/30doctors.html; NY Pub. Health Law § 3080, Art. 30-D (2020).

[26] NY Pub. Health Law § 3080, Art. 30-D (2020).

Organizational Ethics Advisement (OEA).[27] OEAs were advice to leadership at the hospital, university, and system levels, mediating disputes between units, and real-time education about developments in New York State law that might have a bearing on patient care.

Based on an historical review of our case notes, phone logs, and emails, we estimated conservatively that we performed 2,500 SPCIs and OEAs during the six-week period we studied.[28] This was an unprecedented amount of activity, prompted in part by the clinical and regulatory contingency of the situation during the spring surge. While the biology of the coronavirus was a force of nature, the lack of state guidance with respect to crisis standards of care was a consequence of human nature. It would turn out that human nature was more difficult to control than the virus: New York's inability to provide direction to clinicians and institutions during the crisis constituted an abdication of leadership.[29]

IV ABDICATION

In failing to promulgate crisis standards of care, the state stepped away from its responsibilities and failed to fulfill its duty during a crisis. This was especially disheartening to clinicians. In addition to grappling with an unfamiliar disease, they were forced to make ethical choices that turned usual presumptions of care on their head amidst the utilitarian demands of a public health emergency. They felt vulnerable to retrospective critique and legal liability because the regulatory context did not adequately acknowledge this need.[30] In the back of our minds was the experience of doctors following Hurricane Katrina and the question of whether physicians would be vulnerable to prosecution after the crisis had passed.[31]

While the governor did insert the Emergency or Disaster Treatment Protection Act of 2020 into the state budget, which mitigated some concerns about professional liability, the provisions of the Act were ambiguous, at least as viewed by those of us in the clinical community, insofar as it related to questions of resuscitation and the provision of critical care.[32] It did nothing to coordinate services across the state and bring resources to underserved areas, an area of omission that would become more glaring as the pandemic wore on.

At the start of the pandemic, the concerns were more localized to hospital care. Many clinicians wanted more specificity about triage and decisions about unilateral resuscitation. Might it be possible to set limits in the face of three pressing issues:

---

[27] Id.
[28] Id.
[29] Joseph J. Fins, Sunshine is the Best Disinfectant, Especially During a Pandemic, 25 *NY State Bar Ass'n Health L.J.* 141 (2020).
[30] Daniel Callahan, Necessity, Futility, and the Good Society, 42 *J. Am. Geriatrics Soc'y* 866 (1994).
[31] Fink, supra note 21.
[32] NY Pub. Health Law § 3080, Art. 30-D (2020).

(1) overwhelming scarcity; (2) the futility of resuscitation given advanced disease; and (3) the risk of contagion to providers who sought to revive patients. Let us take these three issues in turn.

With respect to scarcity, at the peak of the surge it was not uncommon for multiple patients to be in imminent need of intubation *at the same time*. One anesthesiologist reported that it was not uncommon for him to intubate more than ten patients on a single shift.[33] Under normal conditions this was unheard of, and it placed a strain on the ability to provide timely care as would have been the case pre-pandemic. Some of the patients who were being intubated were certain to die and yet, absent any change in New York State law regarding resuscitation, there was no way to unilaterally write DNR orders if consent could not be obtained from surrogates.[34]

Turning to the question of futility, at that early juncture during the pandemic, patients who had a cardio-pulmonary arrest invariably died. The initial survivor data from Wuhan reported that only 2.9 percent survived.[35] An audit of ICU care in the United Kingdom reported in early April 2020 was similarly dire. The thirty-day mortality of patients who were ventilated in intensive care was 49.9 percent for all patients and 68.1 percent for those 70 and older.[36] So, the issue was one of futility *and* the utility of these interventions, an inter-relationship that is often overlooked when we consider medical interventions.[37]

Finally, there was the question of proportionality and the burdens-to-benefits ratio associated with resuscitation.[38] As just noted, the benefit at that juncture was fleetingly low, approaching zero. In contrast, the risks were exceedingly high for practitioners, who would be exposed to aerosolized secretions during emergent intubations and cardio-pulmonary resuscitation (CPR). This would expose clinicians to the risk of contagion, a danger compounded by the inadequate availability of PPE at the time and the fact that those who were performing intubations might not have been as skilled as those normally called upon to perform that task prior to the pandemic. The risk of contagion was quite real. Spain, which was a few weeks ahead of New York with respect to the course of the pandemic, reported that 18.5 percent of health care workers contracted the coronavirus.[39] This combination of factors, very

---

[33] Fei Shao et al., In-Hospital Cardiac Arrest Outcomes Among Patients with COVID-19 Pneumonia in Wuhan, China, 151 *Resuscitation* 18 (2020).

[34] In these circumstances, it would be unusual for agonal patients to have retained decision-making capacity.

[35] Shao et al., supra note 33.

[36] Intensive Care National Audit & Research Center, ICNARC Report on COVID-19 in Critical Care (Apr. 4, 2020).

[37] Callahan, supra note 30.

[38] Joseph J. Fins & Franklin G. Miller, Proportionality, Pandemics and Medical Ethics, 133 *Am. J. Med.* 1243 (2020).

[39] Red Nacional de Vigilancia Epidemiológica, Informe Num. 22 Sobre la Situación de COVID-19 en España (Apr. 13, 2020), www.isciii.es/QueHacemos/Servicios/VigilanciaSaludPublicaRENAVE/

low benefit coupled with high risk, made the procedure ethically unbalanced given risks outweighed benefits: low benefit to the patient against the risk of contagion to staff. This combination of factors made resuscitation disproportionate.

V FOR WANT OF CRISIS STANDARDS OF CARE

Scarcity, futility, and contagion would seem to argue for a change in resuscitation policy in New York State and the promulgation of some sort of triage mechanism along the lines of the 2015 Ventilator Report utilizing the SOFA mechanism. This seemed to be where the New York State Department of Health (DOH) was headed in late March. Despite the granularity of these conversations, the Department neither promulgated guidelines nor explained their decision not to act – either then or since.

The possible reasons why guidelines were not offered by the DOH are complex and multivariate, and one can only speculate. Politically, it was easier to build up capacity, as they did, rather than admit that resources were limited, as later documented in a report from the US Department of Health and Human Services Office of the Inspector General.[40]

The most objective reason that guidelines were not offered was likely scientific and a question of the prognostic utility of the SOFA methodology with respect to COVID-19 respiratory failure. The 2015 report and the SOFA methodology were designed to respond to an Avian flu pandemic, not COVID-19. Even weeks into the coronavirus pandemic, it became clear that the SOFA methodology was not a perfect fit: The Avian flu had a much quicker time course than did patients with COVID-19. For example, in the context of the Avian flu, patients triaged to one of the SOFA color categories were to be reevaluated at two- to three-day intervals. This was far too soon to evaluate patients with respiratory failure from COVID-19, who could take a month to recover and get off a ventilator.

In our discussions, this prompted the perennial adage of not letting perfect be the enemy of good. Could the SOFA methodology be modified to respond to this emerging disease or would such a modification make the use of SOFA a non-evidence-based approach to ventilator allocation? Or would the use of a modified SOFA methodology be better than an ad hoc approach to rationing ventilators? When the DOH convened in March to discuss this question, the trend was toward modification of intervals with an eye toward data collection and further iteration

EnfermedadesTransmisibles/Documents/INFORMES/Informes%20COVID-19/Informe%20n°%20 22.%20Situación%20de%20COVID-19%20en%20España%20a%2013%20de%20abril%20de%202020 .pdf.; Diego Real de Asúa & Joseph J. Fins, Should Healthcare Workers be Prioritised During the COVID-19 Pandemic? A View from Madrid and New York, *J. Med. Ethics* 1 (2021).

[40] Christi A. Grimm, Hospitals Reported that the COVID-19 Pandemic Has Significantly Strained Health Care Delivery: Results of a National Pulse Survey February 22–26, 2021 (2021), https://oig.hhs .gov/oei/reports/OEI-09-21-00140.pdf.

in order to retrofit the methodology for the current pandemic. Whether or not this would be possible is still a question for debate, with the literature suggesting both the ability *and* inability of SOFA scores to risk stratify and predict mortality from acute respiratory failure from COVID-19.[41]

Another salient objection was that triage policies could be discriminatory. This is a serious objection but my view at the time was that the greater threat was *unregulated* triage, rationing, or priority setting, in which bias would sneak in without the proper oversight and accountability afforded by the law. Explicit guidelines could better protect the civil rights of people with disabilities, something that was in fact at risk during the pandemic, which saw the thirtieth anniversary of the Americans with Disabilities Act. Crisis standards of care, if properly conceptualized and implemented, could (and should) incorporate disability rights as part of any normative and legal framework. People with disabilities would be better off with transparent crisis standards of care that are properly designed and regulated than ad hoc decision-making, which could be discriminatory.

In a more recent analysis, I have argued that the SOFA methodology was indeed flawed when it came to the assessment of people with severe brain injury, but that is getting ahead of what I knew at the time.[42] I have also worried that altering hard-won patient prerogatives about decision-making at the end of life could result in resurgent paternalism and an erosion of norms that we would come to regret.[43] Finally, there is an emerging literature on racism and SOFA scores. As one example, Tolchin and colleagues subsequently analyzed SOFA scores in non-Hispanic Black and Hispanic patients hospitalized in Yale New Haven Health System from March 29 to August 1, 2020. They found that non-Hispanic Black patients had greater odds of having a SOFA score greater than or equal to 6 when compared with non-Hispanic White patients.[44] But all of this was later, *after* the surge and in moments of quiet reflection.

VI SOCIAL JUSTICE AND THE CLINIC

Whatever the reason for the failure to promulgate crisis standards of care, the consequences were significant. Without this guidance, clinicians and institutions were left to their own devices to make judgments unilaterally. This placed practitioners

---

[41] Sijia Liu et al., Predictive Performance of SOFA and qSOFA for In-Hospital Mortality in Severe Novel Coronavirus Disease, 38 Am. J. Emergency Med. 2074 (2020); Robert A. Raschke et al., Discriminant Accuracy of the SOFA Score for Determining the Probable Mortality of Patients With COVID-19 Pneumonia Requiring Mechanical Ventilation, 325 JAMA 1469 (2021).

[42] Joseph J. Fins, Disorders of Consciousness, Disability Rights and Triage During the COVID-19 Pandemic: Even the Best of Intentions Can Lead to Bias, 1 J. Phil. & Disability 211 (2021).

[43] Joseph J. Fins, Pandemics, Protocols, and the Plague of Athens: Insights from Thucydides, 50 Hastings Ctr. Rep. 50 (2020).

[44] Benjamin Tolchin et al., Racial Disparities in the SOFA Score among Patients Hospitalized with COVID-19, 16 PLoS One e0257608 (2021).

under tremendous stress. The stress, however, was not equally distributed. It dispro-portionately burdened clinicians and communities in underserved areas.

By way of an example is correspondence with a physician-ethicist practicing in a hospital in the Bronx.[45] In a brave post on a national bioethics listserv at the height of the pandemic in New York, he wrote of the desperate situation on the ground. Overwhelmed by patients and by an inability to meet their needs, he wrote of uni-lateral decisions to withhold and withdraw life-sustaining therapy made at his city hospital.

He reported that, "we have mostly stopped performing CPR (notwithstanding absence of a DNR order) in cases where there was no chance of survival even with CPR." He invoked the 2015 Task Force Report for guidance to *withdraw* life-sustaining therapy, guidance that – absent DOH crisis standards of care – remained an advisory document without the force of law. He concluded his email with an ethical justification: "Arguably, these withdrawals were acknowledgment of reality, not a true triage."[46] It was unfortunate that a lone clinician had to be placed in this predicament, with its normative burden and associated liability risk.

His professional challenge as a practitioner was reflective of the broader com-munity he served. At that juncture, society was just beginning to comprehend the disproportionate burden that communities of color experienced from COVID-19. A remarkable research letter in *JAMA* in late April 2020 would report that the Bronx had the city's highest COVID-19 morbidity and mortality due to long-standing health inequities, poverty, dense housing, and a disproportionate number of essen-tial workers.[47]

Here, the gritty experience of the clinic, what Foucault called the "medical gaze,"[48] is illustrative of broader social forces: the lack of preparation for the com-ing plague and the endemic health disparities that compounded its consequences. It should not have taken COVID-19 for us to have been prepared, or to recognize and respond to, health inequity. If this lived experience fails to inspire a concerted response, it will only compound the tragedy of the pandemic. There are many les-sons to be learned from this history. We must heed these lessons lest history repeat itself when the next pandemic hits, as it surely will.

45 Fins, supra note 29.
46 E-mail from Dr. James J. Zisfein to author (Apr. 12, 2020, 7:24PM) (on file with author). Dr Zisfein granted permission to Dr. Fins to quote him.
47 Rishi K. Wadhera et al., Variation in COVID-19 Hospitalizations and Deaths Across New York City Boroughs, 323 *JAMA* 2192 (2020).
48 Michel Foucault, *The Birth of the Clinic: An Archaeology of Medical Perception*. A.M. Sheridan (translator) (Routledge 1989).

2

Patients First, Public Health Last

Richard S. Saver

I INTRODUCTION

If a crisis is a terrible thing to waste, the COVID-19 pandemic will hopefully stimulate a needed reexamination of physicians' public health obligations. Law, bioethics, and medical norms consider physicians' duties to individual patients supreme, reflected in the ubiquitous health care mantra of "putting patients first."[1] As a result, public health inevitably ends up last. The generally accepted dominance of patient-centered duties crowds out physician attention to non-patients and the larger public health space. Patient primacy, while appealing for many reasons, is incomplete; addressing problems of collective importance often requires standardized, regulatory approaches and looking beyond relational obligations to patients.[2] This is especially true for public health.

Physicians can all too easily discount community health considerations because their public health duties under the law are confoundingly elusive. At times, the law affirms physicians' special capacity and obligations to improve the health of the community. More often, though, physicians' public health duties are recognized on only a limited, ad hoc basis and without thoughtful justification for the reasons why physicians should have obligations for the health of non-patients. Meanwhile, the directive to put patients first means that physicians have considerable discretion to evade public health laws or disregard the public health implications of their treatment decisions.

Part I of this chapter describes the legal background concerning physicians' duties to patients and to the community. Part II analyzes how bioethics and medical norms amplify the law's patient-primacy directive. Part III illustrates how the elusiveness of physicians' public health duties enables the externalization of health risks from patients to the population at large, considering COVID-19 and other

---

[1] See, for example, Coombes v. Florio, 877 N.E.2d 567, 577 (Mass. 2007); David Orentlicher, The Physician's Duty to Treat During Pandemics, 108 Am. J. Pub. Health 1459, 1459 (2018).

[2] See, for example, William M. Sage, Relational Duties, Regulatory Duties, and the Widening Gap between Individual Health Law and Collective Health Policy, 96 Geo. L. J. 497, 500 (2008).

examples. Part IV evaluates the difficult challenges, as well as countervailing justifications, in making physicians' public health duties more cognizable. The most
important reason is instrumental and policy-driven: physicians play an indispensable role in public health protection. The private physician is strategically embedded between his/her patient, other patients, and society, and performs critical
sentinel, gate keeper, and learned intermediary functions essential to an effective
public health system.

II LEGAL DUTIES TO PROTECT PUBLIC HEALTH

Physicians' public health duties arise from a confusing patchwork of overlapping
sources of legal authority. At times, and seemingly ad hoc, the law acknowledges
that private physicians play an important public health role. Yet the obligations
imposed are hardly robust and, more frequently, the law has difficulty recognizing physicians' duties beyond the relational obligations formed with specific
patients.

A *Relationship-Based Duties, Including Duty of Loyalty*

Physicians' core common law responsibilities – such as the obligation of loyalty
and additional duties of care, nonabandonment, and confidentiality – arise only
from the formation of a treatment relationship with a specific patient.[3] As a quasi-
fiduciary to his/her patient, the physician generally must act for the patient's benefit
and avoid elevating other interests above the patient's welfare unless there has been
proper disclosure. Physicians sometimes act as agents for other parties in addition to
their patients, as in the provision of employment fitness examinations. But this still
offers little leeway for physicians to pursue public health goals with sufficient vigor.
Invariably, the message to physicians in most dual-loyalty scenarios is to restruc-
ture their roles to minimize dual-loyalty conflicts,[4] or to resolve the dual-allegiance
dilemma by putting patients first.[5]

B *Duties to Third Parties*

Common law has, at times, recognized a quasi-public health role for physicians in
considering the welfare of third parties potentially endangered by the patient. When
a patient has a contagious illness, such as tuberculosis or scarlet fever, courts have
traditionally recognized a duty on the physician to address the health risks to the

---

[3] See, for example, Kelley v. Middle Tenn. Emergency Physicians, P.C., 133 S.W.3d 587, 592 (Tenn. 2004).
[4] See, for example, I. Glenn Cohen et al., A Proposal to Address NFL Club Doctors' Conflicts of
Interest and to Promote Player Trust, 46 *Hastings Cent. Rep.* S2 (2016).
[5] See, for example, Solomon R. Benatar et al., Dual Loyalty of Physicians in the Military and in Civilian
Life, 98 *Am. J. Pub. Health* 2161, 2161 (2008).

patient's very close contacts, often family members.[6] Courts seem more likely to sustain claims by infected third parties when there is an underlying disease-reporting law imposing a statutory obligation on the physician to notify public health authorities about the illness.[7]

Courts have at times used seemingly broad language affirming a critical public health role for private physicians. As the Supreme Court of Connecticut recently stated, "[doctor–patient relationship] concerns are at their nadir, and a physician's broader public health obligations are at their zenith, with respect to the diagnosis and treatment of infectious diseases."[8]

However, a more generalized duty to protect public health lacks a clear foundation in common law. First, the infectious disease line of cases typically extends the physician's duty to a specific third party in close nexus to the patient, rather than the public at large. Second, the common law duty described is often narrowly limited to advising or warning the patient about the risk to others, as opposed to requiring broader steps, and courts have often been reluctant "to extend the requirement for affirmative physician interventions *outside the physician-patient relationship*."[9] Third, courts have displayed concern with not overburdening physicians with infeasible liability exposure to many potential plaintiffs.[10]

C Medical Practice Acts/Professional Licensure

Only a handful of state medical practice acts expressly envision the licensed physician engaging in public health protection. Some licensing statutes provide that a physician's failure to comply with infectious disease-reporting laws can trigger licensure discipline. Beyond this link to disease reporting, the situations seem to be ad hoc, such as licensing laws permitting physicians to prescribe opioid antagonists to non-patients to prevent overdoses.[11] There is a noteworthy dearth of physician disciplinary actions involving conduct harming non-patients and the health of the community.[12]

D Other Statutory Duties

Other statutes provide clearer legal foundations for physicians' public health responsibilities, albeit in narrow contexts. First, some statutes impose direct public health surveillance responsibilities on treating clinicians, such as communicable

---

[6] See, for example, Skillings v. Allen, 173 N.W. 663 (Minn. 1919) (scarlet fever); Hofmann v. Blackmon, 241 So.2d 752 (Fla. Dist. Ct. App. 1970) (tuberculosis).

[7] Jones v. Stanko, 160 N.E. 456, 456 (Ohio 1928).

[8] Doe v. Cochran, 210 A.3d 469, 488 (Conn. 2019).

[9] Seebold v. Prison Health Servs., 57 A.3d 1232, 1248 (Pa. 2012) (emphasis added).

[10] McNulty v. City of New York, 792 N.E.2d 162, 166 (N.Y. 2003).

[11] N.C. Gen. Stat. § 90-12.7 (2019).

[12] James M. Dubois et al., Serious Ethical Violations in Medicine: A Statistical and Ethical Analysis of 280 Cases in the United States from 2008 to 2016, 19 *Am. J. Bioethics* 16, 16 (2019).

disease-reporting laws and elder abuse-reporting laws. Failure to comply with reporting obligations can subject a physician to licensure discipline in several states. However, as discussed further later, compliance with disease-reporting laws has been poor and enforcement weak.[13]

Other statutes permit commandeering the services of physicians during a public health crisis.[14] But such commandeering statutes typically apply only in the narrow context of a discrete, declared public health emergency, not daily treatment decisions.

Physicians may also have an obligation to treat individuals during a public health emergency under the federal Emergency Medical Treatment and Active Labor Act.[15] But the Act applies only when individuals present at a hospital emergency room. Outside of the emergency room context, the common law view of the doctor–patient relationship as contractual in nature gives physicians considerable leeway to decline to start a treatment relationship for any reason, with little regard for the impact on public health.

III MEDICAL ETHICS AND PROFESSIONAL NORMS AMPLIFYING PATIENT PRIMACY

Medical ethics and professional norms reinforce and amplify the law's patient-primacy directive, often to the detriment of public health. The nine core principles of the American Medical Association's Code of Medical Ethics (AMA Code) include a seemingly bold endorsement of a robust public health role for the physician: "A physician shall recognize a responsibility to participate in activities contributing to the improvement of the community and the betterment of public health."[16] But significantly undercutting this obligation to non-patients, the AMA Code further instructs physicians to "place patients' welfare above the physician's own self-interest *or obligations to others*."[17]

The AMA Code underwent significant revisions in 2016, including, importantly, a reorganized series of ethics opinions in Chapter 8 that addresses "Ethics for Physicians [and] the Health of the Community."[18] Yet many of the Chapter 8 ethics opinions make clear a physician's public health responsibilities remain necessarily inferior to patient obligations. For example, Ethics Opinion 8.1, dealing with the importance of physician participation in routine universal screening of patients for

---

[13] See infra Section IV.C.

[14] Model State Emergency Powers Act, Dec. 21, 2001 draft, www.aapsonline.org/legis/msehpa2.pdf.

[15] 42 U.S.C. § 1395dd (2018).

[16] Am. Med. Ass'n, Code of Medical Ethics, Principles of Medical Ethics § VII, www.ama-assn.org/about/publications-newsletters/ama-principles-medical-ethics.

[17] Am. Med. Ass'n, Code of Medical Ethics, Ethics Opinion 1.1.1 (emphasis added), www.ama-assn.org/system/files/code-of-medical-ethics-chapter-1.pdf.

[18] Am. Med. Ass'n, Code of Medical Ethics, Chapter 8: Opinions on Physicians and the Health of the Community, www.ama-assn.org/system/files/2020-12/code-of-medical-ethics-chapter-8.pdf.

HIV, assumes that "[p]hysicians' primary ethical obligation is to their individual patients" and thus advises that physicians should respect a patient's informed refusal to be tested for HIV.[19]

The failure of traditional medical ethics to support more robust public health duties for physicians, and its seeming enfeeblement of such duties by obfuscation, should not surprise. Organized medicine has historically had a tense relationship and professional rivalry with public health. Further, public health's more communitarian orientation remains at odds with the emphasis in traditional medical ethics on values such as autonomy, civil liberty, and anti-paternalism.[20]

Medicine's professional norms also slight the health needs of the community in favor of patient primacy. Most medical school graduates take formal pledges to prioritize the patient's welfare, with common language such as "the health and life of my patient will be my first consideration."[21] Public health actions fit awkwardly with this sense of professional mission.

Physician discomfort with public health arises in part from the limited public health education they receive as part of their training.[22] Further, the fact that much physician work is oriented around particular episodes of care makes it harder to adopt population-based perspectives in decision-making. The understandable default is to deal with the patient at hand, case by case.

IV RISK EXTERNALIZATION TO THE PUBLIC

The patient-primacy directive, combined with the otherwise elusiveness of physicians' public health duties, enables the externalization of insidious health risks from patients to the population at large. Several examples across the wide public health space reflect this troubling pattern.

A COVID-19

An important public health strategy deployed during the COVID-19 pandemic was delay of certain procedures. This was intended to minimize virus transmission opportunities and preserve the health care system's limited resources for fighting COVID-19. In March 2020, a growing public health consensus emerged favoring a

---

[19] Am. Med. Ass'n, Code of Medical Ethics, Ethics Opinion 8.1: Routine Universal Screening of HIV, www.ama-assn.org/delivering-care/ethics/routine-universal-screening-hiv.

[20] Daniel Callahan & Bruce Jennings, Ethics and Public Health: Forging a Strong Relationship, 92 *Am. J. Pub. Health* 169, 170 (2002).

[21] See Audiey C. Kao & Kayhan P. Parsi, Content Analyses of Oaths Administered at US Medical Schools in 2000, 79 *Acad. Med.* 882, 882–84 (2004).

[22] Kevin Correll Keith et al., Student Perspectives on Public Health Education in Undergraduate Medical Education, 15 *Diversity & Equity in Health Care* 234, 239 (2018).

pause in nonessential care. The Centers for Disease Control and Prevention (CDC) and professional associations such as the American College of Surgeons issued recommendations along these lines.[23] Eventually, many states imposed restrictions on elective procedures.[24]

Despite the public health guidance, some physicians continued to perform procedures generally considered less essential, such as spinal decompression. They defended their conduct as doing the best for their patients. For example, Dr. Neal ElAttrache, a highly regarded orthopedic surgeon and president of the American Orthopaedic Society for Sports Medicine, performed "Tommy John" surgery on several athletes during this period.[25] Although acknowledging the public health risks, he maintained that he was obligated to treat his patients and remained focused on how delays would affect them personally.[26] Likewise, many dermatology practices remained open in late March of 2020, in defiance of public health calls to limit such in-person care and guidelines from the American Academy of Dermatology to reschedule all nonessential visits or switch to telemedicine.[27]

Undoubtedly, economic considerations likely motivated these providers to keep offering such nonessential services. Many of the dermatology practices that remained open in this period were owned by private equity firms and faced pressures to generate practice revenues for investors.[28] But the physicians' stated reasons, even if somewhat pretextual, predictably referenced doing what was best for their patients.

Thus, it would be wrong to dismiss these physicians as outliers. Because their public health responsibilities were so elusive, these physicians had considerable discretion to downgrade public health concerns to an alarming degree. Meanwhile, the "patients first" rationale was so broad and seemingly beyond reproach that it could obscure financial incentives and other questionable reasons at odds with community health protection.

[23] Am. Coll. of Surgeons, COVID-19: Recommendations for Management of Elective Surgical Procedures (Mar. 13, 2020), www.facs.org/covid-19/clinical-guidance/elective-surgery; Ctrs. for Disease Control & Prevention, Interim Guidance for Healthcare Facilities: Preparing for Community Transmission of COVID-19 in the United States (Feb. 29, 2020), https://stacks.cdc.gov/view/cdc/85502. The CDC's interim guidance was later revised to provide greater flexibility concerning elective procedures. See Ctrs. for Disease Control & Prevention, Managing Healthcare Operations During COVID-19, www.cdc.gov/coronavirus/2019-ncov/hcp/guidance-hcf.html (last updated Feb. 8, 2021).

[24] See, for example, N.Y. Exec. Order No. 202.10 (Mar. 23, 2020), www.governor.ny.gov/sites/default/files/atoms/files/EO_202.10.pdf.

[25] Henry Schulman, Top Tommy John Surgeon Defends Procedures Done During Coronavirus Outbreak, SF Chronicle (Mar. 24, 2020), www.sfchronicle.com/giants/article/Top-Tommy-John-surgeon-defends-procedures-done-15154721.php.

[26] Id.

[27] Katie Hafner, Many Dermatology Practices Stay Open, Ignoring Public Health Pleas, NY Times (Apr. 8, 2020), www.nytimes.com/2020/04/08/health/coronavirus-telemedicine-dermatology.html.

[28] Id.

B *Antibiotic Prescribing*

The "antibiotic paradox" means that prescribing an antibiotic can have dual, contradictory effects – combating targeted illness for one patient while also increasing resistant bacterial strains in the community and therefore jeopardizing the medication's effectiveness when used again for future health threats.[29] Thus, for public health reasons, physicians must sometimes limit the use of antibiotics when the medication might offer only marginal benefit to the patient.

Yet physicians engage in much inappropriate antibiotic prescribing, including over- ordering the drugs by as much as 50 percent.[30] Evidence suggests that physicians privilege their patients and do not attach sufficient weight to public health concerns when deciding on a course of antibiotic therapy. A study of physician attitudes concerning antibiotic prescribing indicated that most physicians placed the societal risk of antibiotic resistance at or very near the bottom of the list of factors (such as side effects, efficacy, and cost to patient) that mattered most in their decision-making.[31]

The law's patient-primacy directive seems to discourage physicians from engaging in antibiotic conservation. For example, informed consent doctrine generally requires a physician to advise the patient about a proposed treatment's material risks. The law is so patient-focused that courts conceive of these risks as the harms that may materialize for the patient, not the populace. A physician is under no legal obligation to inform the patient about the resistance risks and dangers to community health from inappropriate antibiotic use.[32] Fiduciary duty obligations also may be at odds with prudent antibiotic stewardship. A physician arguably may run afoul of the fiduciary's duty of loyalty if the physician restricts the patient from even the marginal benefits of using a medication.

C *Disease Reporting*

Every state has statutory and regulatory requirements that physicians, clinical laboratories, and select other providers report various infectious disease cases to public health authorities. Despite the clear statutory mandates, physicians have historically performed poorly as mandatory reporters.[33] Surveys show compliance rates ranging

---

[29] Stuart B. Levy, The Antibiotic Paradox: How the Misuse of Antibiotics Destroys Their Curative Powers XII-XIV (2002).

[30] Katherine E. Fleming-Dutra, Prevalence of Inappropriate Antibiotic Prescriptions Among US Ambulatory Care Visits, 2010–2011, 315 *JAMA* 1864, 1869 (2016).

[31] Joshua P. Metlay et al., Tensions in Antibiotics Prescribing: Pitting Social Concerns against the Interest of Individual Patients, 17 *J. Gen. Internal Med.* 87, 87 (2002).

[32] Wendy E. Parmet, Unprepared: Why Health Law Fails to Prepare Us for a Pandemic, 2 *J. Health & Biomedical L.* 157, 176 (2006).

[33] Timothy J. Doyle et al., Completeness of Notifiable Infectious Disease Reporting in the United States: An Analytical Review, 155 *Am. J. Epidemiology* 866, 871 (2002).

from about 37 to 57 percent for common sexually transmitted diseases such as chlamydia and AIDS.[34]

Physician non-compliance may seem largely a problem of lax enforcement and insufficient deterrence. But the non-compliance problems indicate deeper problems of physician disengagement. After all, individuals adhere to mandates and statutory obligations, even when infrequently enforced, when they have more intrinsic motivations for compliance.[35]

The stated reasons for physician non-compliance have varied over time, including concerns over patient confidentiality, burdensome time and resource commitments, and physician reliance on other health care team members to make the required reports.[36] Some of the reasons offered for physician non-compliance seem pretextual. For example, complaints about breaching confidentiality are likely overstated. The federal medical privacy law, the Health Insurance Portability and Accountability Act, has a broad public health exception that permits provider reporting of infectious disease incidents.[37]

The varied reasons offered for physician non-compliance obscure a more fundamental problem: public health practitioners and private physicians view disease reporting through very different perspectives. Public health practitioners envision disease reporting as instrumental for necessary surveillance and as part of each provider's shared accountability for the health of the populace. But physicians have been far more wary of disease reporting, in particular how it may intrude upon the "sanctity of their therapeutic relationships."[38]

D *Opioid Epidemic*

The opioid epidemic has multiple root causes, including aggressive marketing and financial incentives offered to prescribers by pharmaceutical companies, flawed reimbursement programs, which encourage prescribing over behavioral alternatives, and inadequate training of physicians in recognizing and treating addiction.[39]

---

[34] Janet S. St. Lawrence et al., STD Screening, Testing, Case Reporting, and Clinical and Partner Notification Practices: A National Survey of US Physicians, 92 *Am. J. Pub. Health* 1784, 1787 (2002).

[35] See, for example, Kristin Underhill, When Extrinsic Incentives Displace Intrinsic Motivation: Designing Legal Carrots and Sticks to Confront the Challenge of Motivational Crowding-Out, 33 *Yale J. Reg.* 213, 220 (2016).

[36] Mary-Margaret A. Fill et al., Heath Care Provider Knowledge and Attitudes Regarding Reporting Diseases and Events to Public Health Authorities in Tennessee, 23 *J. Pub. Health Mgmt. Prac.* 581, 582–83 (2017).

[37] 45 C.F.R. § 164.512(b).

[38] Lawrence O. Gostin, Public Health Law: Power, Duty, Restraint 313 (2d ed. 2008).

[39] See, for example, Mark A. Rothstein, Ethical Responsibilities of Physicians in the Opioid Crisis, 45 *J. L. Med. Ethics* 682, 683 (2017).

But lurking less visibly beneath the surface is a familiar pattern: physicians' underweighting of public health. A blinkered devotion to their individual patients has allowed many physicians to exacerbate the opioid epidemic.

First, physicians prescribe opioids in patterns and amounts that foreseeably permit diversion of the medications to non-patients, fueling potential health dangers for the community. As Dr. Anna Lembke describes in the *New England Journal of Medicine*, one puzzle of the opioid crisis is that "[i]n many instances, doctors are fully aware that their patients are abusing these medications or diverting them to others for nonmedical use, but they prescribe them anyway."[40] Physicians can rationalize such excessive prescribing on the grounds of patient convenience. These well-meaning physicians also allow concerns of patient pain to override attention to the serious community health risks from widespread, chronic use of opioids, such as increased rates of addiction and bloodborne, bacterial, and sexually transmitted infections.

Particularly revealing is physician resistance to prescription drug monitoring programs (PDMPs). PDMPs, electronic databases that track prescriptions of certain medications and require physician query before prescribing, have been implemented by law in many states as a means to combat the opioid epidemic. Yet debates about PDMPs invariably include claims that this form of regulation interferes with the doctor–patient relationship and impedes physicians' ability to provide individually tailored care.[41] Patient welfare becomes deeply intertwined with, and may even provide appealing cover for, underlying anxieties about physicians' professional autonomy.

Further, many public health regulatory interventions, such as PDMPs, rely on uniform, standardized approaches. Physicians, zealously focused on individual patient health, tend to be suspicious of this form of regulation, because "[a]pparent solutions of general applicability may result in individual cases of suboptimal medical care."[42]

V RECALIBRATING PHYSICIANS' PUBLIC HEALTH DUTIES

Considerable obstacles arise in making physicians' public health duties more robust and cognizable under the law. Yet countervailing justifications support this shift, including, most importantly, role indispensability.

---

[40] Anna Lembke, Why Doctors Prescribe Opioids to Known Opioid Abusers, 367 *New Eng. J. Med.* 1580, 1580 (2012).

[41] Mark Barnes et al., Opioid Prescribing and Physician Autonomy: A Quality of Care Perspective, HSS J. 20, 23 (2019), www.ehidc.org/sites/default/files/resources/files/Barnes2019_Article_OpioidPrescribing AndPhysicianAutonomy.pdf.

[42] Id. at 22.

A *Challenges*

1 Too Many Plaintiffs/Liability Without Limits

If the law imposes stronger public health responsibilities, would each physician owe to any member of the public an actionable duty to safeguard community health? This shift might counterproductively move from limited accountability to an even worse state of overdeterrence.

While a challenge, the "too many plaintiffs" problem is not necessarily insurmountable. In other contexts, courts have deployed various doctrinal rules, such as privity, to protect against crushing exposure to liability. Courts in public health disputes likewise could use line-drawing rules. Alternatively, courts and legislators could instead establish that the physician's breach of public health duties is not actionable by individual community members, but only by intermediaries and proxies for the public, such as state attorney generals or state medical boards. These intermediaries would be expected to act as prudent representatives and remain sensitive to overburdening ordinary physicians with inordinate liability exposure.

2 Common Law Reluctance to Impose Affirmative Duties

In relation to non-patients, physicians are arguably in the same position as ordinary individuals and, as such, they generally have no duty unless they are risk-creating or misfeasant.

Doctrinally, therefore, broad public health duties for physicians seemingly run counter to the common law tradition. This is a tradition that emphasizes autonomy and allowing persons to choose to be instruments of good, rather than having them answer to compelled societal obligations and intrusive governmental regulation. Moreover, as a matter of institutional competence, legislatures and regulatory bodies may be better equipped than courts to consider the social and policy consequences of broadening duty rules.

These concerns, while meritorious, do not completely preclude broadening physicians' common law public health duties. At present, with physicians' community health obligations underpowered, the insidious externalization of health risks from patients to the populace occurs unabated. In addition, the distinction between misfeasance and nonfeasance is often arbitrary and misleading. Instead, the extent of physicians' duties should turn more openly on the underlying policy considerations for imposing legal responsibility.

In many public health situations, as explained later, physicians are in the best position to address the community health risk, equivalent to the cheapest-cost-avoider.[43] Their actions and inactions with regard to public health risks have more significant

[43] See infra Section V.B.1

consequences because of their indispensable role in safeguarding the health of the populace. Courts might ultimately justify strengthening physicians' public health duties as a form of "benign commandeering … [where] we impose special altruistic responsibilities on [particular defendant classes such as] health care professionals and places of public accommodation" for overall general welfare.[44]

3 Fiduciary Duty Constraints

Recalibrating physicians' public health duties also runs the risk of eviscerating physicians' fiduciary obligations to patients. However, despite the strong rhetoric surrounding the fiduciary's duty of loyalty, absolute fidelity to the beneficiary is not always required. Fiduciary law has, for example, been applied flexibly to allow deployment of financial incentives directed at physicians for controlling health care costs.[45]

Moreover, the question of physicians' fiduciary duties of loyalty becomes more complex when one recognizes that the typical physician has multiple patients. Some actions taken by a physician to protect community health, such as limiting antibiotic prescriptions, may disfavor the one patient denied access while helping the physician's *other patients* as members of the community who benefit from a reduced risk of antibiotic resistance.

B *Possible Justifications*

Countervailing justifications support strengthening physicians' public health duties.

1 Role Indispensability

Perhaps the strongest reason is the physician's critical and indispensable role in protecting the health of the community. The argument is not that physicians are particularly suited for the role of public health stewards. But, pragmatically, they are still likely better than the alternatives. The conventional medicine/public health divide typically overlooks private physicians as part of the public health space. However, as the COVID-19 pandemic has revealed, traditional public health personnel, such as contact tracers and epidemiologists, are quite limited in number and work for state and local health departments that have been consistently underfunded and understaffed. To a surprising degree, "[t]he rest of the [public health] response is in the hands of thousands of private militias – hospitals, insurers, doctors, nurses, respiratory technicians, pharmacists and so on."[46]

---

[44] Kenneth S. Abraham & Leslie Kendrick, There's No Such Thing as Affirmative Duty, 104 *Iowa L. Rev.* 1649, 1692 (2019).

[45] See, for example, Robert Gatter, Communicating Loyalty: Advocacy and Disclosure of Conflicts in Treatment and Research Relationships, in Oxford Handbook of U.S. Health Law 242–47 (2017).

[46] Donald G. McNeil, Jr., American Public Health Infrastructure Needs an Update, NY Times (June 18, 2020), www.nytimes.com/article/coronavirus-facts-history.html#link-5d80e42a.

Physicians work at the critical nerve center of this private/public response force. Their uniquely advantageous position – strategically embedded between their patient, other patients, and society – makes private physicians' engagement critical for effective public health protection. First, physicians perform a sentinel function. As front-line practitioners, they have the initial opportunity to identify illnesses and patterns that threaten the entire community. Physicians also are usually in the best position to act on alarming information when limited time windows exist.[47]

Second, community physicians perform a key role as gatekeepers. They are in an advantageous position to monitor, influence, and induce demand for health care products and services. There is a clear connection between gatekeeping and public health. For example, the negative downstream effects of indiscriminate opioid prescribing can be understood as community physicians performing poorly as gatekeepers to powerfully addictive medications.

Third, physicians perform key roles as learned intermediaries. Informed consent law and the learned intermediary doctrine under product liability law require that physicians distill and shape complex medical information for their patients' particular situations and needs. As learned intermediaries, physicians can call attention to the public health implications that their patients may not otherwise understand or heed.

Physicians are successful learned intermediaries because they command significant public trust. Of course, a legal shift requiring stronger physician duties for public health protection could erode patient trust if patients perceive that their physicians are no longer as devoted to individual patient welfare. However, powerful intrinsic reasons for patients to have confidence in their physicians exist, even in the face of legal regulation that seemingly threatens trust in the doctor–patient relationship.[48]

2 Social Contract

In addition to the basic benefits every citizen enjoys from the state, physicians are granted a special license to provide professional services. They also receive expensive medical education and graduate medical training that the government significantly subsidizes. Physicians also enjoy high social status and membership in an elite, guild-like profession. In return for these many benefits, physicians arguably have public health obligations.

However, it is debatable whether social contract theory can be relied upon to require broader public health measures of physicians. To the extent that social contract theory arguments heavily depend on some quid pro quo for the societal benefits physicians enjoy, the difficult question is whether physicians understand what their end of the bargain is and voluntarily assume broad public health responsibilities when

---

[47] Fill et al., supra note 36, at 581.
[48] Mark A. Hall, Law, Medicine, and Trust, 55 *Stan. L. Rev.* 463, 507 (2002).

entering the medical profession.[49] Moreover, many physicians could justify their regular patient care activities as fulfilling their end of any implicit social contract bargain.

3 Social Expectations

As legal duties often mirror and reinforce social attitudes, an important consideration is whether imposing more vigorous public health duties on physicians vindicates or frustrates societal expectations about the medical profession. The public and most physicians likely agree on the reassuring dynamic of the faithful doctor who acts zealously for his or her patient. Under this view, physicians who "prioritize public health care ... would devalue the expectations of patients."[50]

On the other hand, social expectations might actually be more nuanced. The public does observe community physicians working to safeguard public health, for example in common activities such as vaccination and assessing impaired patients' fitness to drive. The public likely holds somewhat contradictory, even unrealistic, views about physicians – that clinicians should always do what is best for the patient *and* should vigorously safeguard the health of the community.

4 Equitable Distribution of Physician Burden/Collective Action

Legal recognition of more robust public health duties for physicians would also help address concerns of inequitable physician burden. Combating many public health threats necessarily raises collective action challenges. The efforts of only some community physicians, however vigorous, will not have much effect if other physicians are not on board because public health risks propagate through the interconnectedness of health care system stakeholders. For example, in the case of antibiotic resistance, a few physicians' inappropriate prescribing patterns can introduce strong resistance selection pressures into the community, rendering future uses of medications ineffective, even if other physicians prudently conserve antibiotics.[51] Letting some physicians "off the hook" by not recognizing and uniformly applying more robust public health duties invites further problems of insufficient coordination.

C *Moving Forward*

How should the law move forward with a legal shift in physicians' public health obligations? Admittedly, enhancing physicians' public health duties, while still

---

[49] Russell L. Gruen et al., Physician-Citizens-Public Roles and Professional Obligations, 291 *JAMA* 94, 95 (2004).
[50] Heinz-Harald Abholz, Conflicts Between Personal and Public Health Care: Can One GP Serve Two Masters?, 57 *Br. J. Gen. Prac.* 693, 694 (2007).
[51] David M. Livermore, Bacterial Resistance: Origins, Epidemiology, and Impact, 36 *Clinical Infectious Diseases* S11, S15–S16 (2003).

demanding strong obligations to each patient, may lead to much variability in practice. However, *any* adjustment in physicians' legal duties would still represent an improvement over the status quo.

Next, lawmakers and regulators ideally should, through statutes and regulations, identify clearer pathways whereby private physicians can enter the public health sphere, move beyond their heavy relational orbit with patients, and protect non-patients from health risks. As previously noted, some medical practice acts permit physicians to prescribe opioid antagonists to non-patients to prevent overdoses. Such codification on a broader scale would be welcome to counter perceived barriers because of patient primacy.

Also critical is stronger enforcement of the minimal public health obligations for physicians already existing under the law, such as addressing physicians' poor compliance with obligations to report communicable disease cases. Importantly, higher compliance can be achieved through targeted education, auditing, financial rewards, and leveraging physicians' intrinsic reasons for compliance, not just the threat of heavy sanction.

Finally, non-maleficence serves as a helpful guiding principle for thinking about the dual-loyalty problem between patient welfare and public health. Non-maleficence generally requires that a physician's intervention not harm the patient. In many instances of potential dual-loyalty conflict, physicians could better justify actions taken for public health protection by ensuring that such conduct at least does not further harm their individual patients. This may not be always practicable. When respecting non-maleficence is feasible, however, with concurrent public health protection, physicians' public health duties should be interpreted to incorporate the principle.

VI CONCLUSION

The traditional pattern of patients first, public health last facilitates the externalization of health risks to the community. It has become unavoidably necessary to reconsider physicians' duties and ensure that they pay greater heed to the population's health. The law needs to appropriate physicians for public health protection because, as a practical matter, there are no better choices.

Their unique strategic role, embedded between the patient, other patients, and society, makes physicians indispensable to effective public health protection.

3

Risk, Responsibility, Resilience, Respect

COVID-19 and the Protection of Health Care Workers

William M. Sage and Victoria L. Tiase

I INTRODUCTION

The COVID-19 pandemic has shown us that the health care system we thought we had is not the health care system we actually have, crystallizing concerns (whether long-standing or emerging) over several aspects of health care financing, delivery, and governance. "Preparedness" calls for more than lip service when failures in public health surveillance and response cost over a million lives and threaten a decade of economic prosperity. "Solidarity" has deeper meaning when social divisions accentuated for political advantage undermine consensus behaviors that could prevent disease spread and accelerate immunization. "Innovation" seems more precious when saving lives and livelihoods depends on adaptive clinical methods, novel therapeutics, and rapid development and distribution of vaccines. "Health equity" is more compelling when poor communities of color are among the first to face illness and death but among the last to access treatment and vaccination. And "burnout" has greater salience when fulfillment from dedicated patient service competes with fear and exhaustion among health care professionals and other front-line workers.

Medicine and nursing have long professional traditions of altruism and self-sacrifice, including undertaking not only extreme stress but also personal risk in service of patient care. With exceptions for natural disasters, humanitarian missions, and military service, however, recent concerns about professional "burnout" often have had more to do with organizational tensions than with core clinical circumstances. The COVID-19 pandemic changed that – bringing front and center the close connections between the well-being of health care workers and the well-being of the patients they serve. This chapter describes the COVID-19 experience of health care workers in New York City (NYC) and environs during the spring of 2020, examining what happened, why things went wrong, and how it drew attention and generated responses. This chapter then steps back to consider the root causes of health professionals' physical and psychological vulnerability during COVID-19, such as inequities within the health care system, professional hierarchies, safety system failures, and gaps in business and regulatory practices.

This concluding section also identifies potential improvements, ranging from ethics and advocacy to corporate governance and labor organization, workplace redesign, and regulatory and payment reform.

II PANDEMIC UNPREPAREDNESS AND THE HEALTH CARE WORKFORCE

Over one million Americans have died from COVID-19, with deaths and serious illnesses occurring at higher rates among individuals and communities identifying as Black, Indigenous, and persons of color. Before vaccination became widespread, health care workers accounted for about 6 percent of all US infections, with a distribution that similarly tracks social determinants and ethnic and racial disparities.[1] Infection rates and mortality have been much higher among nurses than among physicians; occupational exposure during patient care is apparently responsible for most cases in those professional categories. Aides and other assistive personnel have suffered from the highest infection rates overall, and have been involved in transmission within nursing homes and congregate care settings, but most of their exposure seems likely to be in their often-vulnerable communities rather than arising from patient care, and their hospitalization rates appear lower. According to a tracking website, over 3,600 US health care workers had died from COVID-19 by the end of April 2021 – a tragic outcome and a continuing source of stress and concern for those who remained at work.[2] In normal times, the health professions regard each patient they treat as the exclusive beneficiary of their attention, with tensions among different patients' interests finessed, interests of potential patients ignored, and outright patient–patient conflicts acknowledged only in specialized contexts (e.g., organ donors and organ transplant recipients). Outside of normal times – on the battlefield, during natural disasters, and certainly in the COVID-19 pandemic – shortages, timing, and other exigencies may require triage decisions, "crisis" (i.e., reduced) standards of care, and even so-called "tragic choices."[3] Depending on the circumstances, these conditions can reinforce professional pride and build teamwork, or can cause profound sadness and inflict moral injury.[4] Health professionals

---

[1]   Michelle M. Hughes et al., Update: Characteristics of Health Care Personnel with COVID-19 – United States, February 12–July 16, 2020, 69 *Morbidity & Mortality Wkly. Rep.* 1364 (Sept. 25, 2020), http://dx.doi.org/10.15585/mmwr.mm6938a3; Anita K. Kambhampati et al., COVID-19-Associated Hospitalizations Among Health Care Personnel – COVID-NET, 13 States, March 1–May 31, 2020, 69 *Morbidity & Mortality Wkly. Rep.* 1576 (Oct. 30, 2020), http://dx.doi.org/10.15585/mmwr.mm6943e3.

[2]   See Jane Spencer, *The Guardian*, and Christina Jewett, Lost on the Frontline: 12 Months of Trauma: More Than 3,600 US Health Workers Died in Covid's First Year, Kaiser Health News (Apr. 8, 2021), https://kffhealthnews.org/news/article/us-health-workers-deaths-covid-lost-on-the-frontline/ (last visited Apr. 9, 2023).

[3]   Inst. of Med., Crisis Standards of Care: A Toolkit for Indicators and Triggers (2013).

[4]   Sonya B. Norman et al., Moral Distress in Frontline Healthcare Workers in the Initial Epicenter of the COVID-19 Pandemic in the United States: Relationship to PTSD Symptoms, Burnout, and Psychosocial Functioning (July 2021), www.ncbi.nlm.nih.gov/pmc/articles/PMC8426909/.

are even less prepared to balance risks of harming patients with risks of harming themselves. Self-sacrifice remains under-developed in both ethical and operational terms. While attention to "burnout" has increased, much of the associated literature (beyond undeniably important concerns over mental health and substance use) has focused on the perceived loss of professional autonomy and control because of organizational, technological, and generational change.[5] Connections to core patient care commitments and long-term clinical performance have been sporadic.[6]

The COVID-19 pandemic reminded the country of health professionals' continued willingness to put themselves in harm's way for the benefit of their patients. Many younger professionals initially embraced self-sacrifice, telling researchers unequivocally that: "We signed up for this!"[7] But in a sustained and serious pandemic, a heroism-based ethical paradigm for accepting personal risk is as misleading as the myth of professional perfection has been for avoiding medical errors. Supportive teams, organizations, families, and communities are essential.

Medical ethics has seldom focused on these issues, generally charging physicians and nurses with furthering the patient's interest even at some personal risk. Because many examples of self-sacrifice reach back in history to infectious diseases that became preventable by the middle of the twentieth century, the point at which professionals may ethically distance themselves from hazardous care is seldom mapped. Recent high-risk exposure has been voluntary, such as traveling to Africa to care for Ebola patients, or hypothetical, such as potential bioterrorism or novel influenza strains that did not ultimately prove that dangerous. COVID-19 presents a very different situation, with high volumes of sick and likely infectious patients across geographies, uncertain prognoses for exposed health care workers, and for many months, neither an effective therapy nor a proven vaccine.

There is little enforceable law to reinforce or guide professional ethics. With only a few exceptions (e.g., duties of nonabandonment, care in emergency departments under the federal Emergency Medical Treatment & Labor Act, various contractual agreements), health professionals are not legally obligated to render care to patients in medical need.[8] This is true even during emergencies, although Section 608(a) of the Model Emergency Powers Act, drafted after the 9/11 attacks, would authorize governors to conscript physicians into service as a condition of professional licensure.[9] A few states have enacted the provision,

---

[5] Nat'l Acads. of Scis., Eng'g, & Med., Taking Action Against Clinician Burnout: A Systems Approach to Professional Well-Being (2019).

[6] Daniel E. Shapiro et al., Beyond Burnout: A Physician Wellness Hierarchy Designed to Prioritize Interventions at the Systems Level, 132 *Am. J. Med.* 556 (2019).

[7] Thomas H. Gallagher & Anneliese M. Schleyer, "We Signed Up for This!" – Student and Trainee Responses to the COVID-19 Pandemic, 382 *New Eng. J. Med.* e96 (2020).

[8] Judith C. Ahronheim, Service by Health Care Providers in a Public Health Emergency: The Physician's Duty and the Law, 12 *J. Health Care L. Pol'y* 195 (2009).

[9] Lawrence O. Gostin et al., The Model State Emergency Health Powers Act: Planning for and Response to Bioterrorism and Naturally Occurring Infectious Diseases, 288 *JAMA* 622 (2002).

but no governor or state official has exercised or requested that authority during the COVID-19 pandemic.

The most developed law and ethics of physician obligation despite personal medical risk relates to the HIV/AIDS epidemic of the 1980s, before patterns of transmission were well established and antiretroviral treatment became routine in developed countries. The American Medical Association issued Ethical Opinion 9.131 in 1992, requiring qualified physicians to treat HIV-positive patients, and courts interpreted the Americans with Disabilities Act of 1990 to prohibit the exclusion of those patients from dental offices and other health care settings.[10] These obligations to care for HIV-positive patients were motivated by concerns about stigma as well as about access to care; HIV cases clustered among groups, such as gay men, who had previously been subject to discrimination. Discrimination also results in disparities during the current pandemic, but the injustices of COVID-19 reflect structural and institutional inequities more than explicit bias.

Tensions between COVID-19 patient care and the well-being of health professionals also reflect the peculiarities of the lavishly funded but only partially industrialized health care system in the United States. The US health care workforce is overwhelmingly deployed in private settings, even though much of its cost is supported by public sources of funding. Each category of licensed health professional is subject to oversight by a dedicated, state-specific licensing board, with little uniformity or coordination. The hospital sector is highly consolidated, and now employs roughly 40 percent of American physicians. Yet physicians retain norms and, in many states, legal rights of self-governance even when they practice within hospitals, are paid from health insurance revenue streams different from those that support health facilities, and may be exempt from the occupational health and safety laws that govern ordinary workplaces. Chronic and long-term care facilities, which also faced a high risk of COVID-19 spread and serious illness, lack the funding, physician and nurse leadership, and public visibility of the hospital sector.

III PROFESSIONAL VULNERABILITY: THE NYC COVID-19 EXPERIENCE

We begin with the experience of NYC hospitals facing a sudden and vicious outbreak of disease in spring 2020, during the first phase of the pandemic in the United States. On March 7, 2020, the governor of New York declared a state of emergency due to the coronavirus pandemic and, by March 20, a stay-at-home order. By the end of March, NYC had become the epicenter of COVID-19, and hospitals were struggling to keep up with the demands placed on them by the pandemic. Immigrant communities in Queens, Brooklyn, and the Bronx were especially afflicted, so much

---

[10]   Bragdon v. Abbott, 524 U.S. 624 (1998).

so that the conditions at NYC Health and Hospital's Elmhurst Hospital in Queens were described as "apocalyptic."[11]

As the crisis advanced, NYC hospitals were faced with an enormous challenge: expanding critical care capacity, increasing critical care staffing, securing supplies and equipment and, most importantly, protecting their front-line workforce.[12] Hospitals with a 300-bed potential intensive care unit (ICU) capacity at baseline had to create space for more than 1,000 ICU patients.[13] Given NYC's preexisting space constraints, hospital administrators used existing infrastructure creatively, converting conference rooms, lobbies, and cafeterias into patient rooms. Procedural areas, such as operating rooms, were used as ICU spaces, with each room supporting two to four patients. Tents were constructed in parking lots and city parks to evaluate lower-acuity patients and decant traditional hospital spaces.

The volume of COVID-19 patients admitted to NYC hospitals, and the speed at which they arrived, placed a significant strain on ICU staffing. This strain was compounded by the number of hospital workers who tested positive for COVID-19, called in sick to care for ill family members, or were hospitalized themselves. At one point, Elmhurst Hospital reported that 8 percent of its workforce had been out sick.

Although the suspension of ambulatory care and elective surgeries freed up some existing staff for COVID-19-related patient care, many remained idle because NYC hospitals recruited critical care staff from other locations rather than retrain local personnel. ICU-trained nurses across the country left jobs in smaller, sometimes rural hospitals to travel to NYC, where they could earn as much as $10,000 per week.[14] Hospitals that were able to afford it therefore supplemented their workforces, while hospitals without as many resources were unable to offer their overworked nursing staff much-needed relief. Over time, this created a shift in nurses to more affluent areas of NYC.

It turned out that not all additional staff had been trained at the necessary level. Reports of improper treatments and overlooked patients dying alone added training of new staff to the burden on existing ICU staff. Non-ICU staff also received

[11] Michael Rothfeld, Somini Sengupta, Joseph Goldstein, & Brian M. Rosenthal. 13 Deaths in a Day: An "Apocalyptic" Coronavirus Surge at an N.Y.C. Hospital, NY Times (Mar. 25, 2020) (updated Apr. 14, 2020). www.nytimes.com/2020/03/25/nyregion/nyc-coronavirus-hospitals.html.

[12] Chris Keeley et al., Staffing Up for the Surge: Expanding the New York City Public Hospital Workforce During the COVID-19 Pandemic, 39 *Health Affs.* 1426 (2020).

[13] Amit Uppal et al., Critical Care and Emergency Department Response at the Epicenter of the COVID-19 Pandemic, 39 *Health Affs.* 1443 (2020).

[14] Hannah Sampson, Travel Nurses Usually See the Country. During the Last Year, Many Saw the Worst of the Pandemic, Wash. Post (Mar. 8, 2021), www.washingtonpost.com/travel/2021/03/08/travel-nurse-covid-pandemic/; Lenny Bernstein, As COVID Persists, Nurses are Leaving Staff Jobs – And Tripling Their Salaries as Travelers, Wash. Post (Dec. 6, 2021), www.washingtonpost.com/health/covid-travel-nurses/2021/12/05/550b15fc-4c71-11ec-a1b9-9f12bd39487a_story.html.

successful training on essential tasks, notably service on manual "proning" teams – those skilled in placing critically ill COVID-19 patients in a downward-facing position to improve gas exchange in the lungs.[15] With proning teams in place, anesthesiologists were redeployed to emergency departments to perform intubations, and pediatric nurses transitioned to adult patient care areas. Tiered staffing structures with a "head" ICU nurse leading non-ICU providers were used to expand capacity, upskilling existing staff in a supervised fashion.[16] Still, some non-ICU nurses reported feelings of inadequacy because they did not know enough to provide independent care, and feared being furloughed.

Having managed inventory for years on a "just-in-time" basis, hospitals facing pandemic caseloads found themselves short of supplies and equipment and were unprepared to acquire them quickly. Delivering the volume of critical care needed by COVID-19 patients at the height of the surge depended on having almost five times the accustomed ICU inventory of ventilators to help patients breathe, infusion pumps for medications, and dialysis machines to treat kidney failure. Disposable supplies such as ventilator tubing, intravenous tubing, dressings, and personal protective equipment (PPE) were also at critically low levels.

With many hospitals competing for the same supplies, systems for tracking, accessing, and distributing supplies and equipment became a paramount need. Given the respiratory nature of COVID-19, the asset management of ventilators was a primary concern. Even hospitals with real-time location tracking systems relied on respiratory therapists to keep count or leveraged patient care data from the electronic health record. Neither workaround was perfect. Busy health care workers had difficulty noting when equipment went out of service or when new equipment was entered into inventory. Electronic health record data were limited by the temporary suspension of charting requirements and delays in documenting ventilator orders by staff who were busy delivering patient care.

Within days of the first reported case in NYC, hospital leaders recognized that front-line staff were exhibiting distress and that protecting them was essential. The suffering took many forms and had many causes. Health care workers feared for their physical safety not only because they might contract COVID-19, but also because they faced targeted discrimination and related stigma. After ending an overnight shift, nurses at one hospital found twenty-two of their vehicles with tires slashed. When some politicians labeled COVID-19 the "China Virus," health care workers of Asian descent were forced to contend with xenophobia, abuse, harassment, and hate crimes. In early April 2020, officials from the World Health

---

[15] Deepa Kumaraiah et al., Innovative ICU Physician Care Models: COVID-19 Pandemic at NewYork-Presbyterian, 1 NEJM Catalyst Innovations in Care Delivery (Apr. 28, 2020), catalyst.nejm.org/doi/full/10.1056/CAT.20.0158.

[16] Neil A. Halpern & Kay See Tan, United States Resource Availability for COVID-19, Society of Critical Care Medicine (2020), www.sccm.org/Blog/March-2020/United-States-Resource-Availability-for-COVID-19.

Organization called for a zero-tolerance approach and established measures to protect health care workers.[17]

Staff were also endangered by supply chain issues involving PPE such as masks, gowns, gloves, and face shields, with many hospitals initiating mandatory conservation measures. Some physicians reused disposable face masks and nurses wore plastic garbage bags instead of gowns.[18] The physical and psychological effects of PPE shortages were worsened by a high degree of uncertainty in the early stages of the pandemic. The Centers for Disease Control and Prevention wavered on when to use single-use N95 respirators versus surgical masks, and on whether COVID-19 required droplet precautions.[19] This confused and misled health care workers.

Psychological pressure took many forms.[20] Health care workers feared that they might bring COVID-19 home to their families or friends. Many stayed in hotels or other isolated residences for months – initially at their own expense but over time as part of additional benefits funded by hospitals (including transportation and childcare). Such isolation, often self-imposed, added to the mental anguish. Some health care workers saw more deaths in a few weeks than they had seen during thirty-year careers. Others held the hands of patients in their final moments because family members were not allowed to visit. In some cases, health care workers made bedside decisions when needed supplies and equipment were not available, raising practical, ethical, and legal questions. But front-line workers wanted to save lives, and they were willing to put themselves in harm's way to do so.

Longer hours at a faster pace, lack of sleep, and emotional exhaustion pushed front-line workers to the breaking point. Although all health care workers were affected, one large study in NYC reported that nurses paid the greatest psychological price.[21] Nurses working double shifts were unable to get groceries for their families, do laundry, or tend to household needs. While many health care workers found solace and respite in healthful activity, the social isolation and other strictures required to contain the pandemic led others down dangerous paths. For some, the price of selflessness was beyond measure. Dr. Lorna Breen, a respected NYC emergency

[17] Stephanie Nebehay, Nurses Must Be Protected from Abuse During Coronavirus Pandemic: WHO, Nursing Groups, Reuters (Apr. 6, 2020), www.reuters.com/article/us-health-coronavirus-nurses/nurses-must-be-protected- from-abuse-during-coronavirus-pandemic-who-nursing-groups-idUSKBN21O317.

[18] Sarah Al-Arshani, Nurse Dies in New York Hospital Where Workers Are Reduced to Using Trash Bags as Protective Medical Gear, Bus. Insider (Mar. 26, 2020), www.businessinsider.com/kious-kelly-hospital-nurse-dies-trash-bags-2020-3#:~:text=A%20nurse%20at%20Mount%20Sinai%20Hospital%20 in%20New,bags%20instead%2C%20according%20to%20photos%20on%20social%20media.

[19] James G. Adams & Ron M. Walls, Supporting the Health Care Workforce During the COVID-19 Global Epidemic, 323 *JAMA* 1439 (2020).

[20] For an extensive qualitative survey of nurses, see Allison Squires et al., "Should I Stay or Should I Go?" Nurses' Perspectives about Working during the COVID-19 Pandemic's First Wave in the United States: A Summative Content Analysis Combined with Topic Modeling, *Int'l J. Nursing Stud.* (July 2022), www.sciencedirect.com/science/article/pii/S0020748922000852#!.

[21] Ari Shechter et al., Psychological Distress, Coping Behaviors, and Preferences for Support Among New York Healthcare Workers During the COVID-19 Pandemic, 66 *Gen. Hosp. Psychiatry* 1 (2020).

room physician and clinical leader, died by suicide after treating patients during the surge and then experiencing symptoms of COVID-19 herself. Other suicides and self-inflicted harms have been reported.[22]

Government uncertainty impacted organizational responses. State and city officials held daily briefings, but sent mixed messages about when health care workers needed to be tested, when exposed staff should return to work, and how to handle reentry for staff recovering from COVID-19. Hospital staff looked to their employers for guidance and protection, not professional associations, not the local government. Although many hospital leaders communicated daily with staff, the shifting guidance was interpreted as a lack of transparency.

Information dissemination also proved challenging: staff were not always working on their usual unit, were sometimes isolated, and left work immediately after shifts. With fewer hospital leaders physically on site, front-line staff also struggled with communicating complaints, articulating needs, and providing feedback on pandemic-related issues. While many hospitals offered financial incentives and free meals to express appreciation for staff, front-line workers indicated a preference for clear communication over extra pay, and some staff reported feeling belittled by bonus payments. At times, staff reported that they were making decisions on-the-fly and running their own units – saying that "anything goes."

IV PRINCIPAL LESSONS AND RECOMMENDATIONS

The COVID-19 pandemic has played out during the unhappy conjunction of the greatest public health threat since 1918 and (with the important exception of vaccine development) the most dysfunctional federal government response to a major social need since the onset of the Great Depression. Yet hospitals and other critical systems of medical care have bent but have not broken – thanks in part to the dedication of millions of health professionals and other essential workers. It is tempting to think that today's performative politics of division is an aberration, that policymaking and public response will return to being based on facts and science, and that the next test of health professional resilience will be milder or more localized. Even so, the COVID-19 experience highlights several aspects of the health care system that bear reexamination and improvement, for the mutual benefit of health care workers and patients.

A *Structural Unfairness*

A first lesson is the profound inequity that characterizes not only the underlying health of communities but also the medical infrastructure available to them. During

---

[22] Charlene Dewey et al., Supporting Clinicians During the COVID-19 Pandemic, 172 *Ann. Intern. Med.* 752 (2020). For a comprehensive description of the mental health effects on nursing from COVID-19, see Brittney Riedel et al., Mental Health Disorders in Nurses During the COVID-19 Pandemic: Implications and Coping Strategies, 9 *Frontiers Publ. Health* 707358 (2021).

the harsh coronavirus spring of 2020, nationally famous facilities – Mount Sinai Hospital, NewYork-Presbyterian Hospital, NYU Langone Health – were undoubtedly stressed. But as was true of prominent health systems elsewhere, they had the cash reserves, influential physicians, wealthy trustees, and scientific connections to hire staff, maintain supply chains, and even fabricate materials not available commercially. By contrast, hospitals owned or operated by New York Health and Hospitals – public institutions typically located in less prosperous neighborhoods and serving mainly poorer persons of color – were overcrowded, understaffed, and short of critical supplies. Unsurprisingly, many patients at those facilities had poor clinical outcomes. These disparities among acute care hospitals were mirrored in the long-term care sector, where facilities serving private-pay, generally White residents and employing a better-compensated workforce with less turnover or moonlighting fared better at preventing coronavirus infection and transmission than facilities with fewer resources serving mainly minority communities.

The governmental response to the pandemic widened rather than narrowed the gap between "have" and "have-not" hospitals, imposing even greater staff burdens at the latter facilities. Federal interventions in domestic policy tend to come mainly as financial support, and the cumulative investment in COVID-19 relief, including economic stimulus, exceeds $10 trillion.[23] The Trump Administration's subsidy programs, including the April 2020 Coronavirus Aid, Relief, and Economic Security Act (which enjoyed broad bipartisan support in Congress), favored larger and wealthier recipients, including among hospitals and other health care enterprises.[24] Even federal emergency management funds were directed more generously at the hospitals that arguably least needed relief.[25] Moreover, state and local governments (which fund most health care programs for the poor and uninsured) were entirely shut out of the relief authorized by Congress during the Trump Administration.

Systemic improvements in health equity may be slow in coming, but measures to stem the inequalities that harmed patients and workers during pandemic surges are possible. An important first step is for hospitals that have consolidated in recent decades – probably raising prices in the process – to act like the systems they purport to be by sharing staff and supplies in an organized and equitable manner. This may

---

[23] COVID Money Tracker, Comm. for a Responsible Fed. Budget, www.covidmoneytracker.org/ (last visited June 25, 2022).

[24] See Karyn Schwartz & Anthony Damico, Distribution of CARES Act Funding Among Hospitals, Kaiser Fam. Found. (May 13, 2020) ("The hospitals in the top 10% based on share of private insurance revenue received $44,321 per hospital bed, more than double the $20,710 per hospital bed for those in the bottom 10% of private insurance revenue"); see also Ben Casselman & Jim Tankersley, $500 Billion in Aid to Small Businesses: How Much Did It Help?, NY Times (Feb. 1, 2021), www.nytimes.com/2021/02/01/business/economy/ppp-jobs-small-business.html. (describing expert consensus that federal Payroll Protection Program funds were received mainly by the businesses that needed them least).

[25] Chad Terhune, Wealthy Hospitals Rake in US Disaster Aid for COVID-19 Costs, Reuters (Dec. 29, 2020), www.aol.com/news/wealthy-hospitals-rake-u-disaster-120452690-125159444.html.

be challenging in hospital systems with both unionized and non-unionized facilities because union rules forbid such shifts. The role of unionization among health care workers merits further study, including with respect to pandemic performance for both patients and personnel. Collective bargaining protects nursing jobs, ensures competitive wages, and enforces whistleblower protections for nurses speaking up against unsafe conditions.[26] However, personnel decisions in a union hospital typically are based on seniority, not job performance, which can dampen patient care innovation and impede workforce flexibility.

Collaboration and collective investment should happen at the community level as well. Throughout the pandemic, core public health functions involving disease detection and response were almost accidentally "outsourced" to private health care providers, even when new waves of infection were readily anticipated. Lack of attention to diagnostics as part of biopreparedness, for example, caused tragic delays in coronavirus testing until the private sector was finally brought in deliberately and productively.[27] This frustrating pattern continues decades-long trends of underinvestment in explicitly public infrastructure for community health. Rebuilding that capacity in connection with preparedness for future pandemics and similar emergencies – reinforcing supply chains, providing for surge capacity, and training and employing critical personnel – will also moderate the adverse consequences of the stark inequities among hospitals that COVID-19 revealed.

B *The Limitations of "Professionalism"*

A second lesson is that professionalism was simultaneously a strength and a weakness in terms of workforce well-being and patient care performance. Even with the recent movement toward interprofessional education and team-based care, the health professions remain individualistic, hierarchical, and generationally deferential, with senior physicians both role models and the principal decision-makers. There is also a broader tension between maintaining traditional but often casual professional control over health care delivery and promoting more structured and rigorous public accountability through direct regulatory oversight of industrial processes.

Directing attention to the collective dedication and resilience of health care workers – particularly to generate material and psychological support through measures such as the "Heroes Act" – was beneficial in the COVID-19 pandemic as rapid

---

[26] Nurses' unions have lobbied to expand workers' compensation programs to encompass COVID-19 infection and have supported a greater role in health care worker safety for the federal Occupational Safety and Health Administration (OSHA). See, for example, Isabel van Brugen, Nurses Union Slams 'Return to Work' COVID Guidelines in California, Newsweek (Jan. 10, 2022), www.newsweek.com/california-covid-return-work-guidelines-nurses-union-1667356.

[27] Carrie Arnold, Why the US Coronavirus Testing Failures Were Inevitable, Nat. Geographic (Mar. 20, 2020), www.nationalgeographic.com/science/article/why-united-states-coronavirus-testing-failures-were-inevitable.

upswings in disease burden bred fear and risked violence against those perceived to be potential carriers of deadly disease. NYC's briefly famous 7 PM "clappy hours," celebrating health care workers and first responders with applause and clattering kitchenware, were also general affirmations of solidarity that helped counter the pervasive reminders of pandemic-induced social isolation as urban life slowed to a silent crawl. But expecting "heroism" of each individual health professional is inviting exhaustion and self-doubt that can become burnout or worse. More generally, perfection in health care is a myth, one that often excuses deception, undervalues collaboration and adaptability, creates a predisposition to error, and fuels backlash.

In general, physicians and nurses and other health care workers pulled together in NYC during spring 2020, avoiding the rivalry and rancor that differences in professional and institutional authority can produce. Even so, those sounding the call to heroism could be tone deaf. In what was probably intended to be a "St. Crispin's Day" call for shared sacrifice as the pandemic exploded, the physician leader of one prominent hospital proclaimed his expectations that essential employees (typically nurses and aides) were expected to do their professional duty in caring personally for COVID-19 patients. It was received very differently, because it was widely recognized among front-line workers that much of his executive team and most senior physicians would be doing their jobs, if at all, from the safety of their suburban or vacation homes. Where physician leadership was absent or invisible – notably in long-term care facilities and other high-risk congregate care settings – chains of communication and accountability were even harder to identify and monitor.

There is also a tension between professionalization and accountability. Government relies on professions such as medicine to self-regulate, exerting far less direct control and applying far fewer performance metrics than it would with respect to any other activity on which lives depend and in which public resources are so massively invested. The American medical profession indeed possesses both expertise and ethics, but delegating public authority to decentralized decision-makers has impeded coordination in cases of collective need and has left personal biases unexamined and consequent health disparities unrepaired. Interventions that must occur prophylactically at the community level – which describes most aspects of pandemic surveillance and control – are also poorly suited to a health care system that looks for leadership to physicians in private practice who by and large are remote, disconnected, and reactive. In domains of health justice, moreover, professional processes continue to neglect the structural and institutional racism that continues to burden communities, patients, and health care workers of color.

COVID-19 therefore is a clarion call to reduce "siloing" in health professional oversight and ethics, building connections among sectors and promoting new forms of collective engagement. One neglected area is collaboration between leaders of health care organizations, who create and sustain the environments in which health professionals practice, and the licensing boards and medical societies that constitute the backbone of the professional regulatory and self-regulatory establishment.

Organizational leadership might also embrace an advocacy role on behalf of the health care workforce when engaging state and federal policymakers, such as the lobbying efforts in behalf of the Dr. Lorna Breen Health Care Provider Protection Act.[28] At the professional level, both educational and practice leaders might build on recent ethical commitments to health equity and health justice to instill and support a broader approach to social engagement and advocacy, encompassing issues such as mass incarceration and climate change.[29] This would offer health professionals opportunities to make collective contributions to the humane values that further community health and social progress, in addition to demonstrating their devotion to individual patient care.

C *Institutional Accountability and Workplace Redesign*

A third lesson for workforce well-being is that over-reliance on professionalism may be accompanied by under-developed institutional authorities and accountability. Employers have both legal duties and moral obligations to prevent workforce harm through open communication, access to PPE, and reasonable duty hours, and to treat harm through practical and emotional support. The physical and psychological effects of COVID-19 are inextricably linked,[30] and sustained COVID-19-related psychological distress is expected to impact health care workers' physical health.[31] Successful intervention requires cultural adaptation: the expectation that health care providers have superhuman qualities – with no pain, no fear, and no need for rest – must change.

Legal duties and associated incentives may derive from state health department oversight, conditions of participation in Medicare and Medicaid, federal and state occupational safety and health regulation, collective bargaining agreements, and workers' compensation insurance requirements.[32] Early in the pandemic, however, PPE shortages were dire and emergencies were declared at multiple levels. Each declaration of emergency altered the legal landscape in ways that challenged both compliance and enforcement in the health care ecosystem, ranging from crisis standards of care to a variety of exemptions, waivers, and legal immunities. As a result, it

---

[28] S. 4349, 116th Cong. (2020)

[29] Donald M. Berwick, The Moral Determinants of Health, 324 *JAMA* 225 (2020).

[30] Anaelle Caillet et al., Psychological Impact of COVID-19 on ICU Caregivers, 39 *Anaesth. Crit. Care Pain Med.* 717 (2020).

[31] See, for example, Riedel et al., supra note 21.

[32] In early 2022, the Supreme Court narrowly upheld regulations by the Department of Health and Human Services requiring vaccination or testing of health care workers in hospitals paid through Medicare. Biden v. Missouri, 142 S. Ct. 647 (2022). Simultaneously, the Court stayed the enforcement of federal occupational safety and health regulations requiring vaccination or testing in general workplaces, with the majority concluding that COVID-19 was not a workplace hazard within the meaning of the Occupational Safety and Health Act. Nat'l Fed'n of Indep. Bus. v. Dep't of Lab., Occupational Safety & Health Admin., 142 S. Ct. 661 (2022).

is not clear what recourse, if any, existed or exists for hospital workers to enforce the obligations of their organizations to protect them. Legal protections are even weaker for long-term care and home health workers.

Staffing and supplies were immediate institutional concerns among NYC hospitals. Nurses struggled to balance compassion toward dying patients and grieving family with necessary practices for infection control, and fears of critical care shortages provoked serious debate over how to allocate ventilators and other potentially life-saving resources. Although NYC hospitals developed innovative approaches to staff and family support, no systematic or lasting connections seem to have been made to the established institutional safety infrastructure.[33] "Communication and resolution" approaches to medical errors and other adverse clinical outcomes, for example, emphasize that what patient safety experts call "Just Culture" consoles and coaches unless behavior has been reckless, and those processes emphasize care for the caregiver even while recognizing that the primary injury remains that of the patient.[34]

Consider lessons from aviation safety, where non-punitive debriefing is a routine, valued practice following an adverse event or near miss. Within twenty-four hours of the miraculous 2009 landing of US Airways Flight 1549 in New York's Hudson River, there was a coordinated, supportive debriefing for crew members and family to prepare them for the emotions they might experience. An air traffic controller needed time off for a month; a flight crew member with thirty-eight years of experience never returned to work. By contrast, usual health care practice involves an explicit or implicit expectation to "go right back in," rather than seek or receive help, which leaves many health care workers feeling psychologically unsafe and fails to measure longer-term staff and patient outcomes. As a medical interviewer of the heroic Captain "Sully" Sullenberger wrote in connecting aviation to health care experience, "[t]he well-being of physicians is tied directly to the well-being of their patients."[35]

Health care organizations should take particular account of workers' COVID-19-related personal circumstances, which may constitute risk factors for distress. The best way to glean this information is to ask, then listen.[36] Risk factors include

---

[33] Eric Wei et al., Coping with Trauma, Celebrating Life: Reinventing Patient and Staff Support During the COVID-19 Pandemic, 39 *Health Affs.* 1597e (2020); Lorri Zipperer, COVID-19: Team and Human Factors to Improve Safety, AHRQ PSNet Patient Safety Primer (July 2020), psnet.ahrq .gov/primer/covid-19-team-and-human-factors-improve-safety.

[34] William M. Sage, Madelene Ottosen, & T. Benjamin Coopwood, A Quiet Revolution: Communicating and Resolving Patient Harm, in *Surgical Patient Care: Improving Safety, Quality, and Value* 649 (Juan A. Sanchez, Paul Barach, Julie K. Johnson, & Jeffrey P. Jacobs eds., 2017); David Marx, Patient Safety and the "Just Culture": A Primer for Health Care Executives (2001).

[35] Marjorie P. Stiegler, What I Learned About Adverse Events from Captain Sully: It's Not What You Think, 313 *JAMA* 361, 361 (2015).

[36] Tait Shanafelt, Jonathan Ripp, & Mickey Trockel. Understanding and Addressing Sources of Anxiety Among Health Care Professionals During the COVID-19 Pandemic, 323 *JAMA* 2133 (2020).

staff who are inexperienced, parents of dependent children, in quarantine or with an infected family member, or lack other resources.[37] As the pandemic recedes, monitoring for ongoing mental health needs should include those returning to their "home" units after being called into critical service during the surge, as their supervisors and colleagues may be unaware of their COVID-19-related experiences.

Financial uncertainty has hindered institutional responses, to the detriment of the health care workforce. To preserve critical care capacity in the spring 2020 surges, especially space and supplies, and to prevent viral spread from non-essential activities, many state governments declared moratoria on elective surgeries and other medical procedures. This had the undesired effect of depriving hospitals and other health care facilities of major payment streams and put already stressed health care workers in peril of furlough or layoff. The underlying causes are structural: hospital business strategies emphasize revenue generation over cost control and negotiate much more lucrative reimbursement rates from private insurers than from government programs. Hospitals doing exactly what they should do in the COVID-19 pandemic – caring for severely ill patients, who are less likely to be privately insured and more likely to be covered by Medicare (the elderly) or Medicaid (the poor) – risked financial collapse. It may take years for health care providers to recover lost revenues, in part because economic distress has shifted patients away from employment-based private coverage.[38] The only lasting solution may be payment reform that reduces the influence of payer mix on provider finances, although in the near term it is likely that the threat of inducing provider insolvency will take many cost-cutting proposals off the table politically.

Workplace redesign that benefits both staff and patients will require cultural change and budgetary flexibility. In addition to support programs, the COVID-19 experience has induced innovation in information systems, workflow, supply chain management, facility design, and space utilization. Unfortunately, NYC hospitals already show signs of returning to old habits and practices. For example, pandemic exigencies yielded long-overdue efficiencies in documentation, such as the ability to omit plan of cares, patient teaching, and other "check the box" requirements with little clinical utility. Almost all have reverted to pre-COVID-19 practice, missing an opportunity to rethink data usability and reduce the continuing burden on clinicians. Instead of building on innovations in virtual visits to make them more accessible to and effective for underserved populations, hospitals are moving back to in-person appointments.[39] While not always perfect, communication from hospital

---

[37] Steve Kisely et al., Occurrence, Prevention, and Management of the Psychological Effects of Emerging Virus Outbreaks on Healthcare Workers: Rapid Review and Meta-Analysis, 369 *BMJ* m1642 (May 5, 2020), www.ncbi.nlm.nih.gov/pmc/articles/PMC7199468/.

[38] Tatyana Deryugina, Jonathan Gruber, & Adrienne Sabety, Natural Disasters and Elective Medical Services: How Big Is the Bounce-Back? (Nat'l Bureau of Econ. Rsch., Working Paper No. 27505, 2020).

[39] See, for example, Ruth Reader, The Telehealth Bubble Has Burst. Time to Figure Out What's Next (Jan. 3, 2022), www.fastcompany.com/90706243/telehealth-in-2021-and-beyond.

leadership to staff reached an unprecedented level of regularity and transparency during pandemic spikes; now, it is again sporadic and limited to when there are "problems."

To help prevent backsliding as the pandemic eases, attention to the corporate, labor, and regulatory environment is required.[40] A high priority for hospital governance is to preserve and eventually reinvent middle management in clinical administration, for whom exhaustion and moral injury are not as readily apparent as among bedside caregivers but who are facing high degrees of burnout and attrition.[41] The urgency of this is heightened by a mass exit of the most senior clinical nurses, often leaving inexperienced recent graduates to train and supervise one another.[42] These staffing failures heighten the risk to patients of medical errors.[43] During COVID-19, mid-level nursing leaders felt squeezed between managing down and managing up, as they tried to cope with being asked constantly to do more with less. Given the pandemic's effect on finances, continuing to use five-year budget cycles that protect senior executive bonuses has had a pernicious effect on mid-level staffing and morale. In addition to more meaningful support for the broader caregiving workforce than "free pizza and free meals," hospitals should assist more senior nurses – many of whom have been leaving the bedside because of COVID-19-induced trauma – in pursuing educational opportunities and transitioning to other valuable roles within health care organizations.[44]

The post-COVID-19 regulatory landscape for hospitals should attempt to bridge health care-specific entities, such as the Joint Commission, to more general governmental mechanisms for workforce safety and support.[45] It should maintain "emergency" authorities under state law that reduced paperwork requirements and empowered health care professionals to work more flexibly. It should also re-examine the self-regulatory privileges that perpetuated professional hierarchies in clinical authority and earning capacity, while also artificially separating professional from institutional oversight in health care.

---

[40] For a systematic discussion of workplace adaptation, see Bernadette Melnyk et al., Associations Among Nurses' Mental/Physical Health, Lifestyle Behaviors, Shift Length, and Workplace Wellness Support During COVID-19: Important Implications for Health Care Systems, 46 *Nursing Admin. Q.* 5 (2022).

[41] Rosanne Raso, Nurse Leader Wellness: What's Changed in 3 Years?: Results of the Second Nursing Management Wellness Survey, 52 *Nursing Mgmt.* 26 (2021).

[42] See Meredith Kells & Karen J. Mathis, Influence of COVID-19 on the Next Generation of Nurses in the United States, *J. Clin. Nursing* (2022).

[43] Stephanie A. Andel et al., Safety Implications of Different Forms of Understaffing Among Nurses During the COVID-19 Pandemic, 78 *J. Adv. Nursing* 121 (2022).

[44] ANA Enter., Pulse on the Nation's Nurses COVID-19 Survey Series: Mental Health and Wellness, www.nursingworld.org/practice-policy/work-environment/health-safety/disaster-preparedness/coronavirus/what-you-need-to-know/mental-health-and-wellness-survey-2/ (last visited Mar. 6, 2021).

[45] Deloitte & Joint Commission Resources, COVID-19 Lessons Learned: A Resource for Recovery (Sept. 18, 2020), www.jcrinc.com/products-and-services/covid-19-lessons-learned-a-resource-for-recovery/.

V CONCLUSION

The COVID-19 pandemic has demonstrated the resilience of the health care work-force but has also exposed its vulnerabilities and has energized efforts to improve the practice and service environment.[46] Some lessons have been learned; for example, NYC hospitals coped far better with record case numbers from the Omicron variant than they had with the smaller initial waves of COVID-19 infection.[47] With careful design and implementation, including research evaluation and as much insulation from partisan politics as possible, these efforts can put meat on the bones of what is often called the "Quadruple Aim." In 2015, leaders at the Institute for Healthcare Improvement added "joy and meaning in the work of health care" to the Institute's path-breaking "Triple Aim" of improving the patient experience of care, improving the health of populations, and reducing per capita health care costs.[48] The core insight of the Triple Aim was its acknowledgment that current health care practice is far from optimal. Rather than accept tradeoffs among cost, access, and quality as unavoidable, self-examination and incremental innovation could yield simultane-ous sustained improvement in all three prongs of the Aim. The pandemic experi-ence confirms that patient experience, population health, and cost are all dependent as well on the fourth prong: an engaged and supported health care workforce.

---

[46] For a structured analysis of health workforce effects in several nations, see Apinya Koontalay et al., Healthcare Workers' Burdens During the COVID-19 Pandemic: A Qualitative Systematic Review, 14 *J. Multidiscip. Healthc.* 3015 (2021).

[47] Sharon Otterman & Joseph Goldstein, How New York City's Hospitals Withstood the Omicron Surge, NY Times (Feb. 5, 2022), www.nytimes.com/2022/02/05/nyregion/omicron-nyc-hospitals.html.

[48] Rishi Sikka, Julianne M. Morath, & Lucian Leape, The Quadruple Aim: Care, Health, Cost and Meaning in Work, 24 *BMJ Qual. Saf.* 608 (2015).

4

Post-Truth Won't Set Us Free

Health Law, Patient Autonomy, and the Rise of the Infodemic

Wendy E. Parmet and Jeremy Paul[*]

> *"Don't it always seem to go*
> *That you don't know what you got 'til it's gone"*
> Joni Mitchell, Canadian-American singer-songwriter

I INTRODUCTION

Numerous interrelated and deep-seated factors helped COVID-19 exact its horrific toll in the United States. Long-standing structural inequities, the depletion of public health departments, a privatized health care system poorly suited to combating a public health disaster, judicial decisions that limited public health powers, and a president who willfully undermined the pandemic response are among the many culprits. Important, too, has been the plethora of misinformation on matters ranging from the value of masks to the purported efficacy of hydroxychloroquine and ivermectin in treating COVID-19. This "infodemic," as the World Health Organization has called it, has also stymied efforts to control the pandemic through vaccination.[1] Misinformation about plagues and vaccines is not new.[2] The current infodemic, however, goes well beyond familiar forms of science skepticism or vaccine rejection. As reports roll in about people eschewing masks and vaccinations and taking unproven and dangerous drugs, it is hard not to wonder whether the United States has been gripped by a more virulent cynicism that questions whether meaningful truth can be – or need be – found at all.

Lee McIntyre and others refer to this alarming mindset as "post-truth."[3] As much as any pathogen, post-truth threatens future efforts to contain pandemics and other public health threats. While many scholars have explored the roots of the post-truth

---

[*] Many thanks to Connor Scholes, Emily Kaiser, Evan Ma, Annika Skansberg, and Hannah Taylor for outstanding research assistance, and to Linda Fentiman and Leslie Francis for their very helpful comments on an earlier draft.
[1] Vivek H. Murthy, Confronting Health Misinformation (2021), www.hhs.gov/sites/default/files/surgeon-general-misinformation-advisory.pdf.
[2] See Heidi J. Larson, Stuck: How Vaccine Rumors Start – and Why They Don't Go Away (2020).
[3] Lee McIntyre, Post-Truth (2018).

problem,[4] we focus on an overlooked piece of the larger puzzle. In particular, we look at developments within health law, generally adopted for important reasons, that may have inadvertently contributed to the post-truth climate. These developments include the creation and evolution of the doctrine of informed consent and the rise of direct-to-consumer advertising (DTCA). These doctrines, which center on patient autonomy, we suggest, may have had the side effect of encouraging individuals to believe that they can and should navigate tough medical questions without guidance from scientific or medical experts. In so doing, these doctrines may have primed people to accept misinformation and reject vaccines and masking. To prevent a similarly bleak outcome during the next pandemic, we need to consider how health law may have contributed to the post-truth problem during COVID-19. This chapter starts that conversation.

We begin in Part II by providing a brief overview of the COVID-19 infodemic. In Part III, we introduce the concept of post-truth and highlight various "attributes" that distinguish it from the healthy skepticism that accompanies critical thinking.[5] We then link the post-truth phenomenon to broader shifts in cultural attitudes toward individual choice and the embrace of subjectivity.

In Part IV, we turn to developments in health law that emphasize individual choice and have led to an erosion in the role of professional expertise. In Part V, we discuss how these developments created fertile ground for post-truth in ways that undermined efforts to mitigate COVID-19. We conclude by suggesting that if we are to avoid the next post-truth pandemic, health law scholars and policymakers must come to grips with the post-truth phenomenon and the practices within health law that may, however inadvertently, encourage it.

II THE COVID-19 INFODEMIC

Since the start of the COVID-19 pandemic, misinformation about the coronavirus, its origins, its dangerousness, and ways to mitigate it has been abundant. The falsehoods started early when President Trump lied to the public about the risks of COVID-19 and touted hydroxychloroquine as a remedy.[6] President Trump,

---

4 Id.; Margaret McCartney, Evidence in a Post-Truth World, 355 *BMJ* i6363 (2016).

5 We leave for another day whether truth can exist independently of the observer's perceptual lenses. See Peter Holtz, Does Postmodernism Really Entail a Disregard for the Truth? Similarities and Differences in Postmodern and Critical Rationalist Conceptualizations of Truth, Progress, and Empirical Research Methods, 11 *Frontiers Psych.* art. 545959 (2020).

6 Alana Wise, Trump Admits Playing Down Coronavirus's Severity, According to New Woodward Book, NPR (Sept. 9, 2020), www.npr.org/2020/09/09/911109247/trump-admitted-to-playing-down-the-coronaviruss-severity-per-new-book; Andrew Solender, All the Times Trump Has Promoted Hydroxychloroquine, Forbes (May 22, 2020), www.forbes.com/sites/andrewsolender/2020/05/22/all-the-times-trump-promoted-hydroxychloroquine; Ana Santos Rutschman, Mapping Misinformation in the Coronavirus Outbreak, *Health Affs.* (Mar. 10, 2020), www.healthaffairs.org/do/10.1377/forefront.20200309.826956/full/.

however, was not alone in spreading misinformation. Conspiracy groups, such as QAnon, popular news outlets, and prominent anti-vaccinationists spread misinformation prolifically, especially via social media.[7] Unfortunately, many Americans believed the deceptions. A Kaiser Family Foundation poll taken in fall 2021 found that 78 percent of adults either believed one or more of eight falsehoods about the pandemic to be true or expressed uncertainty about whether one or more was true.[8] Over one-third of Americans believed that the government had exaggerated the number of COVID-19 deaths, while over one-third either believed or were unsure if the government was hiding the number of vaccine-related deaths.[9] Other polls have found similar or even more alarming findings.[10]

This misinformation has taken its toll. According to the Surgeon General, it has "led people to decline COVID-19 vaccines, reject public health measures such as masking and social distancing, and use unproven treatments."[11] It has also incited "harassment of and violence against" public health workers.[12] As we discuss in Part V, it has spurred litigation against health professionals and public health measures. In short, it has made a very bad situation far worse.

III POST-TRUTH

Although health-related misinformation is not new, its impact during the pandemic has been especially worrisome. One reason is that COVID-19-related misinformation landed in a post-truth environment.

Defining "post-truth" is notoriously difficult, but for our purposes we might encapsulate "post-truth" as the widespread abandonment of any metric by which statements about the world can be judged correct or not. Delving into the nature and causes of the current post-truth environment would require exploring factors that include political polarization, the media environment,[13] loss of faith in experts and institutions,[14] and advances in our understanding of how preconceptions influence

---

[7] Rob Savillo & Tyler Monroe, Fox's Effort to Undermine Vaccines Has Only Worsened, Media Matters (Aug. 9, 2021), www.mediamatters.org/fox-news/foxs-effort-undermine-vaccines-has-only-worsened.

[8] Liz Hamel et al., KFF COVID-19 Vaccine Monitor: Media and Misinformation, Kaiser Fam. Found. (Nov. 8, 2021), www.kff.org/coronavirus-covid-19/poll-finding/kff-covid-19-vaccine-monitor-media-and-misinformation/.

[9] Id.

[10] Observatory on Social Media, Tracking Public Opinion About Unsupported Narratives (June 2021), https://osome.iu.edu/research/white-papers/Tracking%20Public%20Opinion%20Wave%207.pdf.

[11] Murthy, supra note 1, at 4.

[12] Id.

[13] See Mark Jurkowitz et al., U.S. Media Polarization and the 2020 Election: A Nation Divided, Pew Rsch. Ctr. (Jan. 24, 2020), www.journalism.org/2020/01/24/u-s-media-polarization-and-the-2020-election-a-nation-divided.

[14] Tom Nichols, The Death of Expertise: The Campaign against Established Knowledge and Why It Matters (2017).

our perception of the facts.[15] Here, we focus on three key attributes and the forces that helped propel them.

As an illustration, consider the debate over the safety of the measles-mumps-rubella vaccine. A strong scientific consensus affirms that it does not cause autism.[16] Nevertheless, a zealous movement of vaccine skeptics, who spread misinformation across social media and elsewhere, have questioned that consensus.[17]

A political community grounded in truth would ask questions and encourage continued research (which has taken place) and debate the questions raised. In a healthy informational environment, debate would be informed by the best available evidence. To put it another way, the research consensus would matter to and influence skeptics.

Such a search for truth, of course, would not guarantee consensus. On many issues, although not the vaccine–autism link, experts disagree. Moreover, many policy choices blend questions of scientific fact (do vaccines cause autism?) with social/economic/political and value choices (should vaccines be mandated?). Nevertheless, a well-functioning democracy depends upon decision-making processes that include reliance on experts to develop an agreed-upon set of facts and ongoing dialogue among voters and public officials about policy responses.

How might a society slip down the path toward post-truth so that the scientific consensus settles so few questions? Part of the answer may rest in breaches of trust by powerful public and private leaders, as exemplified by the *Pentagon Papers* and the lies leading to the Iraq War.

Deceptions in biomedical research, such as the infamous Tuskegee experiments or Elizabeth Holmes's fantasies about miraculous home blood tests, offer powerful grounds for distrust. Trust can also be undermined when officials offer seemingly inconsistent advice. For example, early statements from government officials, such as Dr. Anthony Fauci,[18] suggesting that masks would not protect the general population (grounded in part by a desire to preserve the limited supply of N95 masks for health care workers) undoubtedly hindered later efforts to encourage masks once scientists knew more about the transmission of COVID-19.

Even the most spectacular fabrications, however, need not generate more than a culture of healthy suspicion. Post-truth also requires the discreditation of science, a process that was fueled by the efforts of powerful industries, such as tobacco

---

[15] See, for example, Jamin Halberstadt et al., Emotional Conception: How Embodied Emotion Concepts Guide Perception and Facial Action, 20 Psych. Sci. 1254 (2009).

[16] Vaccine Safety: Autism and Vaccines, Ctrs. for Disease Control & Prevention, www.cdc.gov/vaccinesafety/concerns/autism.html (last visited Jan. 13, 2021).

[17] See, for example, Michiko Kakutani, The Death of Truth (2018); Larson, supra note 2; David A. Broniatowski et al., Weaponized Health Communication: Twitter Bots and Russian Trolls Amplify the Vaccine Debate, 108 Am. J. Pub. Health 1378 (2018).

[18] Grace Panetta, Fauci Says He Doesn't Regret Telling Americans Not to Wear Masks at the Beginning of the Pandemic, Bus. Insider (July 16, 2020), www.businessinsider.com/fauci-doesnt-regret-advising-against-masks-early-in-pandemic-2020-7.

companies and fossil fuel companies, to undermine the very idea of science in order to deflect criticism and regulation.[19] The resulting loss of confidence in science and the value of a productive exchange of views, informed by the guidance of experts, is the first attribute in the slide toward post-truth.

Our polarized era, however, has fostered an acceleration of a second key attribute of the rise of post-truth: a tendency to make decisions by relying on personal intuition and advice from those who share one's background and values, rather than those who have developed knowledge through lengthy study and professional experience. At first glance, asking people to rely on their own best judgment may seem like good old-fashioned American self-reliance. Personal decision-making founders, however, in the face of challenging aspects of contemporary life. Consumer markets, for example, demand that everyone become educated on multiple topics, from electricity rates to health insurance plans.[20] Mastering the many choices we face is impossible.

Yet, without trust in experts, individuals turn to the Internet and social media to glean information that confirms their previous, often uninformed, predilections. In this environment, the wondrous availability of information that originally promised the democratization of knowledge perversely facilitates the manipulation of preferences. Post-truth flourishes when people who must make more choices than they can rationally handle rely on the counsel of nonexperts whose interests or views they share. Thus, just as consumers rely on advertisements on their favorite channels or media sites to make product choices, they begin to base their health decisions on affinity and political affiliation. How else could the wisdom of wearing masks or being vaccinated turn on party affiliation, an observation confirmed in a Gallup survey revealing that as of mid-September 2021, 92 percent of Democrats had been vaccinated against COVID-19, as compared to only 68 percent of Independents and only 56 percent of Republicans.[21]

It gets worse. As individual choices move from reliance on expertise to group affiliation, choices tend to reinforce themselves. Just as sports fans view referee calls through the lens of their team affiliation,[22] people who identify with a social movement, such as anti-vaxxers, are likely to view new evidence through lenses they have already adopted. Cognitive mechanisms, including confirmation bias and the Dunning-Kruger effect, magnify distortions as people weigh new information that reinforces their predispositions more heavily, and those who know little about a

---

[19]   See Naomi Oreskes & Erik M. Conway, Merchants of Doubt: How a Handful of Scientists Obscured the Truth on Issues from Tobacco Smoke to Climate Change (2010).

[20]   Barry Schwartz, The Paradox of Choice: Why More is Less (2004).

[21]   William A. Galston, For COVID-19 Vaccinations, Party Affiliation Matters More than Race and Ethnicity, Brookings (Oct. 1, 2021), www.brookings.edu/blog/fixgov/2021/10/01/for-covid-19-vaccinations-party-affiliation-matters-more-than-race-and-ethnicity/.

[22]   See Albert H. Hastorf & Hadley Cantril, They Saw a Game: A Case Study, 49 J. Abnormal Psych. 129, 129–34 (1954).

subject are apt to overestimate their knowledge.[23] As people find themselves more deeply attached to the choices of their group, they grow steadily more comfortable with the idea that contestation about which policy to pursue or which health choice to make is more about "winning" the argument than finding the truth. And thus we slide still further toward the third attribute of post-truth: a high comfort level with the idea that there is no such thing as a fact. This "what me, worry?" stance combines rejection of one's civic duty to remain open-minded toward the ideas of experts and fellow citizens with a self-flattering notion that protects people from accepting that they are ever wrong. The result is a world in which people not only believe and act on misinformation, but in which they dismiss contrary evidence, sometimes even on their deathbeds.[24]

IV POST-TRUTH HEALTH – THE RISE OF PATIENT DECISION-MAKING

Why was post-truth so prominent during the pandemic? Why did mounting deaths and overcrowded hospitals not cause more people to follow the advice of experts? In this part, we explore the role that health law and bioethics may have inadvertently played in leading Americans to believe that they, rather than the experts, were both adept at and responsible for making decisions about COVID-19. In so doing, we provide neither a full history nor a critical assessment of the developments we discuss as there is an abundant literature. We also readily acknowledge that many other factors, including the rise of right-wing populism and ideological opposition to legal protections for some rights (e.g., abortion and gay rights), have also fueled doubts about expertise and truth. Nevertheless, accepting that law nurtures and reinforces social norms,[25] we highlight some ways in which legal developments may have altered norms about truth and expertise with respect to health.

A *Informed Consent and Patient Decision-Making*

In the fall of 2021, several COVID-19 patients sought court orders requiring their physicians to give them ivermectin and other non-standard treatments.[26] As we discuss

---

23 See, for example, Justin Kruger & David Dunning, Unskilled and Unaware of It: How Difficulties in Recognizing One's Own Incompetence Lead to Inflated Self-Assessments, 77 *J. Pers. Soc. Psych.* 1121 (1999).

24 Paulina Villegas, South Dakota Nurse Says Many Patients Deny the Coronavirus Exists – Right Up Until Death, Wash. Post (Nov. 16, 2020), www.washingtonpost.com/health/2020/11/16/south-dakota-nurse-coronavirus-deniers/.

25 Michael McCann, Law and Social Movements, Contemporary Perspectives, 2 *Ann. Rev. L Soc. Sci.* 17, 21 (2006).

26 See Jennifer Bard, Legal and Ethical Analysis of Court-Ordered Ivermectin Treatment for COVID-19, Bill of Health (Sept. 2, 2021), https://blog.petrieflom.law.harvard.edu/2021/09/02/court-ordered-ivermectin-covid/.

in Part V, such cases constitute the problematic but logical endpoint of health law's long march to promoting informed consent and patient decision-making.

An important early impetus for this march was the revulsion against the "experiments" by Nazi physicians on concentration camp victims. In 1947, the judges presiding over the doctors' trial issued the Nuremberg Code, which declared that "voluntary consent" of human subjects was "absolutely essential" to the ethical conduct of medical research.[27] The following year, the World Medical Association included patient autonomy as a key component of the "physician's pledge."[28]

Despite these advances, the abuse of human subjects continued. In the United States, the most notable (but hardly only) atrocity was the Tuskegee syphilis study, which tracked, but did not treat or inform, hundreds of Black men who had syphilis, even after the development of antibiotics.[29] Following the uproar that greeted public reports about the study, Congress in 1974 established the National Commission for the Protection of Human Subjects of Biomedical Research.[30] In 1976, the Commission released the *Belmont Report*, which cited informed consent for human subjects as its first ethical principle.[31] This principle featured prominently in the Common Rule, which regulates human subject research conducted with federal funds.[32] Although the Rule has been criticized for insufficiently protecting human subjects,[33] and has been amended to tighten some provisions while providing further exemptions,[34] it helped recalibrate "the power imbalance between researchers and their subjects, and more broadly between physicians and patients."[35]

The law's support for informed consent extends to therapeutic encounters. In 1914, in *Schloendorff v. Society of New York Hospital*,[36] Justice Benjamin Cardozo stated that "every human being of adult years and sound mind has a right to determine what shall be done with his own body."[37] *Schloendorff*, however, did not

---

[27] Evelyne Shuster, Fifty Years Later: The Significance of the Nuremberg Code, 337 *New Eng. J. Med.* 1436, 1436 (1997).

[28] WMA Declaration of Geneva, World Med. Ass'n (July 9, 2018), www.wma.net/policies-post/wma-declaration-of-geneva/.

[29] The Tuskegee Timeline, Ctrs. for Disease Control & Prevention, www.cdc.gov/tuskegee/timeline.htm (last visited Mar. 2, 2020); David M. Smolin, The Tuskegee Syphilis Experiment, Social Change, and the Future of Bioethics, 3 *Faulkner L. Rev.* 229, 229–33 (2012).

[30] Smolin, supra note 29, at 240.

[31] Nat'l Comm'n for the Prot. of Hum. Subjects of Biomed. & Behav. Rsch., The Belmont Report (Apr. 18, 1979), www.hhs.gov/ohrp/sites/default/files/the-belmont-report-508c_FINAL.pdf.

[32] Federal Policy for the Protection of Human Subjects ('Common Rule'), HHS.gov, www.hhs.gov/ohrp/regulations-and-policy/regulations/common-rule/index.html (last visited Sept. 7, 2021).

[33] See Scott Jaschik, New 'Common Rule' for Research, Inside Higher Ed (Jan. 19, 2017), www.insidehighered.com/news/2017/01/19/us-issues-final-version-common-rule-research-involving-humans.

[34] Paul Smith & Andrea Frey, Modernizing the Common Rule: Federal Agencies Revise Rule on the Protection of Human Subjects, 29 *Health L.* 10, 10–11 (2017).

[35] Smolin, supra note 29, at 240.

[36] 105 N.E. 92 (NY 1914).

[37] Id. at 93.

establish a cause of action for informed consent.[38] That came only after the social movements of the 1960s and 1970s invigorated a "profound suspicion and distrust of constituted authority," including medical authority.[39]

In 1972, in *Cobbs v. Grant* and *Canterbury v. Spence*, the Supreme Court of California and the DC Court of Appeals, respectively, held that physicians had a duty to inform patients about the risks relating to treatment that a reasonable patient would find material.[40] Each court rooted this duty in both the patient's right to self-determination and the physician's expertise. The *Cobbs* court explained:

> [T]o the physician whose training and experience enable a self-satisfying evaluation, the particular treatment which should be undertaken may seem evident, but it is the prerogative of the patient, not the physician, to determine for himself the direction in which he believes his interests lie. To enable the patient to chart his course knowledgeably, reasonable familiarity with the therapeutic alternatives and their hazards becomes essential.[41]

True, the tort of informed consent, as opposed to the ethical principle, always promised more to patient autonomy than it delivered.[42] For one thing, not all jurisdictions adopted the "reasonable patient" standard.[43] Moreover, those that did required only that physicians provide the information that a reasonable patient, rather than the actual patient, would find material.[44] Courts also limited claims to cases in which patients could show an adverse health outcome; they also recognized several exceptions, including when physicians believed that obtaining informed consent would be harmful to a patient.[45]

Nevertheless, the doctrine promoted the "ethical shift away from professional paternalism (following the doctor's identification of the patient's best interest) and toward individual autonomy (letting the patient decide, once fully informed, what was best)."[46] This approach was quickly embraced by the burgeoning field of bioethics, which treated autonomy as its most important principle.[47] Ultimately, medical practice and the larger culture adopted this shift.

---

[38] Id. at 95.

[39] David Rothman, The Origins and Consequences of Patient Autonomy: A 25-Year Retrospective, 9 *Health Care Analysis* 255, 256 (2001).

[40] Canterbury v. Spence, 464 F.2d 772, 786–87 (D.C. Cir. 1972); Cobbs v. Grant, 502 P.2d 1, 11 (Cal. 1972).

[41] 502 P.2d at 10.

[42] See Jay Katz, Informed Consent – Must It Remain a Fairy Tale?, 10 *J. Contemp. Health L. Pol'y* 69, 71, 84–85 (1994).

[43] See S. Allan Adelman, The Evolution of Patient Rights: Individual Benefits and Provider Burdens, 10 *J. Health Life Sci. L.* 66, 69 (2017).

[44] See Canterbury, 464 F.2d at 781–82, 785–87; Cobbs, 502 P.2d at 12.

[45] See Katz, supra note 42, at 77–78.

[46] Charity Scott, Why Law Pervades Medicine: An Essay on Ethics in Health Care, 14 *Notre Dame J. L. Ethics Pub. Pol'y* 245, 266 (2000).

[47] Leslie Francis et al., How Infectious Disease Got Left Out – and What This Omission Might Have Meant for Bioethics, 19 *Bioethics* 307, 311–13 (2005); Jonathan F. Will, A Brief Historical and Theoretical Perspective on Patient Autonomy and Medical Decision Making: Part 2: The Autonomy Model, 139 *Chest J.* 1491, 1495–96 (2011).

The embrace of patient autonomy was also evident in the recognition that competent patients could choose whether to continue life-sustaining care, and that the wishes of formerly competent patients should be followed even after they were no longer competent.[48] In *Cruzan v. Director, Missouri Department of Health*, the majority of the justices of the Supreme Court even seemed to accept that the Constitution offered some protection for patient decision-making regarding end-of-life treatment.[49] While states currently employ different ways of respecting private decision-making, the idea that the decision should be reserved to the patient, rather than the physician, is now widely accepted.

B *The Women's Health Movement and Reproductive Rights*

Doctrines that developed in the second half of the twentieth century around reproductive rights furthered the idea that patients should have a right to determine their own health care.

The story begins in 1965, when in *Griswold v. Connecticut* the Supreme Court struck down a Connecticut law prohibiting married couples from using contraceptives as violating the "right to privacy."[50] Eight years later, in *Roe v. Wade*, the Court held that "the right of personal privacy includes the abortion decision."[51] The *Roe* Court, however, did not see that right as one of personal decision-making. Rather, it held that in the first trimester, the choice should be "left to the medical judgment of the pregnant woman's attending physician." Despite the *Roe* Court's attempt to tie the "right to an abortion" to medical judgment, the battle over abortion quickly transformed into one between a "woman's right to choose" and the state's interest in protecting "the right to life."[52] Without recounting those debates and the many doctrinal detours, suffice it to say that, for many, support for abortion became synonymous with the claim that patients have a right to "choose" what happens to their body. At the same, litigation over abortion restrictions has highlighted questions of "expertise and credibility," as abortion opponents began relying on the claim, unsupported by credible science, that abortion harmed women's health.[53] Thus abortion became another arena in which many trumpeted patient decision-making, while science itself became discredited.[54]

---

[48] James Bopp, Jr. & Daniel Avila, Trends in the Law: From Death to Life, 27 *Idaho L. Rev.* 1, 9–10 (1990).

[49] Cruzan v. Dir., Mo. Dep't Health, 497 U.S. 261, 270 (1990).

[50] 381 U.S. 479, 484–85 (1965).

[51] 410 U.S. 113, 154 (1973).

[52] David J. Garrow, Abortion before and after Roe v. Wade: An Historical Perspective, 62 *Albany L. Rev.* 833, 837, 841 (1999).

[53] See Mary Ziegler, Abortion Politics Polarized Before Roe. When It's Gone, the Fighting Won't Stop, Wash. Post (Oct. 22, 2020), www.washingtonpost.com/outlook/2020/10/22/roe-polarize-abortion-politics/.

[54] See Aziza Ahmed, Medical Evidence and Expertise in Abortion Jurisprudence, 41 *Am. J. L. Med.* 85, 89–90, 99–103 (2015). As this chapter was in publication Roe v. Wade was overruled. Dobbs v. Jackson Women's Health Org., 142 S.Ct. 2228 (2022).

Importantly, the women's health movement supported not merely abortion rights but broader access for women to information about their health, sexuality, and reproduction. It also "expressed general dissatisfaction with the treatment of women by a patriarchal, technocratic medical system,"[55] and pressured regulatory agencies to more fully respect women's autonomy. It is not, therefore, surprising that the first foray by the Food and Drug Administration (FDA) into mandating direct-to-consumer labeling concerned oral contraceptives.[56] A few years later, the agency required patient labeling for estrogen replacements.[57] These changes were followed in 1979 by a proposal by the FDA that would have required most prescription drugs to be labeled "in nontechnical language that is directed to the patient."[58]

Courts also began to recognize patients' independent role by holding that drugmakers have a duty to warn patients, and not only their doctors, about the risks associated with birth control. As the Eighth Circuit explained in *Hill v. Searle Laboratories*, "[i]n the case of birth control, ... the patient makes an independent decision as to whether she desires a prescription drug for birth control, and if so, which method she prefers, with only limited input from the prescribing physician."[59] Such doctrinal and regulatory changes helped alter how patients and experts understood their relationship. Where the doctrine of informed consent initially assumed that patients required their physician's help to understand medical information, patients were now deemed capable of comprehending and assessing that information on their own, even as scientific evidence became increasingly contested.

C AIDS Activism and the Right to Treatment

The push for a patient's right to choose a treatment over the objections of medical authority or the state extended beyond reproductive and sexual health. In the 1970s, in a battle that foreshadowed today's fight over ivermectin, some cancer patients began to demand that the FDA approve laetrile, a derivative of apricots that its supporters claimed – without any scientific proof – cured cancer.[60] Protests and hearings were held; court battles ensued. In 1979, the Supreme Court upheld the FDA's determination that laetrile was not reasonably safe or

---

[55] Lewis Grossman, FDA and the Rise of the Empowered Consumer, 66 *Admin. L. Rev.* 627, 638 (2014).

[56] 21 C.F.R. § 310.501 (1970).

[57] Grossman, supra note 55, at 653–54; see also Requirement of Labeling Directed to the Patient, 21 C.F.R. § 310.515 (1977).

[58] Prescription Drug Products; Patient Labeling Requirements, 44 Fed. Reg. 40,016, 40,016 (July 6, 1979). For current regulations related to labeling directed at laypersons, see 21 C.F.R. § 208 et seq.

[59] 884 F.2d 1064 (8th Cir. 1989); see also Odgers v. Ortho Pharmaceutical Corp., 609 F.Supp. 867 (E.D. Mich. 1985).

[60] See generally Politics, Science and Cancer: The Laetrile Phenomenon (Gerald E. Markle & James C. Petersen eds., 2019).

effective.[61] Nevertheless, as Lewis Grossman explains, the controversy "demonstrated how popular movements for freedom of choice could shake FDA to its foundations."[62]

AIDS activists posed a far greater, and more lasting, threat to the FDA's authority. People living with HIV and AIDS and their allies pushed for a dramatic expansion of research into HV/AIDS, as well as a greater role for patients in the design and implementation of clinical trials.[63] Their efforts helped "introduce into the mainstream the argument, now often deployed, that patients, in consultation with their doctors, should be able to perform their own risk-benefit balancing, particularly when fatal and disabling diseases are at issue."[64] Their demands also spurred statutory and regulatory changes diminishing the FDA's gatekeeping role. For example, in 1986, the FDA allowed the investigational AIDS drug AZT to be prescribed outside of clinical trials.[65] The agency also proposed a new rule formalizing the compassionate use of investigational drugs.[66] In 1997, Congress passed the FDA Modernization Act of 1997, which created a new "fast track" procedure to expedite approval of life-saving drugs.[67]

Advocates for patients with other diseases soon followed the "model for direct patient involvement in FDA decision-making employed by AIDS activists.[68] Their combined efforts led to significant expansion of so-called compassionate use policies, culminating in the 21st Century Cures Act, which requires pharmaceutical companies to make those policies publicly available.[69]

Concomitantly, manufacturers worked with consumer groups to push for the Dietary Supplement Health Education Act of 1994, which allowed manufacturers to sell dietary supplements (including herbs, vitamins and botanicals) "without submitting proof of efficacy or safety." Only after several widely reported incidents of harm associated with dietary supplements did Congress in 2007 require manufacturers to report adverse events to the FDA.[70] These regulations still do not require pre-marketing review. They leave it to the consumer to assess the risks and benefits

---

[61] United States v. Rutherford, 442 U.S. 544, 555–59 (1979).

[62] Grossman, supra note 55, at 668. See also Lewis A. Grossman, Choose Your Medicine: Freedom of Therapeutic Choice in America 149–61 (2021).

[63] Raymond A. Smith & Patricia D. Siplon, Drugs into Bodies: Global AIDS Treatment Activism (2006); Steven Epstein, The Construction of Lay Expertise: AIDS Activism and the Forging of Credibility in Reform of Clinical Trials, 20 Sci. Tech. Hum. Values 408, 415–16 (1995).

[64] Grossman, supra note 55, at 673.

[65] Id. at 669.

[66] Id. at 669.

[67] Grossman, supra note 55, at 671–72.

[68] Grossman, Choose Your Medicine, supra note 62 at 192.

[69] 21st Century Cures Act, Pub. L. No. 114-255, § 3032, 130 Stat. 1033, 1100 (2016) (codified at 21 U.S.C. 360bbb-0 (2018)).

[70] Bimal H. Ashar, The Dietary Supplement Health and Education Act: Time for a Reassessment, 170 Arch. Intern. Med. 261, 261 (2010) (discussing Dietary Supplement Health and Education Act of 1994, Pub. L. No. 103-417, 108 Stat. 4325).

associated with a supplement.[71] Yet as Bimal H. Ashar has explained: "for a choice to be truly autonomous, there needs to be a substantial degree of understanding. Research suggests that this level of understanding is not typically present among patients regarding dietary supplement regulation."[72]

D *Commercial Speech*

Even as health law and bioethics promoted patient decision-making, the Supreme Court's evolving commercial speech doctrine handcuffed regulators' ability to oversee health-related information conveyed by commercial entities. The Supreme Court's early commercial speech decisions reflected the same anti-paternalistic sentiments that animated the law of informed consent and the right to make treatment decisions. For example, in one of its earliest commercial speech cases, *State Board of Pharmacy v. Virginia Citizens Consumer Council, Inc.*,[73] the Court emphasized the value of granting individuals access to information about drug costs. In recent years, however, the Court has granted more weight to the interests of commercial speakers and has made it increasingly difficult for regulators to protect the public against potentially harmful information about pharmaceuticals,[74] tobacco,[75] and other potentially dangerous products. The Court has also limited the government's capacity to compel truthful health-related information,[76] even as patients are left with greater responsibility for making decisions related to their health.

The Court's increasing solicitude for commercial speech aligns with a deregulatory agenda that furthers the interests of powerful industries whose products endanger the health of consumers.[77] It has also spurred the FDA to loosen the regulation of commercial speech in the name of patient empowerment.[78] These developments in turn helped to unleash the proliferation of DTCA of pharmaceuticals and other health-related products. By 2005, DTCA comprised 40 percent of total pharmaceutical promotional expenditures.[79]

DTCA allows pharmaceutical companies to bypass physicians as gatekeepers. Ideally, patients use the information they learn through DTCA to communicate

---

[71] Dietary Supplement and Nonprescription Drug Consumer Protection Act, Pub. L. No. 109-462, 120 Stat. 3469 (2006).

[72] George Kennett, Time for Change: Stepping up the FDA's Regulation of Dietary Supplements to Promote Consumer Safety and Awareness, 33 *J. L. Health* 47, 60 (2019).

[73] Ashar, supra note 70, at 262.

[74] 425 U.S. 748 (1976).

[75] Thompson v. Western States Med. Ctr., 535 U.S. 357 (2002).

[76] See, for example, R.J. Reynolds Tobacco Co. v. FDA, 845 F.Supp.2d 266 (D.D.C. 2012).

[77] Nat'l Institute of Fam. & Life Advocs. v. Becerra, 138 S.Ct. 2361 (2018).

[78] See Morgan N. Weiland, Expanding the Periphery and Threatening the Core: The Ascendant Libertarian Speech Tradition, 69 *Stan. L. Rev.* 1389, 1454 (2017).

[79] See Julie Donohue, A History of Drug Advertising: The Evolving Roles of Consumers and Consumer Protection, 84 *Milbank Q.* 659 (2006).

effectively with their physician.[80] Less positively, DTCA can stimulate unwarranted demand for prescriptions and weaken the physician–patient relationship,[81] as patients no longer need to rely on their physicians to learn about treatments. Indeed, in some instances, patients who learn about a medication through DTCA need not even contact (never mind rely on) their health care provider, as advertisers willingly supply them with physicians who will (without any in-person examination or existing relationship) prescribe the advertised medication.[82] In such cases, the original ideal of informed consent – in which physicians provide patients with information they need to know – remains only in form, as health care decisions increasingly become detached from professional expertise.

V POST-TRUTH DURING A PANDEMIC

In early November 2021, Aaron Rodgers, star quarterback for the Green Bay Packers, announced that he had contracted COVID-19. Rodgers, who had previously said he was "immunized" against COVID-19, explained that he was unvaccinated, and that while conferring with his physician, he was also consulting podcast host Joe Rogan, and taking not only monoclonal antibodies (which had been authorized to treat COVID-19) but also ivermectin, hydroxychloroquine, and vitamins, none of which have been shown to be effective.[83] Rodgers' announcement was startling only because of his fame. His reliance on nonexperts and his willingness to take unproven (and potentially harmful) drugs was far too common. Indeed, across the country, COVID-19 patients insisted that their physicians prescribe unapproved elixirs. In at least two dozen cases, patients went to court to force their physicians to provide such "treatments."[84] A few lower court judges granted such orders.[85]

In one sense, such cases are a perversion of informed consent and patient empowerment.

Again, in its initial formulation, informed consent imposed a duty on physicians to share their expertise with patients. It did not dispense with the idea of expertise, or suggest that patients could force physicians to provide treatments that

---

[80] Id.

[81] Id. at 683–85.

[82] Jessica T. DeFrank et al., Direct-to-Consumer Advertising of Prescription Drugs and the Patient-Prescriber Encounter: A Systematic Review, 35 *Health Comm.* 739 (2020); Anna A. Filipova, Relationship of Direct-to- Consumer Advertising to Efficiency of Care, Quality of Care, and Health Outcomes, 42 *J. Healthcare Quality* e18 (2020).

[83] Example, How Do I Get It?, Annovera, www.annovera.com/how-do-i-get-it (last visited Jan. 24, 2021).

[84] Aaron Rodgers Explains Decision to Not Get COVID-19 Vaccination in His First Comments Since Positive Test, NFL (Nov. 5, 2021), www.nfl.com/news/aaron-rodgers-explains-decision-to-not-get-covid-19-vaccination-in-first- comment.

[85] Deepti Hajela, Lawsuits Demand Unproven Ivermectin for COVID Patients, AP News (Oct. 16, 2021), https://apnews.com/article/coronavirus-pandemic-business-health-new-york-lawsuits-7ab397f26 9d1fb9083bb782f9bfc2317.

the profession viewed as harmful. In other ways, however, such cases are a logical extension of legal protections for patient decision-making, which emphasize patients' own agency. Patients' insistence on treatments that their physicians do not recommend also flows naturally from DTCA, where manufacturers bypass physicians to speak directly to patients. Indeed, the web presence of groups such as America's Frontline Doctors,[86] which promotes ivermectin and other unproven treatments, sells tee shirts, and offers to connect patients to physicians who will prescribe ivermectin for a $90 fee, relies on patients expecting to make their own decisions and a legal regime that permits DTCA. Such groups also depend on the erosion of trust of regulatory agencies, such as the FDA and Centers for Disease Control and Prevention (CDC).

Health law's embrace of patient decision-making devoid of expertise has perhaps been most evident in resistance to vaccine and mask mandates. As noted above, misinformation about masking and vaccines has been rampant. More troubling, and more connected to post-truth, is the common refrain that lay individuals should have the "right" to decide the benefits of both masking and vaccines. At times, even CDC director Dr. Rochelle Walensky has seemed to agree, stating, "[w]e really want to empower people to take this responsibility [to mask] into their own hands."[87] Some governors have joined the refrain, arguing that mandates undermine "freedom."[88]

The principle of informed consent has always co-existed uneasily with vaccine mandates.[89] Nevertheless, until COVID-19, their constitutionality was well-established.[90] In the post-truth environment, that is no longer certain, as the cry for individual decision-making has led to a deluge of cases challenging vaccine mandates. Although the legal claims raised and the doctrines implicated vary (and are beyond the scope of this discussion), the plaintiffs share the view that individuals, rather than experts, should decide whether the risks of vaccination outweigh the benefits. Further, they conceptualize vaccination as a personal, rather than a public health, issue. To the plaintiffs, and at least some judges,[91] neither expertise, medical authority, nor the public's welfare seems to count as much as individuals' subjective determination of what is true and false and what they want to do.

---

[86] Id.

[87] America's Frontline Doctors, https://americasfrontlinedoctors.org/.

[88] Ed Yong, The Fundamental Question of the Pandemic Is Shifting; We Understand How This Will End. But Who Bears the Risk that Remains?, Atlantic (June 9, 2021), www.theatlantic.com/health/archive/2021/06/individualism-still-spoiling-pandemic-response/619133/.

[89] Memorandum from Taryn Fenske, Dir. of Commc'ns, Governor Ron DeSantis to Members of the Press, Governor DeSantis Issues an Executive Order Ensuring Parents' Freedom to Choose (July 30, 2021), www.flgov.com/2021/07/30/governor-desantis-issues-an-executive-order-ensuring-parents-freedom-to-choose/.

[90] Wendy E. Parmet, Informed Consent and Public Health: Are They Compatible When It Comes to Vaccines?, 8 J. Health Care L. Pol'y 71 (2005).

[91] Example, Zucht v. King, 260 U.S. 174 (1922); Jacobson v. Massachusetts, 197 U.S. 11 (1905); Does 1-3 v. Mills, 142 S.Ct. 17 (2021) (Gorsuch, J., dissenting).

The outcome of this litigation remains for now uncertain. What is clear is that the proliferation of misinformation and the insistence on the rights of individuals to rely upon it helped to inflame the controversy over vaccination (and masking), adding to COVID-19's death toll. Perhaps even worse, it appears poised to spill over to other well-established public health tools, including vaccine mandates for schoolchildren. A world in which everyone gets to decide, bereft of evidence, which facts are true and which public health measures they should follow is a world endangered.

VI CONCLUSION

So here we are with our post-truth, epistemologically subjective pandemic. In connecting the developments that we have outlined in health law to the post-truth pandemic, we hardly mean to suggest that health law and bioethics are solely or even primarily responsible for this crisis.

Indeed, we believe that the transformation of health law that we have described is as much symptom as cause. Still, this is an important moment for health law scholars to consider how health law and bioethics may have nurtured the seeds of post-truth and complicated our battle against COVID-19 and future threats.

By prioritizing individual choice and castigating paternalism, health law may have helped – however unintentionally – to erode trust in medical and scientific expertise. At the same time, health law has sent the message that each individual must be the decision-maker and therefore must determine what is true and not true regarding their own health, without having to consider the impact of their decisions on others. Faced with such a burden and power, patients understandably rely on their social media "friends," DTCA, and the rabbit holes that algorithms send them down.

We readily acknowledge that there are no easy fixes. We certainly would not suggest that health law should – even if it could – go back to the time when "the doctor knows best." As we have shown, the move to patient empowerment arose in response to significant abuses. We do, however, believe that it is critical to consider how laws that have aimed to enhance patient autonomy and weaken regulatory oversight of markets have facilitated post-truth. We must also explore how autonomy over one's own medical decisions can be respected without endangering public health and undermining respect for expertise. While we should not go back to the bad old days, we need to find a recalibration that values the common good and recognizes that its attainment requires that discourse be informed by science.

What COVID-19 has sadly taught us is that our descent into the post-truth world, augmented by our political divisions, can be deadly. In the wake of the pandemic, not to mention the climate crisis, we need to find ways to reject the epistemological nihilism of post-truth, and the overbearing insistence on an autonomy that elevates uninformed individual choice over the common good. Nature, alas, is not bemused by our subjectivity.

5

Structural Factors Related to COVID-19 Disparities

Saida I. Coreas, Erik J. Rodriquez, and Eliseo J. Pérez-Stable[*]

I INTRODUCTION

In December 2019, an outbreak of severe acute respiratory syndrome coronavirus 2 (SARS-CoV-2) began spreading across the world.[1] Its clinical syndrome, COVID-19, has led to significant morbidity and mortality in the United States.[2] On the one-year anniversary of the pandemic, more than 31 million people had been infected and almost 560,000 people had died due to COVID-19 in the United States;[3] both of these statistics are probably underestimates. Reports have revealed stark disparities in infection, severe illness, and mortality from COVID-19 among racial and ethnic minority populations in the United States, particularly African American and Latino populations, but also American Indian and Alaska Native as well as Native Hawaiian and Pacific Islander populations.[4] The observation of this dramatically disproportionate burden of illness from COVID-19 has shone a bright light on long-standing health disparities in the United States.

The principal reason for excess infections among racial and ethnic minorities is structural. A larger proportion of these populations are employed in essential jobs that require a physical presence in settings such as food markets and public transportation. Working from home and sheltering in place are privileges that are not available to many. In addition, other important factors include: (1) living in single-family homes with spacing between structures, as opposed to densely populated urban

[*] This analysis was supported by the Divisions of Intramural Research at the National Heart, Lung, and Blood Institute and the National Institute on Minority Health and Health Disparities, National Institutes of Health. The authors do not have either conflicts of interest or financial relationships relevant to this article to disclose. The corresponding author is Eliseo J. Pérez-Stable, MD; 6707 Democracy Boulevard, Suite 800, Bethesda, Maryland 20892; eliseo.perez-stable@nih.gov.
[1] Brad Boserup et al., Disproportionate Impact of COVID-19 Pandemic on Racial and Ethnic Minorities, 86 *Am. J. Surg.* 1615 (2020).
[2] Id.
[3] Johns Hopkins Univ. & Med., Coronavirus Resource Center, https://coronavirus.jhu.edu/.
[4] Ankur K. Dalsania et al., The Relationship Between Social Determinants of Health and Racial Disparities in COVID-19 Mortality, 9 *J. of Racial & Ethnic Health Disparities* 288 (2021); Boserup et al., supra note 1.

communities, such as apartment buildings; (2) fewer individuals sharing a household; and (3) larger physical living space. Self-isolation after a potential COVID-19 exposure or initial symptoms becomes almost impossible when extended families of, for example, ten persons share a living space with two bedrooms and one bathroom. Higher poverty rates and less access to broadband Internet, or ownership of a computer, create additional barriers to accessing information and services. Once infected, a higher prevalence of underlying comorbidities, lack of health care insurance or access, and delay or avoidance of medical care has led to persons presenting with more advanced COVID-19 disease, and has led to more hospitalizations and subsequently a higher share of mortality. Such preexisting disparities have been amplified by the pandemic, resulting in worse health outcomes related to COVID-19 among racial and ethnic minority groups. It is important to understand the populations at most risk and the factors that have contributed to COVID-19 disparities.

II WHAT ARE HEALTH DISPARITIES AND WHO IS AFFECTED?

The National Institute on Minority Health and Health Disparities (NIMHD) defines a health disparity as "a health difference, on the basis of one or more health outcomes, that adversely affects disadvantaged populations."[5] Health disparities adversely affect groups of people who have systematically experienced greater obstacles to health based on a social disadvantage, in part due to discrimination or racism and in part due to being underserved in health care.[6] Populations with health disparities include racial and ethnic minorities, as defined by the US Census, underserved rural populations, socioeconomically disadvantaged populations of any background, and sexual and gender minorities.

The complexity of how or why these factors influence health outcomes is at the core of the science of minority health and health disparities. Self-identified race or ethnicity and social class are the fundamental pillars of this science and interact in ways that are not entirely clear in terms of how they produce disparities. Rarely does one factor fully account for the variance in a specific condition or outcome. As an example, data on obesity among youth between the ages of two and nineteen years show differences by race and ethnicity, with 8.6 percent of Asians, 19.5 percent of Blacks, 21.9 percent of Latinos, and 14.7 percent of Whites being obese. When these data are also stratified by the level of education of the head of household, the effects of both fundamental factors become evident. Among youth who live with a head of household who has a college education, 5.5 percent of Asians, 15.4 percent

[5] Jennifer Alvidrez et al., The National Institute on Minority Health and Health Disparities Research Framework, 109 *Am. J. Pub. Health* S16 (2019).

[6] Neeta Thakur et al., The Structural and Social Determinants of the Racial/Ethnic Disparities in the U.S. COVID-19 Pandemic. What's Our Role?, 202 *Am. J. of Respiratory & Critical Care Med.* 943 (2020).

of Blacks, 13.5 percent of Latinos, and 8.5 percent of Whites are obese.[7] Racial and ethnic disparities persist in youth obesity prevalence, even among households with a college-educated head of household.

III RACIAL AND ETHNIC DISPARITIES AND COVID-19

The COVID-19 pandemic has greatly exacerbated existing racial and ethnic disparities among US populations with health disparities and has had a disproportionate impact on these communities across the country.[8] In addition to a higher risk of infection due to structural factors, conditions associated with severe COVID-19-related morbidity and mortality, such as diabetes and cardiovascular diseases, are more prevalent among African American and Latino populations than among Whites, and are more prevalent among sexual and gender minorities than among heterosexual and cisgender individuals.[9] These chronic conditions lead to a higher risk of COVID-19-related hospitalization, exacerbated by less access to health care.[10] Other comorbidities, such as hypertension and severe obesity, are also higher in prevalence among low-income, minority populations.[11]

Within six months of the original outbreak, national data were consistently showing that African American, American Indian and Alaska Native, and Latino populations were much more likely to contract and suffer from COVID-19 than their White counterparts.[12] Despite these three groups representing only about 33 percent of the US population at the time,[13] they constituted more than 50 percent of cases and 45 percent of deaths.[14] National data indicate that American Indians and Alaska Natives, as well as Latinos, have had the highest age-adjusted and standardized prevalence

---

[7] Cynthia L. Ogden et al., Prevalence of Obesity Among Youths by Household Income and Education Level of Head of Household – United States 2011–2014, 67 *Morbidity & Mortality Wkly. Rep.* 186 (2018).

[8] Sonu Bhaskar et al., Call for Action to Address Equity and Justice Divide During COVID-19, 11 *Front Psychiatry* (2020); George B. Cunningham & Lisa T. Wigfall, Race, Explicit Racial Attitudes, Implicit Racial Attitudes, and COVID-19 Cases and Deaths: An Analysis of Counties in the United States, 15 *PLoS One* (2020).

[9] Timothy J. Cunningham et al., Vital Signs: Racial Disparities in Age-Specific Mortality Among Blacks or African Americans – United States, 1999–2015, 66 *Morbidity & Mortality Wkly. Rep.* 444 (2017); Kenneth Dominguez et al., Vital Signs: Leading Causes of Death, Prevalence of Diseases and Risk Factors, and Use of Health Services Among Hispanics in the United States – 2009–2013, 64 *Morbidity & Mortality Wkly. Rep.* 469 (2015).

[10] Dalsania et al., supra note 4.

[11] Boserup et al., supra note 1; J. M. Carethers, Insights into Disparities Observed with COVID-19, 289 *J. of Internal Med.* 463 (2020).

[12] Jazmyn T. Moore et al., Disparities in Incidence of COVID-19 Among Underrepresented Racial/ Ethnic Groups in Counties Identified as Hotspots During June 5–18, 2020–22 States, February-June 2020, 69 *Morbidity & Mortality Wkly. Rep.* 1122 (2020).

[13] US Census Bureau & US Dep't of Com., QuickFacts, www.census.gov/quickfacts/fact/table/US/ PST045219.

[14] Jeremy A.W. Gold et al., Race, Ethnicity, and Age Trends in Persons Who Died from COVID-19 – United States, May-August 2020, 69 *Morbidity & Mortality Wkly. Rep.* 1517 (2020).

of COVID-19 infection: 1.5 times higher for both compared to Whites (Table 5.1).[15] Hospitalization data have shown that African Americans, American Indians and Alaska Natives, and Latinos all experienced a higher age-adjusted and standardized prevalence of COVID-19-related hospitalization than Whites (2.85–3.70 times higher) (Table 5.1).[16]

These disparities have been observed in mortality data as well. Age-specific percentages of COVID-19 deaths by race and ethnicity, compared to the percentage of each racial and ethnic group in the US population, have revealed that Latinos in every age group have been the most affected by COVID-19, followed by African Americans, American Indians and Alaska Natives, and Native Hawaiians and Pacific Islanders.[17] More specifically, the proportion of deaths from COVID-19 among persons aged 25–54 who are Latino is at least 10 percent higher than would be suggested by their overall proportion in the population.[18] For Whites aged 25–54 years, the death rates are lower by as much as 20 percent than would be suggested by their population representation.[19] Latinos had the largest increase in the number of deaths per week in 2020 compared to the average number of deaths per week between 2015 and 2019 (53.9 percent), as compared to Whites (11.9 percent).[20] Asians (36.6 percent), African Americans (32.9 percent), and American Indians and Alaska Natives (28.9 percent) also experienced dramatic increases in deaths per week compared to prior years.[21] Furthermore, COVID-19-related death rates among African Americans, American Indians and Alaska Natives, and Latinos are more than 1.5 times higher those among Whites (Table 5.1).[22] Although national data on COVID-19 among

[15] Ctrs. for Disease Control & Prevention, Risk for COVID-19 Infection, Hospitalization, and Death by Race/Ethnicity, www.cdc.gov/coronavirus/2019-ncov/covid-data/investigations-discovery/hospitalization-death-by-race-ethnicity.html.

[16] Anna M. Acosta et al., Racial and Ethnic Disparities in Rates of COVID-19-Associated Hospitalization, Intensive Care Unit Admission, and In-Hospital Death in the United States from March 2020 to February 2021, 4 *JAMA Network Open* (2021); Ctrs. for Disease Control & Prevention, Coronavirus Disease 2019 (COVID-19) – Associated Hospitalization Surveillance Network (COVID-NET), www.cdc.gov/coronavirus/2019-ncov/covid-data/covid-net/purpose-methods.html.

[17] Nat'l Ctr. for Health Stat. & Ctrs. for Disease Control & Prevention, Health Disparities: Race and Hispanic Origin, Provisional Death Counts for Coronavirus Disease 2019 (COVID-19), fig. 3a, www.cdc.gov/nchs/nvss/vsrr/covid19/health_disparities.htm.

[18] Nat'l Ctr. for Health Stat. & Ctrs. for Disease Control & Prevention, Health Disparities: Race and Hispanic Origin, Provisional Death Counts for Coronavirus Disease 2019 (COVID-19), fig. 3b, www.cdc.gov/nchs/nvss/vsrr/covid19/health_disparities.htm.

[19] Id.

[20] Lauren M. Rossen et al., Excess Deaths Associated with COVID-19, by Age and Race and Ethnicity – United States, January 26-October 3, 2020, 69 *Morbidity & Mortality Wkly. Rep.* 1522 (2020) [hereinafter, Excess Deaths Associated with COVID-19]; Lauren M. Rossen et al., Disparities in Excess Mortality Associated with COVID-19 – United States, 2020, 70 *Morbidity & Mortality Wkly. Rep.* 1114 (2021) [hereinafter, Disparities in Excess Mortality].

[21] Excess Deaths Associated with COVID-19, supra note 20; Disparities in Excess Mortality, supra note 20.

[22] Ctrs. for Disease Control & Prevention, Provisional COVID-19 Deaths by Race and Hispanic Origin, and Age, https://data.cdc.gov/NCHS/Provisional-COVID-19-Deaths-by-Race-and-Hispanic-O/ks3g-spdg.

TABLE 5.1 *Risk of COVID-19 infection, hospitalization, and death by race and ethnicity, updated February 1, 2022*

	American Indian or Alaska Native	Asian	Black or African American	Hispanic or Latino
Cases	1.5x	0.7x	1.0x	1.5x
Hospitalized	3.2x	0.8x	2.5x	2.4x
Deaths	2.2x	0.8x	1.7x	1.9x

Source: www.cdc.gov/coronavirus/2019-ncov/covid-data/investigations-discovery/hospitalization-death-by-race-ethnicity.html

sexual and gender minority populations are not available, there is evidence that risk factors for severe disease are more frequent.[23]

IV THE SOCIAL DETERMINANTS OF HEALTH AND COVID-19

The COVID-19 pandemic has proven that the driving force behind racial and ethnic disparities stems from the social and structural factors that put minority populations at a significant disadvantage. Such factors, labeled the social determinants of health, are powerful drivers of health outcomes, can be influenced by governmental policies, and have been shown to influence COVID-19 disparities.[24] The US Department of Health and Human Services organizes the social determinants of health into the following five key domains: (1) health care access and quality; (2) economic stability; (3) education assets and quality; (4) neighborhood and the built environment; and (5) the social and community context.[25] Demographic characteristics and individually measured factors (e.g., health literacy) are also important to consider. While these disparities have been alarming to many, for others they have illuminated the unfortunate inequities in health and health care that have persisted in the United States for decades. These inequities do not arise on their own and are not independent of other factors. They are driven by underlying causes that contribute to the disproportionate burden of disparities among racial and ethnic minorities.

---

[23] Kristen D. Krause, Implications of the COVID-19 Pandemic on LGBTQ Communities, 27 *J. Pub. Health Mgmt. Prac.* S-69 (2021); Megan M. Ruprecht et al., Evidence of Social and Structural COVID-19 Disparities by Sexual Orientation, Gender Identity, and Race/Ethnicity in an Urban Environment, 98 *J. Urb. Health* 27 (2021).

[24] Ahmad Khanijahani, Racial, Ethnic, and Socioeconomic Disparities in Confirmed COVID-19 Cases and Deaths in the United States: A County-Level Analysis as of November 2020, 26 *Ethnic Health* 22 (2021).

[25] Healthy People 2030 et al., Social Determinants of Health, https://health.gov/healthypeople/objectives-and-data/social-determinants-health.

V HEALTH CARE ACCESS INEQUITIES

It has been well documented that there are inequities and disparities in health care access and quality in the United States.[26] COVID-19 has amplified existing health care disparities in highly visible ways, with issues such as a lack of or inadequate health insurance and hard-to-access health care facilities becoming even more pertinent for racial and ethnic minorities.

Compared to Whites, racial and ethnic minority populations are more likely to experience delays in receiving routine and emergency care and are less likely to have a primary care clinician.[27] Since the start of the pandemic, millions of Latinos have lost access to health care coverage due to the abrupt loss of employment.[28] African American and Latino individuals are less likely to seek care due to cost, lack of insurance, medical mistrust, concerns about immigration status, and a lack of appropriate health care facilities in one's own community.[29] A study in Chicago showed that racial and ethnic minorities and sexual and gender minority populations reported even greater disparities in accessing high-quality, culturally competent care.[30]

Patients with limited English proficiency and health literacy are also more likely to have worse health outcomes.[31] The lack of patient–clinician language concordance, limited access to professional interpreters, and a singular communication type may also contribute to ineffective and/or misunderstood health communication.[32] Part of these concerns were highlighted in a study that found African American men were less likely than White men to have health-related knowledge about the symptoms and the mechanisms of the spread of COVID-19.[33] These findings suggest that public health information may not be disseminated in ways that are equitable or equally understandable to different groups. In fact, due to concerns

[26] Thomas M. Selden & Terceira A. Berdahl, COVID-19 and Racial/Ethnic Disparities in Health Risk, Employment, and Household Composition, 39 *Health Affs.* 1624 (2020); Carethers, supra note 11; Charles Ellis et al., The Impact of COVID-19 on Racial-Ethnic Health Disparities in the US: Now Is the Time to Address the Problem, 113 *J. Nat'l Med. Ass'n* 195 (2020).

[27] Hyunsung Oh et al., Addressing Barriers to Primary Care Access for Latinos in the U.S.: An Agent-Based Model, 11 *J. of the Soc'y for Soc. Work and Rsch.* 165 (2020); Lonnie R. Snowden & Genevieve Graaf, COVID-19, Social Determinants Past, Present, and Future, and African Americans' Health, 8 *J. of Racial & Ethnic Health Disparities* 12 (2021).

[28] Leo Lopez, III et al., Racial and Ethnic Health Disparities Related to COVID-19, 325 *JAMA* 719 (2021).

[29] Allan S. Noonan et al., Improving the Health of African Americans in the USA: An Overdue Opportunity for Social Justice, 37 *Pub. Health Revs.* (2016); Dominguez et al., supra note 9; Oh et al., supra note 29; Snowden & Graaf, supra note 29.

[30] Ruprecht et al., supra note 25.

[31] Lopez, III et al., supra note 30.

[32] Rebecca L. Sudore et al., Unraveling the Relationship Between Literacy, Language Proficiency, and Patient-Physician Communication, 75 *Patient Educ. & Counseling* 398 (2009).

[33] Lopez, III et al., supra note 30; Marcella Alsan et al., Disparities in Coronavirus 2019 Reported Incidence, Knowledge, and Behavior Among US Adults, 3 *JAMA Network Open* (2020).

around COVID-19 exposure, 40.9 percent of US adults, disproportionately African American and Latino adults, persons with disabilities, and persons with underlying health conditions, delayed or avoided seeking medical care for urgent problems.[34] Concerns about COVID-19 exposure, and potentially delays to care once a person becomes ill, could potentially increase the risk of severe illness and death once medical care is sought. Delay or avoidance of medical care, including emergency and routine care, could contribute to reported excess deaths directly or indirectly related to COVID-19.[35]

VI ECONOMIC FACTORS DRIVING DISPARITIES

Due to existing economic inequality, African American and Latino populations have been disproportionately impacted by the social and financial effects of the COVID-19 pandemic.

Across the United States, racial and ethnic minorities are overrepresented in the critical infrastructure workforce, such as food retail and grocery, public transportation, and allied health professions, areas that offer no option to telework, thus making it difficult to physically distance outside of the home and therefore increasing the risk of being exposed to COVID-19.[36] Although racial and ethnic minority populations are at a higher risk of getting infected since they are more likely to be essential workers and, as a result, in constant contact with other people, they are dependent on their jobs in order to financially support themselves and/or their families. Dependency on essential work can pose a serious issue for these populations, particularly when it comes to self-isolation after a potential COVID-19 exposure. After exposure to the virus, symptoms may take from two to fourteen days to appear, although the Omicron variant causes symptoms to appear in one to three days. A variable proportion of infected persons may remain asymptomatic or experience only very mild symptoms.

Many essential workers simply cannot afford to miss any time away from work and may have limited access to at-home antigen tests, or a laboratory test, to establish the presence or absence of COVID-19 infection. Persons who work in essential sectors may also have greater difficulty in following evidence-based guidance, because of structural factors and a lower level of access to COVID-19 testing and care facilities.[37]

The disproportionate representation of racial and ethnic minorities in these employment categories has increased their risk of exposure to the virus and thus led

---

[34] Mark É. Czeisler et al., Delay or Avoidance of Medical Care Because of COVID-19-Related Concerns – United States, June 2020, 69 *Morbidity & Mortality Wkly. Rep.* 1250 (2020).

[35] Id.

[36] Thakur et al., supra note 6.

[37] Bhaskar et al., supra note 8.

to higher COVID-19 infection rates in populations with health disparities. Although some individuals have been able to work remotely or shelter at home, people with lower incomes typically live with at least one household member who is an essential worker, resulting in a higher likelihood of exposure to COVID-19. Furthermore, racial and ethnic minority populations in the United States are more likely to live in more crowded conditions and multi-generational households, making it extremely difficult to isolate if and when a household member becomes exposed to or infected with the virus.[38] One study reported that among Latino adults at high risk of severe illness, about 64 percent lived in households with at least one worker who was unable to work from home, compared to approximately 56 percent among African Americans and 46 percent among Whites.[39]

Distance learning, telework, and access to information has posed its own set of challenges for populations with health disparities. Remote learning and/or work requires a computer and/or a smartphone with an unlimited data plan, broadband Internet access, and the knowledge of how to use such technology.[40] The likelihood of having accessible and reliable home broadband Internet available is lower among non-White individuals, those with a lower income, and individuals living in a rural community.[41] As a result, there is a greater reliance on smartphones for online access among younger adults, Latinos, African Americans, and lower-income individuals.[42] In the first year of the pandemic, this digital divide was dramatic, particularly in distance learning for children. Households without access to the Internet, or that share a smartphone hotspot between multiple family members, had greater difficulties in attending online courses and completing homework assignments. Although some schools and cellphone companies offered mobile hotspots, policy efforts are needed to support affordable access to broadband Internet, particularly in underserved communities. The pandemic has revealed a structural inequity in society that can be addressed by making access to broadband Internet a public good that is managed like a utility, so that low-income households have sufficient access to it.

VII DISPARITIES-RELATED CHALLENGES

As vaccines became more widely available in the United States, there have been significant challenges with vaccine uptake by racial and ethnic minorities. National

---

[38] Thakur et al., supra note 6; Monica Webb Hooper et al., COVID-19 and Racial/Ethnic Disparities, 323 *JAMA* 2466 (2020).

[39] Selden & Berdahl, supra note 28.

[40] Angelica C. Scanzera et al., Teleophthalmology and the Digital Divide: Inequities Highlighted by the COVID-19 Pandemic, 35 *Eye* 1529 (2020); Elisabeth Beaunoyer et al., COVID-19 and Digital Inequalities: Reciprocal Impacts and Mitigation Strategies, 111 *Comp. Hum. Behav.* (2020).

[41] Pew Rsch. Ctr., Internet/Broadband Fact Sheet (2019), www.pewresearch.org/internet/fact-sheet/internet-broadband/.

[42] Id.

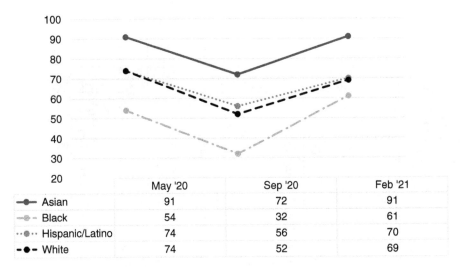

	May '20	Sep '20	Feb '21
Asian	91	72	91
Black	54	32	61
Hispanic/Latino	74	56	70
White	74	52	69

FIGURE 5.1 Percentage of US adults who say they will definitely/probably get a vaccine to prevent COVID-19 or have already received at least one dose
Source: www.pewresearch.org/science/2021/03/05/growing-share-of-americans-say-they-plan-to-get-a-covid-19-vaccine-or-already-have/

surveys showed that African American adults were less likely to say they would get the vaccine in May 2020, with only 54 percent reporting that they would definitely/probably get a vaccine to prevent COVID-19. By September 2020, there was a significant decline in the percentage of US adults who said they would definitely/probably get the vaccine, with the lowest percentage among African Americans compared to all other racial and ethnic groups (Figure 5.1). However, as of February 2021, an increase in the percentage of African Americans who reported they would definitely/probably get a vaccine to prevent COVID-19, or have already received at least one dose, was observed (Figure 5.1). An increase in willingness to get a COVID-19 vaccine could be tied to factors such as change of attitude toward the vaccine.[43] Efforts to increase trust in underserved communities are needed as vaccine willingness among racial and ethnic minorities has not been static over time (Figure 5.1).

Over the course of 2021, vaccination prevalence steadily increased for all racial and ethnic groups, although the prevalence among African Americans generally lagged behind that of other groups.[44] However, during the second half of 2021, the definition of being sufficiently vaccinated started to be questioned. As a new variant of the virus began to circulate, it became clear that a third dose of the vaccine

[43] Jeanine P.D. Guidry et al., Willingness to Get the COVID-19 Vaccine with and without Emergency Use Authorization, 49 *Am. J. Infection Control* 137 (2021).
[44] Nambi Ndugga et al. Latest Data on COVID-19 Vaccinations by Race/Ethnicity (2022), www.kff.org/coronavirus-covid-19/issue-brief/latest-data-on-covid-19-vaccinations-by-race-ethnicity/.

TABLE 5.2 *Main reasons for not intending to get a COVID-19 vaccination if available today at no cost,[a] by race and ethnicity, United States, September 2020*

Reason	All Adults (n = 1,280)		Black or African American (n = 250)		Hispanic or Latino (n = 163)		Other (n = 156)		White (n = 711)	
	Weighted %	95% CI	Weighted %	95% CI	Weighted %	95% CI	Weighted %	95% CI	Weighted %	95% CI
I am concerned about the side effects and safety of the COVID-19 vaccine	23.4	(21.0–26.0)	21.9	(16.9–27.8)	31.5	(24.4–39.4)	29.0	(21.7–37.7)	21.0	(18.0–24.4)
I am concerned that the COVID-19 vaccine has been developed too fast	21.7	(19.4–24.2)	24.4	(19.3–30.3)	17.4	(12.3–24.0)	18.6	(12.6–26.4)	22.4	(19.4–25.8)
I plan to wait and see if it is safe and may get it later	17.9	(15.8–20.3)	16.9	(12.5–22.5)	20.0	(14.4–27.2)	24	(17.1–32.3)	16.9	(14.2–19.9)
I do not trust the government	10.0	(8.2–11.8)	15.0	(11.0–20.2)	9.7	(5.7–16.1)	6.4	(3.4–11.6)	8.8	(6.7–11.3)
Something else	7.3	(5.9–8.8)	6.3	(3.9–10.0)	4.9	(2.5–9.2)	8.0	(4.5–13.3)	8.0	(6.3–10.4)

Abbreviations: CI = confidence interval.

[a] Respondents who indicated that they were not likely to get a COVID-19 vaccination if available today at no cost were asked about the reasons for their lack of intent, and then asked their main reason for not intending to get a COVID-19 vaccination.

Respondents who did not provide a response were excluded from this analysis (n = 79). All reasons included in the survey are listed in the table, except: "I don't know where to get it"; "My doctor has not recommended a COVID-19 vaccine to me"; "I didn't know I needed a vaccine against COVID-19"; "I am concerned about the costs associated with the vaccine (such as office visit costs or vaccine administration fees)"; "I don't like needles"; "I plan to use masks and other precautions instead"; "I don't like vaccines"; "I am not a member of any group that is at high risk from COVID-19"; "COVID-19 is not a serious illness"; "The vaccine could give me COVID-19"; "I think the COVID-19 vaccine will not work"; and "I already had COVID-19 and should be immune."

Source: www.cdc.gov/vaccines/imz-managers/coverage/adultvaxview/pubs-resources/COVID-online-report2020.html (i.e., a booster) would be necessary for individuals to maintain their level of protective immunity. Despite vaccines being widely available from multiple sources, racial and ethnic disparities were observed. As of February 1, 2022, in twelve states, the prevalence of obtaining a booster dose of vaccine was lowest among Latinos, followed by American Indians and Alaska Natives as well as African Americans.[45]

A critical factor in vaccine hesitancy and mistrust is the deep and justified lack of trust many populations have in the health care system and clinical research. This distrust is deeply rooted in decades of well-documented examples of racist exploitations that have affected African Americans,[46] as well as Latinos, American Indians, and Asian populations, who have also experienced unequal care and scientific mismanagement. Other key factors, such as the perceived risk of the disease and the perceived safety of the vaccine, influence an individual's willingness to be vaccinated against COVID-19.[47] Among US adults, the main reason people reported that they were not likely to get vaccinated was due to concerns about the side effects and safety of the COVID-19 vaccine, and these concerns were highest among Latino adults (Table 5.2).[48]

VIII THE NATIONAL INSTITUTES OF HEALTH RESPONSE TO COVID-19 DISPARITIES: THE COMMUNITY ENGAGEMENT ALLIANCE AGAINST COVID-19 DISPARITIES

In response to the pandemic public health emergency and related disparities, NIMHD partnered with the National Heart, Lung, and Blood Institute and the National Institutes of Health (NIH) Office of the Director to develop and launch the Community Engagement Alliance (CEAL) Against COVID-19 Disparities.[49] The initial goal of CEAL was to promote the inclusive participation of underrepresented minorities in the COVID-19 vaccine trials, which were supported by NIH and subsidized by the US government. CEAL leveraged NIH-funded investigators with many years of experience in community-engaged research to form coalitions of community-academic-public health partnerships in eleven states to address misinformation, promote trust in science, and engage communities in the clinical

---

[45] Id.

[46] Noonan et al., supra note 31; Rueben C. Warren et al., Trustworthiness Before Trust – COVID-19 Vaccine Trials and the Black Community, 383 *New Eng. J. Med.* (2020); Crista E. Johnson-Agbakwu et al., Racism, COVID-19, and Health Inequity in the USA: A Call to Action, 9 *J. of Racial & Ethnic Health Disparities* 52 (2020).

[47] Linda C. Karlsson et al., Fearing the Disease or the Vaccine: The Case of COVID-19, 172 *Personality & Individual Differences* (2021).

[48] Kimberly H. Nguyen et al., COVID-19 Vaccination Intent, Perceptions, and Reasons for Not Vaccinating Among Groups Prioritized for Early Vaccination, United States, September 2020, www.cdc.gov/vaccines/imz-managers/coverage/adultvaxview/pubs-resources/COVID-online-report2020.html.

[49] Nat'l Insts. of Health, NIH CEAL, https://covid19community.nih.gov/.

trials. Through the CEAL initiative, the NIH expects to increase the use of mitigation practices that can reduce the spread of COVID-19, disseminate accurate information about the spread of the virus, the safety and efficacy of vaccines and treatments, and increase the public's understanding of how science works.

To address COVID-19 disparities, CEAL needed to address the widespread misinformation about the vaccine and the pandemic with transparent and easy-to-understand facts based on scientific evidence in the communities most affected by COVID-19. The high level of distrust in African American and Latino communities of any governmental-, pharmaceutical-, or university-sponsored study or therapeutic undergoing evaluation through clinical trials necessitated a strong message and campaign to promote trust in science. A key component was to deliver the message clearly and through trusted local messengers that knew their communities. These included clinicians, nurses, faith-based leaders, and leaders from the community who were respected role models. This diverse partnership network was leveraged by all the sites to engage in local and media events with widespread use of social media. CEAL is built on full partnerships with community-based organizations and is guided by the principle of "Move at the Speed of Trust." The CEAL initiative can be used as a model by other governmental and large organizations to develop partnerships with communities in the quest to mitigate COVID-19 disparities. In the future, CEAL may function as a community-engaged research platform to advance health equity by addressing other pandemics.

IX THE NIH RESPONSE TO COVID-19 DISPARITIES: RAPID ACCELERATION OF DIAGNOSTICS FOR UNDERSERVED POPULATIONS

The NIH-wide effort to increase testing for COVID-19 in underserved and vulnerable populations was funded as a community-engaged research initiative in 2020 and named Rapid Acceleration of Diagnostics for Underserved Populations (RADx-UP).[50] Although RADx-UP was part of a larger effort to develop and implement tests for COVID-19, the decision to allocate substantial resources over the course of four years to this effort for underserved populations reflected NIH leadership's commitment to addressing COVID-19 disparities. To date, RADx-UP has funded seventy-nine testing projects in underserved and vulnerable communities, sixteen projects focused on school systems to promote safe return to school, twenty-one research studies on the social, ethical, and behavioral consequences of the pandemic, and a new Coordination and Data Collection Center. Collectively, these sites are in all fifty states, the District of Columbia, Puerto Rico, and the Pacific Island territories. This NIH-wide effort is co-led by NIMHD, the National Institute

---

[50] Bruce J. Tromberg et al., Rapid Scaling Up of COVID-19 Diagnostic Testing in the United States – The NIH RADx Initiative, 383 *New Eng. J. Med.* 1071 (2020).

on Aging, and the NIH Office of the Director. The goal is to understand factors that contribute to the high, disproportionate burden of COVID-19 in underserved communities and to develop strategies for addressing these disparities.

The funded projects are using principles of community-engaged outreach to work closely with communities that have been disproportionately affected by COVID-19. NIH has defined common data elements that all projects will be required to collect using standardized measures to subsequently share data in a common depository for general research use. School projects were funded to generate data on the risk of children returning to school in the 2021–22 school year; all the schools had at least 50 percent of their children who were eligible for free or reduced meals. As the pandemic has evolved, RADx-UP has launched programs that will include addressing vaccine uptake in these communities linked to the testing strategies. Efforts to create synergy between RADx-UP projects and CEAL teams are also underway.

X THE CENTERS FOR DISEASE CONTROL AND PREVENTION RESPONSE TO COVID-19 DISPARITIES: VACCINE AND HEALTH EQUITY

The Centers for Disease Control and Prevention (CDC) has responded to racial and ethnic disparities in COVID-19 by providing funding to jurisdictions, health departments, and organizations to promote COVID-19 vaccination among African Americans and Latinos.[51] Funding has been spread across the United States and its territories, and has included awards to 64 jurisdictions, 108 health departments, and 71 organizations. The purpose of the funding has either been to (1) launch new programs and initiatives to increase vaccine access, acceptance, and uptake in communities disproportionately impacted by COVID-19; (2) support efforts to address COVID-19 health disparities; (3) support COVID-19 prevention and control using community health worker services; or (4) support training, technical assistance, and evaluation to community health worker services involved in COVID-19 response efforts.

Additionally, the CDC has prioritized vaccine equity for racial and ethnic minority groups through funding to thirty-four national, state, tribal, and community organizations through their existing Racial and Ethnic Approaches to Community Health (REACH) program, as well as eight national organizations, four medical organizations, and three national foundations.[52] Originally launched in 1999 and most recently renewed in 2018, the goal of the REACH program has been to improve health, prevent chronic diseases, and reduce health disparities among racial and ethnic populations with the highest risk or burden of chronic

---

[51] Ctrs. for Disease Control and Prevention, COVID-19 Vaccine Equity for Racial and Ethnic Minority Groups, www.cdc.gov/coronavirus/2019-ncov/community/health-equity/vaccine-equity.html.

[52] Id.

disease using culturally tailored interventions to address preventable risk behaviors. By providing vaccine-specific funding through this program, the CDC has leveraged the network of organizations supported by REACH to further address disparities in COVID-19 vaccination.

XI CURRENT AND FUTURE DIRECTIONS

Further efforts must be made to build trust, dispel myths, and directly address the misinformation that exists. This can be done through the effective use of credible messengers within communities who should be credentialed professionals and community members. The key is that the information that is shared must be factual, reliable, and consistent, and generally avoid the subtlety of uncertainty that accompanies academic discourse. Elected representatives, policymakers, economists, educators, public health professionals, faith-based leaders, and local community leaders must join in a multidisciplinary, coordinated effort to actively and systematically advance health equity. Cultural competency training is fundamental to engage all entities, including local community leaders and stakeholders.

We have an obligation to take concrete steps to dismantle systematic inequities in order to improve the lives of people experiencing disparities. To reduce disparities in COVID-19 outcomes, structural and institutional racism and biases in health care systems must be addressed through policy and legal change, and proportionally representative inclusion at all levels of decision-making. Disparities and inequities in health are not caused by one factor and as such cannot be eliminated by a single intervention. Similarly, the root causes of disparities in any health indicator, including COVID-19, are multi-factorial and require both short- and long-term strategies. These strategic interventions and investments should focus not only on broader health insurance coverage and improvements in health care, but also on building healthy communities for all by addressing the social and structural issues affecting the neighborhoods of populations with health disparities; these issues include quality of schools, the availability of jobs paying a living wage, access to broadband Internet, and other structural determinants. The most sustainable impact will be achieved through long-term interventions and investments – those that are designed to achieve equity – that address the social and structural determinants of health.

COVID-19, Disparities, and Vulnerable Populations

Introduction

Asees Bhasin

COVID-19 has claimed over one million lives in the United States alone. The disease transcends race, class, gender, age, and religion, prompting many to refer to it as "the great equalizer." The chapters in Part II of this volume debunk the "level playing field" myth and instead examine how the pandemic lays bare the social fault lines of our society. Each of these chapters delves into a discussion about how COVID-19 disproportionately impacts a specific historically marginalized community or population and exacerbates existing inequities while simultaneously giving rise to new ones.

In Chapter 6, "Tolerating the Harms of Detention: With and Without COVID-19," Dr. Jaimie Meyer, Marisol Orihuela, and Judith Resnik examine the impact of COVID-19 on people in detention and locate the present moment within a historical movement for greater rights for prisoners. This chapter describes the poor spacing, lack of shared spaces and ventilation, and the scarcity of resources in prisons which give rise to "tinderbox situations" that lead to high rates of infections and clusters of outbreaks. It also discusses the legal and public health call for "dedensification" and critiques the institutional response to these demands as well as the limitations of the Eighth Amendment standard of "deliberate indifference to serious medical needs" in questioning conditions of confinement.

In Chapter 7, "A Bend Toward Greater Realized Health Equity and Racial Justice: How the Confluence of the COVID-19 Pandemic and Structural Racism Will Monumentally Shape American Law and Policy," Scott Schweikart, Fernando De Maio, Mia Keeys, Joaquin Baca, Brian Vandenberg, and Dr. Aletha Maybank examine how the inequitable epidemiological burden of COVID-19 falls on Black, Indigenous, and People of Color communities in terms of tangible indicators such as mortality rates and life expectancy, as well as more ancillary indicators such as job loss and decline in employment income. This chapter demonstrates why such disparities cannot be attributed simply to preexisting conditions such as asthma and obesity; instead, a holistic examination of the impact of white supremacy and racism is warranted. Building on Abbe Gluck's position that traditional health law should encompass public law that is defined by the role of the government, this chapter compellingly argues that factors such as structural racism are core areas of law related to the social and structural determinants of health, and further shows how nearly all areas of law could be deemed "health law" due to their impact on health equity.

Govind Persad and Jessica Roberts in Chapter 8, "Access to Vaccines and Critical Care Treatments for Older People and People with Disabilities," take a more theoretical approach, outlining frameworks governing the formal allocation of critical care and vaccines in times of scarcity and exploring whether certain protocols and policies have the result of magnifying disadvantages for older Americans and people with disabilities. This chapter also discusses frameworks that could remediate disadvantages through intentional efforts, but goes on to describe how implementing such approaches could be made difficult due to barriers such as unconscious biases of health care providers and lack of transportation and technology, all of which make it hard for elderly people and people with disabilities to access care.

In Chapter 9, "Humane and Resilient Long-Term Care: A Post-COVID-19 Vision," Nina Kohn details the devastating number of deaths and infections in long-term care facilities and, as does the chapter on incarceration, likens them to tinderboxes. This chapter attributes "preventable suffering" in long-term care facilities to public health failures, such as the lack of mandates for testing residents and staff, a limited supply of personal protective equipment, and a bumpy vaccine rollout. It also concretely identifies the lack of regulation and failure to implement existing regulations as problems made visible by COVID-19.

Each of these chapters reckons with the possibility that the pandemic "is a portal, a gateway between one world and the next," as writer and political activist Arundhati Roy has described it. Chapter 6 on incarceration is less optimistic and exposes the tension between the heightened awareness of health risks to incarcerated populations and the state's continuing appetite for mass incarceration and tolerance for debilitating modes of detention. In Chapter 7, on structural racism, the authors take a more optimistic view, finding that the pandemic's legacy may include expanded health care access, criminal justice reform, and correction of historical redlining – each of which favorably impacts health equity. In Chapter 8, the authors put forth lessons learned from the pandemic, including the need for "debiasing" care and improving access to resources such as vaccines. Chapter 9, on long-term care, also focuses on what can be learned from the pandemic and outlines how financial incentives can be used to improve the quality of care.

Upon perusing these chapters, the reader will understand exactly why it is a mistake to think of the pandemic as an equalizer instead of a multiplier of inequities. That said, the purpose of these chapters is not to encourage despair, but to foster calls to action and make tangible legal and policy recommendations. It is powerful that these authors see this pandemic as an inflection point for more than mere superstructural changes to the policy framework, and intentionally identify deeper issues, such as mass incarceration, racism, ableism, and the lack of community-based care, as impeding us from creating a safer, healthier, and more equitable future for our society's most vulnerable people.

6

Tolerating the Harms of Detention, With and Without COVID-19

Jaimie Meyer, Marisol Orihuela, and Judith Resnik[*]

I INTRODUCTION

What does COVID-19 teach about the lives of people in detention and the obligations of those running such facilities? How should the experiences of this pandemic inform the body politic about COVID-19 and about incarceration?

In a host of ways, COVID-19 has been radically disruptive. Yet, for people in detention, whether housed in jails before trial, in prisons after conviction, or as immigrants potentially subject to deportation, COVID-19 presents challenges that they faced before this pandemic. The loss of free movement and autonomy is what detention in the United States currently is. A risk of contagion accompanies confinement, which too often entails hyper-density as well as profound isolation, if people are held in solitary confinement.

The stunning dysfunction, expense, and racial inequities of the prison system have become topics of national concern. From a variety of vantage points (whether from conservative groups described as "right on crime" or progressive activists), curbing incarceration has become imperative. When COVID-19 hit, some commentators thought that it would provide a new impetus for radical revisions in support of the prison abolition movement. Yet, the heightened risks of COVID-19 atop the other harms incarcerated people face have not, to date, dislodged widespread commitments in the United States to incarceration.

[*] Thanks to Yale Law School students Adela Lilollari, Ellie Driscoll, Sonya Jacobs, and Alexandra Ricks for superb research assistance; to Abbe Gluck, Eunice Cho, Margo Schlanger, and David Fathi for comments; to lawyers in a COVID-19 network chaired by Margo Schlanger, David Fathi, and Sarah Grady; and to Sarah Russell, Alexandra Harrington, Tessa Bialik, David Golub, Jonathan Levine, and clinical students at Quinnipiac School of Law, Yale Law School, and University of Buffalo School of Law who joined on behalf of people incarcerated at the Federal Correctional Institution at Danbury, Connecticut to lessen the harms of COVID-19 and of other health care failures. Under the auspices of Sharon Dolovich at the University of California, Los Angeles, a remarkable database of COVID-19-related detention policies and litigation is available. See COVID Behind Bars Data Project, UCLA Law, https://uclacovidbehindbars.org.

This chapter analyzes how the experiences of COVID-19 for people in detention illuminate both the achievements and the limits of the previous decades. Health care became inscribed as a constitutional right of detained and incarcerated people, yet its implementation remained elusive. COVID-19 underscored the total dependence of detained people on the governments that confine them and made vivid the health care failures endemic before COVID-19 and the degree of connection between prisons and the communities in which they sit. The divisive debates about regulation, government obligations, and the need for joint venturing to reduce the risk of disease have shaped the responses to COVID-19, in and outside the prison gates.

II COVID-19 – IN AND OUT OF PRISON

Congregate settings such as jails and prisons enable the rapid spread of infectious diseases that are transmitted person to person, especially those passed by droplets emitted by coughing and sneezing. People are generally required to share bathrooms, showers, eating areas, and other common spaces. Many facilities are old, dilapidated, and have poor ventilation.

The density of prison populations, before and after the development and availability of COVID-19 testing, vaccines, and treatment, is an obvious problem. Detained people arrive from other institutions, as do visitors and service providers, including full-time staff, contract personnel, vendors, health care professionals, attorneys, and religious leaders. Under usual circumstances, people in need of specialized health care are sent to outside medical facilities.

Once COVID-19 hit, international and national public health organizations began to provide some guidance. In March 2020, the World Health Organization released "Preparedness, Prevention and Control of COVID-19 in Prisons and other Places of Detention."[1] Shortly thereafter, the Centers for Disease Control and Prevention (CDC) put forth its "Interim Guidance on Management of COVID-19 in Correctional and Detention Facilities."[2] Both documents called for operationalizing basic tenets of infection prevention: cleaning and disinfecting, hand hygiene, testing, contact tracing, quarantining, and medical isolation. Yet, and to the dismay of many health care experts, incarcerated people, and their families, the CDC guidelines were silent on an important facet of prevention: lowering prison population density.

Given poor equipment, limited resources and, at times, a lack of commitment, implementation of the guidance provided was uneven. Most facilities lacked

---

[1] World Health Org., Eur. Reg'l Office, Preparedness, Prevention and Control of COVID-19 in Prisons and Other Places of Detention (Mar. 15, 2020), www.euro.who.int/en/health-topics/health-determinants/prisons-and-health/publications/2020/preparedness,-prevention-and-control-of-covid-19-in-prisons-and-other-places-of-detention,-15-march-2020-produced-by-whoeurope.

[2] Ctrs. for Disease Control & Prevention, Interim Guidance on Management of Coronavirus Disease 2019 (COVID- 19) in Correctional and Detention Facilities (June 9, 2021), www.cdc.gov/coronavirus/2019-ncov/community/correction-detention/guidance-correctional-detention.html.

disinfecting supplies and adequately trained personnel to support infection prevention. Despite mandates for soap and hand sanitizer, prisons set time limits on how
long people could use sinks; gave out minimal amounts of free soap; required prisoners to purchase (if they could) more disinfectants; and rejected sanitizers because
they are often alcohol-based, flammable, or potentially ingestible.

Moreover, many facilities did not have spaces for appropriate medical quarantine.
Some people were warehoused in common areas and others put in cells designed to
isolate for punishment. Some institutions imposed lockdowns that cut off access to
outside health care providers and often prevented specialists, as well as lawyers, family,
and other visitors, from coming in. Nonetheless, staff continued to go in and out, and
some facilities admitted new people into detention. In public health terms, the result
was a "tinderbox scenario" in which rampant spread occurred, in and around prisons.

In July 2020, the *New York Times* reported that 80 percent of the largest clusters of
COVID-19 cases had occurred in prisons.[3] By November 2020, the health disparities
between people residing and working in prisons and the general public widened. Staff
in federal and state prisons were 3.2 times more likely to be infected with COVID-19
compared to the US population, and the likelihood for incarcerated people was 1.4
times higher still.[4] As of June 2021, one report identified 398,627 COVID-19 cases
and 2,715 deaths of people confined in prisons.[5] In another model of the impact which
controlled for differences in race and gender, the death rate from COVID-19 in prisons was three times higher than in the general US population.[6] COVID-19 infection
rates in Immigration and Customs Enforcement (ICE) detention were twenty times
higher than in the general population and five times greater than in prisons.[7]

Yet such estimates were an undercount. Not all systems keep high-quality records
or make complete and accurate accountings public. In the summer of 2021, researchers at the University of California, Los Angeles-based *COVID Behind Bars Data
Project* reported that several states had stripped public-facing dashboards of relevant
information on infection and death rates.[8] These statistics have public health implications beyond those facilities. As noted, staff members come in and out, and detained
people rely on area hospitals for acute care. A 2020 modeling study predicted that,

3 Coronavirus in the U.S.: Latest Map and Case Count, NY Times, www.nytimes.com/interactive/2021/
   us/covid-cases.html#clusters (last visited July 2020).
4 Julie A. Ward et al., COVID-19 Cases among Employees of U.S. Federal and State Prisons, 60 *Am. J.
   Preventive Med.* 840, 841 (2021).
5 The Marshall Project, A State-By-State Look at 15 Months of Coronavirus in Prisons (July 1, 2021),
   www.themarshallproject.org/2020/05/01/a-state-by-state-look-at-coronavirus-in-prisons.
6 Brendan Saloner et al., COVID-19 Cases and Deaths in Federal and State Prisons, 324 *JAMA* 602, 603
   (2020).
7 Isabelle Niu & Emily Rhyne, 4 Takeaways from Our Investigation into ICE's Mishandling of
   COVID-19, NY Times (Apr. 25, 2021), www.nytimes.com/2021/04/25/video/immigration-detention-
   covid-takeaways.html.
8 Michael Ollove, Some States Are Cloaking Prison COVID Data, Pew Charitable Trusts: Stateline
   (Oct. 27, 2021), www.pewtrusts.org/en/research-and-analysis/blogs/stateline/2021/10/27/some-states-are-
   cloaking-prison-covid-data.

were every intensive care unit bed made available for sick detainees, COVID-19 outbreaks in nine ICE detention centers would, within three months, overwhelm local intensive care units within a fifty-mile radius, and that the capacity to care for others would be greatly reduced. Other researchers focused on the comparable impacts to the community from COVID-19 in prisons.[9] For example, a multi-county study using data from the summer of 2020 estimated that incarceration contributed to over half a million COVID-19 cases both inside facilities and in the surrounding communities.[10]

III SEEKING THE PROTECTION OF THE LAW

Documentation of detention facilities' health care failures came by way of expert analyses provided to legislatures, government officials, and courts. One overview of the inadequacies in the Federal Bureau of Prisons (BOP), with some 120 facilities across the United States, came from testimony by Homer Venters, a physician and epidemiologist who had served as the Medical Director and Chief Medical Officer of New York City Correctional Health Services, and then as a member of the Biden–Harris COVID-19 Health Equity Task Force.[11] In his April 14, 2021 statement to the US Senate Judiciary Committee, Dr. Venters reported that COVID-19 "revealed a disturbing lack of access to care" in general. To seek care in the BOP, a written request had to be submitted; with and without the pandemic, requests were ignored, mishandled, or received a delayed response.

The consequence, as Dr. Venters reported, was that "when COVID-19 arrived, incarcerated people relied on broken systems of sick call to seek care." Individuals who did report COVID-19 symptoms were often met with delays; that slow response resulted in belated care and isolation, which meant that contagious individuals could unwittingly transmit the virus to others. For people who had other medical issues, the situation became dire. Many described disabling delays – before as well as during acute phases of COVID-19 – in receiving specialized and necessary care. The result, according to Dr. Venters, was that the "pre-existing weakness in the BOP health services worsened the morbidity and mortality of COVID-19."[12]

---

[9] Michael Irvine et al., Modeling COVID-19 and its Impacts on US Immigration and Customs Enforcement (ICE) Detention Facilities, 2020, 97 *J. Urb. Health* 439, 444 (2020); see also Danielle Wallace et al., Is There a Temporal Relationship between COVID-19 Infections among Prison Staff, Incarcerated Persons and the Larger Community in the United States?, 18 *Int'l J. Env't Rsch. Pub. Health* 6873 (2021).

[10] Gregory Hooks & Wendy Sawyer, Mass Incarceration, COVID-19, and Community Spread, Prison Pol'y Initiative (Dec. 2020), www.prisonpolicy.org/reports/covidspread.html#aggregate.

[11] Health Priorities for the Federal Bureau of Prisons: Hearing Before the U.S. Senate Comm. on the Judiciary, 117th Cong. 1, 3 (Apr. 14, 2021) (statement of Dr. Homer Venters), https://s3.documentcloud .org/documents/20616259/ventersbop.pdf.

[12] Id. at 3–4; see also Katie Park, Keri Blakinger, & Claudia Lauer, A Half-Million People Got COVID-19 in Prison. Are Officials Ready for the Next Pandemic?, Marshall Project (June 30, 2021), www.themarshallproject .org/2021/06/30/a-half-million-people-got-covid-19-in-prison-are-officials-ready-for-the-next-pandemic;

Parallels abounded in the states. In October 2021, a California state court judge provided more than 100 pages on the failures in the state. His conclusion was that California's Department of Corrections had caused "the worst epidemiological disaster in California correctional history;" rather than comply with the various recommendations to mitigate harms, "it chose to litigate the matter while people died."[13]

The lawsuit that prompted that account is one marker of significant changes that have been won by people in detention who, in prior centuries, had virtually no legal protection. In the 1960s, incarcerated people around the United States challenged the injustice of their exclusion from constitutional rights. Through political protests, petitions to government officials, and pleadings in courts, incarcerated people pushed the law to make good on what they read the Constitution to promise: the equal protection of the law and a ban on cruel and unusual punishments. Prisoners asserted that they had rights to a modicum of safety, sanitation, and activities and to protection against violence, such as being whipped, starved, stripped, or held in cold bare cells.[14]

The specific issue of health care reached the Supreme Court in 1976 through the efforts of J.W. Gamble, who was incarcerated in Texas. He filed a handwritten petition and told a federal judge that, while working, he had been hit by a 600-pound bale of cotton. Although seen by prison doctors, the prison did not follow through on the doctor's prescriptions and then sent him to solitary confinement as punishment because of his inability to work. Reversing a lower court decision that had thrown Gamble out of court, appellate judges noted the "woefully inadequate" medical services; one facility had a single doctor for 17,000 incarcerated people.[15]

What *does* the Constitution say about health care in prisons? The Fifth and Fourteenth Amendments protect "life, liberty, and property" from deprivations without "due process," and the Eighth Amendment prohibits "cruel and unusual punishments" from being used on those serving a criminal sentence. Before Gamble's case went to the Supreme Court, a few lower courts concluded that, either as a matter of a person's "liberty" or because of the ban on "cruel" punishments, prison officials had to provide some health care, but many judges responded to only the direst situations. Writing for the majority honing in on what the Eighth Amendment required, Justice Thurgood Marshall explained in *Estelle v. Gamble* that the ban on cruel and unusual punishments embodied "broad and idealistic concepts of dignity, civilized standards, humanity, and decency," which required states not to be deliberately indifferent "to serious medical needs."[16]

Eddie Burkhalter et al., Incarcerated and Infected: How the Virus Tore Through the U.S. Prison System, NY Times (Apr. 10, 2021), www.nytimes.com/interactive/2021/04/10/us/covid-prison-outbreak.html.

[13] In re Hall, Nos. SC212933, 213244, 212566 at 112–13 (Cal. Super. Ct. Marin Cnty. Nov. 16, 2021).

[14] See, generally, Judith Resnik et al., Punishment in Prison: Constituting the "Normal" and the "Atypical" in Solitary and Other Forms of Confinement, 115 *Nw. U. L. Rev.* 45 (2020); Margo Schlanger, Beyond the Hero Judge: Institutional Reform Litigation as Litigation, 97 *Mich. L. Rev.* 1994 (1999).

[15] Gamble v. Estelle, 516 F.2d 937, 940 (5th Cir. 1975).

[16] Estelle v. Gamble, 429 U.S. 97, 102, 104 (1976).

Even as this constitutional pronouncement was a major breakthrough, its test raises many questions. If a prison system does not provide adequate care, why should the *intent* – as contrasted with knowledge – of the administrators matter? And why should the burden rest with the incarcerated person? Those points were part of the dissent in *Estelle* by Justice John Paul Stevens, criticizing the majority's "deliberate indifference" requirement.

Losing *and* winning is one way to understand what happened thereafter. That ruling insulated prison officials, who could rebut claims by arguing they did not have the requisite level of intent to be subjected to injunctive orders to make changes or be held liable for monetary damages. Less than nine months after Mr. Gamble "won" in the Supreme Court, the appellate court dismissed his case because he could not meet the "rigorous guidelines" of showing the prison system's indifference to "satisfy" the Supreme Court's standard.[17]

Yet the Supreme Court's decision also opened the courthouse door to arguments about the level and kind of care provided in detention. The opinion has supported a host of court rulings requiring system-wide relief to improve medical and mental health services for people in prison. In 2011, obligations established in *Estelle v. Gamble* were part of another Supreme Court decision upholding the release of people from prison in California because massive overpopulation rendered it impossible to provide minimally adequate health care.[18] *Estelle v. Gamble* also spawned new organizations aiming to improve care.[19] Several private corporations saw the potential for profits. A few have a large market share of lucrative contracts and long lists of complaints about their failures to provide adequate services.

A distinctive feature of the *Estelle v. Gamble* ruling needs to be highlighted. In contrast to the constitutions of many other countries, the Constitution of the United States has rarely been read to require affirmative support from the government. Many commentators see the Constitution as creating "negative liberties" that produce freedom from government intervention rather than "positive rights" of provisioning. Moreover, even as other countries have social policies that provide for universal health care, as well as education and other benefits, the United States currently does not. Yet the Court's 1976 requirement that prisons not be deliberately indifferent to serious medical needs does impose an affirmative obligation to provide health care. Prisons are, therefore, one of the few places in the United States where a form of access to health care has a degree of constitutional protection.

In the decades since *Estelle v. Gamble*, it has become clear that *some* level of health care should not be equated with *high-quality* care. Long before the arrival of COVID-19, an array of reports and lawsuits documented the ongoing failures of

---

[17] Gamble v. Estelle, 554 F.2d 653, 654 (5th Cir. 1977).
[18] Brown v. Plata, 563 U.S. 493 (2011).
[19] See, for example, National Commission on Correctional Health Care, www.ncchc.org/ (last visited Oct. 20, 2021); Community Oriented Correctional Health Services, https://cochs.org/ (last visited Oct. 20, 2021); American College of Correctional Physicians, https://accpmed.org/ (last visited Oct. 20, 2021).

prison systems to provide minimally adequate care as compared to what was available in the community.[20]

IV DE-DENSIFICATION AS A PUBLIC HEALTH STRATEGY AND AS A LEGAL OBLIGATION

This account makes plain that detention itself is a major source of risk of infections. When COVID-19 hit, social distancing, coupled with masks and, as the science developed, testing and vaccines, became the safety protocols for people for whom these were available. In congregate settings, when masks, testing, and vaccines were often not available, "de-densification" was central. One study identified both testing and de-densification as key, as together they reduced transmission by more than 55 percent.[21]

Prison overcrowding is an artifact of decades of social policy. Beginning with the political shifts in the latter part of the twentieth century, a "war on crime," fueled by racist tropes, produced prosecution policies and sentencing laws that resulted in massive numbers of people held in detention.[22] Incarceration rates that had been relatively stable (with about 320,000 people incarcerated nationwide in 1980) rose to record highs.[23] By the end of 2020, the Federal Bureau of Justice Statistics reported that 1.4 million people were incarcerated in prisons, with another 750,000 held in jails. About 58 percent of the US population was categorized as "white," even though only 31 percent of people in prison are white prisoners. In this context, as in many others, the risks of detention are borne disproportionately by people of color.[24]

The public health call to de-densify was in sync with the goals of the decarceration movement, which has been vividly embodied in Angela Davis's call for "prison abolition."[25] Advocates' hope was that COVID-19, along with the myriad harms and costs of incarceration, would widen acceptance of the need to limit incarceration.[26]

---

[20] US Dep't of Just., Office of the Inspector Gen., Review of the Federal Bureau of Prisons' Medical Staffing Challenges (Mar. 2016), https://oig.justice.gov/reports/2016/e1602.pdf; see, for example, Braggs v. Dunn, 257 F.Supp.3d 1171, 1267–68 (M.D. Ala. 2017); Braggs v. Dunn, 367 F.Supp.3d 1340 (M.D. Ala. 2019).

[21] Giovanni Malloy et al., The Effectiveness of Interventions to Reduce COVID-19 Transmission in a Large Urban Jail, 11 *BMJ Open* 1, 6 (2020).

[22] See, for example, Jeremy Travis, Bruce Western & F. Stevens Redburn, The Growth of Incarceration in the United States: Exploring Causes and Consequences 104–29 (2014); Elizabeth Hinton, From the War on Poverty to the War on Crime: The Making of Mass Incarceration in America (2017); Marie Gottschalk, The Prison and the Gallows: The Politics of Mass Incarceration in America (2006).

[23] Bureau of Just. Stat., Prisoners in 1980, at 1 (1981), https://bjs.ojp.gov/content/pub/pdf/p80.pdf.

[24] Ann Carson, Bureau of Just. Stat., Prisoners in 2019, at 2, 6 (2020), https://bjs.ojp.gov/content/pub/pdf/p19.pdf; Zhen Zeng & Todd D. Minton, Jail Inmates in 2019, at 2 (2021), https://bjs.ojp.gov/content/pub/pdf/ji19.pdf; U.S. Census Bureau, Racial and Ethnic Diversity in the United States: 2010 Census and 2020 Census (Aug. 12, 2021), www.census.gov/library/visualizations/interactive/racial-and-ethnic-diversity-in-the-united-states-2010-and-2020-census.html.

[25] Angela Y. Davis, Are Prisons Obsolete? (2011); see also Ruth Wilson Gilmore, Golden Gulag: Prisons, Surplus, Crisis, and Opposition in Globalizing California (2007).

[26] See, for example, Joshua Petersen, James Cavallaro & Andrew Clark, Connecticut at the Crossroads: COVID-19, the State Budget Crisis and the Path Towards Decarceration, Public Safety and

Advocates deployed that movement's slogans (such as "Free Them All") and coined others (such as "Free Them All 4 Public Health") to mark the abolitionist aim.

Whether abolitionist or not, an array of communities and professionals mobilized to try to mitigate the risk COVID-19 caused in detention. People in prison and their lawyers filed hundreds of lawsuits, some seeking individual releases and others class-wide remedies.[27] One theory was that, because COVID-19 infection put a person at risk of illness and death, COVID-19 turned a lawful sentence for a term of years into unlawful detention. The remedy was release, either by "enlarging" the place of custody to permit serving time outside of prison, to admit a person to "bail," or to grant a petition for habeas corpus.[28] Another theory was that, under *Estelle v. Gamble*, prison systems were deliberately indifferent to known medical needs. Some lower court judges agreed and ordered soap, masks, distancing, reduction of time, release of eligible individuals, and more.

These efforts were complicated by a 1996 statute known as the Prison Litigation Reform Act, through which Congress circumscribed judges' authority to respond when prisoners sought relief from conditions of confinement. One line of COVID-19 cases rejected lawsuits because prisoners had not "exhausted" administrative remedies by asking prison officials for action before going to the courts, even though the public health crisis and the limited kinds of relief in prison grievance programs undermined the utility of such requests.[29] Other trial-level judges recognized the need for release and did so by shortening sentences or relocating individuals to spend the remaining time in "home confinement."[30] Some of those rulings remained in place,[31] but appellate courts stayed or reversed others,[32] and in a few instances, the Supreme Court (over dissents) blocked relief.[33] Those decisions generally relied on

Community Investment, Univ. Network for Hum. Rts. (Jan. 2021), https://static1.squarespace.com/static/5b3538249d5abb21360e858f/t/600f29b9d383732f202b08dc/1611606459237/ConnecticutAtTheCrossroads_25Jan21.pdf.

[27] See, for example, Martinez-Brooks v. Easter, 459 F.Supp.3d 411, 418 (D. Conn. 2020); COVID-19 Special Collection, Civil Rights Litigation Clearinghouse, https://clearinghouse.net/results.php?searchSpecialCollection=62 (last visited Oct. 24, 2021).

[28] Brief of Law Professors on the Remedial Powers of Federal Courts as Amici Curiae Supporting Petitioners-Appellees, Hernandez Roman v. Wolf, 829 F.App'x 165 (9th Cir. 2020) (Nos. 20-55436, 20-55662); Wilson v. Williams, 455 F.Supp.3d 467, 478 (N.D. Ohio 2020), enforcement granted, No. 4:20-CV-00794, 2020 WL 2542131 (N.D. Ohio May 19, 2020), vacated and remanded, No. 20-3547, 2020 WL 9813537 (6th Cir. Sept. 17, 2020), and vacated, 961 F.3d 829 (6th Cir. 2020).

[29] See Ross v. Blake, 578 U.S. 632 (2016).

[30] See, for example, Wilson v. Williams, 455 F.Supp.3d 467, 478 (N.D. Ohio 2020), enforcement granted, No. 4:20-CV-00794, 2020 WL 2542131 (N.D. Ohio May 19, 2020), vacated and remanded, No. 20-3547, 2020 WL 9813537 (6th Cir. Sept. 17, 2020), and vacated, 961 F.3d 829 (6th Cir. 2020). But see Money v. Pritzker, 453 F.Supp.3d 1103 (N.D. Ill. 2020) (rejecting this view).

[31] See, for example, Torres v. Milusnic, 472 F.Supp.3d 713 (C.D. Cal. 2020), enforcement granted in part, denied in part, No. 20-4450, 2021 WL 3829699 (C.D. Cal. Aug. 27, 2021).

[32] Valentine v. Collier, 490 F.Supp.3d 1121, 1175 (S.D. Tex. 2020), rev'd, 993 F.3d 270 (5th Cir. 2021), application to vacate stay denied, 140 S.Ct. 1598 (2020).

[33] Ahlman v. Barnes, No. 20-55568, 2020 WL 3547960, at *1 (9th Cir. June 17, 2020), application for a stay granted, 140 S.Ct. 2620 (2020); Valentine v. Collier, 490 F.Supp.3d 1121, 1175 (S.D. Tex. 2020), rev'd, 993 F.3d 270 (5th Cir. 2021), application to vacate stay denied, 141 S.Ct. 57 (2020).

prison officials' arguments that whatever they did to buffer against COVID-19 was sufficient under the test of "deliberate indifference to known medical needs." Thus, after an initial spurt of lower court judges insisting on methods to lessen the risks to people's lives and health, several courts showed their tolerance for the status quo.[34]

Courts were one venue to seek de-densification, executive action another. Many communities called on directors of correctional facilities, governors, federal officials, and legislatures to take affirmative steps to de-densify. One response came from Congress in the Coronavirus Aid, Relief, and Economic Security Act (CARES) Act, which became law in March 2020. That Act authorized the Attorney General, during the Act's covered emergency period, to direct the BOP to expand the number of people eligible for "home confinement" by "lengthen[ing] the maximum amount of time for which the Director is authorized to place a prisoner in home confinement."[35] Thus, people who would otherwise not have met the requirements for reassignment were able – if the BOP acted – to serve the remainder of their sentences at their homes or in halfway houses.[36]

On April 3, 2020, the Attorney General made the relevant finding that the emergency conditions created by COVID-19 materially affected the functioning of the BOP.[37] That decision gave the BOP Director authority to de-densify by letting some people out and lowering the number of people held in close proximity to one another. Yet the BOP used this opportunity less than it could have done. For example, at the sole federal prison in Connecticut, prison officials did little until incarcerated people brought a class-action lawsuit and a federal court issued an order that the prison's warden had likely violated the Eighth Amendment by failing to release people eligible for home confinement.[38] As of October 18, 2021, the agency's website reported that since March 2020, the BOP had released 33,056 people on home confinement and that 7,586 individuals then remained on home confinement status.[39] Those numbers demonstrate that many released individuals would have been eligible for release even without the CARES Act provision, for they were close to the end of their sentences.

Low numbers of releases were also visible in data from states. For example, by the fall of 2020, 10,000 people were confined in Connecticut state prisons and jails, of whom 3,100 were either held before trial or on misdemeanor convictions – all facing the risks that COVID-19 imposed. A lawsuit challenged those failures, but as some

---

[34] See Brandon L. Barrett & Lee Kovarsky, Viral Injustice, 110 *Cal. L. Rev.* 117 (2022).

[35] See Memorandum Opinion for the General Counsel Federal Bureau of Prisons, Home Confinement of Federal Prisoners After the COVID-19 Emergency (Jan. 15, 2021), www.justice.gov/olc/file/1355886/download.

[36] See Coronavirus Aid, Relief, and Economic Security Act, Pub. L. No. 116-136, § 12003, 134 Stat. 281, 516 (2020).

[37] See Attorney General, Memorandum for Director of Bureau of Prisons (Apr. 3, 2020), www.bop.gov/coronavirus/docs/bop_memo_home_confinement_april3.pdf.

[38] Martinez-Brooks v. Easter, 459 F.Supp.3d 411 (D. Conn. 2020).

[39] Bureau of Prisons, COVID-19 Home Confinement Information, www.bop.gov/coronavirus/ (last visited Mar. 28, 2022).

courts took a narrow view of the "deliberate indifference" standard, an agreement was put into place about monitoring conditions rather than releasing individuals.[40]

Lawsuits to protect people detained by immigration were at times somewhat more successful than those brought on behalf of people in state and federal prisons. Several facility-wide class-action lawsuits resulted in the release of significant numbers of people from ICE detention, even when lower court decisions were subsequently modified or reversed.[41] These ICE detention suits did not face the legal hurdles imposed by the Prison Litigation Reform Act, including its exhaustion requirements. Moreover, because people held in ICE detention are "civil" detainees, their right to health care comes from constitutional guarantees of liberty rather than prohibitions on cruel and unusual punishment. A few judges focused on the lack of health care and did not require demonstration of proof of intent ("deliberate indifference"), as courts have done in the post-conviction context.[42]

In terms of the whole country, between January 2020 and January 2021, the number of people held in jails and in prisons declined somewhat in some jurisdictions.[43] Yet rather than resulting from releases of people who were already incarcerated, much of that decline was attributed to COVID-19-induced slowdowns in prosecution and in courts, as well as the appropriate reluctance of some prosecutors and judges to put people in confinement while awaiting trial. Moreover, the benefits of these policies did not inure to people of color as they did to white populations.[44] Atop these front-end shifts, only a few governors exercised their pardon, clemency, parole, or other authority to release people from prison, and when they did, it was typically to release only small numbers. One exception came from North Carolina, where the governor, responding to litigation about prison conditions, issued an order for a plan to release 3,500 people.[45]

Populations declined in the federally run immigration detention system as well. In the winter of 2020, the government held approximately 39,000 non-citizens for potential removal. By April 2021, that number was down to 14,000.[46] Whether the reduction in population was due to decisions by the Department of Homeland

---

[40] Conn. Dep't of Corr. Rsch. Unit, Average Confined Inmate Population and Legal Status (Oct. 2020), https://portal.ct.gov/-/media/DOC/Pdf/MonthlyStat/Stat11012020.pdf.

[41] See, for example, Fraihat v. US Immigr. & Customs Enf't, 445 F.Supp.3d 709 (C.D. Cal. 2020), order clarified, No. EDCV 19-1546, 2020 WL 6541994 (C.D. Cal. 2020), rev'd and remanded, 16 F.4th 613 (9th Cir. 2021); Roman v. Wolf, 977 F.3d 935 (9th Cir. 2021); Savino v. Souza, 459 F.Supp.3d 317 (D. Mass. 2020).

[42] See, for example, Malam v. Adducci, 455 F.Supp.3d 384 (E.D. Mich. 2020), appeal dismissed, No. 20-1977, 2021 WL 1400901, at *1 (6th Cir. Mar. 11, 2021).

[43] Emily Widra, How Much Have COVID-19 Releases Changed Prison and Jail Populations?, Prison Pol'y Initiative (Feb. 3, 2021), www.prisonpolicy.org/blog/2021/02/03/january-population-update/.

[44] Brennan Klein et al., The COVID-19 Pandemic Amplified Long-Standing Racial Disparities in the United States Criminal Justice System, *medRxiv* (2021).

[45] Jordan Wilkie, NC Prisons Settle NAACP Case, Agree to Fast-Track Release of 3,500 Inmates, Carolina Public Press (Feb. 25, 2021), https://carolinapublicpress.org/42883/nc-prisons-settle-naacp-case-agree-to-fast-track-release-of-3500-inmates/.

[46] Dep't of Homeland Sec., ICE Details COVID-19 Impacts on Immigration Enforcement in FY 2020, www.ice.gov/features/ERO-2020 (last visited Oct. 24, 2021).

Security to de-densify is not clear; arrests for immigration violations did decline. Some analysts point to the government's virtual closing of the border as a significant source of the decrease, and this possibility could have more explanatory power than a decrease in arrests inside the country.[47]

In general, the consensus among public health experts on de-densification was not met by adequate responses from a host of governmental officials, the CDC included. A few initiatives aspired to do more. For example, "complete clemency" is the shorthand for providing that all the people released from the federal system through the CARES Act and serving their sentences under home confinement should remain outside prison.[48] In addition, the harms of COVID-19 helped to energize efforts in some jurisdictions to legislate to limit the practice of reincarcerating people who may have violated conditions when on bail, probation, or parole. Violations range from committing new crimes to minor problems such as not showing up on time for a meeting or not completing drug testing and mental health treatment. An initiative in New York called "Less is More" had, since 2017, sought to limit using such violations to put people back into high-risk detention. New York City's Rikers Island provided a horrific example; in the first ten months of 2021, thirteen people – held before trial – died because of an understaffed, lawless, and dangerous facility.[49] New York's legislature passed "Less Is More," which Governor Kathleen Hochul signed in that September 2021.[50]

Parallel concerns helped to close an immigration detention facility, Bristol County House of Corrections in the Northeast. Advocates in New England documented terrible conditions of confinement and provided crucial support and organizing for the class-action litigation brought on behalf of all people detained at the facility.[51] The litigation resulted in a significant reduction of the population at the facility, and, in 2021, the Biden Administration terminated its contract authorizing non-citizens to be detained at the facility.[52] Members of California's congressional delegation, citing COVID-19, called for closing some of the detention facilities there as well.[53]

---

[47] Control of Communicable Diseases; Foreign Quarantine: Suspension of Introduction of Persons into United States from Designated Foreign Countries or Places for Public Health Purposes, 85 Fed. Reg. 16,559 (proposed Mar. 24, 2020) (to be codified at 42 C.F.R. § 71).

[48] Am. C.L. Union, The Redemption Campaign: Embracing Clemency (June 23, 2021), www.aclu.org/news/topic/the-redemption-campaign-embracing-clemency/.

[49] Jan Ransom, Rikers Death Pushes Toll in NYC Jails to 13 This Year, NY Times (Oct. 15, 2021), www.nytimes.com/2021/10/15/nyregion/rikers-death-toll.html.

[50] Less is More Act, S.B. S1144A, 2021-22 Leg. Sess. (NY 2021).

[51] Savino v. Souza, 459 F.Supp.3d 317 (D. Mass. 2020).

[52] Laura Crimaldi, Biden Administration Terminates ICE Contract with Bristol Sheriff Thomas Hodgson, Boston Globe (May 20, 2021), www.bostonglobe.com/2021/05/20/metro/biden-administration-terminates-ice-contract-bristol-sheriff-thomas-hodgson/.

[53] Deepa Fernandes, Congressional Lawmakers Take Aim at Three Immigration Detention Centers in California, SF Chron. (Oct. 22, 2021), www.sfchronicle.com/california/article/Congressional-lawmakers-take-aim-at-three-16552821.php?utm_campaign=CMS%20Sharing%20Tools%20(Premium)&utm_source=t.co&utm_medium=referral.

V COVID-19 VACCINES: THE PROMISE AND CHALLENGES OF DELIVERY IN PRISONS

As is now familiar, COVID-19 prompted a remarkable effort to produce vaccines; the results exceeded many predictions in terms of timing and efficacy. When vaccine supplies were limited, some states put prisoners, along with others in congregate housing such as nursing homes, on the list of priority recipients.[54] Other states did not, and one court ruled that the state's categories for access had to treat prisoners the same as others, similarly situated, and make vaccinations available as the state did for all in congregate settings.[55]

As vaccine availability increased, the issues turned from access to obligations: Who would get vaccinated, and could vaccines be mandated in detention? Available data suggested that, as of February 2022, in those jurisdictions providing information, the percentage of incarcerated people with at least one dose of a COVID-19 vaccine ranged from 52 percent to 94 percent. The rates of prison staff who had received at least one dose ranged from 23 percent to 82 percent.[56]

That variation brought issues of obligation to the fore. In at least one instance, a court directed state facilities to lower the risk of the spread of infection by requiring vaccines for people denoted as "workers" entering the facilities.[57] In the fall of 2021, the White House COVID-19 Action Plan mandated vaccines for federal employees and federal contractors, and applied that requirement to people working for BOP and ICE.[58] In 2022, after the Supreme Court concluded that the Occupational Safety and Health Administration lacked the authority to mandate vaccines and testing for the private sector, the agency substituted guidelines that encouraged those practices and additional care for "at risk" populations.[59] Given the mix of public and private staff in detention facilities, facility administrators became the source of important decisions about how to protect the safety of people in detention and staff.[60]

---

[54] Roni Caryn Rabin, In Massachusetts, Inmates Will Be Among First to Get Vaccines, NY Times (Dec. 18, 2020), www.nytimes.com/2020/12/18/health/coronavirus-vaccine-prisons-massachusetts.html.

[55] See Maney v. Brown, No. 6:20-CV-00570-SB, 2021 WL 354384 (D. Or. Feb. 3, 2021).

[56] COVID Behind Bars Data Project, UCLA Law, https://uclacovidbehindbars.org (last visited Feb. 23, 2022); see also Jaimie P. Meyer, Jaelen King & Alana Rosenberg, Meeting the Moment by Vaccinating Prison Staff Against COVID-19, 3 JAMA Health Forum 1 (2022).

[57] Plata v. Newsom, No. 01-CV-01351, 2021 WL 4448953, at *13 (N.D. Cal. Sept. 27, 2021).

[58] M.D. Carvajal, Director, US Dept. of Just., Fed. Bureau of Prisons, Memorandum for All Staff re Vaccination Mandate (Sept. 29, 2021), https://cdn.govexec.com/media/gbc/docs/pdfs_edit/100521cb1 .pdf; US Immigr. & Customs Enf't, Enforcement and Removal Operations, COVID-19 Pandemic Response Requirements (Oct. 19, 2021), www.ice.gov/doclib/coronavirus/eroCOVID19responseReqs CleanFacilities.pdf.

[59] Nat'l Fed'n of Indep. Bus. v. Dep't of Lab., 142 S.Ct. 661 (2022) (granting stay); US Dep't of Lab., Protecting Workers: Guidance on Mitigating and Preventing the Spread of COVID-19 in the Workplace, www.osha.gov/coronavirus/safework (last visited Mar. 18, 2022).

[60] See Meyer et al., supra note 56.

The question of imposing vaccine mandates for detained people is nested in oppressive histories of detention and of medical experimentation. As discussed, given the lack of care in many facilities, people in prison have many reasons to distrust the system that detains them. Further, informational sources are regulated; incarcerated patients face challenges in making well-informed choices. To respect a modicum of autonomy related to health care, most jurisdictions have not required vaccinations against diseases such as influenza.

COVID-19 contagion put stress on that approach. Innovative responses have aimed to address the challenges of ethical and equitable vaccine distribution in prisons. Public health experts focused on identifying "trusted messengers" who could provide information beyond what staff gave to incarcerated people. Such innovative information campaigns aimed to provide accurate knowledge and counteract misinformation. For example, the National Commission on Correctional Health Care and AMEND, based at the University of California, San Francisco Medical School, provided free materials, developed with input from people in detention, on COVID-19 vaccines.[61] In Rhode Island, handouts shaped by incarcerated people were provided weeks before vaccines arrived to all people in detention in the Rhode Island Department of Corrections.[62] The University of Massachusetts Medical School, through a contract with the Massachusetts Office of Public Safety, developed a "COVID-19 vaccines in prison" information campaign in several languages and included factsheets, posters, and videos; these were distributed to people incarcerated, staff, and state police.[63]

VI COVID-19'S LESSONS

Our account of COVID-19 in US detention from 2020 to 2021 is embedded in the unhealthy (in all senses of that word) attachment to incarceration, which diminishes the well-being of the people required to live in prison, the staff who work there, and the communities and country of which they are a part. The global and national experience of this public health emergency has again underscored that massive incarceration undermines public and personal health. Moreover, even after vaccines rolled out and the end of an acute phase of pandemic came into sight in

---

[61] AMEND, COVID-19 in Correctional Facility: Answers, Advice, and Answers, https://amend.us/covid/ (last visited Oct. 24, 2021); Nat'l Comm. on Correctional Health Care, COVID-19 Coronavirus: What You Need to Know in Corrections, www.ncchc.org/covid-resources (last visited Oct. 24, 2021).

[62] Nat'l Comm. on Correctional Health Care, Rhode Island DOC's Vaccine Acceptance Success Story (Apr. 27, 2021), www.ncchc.org/blog/rhode-island-docs-vaccine-acceptance-success-story; Melanie DaSilva & Kayla Fish, RI Correctional Officers, Inmates Getting Vaccinated Despite Hesitancy in Other States, WPRI (Mar. 17, 2021), https://doc.ri.gov/covid-19.

[63] UMass Med. Sch. Commc'ns, Medical Students Improve Access to COVID-19 Vaccine Information for Multilingual Community, UMASS Chan Med. Sch. (May 5, 2021), www.umassmed.edu/news/news-archives/2021/05/medical-students-improve-access-to-covid-19-vaccine-information-for-multilingual-community/.

the United States, COVID-19 is becoming endemic and the risks it poses to people in congregate settings remain high.

Further, COVID-19 is far from the only risk to health associated with incarceration. Prison is bad for people on a host of dimensions. For example, according to 2020 federal data, people in prison have a 2.5 times higher risk of dying from homicides than those in the community.[64] One lesson that COVID-19 ought to have provided is that the hyper-density of detention (coupled at times with the profound isolation of solitary confinement) is unsafe as well as unwise and unjust.

COVID-19 also underscored the interdependence of communities around the world, including prisons, and the centrality of education in improving public health. The conflicts over collective action to respond to the health emergency of COVID-19 took place in many venues. Divides about mask and vaccine mandates, economic support, eviction bans, and religious exemptions in relationship to COVID-19 are intertwined with conflicts about the government's role in providing help and care more generally. Likewise, insufficient responses to COVID-19 in detention mirrored the lack of sufficient health care in prison for other diseases.

COVID-19 has thus served as a painful reminder that prison is a place where the harms of confinement are known and tolerated. We are "in medias res" – in the middle of understanding the import of the pandemic and in the middle of conflicts about how to generate the political and social will to provide for more safety and to support well-being for all. For people in prison, rethinking detention, with and without COVID-19, is required.

---

[64] Leah Wang & Wendy Sawyer, New Data: State Prisons Are Increasingly Deadly Places, Prison Pol'y Initiative (June 8, 2021), www.prisonpolicy.org/blog/2021/06/08/prison_mortality/.

7

COVID-19 and Racial Justice in America

Scott J. Schweikart, Fernando De Maio, Mia Keeys, Joaquin Baca, Brian Vandenberg, and Aletha Maybank[*]

I INTRODUCTION

In the United States, the impact of COVID-19 is influenced and exacerbated by an embedded social issue: structural racism and its attendant systemic inequities.[1] In this chapter, we address how structural racism – broadly construed as the deeply rooted discriminatory policies and systems that produce the chronic systemic inequities faced by Black, Indigenous, and People of Color (BIPOC) people in American society – have influenced, with notable detriment,[2] COVID-19's impact in the United States. We argue that the pandemic's legal and policy legacy will be one of greater realized health equity and racial justice. The United States is at a pivotal political point. The confluence of an ever-looming pandemic intertwined with racial equity protests and a newly elected president provide the political impetus for monumental legal and social change. Notably, because of the pervasive nature of systemic inequities and structural racism, legal and social changes flowing from this pivot point will influence both health and non-health law realms. Probable changes to American law and policy are likely to be immense – historic in both scope and impact. We broadly examine these possibilities, providing an ultimate assessment of the probable far-reaching legal and policy legacy of COVID-19: naming and challenging the foundation of structural racism in the United States.

II RACISM IN THE EPIDEMIOLOGY OF COVID-19

Understanding the epidemiology of COVID-19 requires one to name racism as a fundamental cause of health inequity, and to acknowledge that racism and white

---

[*] The views expressed are those of the authors and do not necessarily represent American Medical Association policy.

[1] William M. Wiecek, Structural Racism and the Law in America Today: An Introduction, 100 *Ky. L.J.* 1, 5 (2011).

[2] See Ruqaiijah Yearby & Seema Mohapatra, Law, Structural Racism, and the COVID-19 Pandemic, 7 *J. L. Biosciences.* 1 (2020).

supremacy have shaped data systems across the country. This has operated in several ways, including failing to collect critically important data, either through colorblind ideology or through the systemic failure to fund critical public health infrastructure, and manifests in the research questions that are asked and the models that are created to explain population health patterns.

On an empirical level, the inequitable epidemiologic burden of COVID-19 has been well established. The earliest studies, emerging in April 2020, warned of a disproportionate cost for marginalized and minoritized groups.[3] Health equity researchers warned that COVID-19 would amplify existing inequities as it spread throughout the country. As the United States crossed the threshold of 600,000 total deaths from COVID-19, it continued to see the significant inequities that were revealed in the early weeks of the pandemic. The latest data (as of July 2021) show that age-adjusted mortality rates for Latinx and Black people are more than double that of White people (2.3 times and 2.0 times, respectively).[4] Indigenous people have experienced age-adjusted mortality rates 2.2 times higher than for White people; Pacific Islanders have a rate that is 2.7 times higher.[5] This translates into an unprecedented level of excess deaths across the country.[6] If the COVID-19 mortality rate experienced in the White population applied universally to BIPOC communities, more than 21,000 Black, 10,000 Latinx, and 1,000 Indigenous people would still be alive today – estimates that continue to rise every month.[7] This burden is clear in epidemiologic models, and it is clear in empirical data; the latest analysis of national vital statistics data reveal that US life expectancy dropped by a full year in the first half of 2020, from 78.8 years in 2019 to 77.8 years in the first half of 2020.[8] This life expectancy decline was largest among non-Hispanic Black males, whose life expectancy dropped by three years in just one year. Hispanic males also saw a large decrease in life expectancy, with a decline of 2.4 years. Non-Hispanic Black females saw a life expectancy decline of 2.3 years, and Hispanic females faced a decline of 1.1 years.[9]

---

[3] Javis T. Chen & Nancy Krieger, Revealing the Unequal Burden of COVID-19 by Income, Race/Ethnicity, and Household Crowding: US County Versus ZIP Codes Analyses, 27 J. Pub. Health Mgmt. Prac. S43, S43, (2021); Samrachana Adhikari et al., Assessment of Community-Level Disparities in Coronavirus Disease 2019 (COVID-19) Infections and Deaths in Large US Metropolitan Areas, 3 JAMA Network Open e2016938 (2020).

[4] Risk for COVID-19 Infection, Hospitalization, and Death by Race/Ethnicity, Ctrs. for Disease Control & Prevention, (July 16, 2021), www.cdc.gov/coronavirus/2019-ncov/covid-data/investigations-discovery/hospitalization-death-by-race-ethnicity.html.

[5] APM Rsch. Lab Staff, The Color of the Coronavirus: COVID-19 Deaths by Race and Ethnicity in the US, APM Rsch. Lab (Feb. 23, 2021), www.apmresearchlab.org/covid/deaths-by-race.

[6] Steven H. Woolf, Derek A. Chapman & Roy T. Sabo, Excess Deaths from COVID-19 and Other Causes, March-July 2020, 324 JAMA 1562, 1562 (2020); Lauren M. Rossen et al., Excess Deaths Associated with COVID-19, by Age and Race and Ethnicity – United States, January 26–October 3, 2020, 69 Morbidity & Mortality Weekly Rep. 1522, 1522 (2020).

[7] APM Rsch. Lab Staff, supra note 5.

[8] Elizabeth Arias, Betzaida Tejada-Vera & Farida Ahmad, Provisional Life Expectancy Estimates for January through June, 2020, at 1 (2021), www.cdc.gov/nchs/data/vsrr/VSRR10-508.pdf.

[9] Id. at 2.

This hit – driven primarily, but not exclusively, by COVID-19 mortality – adds to an already inequitable picture with excess deaths associated with all-cause mortality.[10]

The disparate impact is also evident regarding problems ancillary to the pandemic, such as the economic recession, which has inflicted a greater toll on BIPOC communities as well. Job and wage losses due to COVID-19 have hit marginalized and minoritized communities hardest; more than half of Hispanic (58 percent) and Black (53 percent) households in the US Census Bureau's Household Pulse Survey reported a decline in employment income since mid-March 2020.[11] Black workers have experienced the highest rates of unemployment and the weakest recoveries since the March-April 2020 unemployment peak.[12]

Early in the pandemic, it became evident that the country's public health infrastructure would strain to meet the demand for timely, granular, and actionable data. In particular, it was clear in the first weeks of the pandemic that despite promises to do so, race/ethnicity data were not being collected in systematic and comprehensive ways. These data are critical for understanding injustice and ensuring the optimal health of all communities – but it was gravely missing from COVID-19 test data throughout the country.[13] These data are also missing from many vaccination records, again hampering efforts to challenge racial injustice and center equity. Despite continued problems with missing race/ethnicity data, the inequitable burden of COVID-19 is well established.[14]

Some have interpreted racial/ethnic inequities in COVID-19 incidence and mortality through behavioral explanations, arguing that patterns are explained by preexisting conditions, including higher levels of obesity, asthma, and heart disease. Yet such logic fails to acknowledge root causes, what epidemiologists call "the causes of the causes."[15] On this point, Data 4 Black Lives is clear: "[W]hy are Black people particularly vulnerable and over-represented among COVID-19 cases and deaths? The conditions that make Black communities vulnerable to the virus are the same conditions that make Black communities vulnerable to the daily harms of structural racism."[16]

---

[10]   Maureen R. Benjamins et al., Comparison of All-Cause Mortality Rates and Inequities Between Black and White Populations Across the 30 Most Populous US Cities, 4 JAMA Network Open e2032086 (2021).

[11]   Sharon Cornelissen & Alexander Hermann, A Triple Pandemic? The Economic Impacts of COVID-19 Disproportionately Affect Black and Hispanic Households, Joint Ctr. for Hous. Stud. Harv. Univ. (July 7, 2020), www.jchs.harvard.edu/blog/a-triple-pandemic-the-economic-impacts-of-covid-19-disproportionately-affect-black-and-hispanic-households.

[12]   Jhacova Williams, Laid Off More, Hired Less: Black Workers in the COVID-19 Recession, RAND Blog (Sept. 29, 2020), www.rand.org/blog/2020/09/laid-off-more-hired-less-black-workers-in-the-covid.html.

[13]   Aletha Maybank, The Pandemic's Missing Data: We Desperately Need to Release the Statistics on Race and Ethnicity, NY Times (Apr. 7, 2020), www.nytimes.com/2020/04/07/opinion/coronavirus-blacks.html.

[14]   Tim F. Liao & Fernando De Maio, Association of Social and Economic Inequality with Coronavirus Disease 2019 Incidence and Mortality Across US Counties, 4 JAMA Network Open e2034578 (2021).

[15]   Michael Marmot, The Health Gap: The Challenge of an Unequal World 52 (2d ed. 2015).

[16]   D4BL (Data for Black Lives), The Impact of COVID-19 on Black Communities, D4BL (Data for Black Lives) (Feb. 22, 2021), https://d4bl.org/covid19-data.html.

And as Rachel Hardeman points out, "[O]ur traditional notions of white supremacy keep us focused on hate groups and vulgar language rather than a culture and ideology born from the premise of Black inferiority and false notions of race as biological that have permeated the ways in which we conduct our research."[17]

One of the lessons from the COVID-19 pandemic has been the need to reexamine the political underpinnings of public health data systems, particularly the ways that racism and white supremacy have inhibited our collective actions. There are new national efforts in this area, with a Robert Wood Johnson Foundation-funded Commission to Transform Public Health Data Systems noting that it "is the time to fundamentally reprioritize our public health data and related health data systems so they work better to ensure equitable outcomes for all."[18]

III POLITICAL PIVOT POINT

A political and social-cultural pivot point has been several years in the making, starting with the Black Lives Matter (BLM) movement,[19] and arguably reaching a crescendo in 2020 with the murder of George Floyd, concurrent with the inequitable hardships inflicted by the COVID-19 pandemic. Some data have indicated that the BLM movement reached new heights in 2020, possibly becoming the largest mass movement in American history.[20] Douglas McAdam, a scholar of social movements, noted that BLM is "setting in motion a period of significant, sustained and widespread social, political change" and that such an achievement by a mass movement is allowing society to experience "a social change tipping point" that is both "rare" and "potentially consequential."[21]

Indeed, public health experts have also noted a "sea change" in America's growing "recognition of racism as a durable feature of US society and of its high cost in Black lives."[22] Moreover, it is important to recognize that the confluence of the BLM protests of 2020 and the COVID-19 pandemic is not accidental; there is a

---

[17] Rachel R. Hardeman & J'Mag Karbeah, Examining Racism in Health Services Research: A Disciplinary Self-Critique, 55 *Health Serv. Rsch.* 777, 777 (2020).

[18] Alonzo Plough & Gail C. Christopher, New Commission to Tackle How National Health Data Are Collected, Shared, and Used, Health Affs. Blog (May 18, 2021), www.healthaffairs.org/do/10.1377/forefront.20210518.409206/full/.

[19] The BLM movement began in 2013 after the acquittal of George Zimmerman in the Trayvon Martin case and gained further national recognition in 2014 after the police killing of Eric Garner. See Howard University Law Library, Black Lives Matter Movement, Howard Univ. Sch. L. (2018), https://library.law.howard.edu/civilrightshistory/BLM; see also Kay Lim, Alicia Garza on the Origin of Black Lives Matter, CBS News (Oct. 18, 2020), www.cbsnews.com/news/alicia-garza-on-the-origin-of-black-lives-matter/.

[20] Larry Buchanan, Quoctrung Bui & Jugal K. Patel, Black Lives Matter May Be the Largest Movement in US History, NY Times (July 3, 2020), www.nytimes.com/interactive/2020/07/03/us/george-floyd-protests-crowd-size.html.

[21] Id.

[22] Zinzi D. Bailey, Justin M. Feldman & Mary T. Bassett, How Structural Racism Works – Racist Policies as a Root Cause of U.S. Racial Health Inequities, 384 *New Eng. J. Med.* 768, 768 (2020).

linkage between the two. If not for the COVID-19 pandemic, the strong momentum, size, and influence of the BLM protests in 2020 following Floyd's death would likely not have materialized to the same extent.[23] Hence, viewed broadly, any outcomes toward equity made by the BLM protests of 2020 could also be viewed as part of the broader legacy of the pandemic.

Also significant is the coupling of the BLM political movement – and its power – with the election of President Biden,[24] and the seismic change transitioning from the Trump Administration to one that is, on the surface, not as hostile to racial and health equity.[25] For example, President Biden has signaled a willingness to protect the Affordable Care Act (ACA),[26] and to implement some reforms called for by BLM activists.[27] Additionally, the Democrats gained control of the Senate,[28] giving the party complete control of both houses of Congress, along with control of the Presidency, at the beginning of 2021. While there is debate about how much progress the Democrats can accomplish toward racial and health equity, the Democrats' goals are more closely aligned with racial and health equity goals, and they provide the BLM movement with actualized political power at the federal level. However, it is important to note that much of the law that impacts health equity also exists at the state and local levels. And while there have been gains made at such levels,[29] local gains vary across the country, as some states are not embracing legal changes advancing health equity. Indeed, there has been significant political pushback. A year after the 2020 election, the scope of gained political power has reached greater uncertainty. Many progressive goals have gone unfulfilled,[30] and the

---

[23] See Maneesh Arora, How the Coronavirus Pandemic Helped the Floyd Protests Become the Biggest in U.S. History, Wash. Post (Aug. 5, 2020), www.washingtonpost.com/politics/2020/08/05/how-coronavirus-pandemic-helped-floyd-protests-become-biggest-us-history/; see also Alan Greenblatt, A Crisis Within a Crisis: How COVID Fueled the Protests, Governing: The Future of States and Localities (June 5, 2020), www.governing.com/now/a-crisis-within-a-crisis-how-pandemic-fueled-the-protests.html.

[24] Mark Sherman, Electoral College Makes It Official: Biden Won, Trump Lost, AP (Dec. 14, 2020), https://apnews.com/article/joe-biden-270-electoral-college-vote-d429ef97af2bf574d16463384dc7cc1e.

[25] Tim Craig & Robert Klemko, Black Lives Matter Movement at a Crossroads as Biden Prepares to Take Office, Wash. Post (Dec. 1, 2020), www.washingtonpost.com/national/black-lives-matter-movement-at-a-crossroads-as-biden-prepares-to-take-office/2020/12/01/8ebb95ce-2f26-11eb-86od-f7999599cbc2_story.html.

[26] Biden Defends Obamacare as Top Court Hears Case, BBC News (Nov. 10, 2020), www.bbc.com/news/world-us-canada-54896663.

[27] Candice Norwood & Daniel Bush, What a Biden Administration Could Mean for Criminal Justice Reform, PBS News Hour (Dec. 14, 2020), www.pbs.org/newshour/politics/what-a-biden-administration-could-mean-for-criminal-justice-reform.

[28] Patricia Zengerle & Susan Cornwell, Democrats Take Narrow Control of the U.S. Senate, Reuters (Jan. 20, 2021), www.reuters.com/article/us-usa-congress/democrats-take-narrow-control-of-u-s-senate-id USKBN29P2SD.

[29] See, for example, Emanuella Evans & Rita Oceguera, Illinois Criminal Justice Reform Ends Cash Bail, Changes Felony Murder Rule, Injustice Watch (Feb. 23, 2021), www.injusticewatch.org/news/2021/illinois-criminal-justice-reform-cash-bail-felony-murder/.

[30] Olive Knox, Biden Enters 2022 With Many Progressive Goals Unmet, Wash. Post (Dec. 17, 2021), www.washingtonpost.com/politics/2021/12/17/biden-enters-2022-with-many-progressive-goals-unmet/.

Republican Party is likely to retake the House in 2022,[31] making the legacy of the political pivot of 2020 somewhat murkier and more nuanced than might have been initially surmised at the height of 2020's political momentum. Still, the political gains and momentum observed in 2020 further solidify the pivot point in which America currently finds itself – a pivot created by an increasingly influential political and social movement coupled with political power gained in Washington, DC.

IV LEGAL AND POLICY IMPACT

Considering the political moment in which the United States currently finds itself – combined with the historic public health crisis – it is both logical and important to question what the legal and policy impact of this pivotal instance in American history will be. While, in a traditional sense, COVID-19's societal impact is most likely to be acutely observed within the lens of health care and medicine (as the crisis is, at its core, a public health and medical problem), the impact of COVID-19 in American society will likely be quite broad, especially with regards to the pandemic's impact on health equity and structural racism. Structural racism – regardless of whether it is directly or tangentially related to health or medicine – has an impact on health, and hence is also key to moving the needle on health equity. For example, police brutality affects health.[32] When evaluating the pandemic's legal impact (especially in the context of health equity and structural racism), it is important to use a broad lens to take account of the multi-faceted way in which health and law interact beyond narrow notions of "health law." This holistic vantage point helps reveal what COVID-19 dramatically exposed – that inequities are structural, engrained, systemic, and inescapable, continually reinforcing flawed systems in all domains of daily life.

A *Law and Health*

The relationship between law and health is complex. One might imagine that the nexus of law and health that produces "health law" would be confined to the directly related jurisprudence, for instance, medical malpractice torts, health insurance contracts, medical privacy, patient autonomy, and informed consent. Abbe R. Gluck notes that these traditional modes of health law are typically "private law," which is focused "on regulating relationships among private parties"

---

[31] Ally Mutnick, *Republican Wave Builds to Take Back the House*, Politico (Nov. 8, 2021), www.politico.com/news/2021/11/08/republican-wave-house-congress-520238.

[32] See Jacob Bor et al, *Police Killings and Their Spillover Effects on the Mental Health of Black Americans: A Population-Based, Quasi-Experimental Study*, 392 *Lancet* 302 (2018); see also, Press Release, Amer. Med. Ass'n, *AMA Policy Recognizes Policy Brutality as a Product of Structural Racism* (Nov. 17, 2020), www.ama-assn.org/press-center/press-releases/ama-policy-recognizes-police-brutality-product-structural-racism.

and has been historically sourced from "states, local governments, and the medical profession itself."[33] However, in our modern society, there is a need to look beyond these traditional relationships between private parties. Gluck notes that health law should encompass a focus on "public law" – in other words, on "a field that is defined by the role of the government" – particularly pointing out the ACA and its outsized role influencing health beyond the traditional "private law" domain.[34]

Additionally, it is important to consider areas of law that may be – on their face – tangential and not directly related to health. However, these "tangential" areas are more than ones merely touching on health care concerns; they are instead truly core areas of law related to the social and structural determinants of health, and have documented impacts on health disparities affecting BIPOC people, including the disparities observed with COVID-19.[35] Social determinants include discrimination, poverty, legal and political systems, housing, and health care.[36] Hence, areas of jurisprudence, such as immigration,[37] employment law,[38] criminal law, education, tax law,[39] and housing/zoning,[40] are relevant to health equity. As previously addressed, criminal justice is a good example, given that the linkage between health and police brutality is now documented.[41] "Mass incarceration" is also a structural determinant of health that has "disproportionality harmed low-income

[33] Abbe R. Gluck, Why Health Lawyers Must Be Public-Law Lawyers: Health Law in the Age of the Modern Regulatory State, 18 J. Health Care L. & Pol'y 323, 324 (2015).

[34] Id.

[35] Emily A. Benfer et al., Health Justice Strategies to Combat the Pandemic: Eliminating Discrimination, Poverty, and Health Disparities During and After COVID-19, 19 Yale J. Health Pol'y, L. Ethics 122, 126 (2020).

[36] Id. at 135. The authors note the wide array of social determinants of health, both structural and intermediary.

[37] See Wendy E. Parmet, The Worst of Health: Law and Policy at the Intersection of Health & Immigration, 16 Ind. Health L. Rev. 211 (2019); see also Wendy E. Parmet, Immigration Law as a Social Determinant of Health, 92 Temp. L. Rev. 931 (2020).

[38] See Ruqaiijah Yearby, The Impact of Structural Racism in Employment and Wages on Minority Women's Health, 43 Hum. Rts. 75 (2018); see also Ruqaiijah Yearby & Seema Mohapatra, Structural Discrimination in COVID-19 Workplace Protections, Health Affs. Blog (May 29, 2020), www .healthaffairs.org/do/10.1377/forefront.20200522.280105/full/.

[39] See Victoria J. Haneman, Contemplating Homeownership Tax Subsidies and Structural Racism, 54 Wake Forest L. Rev. 363 (2019).

[40] See Juliana Maantay, Zoning Law, Health, and Environmental Justice: What's the Connection?, 30 J. L. Med. Ethics 572 (2002); see also Abraham Gutman, Katie Moran-McCabe & Scott Burris, Health, Housing, and the Law, 11 Ne. Univ. L. Rev. 251 (2019); David Oshinsky, A Powerful, Disturbing History of Residential Segregation in America, NY Times (June 20, 2017) (reviewing Richard Rothstein, The Color of Law: A Forgotten History of How Our Government Segregated America (2017)), www .nytimes.com/2017/06/20/books/review/richard-rothstein-color-of-law-forgotten-history.html.

[41] See Bor et al., supra note 32; see also Abigail A. Sewell & Kevin A. Jefferson, Collateral Damage: The Health Effects of Invasive Police Encounters in New York City, 93 J. Urb. Health S42 (2016); Alyasah Ali Sewell et al., Illness Spillovers of Lethal Police Violence: The Significance of Gendered Marginalization, 44 Ethnic Racial Stud. 1089 (2020).

and racial and ethnic minorities."[42] Nearly every aspect of daily life plays a role in constructing one's health. These aspects of daily life – in other words, the conditions where people live, learn, work, and play – are part of the social determinants of health.[43] The law also touches on every aspect of daily life and thus also touches on the social determinants of health. In this way, nearly every area of law could be deemed "health law" and have some influence on societal health equity.

B *Legal Legacy*

COVID-19's imperfect legal legacy on health justice is unfolding before us. A legacy that bends the United States toward greater health equity is possible and can be rooted in several areas of policy and law, such as state and local law, and federal administrative law. In this section, we broadly examine four possible examples of legal legacy: (1) expanded health care access; (2) criminal justice reform; (3) the correction of historical red-lining; and (4) the reformation of administrative enforcement of Title VI of the Civil Rights Act.

First, expanded health care access is a key component of combating health inequities and tackling the pandemic,[44] and expansion is likely to be one of COVID-19's legal legacies.

Expansion will most likely be demonstrated through protecting and expanding the ACA and Medicaid coverage. In 2021, President Biden issued an executive order reopening enrollment to ACA health plans, explicitly noting that doing so would "protect and build on the Affordable Care Act, meet the health care needs created by the pandemic, reduce health care needs created by the pandemic, reduce health care costs, protect access to reproductive health care, and make our health care system easier to navigate and more equitable."[45] President Biden is also signaling an end to the Trump Administration's "health policy goal" of approving state Medicaid waivers to allow work requirements for Medicaid enrollees.[46] Work requirements are state mandates that require Medicaid recipients to work a set number of hours per month

---

[42] Benfer et. al., supra note 35, at 133–34.

[43] Social Determinants of Health: Know What Affects Health, Ctrs. for Disease Control & Prevention (Sept. 30, 2021), www.cdc.gov/socialdeterminants/index.htm.

[44] See Marsha Lillie-Blanton & Catherine Hoffman, The Role of Health Insurance Coverage in Reducing Racial/Ethnic Disparities in Health Care, 24 *Health Affs.* 398, 407 (2005); see also Rene Bowser, The Affordable Care Act and Beyond: Opportunities for Advancing Health Equity and Social Justice, 10 *Hastings Race Poverty L.J.* 69, 79 (2013); Jesse Cross-Call & Matt Broaddus, States That Have Expanded Medicaid Are Better Positioned to Address COVID-19 and Recession (2020), www.cbpp.org/research/health/states-that-have-expanded-medicaid-are-better-positioned-to-address-covid-19-and.

[45] White House Press Office, Fact Sheet: President Biden to Sign Executive Orders Strengthening Americans' Access to Quality, Affordable Health Care (Jan. 28, 2021), www.whitehouse.gov/briefing-room/statements-releases/2021/01/28/fact-sheet-president-biden-to-sign-executive-orders-strengthening-americans-access-to-quality-affordable-health-care/.

[46] Sara Kliff & Margot Sanger-Kate, Biden Administration Moves to End Work Requirements in Medicaid, NY Times (Feb. 12, 2021), www.nytimes.com/2021/02/12/upshot/biden-medicaid-reversing-trump.html.

in order to receive Medicaid benefits.[47] Data have shown that work requirements are harmful and lead to coverage loss.[48] Rolling back work requirements removes a barrier to accessing care. However, a possible pitfall in the expansion of health care is the continuing deadlock in Congress. For example, the Democrat's "Build Back Better" bill contains measures that would help address the expansion of health care, such as closing the Medicaid coverage gap,[49] and reducing high drug prices,[50] among other ambitious priorities. But with the bill stalled and the increasing possibility of the Democrats losing control of Congress in the midterms, the chances of such legislative initiatives succeeding in reducing health inequities are limited.

A second legal legacy is criminal justice reform. Flowing from the political pivot earlier discussed, issues of criminal justice reform have taken on recent impetus. Additionally, criminal justice is a key factor in racial inequity in the United States, and reform is important to reduce health inequities. A recent example of reform comes from Illinois, where the state passed a sweeping reform of criminal law.[51] The law notably makes Illinois the first state to eliminate cash bail and narrows the definition of felony murder, something criminal justice reform advocates have been calling for nationwide for years. Such reforms are critical from a health equity standpoint. Like police brutality, criminal justice and incarceration have notable and recognized links to health and health equity in American society.[52]

A third possible legacy is addressing housing equity. In 2015, the Obama Administration instituted an administrative rule enforcing the Affirmatively Further Fair Housing (AFFH) provision of the Fair Housing Act. The Obama rule conditioned "receipt of HUD [US Department of Housing and Urban Development] funds by local recipients on their [local governmental authorities] looking searchingly at unequal access by community members to housing located in neighborhoods of opportunity."[53] AFFH serves as a federal governmental incentive to influence local government zoning law, where "HUD beneficiaries are required to initiate discussion about how to move toward fair housing for all and then to take action."[54] The Obama-era proposal

---

[47] Jennifer Wagner & Jessica Schubel, States' Experiences Confirm Harmful Effect of Medicaid Work Requirements 1 (2020), www.jstor.org/stable/pdf/resrep27502.pdf.

[48] Id.

[49] Judith Solomon, Build Back Better Legislation Would Close the Medicaid Coverage Gap 1 (2021), www.cbpp.org/research/health/build-back-better-legislation-would-close-the-medicaid-coverage-gap.

[50] Ricardo Alonso-Zaldivar & Lisa Mascaro, Democrats Push to Retool Health Care Programs for Millions, AP (Sept. 19, 2021), https://apnews.com/article/congress-health-care-69c7bb592f8d73232bec1d8e15be82e3.

[51] Ill. Public Act No. 101-0652 (2021); see also Maria Cramer, Illinois Becomes First State to Eliminate Cash Bail, NY Times (Feb. 23, 2021), www.nytimes.com/2021/02/23/us/illinois-cash-bail-pritzker.html; Evans & Oceguera, supra note 29.

[52] George Hobor & Alonzo Plough, Addressing Mass Incarceration to Achieve Health Equity, 110 Am. J. Pub. Health S13 (2020).

[53] Palma Joy Strand, The Invisible Hands of Structural Racism in Housing: Our Hands, Our Responsibility, 96 U. Det. Mercy L. Rev. 155, 157 (2019).

[54] Id. at 158.

was lauded as finally allowing administrative enforcement of the AFFH. However, the Trump Administration terminated the rule, citing it as "unworkable" and a "waste of time."[55] As was widely expected, the Biden Administration reinstated the Obama-era rule, effective July 31, 2021.[56] A return to the Obama-era rule is an important push toward health equity, with HUD Secretary Marcia Fudge noting that the return reflects the fact that "HUD is taking a critical step to affirm that a child's future should never be limited by the ZIP code where they are born."[57] Another key aspect of housing in the realm of health equity is that of the COVID-19 eviction moratorium. In 2020, the Centers for Disease Control and Prevention took the unprecedented step of halting evictions to stop the spread of COVID-19.[58] The moratorium was a positive step toward health equity, while also underscoring broader housing concerns.[59] However, the Supreme Court struck down the moratorium in August 2021.[60] The order doing so was 6-3, along ideological lines, a reminder of another barrier toward effectuating health equity. Considering the substantial change in the federal judiciary over the last few years via the Trump Administration's conservative judicial appointments, ones which lack any meaningful reflection of the nation's diversity,[61] it is important to recognize that this unrepresentative judiciary could imperil equitable progress.

A final example is reformation of administrative enforcement to Title VI of the Civil Rights Act to better effectuate health equity. With the increased recognition and understanding of structural racism and how it is a root cause of health inequities,[62] it makes sense that structural pillars such as federal governmental agencies are part of the structural problem producing inequities that continue into the COVID-19 era. However, reformation of a structural pillar such as administrative enforcement is also a key opportunity to reduce inequities. In the context of health care, "Title VI prohibits health care facilities in receipt of government funding from using racial bias to determine who receives quality health care."[63]

---

[55] Press Release, US Dep't Hous. & Urb. Dev., Secretary Carson Terminates 2015 AFFH Rule: Removal of Rule Returns Power to Localities in Effort to Advance Fair Housing Nationwide (July 23, 2020), https://archives.hud.gov/news/2020/pr20-109.cfm.

[56] 24 C.F.R. 5.151-52, 91.325.

[57] Press Release, US Dep't Hous. & Urb. Dev., HUD Restores Affirmatively Furthering Fair Housing Requirement (June 10, 2021), www.hud.gov/press/press_releases_media_advisories/HUD_No_21_098.

[58] Temporary Halt in Residential Evictions to Prevent the Further Spread of COVID-19, 85 Fed. Reg. 55292, (Sept. 4, 2020).

[59] Emily Benfer et al., Opinion: The Eviction Moratorium Limbo Laid Bare the System's Extreme Dysfunction, Wash. Post (Aug. 12, 2021), www.washingtonpost.com/opinions/2021/08/12/eviction-moratorium-court-cdc-congress/.

[60] Krishnadev Calamur & Chris Arnold, The Supreme Court Will Allow Evictions to Resume. It Could Affect Millions of Tenants, NPR (Aug. 26, 2021), www.npr.org/2021/08/26/1024668578/court-blocks-biden-cdc-evictions-moratorium.

[61] Stacy Hawkins, Trump's Dangerous Judicial Legacy, 67 *UCLA L. Rev. Discourse* 20, 20 (2019).

[62] Zinzi D. Bailey, Justin M. Feldman & Mary T. Bassett, How Structural Racism Works – Racist Policies as a Root Cause of US Racial Health Inequities, 384 *New Eng. J. Med.* 768 (2021).

[63] Ruqaiijah Yearby, When Is a Change Going to Come?: Separate and Unequal Treatment in Healthcare Fifty Years after Title VI of the Civil Rights Act, 67 *SMU L. Rev.* 287, 288 (2014).

The promise of Title VI to eliminate health inequities has not been fulfilled. A key reason is that the "Supreme Court ruled that private parties do not have a right to sue for disparate impact bias under Title VI,"[64] leaving enforcement to the Department of Health and Human Services, whose track record has been "woefully inadequate" in enforcing Title VI to stop segregation and inequities in federally funded health care facilities.[65] Hence, there is an opening for the Biden Administration to prioritize effective Title VI enforcement. With the right leadership and guidance, administrative enforcement can potentially be more effective than private enforcement in the courts, as federal agencies have the "institutional advantages" of "resources" and "expertise" that courts may not have.[66]

V CONCLUSION

The legacy of the pandemic in the context of structural racism is unfolding; its path, while uncertain, contains promise to better effectuate health equity in the United States. How far the pandemic will move the country toward health equity is difficult to predict with precision; however, the unique moment presents the possibility of significant, if not monumental, progress. We believe that the legacy of COVID-19 in the context of American structural racism will be one that yields greater health equity; however, this outcome is not certain because while there are clear forces that can help propel America to greater health equity, opposing forces remain and will mitigate gains. While we offer our analysis as a predictive legacy informed by what has unraveled thus far, we also hope that it inspires and informs key stakeholders of the critical policy and legal areas on which to focus energy in the wake of the "twin crises" of the pandemic and structural racism.[67] Indeed, it is no guarantee that the arc of history will "bend" toward justice; it must be actively steered and pulled toward an equitable destination.[68] The future is in our hands.

[64] Id. at 313; see also Alexander v. Sandoval, 532 US 275 (2001).

[65] Yearby, supra note 63, at 312.

[66] Olatunde C.A. Johnson, Lawyering That Has No Name: Title VI and the Meaning of Private Enforcement, 66 Stan. L. Rev. 1293, 1328 (2014).

[67] Sheryl Gay Stolberg, 'Pandemic within a Pandemic': Coronavirus and Policy Brutality Roil Black Communities, NY Times (June 7, 2020), www.nytimes.com/2020/06/07/us/politics/blacks-coronavirus-police-brutality.html.

[68] Mychal Denzel Smith, The Truth About 'The Arc of the Moral Universe,' Huffington Post (Jan. 18, 2018), www.huffpost.com/entry/opinion-smith-obama-king_n_5a5903e0e4b04f3c55a252a4.

8

Access to Scarce Interventions

Age and Disability

Govind Persad and Jessica L. Roberts[*]

I INTRODUCTION

The COVID-19 pandemic placed older people and people with certain disabilities at especially acute risk of death. This risk did not stem merely from the virus, but from unfair policies during the pandemic. This chapter focuses on two resources that were scarce at different points in the pandemic: (1) critical care interventions; and (2) vaccines. We explore both formal allocation guidelines and their implementation, focusing on older adults and people with disabilities.[1] We conclude that while inclusive, non-discriminatory policies are necessary, they are insufficient alone. True fairness and equality require addressing biases and inequities in implementation.

II CRITICAL CARE RESOURCES

Patients who are severely ill, whether with COVID-19 or other conditions, often need critical care. When need exceeds availability, difficult choices among patients arise. Ventilator scarcity was publicized early in the US pandemic response, but rarely materialized. More common has been scarcity of staff, intensive care unit (ICU) beds, equipment such as dialysis machines, and supplies such as oxygen. This part explores US crisis standards of care, starting with written policies and then turning to implementation.

Crisis standards of care are formalized resource allocation protocols designed to guide health care providers in emergencies. They articulate how scarce, potentially life-saving health care should be distributed when need outstrips availability. How can we ensure that protocols for responding to scarcity treat older people, or people with preexisting medical conditions or disabilities, fairly? Three concerns about protocols should be distinguished: (1) whether an outcome is fundamentally

---

[*] Thanks to Marisa DeForest and Jessie N. Totten for research assistance and Emily Lawson for library support.

[1] Of course, these two categories are not mutually exclusive. People of any age may have disabilities. However, for purpose of our analysis here, we treat age and disability as distinct statuses.

inappropriate to consider; (2) whether considering an outcome may exacerbate disadvantage; and (3) whether predictions regarding an outcome may be inaccurate.

Some fairness concerns may apply more broadly than others. Legally, protections against disparate *treatment* (for instance, exclusion of specific medical conditions) often apply to individuals rather than groups. In contrast, protections against disparate *impact* – protocols that may create unequal outcomes – require considering population-level effects.

A *Benefit-Based Frameworks*

Unfairness charges have been leveled at protocols that aim to achieve three different types of outcomes: (1) quality of life; (2) years of life preserved; and (3) deaths prevented. These aims could be pursued through individualized assessments – for instance, use of Sequential Organ Failure Assessment (SOFA) scores. They could also be pursued through less individualized approaches.[2] We discuss each of these three outcomes in turn.

1 Quality of Life

Outside of scarcity contexts, there is little disagreement that treatments' effect on quality of life matters. That a treatment lacks painful side effects, for instance, is a point in its favor. Almost all recognized frameworks, however, regard using preexisting quality of life to distribute scarce resources among individuals as inadvisable.[3] Individuals are typically best placed to judge their own past and present quality of life, which makes present quality of life a poor basis for choosing among individuals. In addition, distributing scarce resources based on preexisting quality of life will likely worsen disadvantage by providing fewer resources to people whose preexisting quality of life is lower.[4] No states proposed using expected quality-adjusted life-years to allocate critical care treatments. Some, however, initially used criteria that referenced medical conditions, such as intellectual disabilities, that might be thought to reflect quality of life factors. These criteria have now been removed, some after legal challenges were announced though not by court order. One ethically defensible exception to a general rule against using others' quality of life judgments to allocate treatments among individuals under scarcity might involve individuals to whom the concept of a quality of life does not apply, such as those who are persistently unconscious.[5]

---

[2] Janet Malek, Defending the Inclusion of Categorical Exclusion Criteria in Crisis Standard of Care Frameworks, 20 *Am. J. Bioethics* 156, 156–57 (2020).

[3] E.g. Ezekiel J. Emanuel et al., Fair Allocation of Scarce Medical Resources in the Time of COVID-19, 382 *New Eng. J. Med.* 2049, 2052 (2020).

[4] Paul T. Menzel, Bias Adjustment and the Nature of Health-State Utility, 7 *J. L. Biosciences* 8 n.15 (2020).

[5] Ryan H. Nelson & Leslie P. Francis, Justice and Intellectual Disability in a Pandemic, 30 *Kennedy Inst. Ethics J.* 319 (2020).

2 Years of Life Preserved

How much a treatment extends life typically matters greatly in medicine – achieving even an extra year of survival is regarded as a breakthrough. Efforts to prolong life avoid the problem of overriding individual experience involved in attempts to assess quality of life, since individuals are typically not best placed to predict their future life expectancy. But considering future life expectancy may sometimes exacerbate disadvantage. Certain medical conditions tend to decrease future life expectancy, which means that considering future life expectancy may disproportionately exclude people with such conditions. How to weigh the risk of disproportionate exclusion against the preservation of future life is complex. Some take the position that life expectancy should be completely irrelevant to resource allocation. Others believe that where medical resources are scarce, it is ethically defensible to prioritize someone with Down syndrome or cystic fibrosis over someone with a drastically life-shortening condition such as terminal cancer, but not to prioritize someone facing no impediments to lifespan over someone with Down syndrome or cystic fibrosis. Still others do not regard life expectancy as fundamentally irrelevant, but worry that using present health status to estimate future life expectancy is too inaccurate or allows for the introduction of bias.

Although no court has found that considering how much a treatment would extend a patient's life violates the law, several states have elected to remove its consideration from crisis standards of care because of concerns about disproportionately excluding candidates with life-shortening conditions. There is, however, no reported case law rejecting the legality of considering future life expectancy in crisis standards of care to allocate ventilators or other treatments. Some studies have indicated strong public support (upwards of 75 percent) for considering life expectancy,[6] but others suggest lower levels of support.

Notably, using age as a predictor of future life expectancy is less likely to exacerbate overall disadvantage than using health status as a predictor.[7] This is true for several reasons: (1) having already lived a long time means one is less likely to have experienced many years of discrimination or poor health; (2) people who are medically or socially vulnerable are likely to become ill earlier in life, when they still have a long future life expectancy; and (3) it is more disadvantaging to die earlier in life. The outsized toll of lost years of life in US minority communities,[8] for instance, suggests that preserving future life by prioritizing the prevention of early deaths may remediate rather than exacerbate disadvantage.[9] Metrics such as Standardized

[6] Dominic Wilkinson et al., Which Factors Should Be Included in Triage? An Online Survey of the Attitudes of the UK General Public to Pandemic Triage Dilemmas, 10 *BMJ Open*, 2020, at 4.

[7] David Wasserman et al., Setting Priorities Fairly in Response to COVID-19: Identifying Overlapping Consensus and Reasonable Disagreement, 7 *J. Law Biosciences* 44 (2020).

[8] Mary T. Bassett et al., Variation in Racial/Ethnic Disparities in COVID-19 Mortality by Age in the United States: A Cross-Sectional Study, 17 *PLOS Med.*, Oct. 2020, at 5.

[9] Govind Persad & Steven Joffe, Allocating Scarce Life-Saving Resources: The Proper Role of Age, *J. Med. Ethics*, 2020, at 1–2; Govind Persad, Prioritizing the Prevention of Early Deaths during COVID-19, 51 *Hastings Ctr. Rep.* 42, 42 (2021).

Expected Years of Life Lost, which uses the global highest life expectancy at the time of death as a comparator rather than individuals' actual life expectancy, could capture the importance of preventing early deaths without disadvantaging individuals who have life-shortening medical conditions or face shorter life expectancies due to structural racism, and without categorically excluding older adults.[10]

3 Deaths Prevented

To prevent more deaths with a limited supply of resources, many protocols consider recipients' probability of survival, and some also consider the quantity of resources (e.g. time on dialysis) they are expected to need in order to benefit. Almost everyone agrees that preventing more deaths matters. But considering probability of survival or quantity of resources required could also exacerbate some forms of disadvantage, if those who are less likely to benefit or who need more resources also tend to be more disadvantaged. This presents a question about how to weigh saving more lives against not exacerbating disadvantage. In assessing this question, it matters whether some of the additional people saved by considering probability of survival or quantity of resources needed are themselves disadvantaged, as appears plausible given the connection between disadvantage and various health risks. For instance, considering quantity of resources used may not exacerbate disadvantage if more disadvantaged patients (for instance, people needing regular dialysis or ICU care for illnesses other than COVID-19) require fewer resources to obtain the same quantum of benefit, compared to COVID-19 patients who are very sick right now but who were not previously disadvantaged. Predictions about future resource use, which are less certain, may also be differentiable from facts about actual resource use – for instance, whether a patient's condition has improved after seven days of ICU treatment.

B *Benefit-Downplaying Frameworks*

Allocation protocols that completely reject the relevance of quality of life, preserving future life, and preventing more deaths might be termed *benefit-insensitive*: a patient's prospect of benefit is irrelevant to whether they receive treatment. Benefit-insensitive approaches include first-come, first-served and random selection of treatment candidates.[11] While these approaches claim to avoid biased decisions, they countenance more loss of life and do not make individualized judgments. Benefit-insensitive approaches may also fail to prevent the magnification of prior disadvantage because disadvantaged people have been more likely to contract and be

---

[10] Dietrich Plass et al., Quantifying the Burden of Disease Due to Premature Mortality in Hong Kong Using Standard Expected Years of Life Lost, 13 *BMC Public Health* 1, 3 (2013).

[11] Ari Ne'eman, 'I Will Not Apologize for My Needs,' NY Times (Mar. 23, 2020), www.nytimes .com/2020/03/23/opinion/coronavirus-ventilators-triage-disability.html; Diego S. Silva, Ventilators by Lottery: The Least Unjust Form of Allocation in the COVID-19 Pandemic, Chest (Sept. 2020).

hospitalized for COVID-19, meaning that the additional loss of life countenanced by benefit-insensitive approaches may fall disproportionately on disadvantaged people.

An alternative approach might be called *benefit-binary*.[12] Unlike the wholesale rejection of the ability to benefit of the benefit-insensitive model, this approach sorts patients into two categories: "unable to benefit" and "able to benefit." Those able to benefit can be prioritized over those who are unable to do so, but there is no further benefit-based prioritization among those able to benefit – instead, benefit-insensitive approaches such as lotteries or first-come, first-served distribution are used to choose among them. This approach is more individualized and could therefore result in fewer deaths than completely benefit-insensitive approaches. But, because it ignores individual variations in the ability to benefit, it would tolerate substantially more loss of life – again, concentrated among those more exposed to COVID-19 – than benefit-based views. It is also unclear whether benefit-binary approaches will address disadvantage or disability discrimination, since non-COVID-19 patients with disabilities or who are disadvantaged may sometimes be *more* likely to benefit from an intervention (such as a ventilator or dialysis treatment) than previously healthy or advantaged acute COVID-19 patients who are also *able* to benefit but less likely to do so. Last, benefit-binary approaches create a sharp distinction between being "unable" and "able" to benefit that treats people with similar prospect of benefit very differently, and may generate pressure to expand the category of people "unable to benefit," since few patients truly have zero prospect of any benefit from an intervention.

C *Frameworks That Remediate Disadvantage*

Rather than eliminating or reducing consideration of benefit in the hope that doing so will treat disadvantaged people more fairly, disadvantage could instead be addressed through intentional efforts. Some have suggested a "reserve" or categorized priority system that would set aside a subset of available resources for priority access for people who are disadvantaged.[13] Others object to approaches such as reserve systems, however, because they address disadvantage at a community rather than an individual level.[14] Even if a reserve system that considers both disadvantage and prospect of benefit is better for disadvantaged people overall than a

---

[12] Samuel R. Bagenstos, Who Gets the Ventilator? Disability Discrimination in COVID-19 Medical-Rationing Protocols, 130 *Yale L. J. Forum* 1, 4 (2020).

[13] Tayfun Sönmez et al., Categorized Priority Systems: A New Tool for Fairly Allocating Scarce Medical Resources in the Face of Profound Social Inequities, 159 *Chest* 1294, 1297 (2021). This approach has been supported by normative theorists as well. Deborah Hellman & Kate Nicholson, Rationing and Disability: The Civil Rights and Wrongs of State Triage Protocols, 4 *Wash. Lee L. Rev.* 1207 (2021); Govind Persad, Disability Law and the Case for Evidence-Based Triage in a Pandemic, 130 *Yale L. J. F.* 26, 45 (2020).

[14] Ari Ne'eman et al., The Treatment of Disability Under Crisis Standards of Care: An Empirical and Normative Analysis of Change Over Time During COVID-19, 46 *J. Health Pol. Pol'y L.* 831 (2021).

benefit-insensitive approach, those specific individuals who are less likely to benefit from treatment may have better chances of receiving treatment under a benefit-insensitive approach.

For policymakers concerned about the fairness of a purely benefit-based approach, the choice between an approach that explicitly incorporates both harm prevention and addressing disadvantage, such as a reserve system, and one that deemphasizes or removes consideration of either value, as benefit-insensitive approaches do, depends on a more fundamental question. If what policymakers value is protecting from the harms of COVID-19 people who are unfairly disadvantaged, including by ableism or ageism, a reserve system is an appealing modification to benefit-based approaches. Under conditions of scarcity, a reserve system can improve the fairness of distribution compared to a purely benefit-based approach, while averting a similar amount of harm. Or it could give further priority to disadvantaged people while averting modestly less harm than purely benefit-based approaches. Under either design, a reserve system can better address overall disadvantage and avert more harm than an outcome-insensitive approach. But benefit-insensitive approaches are preferable if policymakers instead regard treating everyone identically or providing a treatment to those specific individuals who are less likely to benefit from that treatment (as opposed to providing treatments to individuals who are disadvantaged more broadly) as fundamentally important. Similar questions about the relative priority of disadvantaged communities' interests and individual anti-discrimination claims have arisen elsewhere, such as in debates over allowable health benefit designs.[15]

The widespread use of age as a factor in vaccine allocation, meanwhile, suggests inconsistency with objections to the use of age in critical care allocation. Notably, one recent study suggested that assessments of expected ventilator benefit using the SOFA score were "significantly inferior to simply using age" to prioritize younger patients; another found that a youngest-first allocation both saved more lives and reduced disparities compared to SOFA or random allocation; and yet another concluded that data from a scoring system based on SOFA alone "strongly suggest the score was biased against younger people."[16] While using age as the *sole* basis for allocation is not consistent with current legal guidance, that guidance also explicitly permits the

[15] Compare Lenox v. Healthwise of Kentucky, Ltd., 149 F.3d 453, 457–58 (6th Cir. 1998), and Equal Emp. Opportunity Comm'n v. Staten Island Sav. Bank, 207 F.3d 144, 148 (2d Cir. 2000), with Boots v. Nw. Mut. Life Ins. Co., 77 F.Supp.2d 211, 219 (D.N.H. 1999).

[16] Robert A. Raschke et al., Discriminant Accuracy of the SOFA Score for Determining the Probable Mortality of Patients With COVID-19 Pneumonia Requiring Mechanical Ventilation, *JAMA* (Feb. 17, 2021), https://jamanetwork.com/journals/jama/fullarticle/2776737; S.V. Bhavani et al., Simulation of Ventilator Allocation in Critically Ill Patients with COVID-19, *Am. J. of Respiratory & Critical Care Med.*, Sept. 9, 2021; Sarah M. Kesler et al., Operationalizing Ethical Guidance for Ventilator Allocation in Minnesota: Saving the Most Lives or Exacerbating Health Disparities?, 3 *Critical Care Explorations* 1 (2021), www.ncbi.nlm.nih.gov/pmc/articles/PMC8202637/.

use of age as one factor.[17] If age is predictive of benefit – albeit in opposite directions – for both ventilators and vaccines, it is difficult to defend its use in one context but not the other. Using age as a factor in distributing scarce ICU beds or ventilators could improve benefit while remediating disadvantage, by protecting younger but very ill people – often people with life-shortening disabilities or members of minority communities – who can benefit from treatment and who were excluded by the age-based prioritization of older patients for vaccines and therapeutics. One study concluded that a SOFA-only approach that excluded consideration of age would likely lead to "giving an older person with a poor prognosis a ventilator instead of a younger patient with a better prognosis" and to "prioritizing older White patients at the expense of younger BIPOC [Black, Indigenous, and People of Color] patients."[18]

III VACCINES

As the pandemic progressed, interventions that forestall the need for critical care – ranging from new therapies for COVID-19 patients to vaccines that could prevent COVID-19 infection – became available but were often scarce. This part turns to the allocation of therapeutics and preventatives with a focus on vaccine prioritization and access. In this context, older Americans and Americans with disabilities were often given formal *priority* in written protocols, but this priority often did not translate into actual priority in access.

Few advocated benefit-insensitive (first-come, first-served or random) vaccine distribution. Nor was individualized assessment required: categorical inclusions and exclusions based on health status or age were typical. This likely reflects the fact that vaccines and therapeutics present less tension between addressing disadvantage and preventing harm: those whose disadvantage worsens their prospect of benefit from a ventilator or ICU bed also gain most in relative safety by becoming vaccinated.

Debates over vaccine prioritization focused on the list of categorical inclusions: which medical vulnerabilities would make a person eligible for early vaccination. The Centers for Disease Control and Prevention (CDC) listed specific medical conditions associated with greater COVID-19 risk, and many studies identified similar high-risk conditions.[19] These studies, however, typically focused on infection fatality rates – that is, risk among those infected – rather than risk of exposure to COVID-19.

---

[17] US Dep't of Health & Hum. Servs., Section 1557: Frequently Asked Questions, HHS.gov: Civil Rights, www.hhs.gov/civil-rights/for-individuals/section-1557/1557faqs/index.html (last visited May 18, 2017).

[18] Kesler et al., supra note 16, at 6.

[19] Elizabeth J. Williamson et al., Factors Associated with COVID-19-Related Death Using OpenSAFELY, 584 *Nature* 430, 433 (2020), www.nature.com/articles/s41586-020-2521-4.pdf; Lyudmyla Kompaniyets et al., Underlying Medical Conditions Associated with Severe COVID-19 Illness Among Children, JAMA Network: Open, 4–6 (June 7, 2021), https://jamanetwork.com/journals/jamanetworkopen/fullarticle/2780706.

Considering exposure risk would also recommend prioritizing people living in congregate settings and potentially those whose medical vulnerabilities preclude effective protective measures, such as masking or socially distancing. In contrast, conditions that do not affect exposure risk or risk if infected were not a basis for accelerated eligibility. Just as certain disabilities, such as those affecting mobility, qualify individuals for parking permits but others do not, conditions such as Down syndrome that increase risk of severe outcomes if infected should support early eligibility for COVID-19 vaccines, while conditions that do not increase risk should not.

Most states used an "honor system," requiring only self-attestation of medical risk.[20] This approach avoided the need for documentation. But it allowed people at lower risk who misinterpreted guidance or willfully misrepresented their status to receive vaccines before people at higher risk. Additionally, while some states prioritized people with multiple risk-increasing conditions, few prioritized among risk-increasing conditions, even though certain conditions (such as Down syndrome or cancer) appeared to increase risk much more than others. Some states allowed providers discretion to manage medical eligibility.[21] This approach might be superior to an "honor system" at matching eligibility to actual risk and be more inclusive of people at high risk because of uncommon conditions, but could present challenges for individuals without providers and introduce subjective judgment by providers. An alternative approach would be active outreach and provision of vaccine appointments to people with documented high-risk conditions, rather than requiring individuals to assess their own risk or provide proof.[22] This approach was used in some health systems but presents challenges due to health system fragmentation.

In contrast to many states' total removal of age from critical care distribution protocols, vaccine eligibility was often based on older age alone. Age was a reasonable access criterion given the sharply increasing risk of COVID-19 death at older ages. However, one-size-fits-all age cutoffs, such as 75, were criticized for exacerbating disadvantage and health disparities, given that disadvantaged people and people with certain disabilities face shorter life expectancies and higher COVID-19 risk earlier in life than others.[23] Empirical research also demonstrated that including factors other

[20] WBUR Newsroom, WBUR Town Hall Recap: Ethics and the Vaccine, WBUR News (Mar. 3, 2021), www.wbur.org/news/2021/03/02/vaccine-town-hall-part-3-qa.

[21] Jeffrey Schweers, Florida Hospital to Receive COVID Vaccine for 'Extremely Vulnerable,' Tallahassee Democrat (Feb. 2, 2021), www.tallahassee.com/story/news/local/state/2021/02/01/florida-hospitals-covid-vaccine-coronavirus-extremely-vulnerable/4335840001/.

[22] William F. Parker et al., Four Recommendations to Efficiently and Equitably Accelerate the COVID-19 Vaccine Rollout, *Health Affs.* (Feb. 10, 2021), www.healthaffairs.org/do/10.1377/hblog20210204.166874/full/.

[23] Wendi C. Thomas & Hannah Grabenstein, People Over 75 Are First in Line to Be Vaccinated Against COVID-19. The Average Black Person Here Doesn't Live That Long, ProPublica (Feb. 12, 2021), www.propublica.org/article/people-over-75-are-first-in-line-to-be-vaccinated-against-covid-19-the-average-black-person-doesnt-live-that-long.

than age was both more equitable and prevented more harm than age cutoffs.[24] In response, some states lowered age thresholds or permitted universal eligibility for certain populations, such as Federally Qualified Health Center patients.[25]

A few states even attempted to use age as the only criterion for vaccine access, touting its administrative simplicity and strong correlation with risk.[26] These approaches quickly faced challenges for excluding individuals at high medical risk,[27] and they may have also been inconsistent with regulatory language interpreting the Age Discrimination Act, which prohibits the use of age as the sole determinant of access to treatment. These approaches were either revised or became moot with universal vaccine eligibility.

IV BARRIERS TO IMPLEMENTATION

While attempts to adopt non-discriminatory allocation policies are laudatory, these efforts alone will not be sufficient to ensure that older Americans and Americans with disabilities receive the care that they deserve during a public health crisis.

A *Unconscious Bias*

Even health care providers who lack discriminatory intent may nonetheless make decisions based on unconscious beliefs or attitudes about particular groups.[28] Over the past decade, experts have recognized implicit bias as a potential contributor to health disparities.[29] While race has been the primary research focus,[30] studies have also documented implicit bias on the basis of age and disability in health care.[31] Sadly, the pandemic has further exposed socially pervasive ageism and ableism.

Importantly, research shows that, when health care professionals exhibit implicit bias, it lowers the quality of care that they provide.[32] Unconscious bias against older

---

[24] Elizabeth Wrigley-Field et al., Geographically Targeted COVID-19 Vaccination is More Equitable and Averts More Deaths than Age-Based Thresholds Alone, 7 *Sci. Advances* eabj2099 (2021), www.science.org/doi/pdf/10.1126/sciadv.abj2099.

[25] Federally Qualified Health Centers Can Vaccinate Anyone They Serve, or. Vaccine News (Mar. 31, 2021), https://covidblog.oregon.gov/federally-qualified-health-centers-can-vaccinate-anyone-they-serve/.

[26] Brenda Leon, Some States Drop CDC Guidelines and Vaccinate People By Age Group, NPR: The Coronavirus Crisis (Mar. 3, 2021), www.npr.org/2021/03/03/972973668/some-states-drop-cdc-guidelines-and-vaccinate-people-by-age-group.

[27] Emily Brindley, Disability Rights Connecticut Files Federal Civil Rights Complaint Claiming State's Age-Based Plan for COVID-19 Vaccinations is Discriminatory, Hartford Courant (Feb. 25, 2021), www.courant.com/coronavirus/hc-news-coronavirus-new-rollout-disability-discrimination-complaint-20210225-ybxtwlgdgffs7kzsijgn72dzhq-story.html [https://perma.cc/L7BK-CVGZ].

[28] Chloë FitzGerald & Samia Hurst, Implicit Bias in Healthcare Professionals: A Systematic Review, 19 *BMC Med. Ethics* 1, 1 (2017).

[29] Irene V. Blair et al., Unconscious (Implicit) Bias and Health Disparities: Where Do We Go from Here?, *The Permanente J.*, 2011, at 71, 72–73.

[30] Id. at 71.

[31] FitzGerald & Hurst, supra note 28, at 4, 11.

[32] Id. at 13.

people and people with disabilities could influence seemingly impartial medical judgments about the kinds of resources an individual might require (including potential accommodations during treatment), the prospects of long-term survival, or the effect of permanent disabilities on short-term recovery. Unconscious bias is particularly salient to approaches that allow for physician discretion rather than a formalized scoring system. These biases could influence the outcomes of allocation approaches that incorporate subjective medical judgment or rely on providers' intuition and affect the provision of non-scarce resources to COVID-19 patients throughout their interaction with health systems. Thus, even well-intentioned health care providers who wish to provide inclusive COVID-19 treatment that conforms with applicable standards and policies could still make biased decisions because of their unconscious negative beliefs about older people and people with disabilities.

B *Lack of Access to Technology*

Many public health authorities relied on digital tools to connect eligible individuals with vaccination appointments. For example, states offer online registration systems for eligible residents that promise to notify them of appointments, often by text or email.[33] Interactive, web-based maps allow people to locate nearby vaccine providers.[34] Unfortunately, relying too heavily on these technologies may exclude some of the most vulnerable Americans. While older adults are online more now than ever before, a digital divide still exists between older and younger Americans.[35] Older, poorer, and less educated seniors are even less likely to be comfortable with digital technology.[36] Troublingly, some of these differences fall on racial lines: older Black Americans are significantly less likely to go online or have broadband access.[37]

Preexisting access barriers related to technology may likewise impede vaccination for people with certain kinds of disabilities and health conditions. Despite the Americans with Disabilities Act,[38] much of the Internet remains inaccessible for people with disabilities that affect vision, communication, and dexterity. One study found that 98 percent of the home pages of one million popular websites failed to meet web accessibility standards.[39] Thus, reliance on online tools to help locate vaccine sites and book appointments could inadvertently exclude people with disabilities.

---

[33] See, for example, COVID-19 Vaccinations in Maryland, Md. Dep't of Health, https://coronavirus .maryland.gov/pages/vaccine (last visited Apr. 29, 2021).

[34] See, for example, GISCorps COVID-19 Resources, https://covid-19-giscorps.hub.arcgis.com/ [https:// perma.cc/T4TB-5BZG] (last visited Apr. 6, 2023).

[35] Monica Anderson & Andrew Perrin, Technology Use Among Seniors, *Pew Rsch. Ctr.* (May 17, 2017), www.pewresearch.org/internet/2017/05/17/technology-use-among-seniors/.

[36] Id.

[37] Aaron Smith, African Americans and Technology Use, *Pew Rsch. Ctr.* (Jan. 6, 2014), www.pewresearch .org/internet/2014/01/06/african-americans-and-technology-use/.

[38] 42 U.S.C. §§ 12101 et seq.

[39] The WebAIM Million: An Annual Accessibility Analysis of the Top 1,000,000 Home Pages, WebAim (Mar. 30, 2020), https://webaim.org/projects/million/#facts.

C *Lack of Access to Transportation*

Despite a diversity of locations, both seniors and people with disabilities encounter serious transportation barriers getting to vaccination appointments. Many older adults no longer drive and lack access to convenient public transportation.[40] In fact, in the United States, about 1.6 million adults over 65 are homebound,[41] and over half of homebound older Americans have at least one additional barrier to vaccination, such as living alone or not having access to technology.[42] Complicating matters more, they may also not have friends or family members who can drive them places.[43] Vaccination sites, which are often hospitals or pharmacies, may be prohibitively far for seniors, who generally receive health care through individual physicians or health centers.[44] One study from late 2020 found that, in 12 percent of counties, about half of older adults would have to travel more than ten miles for a vaccine.[45] Again, race is a complicating factor. Only 3 percent of White older adults are homebound, compared to 15 percent of Hispanic older adults and 7 percent of Black older adults.[46]

Similarly, over 25 million Americans with disabilities report travel limitations, and 3.6 million people with travel-limiting disabilities are homebound.[47] As a group, people with disabilities are less likely to drive than people without disabilities, meaning they may need assistance to reach vaccine sites.[48] People with disabilities also encounter barriers in both public transportation and in paratransit.[49] Stations may be inaccessible; lifts and ramps may be inoperable; drivers may not stop for people with visible disabilities; scheduled pick-ups may be difficult to book, run late, or be completely missed; and travel times may be excessively long.[50] In addition, buildings or medical equipment may be inaccessible,[51] and medical facilities may lack

---

[40] Jenni Bergal, Without a Ride, Many in Need Have No Shot at COVID-19 Vaccine, Pew Charitable Tr. (Feb. 1, 2021), www.pewtrusts.org/en/research-and-analysis/blogs/stateline/2021/02/01/without-a-ride-many-in-need-have-no-shot-at-covid-19-vaccine.

[41] Emma Nye & Martin Blanco, Characteristics of Homebound Older Adults: Potential Barriers to Accessing the COVID-19 Vaccine Issue Brief, *US Dep't Health & Hum. Servs.* (Apr. 6, 2021), aspe.hhs.gov/homebound-vaccine-covid.

[42] Id.

[43] Bergal, supra note 40.

[44] Nye & Blanco, supra note 41.

[45] Some States May Lack Facilities for Administering COVID-19 Vaccine to Residents, W. Health (Dec. 16, 2020), www.westhealth.org/press-release/states-lack-facilities-for-administering-covid-19-vaccine/.

[46] Nye & Blanco, supra note 41.

[47] Stephen Brumbaugh, Travel Patterns of American Adults with Disabilities, US Dep't of Transp. (Sept. 2018), www.bts.gov/sites/bts.dot.gov/files/docs/explore-topics-and-geography/topics/passenger-travel/222466/travel-patterns-american-adults-disabilities-11-26-19.pdf.

[48] Id.

[49] Jill L. Bezyak et al., Public Transportation: An Investigation of Barriers for People with Disabilities, 28 *J. Disability Pol'y Stud.* 52 (2017).

[50] Id.

[51] Access to Medical Care for Individuals with Mobility Disabilities, US Dep't of Just. (Feb. 28. 2021), www.ada.gov/medcare_mobility_ta/medcare_ta.htm.

sufficient communication supports such as interpreters, qualified readers, informational materials, and accessible kiosks.[52] These same issues could likewise impede vaccine access, even after a person with a disability manages to secure transportation and arrive at the vaccination site.

V RECOMMENDATIONS

Drawing from the lessons of the pandemic, we make the following recommendations for ensuring the fair allocation of limited health care resources.

A *Debiasing*

Given health care providers' reported biases regarding older adults and people with disabilities and the vulnerability of those populations during the pandemic, debiasing will be essential to ensuring fair treatment and better outcomes. Studies have shown that interventions can effectively reduce ageism and improve attitudes toward older adults.[53] Reducing or eliminating negative stereotypes could then, in turn, reduce the effects of implicit bias, including in the context of health care. Effective strategies consist of education, intergenerational interactions, or some combination of the two.[54] Similarly, incorporating disability perspectives into medical education and practice could have a debiasing effect.[55] In addition, removing barriers to equitable treatment for older adults and their caregivers is essential. These factors, for instance, might support allowing many older adults and patients with certain disabilities to be accompanied by appropriately protected companions, even during a pandemic.

B *Improving Access*

The use of specific disabilities as a priority factor in vaccine allocation is a welcome attempt to address the outsized burdens that people with certain disabilities have borne during the COVID-19 pandemic. Yet simply listing older adults and people with disabilities as priority groups in vaccination plans will not by itself ensure that these populations receive vaccines.

Offering more vaccines in settings used by people with risk-increasing disabilities, and reaching out proactively rather than requiring people to prove eligibility, could have both improved the fairness of allocation and practically eased the process of

---

[52] Health Care and the Americans with Disabilities Act, ADA Nat'l Network, https://adata.org/factsheet/health-care-and-ada (last visited Apr. 29, 2021).

[53] David Burnes et al., Interventions to Reduce Ageism Against Older Adults: A Systematic Review and Meta-Analysis, 109 *Am. J. Pub. Health* e1, e5–e7 (2019).

[54] Id. at e1.

[55] Heidi L. Janz, Ableism: The Undiagnosed Malady Afflicting Medicine, 191 *Canadian Med. Ass'n J.* E478, E479 (2019).

obtaining vaccines for people with disabilities. In March 2021, President Biden took action to improve vaccine access for both older Americans and Americans with disabilities.[56] His plan includes a partnership between the CDC and the Administration for Community Living to provide almost $100 million in grant funding to networks for seniors and people with disabilities across the country with the goal of addressing barriers to vaccination.[57] The Administration for Community Living has already identified a number of promising strategies for combating many of the challenges described above. States, municipalities, and community partners can ensure that websites and materials are accessible and easy to understand, and that hotlines are available as an alternative to schedule appointments.[58] Advocacy organizations and networks can act as partners to help schedule appointments, provide transportation, and offer reminders.[59] Organizations can also help to identify access barriers at vaccination sites and to locate vaccination sites friendly to older adults and people with disabilities.[60] And finally, all stakeholders – states, municipalities, and community partners – can collaborate to facilitate mobile and in-home vaccinations.[61]

VI CONCLUSION

Several states adopted openly discriminatory resource allocation policies, especially in the early days of the pandemic. Much attention was given to these policies, and they were revised before being put into place. Most disparities, however, appeared to stem from problems in implementation. Regardless of crisis standards of care and vaccine distribution policies, older Americans and Americans with disabilities may still experience disparities. These issues do not disappear in the course of a pandemic, when tensions run high and resources run low. We have certainly learned many lessons from the current public health crisis. However, if we are serious about health equity in the future, adopting non-discriminatory and inclusive policies will not be enough. We must address the causes of health disparities in health care delivery to ensure that these laudable standards do not falter at implementation.

---

[56] HHS to Expand Access to COVID-19 Vaccines for Older Adults and People with Disabilities, US Dep't Health & Hum. Servs. (Mar. 29, 2021), http://web.archive.org/web/20210329191126/www.hhs .gov/about/news/2021/03/29/hhs-to-expand-access-to-covid-19-vaccines-for-older-adults-and-people-with-disabilities.html.

[57] Id.

[58] Strategies for Helping Older Adults and People with Disabilities Access COVID-19 Vaccines, Admin. Cmty. Living (Apr. 2021), https://acl.gov/sites/default/files/2021-04/ACLStrategiesVaccineAccess_ Final.pdf.

[59] Id.

[60] Id.

[61] Id.

9

Humane and Resilient Long-Term Care

A Post-COVID-19 Vision

Nina A. Kohn

I INTRODUCTION

Long-term care institutions were ground zero for the COVID-19 pandemic in the United States. The first reported outbreaks in the country were in long-term care institutions; such facilities continued to experience very high rates of infection and death during the first two years of infection, and substantial risk well into 2023.[1]

Long-term care residents make up less than 1 percent of the US population. Yet, by January 2021, before the benefits of the COVID-19 vaccinations had been realized to any significant extent,[2] residents and staff of these institutions accounted for 38 percent of all US deaths from COVID-19,[3] and nursing home residents alone accounted for about 25 percent of confirmed US deaths.[4] A year later, residents and staff of long-term care facilities still represented a very disproportionate share of COVID-19 fatalities – as of January 2022, they accounted for at least 23 percent of all COVID-19 deaths in the United States.[5] This chapter explains the underlying causes of this devastation and what can be learned from it to improve the future quality of long-term care. It shows how the patterns observed in long-term care facilities

---

[1] See Centers for Disease Prevention & Control, Nursing Home Covid-19 Data Dashboard, www.cdc
   .gov/nhsn/covid19/ltc-report-overview.html.
[2] See Priya Chidambaram & Rachel Garfield, COVID-19 Long-Term Care Deaths and Cases Are at
   an All-Time Low, Though a Rise in LTC Cases in a Few States May Be Cause for Concern, Kaiser
   Family Foundation (Apr. 22, 2021), www.kff.org/coronavirus-COVID-19/issue-brief/COVID-19-long-
   term-care-deaths-and-cases-are-at-an-all-time-low-though-a-rise-in-ltc-cases-in-a-few-states-may-be-
   cause-for-concern/ (documenting the link between vaccination rates and the decline in COVID-19
   mortality among residents and staff of long-term care facilities).
[3] More Than One-Third of U.S. Coronavirus Deaths are Linked to Nursing Homes, NY Times, Jan. 12,
   2021, www.nytimes.com/interactive/2020/us/coronavirus-nursing-homes.html (reporting on deaths in
   long-term care, despite the misleading article title).
[4] Center for Medicaid & Medicare Services, COVID-19 Nursing Home Data, https://data.cms.gov/
   stories/s/COVID-19-Nursing-Home-Data/bkwz-xpvg/.
[5] See Priya Chidambaram, Over 200,000 Residents and Staff in Long-Term Care Facilities Have
   Died from COVID- 19, Kaiser Family Foundation (Feb. 3, 2022), www.kff.org/policy-watch/over-
   200000-residents-and-staff-in-long-term-care-facilities-have-died-from-covid-19/ (noting the lack of
   data on the demographic breakdown of these deaths).

are the combined result of an inadequate public health response to the needs of long-term care residents, preexisting regulatory failures that rendered long-term care institutions infection tinderboxes, and policies that steered vulnerable adults into these institutions in the first place. It then suggests the regulatory and cultural shifts needed to create a more humane and resilient model of long-term care.

II THE CRISIS IN LONG-TERM CARE INSTITUTIONS

In the United States, long-term care facilities fall into two major categories. First, there are nursing homes, highly regulated institutions that provide skilled medical and custodial care to adults with substantial chronic-care needs. Second, there are assisted living facilities, which provide a varied combination of housing, meals, and health-related services to adults with a broader range of care needs.

Residents of both types of long-term institutions are highly susceptible to COVID-19, as they are to other infectious diseases. Living in a congregate care setting impedes social distancing, and the flow of staff and visitors in and out of facilities creates many potential vectors of contagion. In addition, residents' underlying health conditions make them highly vulnerable to the effects of infections, increasing the likelihood that they will experience serious illness and death if infected with COVID-19.

However, as detailed in this part, COVID-19's disastrous impact on residents of long-term care institutions cannot be explained simply by residents' susceptibility to infection. Rather, it also reflects an inadequate public health response to COVID-19 in these facilities, as well as a preexisting regulatory failure that left long-term care residents unreasonably vulnerable to pandemic conditions.

A *The Role of Public Health Response Failures*

COVID-19's impact on long-term care residents reflects a slow and inadequate public health response to the heightened risk the virus posed to residents. Testing of nursing home residents and staff was not mandated by the Centers for Medicaid and Medicare Services (CMS), the federal agency that regulates such homes, until September 2020, six months after the start of the pandemic in the United States.[6] Nursing homes were provided with limited personal protective equipment (PPE) by the federal government. However, the Federal Emergency Management Agency (FEMA), which was tasked with provision, provided woefully insufficient amounts of PPE, much of which was simply unusable (e.g., faulty masks, gowns with no armholes) or clearly inappropriate (e.g., condoms as PPE);[7] FEMA never provided the

---

[6] Joe Eaton, Who's to Blame for the 100,000 Covid Dead in Long-Term Care?, AARP (Dec. 3, 2020), www.aarp.org/caregiving/health/info-2020/covid-19-nursing-homes-who-is-to-blame.html.
[7] Id.

N95 masks that workers needed to avoid infecting residents.[8] Of course, testing deficiencies and PPE shortages also occurred in hospital settings, but nursing homes were generally given lower priority than hospitals for testing and PPE allocation, despite their highly vulnerable populations.

The public health response to the needs of assisted living residents was even slower and more haphazard than that to nursing home residents. The Centers for Disease Control and Prevention prioritized all long-term care facilities for the administration of vaccines, and states largely followed this advice. Nevertheless, the rollout to assisted living facilities was slower and bumpier than in nursing homes, in part because the facilities are less equipped to facilitate medical care.[9] Similarly, the federal government provided support to nursing homes in general but provided support only to assisted living communities serving Medicaid-eligible residents (some 16 percent of assisted living facilities).[10]

B *The Role of Regulatory Failure*

The degree of danger that COVID-19 has posed to long-term care residents reflects long-standing problems in how these facilities are operated. The extent of the operational failures, in turn, is shaped by two types of regulatory failure: (1) a failure to mandate certain practices essential to ensuring safe and humane care; and (2) a failure to enforce existing regulations designed to protect residents.

1 Inadequate Regulatory Requirements

The extent to which long-term care institutions are subject to regulations designed to protect residents varies by type of long-term care facility. Nursing homes are highly regulated. Since the adoption of the federal Nursing Home Reform Act as part of the Omnibus Reconciliation Act of 1987, nursing homes certified to receive Medicaid or Medicare funding must have a comprehensive resident assessment and care planning system, meet federal standards related to quality of care and resident safety, and respect and support a litany of residents' rights. By contrast, assisted living facilities, which are home to approximately one million Americans, are regulated almost exclusively at the state level (with significant variation from state to state) and are subject to far fewer regulatory requirements than nursing homes.[11] This difference in

---

[8] Id.

[9] Cf. Kaiser Family Foundation, January 14 Web Event: A Shot in the Arm for Long-Term Care Facilities? Early Lessons from the COVID-19 Vaccine Rollout to High Priority Populations (Jan. 14, 2021), www.kff.org/medicaid/event/january-14-web-event-a-shot-in-the-arm-for-long-term-care-facilities-early-lessons-from-the-COVID-19-vaccine-rollout-to-high-priority-populations/.

[10] See Helena Temkin-Greener et al., COVID-19 Pandemic in Assisted Living Communities: Results from Seven States, 68 J. Am. Geriatrics Soc'y 2727 (2020).

[11] See Alison M. Trinkoff et al., Comparing Residential Long-Term Care Regulations Between Nursing Homes and Assisted Living Facilities, 68 *Nursing Home Outlook* 113 (2019).

regulation can be attributed to several factors, including that: (1) assisted living was developed, at least ostensibly, as a nonmedical model of care; (2) the primary source of funding for assisted living facilities is private payment (unlike nursing homes); and (3) the 1987 Act was enacted prior to the ascendence of the assisted living industry.

Under-regulation of assisted living facilities is a serious concern. Such facilities increasingly take high-needs patients who might otherwise require nursing home care.

Nevertheless, state requirements for staffing – both in terms of the number and qualifications of personnel – are often minimal; assisted living facilities in some states are not even required to have staff present throughout the entire day.[12] A 2016 study found that although the majority of assisted living facilities admit residents who require nursing care, most did not have a licensed care provider on staff; rather, such facilities were staffed primarily by patient care aides, who, on average, were required to have fewer than seventy-five hours of training before they began providing care to residents, and who, in some facilities, were not required to have any formal training before providing resident care.[13] This lack of skilled staffing is often attributed to the use by assisted living facilities of a "social model" of care instead of a "medical model," but it raises serious concerns, by both patient advocates and medical providers,[14] about the ability of assisted living facilities to meet residents' basic needs, even during normal, non-pandemic conditions.[15]

Of particular relevance during the COVID-19 pandemic, infection-control requirements for assisted living facilities are also meager, despite the known risk of infectious disease outbreaks in such facilities.[16] Only approximately one quarter of the states impose specific infection-control requirements on assisted living facilities, and over a third do not even require facilities to have infection-control plans.[17] The result is a lack of proper planning and preparation for preventing transmission of disease. The lack of federal engagement is also a barrier to national-level planning and intervention. For example, assisted living facilities do not report COVID-19 infections and fatalities directly to the federal government,[18] making it more difficult to understand and address the overall risk COVID-19 has posed to their residents.

---

[12] Id.

[13] Kihye Han et. al., Variation Across U.S. Assisted Living Facilities: Admissions, Resident Care Needs, and Staffing, J. Nursing Scholarship (2016); see also Anne S. Beeber et al., Licensed Nursing Staffing and Health Service Availability in Residential Care and Assisted Living, 62 J. Am. Geriatrics Soc'y 805 (2014).

[14] Sheryl Zimerman et al., The Need to Include Assisted Living in Responding to the COVID-19 Pandemic, 21 J. Am. Med. Dirs. Ass'n 572 (2020); Phillip D. Sloane et al., Physical Perspectives on Medical Care Delivery in Assisted Living, J. Am. Geriatrics Soc'y 59 (2011).

[15] Accord Andrew Vipperman, Sheryl Zimmerman & Philip D. Sloane, COVID-19 Recommendations for Assisted Living: Implications for the Future, 22 J. Am. Med. Dirs. Ass'n 933 (2021).

[16] Rachel Kossover et al., Infection Prevention and Control Standards in Assisted Living Facilities: Are Residents Needs Being Met?, 15 J. Am. Med. Dirs. Ass'n 47 (2014).

[17] Debra Dobbs, Lindsay Peterson & Kathryn Hyer, The Unique Challenges Faced by Assisted Living Communities to Meet Federal Guidelines for COVID-19, 32 J. Aging Soc. Pol'y 334 (2020).

[18] Sarah H. Yi et al., Characterization of COVID-19 in Assisted Living Facilities – 39 States, October 2020, 69 Morbidity and Mortality Weekly Report, Ctrs. for Disease Control & Prevention 1730 (Nov. 2020),

While nursing homes are much more highly regulated than assisted living facilities, regulatory gaps still exist. Most importantly, federal regulations governing nursing homes fail to impose minimum staffing ratios. This failure had been identified as a major risk long before COVID-19 hit. It was well recognized that nursing home quality of care was undermined because nursing homes tend to be chronically under-staffed and to over-rely on part-time staff and staff who lack sick leave benefits (and thus are more likely to come to work when ill). There was also widespread agreement among experts that a minimum of 4.1 hours of direct-care staff per resident per day is needed on average to avoid systemic neglect,[19] although most nursing homes provide less.[20] Recent evidence from the COVID-19 pandemic further underscores the danger of this gap by demonstrating the close relationship between staff time and resident well-being. Studies are finding that higher staffing levels (especially nurse staffing levels) are associated with reduced presence of COVID-19 in long-term care facilities,[21] and with increased ability to contain outbreaks when they do occur.[22] In addition, studies have linked over-reliance on part-time and agency staff, as well as lack of paid sick leave, to the spread of COVID-19 both within and among long-term care facilities.

2 Under-Enforcement of Existing Regulations

Whereas the primary regulatory failure in the assisted living context is a failure to mandate necessary practices, the primary failure in the nursing home context is under-enforcement of existing regulations. Under federal law, US nursing homes that accept Medicare or Medicaid funds – virtually all US nursing homes – are required to meet extensive quality-of-care requirements.[23] For example, nursing homes must ensure that their residents receive individualized care in accordance with professional standards of practice and do not experience avoidable harm or avoidable reductions in functional abilities.[24] If such requirements were enforced, the fact that nursing homes are not directly required to use the inputs

---

www.cdc.gov/mmwr/volumes/69/wr/pdfs/mm6946a3-H.pdf (describing the lack of data on assisted living infections); Staff Report on COVID-19 in Assisted Living Facilities (July 2020), www.warren.senate.gov/imo/media/doc/Assisted%20Living%20Facilities%20Staff%20Report.pdf.

19 Charlene Harrington et al., The Need for Higher Minimum Staffing Standards in U.S. Nursing Homes, 9 *Health Servs. Insights* 13 (2016).

20 Id.; see also Maggie Flynn, Registered Nurse Staffing Falls Short in Most Nursing Homes, Skilled Nursing News (Mar. 15, 2018), https://skillednursingnews.com/2018/03/registered-nurse-staffing-falls-short-nursing-homes/.

21 Charlene Harrington, Leslie Ross & Susan Chapman, Nurse Staffing & Coronavirus Infections in California Nursing Homes, Pol'y, Pol., & Nursing Prac. (2020); Rebecca J. Gorges & R. Tamara Konetzka, Staffing Levels and COVID-19 Cases & Outbreaks in U.S. Nursing Homes, 68 *J. Am. Geriatrics Soc'y* 2462 (2020).

22 Gorges & Konetzka, supra note 20.

23 See Ctrs. for Medicare & Medicaid Servs., Nursing Home Data Compendium 2015 edition 1, 10 fig.1.2. (2015).

24 See 42 C.F.R. §§ 483.21, 483.24–25 (2021).

they need to achieve those outcomes (such as sufficient staffing levels) would be of little practical consequence. However, that is not the case: nursing homes are rarely held to account for their failure to comply with regulations designed to protect residents.

This under-enforcement of regulations designed to protect nursing home residents is the combined result of two failures. The first is a failure of state inspectors to identify and accurately assess violations. As the Government Accountability Office has found, state inspectors systematically underreport serious deficiencies, including ones that pose immediate threats to residents' health and safety.[25] Similarly, the Government Accountability Office has criticized regulators for failing to collect the information necessary to protect residents from identified abuse and neglect.[26]

The second type of under-enforcement failure is a failure to correct and penalize identified violations. Regulators have statutory authority to impose significant penalties on facilities – including holds on new admissions or payment, as well as monetary fines. However, CMS has instead taken an approach that imposes no financial consequences for most regulatory violations. When violations are found – even serious violations – facilities are typically simply directed to make corrections and regulators may never assess whether those corrections are actually made.[27] Fines are rare and are reserved for certain categories of violation; they are also typically too small to deter bad behavior.

These problems became more acute during the Trump Administration,[28] in part because the Administration moved away from assessing fines for violations on a per-day basis in favor of assessing them on a per-instance basis.[29] Moreover, the Trump Administration severely curtailed enforcement efforts during the COVID-19 pandemic as CMS suspended a broad array of enforcement actions and waived key regulatory requirements for nursing homes,[30] often as part of broader efforts to ease burdens on

---

[25] See US Gov't Accountability Off., Nursing Homes: Despite Increased Oversight, Challenges Remain in Ensuring High-Quality Care and Resident Safety (2006).

[26] See US Gov't Accountability Off., Improved Oversight Needed to Better Protect Residents from Abuse (2019).

[27] Off. of the Inspector Gen., Dep't of Health & Human Servs., CMS Guidance to State Survey Agencies on Verifying Correction of Deficiencies Needs to Be Improved to Help Ensure the Health and Safety of Nursing Home Residents (2019).

[28] See, generally, Joran Rao, Nursing Home Fines Drop as Trump Administration Heeds Industry Complaints, Kaiser Health Network (Mar. 15, 2019), www.aarp.org/caregiving/health/info-2020/nursing-home-covid-federal-aid-transparency.html.

[29] These changes are the subject of a lawsuit filed by AARP Foundation and Constantine Cannon LLP on behalf of the California Advocates for Nursing Home Reform and the National Consumer Voice for Quality Long-Term Care. See Complaint for Declaratory & Injunctive Relief, Nat'l Consumer Voice for Quality Long-Term Care v. Azar (filed Jan. 18, 2021) (No. 21-162), www.aarp.org/content/dam/aarp/aarp_foundation/litigation/2021/nat-consumer-voice-v-us-dept-hhs-complaint.pdf.

[30] Nina A. Kohn, Addressing the Crisis in Long-Term Care Facilities, The Hill, (Apr. 23, 2020), https://thehill.com/opinion/civil-rights/494337-addressing-the-crisis-in-long-term-care-facilities.

health care providers.[31] In addition, in response to the pandemic, nearly half of the states granted nursing homes (as well as other health care providers, such as hospitals) new immunity from civil liability, either by executive order or by statute.[32] This was despite the much weaker justification for immunity in the nursing home context. As Jessica Roberts and I observed in spring 2020: "Hospitals justify their push for immunity on the grounds that courts should not second-guess the ethically charged resource allocation decisions made rapidly in response to a crush of COVID-19 patients. By contrast, the primary concern for nursing homes is that they will be held liable for inadequate infection control – a problem that typically reflects more deliberative choices over time."[33]

The result is that regulations designed to ensure that nursing homes provide adequate care are treated more like aspirational standards than enforced rules. It should not be surprising, then, that preventable suffering plagues nursing home residents. For example, roughly 20 percent of Medicare beneficiaries in skilled nursing facilities suffered avoidable harm during their stays,[34] and most nursing homes had documented infection-control problems.

III A PATH FORWARD

The problems made visible by COVID-19 suggest the need to improve the regulatory framework governing long-term care facilities.[35] This section outlines regulatory changes that could better align financial incentives with quality of care and advocacy strategies that could help pave the way for such reforms.

A *Align Financial Incentives for Institutions with Quality Indicators*

Improving the overall quality of nursing home care in the United States will require adjusting the regulatory environment to create a much stronger economic incentive for nursing homes to deliver humane, high-quality care.

Economic incentives could take several forms. First, regulators could pursue enforcement approaches that include economically meaningful consequences for

---

[31] See, for example, Dep't of Health & Human Servs., Exceptions and Extensions for Quality Reporting Requirements (Mar. 27, 2020), www.cms.gov/files/document/guidance-memo-exceptions-and-extensions-quality-reporting-and-value-based-purchasing-programs.pdf (waiving certain reporting requirements for a range of health care institutions, including nursing homes).

[32] See Nina A. Kohn & Jessica L. Roberts, Nursing Homes Need Increased Staffing, Not Legal Immunity, The Hill (May 23, 2020), https://thehill.com/opinion/healthcare/499286-nursing-homes-need-increased-staffing-not-legal-immunity.

[33] Id.

[34] Off. of the Inspector Gen., Dep't of Health & Human Servs, Adverse Events in Skilled Nursing Facilities: National Incidence Among Medicare Beneficiaries (Feb. 2014), https://oig.hhs.gov/oei/reports/oei-06-11-00370.pdf.

[35] For further discussion of changing the regulatory framework for nursing homes, see Nina A. Kohn, Nursing Homes, COVID-19, and the Consequences of Regulatory Failure, 110 *Geo. L. J.* 1 (2021).

falling below acceptable standards. This would require making a broader range of violations fineable events and withholding new admissions and payments to facilities that are not in compliance with regulatory requirements. One way to do this would be to substantially expand the Special Focus Facility Program, which puts facilities with consistently high deficiencies on a more frequent inspection cycle and on a path to possible decertification, as legislation introduced in the US Senate in 2021 would do.[36] A more comprehensive approach would be to apply a broader and more robust range of penalties to all facilities – not merely those previously identified as particularly problematic.

Additionally, the Secretary of Health and Human Services might create real consequences for owners or operators with a track record of deficient care by refusing to certify the facilities that they own for participation in Medicare and Medicaid programs,[37] thereby cutting off primary sources of revenue.[38] Given that many facilities are part of large chains, and that chain ownership has been linked to lower quality care,[39] this could have substantial impacts.

Second, public funding for long-term care facilities could be much more closely tied to outcomes. Specifically, a robust pay-for-performance scheme could vary payments to facilities based on metrics of resident well-being. Such an approach would be a significant departure from the status quo. Most nursing home residents in the United States have their care paid for by the Medicaid program. Yet the Medicaid program provides little incentive for nursing homes to provide high-quality care. The precise formulas by which state Medicaid programs reimburse nursing homes for care can be complicated and are largely based on a per-resident, per-day approach, with increases common for patient mix and some limited increases for certain factors related to quality. Nursing homes that provide a high level of personalized care can therefore expect to receive similar levels of compensation as homes that provide woefully substandard care. The result is an insufficient incentive to provide high-quality care and an opportunity for unscrupulous providers to profit at the expense of their residents' well-being.

The United States has never seriously tried a pay-for-performance system. Some states have offered small bonuses for certain improvements – but often these

[36] Sen. 4866, 11th Cong. (2021), www.congress.gov/bill/116th-congress/senate-bill/4866.

[37] See 42 U.S.C. § 1395i-3(d)(1)(A) ("[A] skilled nursing facility must be administered in a manner that enables it to use its resources effectively and efficiently to attain or maintain the highest practicable physical, mental, and psychosocial well-being of each resident (consistent with requirements established under subsection (f)(5))"); 42.
U.S.C. §1395i-3(d)(1)(A) and § 1395i-3(f)(5) (2021) (requiring the Secretary of Health and Human Services to establish criteria for assessing a skilled nursing facility's compliance with the requirement of subsection (d)(1) with respect to, among other things, "its governing body and management").

[38] See Nina A. Kohn et al., Using What We Have: How Existing Legal Authorities Can Help Fix America's Nursing Home Crisis, 65 *William Mary L. Rev.* (forthcoming 2023–2024) (explaining how this would be consistent with the Secretary's statutory authority).

[39] See David C. Grabowski et al., Low-Quality Nursing Homes Were More Likely Than Other Nursing Homes to be Bought or Sold by Chains in 1993–2010, 35 *Health Affairs* (May 2016).

payments are too small to make those improvements economically attractive. Even amid the pandemic, as massive federal relief flowed to nursing homes, this windfall was almost entirely devoid of conditions,[40] and much of it may have never gone to patient care.[41] Indeed, although the Trump Administration offered what it termed a "pay-for-performance" scheme in fall 2020, that scheme created no new requirements or meaningful new incentives. Rather, it simply offered bonus payments to facilities that kept new COVID-19 infections below a certain threshold – something the pay-per-resident model already incentivized. (Even without the payments, especially given shrinking admissions, nursing homes had an incentive to retain existing patients by avoiding lethal infections.)

The pandemic has exposed the need to consider moving to a robust pay-for-performance mechanism for long-term care facilities. Such an approach would encourage such facilities to improve performance and give facilities that make good choices for residents a stronger competitive advantage.

Third, public funding for long-term care facilities could be tied to inputs that research indicates predict quality of care and quality of life. That is, funding could be tied to use of inputs that are proxy measures of performance instead of (or in addition to) tying funding to direct measures of performance, as one would in a traditional pay-for-performance model. For example, funding – or at least increases in funding – should be tied to nursing homes meeting direct-care staffing minimums – including the 4.1 hours of direct-care staffing per day, which experts agree is critical to avoid systemic neglect.

Another way to prompt investment in critical inputs would be to adopt a "medical loss ratio" approach in which providers would be required to use at least a certain percentage of revenue to provide resident care. Much as the Affordable Care Act requires insurance providers to spend at least 80 or 85 percent of premium dollars on providing medical care, the federal government could require long-term care providers that accept Medicaid or Medicare funds to spend a minimum percentage of those funds on direct resident care (and not on administrative costs and profit).

Several states – spurred by concerns exposed by the COVID-19 pandemic – have begun to experiment with this type of spending requirement. In September 2020, Massachusetts announced that nursing homes in the state would be required to spend 75 percent of their revenue on direct-care staffing costs.[42] The following month, New Jersey adopted legislation requiring that its nursing homes spend 90 percent of annual aggregate revenue on direct resident care, potentially broadly

---

[40] Eaton, supra note 5.

[41] Andrew Soergel, *Nursing Homes Are Getting Billions in COVID Aid – Where Is It Going?*, AARP (Nov. 24, 2020), www.aarp.org/caregiving/health/info-2020/nursing-home-covid-federal-aid-transparency.html.

[42] Nursing Facility Accountability and Supports Package 2.0 (Sept. 10, 2020), www.mass.gov/doc/COVID-19-nursing-facility-accountability-and-supports-package-20/download.

defined.[43] New York followed suit in April 2021, when – as part of the state's annual Budget Bill – it adopted a requirement that nursing homes spend at least 70 percent of their revenue on direct patient care.[44]

Ultimately, the success of this type of approach, however, will depend on several factors.

These include how states categorize expenses. New York, for example, defines "direct patient care" to include expenses that arguably do not fit that description (such as "plant operation and management") and thus would allow for less money to be spent on what the lay person might think of as "direct patient care" than the language of its requirement suggests. It will also depend on setting the threshold at the correct level (i.e., higher than the 70 percent New York requires), so that owners do not unreasonably profit at the expense of residents. In addition, it will require imposing transparency requirements that prevent nursing homes from hiding profits as expenses through transactions with related entities.

B *Increase Support for Community-Based Care*

The pandemic revealed the inherent danger posed by the current policy framework, which favors institutional care over community-based care. Currently, Medicaid – the primary funding source for long-term care services in the United States – steers older adults in need of long-term care into institutions by (1) requiring states to use Medicaid funds to cover nursing home care but allowing states to choose whether to pay for most home-based care; and (2) allowing states that cover home-based care services to cap the number of beneficiaries served. Thus, in some states older adults must wait years before they can get home-based care.[45] Even then, care recipients may receive less help than they need because nearly three quarters of states limit how many hours they can get.[46] Thus, Medicaid pushes individuals – especially those with a lower socioeconomic status – into institutions even when they could live healthier and more satisfying lives with in-home help.

This institutional bias cannot be justified on fiscal grounds as it is not clear that steering individuals into facilities reduces public costs; there is some evidence that it may actually increase care-associated costs.[47] Nor can it be squared with the integration

---

[43] See S.B. 4482, 2020–2021 Leg., Reg. Sess. (N.J. 2020) (spelling out New Jersey's provisions, which give executive branch actors substantial discretion in defining "direct patient care").

[44] S.B. 2507-C (NY 2021).

[45] Medicaid and CHIP Payment & Access Commission, State Management of Home- and Community-Based Services Waiver Waiting Lists (Aug. 2020), www.macpac.gov/wp-content/uploads/2020/08/State-Management-of-Home-and-Community-Based-Services-Waiver-Waiting-Lists.pdf.

[46] MaryBeth Musumeci, Molly O'Malley Watts & Priya Chidambaram, Key State Policy Choices About Medicaid Home and Community-Based Services (Feb. 2020), http://files.kff.org/attachment/Issue-Brief-Key-State-Policy-Choices-About-Medicaid-Home-and-Community-Based-Services.

[47] See, for example, Off. of Pol'y Dev. & Rsch., US Dep't of Housing & Urban Dev., Measuring the Costs and Savings of Aging in Place (2013), www.huduser.gov/portal/periodicals/em/fall13/highlight2.html.

mandate of the Americans with Disabilities Act, which prohibits states from unreasonably requiring individuals with disabilities to receive services in a segregated setting when their needs could be reasonably accommodated in the community.[48]

If the devastation that COVID-19 has wrought on residents of long-term care institutions has taught policymakers nothing else, it should teach them this: Medicaid's bias in favor of institutionalization is dangerous and must end. Where a Medicaid beneficiary's long-term care needs could be met in the community, and providing such care in a community-based setting would not be more expensive than providing care in an institutional setting, states should be required to provide coverage for community-based care on at least equal terms with institutional care. States should also be encouraged, even if not required, to cover care in community-based settings when doing so is not prohibitively expensive.

C Change the Narrative

The lack of protection for long-term care residents indicates an underlying willingness on the part of policymakers to tolerate suffering and isolation among older adults. This tolerance, which was present long before the COVID-19 pandemic, has been revealed in stark terms by the crisis itself. Indeed, the pandemic has shown not only how policymakers allowed dangerous conditions and patterns to persist, but also that they are willing to accept unprecedented levels of isolation and suffering. For example, federal and state regulators have responded to the pandemic by barring residents from having family visitors, while doing nothing to reduce the number of staff entering facilities. Limits on family visitors – even those who were serving as caregivers – were accepted in the name of protection, even though it meant condemning residents to conditions akin to solitary confinement. At the same time, not a single state adopted a one-site rule limiting staff to working in one care facility during the pandemic, as Canadian provinces did.[49] Nor did regulators require facilities to make efforts to reduce reliance on part-time and agency staff, despite evidence suggesting that eliminating staff linkages could reduce COVID-19 infections in nursing homes by 44 percent.[50]

This tolerance suggests that public outcry and advocacy for the good care and humane treatment of long-term care residents is not yet sufficiently aligned or effective to support reform. Particularly in the context of a strong nursing home industry lobby – which demonstrated its muscle last year by extracting billions of dollars in payouts, in addition to liability relief from the COVID-19 pandemic – a different narrative and more robust advocacy effort is likely to be needed to significantly change the status quo.

---

[48] See, generally, Olmstead v. LC, 527 US 581 (1999).
[49] See, for example, Ont. Ministry of Long-Term Care, COVID-19 Action Plan: Long-Term Care Homes (May 2020), www.ontario.ca/page/COVID-19-action-plan-long-term-care-homes.
[50] M. Keith Chen, Judith A. Chevalier & Elisa F. Long, Nursing Home Staff Networks & COVID-19 (Oct. 2020), www.pnas.org/content/118/1/e2015455118.

It is instructive to compare policy and advocacy related to institutionalized older adults to that pertaining to children and disabled younger adults. A bias in favor of institutionalization persists for older adults even as it is eroded for younger ones. Although public funding continues to steer older adults into institutions, institutions for children and younger adults (e.g., orphanages, mental hospitals, and institutions for the developmentally and cognitively disabled) are increasingly shuttered, with the money diverted to community-based care. Ageism likely also shapes the willingness to tolerate regulatory violations in nursing homes. As noted above, nursing homes that violate regulations designed to protect residents from harm typically face a mere slap on the wrist. By comparison, childcare centers in violation of state regulations designed to protect children in their care commonly have their licenses revoked and their facilities closed.

Creating the momentum for reforming the status quo will therefore require concerted advocacy efforts to make it clear to policymakers that it is worthwhile to invest the political capital and resources necessary to transform long-term care – that the lives of those who need long-term care are worth it. This, in turn, will likely require creating a vocal, organized constituency for reforming long-term care systems. Advocates have long worked to improve regulations and policy interventions by working with regulators to improve the design and administration of long-term care policy. Little focus, by comparison, has been placed on creating public momentum or awareness of the issues, or on organizing stakeholders, such as family members, to advance reform.

With the consequences of the status quo laid bare by COVID-19, advocates should seize the moment to change the narrative about long-term care. Specifically, advocates must describe over-institutionalization of older adults, and the neglect they receive in facilities, not merely as a policy challenge, but as a civil rights issue of major moral consequence. By embracing a narrative that focuses on rights and morality, advocates may be able to capitalize on the moment to invigorate advocacy efforts and potentially foster a grassroots movement to push for a system of long-term care that is both humane in its approach and resilient to future disruptions.

IV CONCLUSION

The vulnerability of nursing homes and other long-term care facilities to COVID-19 both exposes the failures of current regulatory schemes designed to protect residents and points to what needs to happen to build a humane long-term care system that is resilient to public health disruptions. Fortunately, the policy changes needed to make long-term care resilient and humane are not radical; they would merely bring interventions that have been applied in other health care contexts into the long-term care space. However, making these changes will require confronting not only entrenched financial interests and institutions, but also the underlying attitudes that have enabled systems that normalize isolation and suffering.

PART III

Government Response and Reaction to COVID-19

Prologue

Marcella Nunez-Smith

I COVID-19 AND HEALTH EQUITY

In 2020, the United States experienced a 1.5-year decrease in life expectancy due primarily to the COVID-19 pandemic, the largest decline since World War II.[1] But the toll of the pandemic has not been equal. Rather, it has exposed how our standard pre-pandemic policies and practices were inadequate to meet the needs of many Americans – particularly for people of color and marginalized communities. For Black Americans, life expectancy dropped 2.9 years in the same period, and in the Latinx community, life expectancy fell by a full three years.[2] That Black and Latinx families are more likely to live in more crowded households or multigenerational homes, or hold essential jobs with higher risks of exposure, accounts for some of these disparities. Similarly, Asian/Asian Americans, Native Hawaiians, and Pacific Islanders, those living outside metropolitan areas, and individuals with certain disabilities have experienced staggeringly high rates of COVID-19 infection, hospitalization, and mortality.

COVID-19 is therefore much more than a public health emergency. It is also a convergence of crises. Hospital workforces have long failed to reflect the diversity of the communities they serve, which has contributed to worse health outcomes for people of color. As COVID-19 spread, rural hospitals shuttered. And when vaccines became available, the public and private sectors did not distribute doses equitably or accessibly. Prior to the pandemic, structurally marginalized communities already struggled to access nutritious food, stable and high-quality housing, childcare, health insurance, transportation, and reliable Internet. The pandemic exacerbated these challenges, making it all the more difficult to adhere to public health guidelines around social distancing and quarantine. The inequities that existed before the pandemic were exploited by COVID-19.

---

[1] Jane Greenhalgh, U.S. Life Expectancy Fell by 1.5 Years in 2020, the Biggest Drop since WWII, NPR (July 21, 2021), www.npr.org/sections/coronavirus-live-updates/2021/07/21/1018590263/u-s-life-expectancy-fell-1-5-years-2020-biggest-drop-since-ww-ii-covid.

[2] Id.

II CLOSING COVID-19 EQUITY GAPS:
A VIEW FROM THE FRONT LINES

COVID-19 presented several distinct challenges over time, and I was privileged to advise both the state of Connecticut and the Biden-Harris Administration. In the early months of the pandemic, testing and tracing were key – as was getting accurate data on how COVID-19 was impacting different communities. After vaccines became available, work shifted to the profound challenges of ensuring equitable access to vaccines and gaining the trust of individuals reluctant to take them. The pressing issues of the day became partnering with community leaders and others to meet people where they were, leading conversations with respectful understanding and providing accurate information. We developed solutions based on unique collaborative initiatives. Our collective efforts helped close the equity gap in vaccination and offer lessons for the future.

Data drives health care and policy. However, getting accurate data on COVID-19 was an early challenge. In an August 2020 paper I co-authored with my Yale colleague Cary Gross and others, we were among the first to show that COVID-19 mortality data stratified by race and ethnicity was largely unavailable in state reporting. We also found that when data were available and adjusted for age, the disparities were severe. For example, we found that the risk of dying from COVID-19 was significantly higher for the Black population than for the White population in twenty-two states (along with New York City). An absence of reliable data makes it harder to develop government policies and appropriately target needed resources.

In the early months of the pandemic testing and tracing were core priorities. In Connecticut, where I served on Governor Ned Lamont's Reopen Connecticut Advisory Committee as co-chair of the community subcommittee, protecting people in congregate settings – such as long-term care facilities, carceral settings, homeless shelters, and shared housing – as well as essential workers was a priority. Contact tracing, while effective, proved to have its own difficulties. It is not enough to develop and deploy a successful program; it must be successful in all communities. We focused on ensuring that people had the right economic and basic needs supports, including food, housing (in those cases where separating and isolating from others in a home was not possible), and childcare, to properly quarantine or isolate as necessary. Months later, once vaccines became available, ensuring equitable access and building trust through community partnership became the next major health equity goal across the country.

The Biden-Harris Administration aimed to provide equitable access across the continuum of COVID-19 life-saving resources. I was privileged to serve as co-chair of the Transition COVID-19 Advisory Board and later as Senior Advisor to the White House COVID-19 Response Team and Chair of the Presidential COVID-19 Health Equity Task Force in the Department of Health and Human Services. To reach the hardest-hit and highest-risk individuals, four direct federal vaccine allocation programs were launched in the first three weeks of the Administration. The four programs – Community Health Center Partnerships, the Retail Pharmacy Program, Community Vaccination Centers, and Mobile Vaccination Sites – complemented the work that states were doing and centered equity as a key priority, keeping considerations such as location and extended hours in mind. Further, metrics such as the Centers for Disease Control and Prevention's social vulnerability index were used to help target these resources to communities. And the Administration always centralized the need to work closely with community and faith-based organizations to be most effective in connecting with their clients and members. Federal vaccination centers were barred from inquiring about citizenship and made sure that everyone knew vaccines were free to them. Pharmacy partners were engaged to ensure they were reaching hard-to-reach populations. Collaborations were key, including with community-based organizations, local public health departments, faith-based communities, and others. The Administration partnered with churches, schools, and even barber shops to reach people where they were. Throughout, the approach was guided by an understanding that both the message and the messenger matter. Messages must be tailored to their audience, and messengers must be trusted and trustworthy within a given community.

The Biden-Harris Administration put this understanding into practice through several necessary programs, in addition to the ones already mentioned. I had the opportunity to co-chair the National Public Education Campaign for COVID-19, which included the COVID-19 Community Corps. Starting with approximately 6,000 members before growing substantially, it comprised community leaders and others across the country who came together to get accurate information from Administration officials about vaccines and other pandemic matters on a regular basis. I was also honored to host a series of stakeholder roundtables, organized across multiple agencies and offices in the White House and the Department of Health and Human Services. These roundtables opened clear lines of communication about the pandemic, including about testing and vaccines, with a wide range of constituencies. They were intimate and off the record, and represented a space designed to elevate the wisdom of those with lived experience. Participants told Administration officials what they needed, while offering feedback on which Administration strategies were and were not effective, helping inform next steps. The Administration listened and acted on what they heard.

But bringing vaccines to communities and building confidence that the vaccines were safe and effective was just the beginning. The close relationships we built through dialogue helped us tackle a core problem: getting individuals who were willing to receive the vaccine but unable to access it a path to vaccination. The next issue was addressing structural barriers to vaccination. Through ongoing dialogue with our partners, we learned that people were facing a series of challenges – some did not have access to transportation or childcare, while others did not have paid time off from work. The Administration introduced policies and initiatives that addressed each of these problems – such as giving tax credits to businesses to make sure people got paid time off, supporting the provision of childcare, and encouraging rideshare companies to provide free rides. These solutions came from public–private collaborations. It was essential to ensure that accurate information was always being shared in a respectful way and to engage with community and local public health leaders. Taken together, this collaborative work paid off. By September 2021, we consistently saw that there were no longer gaps by race and ethnicity in adult vaccination rates.

Throughout the pandemic, what set effective interventions apart and really made a difference from prior moments in the health equity space was the presence of political will, stemming from the very top. The personal commitment of President Biden and Vice President Harris to both understand what was needed to close equity gaps in the pandemic and to act on that understanding was transformational.

III THE PANDEMIC'S LEGACY AND LESSONS FOR THE FUTURE

The pandemic has caused incalculable grief, stress, and other mental health challenges. More than 100,000 children have lost caregivers to the pandemic. Black, Brown, and LGBTQIA+ communities have reported skyrocketing rates of anxiety and depression. So, too, have older adults, for whom social isolation and loneliness increases the risk of cognitive dysfunction, heart disease, and mortality. COVID-19 also drove a significant spike in opioid overdoses. Even as mental health worsened in the country, stay-at-home orders and the widespread job-related loss of insurance made it harder for individuals to access behavioral health services. Meanwhile, people of color were more likely than their White counterparts to be essential workers, putting themselves and their families at increased risk.

The disproportionate burden of COVID-19 morbidity and mortality have resulted in a "grief gap" among communities of color and other marginalized populations. A broad lens is necessary to center equity across the groups the pandemic most affects: people living with disabilities, those who are involved with the justice system, cherished elders, rural neighbors, mixed-status families, LGBTQIA+ people, Black and Brown people, Indigenous people, Asian/Asian Americans, Native Hawaiians, Pacific Islander people, and those struggling on the margins of the economy.

The pandemic's lesson is that while high-quality health care is essential, health equity goes beyond health care. It includes housing stability, food and nutrition security, and ensuring equitable access to technology. People need pathways to educational and economic opportunities. The prominence of COVID-19 in the public consciousness has made us aware of its uneven toll on communities of color and other marginalized groups, but there has never been a time in which these communities have not suffered disproportionate burdens of death and disease. To advance health equity, we must urgently address both the historical and contemporary underpinnings of these realities.

Systemic problems require systemic solutions. An effective pandemic response is reliant on people's trust in science and is grounded in meaningful community engagement.

Misinformation, conflicted messaging, and the politicization of science have undermined the pillars of effective response. Therefore, we must also strive toward a new post-pandemic reality, a reality that puts science, reliable communication, community health, and racial/ethnic and social equity at the forefront.

In this rebuilding, we must also remember that although communities are experts in their own needs, we can no longer allow them to shoulder the burdens of establishing health equity alone. We must work toward sustained investment in community-led solutions. The pandemic gave us an opportunity to disrupt patterns of harm and improve inequitable systems and practices.

Looking forward, there are concrete steps that we can take to learn from the pandemic. The final report of the Presidential COVID-19 Health Equity Task Force, which I chaired, lays out fifty-five prioritized recommendations, with five toplines. First, we must invest in community-led solutions to address health equity. Second, we need a data ecosystem that promotes equity-driven decision-making. Third, we must increase accountability for health equity outcomes. Fourth, investing in a diverse and representative health care workforce and increasing equitable access to high-quality health care for all is essential. Finally, leading and coordinating implementation of the COVID-19 Health Equity Task Force's recommendations should take place from a permanent health equity infrastructure in the White House.

We have a once-in-a-generation opportunity for transformational change. But we must acknowledge that advancing health equity will take multisectoral commitment, collaboration, and intention. The legacy of the pandemic is an invitation for us all to envision a new world, one in which the government, the private sector, community leaders, and philanthropists collaborate to achieve health justice.

Introduction

Abbe R. Gluck

In addition to being the great public health challenge of a generation, COVID-19 also will be remembered as one of the most significant governance challenges of our time. The pandemic exposed both the strengths and weaknesses of our fragmentated, federalist system of health care at the same time that it showcased the underappreciated capacity of the Affordable Care Act – the centerpiece of our national health care law – as a highly effective national safety net. The pandemic also revealed the dire costs of ignoring large parts of our public health infrastructure and failing to address the stark inequities in our health care system. And it took far too long for regulators to focus on the risks taken by the hundreds of thousands of essential and frontline workers who kept the nation going in the most uncertain of times. At the same time, the reactions of governments in response to the crisis propelled to the center of legal discourse a century-old landmark Supreme Court decision, *Jacobson v. Massachusetts*,[1] which embodies deference to science-based government decisions in the name of public health.

Jacobson came back to the fore to justify government action in the name of an unprecedented public health crisis at the same moment that some legal experts, including members of the Supreme Court, were mid-battle to shrink the administrative state and unwind decades of doctrine supporting administrative delegations. The chapters in Part III take up these varied and complex questions of the separation of powers, federalism, and regulation.

In Chapter 10, "Federalism, Leadership, and COVID-19: Evolving Lessons for the Public's Health," Nicole Huberfeld complicates earlier critiques of health care federalism, including her own. The failure of the national government under the Trump Administration to act quickly to trigger emergency authorities and use other available regulatory tools created a void that many state governments stepped in to fill. In that sense, 2020 evinced the strengths of a state–federal health care system, like ours, that is decentralized and built on redundancies and overlapping authorities. On the other hand, as the pandemic wore on, those same authorities

---

[1] 197 U.S. 11 (1905).

served as obstacles in many states to the more direct national control that the Biden Administration tried to exert over the pandemic to achieve a more effective and equitable response. By 2021, some states and localities were fiercely resisting federal regulatory moves relating to protective measures such as mask-wearing and vaccination. Huberfeld argues that the US tradition of health policy heterogeneity across the states – not only with respect to pandemic-related safety measures but also in the system's structure, such as in Medicaid and emergency authorities – ultimately produced more inequalities and a more uncoordinated response than a fully centralized national system would have done.

Chapter 11, "Coronavirus Reveals the Fiscal Determinants of Health," by Matthew Lawrence, and Chapter 12, "Legislating a More Responsive Safety Net," by Ariel Jurow Kleiman, Gabriel Scheffler, and Andrew Hammond, are somewhat less sanguine about federal action, with both chapters delving into fiscal preparedness and the safety net. Whereas Huberfeld aptly highlights the pandemic responses of Congress, including major relief bills and making vaccines cost-free, Lawrence criticizes Congress for its earlier inattention to public health. He also describes structural features of our national fiscal system, such as the requirement that legislation be "scored" for its impact on the budget, that discourage long-term investments in areas such as pandemic preparedness, and highlights the risks associated with a public health system that largely relies on annual appropriations rather than permanent funding.

Kleinman, Scheffler, and Hammond focus on a different aspect of the fiscal response: the variety of federal safety-net programs – in areas ranging from tax credits to food support, unemployment insurance, and health care – that did step up with significant support in 2020–21 but that the authors contend should have done more. Refuting the common description of the pandemic as the "great equalizer," they highlight how the pandemic both exacerbated preexisting inequalities and argue for "automatic stabilizers" in critical safety-net programs to bring help more quickly, equitably, and sufficiently in the future.

In Chapter 13, "Eradicating Pandemic Health Inequities: Health Justice in Emergency Preparedness," Ruqaiijah Yearby takes on another aspect of health justice: the failure of both the federal and state governments to focus on essential workers early or completely enough. Arguing through a lens of health (in)justice, Yearby argues that the governments should have designed better workplace protections and ensured other benefits, such as sick leave, for those who became infected. She proposes a new model with more robust community engagement, especially from essential workers themselves, to revise emergency preparedness plans before the next emergency.

These analyses of legislative and executive actions would not be complete without including the third branch of government: the courts. From the beginning of the pandemic, the courts were thrust into disputes on topics ranging from the lockdowns of gun shops, to limits on access to "elective" medical procedures – including abortion – to prohibitions on religious gatherings. At the center of all these cases was a debate about how deferential courts should be to government decisions made in the name of public health, a question until that point controlled by the century-old Supreme Court decision *Jacobson*. In Chapter 14, "The *Jacobson* Question: Individual Rights, Expertise, and Public Health Necessity," Lindsey Wiley details how courts have struggled to reconcile *Jacobson*'s emphasis on the common good and deference to scientific regulatory judgment with the revolution in individual rights which occurred over the intervening century. She argues that courts were wrong to "suspend" ordinary judicial review in the name of the public health crisis. At the same time, she argues that *Jacobson*'s principles of public health necessity, proportionality, and deference to scientific judgment nevertheless remain relevant factors that courts must reintegrate into modern standards of review in order to balance individual rights against government actions like those taken during the pandemic.

The proper role of government has always been one of the dominant questions of health policy and indisputably remains a key question three years into the COVID-19 pandemic. Congress, the executive, the states, and the courts each have unique roles to play, and their varied choices have significant impacts on access to pandemic-related protections, redressing inequalities, and protecting the interests of both individuals and the community. The history continues to be written. As this book goes to press, Congress is fighting over whether to accord additional COVID-19 relief requested by President Biden; proposals abound to close the Medicaid gap that remains in ten states; and more than a year ago, the Supreme Court struck down the Occupational Safety and Health Administration's emergency temporary standard for workplace protection. Like so many other areas covered in this book, the governance challenges highlighted by this set of chapters existed before the pandemic, but COVID-19 has shined a bright light on them which demands attention.

10

Federalism, Leadership, and COVID-19

Evolving Lessons for the Public's Health

Nicole Huberfeld

I INTRODUCTION

The first year of the COVID-19 pandemic distinguished the United States as having the "worst outbreak in the world," with more Americans dying than in World War II, the Korean War, and the Vietnam War combined.[1] By October 2021, COVID-19 deaths exceeded those caused by the former deadliest pandemic, the 1918 influenza virus.[2] Prominent commentators framed the turbulent early pandemic response as a failure of leadership, but this assessment does not tell the complete story.[3] There are structural explanations for the complicated response of the United States too. In particular, a fundamental feature of the American approach to public health – the national governance structure known as federalism – is at least partially responsible for weaknesses in the country's response to the pandemic.

Federalism divides power, responsibility, and capacity for health policies across multiple levels of government, most often between federal and state governments. Though federalism is the default choice for structuring health laws, often it is not a constitutionally required one.[4] States are invited through federal laws to participate in national policies with the promise of money and regulatory guardrails but also policy flexibility. Proponents claim the vertical division of authority between governments fosters tailored policies for local populations, experimentation, and innovation.

---

[1]   Noah Higgins Dunn, The U.S. Has the Worst Coronavirus Outbreak in the World: 'The Numbers Don't Lie,' Dr. Fauci Says, CNBC (Aug. 5, 2020), www.cnbc.com/2020/08/05/dr-fauci-agrees-the-us-has-the-worst-coronvirus-outbreak-in-the-world-the-numbers-dont-lie.html.

[2]   Farida B. Ahmad, Jodi A. Cisewski, and Robert N. Anderson, Provisional Mortality Data — United States, 2021, CDC Morbidity and Mortality Weekly Report (April 29, 2022), www.cdc.gov/mmwr/volumes/71/wr/pdfs/mm7117e1-H.pdf.

[3]   The Editors, Dying in a Leadership Vacuum, 383 New Eng. J. Med. 1479 (Oct. 7, 2020), www.nejm.org/doi/full/10.1056/NEJMe2029812?query=TOC; The U.S. Is Missing Key Opportunities to End the COVID-19 Pandemic, The Dose – Commonwealth Fund (Jan. 15, 2021), www.commonwealthfund.org/publications/podcast/2021/jan/us-is-missing-key-opportunities-end-covid-19-pandemic.

[4]   Abbe R. Gluck & Nicole Huberfeld, What Is Federalism in Healthcare for?, 70 Stan. L. Rev. 1689, 1719–24 (2018).

Yet divided authority also requires more coordination between government officials, which increases complexity in a public health emergency, requiring each leader to act in the right way at the right time and leaving more room for error when they do not.

In public health governance, authority is divided even further, between the federal government and more than 2,800 state, local, and tribal governments. Congress generally must draft emergency and disaster relief bills around state and local efforts; so, under existing laws, an emergency response always builds on the foundation of states' policy choices and is likely to intensify states' preexisting health and economic conditions, which in turn heightens the inequitable impact of an event such as a pandemic.

This is what has happened with the novel coronavirus. Decisions made by leaders at every level, but especially state officials, directly impacted infection and death rates and stymied relief efforts. Early in the pandemic, some state leaders filled the void when expected federal support was not supplied. But throughout the pandemic and especially as it evolved in 2021, state choices regarding containment measures and vaccination rollout decisions, as well as uptake and distribution of federal relief funds and challenges to federal vaccine rules, exacerbated the public health emergency and increased inequitable impacts. Populations already experiencing persistent health disparities, such as Black, Hispanic, Indigenous, and other people of color, as well as low-income and rural populations, suffered greater rates of infection and death.

In short, federalism increases the need for a coordinated response in emergency and disaster relief efforts. In the case of COVID-19, public health federalism quickly complicated dealing with the pandemic in the face of weak early federal leadership, long-underfunded state public health systems and resistance to health reform, and other emergency response policy choices that teed up the "worst outbreak." To reduce unnecessary risk when the next emergency occurs, COVID-19's legacy will need to include building a better governance structure to increase the resilience of individuals, populations, and public health systems.

II FEDERAL AUTHORITY AND EMERGENCY RESPONSE

A public health emergency (PHE) prompts a suite of federal actions, especially if it involves a multi-state or nationwide event. Congress, the President, and multiple federal agencies all must exercise authority under a set of federal laws that address the need for swift reaction in an emergency or disaster. Congress typically addresses national emergencies through legislation designed to assist those harmed on a short-term basis, using "relief bills" to deliver economic and other aid. Congress first responded to the COVID-19 PHE with two relief bills enacted in March 2020: the Coronavirus Aid, Relief, and Economic Security Act (CARES Act);[5] and the Family First Coronavirus Response Act (Families First Act).[6] Both followed prior relief bill

---

[5] Pub. L. No. 116-136, 134 Stat. 281 (2020).
[6] Pub. L. No. 116-127, 134 Stat. 177 (2020).

blueprints by providing loans to struggling businesses, increasing federal funding to cover Medicaid enrollment spikes, and enhancing unemployment insurance benefits. Recognizing Medicaid's countercyclical nature and states' immediate need for support given their balanced budget requirements, the bills offered states and private actors short-term monetary and deregulation measures.

The Families First Act, in Section 6008, provided an enhanced federal Medicaid match during the PHE, along with a requirement of "maintenance of effort" (MOE) so states could not decrease enrollment or eligibility while accepting enhanced federal funds. The Families First Act also allowed states to cover COVID-19 testing and related services for uninsured people through Medicaid with a 100 percent federal match. When the PHE ends, states lose emergency flexibilities, and the Families First Act enhanced match expires. With every state accepting the enhanced federal match, the two relief bills supported a 13.9 percent increase in Medicaid enrollment from the pandemic's beginning in February 2020 through January 2021.[7]

A national emergency also triggers unique presidential power and the need for coordinated action among the President, federal agencies, and state and local officials. Both the President and the Secretary of the Department of Health and Human Services (HHS) must declare an emergency to invoke the full range of federal aid available during a PHE. Under the Stafford Act, the President facilitates disaster and emergency aid by issuing major disaster declarations to individual states, usually after a governor's request, although President Trump also issued a national emergency declaration for COVID-19.[8] A disaster declaration initiates help from agencies such as the Department of Homeland Security and its subagency, the Federal Emergency Management Agency,[9] and triggers federal assistance that coordinates relief to states; provides technical and advisory support to state and local governments, including public health information and data; helps state and local officials with the distribution of food, medicine, and other supplies; and provides direct support to "save lives."[10] The President can provide additional federal assistance if the response is deemed "inadequate … to save lives, protect property and public health and safety, and lessen or avert the threat of a catastrophe."[11] The President also has authority to declare a national emergency under the National Emergencies Act, which triggers other flexibilities, including

[7] Ctrs. for Medicare & Medicaid Servs., Press Release: New Medicaid and CHIP Enrollment Snapshot Shows Almost 10 Million Americans Enrolled in Coverage During the COVID-19 Public Health Emergency (June 21, 2021), www.cms.gov/newsroom/press-releases/new-medicaid-and-chip-enrollment-snapshot-shows-almost-10-million-americans-enrolled-coverage-during.

[8] Robert T. Stafford Disaster Relief and Emergency Assistance Act, 42 U.S.C. § 5191; Cong. Rsch. Serv., The Stafford Act Emergency Declaration for COVID-19 (Mar. 13, 2020), https://crsreports.congress.gov/product/pdf/IN/IN11251.

[9] 42 U.S.C. §§ 5122, 5191–92.

[10] 42 U.S.C. §§ 5121, 5192(a).

[11] 42 U.S.C. § 5192(b).

actions under the Defense Production Act.[12] The national emergency and PHE are relatively short-term declarations and must be renewed if an emergency continues; disaster declarations are open-ended.

The HHS Secretary's declaration of a PHE under the Public Health Service Act prompts regulatory, financial, and other relief that facilitates state emergency response.[13] Using this suite of emergency powers, HHS and other federal agencies issue guidance for dealing with an emergency, deploy federal workers to assist state and local officials, and relax certain rules for Medicaid/Children's Health Insurance Program, Medicare, and some Health Insurance Portability and Accountability Act privacy standards. This labyrinth of emergency authority laws builds federal/state collaboration into a national emergency response. Because state officials can operationalize federal funding and policy guidance on the ground, pragmatically, both executive and legislative emergency actions rely on states and localities to partner in addressing emergencies and disasters.

Though HHS Secretary Alex Azar declared a PHE on January 31, 2020, the President waited to declare a national emergency, with the first declaration effective March 1, 2020; as such, states such as Washington and California facing the pandemic in January and February were responding to a new disease outbreak without the full range of federal assistance.[14] Despite the enhanced executive powers that become available upon declaring a national emergency, President Trump was widely reported to have chosen not to exercise such powers, with the exceptions of imposing international travel restrictions and supporting rapid vaccine development. The kinds of actions President Biden commenced upon entering office provide examples of the authority that went unexercised: mask-wearing requirements on federal property; evidence-based manufacturing enhancements and distribution of personal protective equipment (PPE); opening and promoting a special enrollment period on the federal health insurance exchange ("marketplace") under the Affordable Care Act (ACA) to assist people who had lost jobs in obtaining insurance coverage; and clear vaccine distribution standards, to name a few.

Each presidential decision that reflected an anti-science stance, or that resulted in inaction, increased risks associated with COVID-19, a decidedly anti-public health approach to a PHE. Such choices included the President flouting state and local disease containment rules by ignoring mask-wearing orders during public events,[15] and other noncompliant behavior,[16] leading to his COVID-19 infection

---

[12] National Emergencies Act, 50 U.S.C. §§ 1601–51.

[13] 42 U.S.C. § 247d.

[14] 85 Fed. Reg. 15,337 (Mar. 18, 2020).

[15] Teo Armus, *A GOP County Chair Asked Trump to Wear a Mask to His Rally. Instead, Trump Mocked Pandemic Restrictions*, Wash. Post (Sept. 9, 2020), www.washingtonpost.com/nation/2020/09/09/trump-rally-masks-nc/.

[16] Jess Bidgood, *'If He Believes He Doesn't Need a Mask, Good for Him': Despite Trump's Illness, Supporters Still Aren't Sure about Masks*, Bos. Globe (Oct. 4, 2020), www.bostonglobe.com/2020/10/04/nation/trumps-positive-covid-test-doesnt-change-views-some-supporters-wearing-masks/.

in October 2020.[17] By law, the federal government is responsible for disseminating stockpiled supplies,[18] yet President Trump told governors "we're not a shipping clerk" and shifted to states the work of purchasing and distributing PPE.[19] The White House interfered with information disseminated through key agencies, such as the Centers for Disease Control and Prevention (CDC), to downplay the magnitude of the outbreak.[20] As the pandemic progressed, White House communications were inconsistent and often undermined scientific evidence while simultaneously encouraging rebellion against state and local containment orders – while also pressuring states to curb the outbreak.[21]

This chaotic approach forced states to act alone and to compete with one another and the federal government for PPE. The devolution of executive responsibility tasked states with actions that centralized, coordinated action should have done and would have addressed better.[22] This very situation was meant to be avoided by federal laws that centralize disaster resources, such as by creating a stockpile and enabling emergency authority under the Defense Production Act to ramp up production of necessary supplies.[23]

The "Operation Warp Speed" vaccine development effort both contrasts with and evidences questionable leadership choices in the first year's response. This effort supplied substantial federal funding for researchers and was deemed successful in generating vaccines worthy of Food and Drug Administration (FDA) emergency use approval by the end of 2020.[24] Vaccine distribution, on the other hand, suffered from many of the same flaws as other aspects of the pandemic response. No federal law currently mandates, tracks, or otherwise governs the distribution of adult vaccines in a consolidated fashion. The CDC largely relies on state and local health

---

[17] Michael. C. Bender & Rebecca Ballhaus, Trump Didn't Disclose First Positive COVID-19 Test While Awaiting a Second Test on Thursday, Wall St. J. (Oct. 4, 2020), www.wsj.com/articles/trump-didnt-disclose-first-positive-covid-19-test-while-awaiting-a-second-test-on-thursday-11601844813.

[18] Fed. Emergency Mgmt. Agency, Bringing Resources to State, Local, Tribal & Territorial Governments, www.fema.gov/disasters/coronavirus/governments.

[19] Quint Forgey, 'We're Not a Shipping Clerk': Trump Tells Governors to Step up Efforts to Get Medical Supplies, Politico (Mar. 19, 2020), www.politico.com/news/2020/03/19/trump-governors-coronavirus-medical-supplies-137658; Olivia Ruben et al., Despite Trump Claim, 13 States Say Some Orders for Coronavirus Supplies Still Unfilled, ABC News (July 23, 2020), https://abcnews.go.com/Health/trump-claim-12-states-orders-coronavirus-supplies-unfilled/story?id=71946598.

[20] Aaron Rupar, Dr. Fauci and Dr. Birx Detail How Trump's Coronavirus Response Was Even Worse Than We Thought, Vox (Jan. 25, 2021), www.vox.com/2021/1/25/22249050/fauci-birx-interviews-trump-coronavirus-response.

[21] Lauren de Valle, Man Pleads Guilty in Plot to Kidnap Michigan Gov. Gretchen Whitmer, CNN (Jan. 27, 2021), www.cnn.com/2021/01/27/politics/gretchen-whitmer-kidnapping-plot/index.html.

[22] Michael D. Shear et al., Inside Trump's Failure: The Rush to Abandon Leadership Role on the Virus, NY Times (Sept. 15, 2020), www.nytimes.com/2020/07/18/us/politics/trump-coronavirus-response-failure-leadership.html.

[23] 50 U.S.C. § 4502.

[24] Dan Diamond, The Crash Landing of 'Operation Warp Speed,' Politico (Jan. 17, 2021), www.politico.com/news/2021/01/17/crash-landing-of-operation-warp-speed-459892.

departments and health care providers to supply data; yet the Trump Administration stopped hospitals from reporting directly to the CDC.[25] The lack of centralized decision-making, combined with stymied data collection and skeletal CDC guidance to state and local public health officials for dissemination, meant that vaccine distribution started fitfully, with high variability from state to state, a situation which continued throughout 2021.[26] The incoming Biden Administration found inconsistent information regarding how many vaccine doses existed, and many states had not collected any data regarding their vaccination efforts.[27] Some states implemented vaccine guidelines so strict that doses went to waste (e.g., New York), while others were so lax that a sort of vaccine tourism popped up (e.g., Florida, Utah).

Generally, HHS made more predictable choices. When the coronavirus penetrated national borders, Secretary Azar declared a PHE effective January 27, 2020. The PHE activated the special authority of HHS to issue emergency grants, enter into contracts, access emergency funds, and increase regulatory flexibility. After the President declared a national emergency under the National Emergencies Act, the two declarations – national emergency and PHE – empowered the Secretary to issue emergency-related waivers under Section 1135 of the Social Security Act (SSA). Section 1135 permits modification of specific Medicaid requirements to ensure sufficient health care access during an emergency, for example, waiving licensure requirements for out-of-state providers. HHS made other emergency flexibilities available to states, including provisions to boost Medicaid capacity without legislative action, as the program is a crucial tool for emergency response. For example, states may make limited changes to Medicaid state plans to address access and coverage issues during a PHE and apply for waivers under SSA Section 1115 for temporary coronavirus-related demonstration projects.

HHS could have taken further actions to facilitate nationwide emergency response. If the President and Secretary Azar were not hostile to the ACA, natural choices would have been to encourage states to expand Medicaid eligibility and to open a special enrollment period on the federal exchange, or at least advertise the end-of-year open enrollment period more widely and extend it. Nevertheless, Secretary Azar renewed the PHE declaration throughout 2020, issuing his last declaration on January 7, 2021 (effective January 21, 2021), ensuring the PHE would continue through the first three months of the Biden Administration.

Congress enacted the American Rescue Plan Act of 2021 (ARPA) shortly after President Biden took office,[28] structuring it similarly to the first two relief bills but

---

[25] Sheryl Gay Stolberg, *Trump Administration Strips C.D.C. of Control of Coronavirus Data*, NY Times (July 15, 2020), www.nytimes.com/2020/07/14/us/politics/trump-cdc-coronavirus.html.

[26] Ctrs. for Disease Control & Prevention, *COVID-19 Vaccinations in the United States*, https://covid.cdc.gov/covid-data-tracker/#vaccinations_vacc-total-admin-rate-total.

[27] Alejandro de la Garza & Chris Wilson, *Many States Don't Know Who's Getting COVID-19 Vaccines. That's a Huge Problem for Equity*, Time (Jan. 28, 2021), https://time.com/5934095/covid-vaccine-data/.

[28] Pub. L. No. 117-2, 135 Stat. 3 (2021).

reflecting different priorities. The Biden Administration's early executive orders made use of available statutory authority, recentered scientific evidence, elevated health equity, and committed to vigorously implementing the ACA, including extending the special enrollment period on the federal exchange and maximizing Medicaid expansion.[29] ARPA reflected these leadership choices, for example, providing an enhanced federal match for states to expand Medicaid eligibility, increasing Supplemental Nutrition Assistance Program (SNAP) funding, enhancing emergency rental assistance, and offering money to get elementary and secondary students back to school.

ARPA also built on the federalist structure found in most American social programs, making state and local choices important even with stronger federal leadership and partnership. For example, Florida did not apply for the bump in SNAP funding for schoolchildren's 2021 summer break,[30] and did not submit a plan to the Department of Education to receive ARPA's school funding before the summer ended.[31] All states distributed some portion of ARPA emergency rental assistance funds, yet as of September 2021 states had distributed just 25 percent of the available money. Eighteen states distributed less than 10 percent of available funds, including Florida, Indiana, Iowa, Montana, and Vermont at 9 percent; Alabama and Georgia at 6 percent; and South Dakota and Wyoming at 2 percent.[32] Further, half of states ended ARPA's federally funded unemployment benefits early.[33] Even with federal money available, for administrative, political, or other reasons, some state officials did not perform their PHE implementation role.

III STATE RESPONSES

Public health officials are largely local and state actors, so historically public health in everyday and emergency circumstances has been addressed through a combination of state and local funding and operationalization, combined with federal guidance and money. This structure assumes states both have and use

---

[29] The Biden-Harris Plan to Beat COVID-19, White House, www.whitehouse.gov/priorities/covid-19/.

[30] Kate Santich, Florida Missing Out on Millions of Dollars in Federal Aid for Childhood Hunger, Orlando Sentinel (Aug. 24, 2021), www.orlandosentinel.com/news/os-ne-florida-missing-out-on-millions-for-childhood-snap-benefits-20210824-drdik44j5zd6pfp34ymcx3id5e-story.html.

[31] ARP ESSER State Plans, Dep't of Educ. Off. of Elementary & Secondary Educ., https://oese.ed.gov/offices/american-rescue-plan/american-rescue-plan-elementary-and-secondary-school-emergency-relief/stateplans/ (last visited Sept. 24, 2021).

[32] Nat'l Low Income Hous. Coal., NLIHC Overview and Analysis of Latest Emergency Rental Assistance Spending Data (Sept. 24, 2021), https://nlihc.org/news/nlihc-overview-and-analysis-latest-emergency-rental-assistance-spending-data.

[33] Sarah Chaney Cambon & Danny Dougherty, States that Cut Unemployment Benefits Saw Limited Impact on Job Growth, Wall St. J. (Sept. 1, 2021), www.wsj.com/articles/states-that-cut-unemployment-benefits-saw-limited-impact-on-job-growth-11630488601.

public health expertise and have the capacity to implement it, which sometimes is true. But as already described, states have not always chosen to respond to federal PHE measures.[34]

Nevertheless, the early vacuum of presidential leadership boosted state responsibility – and power – to respond to a disease outbreak posing a greater challenge than any public health event in recent history. A solely state-based response could not have adequately addressed this level of disaster, making national containment measures even more important. Facing little federal assistance and contradictory guidance, it is unsurprising that states initially responded to the pandemic in a highly irregular fashion. Governors found themselves thrust onto the pandemic frontline but also sometimes in a bind. While governors have authority to respond quickly to an emergency, in some states, such as Missouri, they refused to adopt containment measures suggested by federal public health experts, such as Dr. Anthony Fauci, the Director of the National Institute of Allergy and Infectious Diseases, leaving decisions and implementation to local officials.[35] In other states, such as Mississippi, governors limited local authority to issue containment rules, contradicting evidence that such measures were critical to slowing disease spread.[36] With the pandemic raging on, some state legislatures in the 2021 session limited gubernatorial emergency powers, which could impair response to future PHE.[37] This shows how state responsibility for the pandemic reflects a particularly risky brew of short- and long-term policy choices driven by leadership successes and failures.

On the short-term policy front, non-pharmaceutical interventions (NPIs) were the primary tool for controlling the spread of COVID-19 in 2020 and remained important into 2021, even as the FDA's emergency use vaccine approvals began on December 11, 2020.[38] The NPIs recommended by the CDC included individual efforts such as mask-wearing and frequent sanitizing of hands and surfaces; public measures such as physical distance and restricted occupancy in public spaces; limitations on the size of gatherings; state and local stay-in-place orders (SIP); and

[34] Pandemic and All-Hazards Preparedness and Advancing Innovation Act of 2019, Pub. L. No. 116–22, 133 Stat. 905 (2019).

[35] Jim Salter, Missouri's COVID-19 Response in Spotlight at Governor Forum, US News (Oct. 9, 2020), www.usnews.com/news/best-states/missouri/articles/2020-10-09/missouris-covid-19-response-in-spotlight-at-governor-forum.

[36] Adam Gabbatt, Which States Have Done the Least to Contain Coronavirus?, Guardian (Apr. 3, 2020), www.theguardian.com/world/2020/apr/03/coronavirus-states-response-who-has-done-least-alabama-oklahoma-missouri.

[37] David A. Lieb, State Lawmakers Are Pushing to Curb Governors' Virus Powers, Associated Press (Jan. 28, 2021), https://apnews.com/article/state-lawmakers-governor-coronavirus-7d5710f2d8aa4e659c oec68400ad3d3c?utm_source=Sailthru&utm_medium=email&utm_campaign=AP%20Mornin g%20 Wire&utm_term=Morning%20Wire%20Subscribers.

[38] Food & Drug Admin. Press Release, FDA Takes Key Action in Fight Against COVID-19 by Issuing Emergency Use Authorization for First COVID-19 Vaccine (Dec. 11, 2021), www.fda.gov/news-events/press-announcements/fda-takes-key-action-fight-against-covid-19-issuing-emergency-use-authorization-first-covid-19.

business, church, and school closures. Some state officials swiftly implemented NPIs and kept them in place when infection rates spiked, as in California, while others such as Texas responded minimally, reopening quickly after SIPs and resisting further containment. South Dakota and neighboring states had a particularly bad outbreak in the summer of 2020 after resisting most NPIs and allowing a major motorcycle rally to occur.[39]

Indeed, data show that states with the weakest containment measures, such as Florida, Mississippi, Texas, and North Dakota, had the worst outbreaks. Studies have documented containment policy differences, including the kinds of measures, stringency, and duration of implementation, showing that policy heterogeneity and weak containment measures correlated to severity of outbreaks in each state.[40] In addition, temporal dissimilarities contributed to severity of outbreaks. State and local NPIs came in waves, with many states opting for near total lockdown, including closing schools and businesses, in March and April of 2020. But some states reopened with almost no containment measures as summer arrived. State containment laxity facilitated a late summer spike in infections across the Midwest and South, followed by a second wave of NPIs. A third wave of NPIs occurred after Thanksgiving outbreaks again flooded hospitals with COVID-19 cases into the end of 2020.[41]

In 2021, when vaccination promised some normalcy, states relaxed and even limited NPIs, going so far as to ban vaccine verification and indoor mask-wearing requirements. These choices fueled a spike in Delta variant cases in the summer months and as the 2021–22 school year began, especially in Southern states, which have had the lowest vaccination rates. As of September 2021, contrary to CDC guidance, nine states forbade school mask-wearing requirements, or required that families be able to opt out for any reason, some of which courts blocked and school boards ignored (Arizona, Arkansas, Florida, Iowa, Oklahoma, South Carolina, Tennessee, Texas, Utah); nineteen states (and also the District of Columbia) required mask-wearing; and the others left decisions to local officials.[42] Many of the same states also banned vaccine mandates and vaccine verification requirements. These same

---

[39] Rosalind J. Carter et al., CDC COVID-19 Response Team, Widespread Severe Acute Respiratory Syndrome Coronavirus 2 Transmission Among Attendees at a Large Motorcycle Rally and Their Contacts, 30 US Jurisdictions, August–September, 2020, 73 Clinical Infectious Diseases S106-S109 (July 15, 2021).

[40] Coronavirus Government Response Tracker, Univ. of Oxford Blavatnik Sch. of Gov't, www.bsg.ox .ac.uk/research/research-projects/coronavirus-government-response-tracker; Variation in US States' Responses to COVID-19, Version 2.0 (Dec. 2020), www.bsg.ox.ac.uk/sites/default/files/2020-12/BSG-WP-2020-034-v2_0.pdf.

[41] Laura Hallas et al., Variation in US States' Responses to COVID-19 Version 3.0 (May 2021), www.bsg .ox.ac.uk/research/research-projects/coronavirus-government-response-tracker.

[42] State COVID-19 Data and Policy Actions, Kaiser Fam. Found. (Sept. 28, 2021), www.kff.org/report-section/state-covid-19-data-and-policy-actions-policy-actions/#note-2-9; Stacey Decker, Which States Ban Mask Mandates in Schools, and Which Require Masks?, Educ. Week (Sept. 29, 2021), www.edweek .org/policy-politics/which-states-ban-mask-mandates-in-schools-and-which-require-masks/2021/08.

states experienced spikes in COVID-19 infections and deaths while the Delta variant became dominant and vaccine hesitancy took hold in the summer of 2021.[43] Arkansas' governor expressed regret for signing the bill banning mask-wearing as infection and death rates spiked in August 2021.[44] Governors and state attorneys general from these and other states also challenged federal vaccine requirements for federal contractors,[45] and health care providers,[46] issued in response to these state officials' reticence to promote or require vaccination, and federal courts have at least preliminarily agreed.[47] Such state choices limited federal vaccination efforts as the Omicron variant emerged in late 2021.

States' variable outcomes also reflect long-term policy choices; two key pre-pandemic examples demonstrate this. First, nearly all public health spending occurs at the state and local level, and most states have reduced public health spending over the last decade and more, with steep budget cuts initiated during the 2008 Great Recession never rebounding.[48] One study found that states spend less than 3 percent of their annual budgets on public health agencies, translating to $100 per resident annually, but varying widely between states, from a high of $263 per person in Delaware to a low of $32 in Louisiana.[49] Another study estimates that public health spending accounts for less than two cents on every health dollar.[50] Florida has had one of the worst COVID-19 outbreaks and spends less than 2 percent of its budget on public health.[51] Even Massachusetts, which increased public health spending over the last decade, had fewer staff relative to the number of residents.[52] Reduced resources impacted state and local governments, increasing leadership turnover and decreasing the reach of short-staffed public health agencies, impacting, for example,

---

[43] Tracking Coronavirus Vaccinations and Outbreaks in the U.S., Reuters (Sept. 30, 2021), https://graphics.reuters.com/HEALTH-CORONAVIRUS/USA-TRENDS/dgkvlgkrkpb/.

[44] Josie Fischels, Arkansas Governor Wants to Reverse a Law That Forbids Schools to Require Masks, NPR (Aug. 4, 2021), www.npr.org/2021/08/04/1024939859/arkansas-governor-reverse-law-let-schools-require-masks.

[45] Executive Order 14,042 (Sept. 9, 2021); Georgia v. Biden, Case No. 1:21-cv-00163-RSB-BKE, 2021 WL5779939 (S.D. Ga. Dec. 7, 2021).

[46] Ctrs. for Medicare & Medicaid Servs., Medicare and Medicaid Programs; Omnibus COVID-19 Health Care Staff Vaccination, 86 Fed. Reg. 61,555-01 (Nov. 5, 2021).

[47] Missouri v. Biden, Case No. 4:21-cv-01329-MTS, 2021 WL 5564501 (E.D. Mo. Nov. 29, 2021); Louisiana v. Becerra, Case No. 3:21-CV-03970, 2021 WL 5609846 (Nov. 30, 2021).

[48] Y. Natalia Alfonso et al., Neglected: Flat or Declining Spending Left States Ill Equipped to Respond to COVID-19, 40 *Health Affs.* 664 (2021).

[49] Lauren Webber et al., Hollowed-Out Public Health System Faces More Cuts Amid Virus, Kaiser Health News & Associated Press (July 1, 2020),.

[50] Jonathan P. Leider et al., Inaccuracy of Official Estimates of Public Health Spending in the United States, 2000–2018, 110 *Am. J. Pub. Health* 194 (2020), https://ajph.aphapublications.org/doi/full/10.2105/AJPH.2020.305709.

[51] Id.

[52] The Impact of Chronic Underfunding on America's Public Health System: Trends, Risks, and Recommendations, 2021, Trust for America's Health (May 2021), www.tfah.org/wp-content/uploads/2021/05/2021_PHFunding_Fnl.pdf.

routine childhood vaccinations and contact-tracing for infections such as HIV, and reducing capacity to respond to a PHE.

State funding cuts should have been balanced by increased federal funding allocated in the ACA, but Congress decreased funding for the Prevention and Public Health Fund shortly after enacting the ACA. Funding for the CDC was flat for the last decade, and states rely on partnering with the CDC for both funding and expertise, producing layers of underfunded public health in the federalist public health structure.[53] In short, public health was underfunded and understaffed when COVID-19 arrived, demanding a massive containment effort and an extensive vaccine rollout without staff or other resources adequate to the tasks.[54] Long-term fiscal neglect increased the risks associated with a pandemic.

Second, states that expanded Medicaid eligibility under the ACA have more federal funding available than non-expansion states, which has administrative, structural, systemic, and population health implications for states' ability to address the pandemic. For example, expansion states drew down more federal money under the CARES Act: $1,755 per resident compared with $1,198 in non-expansion states.[55] Before the pandemic, expansion states experienced improvements in individual and public health as well as financial benefits for health care providers (especially hospitals) and state budgets.[56] Fourteen states did not expand Medicaid as of January 2020, and their populations have higher rates of chronic conditions and worse overall health;[57] their hospitals are less financially stable and have closed at higher rates;[58] and their budgets have not seen the stabilizing shift that comes with expansion funding.[59] All of these are factors contributing to higher COVID-19 infection and death rates.

[53] David Himmelstein & Steffie Woolhandler, Public Health's Falling Share of US Health Spending, 106 *Am. J. Pub. Health* 56–57 (2016), www.ncbi.nlm.nih.gov/pmc/articles/PMC4695931/; Patient Protection and Affordable Care Act, Pub. L. No. 111-148, 124 Stat. 119 § 4002 (2010).

[54] Nicholas Florko, Trump Officials Actively Lobbied to Deny States Money for Vaccine Rollout Last Fall, STAT News (Feb. 1, 2021), www.statnews.com/2021/01/31/trump-officials-lobbied-to-deny-states-money-for-vaccine-rollout/?utm_source=STAT+Newsletters&utm_campaign=a94a277bf9-MR_COPY_14&utm_medium=email&utm_term=0_8cab1d7961-a94a277bf9-150488781.

[55] Cindy Mann, The COVID-19 Crisis Is Giving States That Haven't Expanded Medicaid New Reasons to Reconsider, Commonwealth Fund (Apr. 15, 2020), www.commonwealthfund.org/blog/2020/covid-19-crisis-giving-states-havent-expanded-medicaid-new-reconsideration.

[56] Madeline Guth, Rachel Garfield & Robin Rudowitz, The Effects of Medicaid Expansion Under the ACA: Updated Findings from a Literature Review, Kaiser Fam. Found. (Mar. 2020), http://files.kff.org/attachment/Report-The-Effects-of-Medicaid-Expansion-under-the-ACA-Updated-Findings-from-a-Literature-Review.pdf.

[57] Jacob Goldin, Ithai Z. Lurie & Janet McCubbin, Health Insurance and Mortality: Experimental Evidence from Taxpayer Outreach (Nat'l Bureau of Econ. Rsch., Working Paper No. 26,533, 2019), www.nber.org/papers/w26533.

[58] Frederic Blavin & Christal Ramos, Medicaid Expansion: Effects on Hospital Finances and Implications for Hospitals Facing COVID-19 Challenges, 40 *Health Affs.* 82 (2021).

[59] Stan Dorn et al., The Effects of the Medicaid Expansion on State Budgets: An Early Look in Select States, Kaiser Fam. Found. (2015), www.kff.org/medicaid/issue-brief/the-effects-of-the-medicaid-expansion-on-state-budgets-an-early-look-in-select-states/.

ACA-resistant states made related long-term policy choices that deepened the crisis for people who lost jobs during the pandemic. For example, Georgia has not expanded Medicaid eligibility and relies on the federal exchange; however, it obtained a federal "Section 1332" waiver to disband the exchange, which HHS approved on November 1, 2020 as the severity of the pandemic was increasing.[60] In June 2021, the Biden Administration asked Georgia for data to support waiver continuation, and the waiver faces a court challenge.[61] But Georgia's approach made it harder for the pandemic's newly jobless to find or renew coverage until the Biden Administration opened and advertised a special enrollment period and enlarged subsidies in ways that increased enrollment under ARPA. Many ACA-resistant states also limited access to social programs that address job loss, such as Temporary Assistance to Needy Families (cash assistance), SNAP/Special Supplemental Nutrition Program for Women, Infants, and Children ("food stamps"), and unemployment insurance, making the economic crisis accompanying the pandemic worse for many people.[62] Many states, such as Florida, made the process of applying for unemployment insurance burdensome and the duration of benefits limited, while also not expanding Medicaid, creating a perfect storm of safety net failures when the emergency hit.[63]

Yet every state used Medicaid's temporary regulatory flexibilities to respond to the PHE, indicating that state leaders sometimes make policy choices that federal lawmakers anticipate. Also, every state claimed the Families First Act enhanced federal match, accepting the condition of meeting MOE requirements for the duration of the PHE: no limits or cuts to Medicaid eligibility, no increased premiums, no disenrollment of current or newly enrolled beneficiaries, and state-sponsored COVID-19 testing and treatment with no cost-sharing. MOE requirements prevented new barriers to coverage and enrollment, which had the effect of pausing waiver initiatives that hindered enrollment and destabilized eligibility, such as work requirements and frequent eligibility determinations. Some parts of the federal–state partnership worked, but many did not.

IV LESSONS LEARNED?

The Biden Administration took office and began pulling all the levers that were at President Trump's disposal, seemingly to make up for a year's worth of delay. During that year, more than 25 million Americans were infected with and more

---

[60] Ctrs. for Medicare & Medicaid Servs., Georgia: State Innovation Waiver Under Section 1332 of the PPACA (Nov. 1, 2020), www.cms.gov/CCIIO/Programs-and-Initiatives/State-Innovation-Waivers/Section_1332_State_Innovation_Waivers-/1332-GA-Fact-Sheet.pdf.

[61] Letter to Governor Brian P. Kemp from CMS Administrator Chiquita Brooks-LaSure (June 3, 2021), www.cms.gov/CCIIO/Programs-and-Initiatives/State-Innovation-Waivers/Downloads/1332-Request-Updated-GA-Analysis-Letter.pdf.

[62] 42 U.S.C. § 503.

[63] Pamela Herd & Donald Moynihan, How Administrative Burdens Can Harm Health, Health Aff. Health Pol'y Brief (Oct. 2020), www.healthaffairs.org/do/10.1377/hpb20200904.405159/full/.

than 429,000 died from COVID-19.[64] Assessing the long-term implications for legal doctrine will be an ongoing project, but some lessons were emerging even as the pandemic continued.

The federalism structure within federal statutes varies from law to law and even within laws.[65] In the field of health law, the federalism structure of Medicaid is different from the decentralized structures within the Public Health Service Act, and these laws are different from the structure of grant-in-aid programs that offer federal money to states for focused purposes, such as family planning under Title X, or limited funding for states to create exchanges. These statutes sometimes provide a federal backup when states resist federal policies, but many do not, leaving gaps when state leaders reject or neglect federal funding, as some did with COVID-19 relief funds, and jeopardizing PHE response.

These laws also reflect congressional assumptions about states' desire to partner with the federal government that do not neatly align with the lived experience of the COVID-19 pandemic. State leaders' persistent anti-science policies during COVID-19, especially as the pandemic surged in 2021 while vaccine and NPI resistance swelled, should be a warning for those implementing future PHEs. Key laws such as the Stafford Act and the National Emergencies Act rely heavily on state and local cooperation and implementation, and these are no longer a given reaction.

If public health, emergency, and disaster laws are reexamined, major questions should arise: Do these laws make accurate assumptions about states' partnership and capacity to implement federal policy, and to what degree is centralized leadership and implementation necessary in addition to money and guidance? This inquiry is not the same as constitutional questions considered by the Supreme Court as to whether the federal government can "coerce" states with money; the issue is not what amount of money states need to implement national goals or whether states need that money, but rather who *should* and who *will* lead a policy effort.[66]

Early state policy heterogeneity may have reflected improvisation and perhaps distrust borne of a lack of federal leadership in 2020. But state defiance of federal policy direction long predated the pandemic and should not be a surprise. States negotiate to get what they want from the federal government, observing how to bargain and lining up for concessions, as exemplified by the dynamic negotiations of Medicaid expansion waivers. Vigorous state negotiation may lead to greater variability and dynamism than Congress envisioned as a tradeoff for policy implementation, an important lesson for public health laws and for broader health reform efforts going forward. Though public health federalism structures provided early backup when state officials filled a federal leadership vacuum, the weaknesses of public health

---

[64] Ctrs. for Disease Control & Prevention, COVID-19 Mortality Overview, www.cdc.gov/nchs/covid19/mortality-overview.htm (last visited Feb. 24, 2021).

[65] Abbe R. Gluck, Intrastatutory Federalism and Statutory Interpretation: State Implementation of Federal Law in Health Reform and Beyond, 121 *Yale L. J.* 534 (2011).

[66] Nat'l Fed'n of Indep. Bus. v. Sebelius, 567 U.S. 519 (2012).

federalism were brought into sharp relief as the pandemic continued. Inadequately funding public health, under-preparation for emergencies and disasters, long-term choices that weakened the social safety net, non-scientific decisions about containment measures and vaccinations necessary to containing a pandemic – these state choices weakened the US public health apparatus.

V CONCLUSION

The legacy of COVID-19 is more than the cost of leadership failures; the pandemic highlighted the costs of the federalist structure, paid in high rates of infection and mortality. The pandemic exposed the room for error that divided governance allows through fragmenting not only responsibility and power but also capacity. Between prior health policy choices, fiscal neglect, and lack of effective coordination between federal and state leaders, it is no wonder that the United States had the world's "worst outbreak."

11

COVID-19 Reveals the Fiscal Determinants of Health

Matthew B. Lawrence

I INTRODUCTION

This chapter describes the ways in which the US fiscal system undermined the country's preparation for and response to the COVID-19 pandemic. It emphasizes that health law scholarship can usefully treat the discovery of a lack of resources to address a particular problem in health or health care as a starting point, not an endpoint, in the identification of legal solutions to policy problems. The fiscal determinants of health – including scorekeeping, fragmentation, fiscal federalism, and forced fragility – contribute to underinvestment in health care and public health. By tracing particular examples of underinvestment back to their fiscal determinants, health law can identify and motivate necessary upstream reforms.

II HEALTH INVESTMENT AND THE PETER/PAUL QUESTION

Health law and policy scholarship are replete with calls for additional investment in health or health care, usually based on careful, persuasive analysis of how such investment would be cost-justified on many dimensions.[1] The COVID-19 pandemic has been no exception. For example, the Network for Public Health Law issued a compilation of scholarly recommendations for steps that state, local, and federal governments might take to mitigate the harms of the pandemic; the unmistakable theme of the recommendations is "more funding."[2] The pervasiveness of

---

[1] Overall, the United Health Foundation estimates a potential, untapped savings of $5.60 for every $1 invested in discrete evidence-based public health programs. United Health Found. Ann. Rep. 85 (2018).

[2] In many cases, the recommendations are explicitly for greater funding. For example, Scott Burris et al., Assessing Legal Responses to COVID-19, Pub. Health L. Watch, at 7 (Aug. 2020) ("Congress should fund ... rapid testing, contact tracing, and isolation"); id. ("Congress should mandate and fund an effort to rebuild CDC's information infrastructure"); id. at 8 ("State legislatures should fund ... ongoing contact tracing"); id. ("Legislators should ... provide sufficient funding to support improved data collection"); id. at 9 ("Local governments should enact paid sick leave policies"). In others, they are for measures that would require federal, state, local, or tribal actors to take resource-intensive actions such as hiring additional full-time employees or hiring subcontractors or consultants. For example, id. at

underinvestment raises the possibility of underlying, systemic causes. Why does US society fail to make worthwhile investments in health and health care?

Prominent explanations include public choice pathologies and racism.[3] From the standpoint of these explanations, there is only so much that health law scholarship can do once scholars identify a particular example of underinvestment, other than to turn directly to political advocacy.

There is another explanation for the nation's tendency to underinvest in health and health care, however: the often-overlooked fiscal system through which the country makes tradeoffs concerning the allocation of its scarce resources. Any suggestion that more funding is needed for a given project will be met by policymakers with the same question: What should I cut to get the money? Just as the "Chicago question" haunts private law ("if it's such a good idea, why aren't private entities already doing it?"), this Peter/Paul question haunts health law. Should policymakers rob Peter to pay Paul? If the country spends too much on treating sickness and not enough on preventing it, should health care entitlements be cut to fund public health investments? If not, where should the money come from: Should it be borrowed? Should taxes be raised – and if they are, will that stifle economic growth and, with it, the revenues available in the future?

The debate over additional pandemic funding in the 2022 Consolidated Appropriations Act illustrated the potency of the Peter/Paul question. In March of 2022, as the pandemic entered its third year, the Biden Administration sought $22.5 billion in additional funding to pay for continued response efforts, including testing, treatment, and vaccination.[4] Congress initially included $15 billion in an omnibus appropriations package to meet this request, but Republicans insisted that any additional funds be offset by reductions elsewhere.[5] A plan to draw such offsets from pandemic funds that had already been appropriated for states, but not yet spent, created controversy and opposition.[6] As a result, the pandemic relief was pulled from the omnibus funding package, which was enacted in March 2022 without it, despite the Administration's predictions of immediate adverse impacts for

---

7 (recommending that the Department of Health and Human Services develop guidance on the spread of communicable disease); id. ("[The] CDC should develop rigorous … guidance for safe operation of schools [and] businesses"); id. ("Congress should require the Department of Health and Human Services to collect and publicly report standardized data"); id. ("Agencies … should coordinate and standardize data collection"); id. at 8 (suggesting that states should "use their police power to promote physical distancing"); id. (recommending that state health departments "seek to identify and address unique barriers and concerns [for] immigrant and migrant populations"); id. at 9 ("Local health departments should collect detailed data on the populations and geographies most affected by COVID-19").

3 Daniel E. Dawes, *The Political Determinants of Health* (2020); Paul A. Diller, Why Do Cities Innovate in Public Health? Implications of Scale and Structure, 91 *Wash. Univ. L. Rev.* 1219 (2014) (discussing public choice explanations).

4 See Cheyenne Haslett & Ben Gittleson, White House Says 1st Cuts to COVID Efforts Will Hit Americans Next Week as Funding Stalls in Congress, ABC News (Mar. 15, 2022).

5 Id.

6 Id.

the nation's pandemic response.[7] At the time of writing, it is not clear whether or when Congress will ever provide the funding, but if it does, it will at least be delayed long enough to cause some of the predicted adverse impacts. As this sequence of events reveals, the question that proved determinative for inclusion of additional pandemic funding in the 2022 Consolidated Appropriations Act was not whether such funding was necessary. The determinative question was how additional funding would be acquired.

As this example makes clear, the Peter/Paul question tends to defuse calls for greater investment by highlighting the tradeoffs forced by such calls. But objections based on tradeoffs are only as good as our system for making them – for deciding where to direct scarce resources. That is not only a story about politics. It is also a story about the complicated system of revenues, expenditures, estimates, and budgets that society uses to make "fiscal" decisions.[8]

III THE FISCAL DETERMINANTS OF HEALTH

The laws, rules, and practices that comprise the US fiscal system load the dice against public health, contributing to the country's failure to make tradeoffs correctly – its failure to allocate resources appropriately for public health and health care. As Professor Westmoreland, whose scholarship has done much to uncover such distortions, put it, "the process is the policy."[9]

The parts that follow elaborate upon how the nation makes tradeoffs about how to allocate scarce resources using a complex fiscal system that: (1) ignores long-term and secondary costs and benefits in estimating the effects of policy; (2) fragments choices into largely arbitrary but outcome-determinative fiscal categories; (3) leaves a flawed federal fiscal apparatus as the main source of essential investments; and (4) forces fragility on public goods. It is useful to think of these tendencies – scorekeeping distortions, fiscal fragmentation, fiscal federalism, and forced fragility – as the "fiscal determinants of health." While the point can be overdone, it highlights the fact that these are distinct causes of unnecessary sickness and suffering embedded in a particular area of law, and that they therefore offer legal levers we might pull to improve outcomes.

The fiscal determinants of health are a promising avenue for legal reform because they are themselves partially the product of law, as described later. Health law scholarship can productively approach individual cases of scarcity it discovers not as an

---

[7] Id. (quoting letter from Shalanda D. Young, Acting Director, OMB & Jeffrey D. Zients, Secretary of the Treasury, to Speaker Nancy Pelosi, Mar. 15, 2022).

[8] Fiscal, Merriam-Webster Dictionary 271 (2016) (deriving from Latin, "basket," often government revenue/expenditure, but also, more broadly, budgeting; "of or relating to taxation, public revenues, or public debt").

[9] Timothy Westmoreland, Standard Errors: How Budget Rules Distort Lawmaking, 95 Geo. L. J. 1555, 1557 (2007).

ending, but as a beginning, tracing them back to underlying fiscal law rules to moti-vate reform. Moreover, this work offers opportunities for engagement with other fields that depend heavily on social ordering through spending, such as education, childcare, and transportation, because fiscal determinants can act as obstacles to investment across these contexts.

The discussion here is not intended to be a comprehensive accounting of the inter-action between fiscal determinants and the nation's preparation for, or response to, the COVID-19 pandemic. Instead, it is intended to illustrate how fiscal rules and practices can undermine health policymaking, drawing on examples from this pandemic.

IV SCOREKEEPING

Scorekeeping is the first fiscal determinant that undermined the country's man-agement of the pandemic. Estimating the costs and benefits of potential policy choices is an essential step in deciding how to allocate scarce resources – without an estimate, there is no way either to assess which allocations are worthwhile or, where many potential allocations seem worthwhile, to make comparisons between them. In a series of articles, Professor Westmoreland has problematized the rules that Congress uses to estimate the costs and benefits of legislation in the budget pro-cess.[10] The closest formal congressional equivalent to cost-benefit analysis of regula-tions, scorekeeping, is the process by which the Congressional Budget Office and the House and Senate Budget Committees estimate the effects of legislation and track its effects for purposes of various budget statutes and points of order.[11]

The scores produced in this process can be incredibly influential. Professor Westmoreland has described how the goal of gaming the "score" distorted a range of health care policies.[12] Professors Westmoreland and William Sage have described how scoring considerations doomed President Clinton's health reform plan and shaped that of President Obama.[13] And Professor Sage has described the importance of scorekeeping considerations for the design of single-payer health reforms such as Medicare for All.[14]

Prophetically, Professor Westmoreland explained how these biases would leave the country unprepared for a viral pandemic years before COVID-19. He pointed out that "[t]he budget process discourages long-term investments" by measuring

---

[10] Id.; Timothy Westmoreland, Invisible Forces at Work: Health Legislation and Budget Processes, in *The Oxford Handbook of U.S. Health Law* 873 (I. Glenn Cohen et al., eds., 2017); Timothy Westmoreland, Can We Get There from Here? Universal Health Insurance and the Congressional Budget Process, 96 Geo. L. J. 523 (2008).

[11] Allen Schick, *The Federal Budget: Politics, Policy, Process* (3d ed. 2007).

[12] Westmoreland, supra note 10, at 1574.

[13] William M. Sage & Timothy M. Westmoreland, Following the Money: The ACA's Fiscal-Political Economy and Lessons for Future Health Care Reform, 48 J. L. Med. Ethics 434, 437–40 (2020).

[14] William M. Sage, Adding Principles to Pragmatism: The Transformative Potential of "Medicare-for-All," 14–15, 23–24 (Feb. 2020) (unpublished manuscript) (available at https://perma.cc/TT5D-FSBT).

both costs and benefits within narrow windows of, at most, ten years.[15] Moreover, estimates exclude so-called "secondary" (dynamic) effects of spending, such as the benefit of reduced Medicare hospital costs associated with measures that promote health or prevent chronic illness.[16] This exclusion is the result of a facially neutral desire for certainty in predictions, but because both costs and market effects are easier to predict than secondary benefits, the facially neutral criterion of certainty in estimates depresses investments in public goods. Furthermore, in what Professor Westmoreland calls an example of "solipsism," federal scorekeeping estimates "place no value on non-federal savings,"[17] "resulting in an underappreciation of public value and public improvement."[18] Because the "widely dispersed benefits of preventing an epidemic would ... remain unscored,"[19] Professor Westmoreland predicted in 2007 that the federal government would fail to invest adequately in pandemic preparedness. Of course, that is precisely what happened.[20]

Scorekeeping most directly undermines health investment when it prevents a bill from being passed or distorts its design. But even when a bill passes, scorekeeping's solipsism and limited time horizons can undermine investment because of the way it interacts with deficit control statutes, such as the Statutory Pay-As-You-Go Act of 2010. When COVID-19 struck, Congress passed major spending legislation to address it, including the Coronavirus Aid, Relief, and Economic Security Act and the American Recovery Plan. It overcame negative scores in doing so, but the Senate refused a permanent exemption from the Pay-As-You-Go Act, instead deferring impacts. The result is that the Act will require a mandatory across-the-board sequestration cut in spending programs in late 2024 or early 2025, unless addressed by Congress through legislation.[21] Even if Congress enacts a measure averting these cuts, their threat, and the votes they force, will increase the fragility of social programs.

Finally, the COVID-19 pandemic also illustrated a blind spot in the US fiscal system: the invisibility of unpaid care work. Some of the most critical work done in this country is the work of caring for those in positions of acute vulnerability, including children and elderly people.[22] Yet, as Professor Noah Zatz points out, this work tends to be ignored in making policy because it is often unpaid and done by women.[23]

---

[15] Westmoreland, supra note 10, at 1590.
[16] Scott Levy, Spending Money to Make Money: CBO Scoring of Secondary Effects, 127 *Yale L. J.* 936 (2018).
[17] Westmoreland, supra note 10, at 1593.
[18] Id. at 1592.
[19] Id. at 1593.
[20] Sage & Westmoreland, supra note 14, at 435.
[21] Ctr. for a Responsible Federal Budget, Upcoming Fiscal Policy Deadlines (Dec. 22, 2021), www.crfb .org/blogs/upcoming-congressional-fiscal-policy-deadlines; S. 610, Protecting Medicare and American Farmers from Sequester Cuts Act, Pub. L. 117–71 (Dec. 10, 2021).
[22] Martha Albertson Fineman, The Nature of Dependencies and Welfare "Reform," 36 *Santa Clara L. Rev.* 287 (1996).
[23] Noah Zatz, Supporting Workers by Accounting for Care, 5 *Harv. L. Pol'y Rev.* 45 (2011).

The COVID-19 response illustrated this blind spot for unpaid care work. Nurses and doctors in hospitals and clinics are usually described as working on the "front lines" of the COVID-19 pandemic,[24] but this framing ignores the fact that most COVID-19 treatment took place in homes across the country and was provided unpaid by family members and loved ones.[25] While the goal of protecting "front-line" professional health care workers from exposure through the provision of personal protective equipment was a leading one throughout the pandemic, protecting home-front health workers was an afterthought.

This oversight proved costly. Household spread appears to have been a key fuel in the COVID-19 pandemic in the United States. While data is still emerging, one study showed that across the country, when symptomatic coronavirus patients were sent home after diagnosis, cohabitating family members quickly contracted the virus (usually within a week) more than 50 percent of the time.[26] This was much higher than results reported in other countries, where the rate was 30 percent or lower.[27] Even congressional efforts to address home care work focused only on workers pulled from the full-time workforce, rather than on those not in that workforce because of their commitment to care work. In the Coronavirus Aid, Relief, and Economic Security Act passed in March 2020, Congress attempted to partially reimburse some home care work, mandating that employers provide their full-time employees with up to six weeks of paid time off to care for dependent children. The measure excluded employees who needed to take time to care for loved ones other than dependent children, including parents and partners,[28] care workers who lacked qualifying full-time employment,[29] and for half of 2020, employees unable to work due to lockdown because of an unlawfully cramped Department of Labor interpretation (which was ultimately overturned).[30]

V FISCAL FRAGMENTATION

The fragmentation of health care costs and benefits into discrete fiscal categories also undermined the nation's handling of the pandemic. Through a dense, interconnected web of property law, contract law, and fiscal law, responsibility for costs associated with sickness and health care in the United States is segmented into

[24] Emily Palmer, Voices from the Pandemic's Front Lines, NY Times (May 11, 2020), www.nytimes .com/2020/05/11/reader-center/coronavirus-healthcare-workers.html.

[25] Kate Power, The COVID-19 Pandemic Has Increased the Care Burden of Women and Families, 16 *Sustainability: Sci., Prac. & Pol'y* 67 (2020).

[26] Carlos G. Grijalva et al., Transmission of SARS-COV-2 Infections in Households – Tennessee and Wisconsin, April-September 2020, 69 *Morbidity & Mortality Wkly. Rep.* 1631 (2020).

[27] Jake Lowary, VUMC Study Finds Faster, Wider Spread of COVID-19 in US Households, *Vand. Univ. Med. Ctr.* (Oct. 30, 2020), https://news.vumc.org/2020/10/30/vumc-study-finds-faster-wider-spread-of-covid-19-in-u-s-households/#:~:text=COVID%2D19%20spreads%20faster%20and,Control%20 and%20Prevention%20(CDC).

[28] Families First Coronavirus Response Act (FFCRA), Pub. L. No. 116–127, 134 Stat. 178 (2020).

[29] Id.

[30] New York v. US Dep't of Lab., 477 F.Supp.3d 1 (SDNY 2020).

categories, such as "public" and "private" and "federal" and "state."[31] They are then further segmented within each category into subcategories – at the federal level, these include "mandatory" expenditures (such as Medicare and Medicaid) and "discretionary" expenditures (most public health funding),[32] and then into programs (Medicare Part A or Medicaid), and so on. Similarly, state spending is separated by department and program; for example, Professor Elizabeth Weeks's recent work has shown the many different components of states and localities that have been impacted financially by the opioid crisis – and the hard work that can be entailed in stitching these segregated categories together to reveal the true costs of the crisis.[33] And, of course, within the private sector, costs are fragmented between and among providers, payers, and patients.[34]

The fragmentation of costs into disparate categories prevents needed investment in public goods by limiting reforms enacted to those that are cost-justified within a given narrow fiscal category or, put differently, by impeding investments that pose costs within one fiscal category but create benefits within another category.[35] At the same time, it facilitates costly and wasteful behaviors that increase overall costs – but create savings for the actor. Take Medicare's readmission penalty. The penalty is an attempt to respond to a problematic phenomenon: fragmentation gives hospitals an economic incentive to discharge patients prematurely because they do not bear the cost of readmissions. In response, Medicare penalizes those hospitals whose patients have the highest readmission rates.[36] In economic terms, fragmentation leads to overproduction of negative externalities and underproduction of positive externalities, necessitating either the coordination required for Coasian bargaining of a Pigouvian subsidy or sanction.[37] In plain English, because decisionmakers may lack either the means or the stakes to take costly actions that reduce health care costs for which they are not responsible, even when those actions are worthwhile from the overall standpoint of the community, such actions will not be taken unless, by contract or government fiat, the benefits of the investment (or costs of foregone investment) are shared with them.

---

[31] See Erin C. Fuse Brown, Matthew B. Lawrence, Elizabeth Y. McCuskey & Lindsay F. Wiley, Social Solidarity in Health Care, American-Style, 48 *J. L. Med. Ethics* 411, 415 (2020).

[32] Federal budgeting laws and rules treat "mandatory" expenditures on programs such as Medicare and Medicaid as distinct from "discretionary" expenditures on annual programs, requiring that increases in mandatory spending be offset by decreases in mandatory spending and that increases in discretionary spending similarly be offset by discretionary decreases. Allen Schick, *The Federal Budget: Politics, Policy, Process* (3d ed. 2007).

[33] Elizabeth Weeks & Paula Sanford, Financial Impact of the Opioid Crisis on Local Government: Quantifying Costs for Litigation and Policymaking, 67 *U. Kan. L. Rev.* 1061 (2019).

[34] Fuse Brown et al., supra note 32.

[35] Id.; see also Fineman, supra note 23 ("It is widely understood that the social safety net is being torn apart by the rhetoric of budget necessity and professed American moral values").

[36] Jordan Rau, Look Up Your Hospital: Is It Being Penalized by Medicare?, Kaiser Health News (Nov. 2, 2020), https://khn.org/news/hospital-penalties.

[37] Wallace E. Oates, *Fiscal Federalism* 66–67 (William J. Baumol ed., 1972) (describing A.C. Pigou's proposed subsidy to counteract positive externalities).

Scholars have noted that an individualized, medical approach to health care does not facilitate the measures needed to address a viral pandemic, such as surveillance testing, quarantine, and expeditious vaccination.[38] The issue is one of means as well as motivation: even if actors might want to further collective interests for the good of society, fiscal fragmentation means they often lack the means: the money to do it.

Through much of the pandemic, the lack of surveillance testing through employers and schools illustrated this problem. From a collective perspective, it makes sense for asymptomatic employees, teachers, and students to be tested before returning to work or school. Doing so can prevent exposure – and cases – for other employees and students, their families, and the broader community. Congress mandated that insurers cover COVID-19 testing, but insurers were able to refuse such testing for employers and schools on the grounds that surveillance testing for an individual was not a "medically necessary" intervention under the insurance contracts.[39] They did so.[40] Workplaces and schools, for their part, refused to pay for such testing themselves in the vast majority of cases. They cited the cost and administrative burden of testing as the primary barriers.[41]

Why would insurers not pay for surveillance testing for employees and schools themselves – indeed for everyone – as a means to curb the pandemic? Why did Congress even have to mandate that insurers cover tests sought by their beneficiaries? In the fragmented US health care system, any one insurer is financially responsible for the medical costs of only a small fraction of the full patient population. Insurers bear 100 percent of the costs of testing their beneficiaries and only a small fraction of the savings (in terms of health care costs) created by preventing viral spread, which are shared among all other insurers: Medicare, Medicaid, and so on.

VI FISCAL FEDERALISM

Fiscal fragmentation can be overcome on issues such as surveillance testing and vaccines by collective action, as it was, to an incomplete extent, by the mandate that insurers cover medically necessary tests. The Coase theorem would predict that community members could bargain with each other to prompt measures in their

---

[38] Example, Emily A. Benfer, Seema Mohapatra, Lindsay F. Wiley & Ruqaiijah Yearby, Health Justice Strategies to Combat the Pandemic: Eliminating Discrimination, Poverty, and Health Disparities during and after COVID-19, 19 *Yale J. Health Pol'y, L. Ethics* 122, 138 (2020).

[39] Julie Appleby, For COVID Tests, the Question of Who Pays Comes Down to Interpretation, Kaiser Health News (July 20, 2020), https://khn.org/news/for-covid-tests-the-question-of-who-pays-comes-down-to-interpretation/.

[40] Id.

[41] Nathaniel L. Wade & Mara G. Aspinall, Facing Uncertainty: The Challenges of COVID-19 in the Workplace, ASU Workplace Commons (Nov. 2020), www.rockefellerfoundation.org/wp-content/uploads/2020/11/ASU_Workplace_Commons_Nov2020_FINAL.pdf (showing that a significant majority of more than 1,100 employers surveyed refused to test asymptomatic employees, citing cost and administrative complexity as reasons).

collective self-interest.[42] And while ordinarily the coordination entailed in such an effort might itself be a barrier to such collective effort,[43] for a universal threat such as COVID-19, government can be the vehicle for compromise and collective choices.

Fiscal federalism is an impediment to many collective responses to fiscal fragmentation.

As Professor David Super has pointed out, states and localities themselves are tightly limited as a source of costly, collective interventions. Not only are most constitutionally prohibited from deficit spending,[44] but during a recession (such as the one brought on by the pandemic), their revenues decrease (due to reduced spending and income), while their expenditures increase (due to heightened demand for social services, such as unemployment benefits).[45]

That leaves the federal government as the primary source for high-cost collective measures. But, as the pandemic revealed, the risk that the federal government will fail to make appropriate interventions is significant. This is in part a question of leadership,[46] of course, but scorekeeping distortions (discussed earlier) also hamper federal investment, even where it is an essential backstop, as does forced fragility (discussed later).

Personal protective and medical equipment offer one example of the federal government's limitations. The George W. Bush Administration's influenza pandemic plan acknowledged that the federal government is best positioned to supply sufficient stock of these measures to respond quickly to a pandemic.[47] The federal government fell short in doing so, however, due to both a lack of preparation and a lack of leadership.[48] States then demonstrated the challenges of fiscal federalism in real time. They competed over scarce supplies, driving up prices, creating an appearance of chaos, and channeling supplies to the best-resourced and best-connected states, rather than those that most needed it.[49]

---

[42] R.H. Coase, The Problem of Social Cost, 3 *J.L. & Econ.* 1 (1960).

[43] Id.

[44] David A. Super, Rethinking Fiscal Federalism, 118 *Harv. L. Rev.* 2544, 2616 (2005).

[45] Id. at 2611–14.

[46] See David Pozen & Kim Lane Scheppele, Executive Underreach, in Pandemics and Otherwise, 114 *Am. J. Int'l L.* 608 (2020).

[47] Homeland Sec. Council, National Strategy for Pandemic Influenza: Implementation Plan 10 (2005) (indicating that the federal government would "[s]tockpil[e] and coordinat[e] the distribution of necessary countermeasures, in concert with states and other entities").

[48] See Scott Burris et al., The Legal Response to COVID-19: Legal Pathways to a More Effective and Equitable Response, 27 *J. Pub. Health Mgmt. Prac.* S72 (2020) (arguing that the federal government "encouraged a Darwinian competition among states for scarce resources").

[49] See Examining the National Response to the Worsening Coronavirus Pandemic: Hearing Before the H. Comm. on Homeland Sec., 116th Cong. (2020) (statement of Hon. Jay Robert Pritzker, Governor of Illinois) (indicating that the state "paid $5 for masks that usually cost 85 cents"); Reviewing Federal and State Pandemic Supply Preparedness and Response: Hearing Before H. Comm. on Homeland Sec., 116th Cong. (2020) (statement of Xochitl Torres Small, Subcommittee Chairwoman) (stating that "[t]he competition for limited resources [among states] drove up prices and attracted new brokers into the marketplace that were inexperienced and unreliable").

VII FORCED FRAGILITY

A fourth aspect of the fiscal system that undermines health investment has to do not with who makes decisions (the domain of fragmentation and fiscal federalism) or how they make them (the domain of scorekeeping), but with how durable those decisions are once made – an intertemporal question. As used here, fragility refers to a program's susceptibility to disruption or abandonment; it is the inverse of durability (sometimes known as entrenchment). Laws, rules, and norms force fragility even when substantive policy considerations counsel stability.

A critical choice in policymaking is how resistant to change to make a decision – how durable or fragile. Flexibility is often desirable, as it permits change with circumstances or new information (though Professor Super has pointed out that flexibility's benefits are often overstated).[50] On the other hand, stability can often be desirable, too, to engender reliance and long-term investment.[51] The appropriate balance between these considerations depends, of course, on the circumstances.

Several aspects of the US fiscal system interfere with decisions about whether to make a decision flexible or stable. The Constitution interferes with balancing by policymakers of the benefits of stability versus those of flexibility over a wide range of subjects. The Takings and Due Process Clauses insist on stability for resource commitments that trigger their protections, such as ownership of real property.[52] Meanwhile the Appropriations Clause encourages fragility for resource commitments that take the form of government spending, encouraging Congress to leave those commitments dependent on annual appropriations, whether stability is warranted or not, in order to secure the "power of the purse" for itself and its committees.[53] Congressional rules carry forward this encouragement of temporary spending enactments.[54] Separation of powers norms endorsed by courts, commentators, and legislators further encourage Congress to fund spending programs annually to preserve power.[55] And federal statutes, including the debt ceiling and the Pay-As-You-Go-Act, threaten disruption to spending programs across-the-board, serving as a blanket source of instability in service of fiscal or separation of powers goals.

These laws, rules, and norms motivated by fiscal concerns and the separation of powers force fragility in federal public good investments – such as pandemic

---

[50] See David A. Super, Against Flexibility, 96 *Cornell L. Rev.* 1375, 1411 (2011).

[51] See id.

[52] Matthew B. Lawrence, Subordination and the Separation of Powers (unpublished manuscript) (on file with author).

[53] Matthew B. Lawrence, Congress's Domain: Appropriations, Time, and Chevron, 70 *Duke L. J.* 1057, 1072 (2021).

[54] Congressional Budget and Impoundment Control Act of 1974, H.R. 7130, 93rd Cong. § 401 (1973–74); 2 U.S.C. 651 (points of order for mandatory spending or budget authority beyond control of appropriations committees).

[55] See Lawrence, supra note 54.

preparedness – even when the goals of such investments would be better served by stability. As a result, public health programs in the United States are less able to engender meaningful health investment because of constant threats to funding and recurrent disruptions.[56]

Again, the nation's preparation for coronavirus was undermined by forced fragility.

Senator Clinton recognized the problem posed by a lack of stable public health funding in the United States, proposing with Jeanne Lambrew a "wellness trust" as a permanent public health funding source.[57] These efforts culminated in the Prevention and Public Health Fund (PPHF) in the Patient Protection and Affordable Care Act (ACA) of 2010. Section 4002 of the ACA created the $18.75 billion PPHF in mandatory, permanent law, with the sole purpose of preparing for public health crises, including pandemics.[58]

Although Congress and the President could make the PPHF permanent, insulating it from the vicissitudes of the annual appropriations process, they could not entrench it against change in future legislation. Spending on public health is a collective benefit, not "property" that anyone owns or a contract with performance owed to any particular business – so existing avenues of constitutional entrenchment were closed.[59] Moreover, as "mandatory" spending, the PPHF was in the same fiscal category as more constitutionally and politically entrenched spending programs, such as Medicare and Social Security, as Professors Westmoreland and Sage explain.[60] That meant that when Congress wanted to make subsequent costly changes in the "mandatory" category, the PPHF was an easy target as a source of funds. Congress repeatedly raided the fund, paying for new expenditures (the Medicare "doc fix") and reduced revenues (the 2017 Tax Cuts and Jobs Act).[61]

The PPHF's fragility thus significantly limited its usefulness. As the fund was raided, fiscally aware onlookers once again made prophetic predictions. "[W]ithout funding, the CDC won't be able to protect us," former CDC Director Tom Frieden

---

[56] Example, Sage & Westmoreland, supra note 14.

[57] See Jeanne M. Lambrew, A Wellness Trust to Prioritize Disease Prevention 21, Brookings Inst. (Apr. 1, 2007), www.brookings.edu/research/a-wellness-trust-to-prioritize-disease-prevention/ (calling for permanent funding source); S. 3674, Twenty-First Century Wellness Trust Act, § 39900(c)(3), 110th Cong. (2008) (proposed legislation).

[58] Patient Protection and Affordable Care Act § 4002, Pub. L. No. 111–148, 124 Stat. 119 (2010); 42 U.S.C. § 300u- 11 (purpose of "expanded and sustained national investment in public health programs").

[59] See Christopher Serkin, Public Entrenchment Through Private Law: Binding Local Government, 78 U. Chi. L. Rev. 879, 882 (2011) (describing means of entrenchment).

[60] Sage & Westmoreland, supra note 14, at 436.

[61] Id. at 441; Michael R. Fraser, A Brief History of the Prevention and Public Health Fund: Implications for Public Health Advocates, 109 Am. J. Pub. Health 572 (2019), https://ajph.aphapublications.org/doi/pdf/10.2105/AJPH.2018.304926?casa_token=ov8zgOdGCsgAAAAA:GDHPZ MM7uWkqRfR-USRmj VJ1JQcZqfQf6ZtVkn8t7ob6PajdPy6fiE7bK-rXzd82rGJHPWiz5WV7.

observed in 2018. "We're more likely to have to fight dangerous organisms here in the U.S."[62] Sadly, Director Frieden's prognosis proved correct.

VIII CONCLUSION

Unlike other barriers to health investment, the fiscal determinants of health are largely a product of law – and so can be changed through legislative, regulatory, and litigation pathways. This effort is not hopeless. Recognizing the importance of fiscal determinants, Democrats in Congress in 2021 amended House procedures to reduce budgetary barriers to future legislation addressing COVID-19 "or public health consequences resulting from climate change."[63] Representative Ocasio-Cortez described the rule change on Twitter as "a big deal – and not only on health care." "They are structural changes in the House that level the playing field for a full SUITE of flagship legislation."[64] This change is closely related to reforms pressed by Professor Westmoreland, discussed earlier.[65]

Health law scholars and policymakers should not see scarcity as inevitable, or fiscal law as beyond health law. It is possible to identify and motivate needed fiscal system reforms by tracing particular instances of harm not only to the lack of investment that contributed to them, but also to the upstream fiscal determinants that contributed to that lack of investment.

---

[62] Ashley Yeager, Cuts to Prevention and Public Health Fund Puts CDC Programs at Risk, TheScientist (Feb. 9, 2018), www.the-scientist.com/daily-news/cuts-to-prevention-and-public-health-fund-puts-cdc-programs-at-risk-30298.

[63] See H.R. Res. § 3(v)(2) (2021), www.congress.gov/bill/117th-congress/house-resolution/8/text ("The Chair of the Committee on the Budget may adjust an estimate … to … exempt the budgetary effects of measures" related to COVID-19 or "public health consequences resulting from climate change.").

[64] Alexandria Ocasio-Cortez (@AOC), Twitter (Jan. 3, 2021, 9:09 PM), https://twitter.com/aoc/status/1345190548815142918?lang=en.

[65] Westmoreland, supra note 10, at 1604–10 (suggesting changes).

12

Legislating a More Responsive Safety Net

Andrew Hammond, Ariel Jurow Kleiman, and Gabriel Scheffler

I INTRODUCTION

The COVID-19 pandemic underscored glaring weaknesses in the ability of American safety net programs to adequately respond to a national crisis. The pandemic and ensuing economic recession left millions of Americans struggling with joblessness, hunger, unstable housing, and insufficient access to health care. Government action was often either short-lived or long-delayed. Policymakers can learn from these mistakes. They must reform safety net policies to ensure that American families can survive future crises. This chapter charts a path for how they can do so.

First, we start by summarizing how Congress and federal agencies responded to the COVID-19 pandemic through various changes to safety net programs.[1] Second, we explore how existing safety net programs proved inadequate in the face of such a catastrophic and sustained crisis, and how Congress can remedy the systemic flaws underlying this inadequate response. We argue that Congress should enact mechanisms – often called "automatic stabilizers" – to ensure that safety net programs respond more immediately and effectively to future emergencies. Third, we defend strengthening automatic stabilizers on democratic grounds, arguing that doing so would increase transparency, limit delegation, and heighten responsiveness.

II PANDEMIC-RELATED CHANGES TO SAFETY NET PROGRAMS

The COVID-19 pandemic was both epidemiological and economic in nature. It resulted in a breathtaking loss of life, leaving over a million Americans dead and many others suffering from debilitating and perplexing long-term symptoms. Meanwhile, the pandemic's economic effects shattered many Americans' financial security. Yet although the pandemic was initially hailed by some as "the great

---

[1] This part of the discussion draws from our previously published essay. Andrew Hammond, Ariel Jurow Kleiman & Gabriel Scheffler, How the COVID-19 Pandemic Has and Should Reshape the American Safety Net, 105 *Minn. L. Rev.* Headnotes 154 (2020).

equalizer," it was anything but. The pandemic both reflected and augmented preexisting social inequalities. Low-income people and people of color in particular were disproportionately harmed by its economic and health impacts.

To address these twin crises, the federal government enacted six major pieces of legislation between March 2020 and March 2021.[2] The most prominent and largest of these were the Families First Coronavirus Response (Families First) Act, the Coronavirus Aid, Relief, and Economic Security (CARES) Act, the Consolidated Appropriations Act, 2021, and the American Rescue Plan Act (ARPA). These laws altered the US safety net in various ways, including through bolstering cash transfers, food support, medical assistance, and job-related support.

This part briefly describes some of the most important changes, though our discussion is necessarily incomplete, given its brevity. We focus in particular on the federal response, due to the federal government's important role in funding these programs and setting their requirements. However, state and local governments likewise play key roles in funding and administering safety net programs, and we highlight these roles as appropriate.[3]

A *The Tax System*

The CARES Act directed the Internal Revenue Service to send "recovery rebate" checks of $1,200 per adult, and $500 per child, to millions of American households.[4] The Consolidated Appropriations Act and ARPA authorized additional payments of $600 and $1,400, respectively, to all adults and children.[5] All payments phased out for incomes above $75,000 ($150,000 for married couples). The Consolidated Appropriations Act also temporarily modified the Earned Income Tax Credit (EITC) and Child Tax Credit to ensure that taxpayers would not be penalized for losing their jobs during the pandemic. The provision allowed taxpayers to use either 2019 or 2020 income to calculate the credit amount for 2020.[6] This change ensured that taxpayers did not receive a smaller credit if they lost work due to the pandemic, since both tax credits phased in at low income levels in tax year 2020.

---

[2] Coronavirus Preparedness and Response Supplemental Appropriations Act, Pub. L. No. 116-123, 134 Stat. 146 (2020); Families First Coronavirus Response Act, Pub. L. No. 116–127, 134 Stat. 178 (2020); Coronavirus Aid, Relief, and Economic Security Act, Pub. L. No. 116–136, 134 Stat. 281 (2020); Paycheck Protection Program and Health Care Enhancement Act, Pub. L. No. 116–139, 134 Stat. 620 (2020); Consolidated Appropriations Act, 2021, Pub. L. No. 116–260, 134 Stat. 1182; American Rescue Plan Act of 2021, Pub. L. No. 117–2, 135 Stat. 4.

[3] See, generally, Andrew Hammond, Welfare and Federalism's Peril, 92 *Wash. L. Rev.* 1721 (2017) (critiquing the devolution of control over safety net programs to the states).

[4] IRC § 6428 (West 2020).

[5] Consolidated Appropriations Act, 2021, Pub. L. No. 116–260, div. N, § 203, 134 Stat. 1182, 1953; American Rescue Plan Act § 9601.

[6] Consolidated Appropriations Act, § 211.

With ARPA, Congress temporarily expanded the Child Tax Credit by making it available to all families, regardless of employment status, and by increasing the credit amount from $2,000 to $3,000 per child (or $3,600 for children under six).[7] Congress also temporarily increased the maximum EITC for childless workers, from about $540 to just over $1,500.[8] These expansions expired at the start of 2022.

B *Unemployment Insurance*

Unemployment insurance (UI) is a joint federal–state program that states administer pursuant to federal guidelines. The CARES Act, Consolidated Appropriations Act, and ARPA temporarily expanded the amount, duration, and scope of UI benefits for those who lost work during the COVID-19 pandemic. With the CARES Act, Congress provided a $600 per week supplement to be paid on top of state UI benefits through July 31, 2020. It also extended the duration of benefits by funding additional weeks of support for workers who had exhausted all state benefits.[9] The CARES Act also expanded UI eligibility by providing federal funding for states to pay benefits to workers who lost hours (even if they retained their jobs), as well as to "gig workers" and other non-employee workers who would otherwise be excluded from UI programs.[10] Congress extended these various provisions with the Consolidated Appropriations Act and then ARPA, and further authorized a $300 weekly UI supplement through September 6, 2021.[11]

C *Food Assistance*

In the Families First Act, Congress authorized the Department of Agriculture to allow states to create "Pandemic E B T [Electronic Benefit Transfer]" programs.[12] Pandemic EBT was created for families with children who were missing out on free or reduced-price meals as a result of school closures.[13] Congress also allowed states to make "emergency allotments" for households receiving Supplemental Nutrition Assistance Program (SNAP) benefits; however, this provision excluded the poorest Americans, who were already receiving maximum benefits. In the Families First Act, Congress also made emergency appropriations to the Special Supplemental Nutrition Program for Women, Infants, and Children (WIC), the

---

7 American Rescue Plan Act § 9611.

8 Id. § 9621.

9 Coronavirus Aid, Relief, and Economic Security Act, Pub. L. No. 116–136, § 2104, 134 Stat. 281, 318–21 (2020).

10 Id. §§ 2102, 2108–09.

11 American Rescue Plan Act §§ 9011–18, 9021–22.

12 Families First Coronavirus Response Act, Pub. L. No. 116–127, § 1101(b)-(i), 134 Stat. 178, 179–80 (2020).

13 Food & Nutrition Serv., US Dep't Agric., State Plan for Pandemic EBT (P-EBT) (June 2, 2020), www.fns.usda.gov/snap/state-guidance-coronavirus-pandemic-ebt-pebt.

Emergency Food Assistance Program (one of the commodity food programs), and the nutrition assistance block grants for the three territories (Commonwealth of the Northern Mariana Islands, American Samoa, and Puerto Rico) that federal law excludes from SNAP.[14] Finally, Congress addressed ongoing efforts by the Trump Administration to restrict access to food assistance for roughly 750,000 SNAP recipients.[15] Even though a federal court had enjoined the Trump Administration's regulation before it could go into effect, Congress suspended all SNAP work requirements until a month after the end of the COVID-19 emergency declaration.[16]

Subsequent COVID-19-related legislation made additional appropriations and built on the Families First Act's food assistance provisions. In the CARES Act, Congress increased federal funding of SNAP assistance by over $16 billion.[17] In the Consolidated Appropriations Act, the stimulus passed at the very end of the Trump Administration, Congress strengthened food assistance in the same manner that it did at the start of the Great Recession. It increased SNAP for all food stamp beneficiaries by 15 percentage points.[18] Through ARPA, Congress extended that increase through September 2021.[19] In passing ARPA, Congress also made additional appropriations for SNAP, WIC, and the nutrition block grants to the three territories.[20] ARPA contained provisions strengthening Pandemic EBT as well. Congress removed date limits to the program, explicitly allowed its operation in summer months, and expanded the program to cover children in schools with reduced hours, as well as children in SNAP households who were enrolled in child care facilities affected by pandemic closures and reduced hours.[21]

D *Medical Assistance*

The federal government took an array of legislative and administrative actions to address the cost of COVID-19-related medical care for patients, health care providers, and states. For instance, through the Families First Act and the CARES Act, Congress generally required most private health plans, Medicare, and Medicaid to cover testing for COVID-19 during the public health emergency.[22]

---

[14] Families First Coronavirus Response Act, Title I (authorizing $500 million for WIC and $400 million for Emergency Food Assistance Program through September 30, 2021); id. §§ 1102,

[15] Id. § 2301(a).

[16] District of Columbia v. US Dep't of Agric., 20-cv-119 (D.D.C. May 12, 2020). See also Families First Coronavirus Response Act § 2301(a).

[17] H.R. Rep. No. 116–146, at 73 (2020).

[18] Consolidated Appropriations Act, 2021, Pub. L. No. 116–260, div. A, Title IV, 134 Stat. 1182, 1209–10.

[19] American Rescue Plan Act of 2021, Pub. L. No. 117–2, § 1101(a), 135 Stat. 4, 115.

[20] Id. §§ 1101, 1103, 1105–06.

[21] Id. § 1108.

[22] Families First Coronavirus Response Act, Pub. L. No. 116–127, §§ 6001–04, 134 Stat. 178, 201–07 (2020); Coronavirus Aid, Relief, and Economic Security Act, Pub. L. No. 116–136, §§ 3201–02, 134 Stat. 281, 366–67 (2020).

The CARES Act – together with the Paycheck Protection Program and Health Care Enhancement Act and the Consolidated Appropriations Act – provided $178 billion in funding for hospitals and other health care entities struggling with the cost of COVID-19-related care and the cancellation of elective procedures.[23] In addition, to help defray the costs of rising Medicaid enrollment and prevent states from cutting benefits (the Medicaid program is jointly funded by the federal government and the states), the Families First Act temporarily increased the Federal Medical Assistance Percentage (FMAP) for state and territorial Medicaid programs by 6.2 percentage points until the end of the public health emergency.[24] States were required to meet various conditions to be eligible for the increased matching funds, including not imposing more restrictive Medicaid eligibility standards or procedures, increasing premiums, and terminating beneficiaries from the program involuntarily.[25] ARPA also provided additional funding for COVID-19 public health activities, including vaccine distribution, contact tracing, and supporting the public health workforce.[26]

ARPA included several reforms that built on the coverage expansions of the Affordable Care Act (ACA), and went beyond paying specifically for COVID-19-related medical care. For instance, ARPA provided that states that newly adopted the ACA's Medicaid expansion for low-income adults would receive a 5 percentage point increase in their FMAP rate for two years, giving the holdout states that had not yet adopted the Medicaid expansion additional incentives to do so.[27] The law also temporarily created an option for states to extend postpartum coverage in Medicaid and the Children's Health Insurance Program (CHIP) for twelve months.[28] In addition, ARPA temporarily offered enhanced premium tax credits for individuals who enrolled in private health insurance coverage through the ACA's health insurance marketplaces, for the plan years 2021 and 2022. Previously, the tax credits had been generally available only for people with a modified adjusted gross income between 100 percent and 400 percent of the federal poverty level (FPL), and even people at the poverty level had to make some premium payments. ARPA both offered increased subsidies for individuals making between 100 percent and 400 percent of the FPL (who were already eligible for subsidized coverage) and expanded the subsidies so that people with incomes above 400 percent of the FPL were newly

23 CARES Act Provider Relief Fund, US Dep't of Health and Hum. Servs., www.hhs.gov/coronavirus/cares-act-provider-relief-fund/index.html; Karyn Schwartz & Tricia Neuman, Funding for Health Care Providers During the Pandemic: An Update, Kaiser Fam. Found. (Feb. 11, 2021), www.kff.org/policy-watch/funding-for-health-care-providers-during-the-pandemic-an-update/.

24 Families First Coronavirus Response Act § 6008.

25 Id.

26 Jennifer Kates, What's in the American Rescue Plan for COVID-19 Vaccine and Other Public Health Efforts?, Kaiser Fam. Found. (Mar. 16, 2021), www.kff.org/policy-watch/whats-in-the-american-rescue-plan-for-covid-19-vaccine-and-other-public-health-efforts/.

27 American Rescue Plan Act of 2021, Pub. L. No. 117–2, § 9814, 135 Stat. 4, 215.

28 Id. § 9812.

eligible for assistance.[29] In addition, ARPA included temporary subsidies to defray the cost of Consolidated Omnibus Budget Reconciliation Act premiums for people who had lost employer-sponsored insurance.[30]

III MAKING THE SAFETY NET MORE RESPONSIVE

A *The Pandemic Revealed Structural Flaws in the Safety Net*

Although it provided essential support, the federal government's response to the COVID-19 pandemic was inadequate in numerous ways. For one, because Congress chose to provide benefits through existing safety net programs, the response excluded the same people these programs have excluded from the beginning. These include childless adults, immigrant families, and those with unstable ties to the labor market. Meanwhile, other stimulus bill provisions – and the ways that agencies implemented those provisions – directed huge sums of money to wealthy individuals and hospitals, and large businesses.[31] In addition, the Families First Act's FMAP increase provided less Medicaid funding than states needed and did not apply to enrollees covered through the ACA's Medicaid expansion.[32] The COVID-19-testing coverage provisions in the Families First Act and CARES Act also had loopholes which caused some Americans to remain on the hook for testing-related out-of-pocket costs.[33]

Second, administrative complexity and technological problems common to safety net programs hampered the speed and efficiency of the pandemic response. As one example, many states' UI systems simply were not equipped to handle a large influx of claims. Claimants faced network crashes and confusing messaging; many failed to access benefits as a result.[34] As another example, six months after the passage of the CARES Act, approximately nine million people still had not received their rebate checks because the Internal Revenue Service lacked their

---

[29] Id. §§ 9661–63.

[30] Id. § 9501.

[31] Example, Clint Wallace, The Troubling Case of the Unlimited Pass-Through Deduction: Section 2304 of the CARES Act, *U. Chi. L. Rev.* Online (2020), https://lawreviewblog.uchicago.edu/2020/06/29/cares-2304-wallace/ [https://perma.cc/Y78T-KSL3]; Jesse Drucker, Jessica Silver-Greenberg & Sarah Kliff, Wealthiest Hospitals Got Billions in Bailout for Struggling Health Providers, NY Times (May 25, 2020), www.nytimes.com/2020/05/25/business/coronavirus-hospitals-bailout.html.

[32] See Aviva Aron-Dine et al., Larger, Longer-Lasting Increases in Federal Medicaid Funding Needed to Protect Coverage, *Ctr. on Budget & Pol'y Priorities* (May 5, 2020), www.cbpp.org/sites/default/files/atoms/files/5-5-20health.pdf.

[33] See Karyn Schwartz et al., Gaps in Cost Sharing Protections for COVID-19 Testing and Treatment Could Spark Public Concerns About COVID-19 Vaccine Costs, *Kaiser Fam. Found.* (Dec. 18, 2020), www.kff.org/health-costs/issue-brief/gaps-in-cost-sharing-protections-for-covid-19-testing-and-treatment-could-spark-public-concerns-about-covid-19-vaccine-costs/.

[34] Ben Zipperer & Elise Gould, Unemployment Filing Failures: New Survey Confirms that Millions of Jobless Were Unable to File an Unemployment Insurance Claim, *Econ. Pol'y Inst.* (Apr. 28, 2020), www.epi.org/blog/unemployment-filing-failures-new-survey-confirms-that-millions-of-jobless-were-unable-to-file-an-unemployment-insurance-claim/ [https://perma.cc/89HW-2FG3].

contact information.[35] Many of these overlooked individuals had incomes below the tax-filing threshold and thus were particularly vulnerable.

Third, while Congress acted quickly to pass the first round of stimulus relief, some relief came too late, while other relief ended too early. For instance, Congress did not increase SNAP benefits for all beneficiaries until ten months into the crisis.[36] The delay left millions of families in need. Meanwhile, although Congress initially expanded UI benefits, the expansion ended on July 31, 2020, just as the virus began surging around the country. Congress did not renew the expansion until December 2020 (and then again in March 2021). The legislative process throughout was rushed and chaotic, then partisan and unproductive. Both modes left little room for community participation, but plenty of room for well-heeled lobbyists. Congress ultimately delayed far too long to provide additional support after the first round of relief bills, each side blaming the impasse on the recalcitrance of the other. Meanwhile, poverty, hunger, and despair deepened.

The COVID-19 pandemic was unexpected and, in some ways, unprecedented. Although the federal government's response was essential, it was also flawed. We can learn from this experience to improve crisis lawmaking in the future. The next section describes how.

B *Principles to Improve Future Crisis Response*

The flawed response of Congress to the pandemic points to several key principles that should inform how policymakers react to future crises. These principles apply to safety net reforms that seek to address not only national emergencies, but state and local emergencies as well.

When future crises occur, safety net program expansions and emergency responses should be:

Immediate. Crises deepen as government delays. While Congress can act quickly, it may not always do so. And, as the COVID-19 response shows, it may not do so comprehensively. Linking temporary program expansions to economic indices or other automatic triggers is one possible way to ensure an immediate response.

Inclusive. The US social safety net has long been and remains exclusionary, especially for Black Americans, immigrants and their families, Indigenous Americans, and Americans living in the territories. During normal times, political pressure and concern over scarce resources may overshadow calls for inclusivity. Yet improving the inclusivity of safety net programs during normal times will ensure that federal programs can reach everyone during hard times.

---

[35] Michelle Singletary, *IRS Is Trying to Reach 9 Million People Who Haven't Collected Their Stimulus Payments*, Wash. Post (Sept. 11, 2020), washingtonpost.com/business/2020/09/11/irs-stimulus-check-letter/ [https://perma.cc/D7SJ-H8KS].

[36] Consolidated Appropriations Act, 2021, Pub. L. No. 116–260, div. A, Title IV, 134 Stat. 1182, 1209–10.

Targeted. Programs must deliver support to the places and people that need it most. In the context of extreme weather events, for instance, federal programs must deliver support to a specific region only. State and local indices should therefore drive automatic responses.

Sustained. Program changes triggered during a crisis must continue until the crisis is truly over. In some places, the economic fallout of a crisis might last several years, as was true after the Great Recession. Once again, automated, quantitative indices will provide a more accurate measure of continued need than a politicized decision-making process.

C *Strengthening Program Responsiveness*

Experts have advocated improved crisis lawmaking for some time. Many such proposals focus on automatic stabilizers – governmental mechanisms that do not require legislative approval and that increase spending or decrease taxes when the economy slows.[37] In other words, they automatically inject money into the economy during contractions. Of course, some safety net programs already *are* automatic stabilizers; for instance, SNAP, UI claims, and Medicaid enrollment tend to increase during recessions. In doing so, they help to protect individuals and families from the worst financial and health effects of economic downturns, as well as to mitigate the downturns themselves through stimulating aggregate economic demand.[38] Yet policymakers can improve these stabilizing effects. This section surveys various proposed reforms that aim to improve how well safety net programs respond to crises, focusing on automatic responses that obviate the need for approval from Congress.

1 Tax Credits

The EITC provides cash transfers to low-income families and childless workers, targeting households living near and just above the poverty line. It therefore operates as an automatic stabilizer by providing cash support to households when incomes drop. However, the work-incentive structure of the EITC mitigates this automatic stabilizer effect. Specifically, the program excludes non-working individuals; further, below a certain income level, benefits decrease as income decreases. This design feature means that a recession can cause many people to lose their benefits or receive a smaller benefit amount if they lose work entirely or lose enough hours to place them in the phase-in range. Imagine a server who works fewer hours when a recession causes her restaurant to cut shifts. This worker could face the double harm

---

[37] Vivien Lee & Louise Scheiner, *What Are Automatic Stabilizers?*, Brookings Inst. (2019), www.brookings.edu/blog/up-front/2019/07/02/what-are-automatic-stabilizers/.

[38] Id.

of reduced wages as well as a smaller EITC. To prevent this procyclical effect, tax policy experts have urged Congress to accelerate how quickly the benefit phases in at low income levels or to eliminate the phase-in entirely.[39]

Outside of ARPA's temporary tax credit expansions, childless workers receive only a small EITC compared to families with children. ARPA's expansion expired after one year. Tax experts and policymakers have routinely called for permanently increasing the benefit provided to childless workers, or to *all* workers, which would strengthen the program's ability to shore up the economy during recessions.[40]

2 Unemployment Insurance

UI is already a vital automatic stabilizer. Even so, Congress and state policymakers can improve the programs' ability to support struggling workers during economic downturns. To start, UI systems have historically excluded certain "nontraditional" workers from coverage – including part-time, temporary, and non-employee workers – leaving them without protection and undermining the systems' ability to act as a safety net during recessions. This exclusion is becoming increasingly untenable considering that such jobs have dominated job-growth figures over the past decade.[41] Since the Great Recession, experts have called on Congress and state legislators to expand UI coverage for self-employed workers and workers who lose hours while retaining their jobs.[42] Although Congress did so in response to the pandemic, the changes were only temporary.

Additionally, states' budgets are often overburdened during economic downturns, since demand for public assistance tends to increase just as tax revenue decreases.[43] Instead of relying on Congress to expand UI funding during each economic downturn, experts have urged Congress to legislate automatic increases.[44] For instance, federal UI funding could increase automatically when a state's unemployment rate increases rapidly or exceeds a threshold level.[45]

---

[39] See Elaine Maag & Donald Marron, Design Changes Can Strengthen the EITC During Recessions, *Urban- Brookings Tax Pol'y Ctr.* 9 (2020), www.taxpolicycenter.org/publications/design-changes-can-strengthen-eitc-during-recessions/full.

[40] Id.

[41] Jason Furman, Chairman, Council of Econ. Advisers, The Economic Case for Strengthening Unemployment Insurance, Remarks at the Center for American Progress, Washington, DC, at 4 (July 11, 2016), https://obamawhitehouse.archives.gov/sites/default/files/page/files/20160711_furman_uireform_cea.pdf [https://perma.cc/Z7YK-L3RS].

[42] See, for example, id.

[43] Matthew Fiedler, Jason Furman & Wilson Powell III, Increasing Federal Support for State Medicaid and CHIP Programs in Response to Economic Downturns, Brookings Inst. (2020), www.brookings.edu/research/increasing- federal-support-for-state-medicaid-and-chip-programs-in-response-to-economic-downturns/ [https://perma.cc/8ENB-P88W].

[44] Example, Furman, supra note 41, at 11.

[45] Id.

3 SNAP

SNAP has a well-earned reputation in Washington, DC for its countercyclical track record. Policymakers know the program can expand quickly during recessions and crises.[46] That is in part because states contribute to the administrative costs of the program, but the federal government pays 100 percent of the substantive benefits.[47] But while SNAP excels at enrolling people who are newly eligible because of unemployment, extreme weather events, or pandemics, it could be made stronger for both new and existing recipients in times of acute need.[48] Experts have called on Congress to amend the Food and Nutrition Act so that SNAP benefits increase automatically when certain economic data suggest a national, regional, state-wide, or even intra-state surge in need.[49] Such a change would have prevented Congress's nine-month delay in enacting such an increase during the pandemic. In fact, the federal statutes governing SNAP already let economic data drive eligibility for a certain segment of recipients.[50] The Food & Nutrition Service allows states to waive statutory work requirements for certain childless adults when the Bureau of Labor Statistics reports specified unemployment levels for a state or intra-state region.[51] Congress could simply automate these increases in benefit amounts and expansions in eligibility.

4 Medicaid

Medicaid is another essential automatic stabilizer. Enrollment in Medicaid increased significantly during the COVID-19 pandemic and likely helped to offset the effects of people losing employer-sponsored insurance.[52]

Yet this stabilizing function should be strengthened. Because states typically must balance their budgets annually, they face significant pressure to cut spending on Medicaid during economic downturns – by making eligibility requirements more

---

[46] In the depths of the 2008 financial crisis, White House advisers relied on the macroeconomic multiplier effect of SNAP. See Peter Ganong & Jeffrey B. Liebman, The Decline, Rebound, and Further Rise in SNAP Enrollment: Disentangling Business Cycle Fluctuations and Policy Changes, 10 *Am. Econ. J.* 153, 154 (2018).

[47] See 7 U.S.C. §§ 2013(a), 2019, 2025(a); 7 C.F.R. §§ 277.1(b), 277.4.

[48] See Ganong & Liebman, supra note 46 at 168.

[49] Hilary Hoynes & Diane Whitmore Schanzenbach, Strengthening SNAP as an Automatic Stabilizer, in *Recession Ready: Fiscal Policies to Stabilize the American Economy* 235 n.5 (Heather Boushey, Ryan Nunn & Jay Shambaugh eds., 2019).

[50] 7 U.S.C. § 2015(o)(4). For Able-Bodied Adults without Dependents, waivers already rely on unemployment data from the Department of Labor.

[51] 7 C.F.R. § 273.24(f)(2). The Trump Administration unsuccessfully tried to make it more difficult for states to obtain these waivers. See Supplemental Nutrition Assistance Program: Requirements for Able-Bodied Adults Without Dependents, 84 Fed. Reg. 66782, 66802 (Dec. 5, 2019). But see District of Columbia, 20-cv-119 (enjoining the rule).

[52] See Daniel McDemott et al., How Has the Pandemic Affected Health Coverage in the U.S.?, Kaiser Fam. Found. (Dec. 9, 2020), www.kff.org/policy-watch/how-has-the-pandemic-affected-health-coverage-in-the-u-s/.

stringent, reducing the scope of covered benefits, or reducing the amount that they pay providers.[53] These cuts in turn not only limit health benefits for low-income Americans at a time when they are especially vulnerable, but also have deleterious economic consequences.[54]

During recent economic downturns, including the COVID-19 recession, Congress has legislated one-off temporary increases to the Medicaid matching rates to prevent such negative outcomes.[55] Yet these increases have sometimes been too small or come too late.[56] To strengthen Medicaid's role as a stabilizer, economists Matthew Fiedler, Jason Furman, and Wilson Powell III have proposed that Congress automatically increase the federal share of spending for Medicaid and the Children's Health Insurance Program once a state's unemployment rate exceeds a threshold level.[57] The Government Accountability Office has likewise proposed automatically increasing Medicaid matching rates during national economic downturns.[58] Either of these approaches would help to mitigate the damaging consequences of future economic downturns, and would help to ensure that the Medicaid program can provide support when Americans need it most.

IV STRENGTHENING DEMOCRATIC NORMS

Until now, most of the arguments in favor of strengthening automatic stabilizers have been made on welfare grounds: that doing so would bolster important protections for vulnerable groups and cushion the impact of economic downturns.[59] Yet, perhaps counterintuitively, we believe that augmenting automatic stabilizers would also help to strengthen democratic norms. Before the COVID-19 pandemic ravaged the United States, scholars had repeatedly criticized the decreasing capacity and increasing dysfunctionality of Congress.[60] In particular, researchers identified how Congress's increasing incapacity to legislate raises concerns about its democratic legitimacy. Relatedly, some scholars have critiqued Congress's reliance on infrequent and unorthodox lawmaking as well as its broad delegations to agencies on

---

[53] Fiedler, Furman & Powell, supra note 43 at 99–100; Matthew Fiedler, States Are Being Crushed by the Coronavirus. Only This Can Help., NY Times (Apr. 22, 2020), www.nytimes.com/2020/04/22/opinion/coronavirus-states-budgets.html.

[54] See Gabriel Chodorow-Reich et al., Does State Fiscal Relief During Recessions Increase Employment? Evidence from the American Recovery and Reinvestment Act, 118 *Am. Econ. J. Econ. Pol.* 118, 121 (2012).

[55] Alison Mitchell, Cong. Res. Serv., Medicaid Recession-Related FMAP Increases (2020).

[56] See Fiedler, Furman & Powell, above note 43, at 99.

[57] Id.

[58] Gov't Accountability Off., Medicaid: Prototype Formula Would Provide Automatic, Targeted Assistance to States during Economic Downturns (2011).

[59] See, generally, *Recession Ready: Fiscal Policies to Stabilize the American Economy* (Heather Boushey, Ryan Nunn & Jay Shambaugh eds., 2019).

[60] See, for example, *Congress Overwhelmed: The Decline in Congressional Capacity and Prospects for Reform* (Timothy M. LaPira, Lee Drutman & Kevin R. Kosar eds., 2020).

the basis that they make the US national legislature less accountable. Here, we offer some preliminary thoughts on the extent to which legislating automatic stabilizers can address the prevailing ills that afflict Congress.

This section tentatively makes a case for automatic stabilizers because of their democracy-protecting potential. In particular, we defend automatic stabilizers on three grounds: transparency, delegation, and responsiveness.[61]

A *Transparency*

The status quo of legislating one-off emergency packages to temporarily bolster safety net programs raises concerns about transparency. Because Congress is under intense time pressure to pass such packages, they tend to do so in ways that bypass traditional procedures – such as committee deliberation and report-writing – that promote transparency.[62] The speed, opacity, and complexity associated with such emergency legislation serve in turn to advantage well-resourced business interests, while making it more difficult for public interest groups and individual members of the public to participate in the legislative process.[63]

By contrast, if Congress were to enact, in a non-emergency context, a set of pro-spective rules governing how safety net programs would automatically adjust dur-ing future economic downturns, there would be ample time to follow the standard legislative procedures that enhance transparency and accountability. Public interest groups and members of the public would be better able to understand and par-ticipate in the legislative process, and to hold members of Congress accountable for their decisions. It seems plausible, therefore, that enacting automatic stabilizers would actually strengthen – rather than weaken – democratic values.

B *Delegation*

One concern about strengthening automatic stabilizers is that doing so would weaken the democratic legitimacy of statutes by allowing legislators to escape taking responsibility for decisions about the safety net.[64] This concern is related to a more general critique that has been levied against broad delegations to administrative agencies: that such delegations enable members of Congress to avoid taking public

---

[61] We explore some of these issues in greater depth in our forthcoming article, Andrew Hammond, Ariel Jurow Kleiman & Gabriel Scheffler, The Future of Anti-Poverty Legislation, 112 *Geo. L. J.* (forthcom-ing 2023).

[62] Abbe R. Gluck, Anne Joseph O'Connell & Rosa Po, Unorthodox Lawmaking, Unorthodox Rulemaking, 115 *Colum. L. Rev.* 1789, 1808 (2015).

[63] See Steven M. Teles, Kludgeocracy in America, Nat. Aff. 98–103 (Fall 2013); Eric Lipton, Special Interests Mobilize to Get Piece of Next Virus Relief Package, NY Times (Jul. 19, 2020), www.nytimes .com/2020/07/19/us/politics/coronavirus-relief-lobbyists-special-interests.html.

[64] See, for example, Michael J. Teter, Congressional Gridlock's Threat to Separation of Powers, 2013 *Wis. L. Rev.* 1097, 1143 (2013).

positions on consequential matters of public policy, and thereby render it more difficult for voters to hold them accountable.[65] Leaving aside the question of whether this more general line of criticism is persuasive, we believe that automatic stabilizers should actually appeal to those who are concerned about excessive delegation.[66] When Congress enacts automatic stabilizers, it dictates how agencies must act and how programs must respond to future crises. This strict control contrasts with a status quo that, in some cases, gives broad authority to federal agencies to choose the best policy response during a crisis. In short, by choosing an automatic stabilizer, Congress decides ahead of time how safety net programs will respond to the next crisis, and in so doing serves to limit the scope of delegations to agencies.

C *Responsiveness*

Currently, the American safety net is insufficiently responsive to the needs of the American public. The Electoral College, state representation in the Senate, and gerrymandered districts in the House skew incentives and lead politicians to focus disproportionately on helping certain swing states or vulnerable members, while ignoring others. Politicized assignment to congressional committees, seniority, alliances with formal caucuses and informal voting blocs, and other legislature features confer unequal power on certain states' federal representatives.[67] Intransigent state policymakers hold up needed assistance or refuse federal support, undermining the federal government's intention to shore up the national economy.[68] Various features of the legislative process, particularly the filibuster, contribute to legislative gridlock and prevent Congress from addressing major social problems on which there is a broad public consensus.

The poor and middle class have less influence on policy outcomes than the rich.[69] Strengthening automatic stabilizers would enable a more equitable, less politicized distribution of benefits to the people and places that need it most and make the safety net more responsive to the needs and circumstances of the electorate as a whole.

V CONCLUSION

The COVID-19 pandemic revealed significant weaknesses in the US social safety net. Despite the scale of the federal government's response, Congress failed to

---

[65] See, for example, David Schoenbrod, *Power Without Responsibility: How Congress Abuses the People Through Delegation* (1993).

[66] For a defense of broad delegations to agencies, see Jerry L. Mashaw, Prodelegation: Why Administrators Should Make Political Decisions, 1 J. L. Econ. Org. 81 (1985).

[67] See Susan Milligan, Playing Games with a Disaster, US News & World Rep. (Sept. 30, 2016), www.usnews.com/news/articles/2016-09-30/the-partisan-politics-of-disaster-relief.

[68] See, for example, Grant Schulte, Ricketts Stands by Decision to Discontinue Emergency SNAP, AP (Sept. 24, 2020), https://apnews.com/article/virus-outbreak-pete-ricketts-omaha-nebraska-archive-dfb8dao712f6f4cb9307412049ab29a2.

[69] See, generally, Martin Gilens, *Affluence and Influence* (2014).

provide adequate assistance to many Americans as it channeled benefits through existing safety net programs. Moreover, although Congress acted relatively quickly by its standards, relief came too late – and ended too early – for many Americans.

This experience underscores the need to legislate a more responsive safety net. During a major crisis, relief should be immediate, inclusive, targeted, and sustained. To achieve these goals, policymakers should strengthen the stabilizing effects of existing safety net programs such as the EITC, UI, SNAP, and Medicaid. Doing so would serve to protect vulnerable populations during economic downturns and to mitigate the downturns themselves. In addition, we defend strengthening automatic stabilizers on democratic grounds, arguing that doing so would increase transparency, limit delegation, and heighten responsiveness.

The COVID-19 pandemic will not be the last major crisis that necessitates temporarily strengthening the safety net. Rather than waiting until the next crisis, Congress should act now to make the safety net more secure and responsive for the future.

13

Eradicating Pandemic Health Inequities

Health Justice in Emergency Preparedness

Ruqaiijah Yearby

I INTRODUCTION

During the 2009 H1N1 flu (Swine flu) pandemic, the Centers for Disease Control and Prevention (CDC) recommended that those exhibiting symptoms practice social distancing and stay at home rather than go to work for seven to ten days.[1] A national survey showed that many low-wage and racial and ethnic minority workers were unable to practice social distancing or stay at home during the H1N1 pandemic because they could not work from home, take time off work, or lacked paid sick leave.[2] These workers were also not provided with protections against the spread of airborne diseases in the workplace. As a result, they had an increased risk of exposure to H1N1 within the workplace, which was associated with their higher rates of infections, hospitalizations, and deaths.[3] In response to racial and ethnic inequities "in illness, hospitalization and death compared to whites" during the H1N1 pandemic and other emergency situations, such as Hurricane Katrina, the Department of Health and Human Services' (HHS) Office of Minority Health published *Guidance for Integrating Culturally Diverse Communities into Planning for and Responding to Emergencies: A Toolkit,*[4] and a 2012 report regarding health equity and pandemics.[5] The toolkit and the report were outgrowths of a National

---

[1] Supriya Kumar et al., The Impact of Workplace Policies and Other Social Factors on Self-Reported Influenza-Like Illness Incidence During the 2009 H1N1 Pandemic, 102 *Am. J. Pub. Health* 132, 134, 135–39 (2012) (citing Ctrs. for Disease Control & Prevention, CDC Recommendations for the Amount of Time Persons with Influenza-Like Illness Should Be Away From Others, www.cdc.gov/h1n1flu/guidance/exclusion.htm [last visited June 13, 2021]); Ctrs. for Disease Control & Prevention, 2009 H1N1 Flu ("Swine Flu") and You, www.cdc.gov/h1n1flu/qa.htm (last visited June 13, 2021).

[2] Kumar et al., supra note 1, at 134, 135–39.

[3] Id.; Sandra Crouse Quinn et al., Racial Disparities in Exposure, Susceptibility, and Access to Health Care in the US H1N1 Influenza Pandemic, 101 *Am. J. Pub. Health* 285, 285–90 (2011).

[4] Dennis Andrulis, Nadia Siddiqui & Jonathan Purtle, Guidance for Integrating Culturally Diverse Communities into Planning for and Responding to Emergencies: A Toolkit (Feb. 2011), www.aha.org/system/files/content/11/OMHDiversityPreparednessToolkit.pdf.

[5] Dennis Andrulis et al., H1N1 Influenza Pandemic and Racially and Ethnically Diverse Communities in the United States: Assessing the Evidence of and Charting Opportunities for Advancing

Consensus Panel made up of national, state, and local experts from public health; emergency management, response, and relief; and racial and ethnic communities.[6] Building on existing resources and evidence-based research, the toolkit and report acknowledged that there were social factors outside an individual's control, such as lack of paid sick leave, that led to pandemic health inequities. They also recommended establishing sustainable community partnerships to, among other things, measure and evaluate emergency plans and actions before, during, and after the emergency was over.

In 2010, the Department of Labor's Occupational Safety and Health Administration (OSHA) began working on an airborne infectious disease rule that would require employers to conduct a worksite hazard assessment to determine how an airborne infectious disease can spread within the worksite or to adopt specific measures to limit the spread of the airborne infectious disease there.[7] Even though the recommendations of HHS and OSHA's proposed rule were created specifically to improve the government's emergency preparedness response and address pandemic health inequities, many of the federal and state government COVID-19 emergency preparedness laws and plans have not incorporated these recommendations or protections. In particular, many of the federal, state, and local laws do not provide paid sick leave for all essential workers or adopt protections from OSHA's proposed airborne infectious disease rule, which has led to pandemic health inequities in COVID-19 infections and deaths for essential workers.[8] In 2021, the Biden Administration,[9] and many employers, began to implement mandatory vaccine policies that required workers to get vaccinated or submit to testing.[10] However, it is unclear how vaccine mandates would work or be applied to industries that have a high number of undocumented immigrants, who have

Health Equity, US Dep't of Health & Hum. Servs., Off. of Minority Health, at 13 (Sept. 2012), www.researchgate.net/publication/340390150_H1N1_Influenza_Pandemic_and_Racially_and_Ethnically_Diverse_ Communities_in_the_United_States_Assessing_the_Evidence_and_Charting_Opportunities_for_Advancing_Health_Equity.

6 Id. at 4.

7 US Dep't of Lab., Occupational Safety & Health Admin., 2010 Infectious Diseases SER Background Document (2010) (on file with author) (hereinafter, Infectious Diseases Rulemaking); Summary of Stakeholder Meetings on Occupational Exposure to Infectious Disease (July 29, 2011), https://apic.org/Resource_/TinyMceFileManager/Advocacy-PDFs/Official_Summary_of_July_2011_OSHA_Meeting.pdf; US Dep't of Lab., Infectious Diseases SER Background Document (July 29, 2011) (on file with author).

8 Ruqaiijah Yearby & Seema Mohapatra, Systemic Racism, The Government's Pandemic Response, and Racial Inequities in COVID-19, 70 *Emory L. J.* 1419, 1433–51 (2021) (hereinafter, Yearby & Mohapatra, Systemic Racism).

9 Medicare & Medicaid Programs, Omnibus COVID-19 Health Care Staff Vaccination (2021); 29 C.F.R. § 1910.501 (2021).

10 Haley Messenger, From McDonald's to Goldman Sachs, Here are the Companies Mandating Vaccines for All or Some Employees, NBC News (Nov. 16, 2021), www.nbcnews.com/business/business-news/here-are-companies-mandating-vaccines-all-or-some-employees-n1275808; James Beck, Not Breaking News: Mandatory Vaccination Has Been Constitutional for over a Century, Am. Bar

limited access to vaccines.[11] Furthermore, the Supreme Court has prevented the Biden Administration's vaccine mandate for non-health care workers from coming into effect,[12] and many employers have begun to roll back their requirements.[13] Thus, there is still a need for paid sick leave and workplace protections for essential workers, which is the focus of this chapter.

More than 55 million Americans were labeled "essential workers" during the COVID-19 pandemic.[14] Health care workers have provided critical medical care to patients, while housekeeping and cleaning workers kept these institutions clean.[15] Grocery store workers, farm workers, and meat processing workers have continued to feed the country. Warehouse, postal, transport, and airline workers have ensured the public receives their essential goods, while utility and communications workers have sustained access to the fundamental human needs of water, electricity, and the Internet.

Nationwide, these jobs have been associated with increased percentages of COVID-19 deaths.[16] Specifically, research showed that working in the health care,

Ass'n (Oct. 28, 2021), www.americanbar.org/groups/litigation/committees/mass-torts/articles/2021/winter2022-not-breaking-news-mandatory-vaccination-has-been-constitutional-for-over-a-century/.

[11] Samantha Artiga, Nambi Ndugga & Olivia Pham, Immigrant Access to COVID-19 Vaccines: Key Issues to Consider, Kaiser Fam. Found. (Jan. 13, 2021), www.kff.org/racial-equity-and-health-policy/issue-brief/immigrant-access-to-covid-19-vaccines-key-issues-to-consider/; Shayna Greene, Fact Check: Are Undocumented Immigrants Ineligible for the COVID-19 Vaccine?, Newsweek (Jan. 15, 2021), www.newsweek.com/fact-check-are- undocumented-immigrants-ineligible-covid-19-vaccine-1562061.

[12] The mandatory vaccine requirement for all workers was found unconstitutional by the Supreme Court, while the requirement for health care workers was upheld. Nat'l Fed'n of Indep. Bus. v. Dep't of Labor, Occupational Safety & Health Admin., 142 S.Ct. 661 (2022) (all workers); Biden v. Missouri, 142 S.Ct. 647 (2022) (health care workers).

[13] Disney Halts Vaccine Mandate for Theme Park Workers After Florida Ban, NY Times (Nov. 23, 2021), www.nytimes.com/live/2021/11/20/world/covid-boosters-vaccines-cases-mandates; Elizabeth Chuck, Growing Number of Companies Suspend Vaccine Mandates, Including Hospitals and Amtrak, NBC News (Dec. 16, 2021), www.nbcnews.com/news/us-news/companies-suspend-vaccine-mandates-hospitals-amtrak-rcna8903.

[14] Celine McNicholas & Margaret Poydock, Who Are Essential Workers? A Comprehensive Look at Their Wages, Demographics, and Unionization Rates, Econ. Pol'y Inst.: Working Econ. Blog (May 19, 2020), www.epi.org/blog/who-are-essential-workers-a-comprehensive-look-at-their-wages-demographics-and-unionization-rates.

[15] Petition for Emergency Rulemaking and Action to Allocate, Finance, and Compel the Manufacture of Personal Protective Equipment and Other Critical Materials to Safeguard Frontline Workers in the COVID-19 Crisis Pursuant to the Defense Production Act (Aug. 11, 2020), https://biologicaldiversity.org/programs/energy-justice/pdfs/2020-08-11-APA-Petition-re-PPE-with-AFL.pdf; Complaint for Declaratory and Injunctive Relief, Amalgamated Transit Union v. Azar, Case No. 20-cv-02876, 2020 WL 5983963 (D.D.C. Oct. 8, 2020).

[16] Justin Feldman, Coronavirus Is an Occupational Disease that Spreads at Work, Jacobin (Jan. 19, 2021), https://jacobinmag.com/2021/01/covid-19-business-work-public-health; Ruqaiijah Yearby, Meatpacking Plants Have Been Deadly COVID-19 Hot Spots – But Policies that Encourage Workers to Show Up Sick Are Legal, The Conversation (Feb. 26, 2021), https://theconversation.com/meatpacking-plants-have-been-deadly-covid-19-hot-spots-but-policies-that-encourage-workers-to-show-up-sick-are-legal-152572; Tiana Rogers et al., Racial Disparities in COVID-19 Mortality among Essential Workers in the United States, 12 *World Med. & Health Pol'y* 311, 318 (2020).

transportation, food preparation, cleaning, and service industries was strongly associated with a high risk of contracting COVID-19 and dying. Low-wage and racial and ethnic minority workers are disproportionately employed in these jobs.[17] In fact, "Blacks disproportionately occupied the top nine occupations that placed them at high risk for contracting COVID-19 and potentially infecting their households."[18]

Therefore, to put an end to health inequities in COVID-19 infections and deaths, the government should adopt the health justice framework, which provides a community-led approach for transforming the government's emergency preparedness response. Based in part on principles derived from the reproductive justice, environmental justice, food justice, and civil rights movements, the health justice framework offers three principles to improve the government's emergency preparedness response: (1) truth and reconciliation; (2) community engagement and empowerment; and (3) structural remediation and financial support.[19] By adopting these principles, the government can not only acknowledge and fix the harm caused, but also improve its emergency preparedness response by providing essential workers with the power to develop and implement more effective laws and plans.

II EMERGENCY PREPAREDNESS AND THE COVID-19 PANDEMIC

In response to the COVID-19 pandemic, forty states and the District of Columbia issued stay-at-home or lockdown orders, which included social distancing measures.[20] Generally, these orders have relied on individuals to change their behavior to stop the spread of COVID-19.[21] However, some individuals, such as essential workers, were not always protected by social distancing measures. For example, the St. Louis City stay-at-home order included social distancing mandates and other measures to stop the community spread of COVID-19.[22] These requirements for

---

[17] Rogers et al., supra note 16, at 319.

[18] Id.

[19] Yearby & Mohapatra, Systemic Racism, supra note 8, at 1433–51; Emily A. Benfer, Seema Mohapatra, Lindsay F. Wiley & Ruqaiijah Yearby, Health Justice Strategies to Combat the Pandemic: Eliminating Discrimination, Poverty, and Health Inequities During and After COVID-19, 19 *Yale J. Health Pol'y, L. Ethics* 122, 136–41 (2020); Emily A. Benfer & Lindsay F. Wiley, Health Justice Strategies to Combat COVID-19: Protecting Vulnerable Communities During a Pandemic, Health Affs. (Mar. 19, 2020), www.healthaffairs.org/do/10.1377/hblog20200319.757883/full/; Amber Johnson, Truth and Reconciliation in Health Care: Addressing Medical Racism Using a Health Justice Framework, Bill of Health (Sept. 21, 2021), https://blog.petrieflom.law.harvard.edu/2021/09/21/truth-and-reconciliation-health-justice/.

[20] State COVID-19 Data and Policy Actions, Kaiser Fam. Found., www.kff.org/report-section/state-covid-19-data-and-policy-actions-policy-actions/#socialdistancing (last updated Feb. 10, 2022).

[21] Lindsay Wiley & Samuel Bagenstos, The Personal Responsibility Pandemic: Centering Solidarity in Public Health and Employment Law, 52 *Ariz. State L. J.* 1235, 1235–36 (2020).

[22] St. Louis City Dep't of Pub. Health, 2019 Novel Coronavirus ("COVID-19"), Safer At Home Order (Mar. 21, 2020), www.stlouis-mo.gov/government/departments/health/communicable-disease/covid-19/orders/health-commissioner-order-5.cfm.

social distancing were not applied to essential businesses, and thus did not protect essential workers. Furthermore, neither the federal nor state emergency preparedness laws and plans provided all essential workers with paid sick leave or workplace protections from exposure to COVID-19.[23] As a result, many essential workers were left unprotected against workplace COVID-19 infections, leading to pandemic health inequities.

A Paid Sick Leave

During the COVID-19 pandemic, most essential workers were employed in the health care (30 percent) and in the food and agricultural (21 percent) industries, which experienced high rates of COVID-19 infections and deaths.[24] These cases and deaths have disproportionately harmed racial and ethnic minority essential workers. As of June 25, 2021, more than 513,773 health care personnel have tested positive for COVID-19, and 1,683 have died, a figure which is not broken down by occupation or race.[25] Yet a National Nursing Union report shows that nurses of Filipino descent comprise 31.5 percent of nurse deaths from COVID-19, but only account for 4 percent of the nursing population.[26] COVID-19 has not only harmed essential workers, but also their families and the communities in which they live.

In 2020, data associated Latino and Black children's higher risk of COVID-19-related hospitalizations with social factors, such as the employment conditions of their parents (e.g., serving as an essential worker).[27] Moreover, in Boston, data showed that the highest number of COVID-19 cases are concentrated in communities with a "very high proportion of both COVID-19-essential workers and residents of color."[28] These pandemic health inequities are in part due to essential workers' lack of paid sick leave, which increases essential workers' exposure to infectious diseases, such as COVID-19, because they must go to work sick, often infecting other workers as a consequence.[29]

---

[23] Lindsay Wiley, Ruqaiijah Yearby & Andrew Hammond, Lex-Atlas US COVID-19 Response Report, in Oxford Compendium of National Legal Responses to COVID-19 (2021), https://lexatlas-c19.org/usa/.

[24] McNicholas & Poydock, supra note 14.

[25] Ctrs. for Disease Control & Prevention, Cases & Deaths among Healthcare Personnel, https://covid.cdc.gov/covid-data-tracker/#health-care-personnel (last visited June 27, 2021).

[26] Allana Akhtar, Filipinos Make up 4% of Nurses in the US, but 31.5% of Nurse Deaths from COVID-19, Bus. Insider (Sept. 29, 2020), www.businessinsider.com/filipinos-make-up-disproportionate-covid-19-nurse-deaths-2020-9.

[27] Chelsea Janes, Hispanic, Black Children at Higher Risk of Coronavirus-Related Hospitalization, CDC Finds, Wash. Post (Aug. 7, 2020), www.washingtonpost.com/health/2020/08/07/hispanic-black-children-higher-risk-coronavirus-related-hospitalization-cdc-finds/.

[28] Lauren Chambers, Data Show COVID-19 Is Hitting Essential Workers and People of Color Hardest, ACLU Massachusetts (2020), https://data.aclum.org/2020/04/07/covid-19-disproportionately-affects-vulnerable-populations-in-boston/.

[29] Quinn et al., supra note 3, at 285–90; Kumar et al., supra note 1, at 134, 135–39.

Research shows that without paid sick leave, working people are one and a half times more likely to go to work with a contagious disease and three times more likely to go without medical care compared to those with paid sick days.[30] Many essential workers, including some nursing home workers, home health workers, and food and agriculture workers, do not have paid sick leave.[31] Furthermore, compared to White workers, Black workers are less likely to have paid sick leave,[32] even after federal and state action to address COVID-19.

The federal government enacted four major COVID-19 laws providing economic relief: the Families First Coronavirus Response Act; the Coronavirus Aid, Relief, and Economic Security Act; the Consolidated Appropriations Act; and the American Rescue Plan Act.[33] These laws provided paid sick leave for workers employed at businesses with fewer than 500 workers.[34] Many essential businesses employ more than 500 workers, so their workers are not covered. The laws also did not cover home health workers and undocumented immigrants, even though they were often designated as essential workers. Some states, such as California and New York, did enact paid sick leave laws, yet many essential workers were still left without paid sick leave.[35] The far-reaching impact of pandemic health inequities due to the lack of paid sick leave is best shown by reference to the food and agriculture industry.

Most meat and processing workers do not have paid sick leave and the economic relief bills did not apply to them because meat and poultry processing plants tend to employ more than 500 workers. As of August 31, 2021, 91,642 food and agriculture workers were infected with COVID-19, and at least 465 workers had died.[36] Racial and ethnic minority workers represent most of these cases and deaths. The CDC noted in May 2020 that there were 16,233 confirmed cases of COVID-19 infections for meat and poultry processing workers and 86 COVD-19-related deaths in 239 plants.[37] Of the 9,919 (61 percent) cases with racial and ethnic data, 56 percent of

---

[30] Benfer & Wiley, supra note 19.

[31] Yearby & Mohapatra, Systemic Racism, supra note 8; Ruqaiijah Yearby & Seema Mohapatra, Law, Structural Racism, and the COVID-19 Pandemic, 7 *Oxford J. L. Biosciences* 1 (2020); Ruqaiijah Yearby, Gaps in Worker Protections that Increase Essential Workers' Exposure to COVID-19, in COVID-19 Policy Playbook: Legal Recommendations for a Safer, *More Equitable Future*, 193, 194–95 (2020), https://static1.squarespace.com/static/5956e16e6b8f5b8c45f1c216/t/6058f406daa8245f7d98ae77/16164 42374635/C hp30-Yearby_COVIDPolicyPlaybook-March2021.pdf; Phillip Sloane et al., Addressing Systemic Racism in Nursing Homes: A Time for Action, 22 *JAMDA* 886, 887 (2021).

[32] Elise Gould & Valerie Wilson, Black Workers Face Two of the Most Lethal Preexisting Conditions for Coronavirus – Racism and Economic Inequality, *Econ. Pol'y Inst.* (June 1, 2020), www.epi.org/publication/black-workers-covid/.

[33] Wiley, Yearby & Hammond, supra note 23.

[34] Yearby & Mohapatra, Systemic Racism, supra note 8; Yearby & Mohapatra, Law, Structural Racism, and the COVID-19 Pandemic, supra note 31.

[35] Wiley, Yearby & Hammond, supra note 23.

[36] Food & Env't Reporting Network, Mapping COVID-19 Outbreaks in the Food System, https://thefern.org/2020/04/mapping-covid-19-in-meat-and-food-processing-plants/ (last visited Aug. 31, 2021).

[37] Michelle A. Waltenburg et al., Update: COVID-19 Among Workers in Meat and Poultry Processing Facilities – United States, April–May 2020, 69 *Morbidity & Mortality Wkly. Rep.* 887, 888 (2020).

COVID-19 cases occurred in Latinos, 19 percent in non-Latino Blacks, 13 percent in non-Latino Whites, and 12 percent in Asians.[38] These infections have also impacted the communities in which these workers live and, more broadly, the entire nation.

Research shows that having a meat or poultry processing plant in the county is associated with a 51–75 percent increase in COVID-19 cases and a 37–50 percent increase in deaths of all people in the county, not just those who worked at the plant.[39] The same research shows that between 3 and 4 percent of all COVID-19 deaths and 6–8 percent of all COVID-19 cases in the United States are tied to meat and poultry processing plants.[40] Infections tied to the lack of paid sick leave are further exacerbated by the government's failure to enforce worker health and safety protections.

B *Lack of Worker Health and Safety Protections*

Neither the federal government nor the states have adequately protected essential workers against workplace exposure to COVID-19. OSHA, and the twenty-one states with OSHA-approved plans,[41] have the power to require employers to provide employees with personal protective equipment, such as masks, and develop a respiratory protection standard to prevent occupational disease.[42] Moreover, employers have a "general duty" to provide employees with a place of employment free from recognized hazards that are causing or likely to cause death or serious harm.[43]

However, the respiratory standard and the "general duty" protections do not apply to some nursing home, home health, and agricultural workers because they are classified as independent contractors. Even if the protections apply, they are insufficient to address COVID-19 because neither the respiratory standard nor the General Duty Clause requires employers to conduct a worksite hazard assessment to determine how an airborne infectious disease can spread within the worksite or adopt specific measures to limit the spread of the airborne infectious disease there. OSHA noted the inadequacies of these laws to address airborne infectious diseases when discussing its 2010 proposed airborne infectious disease rule.[44]

---

[38] Id.

[39] Charles Taylor, Christopher Boulos & Douglas Almond, Livestock Plants and COVID-19 Transmission, Proceedings of the National Academy of Sciences 1–2 (2020), www.pnas.org/content/early/2020/11/25/2010115117.long.

[40] Id.

[41] The twenty-one states include Alaska, Arizona, California, Hawaii, Indiana, Iowa, Kentucky Maryland, Michigan, Minnesota, Nevada, New Mexico, North Carolina, Oregon, South Carolina, Tennessee, Utah, Vermont, Virginia, Washington, and Wyoming. Occupational Safety and Health Act of 1970, 29 U.S.C. §§ 651 et seq. (1970); 29 C.F.R. § 1910.134 (2011).

[42] Occupational Safety and Health Act of 1970, 29 U.S.C. §§ 651 et seq. (1970); 29 C.F.R. § 1910.134 (2011).

[43] 29 U.S.C. § 654.

[44] Infectious Diseases Rulemaking, supra note 7; Summary of Stakeholder Meetings on Occupational Exposure to Infectious Disease, supra note 7; Infectious Diseases SER Background Document, supra note 7.

Instead of adopting the protections in the proposed rule, OSHA, in partnership with the CDC, has issued numerous advisory worker health and safety guidance. All the guidance discusses very similar issues, such as the potential for workplace exposure and the need to create a COVID-19 assessment and control plan. Nevertheless, the guidance does not *require* the adoption of specific measures to limit the spread of COVID-19 in the workplace. Additionally, neither the guidance nor OSHA require employers to report infected workers or test all workers exposed to COVID-19.

In 2014, OSHA adopted a rule requiring the recording and reporting of occupational illness and injury.[45] Under the rule, all employers with more than ten employees, who are covered under the Occupation Safety and Health Act, must report work-related fatalities to OSHA within eight hours of the event. The employers also must report all work-related, in-patient hospitalizations to OSHA within twenty-four hours of the event.[46] However, during the COVID-19 pandemic, OSHA requires employers to report worker hospitalizations for COVID-19 *only if* the hospitalization occurs within 24 hours of their workplace exposure to the virus.[47] Furthermore, employers need to report worker infections and hospitalizations *only if* the worker can show that the infection occurred in the workplace. Limiting reporting of worker infections based on when the hospitalization occurred or where the exposure occurred keeps the government from being able to prevent, mitigate, and contain the spread of COVID-19.

Identifying all workers infected with COVID-19 and mandating the testing of all exposed workers is necessary to track infections and protect workers from being exposed to COVID-19 in the workplace. The pandemic health inequities caused by these gaps in enforcement and reporting are best illustrated by the high rates of COVID-19 infections and deaths of essential workers. In June 2020, the owner of a pistachio farm in Wasco failed to report worker COVID-19 cases to the government or test exposed workers. Consequently, workers at the farm, many of whom were racial and ethnic minorities, did not know other workers had tested positive for COVID-19 until they learned it from the media. By that time, 150 workers and 65 family members had tested positive.[48] After the announcement, the farm started to make masks available free of cost, whereas before they were charging workers $8 per mask.[49]

---

[45] 29 C.F.R. § 1904 (2014).

[46] 29 C.F.R. § 1904.39.

[47] 29 C.F.R. § 1904; US Dep't of Lab., Occupational Safety & Health Admin., Reporting COVID-19 Fatalities and In-patient Hospitalizations to OSHA, www.osha.gov/sites/default/files/publications/OSHA4129.pdf (last visited May 15, 2022).

[48] Associated Press, Farmworkers at Central California Pistachio Farm Strike After Dozens Test Positive for the Coronavirus, LA Times (June 25, 2020), www.latimes.com/california/story/2020-06-25/farmworkers-at-central-california-pistachio-strike-after-dozens-test-positive-for-the-coronavirus; Jacqueline Garcia, Dozens of Pistachio Plant Workers Infected with COVID-19, KQED (July 6, 2020), www.kqed.org/news/11827498/dozens-of-pistachio-plant-workers-infected-with-covid-19; Dale Yurong, Protest Held After Dozens of Farmworkers Test Positive for COVID-19 at Wasco Packing House, ABC30 Fresno (July 16, 2020), https://abc30.com/wasco-coronavirus-covid-packing-house-primex-farms/6321004/.

[49] Associated Press, supra note 48.

Moreover, although workers across the United States have filed over 5,000 complaints regarding workplace hazards that increase the risk of COVID-19 infection, OSHA has only issued one citation related to the pandemic and closed many of these complaints without in-person inspections.[50] Instead, OSHA has relied on employers to make a "good faith" effort to comply with its advisory worker health and safety guidance rather than issue mandatory requirements or conduct in-person inspections. Under the Biden Administration, OSHA has issued an emergency temporary standard to provide mandatory workplace COVID-19 protections for health care workers,[51] but this leaves many essential workers unprotected.

For example, a COVID-19 outbreak at the Farmer John pork processing plant in California began in 2020 and continued for nearly a year, "with more than 300 cases reported in January (2021) alone."[52] Moreover, an April 2021 report showed that essential workers in California accounted for 87 percent of the COVID-19 deaths in adults aged 18 to 65.[53] Warehouse workers "had the highest statewide increase in pandemic related deaths (57 percent)," compared to a 25 percent increase for those not working.[54] Other California industries with high rates of worker deaths include agriculture (47 percent), food processing (43 percent), and nursing homes (39 percent).[55]

III HEALTH EQUITY: SOCIAL DETERMINANTS OF HEALTH AND HEALTH JUSTICE

To eradicate pandemic health inequities, the federal and state governments should revise their emergency preparedness laws and plans, using the three principles of the health justice framework: (1) truth and reconciliation;[56] (2) community engagement and empowerment; and (3) structural remediation and financial support.[57]

---

[50] Ted Knutson, OSHA has Issued Just One COVID-19 Enforcement Action After 5,00 Complaints, House Dems Claim, Forbes (May 28, 2020), www.forbes.com/sites/tedknutson/2020/05/28/osha-is-covid-19-invisible-1-enforcement-after-5000-complaints-charge-dems/; US Dep't of Lab., Office of Inspector Gen., COVID-19: Increased Worksite Complaints and Reduced OSHA Inspections Left US Workers' Safety at Increased Risk (Feb. 25, 2021), www.oig.dol.gov/public/reports/oa/2021/19-21-003-10-105.pdf.

[51] 29 C.F.R. §§ 1910.502, 1910.504, 1910.505, 1910.509 (2021).

[52] Leah Douglas & Georgia Gee, A COVID Outbreak at a California Meatpacking Plant Started a Year Ago – and Never Went Away, Mother Jones (Mar. 16, 2021), www.motherjones.com/food/2021/03/a-covid-outbreak-at-a-california-meatpacking-plant-started-a-year-ago-and-never-went-away/.

[53] Univ. of Cal. Merced, Fact Sheet: The Pandemic's Toll on California Workers in High Risk Industries (Apr. 2021), https://clc.ucmerced.edu/sites/clc.ucmerced.edu/files/page/documents/fact_sheet_-_the_pandemics_toll_on_california_workers_in_high_risk_industries.pdf.

[54] Id.

[55] Id.

[56] Maya Sabatello et al., Structural Racism in the COVID-19 Pandemic: Moving Forward, 21 Am. J. Bioethics 56, 56–58 (2021).

[57] Yearby & Mohapatra, Systemic Racism, supra note 8, at 1433–51; Benfer, Mohapatra, Wiley & Yearby, supra note 19, at 136–41; Benfer & Wiley, supra note 19; Johnson, supra note 19.

A *Recommendations*

First, the process of developing and implementing new emergency preparedness laws and plans must include a truth and reconciliation process that provides an opportunity for communities to heal and build trusting and respectful relationships with the government, which is necessary for meaningful community engagement. As the W. K. Kellogg Foundation notes, transformational and sustainable change must include "ways for all of us to heal from the wounds of the past, to build mutually respectful relationships across racial and ethnic lines that honor and value each person's humanity, and to build trusting intergenerational and diverse community relationships that better reflect our common humanity."[58]

Providence, Rhode Island adopted a truth and reconciliation process to address racial inequities, beginning with the mayor and a group of advisers meeting to develop "a plan for sharing the state's role throughout history in the institution of slavery, genocide of Indigenous people, forced assimilation[,] and seizure of land." This was followed by city leaders reviewing laws and policies that resulted in discrimination against Black and Indigenous people and concluded with community discussion about the "state's history and the ways in which historical injustices and systemic racism continue to affect society today."[59] This process should be used as a model to provide essential workers and their communities with an opportunity to share their experiences and stories with the government, particularly policymakers and regulators.

Second, essential workers, particularly low-wage and racial and ethnic minority workers, must be empowered and engaged as leaders in the development and implementation of new emergency preparedness laws and plans. Community engagement is a key priority of public health. In fact, the HHS 2011 toolkit and 2012 report noted that "effective preparedness and response requires the ongoing and active engagement of diverse communities" before, during, and after an emergency, through "sustainable partnerships between community representatives and the public health preparedness systems"; only then "can plans and programs be tailored to a community's distinct social, economic, cultural, and health-related circumstances."[60] The government must engage communities and give them the power to lead the process of revising, implementing, and evaluating emergency preparedness laws and plans before, during, and after an emergency.[61] For example, there

---

[58] W. K. Kellogg Foundation, Truth, Racial Healing and Transformation, https://healourcommunities .org/ (last visited June 28, 2021).

[59] Madeleine List, Providence Mayor Signs Order to Pursue Truth, Reparations for Black, Indigenous People, Providence J. (July 16, 2020), www.providencejournal.com/story/news/2020/07/16/ providence-mayor-signs-order-to-pursue-truth-reparations-for-black-indigenous-people/42496067/.

[60] Andrulis, Siddiqui & Purtle, supra note 4, at 5.

[61] Athena K. Ramos et al., "No Somos Maquinas" (We Are Not Machines): Worker Perspectives of Safety Culture in Meatpacking Plants in the Midwest, 64 Am J. Indus, Med 84, 90–92 (2021); Yearby & Mohapatra, Systemic Racism, supra note 8; Yearby & Mohapatra, Law, Structural Racism, and the COVID-19 Pandemic, supra note 31.

should be a community-led, employee safety board that consults the White House and assists in the development and implementation of an emergency preparedness worker protection agenda. There should also be community-led, employee safety boards that advise HHS, OSHA, and the states in the creation, implementation, tracking, and evaluation of new emergency preparedness laws and plans.[62]

The Los Angeles County supervisor is already empowering essential workers to play a central role in COVID-19 mitigation efforts. The county unanimously approved a program in which workers from certain sectors (the food and apparel manufacturing, warehousing and storage, and restaurant industries) will form public health councils to help ensure that employers follow coronavirus safety guidelines.[63] Communities and individual community members involved in this process of revising, implementing, and evaluating emergency preparedness laws and plans should also be paid. For instance, President Biden issued a *National Strategy for the COVID-19 Response and Pandemic Preparedness* that has directed the federal government to use and pay community members and community health workers as part of the COVID-19 pandemic response.[64]

Third, emergency preparedness laws and plans must change the structure of the emergency preparedness response by incorporating measures to address employment factors and providing financial support for essential workers, their families, and the communities in which they live. In particular, the emergency preparedness laws and plans must mandate that employers who employ essential workers provide them with health and safety protections to prevent the workplace spread of disease during a pandemic. This could be accomplished by OSHA and the OSHA-approved states adopting the 2010 proposed airborne infectious disease rule.[65]

Furthermore, all federal and state emergency preparedness laws and plans must mandate that if an individual is employed in an essential job during a pandemic, that individual should automatically receive paid sick leave – without exception. Paid sick leave "reduces costly spending on emergency health care, reduces the rate of influenza contagion, and saves the US economy $214 billion annually in increased productivity and reduced turnover."[66] Some cities, such as Oakland,

---

[62] David Michaels & Gregory R. Wagner, Halting Workplace COVID-19 Transmission: An Urgent Proposal to Protect American Workers, Century Found. (Oct. 15, 2020), https://tcf.org/content/report/halting-workplace-covid-19-transmission-urgent-proposal-protect-american-workers/.

[63] Leila Miller, LA County Approves Program for Workers to Form Public Health Councils to Curb Coronavirus Spread (Nov. 10, 2020), www.latimes.com/california/story/2020-11-10/la-me-la-county-public-health-councils.

[64] President Joe Biden, National Strategy for the COVID-19 Response and Pandemic Preparedness (Jan. 2021), www.whitehouse.gov/wp-content/uploads/2021/01/National-Strategy-for-the-COVID-19-Response-and-Pandemic-Preparedness.pdf.

[65] Infectious Diseases Rulemaking, supra note 7; Summary of Stakeholder Meetings on Occupational Exposure to Infectious Disease, supra note 7; Infectious Diseases SER Background Document, supra note 7.

[66] Benfer & Wiley, supra note 19.

California, are already requiring that employers provide paid sick leave to essential workers during the pandemic.[67]

Additionally, until the end of the COVID-19 pandemic, the government should provide essential workers with financial support, such as hazard pay, savings accounts, and survivorship benefits for their families. This will ensure essential workers receive compensation for risking their lives and that their families are provided for if the essential worker dies. Additionally, based on suggestions from a coalition of South Dakota meat plant workers, the state and federal government should use federal COVID-19 economic relief funds to invest directly in low-income communities and "communities of color severely and disproportionately impacted by the deadly virus."[68] This can be accomplished through the implementation of a guaranteed basic income until the end of the pandemic for these communities.[69] The mayors of Mount Vernon, New York and St. Paul, Minnesota have already used part of their federal economic relief money to provide a guaranteed income program for some residents. The federal and state government already have the power, tools, and money to implement these changes.

B *Implementation*

During the COVID-19 pandemic, Congress enacted economic relief bills that either provided authority or left room for the President, HHS, and the states to shift these funds to support states' individual responses to COVID-19. In particular, HHS has the authority under the federal economic relief bills to regulate the distribution of some of the funds. HHS has used this authority to approve the use by Arkansas and New Hampshire of relief funds to provide hazard pay to home health workers.[70] HHS should use this authority to direct all states to provide paid sick leave to essential workers left out of the bills, including home health care workers. President Biden has the authority to address the lack of workplace protections for essential workers. On January 21, 2021, President Biden issued an executive order concerning worker health and safety, as well as a COVID-19 plan with recommendations

---

[67] Bay City News, Oakland City Leaders OK Paid Sick Leave for Essential Workers, NBC Bay Area (May 13, 2020), www.nbcbayarea.com/news/local/oakland-city-leaders-ok-paid-sick-leave-for-essential-workers/2289529/.

[68] Letter from Taneeza Islam, Exec. Dir., S.D. Voices for Peace, to Kristi Noem, Gov. of S.D. (Apr. 30, 2020), www.argusleader.com/story/news/2020/04/30/letter-asks-noem-meet-meatpacking-workers-before-smithfield-plant-reopens/3058042001/.

[69] Kimberly Amadeo & Thomas J. Brock, What is Universal Basic Income? Pros and Cons of a Guaranteed Income, The Balance (Aug. 19, 2020), www.thebalance.com/universal-basic-income-4160668.

[70] Elisha Morrison, CMS Approves Some Healthcare Worker Bonuses, Benton Courier (Apr. 16, 2020), www.bentoncourier.com/covid-19/cms-approves-some-healthcare-worker-bonuses/article_3946 adc8-800c-11ea-944a-1b151690787e.html; KATV, Governor Announces Bonus Pay for Some Health Workers; COVID-19 Death Toll Rises to 34, ABC7 (Apr. 15, 2020), https://katv.com/news/local/governor-announces-bonus-pay-for-health-workers-at-long-term-care-facilities.

to address worker safety issues.[71] As a result, OSHA adopted mandatory COVID-19 workplace protections for health care workers. The President should issue another executive order directing OSHA to publish and adopt the 2010 airborne infectious disease rule for all workers.

Moreover, with the enactment of the Public Health Security and Bioterrorism Preparedness and Response Act of 2002, Congress directed the Secretary of HHS to coordinate a strategy for developing and implementing a national emergency preparedness response for public health emergencies and bioterrorism.[72] In 2006, Congress amended the Public Health Services Act directing the Secretary of HHS to lead "all federal public health and medical response to public health emergencies and incidents."[73] These acts expanded federal authority for responding to public health emergencies and provided funding for federal and state emergency preparedness plans. Thus, the Secretary of HHS has, and should use, the authority to develop and implement a revised national emergency preparedness response for public health emergencies and bioterrorism that includes addressing employment factors. Using the funding power, HHS should require states that receive funding for emergency preparedness under the Public Health Services Act to implement a truth and reconciliation process as well as to engage communities in the revision of emergency preparedness laws and plans.

These are just a few suggestions for eradicating pandemic health inequities experienced by essential workers. However, to fully address pandemic health inequities, the federal and state government must ensure that essential workers, particularly low-income and racial and ethnic minority workers, are guiding the ongoing process to revise emergency preparedness laws and plans, even when there is not an emergency situation.

---

[71] Exec. Order No. 13,999, 86 Fed. Reg. 7,211 (Jan. 21, 2021); Biden, supra note 64.
[72] Pub L. No. 107-188, 116 Stat. 594.
[73] Pub. L. No. 109-417, 120 Stat. 2832.

14

The *Jacobson* Question

Individual Rights, Expertise, and Public Health Necessity

Lindsay F. Wiley

I INTRODUCTION

Individuals and organizations asserting their personal liberty and economic interests have always challenged public health authority. Since the founding of the republic, state legislatures have used their police power to enact sweeping public health statutes.[1] State and local executive branch officials (some of them appointed for their particular expertise) have used the broad authority granted to them by statutes to issue regulations and orders to protect the public's health. People and organizations affected by these public health laws (statutes, regulations, and orders) have called on the judicial branch to review them – to determine whether the legislative and executive branches have complied with constitutional and statutory limits on their power.

Some litigants claim that public health laws violate the civil liberties protected by constitutional provisions and certain statutes. Some litigants rely on the separation of powers enshrined in the structure of the federal and state constitutions to claim that executive branch officials have overstepped the bounds of authority properly delegated to them by statutes.

Since 1905, *Jacobson v. Massachusetts* has guided courts when they adjudicate challenges to public health laws.[2] *Jacobson* upheld a state statute that authorized local health boards to make smallpox vaccination compulsory if, in the opinion of the medical experts on the board, it was necessary for public health. *Jacobson* supported public health necessity as a counterweight that justifies encroachments on civil liberties under at least some circumstances. It also recognized the constitutional authority of state legislatures to protect the public's health – including by delegating power to executive branch officials – without unwarranted interference from federal judges.

---

[1] A state's police power is its inherent authority to exercise reasonable control over people and property, within its jurisdiction, for the protection of the general public's health, safety, and welfare, subject to limits imposed by the Constitution. Public health laws are a subset of police power regulations.

[2] 197 U.S. 11 (1905).

In 2020, legal disputes over COVID-19 emergency orders put *Jacobson* to the test.[3] In one of the first major lawsuits challenging a COVID-19 restriction, the Fifth Circuit Court of Appeals developed a novel interpretation of *Jacobson*. The Fifth Circuit (and the many courts that followed its lead) held that during a public health emergency, *Jacobson* requires judges to suspend the standards they would ordinarily apply to civil liberties claims and instead apply the specific (and highly deferential) standard the Supreme Court set forth in 1905. In this chapter, I refer to the Fifth Circuit's 2020 interpretation of *Jacobson* as the "public health emergency suspension doctrine," or the "suspension doctrine" for short.[4] From April to November 2020, judges relied on the suspension doctrine in dozens of cases upholding orders prohibiting gatherings, restricting business operations, limiting interstate travel, requiring people to stay at home, and mandating face masks. On November 25, 2020, the Supreme Court weighed in on the question of which level of deference the courts should give to executive orders in a public health emergency. It rejected the suspension doctrine and cast doubt on the future of *Jacobson* as a modern precedent.

In the post-2020 era, litigants are calling on courts to answer the *Jacobson* question: Is *Jacobson v. Massachusetts* still a valid precedent?[5] This chapter argues that the foundational principles enshrined in *Jacobson* endure, but public health advocates will need to craft new arguments that incorporate these principles within modern (and sometimes less deferential) standards of judicial review.

II THE EVOLUTION OF JACOBSON

Prior to 2020, *Jacobson* was not on the short list of cases famous among non-lawyers. It was not even particularly well known among the wider legal community. But for more than a century, specialists have revered *Jacobson* as the foundational authority for laws that protect the public's health.

In 2020, a flood of lawsuits challenging COVID-19 mitigation efforts put *Jacobson* in the public spotlight. Hundreds of news stories, op-eds, and podcasts mentioned the case by name.

Beginning in April 2020, many federal judges interpreted *Jacobson* in a novel way, relying on it as the basis for a new doctrine governing the level of deference that courts should grant executive branch officials and legislatures during a public health emergency. These courts set aside modern precedents and suspended ordinary standards of judicial review, using *Jacobson* as a shortcut for upholding

---

[3] Wendy E. Parmet, Rediscovering Jacobson in the Era of COVID-19, 100 *B.U.L. Rev. Online* 117 (2020).

[4] Lindsay F. Wiley & Stephen I. Vladeck, Coronavirus, Civil Liberties, and the Courts: The Case Against "Suspending" Judicial Review, 133 *Harv. L. Rev. F.* 179, 181.

[5] See, for example, Klaassen v. Trs. of Ind. Univ., 7 F.4th 592 (7th Cir. 2021).

COVID-19 mitigation orders without grappling with the thorny legal questions that some of these orders raised. In November 2020, when the Supreme Court rejected this interpretation of *Jacobson*, it cast a shadow on the continued vitality of the case as a whole.

To protect *Jacobson* as a precedent for current and future disputes, public health advocates must parse its meaning carefully. In this section, I provide a chronology of *Jacobson*'s evolution, identifying the specific interpretation of it that the Supreme Court majority rejected in 2020 and separating that from foundational principles that courts can and should rely on in the post-2020 era.

A Jacobson *in 1905*

Around the turn of the twentieth century, life-threatening communicable diseases put the public's health in more or less constant peril. To control the spread of disease, state and local officials routinely brought their police power to bear against businesses and individuals. For smallpox, the availability of an effective vaccine – the first ever developed – prompted state and local governments to require individuals to submit to vaccination under penalty of fines, exclusion from school, and even by force.[6] To cope with frequent smallpox outbreaks, the Massachusetts legislature passed a statute authorizing local health boards to require residents to be vaccinated if, in the opinion of the medical experts on the board, it was "necessary for the public health."[7] The statute imposed a penalty of five dollars for anyone over the age of twenty-one who failed to comply with a local health board's vaccination requirement. In 1902, the board of health of the city of Cambridge, Massachusetts adopted a regulation requiring smallpox vaccination in response to a worsening outbreak. Henning Jacobson, the pastor of a church in Cambridge, refused to be vaccinated. In a criminal proceeding the city initiated to collect the fine, Jacobson claimed that requiring vaccination violated the Due Process Clause of the Fourteenth Amendment, among other provisions.[8] Jacobson argued that the state vaccination law was "unreasonable, arbitrary, and oppressive, and, therefore, hostile to the inherent right of every freeman to care for his own body and health in such way as to him seems best."[9] The case eventually made its way to the Supreme Court, resulting in one of the first major decisions where the Court applied the Fourteenth Amendment to a police power regulation.

---

[6] Parmet, supra note 3, at 121.

[7] Jacobson, 197 U.S. at 12 (quoting the applicable statute).

[8] The Due Process Clause of the Fourteenth Amendment prohibits states from "depriv[ing] any person of life, liberty, or property, without due process of law." In 1915, the Supreme Court was still decades away from holding that the First Amendment's proscription against laws "prohibiting the free exercise of religion" applied to state governments at all. Therefore, Jacobson's argument that the law violated his religious freedom did not get very far, and the Supreme Court did not address it.

[9] Jacobson, 197 U.S. at 26.

The Supreme Court rejected Jacobson's arguments and upheld the state vaccination law. In an opinion written by Justice John Marshall Harlan, the *Jacobson* Court recognized that the Fourteenth Amendment does impose limits on the state's police power. Harlan reasoned that the

> power of a local community to protect itself against an epidemic ... might be exercised in particular circumstances and in reference to particular persons in such an arbitrary, unreasonable manner, or might go so far beyond what was reasonably required for the safety of the public, as to authorize or compel the courts to interfere for the protection of such persons.[10]

The Court directed that judges should overturn police power laws only in cases where "a statute purporting to have been enacted to protect the public health, the public morals, or the public safety, has no real or substantial relation to those objects, or is, beyond all question, a plain, palpable invasion of rights secured by the fundamental law."[11] Yet the Court reasoned that "liberty regulated by law"[12] subjects individual rights to "restraint, to be enforced by reasonable regulations, as the safety of the general public may demand."[13] Under the circumstances, the Massachusetts vaccination law was reasonable, proportionate to the threat, and consistent with public health necessity; consequently, the Court upheld the statute.

Although the Cambridge Board of Health had acted in response to a smallpox outbreak, the *Jacobson* Court did not clearly limit its holding to public health emergencies – or even to public health regulations. The standard of judicial review that the Court articulated and applied in *Jacobson* was, at the time, commonly applied by state courts in challenges to police power regulations generally (of which public health laws are a subset).[14] In a dissenting opinion that Justice Harlan authored shortly after *Jacobson*, he argued that the definitive standard of review for any police power regulation was the one set forth in *Jacobson*.[15] Several months later, in a case upholding state regulations governing the sale of milk, the Court's majority opinion cited *Jacobson* for the proposition that "the state has a right, by reasonable regulations, to protect the public health and safety," without any reference to epidemics or other exigencies.[16] *Jacobson* was "the Court's first systematic statement of individual rights as limitations imposed on government."[17] It is best understood as having "established a floor of constitutional protection" that courts have subsequently

---

[10] Id. at 28.

[11] Id. at 31.

[12] Id. at 27.

[13] Id. at 29.

[14] See, for example, Keith v. Johnson, 59 S.W. 487, 488 (Ky. 1900); State v. Dist. Ct. of Wyman Co. 103 N.W. 744, 744 (Minn. 1905).

[15] Lochner v. New York, 198 U.S. 45, 67 (1905) (Harlan, J., dissenting).

[16] New York v. Van De Carr, 199 U.S. 552 (1905).

[17] Lawrence O. Gostin & Lindsay F. Wiley, *Public Health Law: Power, Duty, Restraint* 214 (3d. ed. 2016).

built upon in cases ranging far beyond the epidemic context in which the regulation upheld in *Jacobson* was adopted.[18]

When *Jacobson* was decided, the Supreme Court had not yet developed the tiered levels of review (rational basis review, intermediate scrutiny, and strict scrutiny) that courts now use to adjudicate federal constitutional rights. Beginning in the mid-twentieth century, the Court developed these varying levels of judicial review for different types of civil liberties claims.[19] The intermediate and strict scrutiny standards that now determine the outcome in some types of cases are far less deferential to the factual determinations and policy choices of the legislative and executive branches. In modern cases that infringe on fundamental rights, judges are supposed to probe the government's asserted interests and the suitability of fit between its chosen means and stated ends more deeply, rather than refraining from overturning any law that is arguably reasonable.

B Jacobson *in 2020*

In the early weeks of the COVID-19 pandemic, state and local officials across the United States issued hundreds of unprecedented executive orders closing businesses, restricting travel, ordering the general public to stay at home, and implementing other measures in hopes of avoiding the devastation experienced in Wuhan, Lombardy, and New York City. Coronavirus mitigation measures adopted in 2020 and 2021 differed from those implemented in the 1918 flu pandemic and mid-century polio outbreaks in important ways. Relying on authority delegated in general emergency and disaster management statutes that largely date to the 1960s and 1970s, governors, not boards of health, typically took the reins on coronavirus mitigation orders.[20] Many coronavirus mitigation orders remained in place longer than the average length of closures in 1918. In addition, coronavirus mitigation orders included innovative measures that had not been implemented in response to previous epidemics.

One innovation was restrictions on elective medical procedures. Most governors either ordered or recommended that health care providers cease procedures deemed elective, nonessential, or not lifesaving. These measures were intended to reduce close contacts among people who could transmit infection and to preserve medical resources for the treatment of COVID-19 patients. In Texas, the state attorney general interpreted Governor Abbott's executive order to effectively bar all abortions as elective medical procedures. Providers and patients filed suit challenging the order's constitutionality.

---

[18] Id.

[19] Wiley & Vladeck, Coronavirus, Civil Liberties, and the Courts: The Case Against "Suspending" Judicial Review, supra note 4, at 193 (citing United States v. Carolene Prods. Co., 304 U.S. 144, 152, n.4 [1938]).

[20] Lindsay F. Wiley, Democratizing the Law of Social Distancing, 19 *Yale J. Health Pol'y, L. Ethics* 50, 69 (2020).

In re Abbott, decided by the Fifth Circuit in April 2020, was one of the first major court decisions upholding a COVID-19 mitigation order.[21] The plaintiffs were abortion providers who filed a lawsuit arguing that to the extent that the Texas emergency order banned abortions, it violated the Fourteenth Amendment's Due Process Clause. The district court judge who initially heard the case granted a temporary restraining order to the plaintiffs (barring Texas from enforcing its prohibition on abortions while litigation continued) without referencing *Jacobson* at all.[22] The judge held that under the Supreme Court's abortion precedents dating back to *Roe v. Wade*, "[t]here can be no outright ban on such a procedure."[23] He referred only obliquely to the defendant's argument that *Jacobson* supplied the correct standard, not *Roe* or subsequent cases establishing abortion rights: "This court will not speculate on whether the Supreme Court included a silent 'except in a national emergency clause' in its previous writings on the issue [of abortion]."[24]

The Fifth Circuit stepped in to stay the lower court's decision, effectively lifting the restraining order and permitting the state to enforce its restrictions on abortion while litigation continued. The appellate court accepted the defendant's argument and interpreted *Jacobson* in a new way. Describing *Jacobson* as imposing "the controlling standards, established by the Supreme Court more than a century ago, for adjudging the validity of emergency measures," the majority set aside the prevailing test for abortion laws – that is, whether the regulation at issue imposes an "undue burden" on the right to choose an abortion. The court suspended the standard of review that would ordinarily apply to restrictions on abortion in favor of a rule that "the scope of judicial authority to review rights-claims" during "a public health crisis" is limited to cases where "a statute purporting to have been enacted to protect the public health, the public morals, or the public safety, has no real or substantial relation to those objects, or is, beyond all question, a plain, palpable invasion of rights secured by the fundamental law."[25] In dicta, the court suggested that this minimal level of scrutiny applies equally to "one's right to peaceably assemble, to publicly worship, to travel, and even to leave one's home."[26] The appellate court turned the lower court's reasoning on its head, arguing that if the Supreme Court had intended for *Roe* or its subsequent cases on abortion rights to be exceptions to the general rule that in a public health emergency the *Jacobson* test applies, it would have said so in specific terms.[27] In the months that followed, dozens of

[21] In re Abbott, 954 F.3d 772 (5th Cir. 2020), vacated, Planned Parenthood Ctr. for Choice v. Abbott, 141 S.Ct. 1261 (2021).
[22] Planned Parenthood Ctr. for Choice v. Abbott, 450 F.Supp.3d 753 (W.D. Tex. 2020).
[23] Id. at 758.
[24] Id.
[25] In re Abbott, 954 F.3d at 784 (quoting Jacobson, 197 U.S. at 31).
[26] Id. at 778.
[27] Id. at 786.

additional courts adopted the *Jacobson* suspension doctrine to uphold orders closing businesses, limiting gatherings, directing the general public to stay at home, and
restricting interstate travel.

In brief opinions accompanying a series of preliminary orders beginning in May
2020, individual Supreme Court justices revealed their positions on *Jacobson's* relevance to COVID-19 disputes. In the first such case, *South Bay United Pentecostal
Church v. Newsom,*[28] Chief Justice John Roberts authored an opinion concurring
with the majority's decision to leave California's limits on religious services in place
while litigation continued. Roberts cited *Jacobson* favorably for the general proposition that "[o]ur Constitution principally entrusts '[t]he safety and the health of the
people' to the politically accountable officials of the States 'to guard and protect.'"[29]
His opinion indicated that he believed California's restrictions would pass muster under ordinary standards of review. Justice Brett Kavanaugh wrote a dissenting
opinion, joined by Justices Clarence Thomas and Neil Gorsuch. The Kavanaugh
dissent indicated that these three justices would have provided injunctive relief to
the plaintiff church because they believed that California's restrictions failed to satisfy ordinary standards of review. Neither of the opinions discussed the suspension
doctrine that had taken hold among many lower courts.

In a similar case in July, the Supreme Court again denied preliminary injunctive
relief to a church challenging COVID-19 restrictions. In his dissenting opinion in
Calvary Chapel Dayton Valley v. Sisolak, Justice Samuel Alito explicitly discussed
the suspension doctrine. Alito (writing for himself, Kavanaugh, and Thomas)
argued that "it is a mistake to take language in *Jacobson* as the last word on what the
Constitution allows public officials to do during the COVID-19 pandemic."[30]

In October, the Court refused to stay a lower court order enjoining limits on
mail-in voting. In *Democratic National Committee v. Wisconsin State Legislature,*[31]
Kavanaugh (writing in dissent to indicate that he would have overturned the lower
court decision and let the limits on mail-in voting stay in place) endorsed "a limited
role of the federal courts in COVID-19 cases."[32] Kavanaugh quoted Roberts's earlier
invocation of a basic principle from *Jacobson,* but without attribution to Roberts or
Jacobson. His version replaced "officials" with "legislatures."[33]

In November 2020, shortly after Justice Amy Coney Barrett replaced the late
Justice Ruth Bader Ginsburg on the Court, the new majority changed the course of
the Court's religious liberty jurisprudence and rejected the suspension doctrine – for

---

[28] South Bay United Pentecostal Church v. Newsom, 140 S.Ct. 1613 (2020).
[29] Id. at 1613 (Roberts, C.J., concurring) (quoting Jacobson, 197 U.S. at 38).
[30] Calvary Chapel Dayton Valley v. Sisolak, 140 S.Ct. 2603, 2608 (Alito, J., dissenting).
[31] Democratic Nat'l Comm. v. Wis. State Legislature, 141 S.Ct. 28 (2020).
[32] Id. at 32, 34 (Kavanaugh, J., concurring).
[33] Id. at 28, 32 (Kavanaugh, J., concurring) ("This Court has consistently stated that the Constitution
     principally entrusts politically accountable state legislatures, not unelected federal judges, with the
     responsibility to address the health and safety of the people during the COVID-19 pandemic.").

First Amendment religious liberty claims, at least.[34] In *Roman Catholic Diocese of Brooklyn v. Cuomo*,[35] the Court granted preliminary relief to the houses of worship who filed suit, enjoining New York from enforcing occupancy limits on religious services. In a per curiam (unsigned) opinion, the majority applied strict scrutiny – the highest standard of review. Under the suspension doctrine, the Court would not have applied strict scrutiny. But it need not have done so under ordinary standards of review either. To trigger strict scrutiny, the majority found that New York's COVID-19 mitigation orders were not neutral laws of general applicability, but rather "single[d] out houses of worship for especially harsh treatment."[36] This determination departed from the Court's past religious liberty precedents. It also misrepresented the facts on the ground.

The majority opinion did not discuss *Jacobson* or the suspension doctrine explicitly, but several justices did discuss it in their concurrences and dissents. Gorsuch concurred in the decision to grant injunctive relief. In an opinion joined by no other justice, Gorsuch harshly criticized the suspension doctrine and accused Roberts of endorsing it by citing *Jacobson* in his *South Bay* concurrence. Gorsuch argued that "*Jacobson* didn't seek to depart from normal legal rules during a pandemic, and it supplies no precedent for doing so. Instead, *Jacobson* applied what would become the traditional legal test associated with the right at issue."[37] Gorsuch implied that rational basis review would be the proper test for a Fourteenth Amendment challenge to a vaccination law under modern precedents because a requirement to get vaccinated, pay a fine, or establish that one qualified for an exemption would not implicate a fundamental right that would trigger heightened review.

In their *Roman Catholic Diocese of Brooklyn* dissent, Justices Stephen Breyer, Elena Kagan, and Sonia Sotomayor quoted Roberts' *South Bay* concurrence (from May 2020) favorably. They appeared to agree with Roberts "that courts must grant elected officials 'broad' discretion when they 'undertake to act in areas fraught with medical and scientific uncertainties.'"[38]

Roberts wrote a separate dissent in *Roman Catholic Diocese of Brooklyn* to distinguish between the suspension doctrine and the basic principles of *Jacobson* that he had previously endorsed in *South Bay*. He defended himself against Gorsuch's accusations. Arguing that "the actual proposition [he] asserted" (and cited *Jacobson* in support of) in his *South Bay* concurrence "should be uncontroversial," Roberts concluded that Gorsuch's "concurrence must reach beyond the

---

34 Several justices who have discussed the suspension doctrine have specifically confined their analysis to First Amendment claims. It is possible they would endorse the use of *Jacobson*'s highly deferential standard of review for Fourteenth Amendment claims (including claims asserting abortion rights that the same justices disfavor).

35 Roman Catholic Diocese of Brooklyn v. Cuomo, 141 S.Ct. 63 (2020).

36 Id. at 66.

37 Id. at 70 (Gorsuch, J., concurring).

38 Id. at 78 (Kagan, J., dissenting).

words themselves to find the target it is looking for."[39] Roberts appeared eager to distinguish his own view of *Jacobson* from that of the lower courts who had adopted the suspension doctrine.

In my view, the Supreme Court was correct to reject the suspension doctrine in favor of applying ordinary standards of review.[40] The point is not that the emergency orders were not justified; rather, suspending ordinary judicial review is the wrong way to evaluate them. I strenuously object to the Fifth Circuit's novel interpretation of *Jacobson*, which I have characterized in previous work with constitutional law expert Steve Vladeck as deeply misguided.[41] We argued that the vast majority of COVID-19 mitigation orders (but probably not the across-the-board ban on abortions challenged in *In re Abbott*) would have passed muster under ordinary standards of review. Subsequent cases bore out this prediction. The vast majority of COVID-19 cases that rejected the suspension principle and applied modern standards of review ultimately upheld emergency measures.

The balancing and proportionality tests that modern standards direct the courts to employ are adaptable to emergency conditions. During an emergency, the government's purpose becomes far more compelling and the evidence a court will expect it to present will understandably and appropriately be less well developed. By interpreting *Jacobson* as a directive to suspend ordinary standards of judicial review during a public health emergency, many lower courts in 2020 sidestepped important legal questions. They abdicated their constitutional responsibility for "forc[ing] the government to do its homework – to communicate not only the purposes of its actions, but also how the imposed restrictions actually relate to and further those purposes."[42] Ironically, by using *Jacobson* as a kind of rubber stamp and failing to require government officials to justify their orders in the ordinary way, these courts robbed government officials of firm precedents to support similar orders in the future.

Fortunately, some lower courts rejected the suspension principle and applied ordinary standards of review throughout 2020. As a result, when the Supreme Court rejected the suspension doctrine in November 2020, at least some federal courts had already upheld every major type of COVID-19 mitigation order pursuant to ordinary standards of review.[43]

---

[39] Id. at 76 (Roberts, C.J., dissenting).

[40] As discussed above, I believe the majority in *Roman Catholic Diocese of Brooklyn* was wrong about which ordinary standard of review to apply, because I do not believe the challenged restrictions singled out religious services for particularly harsh treatment relative to comparable gatherings.

[41] Lindsay F. Wiley & Steve Vladeck, COVID-19 Reinforces the Argument for "Regular" Judicial Review—Not Suspension of Civil Liberties—In Times of Crisis, *Harv. L. Rev. Blog* (Apr. 9, 2020), https://blog.harvardlawreview.org/covid-19-reinforces-the-argument-for-regular-judicial-review-not-suspension-of-civil-liberties-in-times-of-crisis/; Wiley & Vladeck, Coronavirus, Civil Liberties, and the Courts: The Case Against "Suspending" Judicial Review, supra note 4.

[42] Wiley & Vladeck, COVID-19 Reinforces the Argument for "Regular" Judicial Review—Not Suspension of Civil Liberties—In Times of Crisis, supra note 41.

[43] Wiley, supra note 20, at 86.

III THE ENDURING MEANING OF *JACOBSON* IN 2021 AND BEYOND

Jacobson's specific formulation of the standard that should guide judicial review may have been characteristic of a bygone era of constitutional jurisprudence, but it has enduring relevance to contemporary disputes. Indeed, lower courts have continued to rely on it to uphold vaccination requirements in the aftermath of *Roman Catholic Diocese*. They have applied the modern standard of rational basis review (which is similar to, but not entirely synonymous with, the standard applied in *Jacobson*) to cases that do not involve religious liberty challenges.[44]

Jacobson should be known (as it was among public health law experts prior to 2020) not for its specific (and outdated) description of the standard for judicial review, but for its assertion of the common good as a counterweight to individual liberties. It also provides support for legislative delegations of broad authority to local boards of health guided by the standard of public health necessity.

A *The "Second Language" of Community*

Advocates often struggle to build support for public health interventions because individualistic cultural norms tend to dominate political debates. Robert Bellah and colleagues have described individualism as the "first language" of American culture, "centered on the values of freedom, self-determination, self-discipline, personal responsibility, and limited government."[45] Public health scholars have noted that the "second language" of America identified by Bellah et al. – "a language of inter-connectedness[,] egalitarian and humanitarian values, of interdependence and community" – is the "first language" for public health.[46] *Jacobson* is a Rosetta Stone by which these two languages are connected in American public health jurisprudence.

The enduring meaning of Justice Harlan's "nuanced and Delphic opinion" in *Jacobson* is that in emergencies,[47] as in routine times, individual liberties should be balanced against collective needs. The Court put "the duty" of "every well-ordered

---

[44] Klaassen, 7 F.4th (declining to enjoin a vaccination requirement for COVID-19 for public university students); W.D. v. Rockland Co., 521 F.Supp.3d 358 (S.D.N.Y. 2021) (upholding an emergency order excluding children who had not been vaccinated for measles from school, public gatherings, and places of public accommodation); Dahl v. Bd. of Trs. of W. Mich. Univ., No. 1:21-cv-757, 2021 WL 3891620 (WD Mich. Aug. 31, 2021), appeal denied, 15 F.4th 728 (6th Cir. 2021) (applying rational basis review to an employee's claim that infection-acquired immunity should exempt her from a vac-cination requirement for COVID-19 but applying strict scrutiny to student athletes' claims that they should be given a religious exemption).

[45] Lawrence Wallack & Regina Lawrence, Talking About Public Health: Developing America's "Second Language," 95 *Am. J. Pub. Health* 567, 567 (2005) (citing Robert N. Bellah et al., Habits of the Heart [2d. ed. 1996]).

[46] Id.

[47] Parmet, supra note 3, at 119 (2020).

society" to "conserv[e] the safety of its members" on an equal footing with the right of "the individual" to "assert the supremacy of his own will" and to "dispute the authority ... of any free government existing under a written constitution, to interfere with the exercise of that will."[48] *Jacobson* offered a ringing endorsement of the social compact in which cooperative efforts to ensure the public's health and safety are important counterweights to individual rights. "There are manifold restraints to which every person is necessarily subject for the common good," the Court reasoned.[49] "On any other basis organized society could not exist with safety to its members."[50]

Even if *Jacobson*'s highly deferential standard no longer applies to laws that infringe on fundamental rights under modern precedents, the basic principles of public health necessity and proportionality that the *Jacobson* Court set forth remain relevant.[51] Modern standards of review may calibrate the scales differently, but collective necessities still serve as counterweights when courts exercise their duty to protect individual rights. In the post-2020 era, public health advocates will need to craft new arguments that incorporate the basic principle that collective needs may outweigh individual rights within the bounds of modern standards of review that require the government to articulate in more compelling terms its purpose and why the means it has chosen are likely to further that end.

B *Deference to Democratic Delegation*

Though it has primarily been relied on in cases asserting individual liberties, *Jacobson* also offers enduring counsel for courts adjudicating claims that public health measures violate the structural constraints imposed by constitutional commitments to separation of powers.[52] Concluding that "[t]he authority to determine for all what ought to be done in such an emergency must have been lodged somewhere or in some body," the Court in *Jacobson* approved the legislature's choice "to refer that question, in the first instance, to a board of health composed of persons ... appointed ... because of their fitness to determine such questions."[53] Thus, the Court endorsed judicial deference to the scientific findings of experts exercising delegated authority, noting that the statutory standard authorized local officials to

---

[48] Jacobson, 197 U.S. at 29.

[49] Id. at 26.

[50] Id.

[51] Wiley & Vladeck, Coronavirus, Civil Liberties, and the Courts: The Case Against "Suspending" Judicial Review, supra note 4, at 182–83.

[52] Gostin & Wiley, supra note 17, at 126 ("In balancing individual rights against the common good, the Court in *Jacobson* relied on separation of powers and federalism to stake out a deferential stance toward the legislative branch and the states.").

[53] Id. at 27; see also Van De Carr, 199 U.S. at 561 (describing *Jacobson* as having "sustained a compulsory vaccination law which delegated to the board of health of cities or towns the determination of the necessity of requiring the inhabitants to submit to compulsory vaccination").

make vaccination compulsory "only when, in the opinion of the board of health, that was necessary for the public health or the public safety."[54]

As a statutory guardrail, the standard of public health necessity has an impressive pedigree. State public health statutes typically delegate authority to health officials to take measures they deem "necessary" to prevent or slow the spread of communicable disease during a declared emergency. Indeed, the public health necessity standard provides more guidance to executive branch officials (and the courts reviewing their actions) than many of the general emergency or disaster management statues on which governors frequently relied during the COVID-19 pandemic. Some governors used general emergency management statues to prohibit local government measures – and even private business policies – that were more protective of public health than the governor preferred, arguing that these statutes give unfettered discretion to the state executive to manage emergencies as they see fit.[55] Courts have not typically relied on *Jacobson* in recent cases interpreting the breadth of officials' authority under these provisions and whether they run afoul of the constitutional doctrine that legislatures cannot delegate their authority to the executive branch without providing sufficient principles to guide officials' exercise of discretion. But the courts can and should rely on the basic principles set forth in *Jacobson* when they are called on to interpret public health statutes.

IV CONCLUSION

As Lawrence Gostin and I have previously commented: "[p]ublic health has always been politically controversial. And public health law – which concerns the extent of government authority to intervene to protect the public's health – lives in the thick of this controversy."[56] There have been many calls throughout the COVID-19 pandemic for elected leaders to "follow the science" and for judges to defer to them when they do. But public health policy cannot be determined exclusively through scientific methods. Decisions about the public health goals that we collectively pursue and how we pursue them should be informed by scientific risk assessments, but these decisions also involve assessments of competing values and interests that require open, forthright, and inclusive deliberation. Delegations of authority to health officials who have been appointed in part based on their scientific expertise embody this balance between science and policy and are wholly consistent with the structural constraints embodied in the federal and state constitutions. The limits

---

[54] Jacobson, 197 U.S. at 27.
[55] See, for example, Tex. Exec. Order GA-15 (Apr. 17, 2020); Tex. Exec. Order GA-25 (Apr. 5, 2021) (relying on the Texas Disaster Act of 1975, which empowers the governor to meet "the dangers to the state and people presented by disasters," to preempt local authority to impose social distancing requirements and vaccination mandates, and to prohibit private businesses from asking patrons to provide proof of vaccination).
[56] Gostin & Wiley, supra note 17, at 532.

that judicial protection of individual rights imposes on majoritarian rule are not absolute. They are flexible and adaptable. Setting aside ordinary standards of review, rather than articulating how they apply under exigent circumstances, disserves the social compact that is at the heart of *Jacobson*. The ability of a free, democratic society to rise to the challenge of taking "action in concert" (during an emergency and after it has ended) is dependent upon, rather than being hindered by, respect for individual rights and the rule of law.[57]

---

[57] Bonnie Honig, Emergency Politics: Paradox, Law, Democracy xv (2009).

PART IV

Innovation During COVID-19

Introduction

I. Glenn Cohen

The three chapters in Part IV all deal with innovation in two senses: (1) the innovation ecosystem that gave us COVID-19 vaccines, diagnostics, and anti-virals; and (2) the innovation *in* the structures that produced those products. Behind the scenes of these chapters, I would argue, is a related but distinct conversation: Are these flaws in the legal system that the COVID-19 pandemic exposed or is this a story about how an exceptional "perfect storm" brought on by the COVID-19 vaccine foundered on the shoals of otherwise good regulatory structures?

In Chapter 15, "Innovation Law and COVID-19: Promoting Incentives and Access for New Health Care Technologies," Rachel Sachs, Lisa Larrimore Ouellette, W. Nicholson Price II, and Jacob Sherkow give a 10,000-foot view of the legal structures that led to these developments and what can be changed. They use the case of COVID-19 testing to show the way conflict and lack of coordination in the legal regimes of three sub-agencies of the Department of Health and Human Services – the Centers for Disease Control and Prevention (CDC), the Food and Drug Administration (FDA), and Centers for Medicare and Medicaid Services – led to problems in the production, approval, and quality of COVID-19 diagnostic tests in the first phase of the pandemic. While interagency problems are not perhaps unique to COVID-19, as more cooperation between agencies/sub-agencies would always be helpful, it is fair to characterize the contribution of this chapter as being about COVID-19's perfect storm, or maybe pandemics more generally, rather than a general critique of how these agencie/sub-agencies work together. The authors then examine the FDA's emergency use authorization (EUA) grants for several COVID-19 treatments, most notably hydroxychloroquine, remdesivir, and convalescent plasma. Here, the critique is more about how COVID-19 shines a spotlight on a deep, preexisting tension – the way in which faster approval or access programs, not just EUAs but the expanded access program, affect "the ability to generate high-quality clinical trial data to confirm or reject preliminary evidence of safety and efficacy" and the need for these programs to be designed with this tradeoff in mind. The final section of this chapter, which looks at government funding for vaccine development in COVID-19, falls between the two poles described here. On the one hand, the authors recognize that Operation Warp Speed's success was in part the result of an unusual configuration in medical research, where "public funding of COVID-19 vaccines focused more on covering the final stages of development and manufacturing costs, building on substantial private investments in early-stage research." On the other hand, some of what they discuss, such as advance purchase commitments as an innovation lever, could be more easily adapted for the next pandemic, which they ominously suggest is certain to come eventually.

In Chapter 16, "Addressing Exclusivity Issues During the COVID-19 Pandemic and Beyond," Dr. Michael Sinha, Sven Bostyn, and Timo Minssen focus on intellectual property rights related to COVID-19 vaccines and therapeutics with a particular focus on regulatory exclusivities. They describe, in general, the marketing authorization rules in Europe, especially the conditional marketing authorization process, and compare them with the EUA pathway in the United States. They then show how these pathways operated for vaccines and therapeutics. For vaccines they find a story in both places that is fairly exceptional. As they note, "[v]accine R&D over the last few decades has largely occurred within small and medium-sized companies" and successfully navigating clinical trials "is often dependent on additional federal funding or acquisition by larger firms," with many products languishing if "funding runs dry or large vaccine manufacturers decline to conduct further studies or pursue" authorization. The COVID-19 vaccine situation is very different. As in the previous chapter, the authors zero in on public funding and advance purchase commitments, but they also point to the intellectual property protection over mRNA vaccine platforms, patent libraries, and trade secrets as creating a much more secure environment for the pioneer companies here. But a quirk of how exclusivity periods run in the United States and Europe make a big difference for COVID-19 in comparing the two regimes: in Europe, the time-limited exclusivity period begins to run when conditional authorization is given, whereas in the United States the period is not triggered by the EUA, only by the Biologics Licensing Application (BLA), which they argue disincentivized the companies to rush to get a BLA approval (often thought of as a "full approval" by the public). They also review how voluntary sharing of technology and data, patent pools, and compulsory licensing have worked out in ensuring equitable vaccine access to poorer countries; the short answer, they conclude, is not very well. Here, it is hard to diagnose whether this represents a persistent problem baked into the system or one that is particularly bad for COVID-19 vaccines. The combination of large numbers of patents, the complexity of the technology and the trade secrets surrounding it, and the vaccine nationalism which prompted rich countries to make sure to secure their share first all made COVID-19 a bad if not worst-case scenario. Some of the changes they examine might be more palatable with respect to other global health needs or other technologies.

In Chapter 17, "Vulnerable Populations and Vaccine Injury Compensation: The Need for Legal Reform," Katharine Van Tassel and Sharona Hoffman examine the strange situation arising from the fact that the United States runs two distinct programs relevant to vaccine injuries (a sad but inevitable result of even very safe vaccines administered to so many): (1) the National Vaccine Injury Compensation Program (VICP), which covers most vaccines given in the United States; and (2) the Countermeasures Injury Compensation Program (CICP), far less generous and more difficult to access, which applies when vaccines are administered as countermeasures. Importantly, during the period when vaccines in the United States were administered under an EUA status, as they were for much of the early months of vaccine availability, those injured could access compensation only under the CICP. The authors nicely show how the CICP coverage interfaced problematically with several – if not exceptional then at least fairly distinct – features of the COVID-19 vaccination scenario: high levels of vaccine hesitancy in poor and minority communities, and the fact that these same populations were both at high risk of COVID-19 infection and also the least financially able to withstand a vaccine-related injury.

The authors argue that an important innovation in policy is needed for future pandemics – a vaccine-specific carve-out (i.e., not drugs or devices) that would "establish that all vaccines that the FDA approves and the CDC recommends to ameliorate a [public health emergency] will be covered by the VICP, regardless of whether they are to be administered to pregnant women or children," thereby shifting all EUA-approved vaccines into the program.

The pandemic is not over, but it is entering a phase where the public is more interested in reviewing what has happened thus far. There is increasing talk in the United States of something like the 9/11 Commission, a full review of what we did and how it went. These chapters are an excellent guide to beginning that discussion. They also present the possibility of leveraging what went wrong with COVID-19, especially regarding access for the worst off globally, into more systemic changes to our innovation ecosystem.

15

Innovation Law and COVID-19

Promoting Incentives and Access for New Health Care Technologies

Rachel E. Sachs, Lisa Larrimore Ouellette, W. Nicholson Price II, and Jacob S. Sherkow

I INTRODUCTION

As the devastating COVID-19 pandemic first swept the globe, it posed a crucial test of biomedical innovation institutions. Containing the virus required developing new technologies including diagnostics, pharmaceuticals, and vaccines; manufacturing them at enormous scale; and rapidly distributing them globally. This, in turn, required mobilizing and coordinating scientists, industry, and government at levels not seen since World War II. Underlying the successes and failures of these efforts was the complex legal architecture of biomedical innovation and access.

This chapter considers how this legal architecture both encouraged and impeded the development and allocation of new technologies in the fight against COVID-19 – and provides lessons about how it might be better deployed for future pandemics. This chapter focuses on three key areas of innovation law: biopharmaceutical regulation; health care reimbursement; and government subsidies for research and development (R&D). The first part of this chapter discusses the need to coordinate government agencies in a public health emergency, especially pertaining to developing, validating, and distributing diagnostic tests. The second part counsels agencies to ensure that early access to therapies in a public health crisis does not obviate developers' ability (or incentive) to generate robust information about such therapies' safety and efficacy. The third relays lessons about the successes of incentives for COVID-19 vaccine development – and their failures for vaccine distribution. Addressing the flaws in US biomedical innovation institutions that have been highlighted by COVID-19 will help avoid repeating these failures during the next pandemic.

II COORDINATING AGENCIES IN A PUBLIC HEALTH EMERGENCY

Fostering interagency coordination at the federal level is a key element of innovation policy, driving both incentives to develop new products and allocation mechanisms to disseminate them.[1] Early in the COVID-19 pandemic, however, federal agencies failed to collaborate and coordinate in the development and rollout of diagnostic testing. As a result, public health officials were unable to identify where the virus was spreading, hindering their ability to contain it. This lack of interagency coordination resulted in unnecessary delays in the dissemination and scale-up of accurate tests for COVID-19.

A *Delayed COVID-19 Diagnostics Due to a Lack of Interagency Coordination*

The delayed development and rollout of diagnostic testing for COVID-19 illustrates problems that can arise when interagency relationships are not carefully considered in the innovation process. Three federal agencies – the Centers for Disease Control and Prevention (CDC), the Food and Drug Administration (FDA), and the Centers for Medicare and Medicaid Services (CMS) – should have worked together from the beginning of the pandemic to facilitate the creation of more robust testing capacity. Instead, the actions of each agency independently slowed the development and scale-up of diagnostic testing.

In January 2020, as concern regarding the virus that would later be named SARS-CoV-2 began to emerge in the United States, the CDC developed a diagnostic test for the disease and obtained the FDA's permission to share the kit with state public health laboratories. However, the CDC quickly discovered a problem with the kits' negative controls and instructed states to stop using them.[2] The CDC was unable to solve this problem for more than a month. Although the agency finally announced, on February 28, that states could restart testing using the CDC kits, many states would not begin doing so until March. Although there was certainly communication between the CDC and its fellow health agencies – the FDA had granted emergency authorization for the test in early February – there were also periods of miscommunication. Perhaps most notably, the CDC temporarily blocked an FDA official from visiting the agency to help address the testing issues, reportedly due to "a scheduling misunderstanding."[3] Acting separately, the FDA likely also inadvertently slowed the emergence of nationwide testing capacity. Under an emergency declaration from Health and Human Services (HHS) Secretary Alex Azar, the FDA used its emergency use authorization (EUA) powers to permit test manufacturers to enter the market with fewer pre-market review requirements than usual. But even these more limited evidentiary requirements slowed products' entry into the market,

---

[1] Rachel E. Sachs, Administering Health Innovation, 39 Cardozo L. Rev. 1991 (2018); Jody Freeman & Jim Rossi, Agency Coordination in Shared Regulatory Space, 125 *Harv. L. Rev.* 1131 (2012).

[2] James Bandler et al., Inside the Fall of the CDC, ProPublica (Oct. 15, 2020), www.propublica.org/article/inside-the-fall-of-the-cdc.

[3] Dan Diamond, CDC Blocked FDA Official from Premises, Politico (Mar. 3, 2020), www.politico.com/news/2020/03/03/cdc-blocked-fda-official-premises-119684.

particularly given both the FDA and companies were dealing with a novel pathogen. Companies spent weeks working with the agency before receiving their EUAs, during which the virus was spreading largely unseen. For laboratory-developed tests, such as those developed by academic medical centers (as contrasted with firms who make kits for others' use), the FDA's EUA requirements represented an *increase* over their usual level of review,[4] further slowing dissemination. There are, of course, important reasons for the FDA to maintain evidentiary standards during a pandemic, as later demonstrated by the FDA's overly permissive authorizations for antibody tests.[5] But the FDA's heightened scrutiny for diagnostics at the beginning of the pandemic meant that other laboratories could not readily fill the space left by the CDC's delays.

At the same time, laboratory certification requirements imposed by the CMS likely also limited the number of labs even eligible to obtain FDA authorization for their own tests. The CMS independently regulates clinical laboratories under the Clinical Laboratory Improvement Amendments of 1988 (CLIA). Many academic laboratories with the technical ability to perform COVID-19 diagnostic tests could not do so legally because they lacked CLIA certification and found it challenging to work with labs possessing such certification.[6] Stronger coordination between these three agencies could have helped address these delays. As head of the parent agency for the CDC, the FDA, and the CMS, HHS Secretary Azar could have worked to mediate disputes and identify where agency policies were delaying the diagnostic rollout. Reporting suggests that the CDC and the FDA waited weeks for Secretary Azar to even approve fallback plans for diagnostic testing.[7] More actively, Secretary Azar could have directed the CDC and the FDA to move forward collaboratively to adapt and authorize the public testing protocol developed by the World Health Organization (WHO), which was in use in many other countries.[8] White House officials could also have taken a stronger hand in coordinating issues that arose.

However, it is possible that these officials were not sufficiently aware of the different legal issues at play – FDA Commissioner Stephen Hahn and CMS Administrator Seema Verma were not even added to the COVID-19 Task Force until well after these testing failures were known.

---

[4]   Barbara J. Evans & Ellen Wright Clayton, Deadly Delay: The FDA's Role in America's COVID-Testing Debacle, 130 *Yale L. J. F.* 78, 88 (2020).

[5]   See Jeffrey Shuren & Timothy Stenzel, The FDA's Experience with COVID-19 Antibody Tests, 384 *New Eng. J. Med.* 592 (2021).

[6]   Amy Maxmen, Thousands of Coronavirus Tests Are Going Unused in US Labs, Nature (Apr. 9, 2020), www.nature.com/articles/d41586-020-01068-3.

[7]   Dan Diamond & Adam Cancryn, Azar in the Crosshairs for Delays in Virus Tests, Politico (Mar. 2, 2020), www.politico.com/news/2020/03/02/azar-crosshairs-delays-coronavirus-tests-118796.

[8]   David Willman, The CDC's Failed Race Against COVID-19: A Threat Underestimated and a Test Overcomplicated, Wash. Post (Dec. 26, 2020), www.washingtonpost.com/investigations/cdc-covid/2020/12/25/c2b418ae-4206-11eb-8db8-395dedaaa036_story.html.

B *Encouraging Interagency Cooperation Going Forward*

Establishing strong norms of interagency coordination can help avoid harms like these and others that have arisen during the pandemic (such as those related to shortages of N95 respirators).[9] Additionally, such coordination can be used to accomplish more affirmative innovation policy goals. Different policymakers have different tools for encouraging interagency coordination, and different strategies may be useful depending on the situation and the goal to be achieved.

Congress can encourage interagency collaboration either by requiring it or just by signaling that collaboration is an important policy goal. For instance, Congress requires the National Institutes of Health (NIH) to report annually on its activities "involving collaboration with other agencies" within HHS.[10] Some of these activities – of which there are several hundred – are congressionally mandated, such as the Interagency Pain Research Coordinating Committee.[11] But most of the NIH's interagency collaborations are not legally required. Instead, Congress has emphasized the importance of interagency collaboration while leaving the areas and form of such collaboration largely to the expert agencies.

Administrative solutions might differ depending on whether structural barriers, personnel, or political considerations are the primary impediments to coordination. Where structural barriers exist, options might involve forcing interagency collaboration either through HHS (as the parent agency for many relevant agencies) or the White House (where a whole-of-government response is needed).[12] A White House-led initiative has been effective at driving innovation in some areas of technology where there is sufficient political will, such as with the focus of Operation Warp Speed on vaccine development, discussed further in Section IV.

Generally, it will be easier to foster novel interagency collaborations if there is already a culture of cooperation within each agency. The more existing collaborations there are, the more potential channels there may be for communicating potential interagency challenges going forward.

III DEVELOPING NEW EVIDENCE WHILE ALLOWING EXPERIMENTAL USE

The FDA balances the goal of making new health care technologies quickly available to the public with the need for sufficient evidence that those technologies are

---

[9] Lisa Larrimore Ouellette et al., Regulatory Responses to N95 Respirator Shortages, Written Description (Apr. 21, 2020), https://writtendescription.blogspot.com/2020/04/regulatory-responses-to-n95-respirator.html.

[10] 42 U.S.C. § 283a(a).

[11] 42 U.S.C. § 284q(b).

[12] Stuart Minor Benjamin & Arti K. Rai, Fixing Innovation Policy: A Structural Perspective, 77 Geo. Wash. L. Rev. 1 (2008).

safe and effective – evidence which is costly and time-consuming to gather. Striking this balance is contentious and has been the subject of substantial scholarship. The pandemic placed greater demands on the agency to make decisions on the basis of very little evidence, sometimes in ways that jeopardized the development of further evidence on the topic. In particular, the agency allowed access to COVID-19-targeted therapeutics using both its Expanded Access (EA) and EUA pathways, each of which requires much lower evidentiary standards than traditional approval or clearance.[13] These cases illustrate the importance, even when prioritizing speed, of ensuring that high-quality data will continue to be collected and evaluated once technologies are available.

A *Quick Authorizations and Limited Evidence for COVID-19 Therapeutics*

The FDA granted EUAs for several COVID-19 treatments, most notably hydroxychloroquine, remdesivir, and convalescent plasma. The standard for granting an EUA is low; under 21 USC § 360bbb-3, the FDA must determine, based on the "totality of the scientific evidence" available, that it is "reasonable to believe" that the drug "may be effective" in treating the disease and that the known and potential benefits outweigh the known and potential risks.

This evidence may – or may not – include randomized controlled clinical trials, which are key elements of the typical FDA approval standard.

After the FDA issued an EUA for hydroxychloroquine to treat COVID-19 on March 28, 2020, prescriptions soared.[14] The EUA came after President Trump repeatedly touted its benefits based on relatively little evidence, leading to it being asked whether there had been political pressure on the FDA. Nevertheless, when the FDA issued the EUA, multiple clinical studies of hydroxychloroquine were ongoing, presenting the agency with another opportunity to look at the drug's safety and efficacy, and potentially revise its decision. Once those studies finished, the evidence was strong that hydroxychloroquine does *not* work to treat COVID-19; indeed, it is affirmatively harmful in some instances.[15] On June 15, 2020, the FDA revoked the EUA on the basis of these data.

Convalescent plasma presents an even more troubling story. On April 3, 2020, the FDA permitted the use of convalescent plasma in clinical trials as an Investigational New Drug and immediately launched a nationwide EA program. Under the program, patients anywhere in the United States could receive convalescent plasma

---

[13] Jacob S. Sherkow, Regulatory Sandboxes and the Public Health, 2022 *U. Ill. L. Rev.* 357.

[14] Lara Bull-Otterson et al., Hydroxychloroquine and Chloroquine Prescribing Patterns by Provider Specialty Following Initial Reports of Potential Benefit for COVID-19 Treatment—United States, January–June 2020, 69 *Morbidity & Mortality Wkly. Rep.* 1210 (2020).

[15] Caleb P. Skipper et al., Hydroxychloroquine in Nonhospitalized Adults with Early COVID-19: A Randomized Trial, 173 *Ann. Intern. Med.* 623 (2020); The RECOVERY Collaborative Grp., Effect of Hydroxychloroquine in Hospitalized Patients with COVID-19, 383 *New Eng. J. Med.* 2030 (2020).

through the Mayo Clinic without participating in clinical trials.[16] Unsurprisingly, faced with the choice between participating in a clinical trial – and running the risk of receiving a placebo – or definitely receiving convalescent plasma, patients overwhelmingly participated in the EA program. Accordingly, randomized controlled trials floundered as they were unable to enroll enough patients, and the efficacy of convalescent plasma remained unvalidated for months.[17] Despite this, in August 2020, on the basis of weak observational evidence – and under substantial pressure from President Trump – the FDA issued an EUA for convalescent plasma.[18] Evidence remains minimal and mixed; several studies found no significant benefit from plasma,[19] though one study published in January 2021 found positive effects for plasma when it was administered very early in the course of infection.[20] In February 2021, the FDA narrowed the EUA for convalescent plasma based on evidence that it was useful only in limited circumstances.[21]

B *Planning for Adequate Data Collection After Approval or Authorization*

The tension between speed and evidence in FDA approvals is not new.[22] For some time now, the needle-threading solution has been to pair various forms of faster access with commitments to generate information after access has already begun.[23] The COVID-19 pandemic and its stumbles along this path cast this strategy into a harsher light. In emergency contexts, policymakers should ensure that the FDA is considering the impact of its access decisions – whether an EUA, an EA program, or something else – on the ability to generate high-quality clinical trial data to confirm or reject preliminary evidence of safety and efficacy. Although some emergencies may end before such high-quality data are ever generated – witness the short-lived Middle East Respiratory Syndrome outbreak of 2012 – policymakers should not assume such a flameout.

---

[16] Coronavirus (COVID-19) Update: FDA Coordinates National Effort to Develop Blood-Related Therapies for COVID-19, Food & Drug Admin. (Apr. 3, 2020), www.fda.gov/news-events/press-announcements/coronavirus-covid-19-update-fda-coordinates-national-effort-develop-blood-related-therapies-covid-19.

[17] Katie Thomas & Noah Weiland, As Trump Praises Plasma, Researchers Struggle to Finish Critical Studies, NY Times (Aug. 4, 2020), www.nytimes.com/2020/08/04/health/trump-plasma.html.

[18] Rachel E. Sachs, Understanding the FDA's Controversial Convalescent Plasma Authorization, Health Affs. Blog (Aug. 27, 2020), www.healthaffairs.org/do/10.1377/hblog20200827.190308/full/.

[19] Louis M. Katz, (A Little) Clarity on Convalescent Plasma for COVID-19, 384 *New Eng. J. Med.* 666 (2021).

[20] Romina Libster et al., Early High-Titer Plasma Therapy to Prevent Severe COVID-19 in Older Adults, 348 *New Eng. J. Med.* 610 (2021).

[21] FDA Updates Emergency Use Authorization for COVID-19 Convalescent Plasma to Reflect New Data, Food & Drug Admin. (Feb. 4, 2021), www.fda.gov/news-events/fda-brief/fda-brief-fda-updates-emergency-use-authorization-covid-19-convalescent-plasma-reflect-new-data.

[22] FDA in the Twenty-First Century, pt. IV (Holly Fernandez Lynch & I. Glenn Cohen, eds. 2015).

[23] W. Nicholson Price II, Drug Approval in a Learning Health System, 102 *Minn. L. Rev.* 2413 (2018).

Problematic incentives hamper both the generation and the use of post-market information generally. For traditional biopharmaceutical products made by a single manufacturer charging supra-competitive prices, incentives to generate costly information on safety and effectiveness are sharply lowered once the product can be sold. Additional positive information on safety or efficacy in subpopulations is realistically unlikely to lead to greater sales. Negative information, meanwhile, could lead to problems, lawsuits, or even withdrawal from the market. These structural problems loom larger in emergencies where products are allowed on the market with less evidence in the first place.

On the use side, the FDA has historically faced difficulty acting on negative post-market information.[24] Patient groups exert substantial pressure against withdrawing drugs from the market. And in the case of EUAs for a second use of an existing product, such as hydroxychloroquine, withdrawing an EUA does not even remove the product from the market. Doctors remain free to prescribe the product off-label.

At least two potential avenues exist to improve the generation of post-market information, especially in emergencies. The first, and most straightforward, is a simple mandate. The agency should release clear statements about what circumstances will lead EUAs to be expanded, revoked, or modified. Such statements should include not only triggers for what evidence will lead to what result (e.g., certain efficacy signals leading to expansion, or certain safety signals leading to revocation), but also how much evidence must be generated.[25]

Unfortunately, such mandates work much better for products with a single, identified manufacturer. The Moderna and BioNTech-Pfizer vaccines fit neatly into this category; the companies have incentives to ensure that the vaccines remain on the market and are actually approved rather than just authorized, with the difference impacting reimbursement and potentially vaccination mandates. For products made by many entities, such as hydroxychloroquine (generic manufacturers) or convalescent plasma (hospitals), incentives are diffuse and a mandate would not have a clear focus. It is hard to see whose behavior would change had the FDA made the convalescent plasma EA program or EUA conditional on the timely generation of high-quality clinical trial data. Data on convalescent plasma were limited by the lack of interested research participants (as several clinical trials closed due to inadequate enrollment), not a lack of clarity or incentive regarding the scope of their EUAs.

Second, government investment could make information generation less costly so that incentives to generate information do not need to be as strong. Research grants can support the costs of pandemic-focused clinical trials, for instance – a

---

[24] US Gov't Accountability Off., Drug Safety: Improvement Needed in FDA's Postmarket Decision-making and Oversight Process 5 (2006).
[25] Sherkow, supra note 13, at 40–41.

non-excludable knowledge good when conducted on already marketed products or generic drugs.[26] But, as noted, trials must also be able to enroll sufficient patients, something that can be aided with government coordination.[27] Reducing the costs of generating higher-quality observational data could also help. Although observational data are typically less dispositive than randomized controlled trial data, learning health systems that systematically collect large amounts of data can help fill evidentiary gaps, particularly in pandemic emergencies when controlled studies must compete for finite patients over short time horizons. Infrastructure for the ongoing collection of such data could help reduce the information problem of rapidly authorized therapeutics. Finally, policymakers could facilitate the use of intermediate protocols that are less costly than patient-level randomization but generate better data than observational studies, such as randomization at the hospital or county level.

Sometimes, though, the tension between the need for high-quality data and the need for broad, early access to novel therapeutics may be irreconcilable. Indeed, for COVID-19 vaccines, the FDA seems to have reached exactly this conclusion, announcing EUA standards in the summer of 2020 that foreclosed the possibility of early access based on the typical relaxed EUA data standard. While policymakers can improve the generation of post-market data, sometimes the best answer is to do it right the first time.

IV REWARDING VACCINES FOR DISEASES WITH PANDEMIC POTENTIAL

Vaccine development in the United States is rife with both political and market failures.[28] But in the COVID-19 context, the record-breaking speed of vaccine development has been the biggest success story. Most notably, policymakers aggressively implemented several reward structures to advance the development and dissemination of new vaccines. Unfortunately, SARS-CoV-2 will not be the last devastating infectious disease, so it is worth considering how the approaches used in this context can be applied more broadly.

---

[26] Lisa Larrimore Ouellette et al., Nonexcludable Innovations and COVID-19, Written Description (May 27, 2020), https://writtendescription.blogspot.com/2020/05/nonexcludable-innovations-and-covid-19.html; Amy Kapczynski & Talha Syed, The Continuum of Excludability and the Limits of Patents, 122 *Yale L. J.* 1900 (2013).

[27] Michelle N. Meyer et al., An Ethics Framework for Consolidating and Prioritizing COVID-19 Clinical Trials, 18 *Clinical Trials* 226 (2021).

[28] Daniel J. Hemel & Lisa Larrimore Ouellette, Valuing Medical Innovation, 75 *Stan. L. Rev.* 517 (2023) Michael Kremer & Christopher M. Snyder, Preventatives Versus Treatments, 130 *Q. J. Econ.* 1167 (2015); Ana Santos Rutschman, The Vaccine Race in the 21st Century, 61 *Ariz. L. Rev.* 729 (2019); Q. Claire Xue & Lisa Larrimore Ouellette, Innovation Policy and the Market for Vaccines, 7 *J. L. Biosciences* (2020).

A *COVID-19 Vaccines at Warp Speed*

Effective COVID-19 vaccines reached the public with record-breaking speed. Less than a year after China announced that an outbreak in Wuhan was caused by a novel coronavirus in January 2020, the FDA issued EUAs for the first two vaccines, from BioNTech-Pfizer (on December 11) and Moderna (on December 18). By contrast, the development of most vaccines takes over a decade, while the prior record was four years (for mumps).

How were COVID-19 vaccines developed so quickly? Part of the story is getting lucky with science: researchers were able to build on years of work on the novel mRNA platform that supported both the BioNTech-Pfizer and Moderna vaccines. Part of the story is effective FDA regulation: clinical trials were allowed to proceed more quickly than usual, and the agency set clear approval standards in advance so that companies had certainty about what would be required for authorization.[29] But perhaps the most important part of the story is that governments committed substantial public resources to the effort.

In a reverse of typical funding patterns, public funding of COVID-19 vaccines focused more on covering the final stages of development and manufacturing costs, building on substantial private investments in early-stage research.[30] Both Massachusetts-based Moderna and German-based BioNTech did receive some government and non-profit funding for developing their mRNA platforms pre-pandemic, but from 2017 through 2019, grants constituted less than 4 percent of Moderna's $1.4 billion in R&D expenses and less than 2 percent of the €450 million spent by BioNTech. By the end of 2019, each firm had been working on mRNA technology for about a decade and had incurred net losses every year, with accumulated losses of $1.5 billion for Moderna and €425 million for BioNTech. But because of these investments, both startups could quickly pivot to applying their platform to COVID-19.

In Moderna's case, a key partner was the NIH, which launched the first human clinical trial on March 16. The following day, BioNTech announced a collaboration with pharmaceutical giant Pfizer, and they launched their own human trial on April 23. In April, Moderna received $483 million from the Defense Department's Biological Advanced Research and Development Authority to support clinical trials and manufacturing; this was later increased to a maximum of $955 million. In May, the firm raised $1.3 billion in private equity to help contract with additional manufacturers. BioNTech funded development through both Pfizer's large cash reserves and a €375 million grant from the German government. The primary goal of this funding

[29] Rachel Sachs et al., How Will the FDA's New COVID-19 Vaccine Guidance Affect Development Efforts?, Written Description (July 10, 2020), https://writtendescription.blogspot.com/2020/07/how-will-fdas-new-covid-19-vaccine.html.

[30] Moderna, Inc., Annual Report (Form 10-K) (Feb. 27, 2020), www.sec.gov/Archives/edgar/data/1682852/000168285220000006/moderna10-k12312019.htm; BioNTech SE, Annual Report (Form 20-F) (Mar. 31, 2020), https://investors.biontech.de/node/7381/html.

was to reduce developers' risks so that steps that usually would depend on the success of earlier stages – such as building manufacturing capacity – could proceed in parallel.

Another critical source of funding for COVID-19 vaccine development was from governments committing to purchase vaccines before clinical trials were completed. In the United States, this effort was coordinated through Operation Warp Speed (OWS), a multi-agency effort primarily run through HHS and the Department of Defense. By mid-August, OWS had already committed to purchasing 800 million doses from six developers if those vaccines ultimately proved effective, including 100 million doses from Moderna (for milestone payments up to $1.5 billion), and 100 million doses from BioNTech-Pfizer (for $1.95 billion).[31] These pre-commitments were both an effective spur to innovation and a form of "vaccine nationalism" that secured early US access to the resulting products, at the expense of other nations.[32] The Biden Administration continued to increase its purchases of vaccines from both BioNTech-Pfizer and Moderna even after the vaccines' authorization, including hundreds of millions of doses for both domestic boosters and global distribution.

Advance vaccine purchases were not completely novel: a 2007 $1.5 billion advance market commitment for pneumococcal disease vaccine doses had been used to spur development and dissemination, resulting in the immunization of over 150 million children in low-income countries.[33] And guaranteeing or increasing reimbursement through health insurance functions as a similar pull incentive for innovation.[34] Indeed, the first empirical study showing that policies to expand health care use can increase R&D was in the vaccine context.[35] But as a whole-of-government push for vaccine development and dissemination, OWS was relatively novel.

Although OWS largely succeeded in getting vaccines through FDA authorization in record-breaking time, vaccines are not vaccinations, and the initial US rollout of the vaccines was tragically slow. Vaccine distribution initially received insufficient attention from the federal government, either in terms of resources or coordination.[36]

---

[31] Jacob S. Sherkow et al., Multi-Agency Funding for COVID-19 Vaccine Development, Written Description (Aug. 19, 2020), https://writtendescription.blogspot.com/2020/08/multi-agency-funding-for-covid-19.html.

[32] Nicholson Price et al., Are COVID-19 Vaccine Advance Purchases a Form of Vaccine Nationalism, an Effective Spur to Innovation, or Something in Between?, Written Description (Aug. 5, 2020), https://writtendescription.blogspot.com/2020/08/are-covid-19-vaccine-advance-purchases.html.

[33] Michael Kremer et al., Advance Market Commitments: Insights from Theory and Experience, 110 *AEA Papers & Proc.* 269 (2020); Daniel Hemel & Lisa Larrimore Ouellette, Want a Coronavirus Vaccine, Fast? Here's a Solution, Time (Mar. 4, 2020), https://time.com/5795013/coronavirus-vaccine-prize-challenge.

[34] Rachel E. Sachs, Prizing Insurance: Prescription Drug Insurance as Innovation Incentive, 30 *Harv. J. L. Tech.* 153 (2016); Mark A. Lemley, Lisa Larrimore Ouellette & Rachel E. Sachs, The Medicare Innovation Subsidy, 95 *N.Y.U. L. Rev.* 75 (2020).

[35] Amy Finkelstein, Static and Dynamic Effects of Health Policy: Evidence from the Vaccine Industry, 119 *Q. J. Econ.* 527 (2004).

[36] Lisa Larrimore Ouellette et al., What Can Policymakers Learn from the Disastrously Slow COVID-19 Vaccine Rollout?, Written Description (Jan. 12, 2021), https://writtendescription.blogspot.com/2021/01/what-can-policymakers-learn-from.html.

Even after COVID-19 vaccines became widely available in the United States, vaccine hesitancy limited uptake domestically. And internationally, vaccine inequity remains a global tragedy: one year after vaccines became available, less than 1 percent of doses had been administered in low-income countries.

B *Vaccines for the Next Pandemic*

Part of the reason the COVID-19 pandemic wrought as much devastation as it did was inadequate preparation, including "insufficient R&D investment and planning for innovative vaccine development and manufacture."[37] Properly rewarding vaccine developers and distributors during the COVID-19 pandemic is important not only for controlling this pandemic, but also for being better prepared for the next one.

Most importantly, policymakers should work to increase public funding for vaccine R&D and to increase incentives for private funding. Research on vaccines for diseases with pandemic potential has enormous social value; ideally, R&D investments should be made up to the point that the marginal social benefit equals the marginal cost. But the vaccine sector has been beset by both political and market failures. Market incentives are insufficient because vaccines are preventatives and because individual prices do not account for societal benefits, such as herd immunity; political incentives are insufficient because payoffs from these investments span electoral cycles, and voters do not pay much attention to problems that were successfully averted.[38]

Even with the mobilization of public funding during COVID-19, the all-in prices paid by the United States to Moderna and to BioNTech-Pfizer are only a small fraction of a low-end estimate of their vaccines' social value.[39] But hopefully these rewards for the firms' private investments and the salience of the costs of an unchecked pandemic will help spur greater private and public investment going forward.

Additionally, we hope that academics, patient advocates, and politicians can use the COVID-19 experience to broaden conventional understandings of the policy playbook for promoting access to medicines. The importance of widespread access to COVID-19 vaccines led some commentators to argue for limits on profits and patent rights for vaccine developers; for example, both Moderna and BioNTech-Pfizer were criticized for rejecting calls to sell their vaccines for no profit. But out-of-pocket costs paid by patients represent an entirely separate question from financial

---

[37] Global Preparedness Monitoring Bd., A World at Risk: Annual Report on Global Preparedness for Health Emergencies 6, 28 (2019), www.gpmb.org/annual-reports/annual-report-2019.

[38] Hemel & Ouellette, supra note 28.

[39] Carsten Fink, Calculating Private and Social Returns to COVID-19 Vaccine Innovation (WIPO Economic Research Working Paper No. 68, 2022), www.wipo.int/publications/en/details.jsp?id=4595.

rewards for developers.[40] Vaccines can be free to patients even if developers receive enormous financial rewards, and access-to-medicines advocates should look for policies that reduce patient costs while still aligning profits with social value.

Even if policymakers recognize that social value is the right lodestar for R&D spending, numerous questions remain about optimal innovation policy design. How should rewards be divided between competing vaccine developers? Between developers and distributors? Who should estimate value? Could more vaccine development or distribution be conducted in-house by the federal government? Many of these questions parallel ones that legal scholars have long grappled with in the patent law context. But for vaccines, rewards are substantially shaped by government decisions on issues such as direct R&D funding, coverage requirements, and market subsidies, requiring these questions to be considered anew.

The critical role of government health agencies in vaccine innovation is a challenge, but it is also an opportunity. COVID-19 has led to an outpouring of scholarship on how to improve vaccine incentives.[41] Now the United States needs the political will to make it happen.

V CONCLUSION

The triumphs and sorrows of the COVID-19 pandemic in the United States ultimately have significant roots in innovation policy. A lack of agency coordination and cooperation regarding diagnostics delayed the country's ability to identify where the virus was spreading. A rush to questionable therapeutics – by enthusiasm, by demand, by political pressure – without developing robust information about their safety and efficacy hampered providers' ability to treat patients. And even while the creation of COVID-19 vaccines was a success story – thanks to advances in science, market incentives, and luck – the failure to rapidly deploy them when the virus was at its peak was a tragedy.

The COVID-19 pandemic has been a truly exceptional event: a rapidly spreading, deadly disease plagued by the failures of political administration and exacerbated by a diminishing trust in science. But pandemics and social failures have long been part of the fabric of history, from the Plague of Athens following the Peloponnesian War to now. New pandemics will emerge, and in less than ideal political circumstances. Innovation policymakers should take lessons from this crisis to guard against history repeating itself.

[40] Daniel J. Hemel & Lisa Larrimore Ouellette, Innovation Policy Pluralism, 128 *Yale L. J.* 544 (2019); Daniel Hemel & Lisa Larrimore Ouellette, Pharmaceutical Profits and Public Health Are Not Incompatible, NY Times (Apr. 8, 2020), www.nytimes.com/2020/04/08/opinion/coronavirus-drug-company-profits.html.
[41] Amrita Ahuja et al., Preparing for a Pandemic: Accelerating Vaccine Availability, 111 *AEA Papers & Proc.* 331 (2021); Matthew Goodkin-Gold et al., Optimal Vaccine Subsidies for Endemic Diseases, 84 *Int'l J. Indus. Org.* 102840 (2022).

16

Addressing Exclusivity Issues: COVID-19 and Beyond

Michael S. Sinha, Sven J.R. Bostyn, and Timo Minssen[*]

I INTRODUCTION

Almost every aspect of the COVID-19 response, from vaccines, diagnostics, and therapeutics to medical equipment, tracking systems, software, and other innovations, are or will become subject to some form of exclusive rights.[1] Many of these involve intellectual property rights (IPRs).[2] By offering innovators the exclusive right to exploit their innovations while recouping research and development (R&D) costs and other expenditures, IPRs may incentivize the development of new technologies.[3] But IPRs may also preclude others from important research, manufacturing, and distribution.[4] In the same vein, these exclusionary rights allow right holders to set prices in the absence of competition. Since this may limit access to innovations that are crucial for tackling pandemics, IPRs are a key factor in pandemic response and preparedness.

Consequently, IPRs have generated much controversy around the globe. Many of these debates have focused on traditional IPRs, particularly patent rights. Numerous existing patent claims cover new chemical or molecular entities. Patents are also filed for repurposed drugs and vaccine platforms (e.g., COVID-19 mRNA platforms), with separate patent protection for the vaccine and its elements, including viral particles, adjuvants, and vaccine boosters. Even in situations where no patent

---

[*] This work was supported by a Novo Nordisk Foundation grant for a scientifically independent collaborative research program in biomedical innovation law (grant number NNF17SA0027784).

[1] Frank Tietze et al., Crisis-Critical Intellectual Property: Findings From the COVID-19 Pandemic, Inst. of Elec. & Elecs. Eng'rs Transactions Eng'g Mgmt. (2020), https://ieeexplore.ieee.org/stamp/stamp.jsp?tp=&arnumber=9120047; see also Cynthia Liu et al., Research and Development on Therapeutic Agents and Vaccines for COVID-19 and Related Human Coronavirus Diseases, 6 ACS Central Sci. 315 (2020); Sven J.R. Bostyn, Access to Therapeutics and Vaccines in Times of Health Pandemics: How Exclusivity Rights Can Affect Such Access and What We Can Do About It, 2020 Intell. Prop. Q. 227-70 (2020).

[2] Intellectual property rights include patents, copyrights, and similar forms of legal protection, such as trade secrets.

[3] Jorge L. Contreras et al., Pledging Intellectual Property for COVID-19, 38 Nat. Biotechnol. 1146 (2020).

[4] Id.

protection is available, many COVID-19 therapeutics and vaccines will also obtain regulatory, data, and market exclusivities.

Consequently, the design and application of regulatory exclusivities have become increasingly important in general innovation policy debates.[5] This chapter addresses exclusivity issues, with a particular emphasis on regulatory exclusivities for vaccines and therapeutics. We begin with a basic overview of the current regulatory exclusivity landscape in Europe and the United States, followed by a discussion of current developments in COVID-19 vaccines and therapeutics. Next, we describe the influence of these technological developments on debates surrounding regulatory exclusivities while describing their relationship to other forms of exclusivities. From these assessments, we draw some lessons for market exclusivity, innovation, and access during the COVID-19 pandemic and beyond.

II CURRENT REGULATORY EXCLUSIVITY LANDSCAPE

A *Two Forms of Exclusivity*

Two forms of exclusivity are particularly relevant to the treatment and prevention of pandemics: patent and regulatory. In the European and US systems of regulatory exclusivity, data and marketing exclusivities do not depend on patents but are often cumulative with patent protection.[6]

1 Europe

Patents in Europe last twenty years from the date of filing. Patent-like protection can be sustained beyond twenty years by a Supplementary Protection Certificate (SPC),[7] which compensates for regulatory approval procedures by adding a maximum of five years to the patent term. Six additional months of SPC extension can be obtained for conducting studies in compliance with a pediatric investigation plan.[8] SPCs apply only to patent-protected products and cannot be added to regulatory exclusivities.

European legislation also offers patent-independent regulatory exclusivity under the 8+2+1 principle for both small molecule drugs and biologics such as vaccines.[9]

---

[5] See, generally, Timo Minssen, Assessing the Inventiveness of Bio-Pharmaceuticals under European and US Patent Law at 7, 315, 321, 323–24 (Nov. 16, 2012) (Ph.D. dissertation, Lund University Faculty of Law) (on file with author).

[6] Sven J.R. Bostyn et al., Effects of Supplementary Protection Mechanisms for Pharmaceutical Products, Technopolis Grp. 61, 61–73 (May 2018), www.technopolis-group.com/report/effects-of-supplementary-protection-mechanisms-for-pharmaceutical-products/; see also Directive 2001/83, of the European Parliament and of the Council of Nov. 6, 2001 on the Community Code Relating to Medicinal Products for Human Use, art. 10(1) (hereinafter, Directive 2001/83/EC).

[7] Council Regulation 469/2009 of May 6, 2009, Supplementary Protection Certificates for Medicinal Products.

[8] Id. at art. 13(3); see also Bostyn et al., supra note 6, at 30–60.

[9] Directive 2001/83/EC, supra note 6.

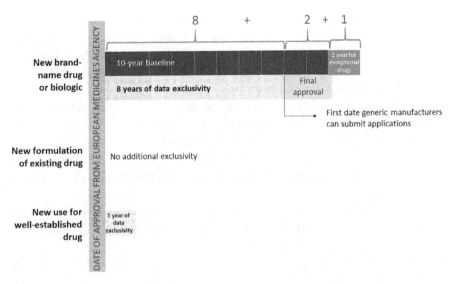

FIGURE 16.1 MA process in Europe

Once approved, a drug obtains automatic data protection for eight years, provided it is the first marketing authorization (MA) for that active ingredient in Europe. During this period, no third party can refer to the data in the regulatory dossier of the reference medicinal product, including competitors seeking to file an abridged generic application. An approved drug also receives ten years of marketing exclusivity starting from the date of approval, protecting the reference product against market entry by third parties during the term. There are also three options for obtaining one additional year of exclusivity.[10] The various types of exclusivities available in Europe are illustrated in Figure 16.1.

This Global Marketing Authorization is issued only once for a given drug product and cannot be renewed or extended for any additional strengths, forms, routes of administration, or presentations, or for any future variations and extensions.[11] Subsets of genetic profiles requiring specific treatment for COVID-19 might lead to the development of drugs for which orphan designation and MA can be obtained.[12]

In Europe, there are three main categories for obtaining an MA: central, decentralized, and mutual recognition procedure. For biologics, including vaccines, and new

---

[10] Id. One additional year of marketing exclusivity may be granted for new therapeutic indications showing significant clinical benefit in comparison with existing therapies (art. 10(1), para. 4); one year of data protection for new indications of well-established substances (art. 10(5)); and one year of protection for data supporting a change of classification (e.g., from prescription drug to over-the-counter) (art 74a). These additional terms of exclusivity are not cumulative, so the total duration of protection cannot exceed eleven years.

[11] Id., art. 6(1), para 2; see also Bostyn et al., supra note 6, at 65.

[12] Ten years of marketing exclusivity is awarded for orphan drugs; see Council Regulation 141/2000 of Dec. 16, 1999, Orphan Medicinal Products, art. 8.

small molecules for viral diseases, the central procedure at the European Medicines Agency (EMA) must be followed.[13] For new indications for already existing small molecules, the decentralized and mutual recognition procedure can be followed.

The main categories of MAs are full and conditional.[14] To date, COVID-19 vaccines and therapeutics have all been issued conditional MAs, which are applied to products aimed at treating, preventing, or diagnosing seriously debilitating or life-threatening diseases. Other medicinal products falling within the scope of the regulations are orphan drugs and medicinal products to be used in emergency situations, in response to public health threats recognized either by the World Health Organization (WHO) or by the European Community in the framework of Decision No. 2119/98/EC.[15]

Conditional MAs may be granted in emergency situations if the EMA Committee for Medicinal Products for Human Use finds that all the following requirements are met: (1) the benefit–risk balance of the product is positive; (2) it is likely that the applicant will be able to provide comprehensive data; (3) unmet medical needs will be fulfilled; and (4) the benefit to public health of the medicinal product's immediate availability on the market outweighs the risks due to need for further data.[16]

2 United States

In the United States, the Patent Act, the Hatch-Waxman Act, and related legislation defines marketing exclusivity periods for pharmaceuticals and biologics.[17] Patent protection for pharmaceutical products in the United States is comparable to that of Europe: twenty years of patent protection, with a patent term restoration period of up to five years for time spent during the regulatory process, and a pediatric exclusivity period of six months for certain drugs studied in pediatric populations pursuant to a written request.[18]

Regulatory exclusivity for new drug application (NDA) applicants exists as a five-year New Chemical Entity exclusivity, a three-year new clinical investigation exclusivity, a seven-year orphan drug exclusivity under the Orphan Drug Act,

---

[13] Council Regulation 726/2004 of Mar. 31, 2004, Community Procedures for the Authorization and Supervision of Medicinal Products for Human and Veterinary Use and Establishing a European Medicines Agency, art. 3(1), annex.

[14] Commission Regulation No 507/2006 of Mar. 29, 2006, Conditional Marketing Authorization for Medicinal Products for Human Use Falling within the Scope of Regulation (EC) No. 726/2004 of the European Parliament and of the Council.

[15] Id., art. 2.

[16] Id., art. 4.

[17] Aaron S. Kesselheim, Michael S. Sinha & Jerry Avorn, Determinants of Market Exclusivity for Prescription Drugs in the United States, 177 JAMA Intern. Med. 1658, 1658 (2017).

[18] Id.; see also Michael S. Sinha et al., Labeling Changes and Costs for Clinical Trials Performed Under the US Food and Drug Administration Pediatric Exclusivity Extension, 2007 to 2012, 178 JAMA Intern. Med. 1458, 1458 (2018).

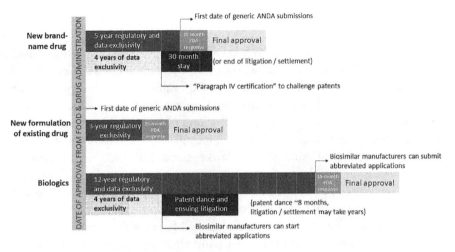

FIGURE 16.2 MA process in the United States

or a twelve-year biologic exclusivity under the Biologics Price Competition and Innovation Act.[19] There is no comparable process of conditional approval.

For new chemical entities, data exclusivity extends for five years as well, though generic manufacturers can begin utilizing originator data after four years for the preparation of generic drug applications. Unlike in Europe, the United States does offer three-year periods of exclusivity for new formulations of existing drugs, though no data exclusivity applies. For biologics, data exclusivity protections run for twelve years, but biosimilar manufacturers can begin using data after the fourth year to develop competing products.[20] Review time by the FDA for generic products is approximately fifteen months. Drugs and vaccines for COVID-19 were evaluated through a relatively new regulatory process known as Emergency Use Authorization (EUA).

EUAs are a byproduct of several post-9/11 laws, including the Project Bioshield Act of 2004 and the Pandemic and All-Hazards Preparedness Act of 2013. When invoked during a public health emergency such as COVID-19, an EUA permits broad use of unlicensed products as long as the benefits outweigh risks.[21] The particulars of available regulatory exclusivities under US law are illustrated in Figure 16.2.

[19] Drug Price Competition and Patent Term Restoration Act of 1984, Pub. L. No. 98-417, 98 Stat. 1585 (codified as amended in scattered sections of 21 U.S.C.); Orphan Drug Act of 1983, Pub L. No. 97-414, 96 Stat. 2049 (codified as amended in scattered sections of 21 U.S.C., 26 U.S.C., and 42 U.S.C.); Patient Protection and Affordable Care Act, Pub. L. No. 111-148, 124 Stat. 119 (2010) (codified as amended in scattered sections of 26 U.S.C. and 42 U.S.C.).

[20] See Timo Minssen & Justin Pierce, Big Data and Intellectual Property Rights in the Health and Life Sciences, in Big Data, Health Law, and Bioethics 311 (I. Glenn Cohen et al., eds., 1st ed. 2018).

[21] See Food & Drug Admin., Guidance Document: Emergency Use Authorization of Medical Products and Related Authorities (Jan. 2017), www.fda.gov/regulatory-information/search-fda-guidance-documents/emergency-use-authorization-medical-products-and-related-authorities.

B COVID-19 Vaccines

Pandemics create a time pressure to develop vaccines as quickly as possible, which concentrates the cost of development over a very short time window. Given the crippling effects of pandemics on the economy and health care systems, governments are often extremely willing to commit capital to accelerate vaccine development. Government funding will typically be in the form of push incentives (e.g., funding R&D in developing new vaccines) and pull incentives (e.g., in the form of advance purchase agreements or other advance market commitments).[22] Yet the exclusive rights structure after regulatory clearance or approval remains unchanged, and final vaccines are fully owned by pharmaceutical companies, even those developed with significant government funding and collaboration.

In Europe, the European Commission joined forces with several countries to collect research funding under the Coronavirus Global Response, which strives for "universal access to affordable coronavirus vaccination, treatment[,] and testing,"[23] as part of the WHO's global call for action.[24] In the United States, investment in vaccine development largely occurred through a federal initiative known as Operation Warp Speed, though execution was largely in conjunction with federal agencies such as the National Institutes of Health. Agencies within the Department of Defense, including the Biomedical Advanced Research and Development Authority and the Defense Advanced Research Projects Agency, have historically been involved in vaccine development as well; the former agency contributed nearly $6 billion each to the Pfizer and Moderna COVID-19 mRNA vaccines.[25]

Vaccine R&D over the last few decades has largely occurred within small and medium-sized companies.[26] Therefore, pushing vaccine candidates through clinical trials and scaling up production is often dependent on additional federal funding or acquisition by larger firms; between 1990 and 2012, small and medium-sized

[22] Rachel Sachs, Lisa Larrimore Ouellette, W. Nicholson Price II & Jacob S. Sherkow, Innovation Law and COVID-19: Promoting Incentives and Access for New Health Case Technologies (Chapter 15 in this book).

[23] Participating countries include Canada, France, Germany, Italy, Japan, Saudi Arabia, Norway, Spain, and the United Kingdom. The United States declined to participate.

[24] See World Health Org., Coronavirus Global Response (2020), https://global-response.europa.eu/index_en. Around €16 billion have been pledged, with €15 billion coming from EU member states. Funding recipients include the Coalition for Epidemic Preparedness Innovation, for vaccines; Gavi, the Vaccine Alliance, for vaccine deployment (related to coronavirus); Therapeutics Accelerator, for therapeutics; UNITAID, for therapeutics deployment; the Foundation for Innovative New Diagnostics, for diagnostics; the Global Fund, for diagnostics deployment; and the WHO, for health systems.

[25] Michael S. Sinha et al., Expansion of the Priority Review Voucher Program under the 21st Century Cures Act: Implications for Innovation and Public Health, 44 *Am. J. Law Med.* 329, 329 (2018); see also US Cong. Budget Off., Research and Development in the Pharmaceutical Industry (Apr. 2021), www.cbo.gov/file-download/download/private/161984.

[26] Thomas J. Hwang & Aaron S. Kesselheim, Vaccine Pipeline Has Grown During The Past Two Decades With More Early-Stage Trials From Small And Medium-Size Companies, 35 *Health Affs.* (Millwood) 219, 219 (2016).

companies accounted for 71 percent of Phase I vaccine trials but only 38 percent of Phase III trials.[27] Many products will languish if funding runs dry or large vaccine manufacturers decline to conduct further studies or pursue an MA. For emerging infectious diseases, this has historically been termed the "valley of death." Even with an urgent push to develop a vaccine – as was the case with the Ebola epidemic – waning interest in the face of a geographically limited outbreak can result in the shelving of important projects prior to clinical testing and approval.[28]

To date, this has not been the story of COVID-19 vaccines. Global R&D efforts and advance market commitments have yielded several promising vaccines, but the issue of exclusive rights has unfortunately been pushed aside. Apart from the fact that the vaccine itself is subject to patent protection and/or regulatory exclusivities, many of the COVID-19 vaccines are based on proprietary platforms. Moderna has a large patent portfolio covering their mRNA vaccine platform, boasting on its website that it "has been granted over 100 patents in the [United States], Europe, Japan[,] and other jurisdictions, protecting fundamental inventions in the mRNA therapeutics space, with several hundred additional pending patent applications covering key advances in the field."[29] Similar patent libraries protect the Pfizer/BioNTech and CureVac mRNA platforms, to the extent that "Moderna, CureVac, BioNTech[,] and GSK collectively own nearly half of the mRNA vaccine patent applications."[30] Trade secrets will also play an important role when it comes to vaccine manufacturing methods.[31] See Table 16.1 for more about COVID-19 vaccines in use and in development.

Focusing on regulatory exclusivities, we can discern different dynamics in Europe and the United States. All vaccines, as new biological products, will be able to benefit from regulatory exclusivities. In Europe, all vaccines approved have received conditional market approval; the regulatory exclusivity period of 8+2 years starts running immediately. In the United States, the vaccines that have currently received an EUA follow a different regulatory path.[32] A Biologics Licensing Application (BLA) would secure permanent regulatory approval of the vaccine by the FDA, but EUAs are temporary and typically expire once the public health emergency ends.[33]

---

[27] Id.

[28] Denise Grady, Ebola Vaccine, Ready for Test, Sat on the Shelf, NY Times (Oct. 23, 2014), www.nytimes.com/2014/10/24/health/without-lucrative-market-potential-ebola-vaccine-was-shelved-for-years.html.

[29] Moderna's Intellectual Property, www.modernatx.com/mrna-technology/modernas-intellectual-property.

[30] See Cecilia Martin & Drew Lowery, mRNA Vaccines: Intellectual Property Landscape, 19 *Nature Rev. Drug Disc.* 578, 578 (2020).

[31] W. Nicholson Price II & Arti K. Rai, How Logically Impossible Patents Block Biosimilars, 37 *Nat. Biotechnol.* 862, 862 (2019).

[32] US Food & Drug Admin., COVID-19 Vaccines, www.fda.gov/emergency-preparedness-and-response/coronavirus-disease-2019-covid-19/covid-19-vaccines.

[33] See Food & Drug Admin., supra note 21.

TABLE 16.1 *Regulatory status and launch prices of COVID-19 vaccines*[34]

Manufacturer	Product Name	Product Type	Dosing Regimen	Approval Status (EU)	Launch Price per Dose (EU)	Approval Status (US)	Launch Price per Dose (US)
Pfizer/ BioNTech	Comirnaty	mRNA (modified nucleoside)	2 doses 3 weeks apart	Conditional approval 12/21/2020	€12	Full approval 8/23/2021	$19.50
Moderna	Spikevax	mRNA (modified nucleoside)	2 doses 4 weeks apart	Conditional approval 1/6/2021	€15	Full approval 1/31/2022	$15
Oxford/ AstraZeneca	Vaxzevria/ Covishield	Viral vector	2 doses 4 to 12 weeks apart	Conditional approval 1/29/2021	£1.61	To be determined	$3–4
J&J/Janssen	Janssen COVID-19 Vaccine	Viral vector	1 dose	Conditional approval 3/11/2021	£6.30	EUA 2/27/2021	$10
Novavax	NVX-CoV2373	Protein subunit	2 doses 3 weeks apart	Conditional approval 12/20/2021	€17.80	EUA 7/13/2022	$16
Sanofi/GSK					€7.56	To be determined	$10.50

[34] EU Prices: Sarah Boseley, Belgian Minister Tweets EU's COVID Vaccine Price List to Anger of Manufacturers, Guardian (Dec. 18, 2020), www.theguardian.com/world/2020/dec/18/belgian-minister-accidentally-tweets-eus-covid-vaccine-price-list; US Prices: Owen Dyer, COVID-19: Countries are Learning What Others Paid for Vaccines, 372 *Brit. Med. J.* n.281 (2021); see also C. Buddy Creech et al., SARS-CoV-2 Vaccines, 325 *J. Am. Med. Ass'n.* 1318, 1319 (2021) (data updated as of July 20, 2022).

Importantly, EUAs do not trigger the beginning of regulatory exclusivity windows, meaning that the Moderna and Pfizer vaccines, which have been distributed to hundreds of millions of Americans, received their full twelve-year marketing and data exclusivity periods only after BLA approval. When it developed statutory provisions granting regulatory exclusivity, Congress likely did not anticipate a scenario in which millions of vaccines could be distributed, and billions of dollars in revenues earned, without triggering regulatory exclusivity periods.

The director of the FDA's Center for Biologics Evaluation and Research, Dr. Peter Marks, described the EUA process as an "EUA-plus," noting that a vaccine EUA "is going to be closer" to full BLA approval.[35] The FDA's "EUA-plus" standard for vaccines seems more aligned with conditional approval in Europe, except that in Europe the clock has already started running on regulatory exclusivities.

With this in mind, vaccine manufacturers are arguably incentivized to delay full BLAs until the public health emergency ends and the EUA is not reauthorized. Indeed, EUAs for past infectious disease outbreaks have been renewed several times, with no guarantee of a later-filed full licensing application.[36]

C COVID-19 Therapeutics

Therapeutics are largely governed by the same rules as vaccines. Upon approval, new chemical entities receive full regulatory periods in both Europe and the United States, governed by the rules set out in Section II. A. In Europe, the clock begins at the time of conditional approval. In the United States, an EUA does not trigger the initiation of regulatory approval periods.

For new uses of existing drugs, regulatory exclusivities may apply even if no patent protection can be obtained. In Europe, options to gain additional regulatory exclusivity protection for repurposed drugs are quite limited. Repurposing could be patent protected in Europe as a so-called further medical indication patent,[37] but under the Global Marketing Authorization, with a few notable exceptions,[38] no renewal or extension of regulatory exclusivities is possible. In the United States, periods of guaranteed market exclusivity can be obtained regardless of patent status; this includes reformulated drug products, which may obtain NDAs or supplemental NDAs.

---

[35] Sarah Owermohle, Marks: Prepare for 'EUA-plus' for COVID Vaccines, Politico (Sept. 11, 2020), www.politico.com/newsletters/prescription-pulse/2020/09/11/marks-prepare-for-eua-plus-for-covid-vaccines-790343.

[36] US Food & Drug Admin., Emergency Use Authorization, www.fda.gov/emergency-preparedness-and-response/mcm-legal-regulatory-and-policy-framework/emergency-use-authorization.

[37] Convention on the Grant of European Patents, art. 54(5), Oct. 5, 1973, 1065 U.N.T.S. 199; see also Sven J.R. Bostyn, Personalised Medicine, Medical Indication Patents and Patent Infringement: Emergency Treatment Required, *Intell. Prop. Q.* 151, 155–58 (2016); Christopher M. Holman, Timo Minssen & Eric M. Solovy, Patentability Standards for Follow-On Pharmaceutical Innovation, 37 *Biotechnology Law Rep.* 131 (2018).

[38] Directive 2001/83/EC, art. 6(1), para. 2.

In the United States, Operation Warp Speed invested far more into COVID-19 vaccines as compared to therapeutics. Globally, the trend is similar: 95 percent of all investments have gone into vaccines, with only 5 percent devoted to therapeutics.[39] Some clinical trials have evaluated the efficacy of marketed antivirals in the fight against COVID-19.

In Europe, remdesivir (Veklury) was conditionally authorized by the EMA for the treatment of COVID-19; in the United States, remdesivir received full FDA approval. The WHO raised issues about remdesivir's efficacy, amending its guidelines accordingly,[40] but in Europe, the drug remains conditionally approved while the EMA continues to evaluate the data. Despite questions about its efficacy, remdesivir is FDA-approved in the United States and costs $3,120 for a five-day course of treatment when purchased by private insurers ($2,340 when purchased by public payers such as Medicare and Medicaid).[41] The drug is still under patent protection: its primary US patent will lapse in 2031 and in Europe in 2035. Other antivirals are being studied, including favipiravir, which is authorized in Japan for the treatment of influenza.[42] Merck recently reported that its antiviral drug molnupiravir "reduced the risk of admission to hospital or death by around 50 percent in non-hospitalized adults who had mild to moderate COVID-19 and were at risk of poor outcomes"; it has requested an EUA from the FDA.[43] Pfizer initiated clinical studies of PF-07321332, its investigational COVID-19 antiviral drug, in August 2021.[44] The drug, later named nirmatrelvir (Paxlovid), received an EUA in December 2021 and has since become a mainstay in COVID-19 treatment in the United States.[45]

The injectable corticosteroid dexamethasone, an older medication that has no patent or regulatory protection, showed considerable promise in treating COVID-19.[46] However, the lack of exclusivities for dexamethasone in the United States and Europe give pharmaceutical companies little incentive to rigorously study its use

---

[39] Governments Spent at Least €93bn on COVID-19 Vaccines and Therapeutics During the Last 11 Months, Bus. Wire (Jan. 11, 2021), www.businesswire.com/news/home/20210110005098/en/Governments-Spent-at-Least-%E2%82%AC93bn-on-COVID-19-Vaccines-and-Therapeutics-During-the-Last-11-Months.

[40] World Health Org., Therapeutics and COVID-19: Living Guideline (Mar. 31, 2021), www.who.int/publications/i/item/therapeutics-and-covid-19-living-guideline.

[41] Allison Inserro, Gilead Sciences sets US Price for COVID-19 Drug (June 29, 2020), www.ajmc.com/view/gilead-sciences-sets-us-price-for-covid19-drug-at-2340-to-3120-based-on-insurance.

[42] Glenmark Begins Phase III Trials of Favipiravir for COVID-19 in India, Clinical Trials Arena (May 13, 2020), www.clinicaltrialsarena.com/news/glenmark-favipiravir-trial-begins/.

[43] COVID-19: Molnupiravir Reduces Risk of Hospital Admission or Death by 50% in Patients at Risk, MSD Reports, 375 *Br. Med. J.* n.242 (2021).

[44] A Study of PF-07321332/Ritonavir in Non-Hospitalized Low-Risk Adult Participants With COVID-19, ClinicalTrials.gov, https://clinicaltrials.gov/ct2/show/NCT05011513.

[45] Spencer Kimball, Paxlovid Prescriptions to Treat COVID Increased Tenfold in U.S. Since Late February, Pfizer Says, CNBC (May 3, 2022), www.cnbc.com/2022/05/03/pfizer-paxlovid-prescriptions-to-treat-covid-increased-tenfold-in-us-since-late-february.html.

[46] RECOVERY Collaborative Group et al., Dexamethasone in Hospitalized Patients with COVID-19, 384 *N. Engl. J. Med.* 693 (2020).

in COVID-19. That said, a significant benefit of dexamethasone is its low cost, which is driven by the existence of multiple generic manufacturers for the product.[47]

Various antibody treatments have also been studied in clinical trials.[48] For instance, the Regeneron antibody cocktail contains human antibodies harvested from COVID-19 patients combined with mouse monoclonal antibodies against the spike protein.[49] Initially available in the United States only via compassionate use or participation in clinical trials, several monoclonal antibodies have since been granted EUAs.

III IMPACT OF REGULATORY EXCLUSIVITIES ON ACCESS TO COVID-19 MEDICAL TREATMENTS

The list of drug and vaccine candidates for COVID-19 that are authorized or in various stages of development is extensive; many are protected by patents or eligible for regulatory exclusivities. These exclusive rights allow manufacturers to determine access and price in the absence of suitable substitutes. COVID-19 vaccines have yet to compete on price because the manufacturers contract with the government for certain quantities of vaccine at fixed prices; those prices, in fact, have risen over time. Exclusive rights offer a significant incentive for the development of vaccines and therapeutics for COVID-19.

Even though the effects of exclusive rights on access are similar for therapeutics and vaccines, the situation is more complicated for vaccines, as there are more parameters to consider: vaccine platforms, vaccine adjuvants, the vaccines themselves, and the complex manufacturing processes for those vaccines, which are often shrouded in trade secrecy. The broadly patented vaccine platforms may slow the development of other vaccines as third parties, unable to make use of patented platforms, are either blocked from entering the market or require a costly licensing agreement. Early on, manufacturers declared their intent not to engage in price gouging,[50] meaning that prices would not rise during the "crisis" phase – presumably the duration of the public health emergency. Yet taxpayers have little information regarding the costs and conditions of vaccine purchasing agreements. The prices listed in Table 16.1 have already started to increase as manufacturers move away from "pandemic pricing" limits.[51] Indeed, Pfizer and Moderna have

---

[47] Id. at 702.

[48] See Bostyn, supra note 1, at 250–53.

[49] Johanna Hansen et al., Studies in Humanized Mice and Convalescent Humans Yield a SARS-CoV-2 Antibody Cocktail, 369 *Sci.* 1010 (2020).

[50] Andrew Dunn, The CEO of the Buzzy Biotech That's Working on a Potential Coronavirus Vaccine Just Pledged He Won't Set a High Price for the Shot, Bus. Insider (Mar. 4, 2020), www.businessinsider.com/moderna-ceo-stephane-bancel-interview-coronavirus-vaccine-price-2020-3.

[51] Deborah Abrams Kaplan & Peter Wehrwein, The Price Tags on the COVID-19 Vaccines, 31 *Managed Healthcare Exec.* 26 (2021) ("During an earnings call in early February, Pfizer CFO Frank D'Amelio described Pfizer's $19.50-per-dose price as 'pandemic pricing' and 'that's not a normal price like we typically get for a vaccine, $150, $175 per dose.'").

increased the prices of their vaccines, including for Omicron-adapted versions, in both Europe and the United States.[52] Though such price increases are good news for investors, they do not bode well for global access.[53]

The presence of extensive patent, regulatory exclusivities, and trade secrets also positions manufacturers in opposition to compelled licensing agreements. We see this already playing out with the shortage of supplies in vaccines. Unwillingness to license vaccine manufacturing to third parties – and limited leverage among payers to compel such licensing – makes patients very vulnerable to delays and disruptions in manufacturing, as we have seen with the AstraZeneca vaccine in Europe.[54]

Even though voluntary sharing of technology is always an option, there is little evidence this is happening for most COVID-19-related technology.[55] AstraZeneca has a licensing agreement in place with Serum Institute India to produce and distribute one billion doses of the AZ/Oxford COVID-19 vaccine;[56] a similar license is in place with Dutch company Halix BV.[57] For the other authorized vaccines, no production licensing agreements are in place. The Medicines Patent Pool, a United Nations-backed public health organization working to increase access to, and facilitate the development of, life-saving medicines for low- and middle-income countries,[58] has extended its mission to include COVID-19 products, but has yet to negotiate licensing agreements. Similarly, the WHO COVID-19 Technology Access Pool (C-TAP) has not led to sufficient sharing of technology or treatments. Though patents present a significant obstacle for technology sharing, their issuance depends on full disclosure and enablement; even if patented technology is licensed, institutional expertise held as trade secrets likely poses greater barriers to the sharing and scale-up of vaccine technology.[59]

---

[52] Fraiser Kansteiner, Pfizer, Moderna Hike COVID-19 Vaccine Prices in New European Supply Deals: Report, Fierce Pharma (Aug. 2, 2021), www.fiercepharma.com/pharma/pfizer-moderna-turn-up-covid-19-vaccine-prices-europe-as-companies-plot-deliveries-into-2022; Fraiser Kansteiner, Pfizer's Latest $3.2b Pandemic Vaccine Contract Suggests Private Market Still a Ways Off: Analysts (June 30, 2022), www.fiercepharma.com/pharma/pfizers-latest-32b-pandemic-vaccine-contract-suggests-private-market-still-ways-analysts ("[T]he U.S. has laid out $3.2 billion for another 105 million doses of Pfizer-BioNTech's mRNA shot Comirnaty[;] … [t]he deal breaks down to around $30.50 per dose.").

[53] Josh Nathan-Kazis, Pfizer Raises COVID Vaccine Price 27%. What It Means for the Stock, Barron's (June 30, 2022), www.barrons.com/articles/pfizer-stock-covid-vaccine-price-increase-51656594199.

[54] Rob Davies, Why the EU and AstraZeneca Are Stuck in a COVID Vaccines Row, Guardian (Jan. 27, 2021), www.theguardian.com/business/2021/jan/27/eu-covid-vaccines-row-astrazeneca-boss-reveals-problems.

[55] See Bostyn, supra note 1, at 230–58.

[56] AstraZeneca Takes Next Steps Towards Broad and Equitable Access to Oxford University's COVID-19 Vaccine (June 4, 2020), www.astrazeneca.com/content/astraz/media-centre/press-releases/2020/astrazeneca-takes-next-steps-towards-broad-and-equitable-access-to-oxford-universitys-covid-19-vaccine.html.

[57] HALIX Signs Agreement With AstraZeneca For Commercial Manufacture of COVID-19 Vaccine (Dec. 8, 2020), www.halix.nl/2020/12/08/halix-signs-agreement-astrazeneca-commercial-manufacture-covid-19-vaccine/.

[58] Medicines Patent Pool, https://medicinespatentpool.org/.

[59] Adam Houldsworth, No, IP rights Are Not the Barrier to COVID-19 Vaccine Supplies, IAM (Feb. 6, 2021), www.iam-media.com/coronavirus/covid-vaccine-supply-not-about-ip-saturday-opinion.

Another solution to guarantee access to vaccines and therapeutics at reasonable prices is to grant compulsory licenses. In Europe, all Patent Acts provide for compulsory licensing, even though the conditions under which they can be granted may differ across nations.[60] In the United States, Section 1498 enables the federal government to step in and use patents in exchange for reasonable compensation, but this authority has never been invoked in any context, let alone for COVID-19.[61] Compulsory licensing is deeply unpopular in both Europe and the United States, and these statutory schemes are rarely invoked. However, a global pandemic is as good a moment as any to begin using these approaches of last resort.[62]

The Agreement on Trade-Related Aspects of Intellectual Property Rights (TRIPs Agreement) also allows for compulsory licensing,[63] and during health crises, it suspends the usual requirement of exhausting voluntary licensing options prior to the grant of a compulsory license.[64] The details of that framework, however, apply predominantly to domestic supply,[65] except for export to the least-developed countries – those that lack production infrastructure.[66] Even in high-income countries, the technical infrastructure may not exist for manufacturing vaccines, especially vaccines as complex as the COVID-19 mRNA vaccines. The more complex the manufacturing process, the less likely that addressing the intellectual property and regulatory issues alone will enable rapid scale-up of production.[67] More effective mechanisms for transferring the necessary know-how will also have to be considered.[68] A refined statutory framework may be needed to allow for global manufacturing via compulsory licensing. In spite of US support, the United Kingdom and the European Union continue to oppose waivers of IPRs during the pandemic.[69] Given the time required for vaccine scale-up, compulsory licensing needs to occur at earlier stages in development.

Compulsory licenses might resolve patent rights issues and guarantee manufacturing of vaccines and therapeutics, but only if regulatory exclusivities are waived or deferred, an option that does not currently exist.[70] Deferring the practical

---

[60] See Bostyn, supra note 1, at 262.

[61] Christopher Morten & Charles Duan, Who's Afraid of Section 1498? A Case for Government Patent Use in Pandemics and Other National Crises, 23 *Yale J. L. Tech.* 1 (2020).

[62] See Bostyn, supra note 1, at 261–67.

[63] Agreement on Trade-Related Aspects of Intellectual Property Rights (TRIPS), art. 31, Apr. 15, 1994, 1869 U.N.T.S. 299.

[64] Id. at art. 31(b).

[65] Id. at art. 31(f).

[66] Id. at art. 31(b).

[67] See Derek Lowe, In the Pipeline Blog: Myths of Vaccine Manufacturing, Sci. Translational Med. (Feb. 2, 2021), www.science.org/content/blog-post/myths-vaccine-manufacturing.

[68] See W. Nicholson Price II, Arti K. Rai & Timo Minssen, Knowledge Transfer for Large-Scale Vaccine Manufacturing, 369 *Sci.* 912 (2020).

[69] Adam Lidgett, Groups Warn COVID IP Waiver Could Hurt Pandemic Efforts, Law360 (Mar. 31, 2021), www.law360.com/articles/1370726/groups-warn-covid-ip-waiver-could-hurt-pandemic-efforts.

[70] See Ellen F. M. 't Hoen, Pascale Boulet & Brook K. Baker, Data Exclusivity Exceptions and Compulsory Licensing to Promote Generic Medicines in the European Union: A Proposal for Greater Coherence in European Pharmaceutical Legislation, 10 *J. Pharm. Pol'y Prac.* 19 (2017).

application of regulatory exclusivities, including data exclusivity, would similarly require statutory change. The benefit of a deferral is that those rights could be paused, to be invoked at a later date. Yet deferring exclusivity to a "less acute" period of the COVID-19 pandemic would permit manufacturers to profit now without curtailing the period where they can charge higher prices. This is the situation in the United States: EUAs have slowed momentum toward full approval and licensure of vaccines, and as a result, regulatory exclusivity periods for many vaccines and therapeutics have yet to start.

Vaccine nationalism further complicates the matter by exacerbating disparities in vaccine access – scarce supply goes to the highest bidder, while the rest of the world waits indefinitely.

The United States has committed to more vaccines than it needs, while in low-income countries, access to vaccines has been limited. COVID-19 Vaccines Global Access (COVAX), which is co-led by Gavi,[71] the Coalition for Epidemic Preparedness Innovations, and the WHO, aims to accelerate the development and manufacture of COVID-19 vaccines, and to guarantee fair and equitable access for every country in the world.[72] By early September 2021, COVAX had delivered 240 million doses to 139 countries.[73] Yet even COVAX seems willing to sell vaccines to the highest bidder.[74] Finally, advance purchase agreements could be conditioned on commitments from manufacturers to voluntarily license technology to third-party manufacturers in order to shore up global supply, though this might limit the power of the advance purchase agreement as a pull incentive for innovation.

IV LESSONS FOR THE FUTURE

During the COVID-19 pandemic, the global biopharmaceutical industry has invested considerable time and resources in the development of treatments and vaccines. Since rapid success was so crucial, the industry also received massive support from public resources and investments around the globe, including US and EU public authorities and EU member states. As a result, millions of people have received highly effective vaccines, several promising vaccine candidates are on the horizon, and some therapeutics show promise in mitigating the severity of SARS-CoV-2 infection. In spite of these successes, challenges to global access and affordability remain due to widespread and ongoing inequities. Few of these inequities have been adequately addressed during the COVID-19 pandemic and

---

[71] Gavi, the Vaccine Alliance, www.gavi.org.
[72] COVAX Facility, www.gavi.org/covax-facility.
[73] See Joint COVAX Statement on Supply Forecast for 2021 and Early 2022 (Sept. 8, 2021), www.unicef.org/press-releases/joint-covax-statement-supply-forecast-2021-and-early-2022.
[74] Paul Karp, Australia's Pfizer Purchase from Vaccine-Sharing Covax Stockpile under Fire, Guardian (Aug. 16, 2021), www.theguardian.com/australia-news/2021/aug/17/australia-pfizer-purchase-from-vaccine-sharing-covax-stockpile-under-fire.

remain substantial obstacles in addressing future pandemics.[75] Inequities have contributed substantially to the prolongation of this pandemic as new SARS-CoV-2 variants continue to emerge for which new booster inoculations will likely be necessary. New variants of contagious viruses are a hallmark of every pandemic, present and future.

This chapter shows that resolving the devastating health issues caused by pandemics tend to follow a similar scenario, convincing those in higher-income nations to subsidize – via pull and push mechanisms – R&D in vaccines and therapeutics. Despite massive public spending, the vaccines and therapeutics are subject to a dense thicket of exclusive rights, in the form of patents, regulatory exclusivities, and trade secrets. The COVID-19 pandemic is no exception.

That web of exclusive rights allows the holders of those rights to act as gatekeepers, restricting access to, and setting the price of, the technology needed to produce vaccines and therapeutics.[76] Despite the existence of competition in the COVID-19 vaccine space, the need to vaccinate billions of people across the globe still gives substantial leverage to the holders of those exclusive rights and presents barriers to access. The recent push to waive IPRs for COVID-19 vaccines illustrates the rather belated realization of the importance of exclusive rights during pandemics.[77] Presumably, a waiver would free those vaccines from their exclusive rights, which could clear a path for third parties to manufacture them – thereby increasing volume while lowering price.[78] Though there are other complex supply chain issues as well, discussions of intellectual property waivers for COVID-19 vaccines understate the complexities of the exclusive rights involved.[79] As noted earlier, COVID-19 vaccines are protected by hundreds of patents, including those that cover the vaccine platforms, and many of the vaccine manufacturing processes are closely guarded

---

[75] Olivier J. Wouters et al., Challenges in Ensuring Global Access to COVID-19 Vaccines: Production, Affordability, Allocation, and Deployment, 397 *Lancet* 1023 (2021).

[76] Aisling McMahon, Global Equitable Access to Vaccines, Medicines and Diagnostics for COVID-19: The Role of Patents as Private Governance, 47 *J. of Med. Ethics* 142 (2021).

[77] World Trade Org., Council for Trade-Related Aspects of Intellectual Property Rights, Waiver From Certain Provisions of the Trips Agreement for the Prevention, Containment and Treatment of COVID-19, WTO Doc. IP/C/W/669 (2020), revised version WTO Doc. IP/C/W/669/Rev.1 (2021). This has finally been watered down by the Ministerial Decision of June 17, 2022 to an Art. 31bis TRIPS style of compulsory licensing patent waiver, WT/MIN(22)/30 – WT/L/1141.

[78] Siva Thambisetty et al., The TRIPS Intellectual Property Waiver Proposal: Creating the Right Incentives in Patent Law and Politics to End the COVID-19 Pandemic (LSE Legal Studies, Working Paper No. 06/2021, 2021), https://ssrn.com/abstract=3851737.

[79] Sven J.R. Bostyn, Why a COVID IP Waiver Is Not a Good Strategy 5-13 (May 10, 2021), https://ssrn.com/abstract=3843327; Reto M. Hilty et al., COVID-19 and the Role of Intellectual Property Position. Statement of the Max Planck Institute for Innovation and Competition of 7 May 2021, www.ip.mpg.de/fileadmin/ipmpg/content/stellungnahmen/2021_05_25_Position_statement_Covid_IP_waiver.pdf; Duncan Matthews & Timo Minssen, US U-turn on COVID IP Waiver Alone Will Not Solve Vaccine Crisis – Intellectual Property Is an Important Part of the Debate, but Greater Transparency Is Required (May 2021), https://privpapers.ssrn.com/sol3/papers.cfm?abstract_id=3881020.

as trade secrets.[80] Finally, regulatory exclusivities are only partially governed by the TRIPS Agreement and would not entirely fall within the scope of the waiver.

Safeguards are needed to guarantee global access to sufficient vaccines at reasonable prices. Such solutions are even more urgent given the emergence of new SARS-CoV-2 variants. If new booster shots against the variants become necessary, current vaccine-related inequities will surely be replicated if nothing is done. That might require statutory change, such as waiving regulatory exclusivities in compulsory licensing arrangements. Moreover, the use of compulsory licensing should become part of a more sophisticated approach to contractual arrangements, such as in advance purchasing agreements. If negotiated equitably, vaccine developers and manufacturers could be contractually obligated to supply more (as opposed to "best effort" commitments) while granting licenses to third parties that can scale up vaccine production in facilities abroad – with appropriate guarantees of safety and quality. Those contractual arrangements could also require vaccine developers to supply the COVAX system directly, with a view toward eliminating inequities in low- and middle-income countries.

As the development and manufacturing of COVID-19 vaccines (and to some extent COVID-19 therapeutics) has largely been financed by public resources,[81] governments have the leverage to use these tools. This may contrast with other areas of drug development, in which the role of public funding might be more limited. Greater effort should be made toward pooling of vaccine and therapeutics technology, including manufacturing processes; C-TAP has not been optimally utilized during COVID-19.

Although more research is needed, our analysis offers a starting point for broader discussions of the nature of these incentives in Europe and the United States. Our proposed solutions may enable global access to products essential for resolving the COVID-19 pandemic, but can also be broadly applied to future global crises. Careful analyses of the complex dynamics that drive innovation, global manufacturing scale-up, and access are essential for improving pandemic preparedness, pharmaceutical innovation, and global access issues in the future.

---

[80] See Bostyn, supra note 79, at 6–9; Matthews & Minssen, supra note 79 at 1–2; Ana Santos Rutschman & Julia Barnes-Weise, The COVID-19 Vaccine Patent Waiver: The Wrong Tool for the Right Goal, Bill of Health (May 5, 2021), https://blog.petrieflom.law.harvard.edu/2021/05/05/covid-vaccine-patent-waiver/.

[81] Hussain S. Lalani, Jerry Avorn & Aaron S. Kesselheim, US Taxpayers Heavily Funded the Discovery of COVID-19 Vaccines, 101 *Clin. Pharmacol. Ther.* 542 (2021); see also Bostyn, supra note 79, at 14–16; Duncan Matthews & Timo Minssen, The Prospects for an IP Waiver Under the TRIPS Agreement, Bill of Health (July 6, 2021), https://blog.petrieflom.law.harvard.edu/2021/07/06/the-prospects-for-an-ip-waiver-under-the-trips-agreement/.

17

At-Risk Populations & Vaccine Injury Compensation

Katharine Van Tassel and Sharona Hoffman[*]

I INTRODUCTION

Developing a new vaccine takes, on average, ten years.[1] In the case of COVID-19, however, the pharmaceutical industry developed vaccines in a matter of months, and three quickly received emergency use authorization (EUA).[2] As discussed in Chapter 15, by Sachs, Ouellette, Price, and Sherkow, and in others in this volume, this record-breaking pace of development raised concerns regarding rare undetected side effects and ones that would manifest only in the long term.

This chapter argues that the potential for vaccine-related harms raises acute concerns for vulnerable populations. These harms have a disparate impact on low-income people, who are disproportionately non-White, and who have limited financial resources to obtain medical care, weather job losses, and pursue injury compensation. When a vaccine is given as a countermeasure during a declared public health emergency (PHE), the problem is acute because of the limited availability of injury compensation.

This chapter reviews and assesses the two existing mechanisms to which injured parties can turn for remedies: (1) the National Vaccine Injury Compensation Program (VICP), which applies to most vaccines given in the United States; and (2) the far less generous and less accessible Countermeasures Injury Compensation Program (CICP), which applies to vaccinations given as

---

[*] This chapter is based in part on Katharine Van Tassel, Carmel Shachar & Sharona Hoffman, COVID-19 Vaccine Injuries – Preventing Inequities in Compensation, 384 *New Eng. J. Med.* e34 (2021).

[1] The Coll. of Physicians of Phila., Vaccine Development, Testing, and Regulation, HistoryofVaccines. org, www.historyofvaccines.org/content/articles/vaccine-development-testing-and-regulation (last updated Jan. 17, 2018).

[2] US Food & Drug Admin., FDA Takes Additional Action in Fight Against COVID-19 by Issuing Emergency Use Authorization for Second COVID-19 Vaccine (Dec. 18, 2020), www.fda.gov/news-events/press-announcements/fda-takes-additional-action-fight-against-covid-19-issuing-emergency-use-authorization-second-covid; Jen Christensen, Johnson & Johnson's COVID-19 Vaccine Gets Emergency Use Authorization From FDA, CNN (Feb. 27, 2021), www.cnn.com/2021/02/27/health/johnson-johnson-covid-19-vaccine-fda-eua/index.html.

countermeasures during PHEs.[3] It highlights the health and financial disparities suffered by vulnerable populations during a pandemic and its aftermath, and how the CICP intensifies these disparities. This chapter then develops a proposal for legal reform to the injury-compensation and vaccine-approval processes that aims to protect the disadvantaged and enhance equity.

II VACCINE SIDE EFFECTS

During the COVID-19 pandemic, Pfizer/BioNTech and Moderna enrolled 44,000 and 30,000 subjects, respectively, in the studies upon which they relied to obtain initial EUA from the Food and Drug Administration (FDA).[4] With tens of thousands of trial participants, common side effects that occur fairly soon after vaccination were identified.[5] But there was little opportunity to identify adverse events that might appear in the longer term or that are rare enough that they would be discovered only after a significant percentage of the public had been vaccinated. Such side effects could include joint pain, anaphylaxis, and neurological conditions such as encephalitis, transverse myelitis, or Guillain-Barré Syndrome, which are known to occur with other vaccines.[6] A case in point is the National Swine Flu Immunization Program. In 1976, the federal government decided to protect the public from swine flu and quickly advanced the administration of a vaccine. Forty million vaccines were administered in just a few months. Unfortunately, 450 vaccinated people developed Guillain-Barré Syndrome, a rare and serious neurological disorder that can result in muscle weakness and paralysis.[7] The program was quickly suspended, but the harm was done. Regrettably, it triggered an enduring public

---

[3] A countermeasure is defined as a "vaccination, medication, device, or other item recommended to diagnose, prevent or treat a declared pandemic, epidemic or security threat." Health Res. & Servs. Admin., Countermeasures Injury Compensation Program (CICP), www.hrsa.gov/cicp (last visited Nov. 2020).

[4] Denise Grady & Katie Thomas, Moderna and Pfizer Reveal Secret Blueprints for Coronavirus Vaccine Trials, NY Times (Sept. 17, 2020), www.nytimes.com/2020/09/17/health/covid-moderna-vaccine.html.

[5] Helen Branswell, Comparing the Covid-19 Vaccines Developed by Pfizer, Moderna, and Johnson & Johnson (February 2, 2021), www.statnews.com/2020/12/19/a-side-by-side-comparison-of-the-pfizer-biontech-and-moderna-vaccines/.

[6] Health Res. & Servs. Admin., Vaccine Injury Table, www.hrsa.gov/sites/default/files/hrsa/vaccine-compensation/vaccine-injury-table.pdf (last visited Jan. 5, 2021). For example, the possibility that the AstraZeneca and Johnson & Johnson vaccines could cause extremely rare, life-threatening blood clots was not discovered until millions of people had been vaccinated. Angela Dewan, et. al., Here's What to Know About the Risk of Blood Clots and the AstraZeneca Vaccine, CNN (Apr. 3, 2021), www.cnn.com/2021/04/02/health/astrazeneca-blood-clots-explainer-intl-cmd-gbr/index.html; Anne Flaherty, Rare Reactions to Johnson & Johnson Vaccine Remain a Mystery, Putting Many Women on Edge, ABC News (Apr. 17, 2021), https://abcnews.go.com/Politics/rare-reactions-johnson-johnson-vaccine-remain-mystery-putting/story?id=77092178.

[7] Rebecca Kreston, The Public Health Legacy of the 1976 Swine Flu Outbreak, Discover Mag. (Sept. 30, 2013), www.discovermagazine.com/health/the-public-health-legacy-of-the-1976-swine-flu-outbreak.

mistrust of flu vaccinations and often appears as part of the anti-vaccination movement's narrative.[8]

III VACCINE INJURY COMPENSATION PROGRAMS

The United States is fortunate to have a robust system to compensate individuals who suffer vaccine injuries. This system, however, is not available to those vaccinated with a countermeasure during a declared PHE.

A *The National Vaccine Injury Compensation Program*

The VICP is normally available to anyone who is injured by a vaccine after the FDA approves it and the Centers for Disease Control and Prevention (CDC) recommends it for children or pregnant women.[9] The VICP covers most vaccines administered in the United States. This no-fault program was created in the 1980s to ensure relatively quick and fair compensation for vaccine injuries and to insulate manufacturers from liability as an incentive for them to pursue vaccine development.[10] Claimants who develop recognized symptoms of injuries listed in the Vaccine Injury Table within a certain amount of time after vaccination need not prove that the injuries were caused by the vaccine. Rather, they present evidence only about the extent of their damages.[11] When an injury is not listed in the Vaccine Injury Table, petitioners must prove that it was caused or exacerbated by the vaccine.[12] Claim denials can be appealed to the Court of Federal Claims.[13]

The VICP offers up to $250,000 for pain, suffering, and emotional distress,[14] as well as attorneys' fees and legal expenses to good-faith claimants.[15] At the end of

---

[8] Id.

[9] Health Res. & Servs. Admin., Covered Vaccines, www.hrsa.gov/vaccine-compensation/covered-vaccines/index.html (last visited Dec. 2020).

[10] Health Res. & Servs. Admin., About the National Vaccine Injury Compensation Program, www.hrsa.gov/vaccine-compensation/about/index.html (last visited Dec. 2020) (hereinafter, About VICP); Health Res. & Servs. Admin., National Vaccine Injury Compensation Program, www.hrsa.gov/vaccine-compensation/index.html (last visited Nov. 2020).

[11] Health Res. & Servs. Admin., Who Can File a Petition?, www.hrsa.gov/vaccine-compensation/eligible/index.html (last visited Dec. 2020); Health Res. & Servs. Admin., Frequently Asked Questions, www.hrsa.gov/vaccine-compensation/faq (last reviewed Apr. 2023).

[12] The Off. of Special Masters, US Ct. of Fed. Claims, Guidelines for Practice Under the National Vaccine Injury Compensation Program 47 (2020), www.uscfc.uscourts.gov/sites/default/files/Guidelines-4.24.2020.pdf.

[13] Id.

[14] Health Res. & Servs. Admin., What You Need to Know About the National Vaccine Injury Compensation Program (VICP), 12 (2019), www.hrsa.gov/sites/default/files/hrsa/vicp/about-vaccine-injury-compensation-program-booklet.pdf.

[15] Health Res. & Servs. Admin., How to File a Petition, www.hrsa.gov/vaccine-compensation/how-to-file/index.html (last visited Dec. 2020). Prior to 2017, the average time to resolve a VICP case was 575 days, or approximately 1.5 years. In 2017, HHS adopted a final rule that added Shoulder Injury Related to Vaccine Administration (SIRVA) injuries to the Vaccine Injury Table. SIRVA injuries are injuries

2022, the Vaccine Injury Compensation Trust Fund (VICTF) was valued at over $4 billion.[16] The VICTF is funded by a seventy-five-cent excise tax on each vaccine dose, which is paid by the manufacturers.[17] From 2006 through 2018, the VICP approved about 70 percent of claims.[18] Since 2015, the fund has paid out an average of $216 million per year to an average of 615 claimants per year.[19]

B *The Countermeasures Injury Compensation Program*

The benefits offered under the VICP are not available to people injured by vaccines given as countermeasures during declared PHEs.[20] When the Department of Health and Human Services (HHS) declares a PHE, it triggers the Public Readiness and Emergency Preparedness (PREP) Act.[21] This federal law requires that claimants bring claims relating to countermeasures that are used during a PHE exclusively under the CICP.[22] Such countermeasures include not only vaccines, but also drugs, equipment, and more. Awards under the CICP are paid by the Covered Countermeasures Process Fund (CCPF). Congress funds the CCPF through emergency appropriations to HHS that HHS may transfer to the CCPF.[23] Manufacturers do not contribute to this fund as they do to the VICTF.

---

related to the intramuscular injection of a vaccine. Adding these SIRVA claims "dramatically" increased the number of claims filed in the VICP. Since 2017, the average amount of time for a VICP case to finally resolve has increased significantly, to 751 days, or approximately two years. National Vaccine Injury Compensation Program: Revisions to the Vaccine Injury Table, 85 Fed. Reg. 43794 (proposed July 20, 2020) (to be codified at 42 C.F.R. pt. 100), www.federalregister.gov/documents/2020/07/20/2020-15673/national-vaccine-injury-compensation-program-revisions-to-the-vaccine-injury-table.

[16] United States Department of the Treasury, Vaccine Injury Trust Fund, Nov. 2022, www.treasurydirect.gov/ftp/dfi/tfmb/dfivi1122.pdf, at 6.

[17] About VICP, supra note 10 ("Trivalent influenza vaccine … is taxed $.75 because it prevents one disease; measles-mumps-rubella vaccine, which prevents three diseases, is taxed $2.25.").

[18] Ken Alltucker, Consumers Filed 106 Injury Claims From COVID-19 Vaccines, Ventilators and Hydroxychloroquine. Here's Why None Have Been Paid, USA Today (Mar. 28, 2021), www.usatoday.com/story/news/health/2021/03/28/covid-19-vaccines-hydroxychloroquine-generate-dozens-injury-claims/6995509002/.

[19] Tom Hals, COVID-19 Era Highlights U.S. 'Black Hole' Compensation Fund for Pandemic Vaccine Injuries, Reuters (Aug. 21, 2020), www.reuters.com/article/us-health-coronavirus-vaccines-liability/covid-19-era-highlights-u-s-black-hole-compensation-fund-for-pandemic-vaccine-injuries-idUSKBN25H1E8.

[20] Cong. Rsch. Serv., The PREP Act and COVID-19: Limiting Liability for Medical Countermeasures (Sept. 21, 2020), https://crsreports.congress.gov/product/pdf/LSB/LSB10443.

[21] 42 U.S.C. § 247d-6d.

[22] Cong. Rsch. Serv., supra note 20.

[23] Id. Both the Coronavirus Aid, Relief, and Economic Security (CARES) Act and the Coronavirus Preparedness and Response Supplemental Appropriations Act (CPRSA) appropriate funding that HHS may use for the Covered Countermeasure Process Fund. "CPRSA appropriates $3.1 billion to the Secretary to respond to COVID-19, including the development and purchase of countermeasures and vaccines, while allowing these funds to 'be transferred to, and merged with' the Covered Countermeasure Process Fund. Similarly, the CARES Act appropriates $27 billion to the Secretary for similar purposes, again providing that the Secretary may transfer these funds to the Covered Countermeasure Process Fund." Id.

The CICP is far less generous than the VICP.[24] It compensates people only for serious injuries,[25] requires a heightened burden of proof regarding injury causation,[26] and has a one-year statute of limitations following the date of vaccination.[27] Individuals are bound by the one-year filing deadline regardless of when their symptoms appear or are determined to be associated with the vaccine. Furthermore, the deadline applies to pregnant women, who must file claims on behalf of their babies within one year of being themselves vaccinated, leaving parents with only a few months to discover any injuries after their baby is born.[28] The CICP also limits damages awards.[29] For example, under the CICP, claimants can recover a maximum of only $50,000 in lost income for each year out of work. The CICP also denies any compensation for pain, suffering, and emotional distress, as well as for attorneys' fees and costs.[30] There is no opportunity to appeal claim denials.[31]

Furthermore, the CICP process for pursuing compensation is lengthier, more difficult, and more expensive because of the absence of reimbursement for attorneys' fees and costs.[32] It is important to note that those receiving countermeasure vaccines

---

[24] Health Res. & Servs. Admin., Comparison of Countermeasures Injury Compensation Program (CICP) to the National Vaccine Injury Compensation Program (VICP), www.hrsa.gov/cicp/cicp-vicp (last viewed Nov. 2020).

[25] Serious injuries are generally those that warrant hospitalization or lead to a significant disability, loss of function, or death. 42 C.F.R. § 110.3(z). Some of the most common injuries caused by *all* vaccines, including COVID-19 vaccines, which are not likely to be viewed as "serious" and will not warrant compensation under the CICP, are SIRVA injuries. National Vaccine Injury Compensation Program: Revisions to the Vaccine Injury Table, supra note 15. SIRVA injuries are injuries related to the intramuscular injection of a vaccine. Id. The costs associated with these shoulder injuries can be significant as these injuries can prevent those whose jobs involve lifting from being able to work for, potentially, long periods of time. Examples of positions that involve lifting include nurses, nursing aids, grocery workers, meat processors, firefighters, and custodial staff, just to name a few. Many of these front-line positions are filled by people from low-income and minority populations. The CICP's narrow compensation scheme results in these workers being left to bear the cost of the losses associated with these SIRVA injuries as they will never be compensated for these injuries if they were vaccinated during the PHE.

[26] Determinations of causation must be "based on compelling, reliable, valid, medical and scientific evidence." 42 U.S.C. § 247d–6e(b)(4).

[27] 42 C.F.R. § 110.42.

[28] 42 C.F.R. § 110.3(n)(1)(3); Countermeasures Injury Compensation Program (CICP): Administrative Implementation, Interim Final Rule, 75 Fed. Reg. 63666 (Oct. 15, 2010) (codified at 42 C.F.R. pt. 110) (corrected by Countermeasures Injury Compensation Program (CICP): Administrative Implementation, Interim Final Rule, 758 Fed. Reg. 64955 (Oct. 21, 2010)), www.federalregister.gov/documents/2010/10/15/2010-25110/countermeasures-injury-compensation-program-cicp-administrative-implementation-interim-final-rule.

[29] Health Res. & Servs. Admin., Countermeasures Injury Compensation Program Request for Benefits Form Instructions 1–2, www.hrsa.gov/sites/default/files/hrsa/cicp/cicp-request-form-instructions.pdf (last updated Mar. 2020).

[30] Health Res. & Servs. Admin., About CICP, www.hrsa.gov/cicp/about (last visited Nov. 2020); Nicholas M. Pace et al., COVID-19 Vaccine Campaign Must Include Fair Compensation for Side Effects, The Hill (Dec. 17, 2020), thehill.com/opinion/healthcare/530546-the-compensation-system-for-potential-side-effects-is-an-important-part-of.

[31] 42 U.S.C. § 247d–6d(b)(5)(C).

[32] See supra text accompanying notes 30.

during a declared PHE can never pursue injury claims under the VICP, even if their symptoms appear or are linked to the vaccine after the declaration is lifted.[33] If they were vaccinated during a declared PHE, they are forever barred from the VICP with respect to the injection in question.

The CICP was first implemented in 2010.[34] Up until 2020 and the declared COVID-19 PHE, the CICP received 485 claims (mostly related to the H1N1 vaccine approved in 2009) but awarded compensation to only 39 people, for a total of $5.7 million.[35] While the VICP has a 70 percent payment rate for claims filed from 2006 through 2018, the CICP has rejected 90 percent of injury claims since it was created.[36] As of the end of March 2023, 11,252 COVID-19-related claims were filed with the CICP.[37] As of March 1, 2023, the CICP rendered decisions on 630 COVID-19 claims. Twenty-one claims were granted, and 630 were denied.[38] Over two-thirds of the claims were for vaccines, with the remainder relating to other COVID-19 treatments.[39]

IV PUBLIC READINESS AND EMERGENCY PREPAREDNESS ACT TRADEOFFS

PREP Act immunity for all countermeasures is designed to accomplish two main goals. First, this immunity encourages manufacturers to speed innovative treatments to market during declared PHEs when there are no other viable treatments. Manufacturers are more willing to skip the usual time it takes to invest in safety through testing when they are given immunity from liability.

Second, PREP Act immunity is an attempt to manage the risk that quickly designed and produced countermeasures might cause a large number of injuries. At the same time that manufacturers are being encouraged to forego their usual testing protocols, PHEs drive the FDA to speed the temporary licensure of countermeasures using a lower standard of safety and effectiveness through its fast-track EUA process.[40] Together, these measures hold the potential to increase the number and seriousness of any unintended countermeasure injuries.

---

[33] Countermeasures Injury Compensation Program (CICP): Administrative Implementation, Interim Final Rule, 75 Fed. Reg. at 63,666.

[34] Health Res. & Servs. Admin., HHS Sets Regulations to Implement Countermeasures Injury Compensation Program (Oct. 15, 2010), www.hrsa.gov/about/news/press-releases/2010-10-15-cicp.html.

[35] Hals, supra note 19.

[36] Alltucker, supra note 18.

[37] Health Res. & Serv. Admin, Countermeasures Injury Compensation Program (CICP) Data, https://www.hrsa.gov/cicp/cicp-data#table-1 (last visited April 5, 2023).

[38] Id.

[39] Id.

[40] Under § 564(a)(1) of the Federal Food, Drug, and Cosmetic Act, the FDA can issue an EUA when the product *may* be effective in diagnosing, treating, or preventing the disease or condition; the known *and potential* benefits outweigh the known *and potential* risks; and there is no adequate, approved, and available alternative to the product for diagnosing, treating, or preventing such disease or condition. Guidance for Industry, Emergency Use Authorization of Medical Products and Related Authorities, 82 FR 4362 (Jan. 13, 2017), www.federalregister.gov/documents/2017/01/13/2017-00721/emergency-use-authorization-of-medical-products-and-related-authorities-guidance-for-industry-and.

The tradeoffs that are the centerpiece of the PREP Act may make some sense for most countermeasures, but they do not appear to do so for vaccines. First, countermeasures that have the greatest potential to cause injuries are treatments such as drugs and devices (e.g. antiviral medication and ventilators), which will be used to treat those who have fallen ill from pandemic-triggering diseases. The manufacturers of these countermeasures have no immunity absent the PREP Act. Consequently, granting these manufacturers immunity to encourage their speed to market, while providing sick consumers with quick access to possible treatments, provides a positive tradeoff for consumers for the loss of access to compensation for all but the most serious of injuries.

In contrast, vaccines, as preventatives, fall into a different category. First, the target population for vaccines is healthy people. As such, there is no "access to treatment" benefit for this population that provides a tradeoff for withholding compensation for injuries. Second, in the context of vaccines, there already is a system, the VICP, that, in the absence of the PREP Act, offers immunity to manufacturers to encourage speed to market while adequately compensating *all* people who are injured by vaccines. It is simply unethical to severely limit compensation for healthy consumers who are injured after agreeing to be vaccinated with an experimental vaccine. They often do so not only for their own benefit, but also for the good of society in that their vaccination promotes herd immunity.

V VULNERABLE POPULATIONS AND THE VACCINE INJURY COMPENSATION PROBLEM

People are less likely to obtain compensation for injuries arising from vaccines they received as countermeasures during a declared PHE than they are for injuries associated with vaccines included in the VICP. Furthermore, the CICP process for pursuing compensation is more burdensome.[41] Those receiving countermeasure vaccines during a declared PHE can never pursue injury claims under the VICP, even if their symptoms appear or are linked to the vaccine after the declaration is lifted.[42]

These concerns are particularly acute for low-income people and people of color because these groups typically endure the greatest difficulties during public health disasters and their aftermaths. During the COVID-19 pandemic, racial and ethnic minorities suffered a death rate that was more than double that of White people.[43]

---

[41] See supra text accompanying notes 30–31.

[42] Countermeasures Injury Compensation Program (CICP): Administrative Implementation, Interim Final Rule, 75 Fed. Reg. at 63,666.

[43] Nat'l Urb. League, State of Black America Unmasked: 2020 Executive Summary 12, http://sobadev .iamempowered.com/sites/soba.iamempowered.com/files/NUL-SOBA-2020-ES-web.pdf (last visited Dec. 30, 2020); Dylan Scott & Christina Animashaun, COVID-19's Stunningly Unequal Death Toll in America, in One Chart, Vox (Oct. 2, 2020), www.vox.com/coronavirus-covid19/2020/10/2/21496884/ us-covid-19-deaths-by-race-black-white-americans.

Likewise, infection rates were significantly higher in economically disadvantaged areas than in wealthier ones.[44] Similar patterns were evident in past disasters, such as the 1918 Spanish influenza pandemic.[45] Vaccinating members of minority and low-income populations during pandemics should therefore be a high priority.

A *Vaccine Hesitancy and Lack of Access to Compensation*

At the same time, however, there are high levels of vaccine skepticism and reluctance to be vaccinated in poor and minority communities.[46] In some cases, vaccine hesitancy may stem from long-standing inequities in medical treatment and abuses that have resulted in general mistrust of government. A well-known example is the infamous Tuskegee Study.[47] In this study, which lasted from 1932 until 1972, researchers deprived African American men of penicillin for syphilis, without informing them that a cure was available, because they wanted to study the natural course of the disease.[48]

In a Kaiser Family Foundation poll conducted in August and September 2020, 49 percent of Black respondents stated that they would probably not or definitely not accept a COVID-19 vaccine, compared with 33 percent of White respondents.[49] Similarly, a Pew Research Center poll conducted in November 2020 revealed that while 71 percent of Black respondents knew someone who had been hospitalized or died because of COVID-19, only 42 percent planned to obtain a COVID-19 vaccine.[50]

During 2021, overall hesitancy dropped as more information was gathered regarding the effectiveness and safety of the COVID-19 vaccines.[51] However, hesitancy continued to be a significant concern among all groups.[52] If the media had covered stories

---

[44] Phillip Reese, High-Poverty Neighborhoods Bear the Brunt of COVID's Scourge, Kaiser Health News (Dec. 15, 2020), https://khn.org/news/article/high-poverty-neighborhoods-bear-the-brunt-of-covids-scourge/.

[45] Clare Bambra et al., The COVID-19 Pandemic and Health Inequalities, 74 J. *Epidemiol. Community Health* 964, 964 (2020).

[46] Shadim Hussain, We Need 'Horizontal' Trust to Overcome Vaccine Skepticism, Wired (Nov. 21, 2020), www.wired.com/story/we-need-horizontal-trust-to-overcome-vaccine-skepticism/.

[47] Rueben C. Warren et al., Trustworthiness Before Trust – COVID-19 Vaccine Trials and the Black Community, 383 *New Eng. J. Med.* e121, e121 (2020).

[48] Ctrs. for Disease Control & Prevention, The Tuskegee Timeline, www.cdc.gov/tuskegee/timeline .htm (last visited Mar. 2, 2020).

[49] Liz Hamel et al., Race, Health, and COVID-19: The Views and Experiences of Black Americans, Kaiser Fam. Found. 17 (Oct. 2020), http://files.kff.org/attachment/Report-Race-Health-and-COVID-19-The-Views-and-Experiences-of-Black-Americans.pdf.

[50] Cary Funk & Alec Tyson, Intent to Get a COVID-19 Vaccine Rises to 60% as Confidence in Research and Development Process Increases, *Pew Rsch. Ctr.* 6, 8 (Dec. 2020), www.pewresearch.org/science/wp-content/uploads/sites/16/2020/12/PS_2020.12.03_covid19-vaccine-intent_REPORT.pdf.

[51] Emmarie Huetteman, Covid Vaccine Hesitancy Drops Among All Americans, New Survey Shows, Kaiser Health News (Mar. 30, 2021), https://khn.org/news/article/covid-vaccine-hesitancy-drops-among-americans-new-kff-survey-shows/.

[52] Reuters Staff, COVID-19 Vaccine Hesitancy Among Black Americans Drops – Poll, Reuters (Mar. 30, 2021), www.reuters.com/article/us-health-coronavirus-vaccine-hesitancy-idUSKBN2BM0WY.

of individuals who were injured and not adequately compensated, vaccine hesitancy might have intensified. As the Presidential Commission for the Study of Bioethical Issues pointed out in the context of clinical trials generally, people may be more willing to participate in research if they are assured that they will be compensated if injured.[53] Similarly, people may be more willing to participate in mass vaccination programs if they know they will be taken care of in the event that they are harmed. Conversely, knowing that they will not be compensated may discourage participation.

B *Compensation Inequities and Structural Racism*

After an emergency declaration is lifted, newly vaccinated individuals can be eligible for VICP compensation if the CDC has recommended the vaccine for routine administration to children or pregnant women.[54] However, delaying vaccination until the end of a declared PHE can be particularly dangerous for minority and lower-income workers, including many essential workers. Many suffer from chronic conditions, such as asthma, heart disease, and diabetes, that make it more likely that they will suffer more severely from infectious diseases.[55] In addition, those with a lower socioeconomic status often have the highest risk of infection because they come in close contact with others at work, while taking public transportation, or while living in crowded households. In fact, employees working in person may have no choice as to whether to receive a vaccine once it is available. Employers may require workers to obtain vaccines. The US Equal Employment Opportunity Commission has determined that such employer mandates are lawful.[56]

At the same time, low-income people who most need to be vaccinated are the most financially at risk. A serious vaccine injury could thus be catastrophic for them if they are not appropriately compensated. Having access only to the CICP rather than the VICP can thus have a disproportionate adverse impact on poor communities.

By contrast, the people who can afford to wait for vaccinations until an emergency declaration has ended, triggering VICP availability, will tend to be more

---

[53] Presidential Comm'n for the Study of Bioethical Issues, Moral Science: Protecting Participants in Human Subjects Research 61 (Dec. 2011; updated edition June 2012), https://bioethicsarchive .georgetown.edu/pcsbi/sites/default/files/Moral%20Science%20June%202012.pdf.

[54] Health Res. & Servs. Admin., Frequently Asked Questions, www.hrsa.gov/cicp/faq (last visited Dec. 2020).

[55] Ctrs. for Disease Control & Prevention, People with Certain Medical Conditions, www.cdc.gov/ coronavirus/2019-ncov/need-extra-precautions/people-with-medical-conditions.html (last updated Dec. 29, 2020); Kenneth E. Thorpe et al., The United States Can Reduce Socioeconomic Disparities by Focusing on Chronic Diseases, Health Affs. Blog (Aug. 17, 2017), www.healthaffairs.org/do/10.1377/ hblog20170817.061561/full/.

[56] US Equal Emp. Opportunity Comm'n, What You Should Know About COVID-19 and the ADA, the Rehabilitation Act, and Other EEO Laws (Dec. 16, 2020), www.eeoc.gov/wysk/what-you-should-know-about-covid-19-and-ada-rehabilitation-act-and-other-eeo-laws; Vimal Patel, Employers Can Require Workers to Get COVID-19 Vaccine, U.S. Says, NY Times (Dec. 18, 2020), www.nytimes .com/2020/12/18/us/eeoc-employers-coronavirus-mandate.html.

privileged. This group will probably consist largely of people who can work remotely and socially isolate until they feel confident about the vaccine's safety profile. They tend to be disproportionately well educated, high earners, and White.[57] If those with socioeconomic advantages choose to wait for vaccines while their working-class counterparts cannot, they may be compensated far more liberally for the same types of vaccine injuries. Differences between the VICP and CICP could therefore reinforce long-established inequities rooted in income, race, and ethnic identity.

VI PROPOSALS FOR LEGAL REFORM

We argue that anyone who receives a vaccine that is a countermeasure to a PHE should have immediate access to the VICP. Disadvantaged people with the greatest need for vaccination, who are also the most at risk of financial harm, should benefit from an efficient and fair system of injury compensation. Moreover, penalizing early recipients of vaccines could undermine the important public health goal of vaccinating as many people as possible as quickly as possible in order to achieve herd immunity.

Experts predict that the world will face future global pandemics, and many have long worried about bioterrorism attacks.[58] Establishing the correct incentives and relief mechanisms for people who receive vaccinations is therefore of critical importance.

A straightforward modification to address the inequities that the CICP propagates is to amend the PREP Act. Under this approach, lawmakers would establish that all vaccines that the FDA approves and the CDC recommends to ameliorate a PHE will be covered by the VICP, regardless of whether they are to be administered to pregnant women or children.[59] This would include vaccines receiving an EUA.[60]

The carve-out would not impact any other countermeasures, such as drugs and devices, that have an EUA. Injury claims related to those countermeasures would

---

[57] Matt Simon, Your Income Predicts How Well You Can Socially Distance, Wired (Aug. 5, 2020), www.wired.com/story/your-income-predicts-how-well-you-can-socially-distance/; Vasil Yasenov, Who Can Work from Home?, IZA – Inst. of Lab. Econ. (May 4, 2020), www.iza.org/publications/dp/13197/who-can-work-from-home.

[58] Reduce Risk to Avert 'Era of Pandemics,' Experts Warn in New Report, UN News (Oct. 29, 2020), https://news.un.org/en/story/2020/10/1076392; Greater Risk of Bioterrorism Post-Corona, Deutsche Welle (May 25, 2020), www.dw.com/en/coronavirus-experts-warn-of-bioterrorism-after-pandemic/a-53554902.

[59] The provision to be amended is 42 U.S.C. § 247d–6d (i)(1). The following language could be added at the end of subparts (A) and (C) of this provision: "except that all vaccines that are recommended by the CDC for children or pregnant women are excluded from this Act and claims for injuries from these vaccines can be pursued under the Vaccine Injury Compensation Program."

[60] Federal law empowers the FDA Commissioner to "allow unapproved medical products or unapproved uses of approved medical products to be used in an emergency to diagnose, treat, or prevent serious or life-threatening diseases or conditions ... when there are no adequate, approved, and available alternatives." US Food & Drug Admin., Emergency Use Authorization, www.fda.gov/emergency-preparedness-and-response/mcm-legal-regulatory-and-policy-framework/emergency-use-authorization (last updated Jan. 25, 2022); 21 U.S.C. § 360bbb–3 (2010).

still be submitted to the CICP. The vaccine carve-out is justified because vaccines are given to healthy people in part for the good of society in that they protect the collective. By contrast, drugs and devices approved under an EUA are provided to unhealthy individuals to treat and cure their individual maladies. As this proposal deals solely with the liability of vaccine manufacturers, it also would not impact state and federal measures that provide immunity from liability to health care providers who administer vaccines.

The second element of this proposal is that Congress should require manufacturers to pay a seventy-five-cent excise tax per dose for all vaccines that the FDA approves and that the CDC recommends as PHE countermeasures. This excise tax will serve to ensure that the VICTF is adequately financed. As noted in Section III, such a tax already applies to vaccines included in the VICP.[61] During a PHE, when the government purchases vaccines and then distributes them to the public without charge, part of this purchase price can be allocated to cover the excise tax. This action will provide immediate funding for the VICP to cover any increase in the number of claims. In addition, Congress should expand the number of special masters who handle VICP cases because this docket is likely to grow significantly.[62] This measure will ensure that claims will be processed expeditiously.

VII CONCLUSION

Even the most carefully developed and tested vaccine can lead to injuries. Such injuries can disproportionately affect vulnerable populations who are most in need of vaccinations but are also at risk of financial ruin if harmed by a vaccine. Fortunately, injured parties can usually attain appropriate recovery through the generous and accessible VICP. However, during a declared PHE, individuals receiving vaccines that are countermeasures can turn only to the much less robust CICP if they are injured.

This difference is not simply technical. It can have severe ramifications, especially for disadvantaged populations. In some cases, people in high-risk communities may struggle to decide whether they should forego a vaccine and risk becoming infected, or risk a vaccine injury for which they could receive little if any compensation.

This chapter has proposed legal changes to rectify this wrong. It argues that the PREP Act should be amended to ensure that relevant vaccines are covered by the VICP rather than the CICP. Rendering the VICP available to all injured parties, including members of vulnerable communities, would advance multiple goals. It would promote public health by encouraging the public to pursue early vaccination, enhance equity, and increase the likelihood of adequate relief in all injury cases.

---

[61] See supra note 17 and accompanying text.
[62] US Ct. of Fed. Claims, Vaccine Claims/Office of Special Masters, www.uscfc.uscourts.gov/vaccine-program-readmore (last visited Jan. 17, 2021).

Opening New Pathways for Health Care Delivery and Access

Introduction

Katherine L. Kraschel

The chapters that follow in Part V of this volume illustrate how COVID-19's disruptive pressure on health care delivery and access served as a catalyst for change. These chapters show that the analogy to a catalyst in a chemical reaction is apropos, demonstrating how COVID-19:

(1) sped up but did not create novel modalities of health care delivery and treatment; (2) created new pathways to care through various legal and policy changes; and (3) ushered in changes that may or may not have sustained impact.

First, in chemistry, a catalyst speeds up a reaction but does not create one itself. Each of the chapters in Part V describes an innovation in delivery or pathway around barriers to access that existed prior to COVID-19 but whose uptake was sped up in the face of the pressures of COVID-19. In Chapter 18, "Telehealth Transformation in COVID-19," Ryan Knox, Laura Hoffman, Asees Bhasin, and Abbe Gluck emphasize that telehealth has existed for more than seventy years and describe the long-standing barriers to embracing it – from payment to licensing, prescribing, and privacy laws, and more. In Chapter 19, "Changes in the Provision of Take-Home Methadone for People with Opioid Use Disorder During the COVID-19 Pandemic: Implications for Future Policymaking," Dr. Zoe Adams, Taleed El-Sabawi, Dr. William Coe, Hannah Batchelor, Janan Wyatt, Mona Gandhi, Dr. Ida Santana, and Dr. Ayana Jordan point to evidence supporting the safety and effectiveness of methadone to treat opioid use disorder (OUD) that predate the pandemic. In Chapter 20, "Reproductive Justice After the Pandemic: How 'Personal Responsibility' Entrenches Disparities and Limits Autonomy," Rachel Zacharias, Elizabeth Dietz, Kimberly Mutcherson, and Josephine Johnston describe the prepandemic consensus that in-person requirements for medication abortion provision were unnecessary. Similarly, in Chapter 21, "Abortion At-Home and At-Law During a Pandemic," Joanna Erdman describes the unrealized revolutionary potential of medication abortion that has been lying in wait since its first uses in the 1980s.

The first three chapters in Part V point to problematic sources of regulatory barriers to access. As Dr. Adams and her coauthors state, "[r]ooted in racialized understandings of criminality, methadone has been regulated for protection of 'the public,' rather than for the safety, efficacy, and treatment of people with OUD." In addition, Zacharias, Dietz, Mutcherson, and Johnston depict the entrenched notions of personal responsibility and blameworthiness that took a backseat in the name of reducing the risk of viral spread and uncover readily available, reproductive justice-enhancing alternatives.

Second, a catalyst speeds up a reaction by creating lower energy pathways to the end state of the reaction. The chapters in Part V show where the system was before COVID-19, including the legal, regulatory, and political structures in place, and how racism and sexism manifest as barriers to effective care. They also detail how government responses elicited by COVID-19 shepherded changes, creating new pathways. Knox and his coauthors detail the rapid change to both state and federal laws that allowed the unprecedented growth of telehealth, largely in a synergistic way between federal law, governing issues such as Medicare reimbursement and privacy, and state laws, governing licensure. The other three chapters in Part V tell a slightly different story of how state and federal laws can work against one another – one looking to maintain the status quo, the other forging a new pathway to access. They show us how COVID-19 acted as a catalyst to motivate government actors to open new pathways to an end state that mitigates some of the pitfalls of the system at the outset and provides a roadmap for similar models in the future.

Finally, a catalyst's effect depends upon whether the reaction is reversible or irreversible. If it is irreversible, the catalyst speeds up the reaction and results in newly formed substances that cannot react with one another to return to the pre-reaction state. If the reaction is reversible, the catalyst serves to move the reaction along more quickly, but to an equilibrium in which some of the new products react to return to the original state. Taken collectively, the chapters in Part V tell a story of accelerated uptake of forward-looking models of care. Some show how COVID-19 expedited the demolition of barriers to care that were largely unsupported by evidence and based in racism and sexism. They also illustrate the precariousness of their longevity and the complexities of laws governing health care. Knox and his coauthors note that the Centers for Medicare and Medicaid Services have made some changes permanent by adding several telehealth services to the list of covered services, while noting that many other changes have sunsetted or are slated to sunset. They also discuss the remaining challenges for telehealth, including perpetuating disparities in accessing care and fraud, and call for continued research and regulatory innovation. Dr. Adams and her research team summarize the growing body of peer-reviewed literature and share their own study that provides concrete evidence of the safety and patient satisfaction of take-home doses of methadone for patients with OUD. Zacharias and her coauthors argue for the reproductive justice-enhancing changes

COVID-19 facilitated to serve as proof of concept for further, long-lasting reforms. Finally, Erdman describes how COVID-19 brought abortion into the home and contemplates the feedback loop that will continue between abortion at-home and laws that govern its provision.

What these chapters make abundantly clear is that no one law, no one body – legislative, regulatory, executive, or judicial – can work in isolation to maintain the gains realized during the pressures of the pandemic. Similarly, no entity alone can ensure lasting improvements or that the barriers removed during COVID-19 are not reconstructed. Time will tell whether COVID-19's catalytic power to reform health care delivery and remove barriers to access will be a lasting legacy of change or a brief snapshot in time.

18

Telehealth Transformation in COVID-19

Ryan P. Knox, Laura C. Hoffman, Asees Bhasin, and Abbe R. Gluck

I INTRODUCTION

Telehealth surged to the forefront of health care delivery during the COVID-19 pandemic. Though it has existed for years, telehealth has long faced legal, regulatory, and economic barriers to widespread adoption in the United States. The COVID-19 pandemic forced the health care system to rapidly adapt to overcome significant challenges, including those relating to reimbursement rules, regulation of online prescribing, privacy laws, and licensing requirements.

The policy changes implemented during the pandemic allowed for the adoption of telehealth at lightning speed and are in many ways unlikely to be rolled back even after the pandemic concludes. Yet while this natural experiment with telehealth demonstrated its overall effectiveness and received high patient satisfaction, concerns remain regarding telehealth's appropriateness in some health care contexts, its cost-effectiveness, its potential for exacerbating existing health disparities, and its risks of fraud and abuse. Further, many of the policy changes implemented during the pandemic were temporary; failure to make changes permanent will limit telehealth's future success.

This chapter engages with the transformation of telehealth use and regulation during the COVID-19 pandemic. After examining the historical and current barriers to telehealth adoption, we detail the explosive growth of telehealth during the pandemic, as well as the challenges that remain for the field's future success.

II BACKGROUND

Telehealth, sometimes referred to as telemedicine, is the provision of medical, public health, and health education services remotely – when a patient and provider are in different locations – using technology. Telehealth may involve real-time communications with a provider using audio-video or audio-only devices, the transmission of health information manually or through a medical device, or data tracking using a mobile health application.

Telehealth has existed in some form for more than seventy years and has grown significantly in recent decades. Radiological images were first sent by telephone in 1948, from West Chester, Pennsylvania to Philadelphia. In 1959, the Nebraska Psychiatry Institute began providing psychiatric consultations by videoconference. The National Aeronautics and Space Administration started telehealth projects in the 1970s, providing telehealth to rural patients in at least six states. Many large telehealth companies formed in the 2000s, providing services to patients directly or through partnerships with insurers or health systems.

Despite its long history and growth before the COVID-19 pandemic, telehealth's role in the US health care system was limited. Telehealth use was increasing by 30–50 percent per year prior to the pandemic, but adoption rates were still very low.[1] Only 0.25 percent of Medicare beneficiaries had used a telehealth service in 2016, and only 840,000 Medicare fee-for-service telehealth visits occurred in 2019.[2] For large employer plans, only 0.8 percent of beneficiaries in 2016 and 2.4 percent of beneficiaries in 2018 had used a telehealth service.[3] In February 2020, fewer than six services per 1,000 Medicaid and Children's Health Insurance Program beneficiaries were delivered via telehealth.[4]

Many factors contributed to telehealth's limited success. First, limited telehealth coverage and reimbursement by payers, or even a complete lack thereof, as well as lower rates of reimbursement as compared to in-person visits, deterred patient and provider adoption. Second, licensing laws have traditionally been barriers to telehealth adoption, as most states and Medicare require providers be licensed in the state where the patient is located. Third, state laws and federal health regulations restricting the creation of a doctor–patient relationship via telehealth, often requiring an initial in-person encounter, have prevented or discouraged telehealth adoption. Fourth, telehealth prescribing of certain medications was restricted by federal laws and regulations prohibiting prescribing without an in-person evaluation or requiring in-person dispensing. Last, health privacy laws have limited the

---

[1] Ateev Mehrotra et al., Telemedicine: What Should the Post-Pandemic Regulatory and Payment Landscape Look Like?, The Commonwealth Fund (Aug. 5, 2020), www.commonwealthfund.org/ publications/issue-briefs/2020/aug/telemedicine-post-pandemic-regulation.

[2] Information on Medicare Telehealth, Ctrs. for Medicare & Medicaid Servs. (Nov. 15, 2018), www .cms.gov/About-CMS/Agency-Information/OMH/Downloads/Information-on-Medicare-Telehealth-Report.pdf; Lok Wong Samson et al., Medicare Beneficiaries' Use of Telehealth in 2020: Trends by Beneficiary Characteristics and Location 1 (Assistant Sec'y for Plan. & Evaluation, US Dep't of Health & Human Servs. Dec. 2021), https://aspe.hhs.gov/sites/default/files/documents/a1d5d81ofe3433e 18b192be42dbf2351/medicare-telehealth-report.pdf.

[3] Matthew Rae et al., Coverage and Utilization of Telemedicine Services by Enrollees in Large Employer Plans, Peterson-KFF Health System Tracker (Mar. 3, 2020), www.healthsystemtracker.org/ brief/coverage-and-utilization-of-telemedicine-services-by-enrollees-in-large-employer-plans/.

[4] Rose C. Chu et al., State Medicaid Telehealth Policies Before and During the COVID-19 Public Health Emergency 1 (Assistant Sec'y for Plan. & Evaluation, US Dep't of Health & Human Servs. July 2021), https://aspe.hhs.gov/sites/default/files/2021-07/medicaid-telehealth-brief.pdf.

technologies that can be used for telehealth, prohibiting the most commonly used and easily accessible platforms, such as Zoom or FaceTime.

III CHANGES TO TELEHEALTH REGULATION IN COVID-19

The COVID-19 pandemic demanded rapid changes virtually overnight. Medical providers suspended non-essential in-person appointments and procedures to curb the spread of the virus and to reduce the burden on a medical system under unprecedented pressure. Both government and health care stakeholders across the country implemented new laws and policies to resolve many barriers to the use of telehealth.

A *Coverage Parity*

Government and private payers moved quickly to increase telehealth coverage and reimbursement. Historically, Medicare covered telehealth only if the patient was in a rural area, and even then required patients to go to an "originating site" to receive the care (typically a provider's office).[5] In March 2020, the Department of Health and Human Services (HHS) used its authority under Section 1135 of the Social Security Act to issue a waiver lifting this restriction by permitting non-rural patients to receive telehealth services and the patient's home to be an "originating site" of care.[6] Medicare also had previously required telehealth be delivered in real time using both audio and video technologies. While this requirement largely remained, the Centers for Medicare and Medicaid Services (CMS) issued a rule allowing reimbursement for behavioral health and patient education services provided via telehealth when patients only have audio-only phones.[7] CMS also added 144 additional telehealth services to its covered services list.[8] Many of these services were temporarily covered through the duration of the public health emergency. CMS extended permanent coverage to many behavioral telehealth services, including audio-only telehealth services, and temporary coverage to several other telehealth services through December 31, 2024, allowing the agency additional time

---

[5] 42 C.F.R. § 410.78 (2001).

[6] Medicare Telemedicine Health Care Provider Fact Sheet, Ctrs. for Medicare & Medicaid Servs. (Mar. 17, 2020), www.cms.gov/newsroom/fact-sheets/medicare-telemedicine-health-care-provider-fact-sheet.

[7] Trump Administration Issues Second Round of Sweeping Changes to Support U.S. Healthcare System During COVID-19 Pandemic, Ctrs. for Medicare & Medicaid Servs. (Apr. 30, 2020), www.cms.gov/newsroom/press-releases/trump-administration-issues-second-round-sweeping-changes-support-us-healthcare-system-during-covid (hereinafter, Second Round Changes).

[8] Trump Administration Finalizes Permanent Expansion of Medicare Telehealth Services and Improved Payment for Time Doctors Spend with Patients, Ctrs. for Medicare & Medicaid Servs. (Dec. 1, 2020), www.cms.gov/newsroom/press-releases/trump-administration-finalizes-permanent-expansion-medicare-telehealth-services-and-improved-payment.

to evaluate whether to cover those services permanently.[9] States and private health plans also removed many telehealth coverage restrictions. Medicaid programs in all fifty states and the District of Columbia covered some telehealth services prior to the pandemic, but only nineteen states permitted beneficiaries to receive services at home and very few covered audio-only services.[10] During the pandemic, the majority of states issued emergency policies expanding Medicaid telehealth coverage, most permitting beneficiaries to access telehealth in their home and some audio-only telehealth visits. More than forty states already had laws regulating telehealth coverage, though only about half of them required private insurers to cover telehealth services to the same extent as in-person visits (i.e., coverage parity).[11] During the pandemic, at least six additional states required coverage parity, with another dozen states requiring some level of expanded telehealth coverage.[12] Many states also took steps to expand access to audio-only telehealth services for individuals with private insurance, with only three states requiring plans to cover audio-only services prior to the pandemic and an additional eighteen states requiring private plan coverage of audio-only services permanently or temporarily during the pandemic.[13]

B *Payment Parity*

In addition to expanding coverage, payers also increased reimbursement rates for telehealth services. Medicare reimbursed all audio-video telehealth services and most audio-only telehealth services at the same rate as in-person visits (i.e., payment parity).[14] This was extended and is set to expire at the end of 2023.[15] In at least forty-five states, Medicaid adopted payment parity for audio-video and audio-only telehealth visits – reimbursing both in-person and telehealth service at the same or

[9] Calendar Year (CY) 2023 Medicare Physician Fee Schedule Final Rule, Ctrs. for Medicare & Medicaid Servs. (Nov. 1, 2022), www.cms.gov/newsroom/fact-sheets/calendar-year-cy-2023-medicare-physician-fee-schedule-final-rule (hereinafter, 2023 Medicare Physician Fee Schedule).

[10] Gabriela Weigel et al., Opportunities and Barriers for Telemedicine in the U.S. During the COVID-19 Emergency and Beyond, Kaiser Fam. Found. (May 11, 2020), www.kff.org/womens-health-policy/issue-brief/opportunities-and-barriers-for-telemedicine-in-the-u-s-during-the-covid-19-emergency-and-beyond/.

[11] Nathaniel M. Lacktman et al., 50-State Survey of Telehealth Commercial Insurance Laws, Foley & Lardner LLP (Feb. 2021), www.foley.com/-/media/files/insights/publications/2021/02/21mc30431-50state-telemed-reportmaster-02082021.pdf; Weigel et al., supra note 10.

[12] State COVID-19 Data and Policy Actions, Kaiser Fam. Found. (Jan. 12, 2022), www.kff.org/report-section/state-covid-19-data-and-policy-actions-policy-actions/.

[13] JoAnn Volk et al., States' Actions to Expand Telemedicine Access During COVID-19 and Future Policy Considerations, The Commonwealth Fund (June 23, 2021), www.commonwealthfund.org/publications/issue-briefs/2021/jun/states-actions-expand-telemedicine-access-covid-19.

[14] Medicare Telemedicine Health Care Provider Fact Sheet, supra note 6; Second Round Changes, supra note 7.

[15] Susan Morse, Telehealth payment parity only good through 2023, Healthcare Finance (Jan. 27, 2023), www.healthcarefinancenews.com/news/telehealth-payment-parity-only-good-through-2023.

comparable rates.[16] At least eighteen states also adopted policies temporarily requiring telehealth payment parity for private health plans.[17] Several states have since made these changes permanent.[18]

C Licensing

Regulators temporarily eliminated state licensing requirements preventing telehealth adoption. For most states and Medicare, providers must be licensed in the state where the patient is located. CMS used its waiver authority to waive licensing requirements, permitting providers with out-of-state licenses to practice via telehealth if they met certain requirements.[19] All fifty states and the District of Columbia also waived certain licensing requirements during the pandemic, with some offering a fast track licensure pathway for out-of-state providers.[20] Some of these waivers applied only to doctors, while many others also included nurses, nurse practitioners, physical therapists, other mental health professionals, or inactive or retired licensees.[21] Most of these waivers were temporary, with about thirty state waivers having expired at the end of 2021 and only three remaining in place in April 2023. States have taken further action,

[16] Kathleen Gifford et al., States Respond to COVID-19 Challenges but Also Take Advantage of New Opportunities to Address Long-Standing Issues: Results From a 50-State Medicaid Budget Survey for State Fiscal Years 2021 and 2022, Kaiser Fam. Found. (Oct. 27, 2021), www.kff.org/report-section/states-respond-to-covid-19-challenges-but-also-take-advantage-of-new-opportunities-to-address-long-standing-issues-benefits-and-telehealth/.

[17] Jared Augenstein et al., Executive Summary: Tracking Telehealth Changes State-by-State in Response to COVID-19, Manatt Health (Dec. 16, 2021), www.manatt.com/insights/newsletters/covid-19-update/executive-summary-tracking-telehealth-changes-stat.

[18] State Telehealth Laws and Reimbursement Policies Report, Fall 2022, Ctr. for Connected Health Policy (Oct. 2022), www.cchpca.org/resources/state-telehealth-laws-and-reimbursement-policies-report-fall-2022/.

[19] COVID-19 Emergency Declaration Blanket Waivers for Health Care Providers, Ctrs. for Medicare & Medicaid Servs., www.cms.gov/files/document/summary-covid-19-emergency-declaration-waivers.pdf (last updated May 24, 2021).

[20] U.S. States and Territories Modifying Requirements for Telehealth in Response to Covid-19, Fed'n of State Med. Bds., www.fsmb.org/siteassets/advocacy/pdf/states-waiving-licensure-requirements-for-telehealth-in-response-to-covid-19.pdf (last updated Apr. 12, 2023). Licensing across state lines, U.S. Dep't of Health & Human Servs., https://telehealth.hhs.gov/licensure/licensing-across-state-lines (last updated May 11, 2023).

[21] COVID-19 State Emergency Response: Temporarily Suspended and Waived Practice Agreement Requirements, Am. Ass'n of Nurse Practitioners, www.aanp.org/advocacy/state/covid-19-state-emergency-response-temporarily-suspended-and-waived-practice-agreement-requirements (last updated Jan. 18, 2022); State Licensure Exemptions and Requirements for PTs and PTAs During COVID-19, Fed'n of State Bds. of Physical Therapy, www.fsbpt.org/Portals/o/documents/news-events/Jurisdiction_Licensure_Exemptions_Requirements_Waivers_during_COVID-19.pdf (last updated May 8, 2020); COVID-19 State Resources: State Actions on Telebehavioral Health, Am. Counseling Ass'n (Sept. 1, 2021), www.counseling.org/docs/default-source/grad-stu-volunteers/telehealth-updates-by-state_september-2021_final.pdf; US States and Territories Expediting Licensure for Inactive/Retired Licensees in Response to COVID-19, Fed'n of State Med. Bds., www.fsmb.org/siteassets/advocacy/pdf/states-expediting-licensure-for-inactive-retired-licensees-in-response-to-covid19.pdf (last updated Jan. 19, 2022).

however, to ease telehealth licensing requirements, including temporary practice laws, interstate licensing compacts, and telehealth practice licensure (https://telehealth.hhs .gov/licensure/licensing-across-state-lines.).

D *Doctor–Patient Relationships*

While many states permitted the creation of a doctor–patient relationship via telehealth before the pandemic, some required an in-person examination or an existing doctor–patient relationship before allowing the provision of telehealth services. During the pandemic, some states suspended laws requiring a doctor–patient relationship to be formed through an in-person visit.[22] Similarly, Medicare previously required that a telehealth provider had an existing relationship with the patient and had treated the patient in-person within the past three years.[23] CMS waived these requirements for the duration of the COVID-19 public health emergency.[24] Medicare requirements for in-person visits within six months of the first behavioral health encounter and annually thereafter were also waived through December 31, 2024.[25]

E *Prescribing*

Historically, federal laws have prohibited telehealth prescribing of certain controlled substances without an in-person evaluation. Prior to the pandemic, most states required a patient–provider relationship before certain drugs (the list of drugs varies by state) could be prescribed remotely, and in at least fifteen states a physical exam would be required – in person, by live video, or by a referring physician.[26] During the pandemic, however, at least fifteen states issued emergency orders removing such in-person requirements. The Secretary of HHS and the Drug Enforcement Administration (DEA) invoked the "telemedicine exception" of the Controlled Substances Act, which permits health care providers to prescribe controlled substances, including opioids, via a real-time video telehealth visit without a prior in-person visit. The DEA also exercised enforcement discretion to permit prescribing of buprenorphine, an opioid use disorder treatment, over the phone without an in-person or video consultation.[27] While the in-person evaluation requirement remained for new patients being treated with methadone,

---

[22] U.S. States and Territories Modifying Requirements for Telehealth in Response to COVID-19, supra note 20.

[23] Weigel et al., supra note 10.

[24] Medicare Telemedicine Care Provider Fact Sheet, supra note 6.

[25] Telehealth policy changes after the COVID-19 public health emergency, U.S. Dep't Health & Human Servs., https://telehealth.hhs.gov/providers/telehealth-policy/policy-changes-after-the-covid-19-public-health-emergency (last updated June 7, 2023).

[26] Weigel et al., supra note 10.

[27] FAQs: Provision of Methadone and Buprenorphine for the Treatment of Opioid Use Disorder in the COVID-19 Emergency, Substance Abuse & Mental Health Servs. Admin. (Apr. 21, 2020), www .samhsa.gov/sites/default/files/faqs-for-oud-prescribing-and-dispensing.pdf.

Opioid Treatment Programs were permitted to dispense both buprenorphine and methadone based on a telehealth evaluation, including an audio-only evaluation. Congress since eased telehealth prescribing of buprenorphine by passing the Mainstream Addiction Treatment Act in 2022.[28] The DEA took further steps, announcing proposed permanent rules that would permit telehealth prescribing of buprenorphine and non-narcotic Schedule III, IV, and V controlled substances under certain circumstances, in some cases without an in-person evaluation.[29]

Similarly, Food and Drug Administration (FDA) regulations requiring in-person visits or laboratory tests for the dispensation of certain medications have historically restricted telehealth prescribing. During the pandemic, the FDA exercised enforcement discretion over in-person testing and dispensing requirements for certain medications, but controversially did not initially waive in-person dispensing requirements for mifepristone, part of a medication abortion regimen.[30] While a Maryland federal court issued two injunctions prohibiting the FDA from enforcing in-person requirements for mifepristone, the Supreme Court stayed enforcement of the Court's decision in January 2021, allowing the FDA to continue enforcing the requirements.[31] The FDA under the Biden Administration later lifted these restrictions, first temporarily in April 2021 and then permanently in January 2023, thereby permitting online prescribing of mifepristone as well.[32] The policy change remains controversial, with an ongoing court battle challenging FDA's approval of and safety requirements for mifepristone.[33] This controversy is exacerbated by the Supreme Court's decision in Dobbs v. Women's Whole Health Organization and states' efforts to both protect and restrict access to abortion. While some states permit telehealth to access medication abortions, other states have required in-person visits or in-person dispensing to limit access.[34]

---

[28] Sheri Doyle & Vanessa Baaklini, President Signs Bipartisan Measure to Improve Addiction Treatment, Pew Charitable Trusts (Dec. 30, 2022), www.pewtrusts.org/en/research-and-analysis/articles/2022/12/30/president-signs-bipartisan-measure-to-improve-addiction-treatment.

[29] Telemedicine Prescribing of Controlled Substances When the Practitioner and the Patient Have Not Had a Prior In-Person Medical Evaluation, 88 Fed. Reg. 12875 (Mar. 1, 2023); Expansion of Induction of Buprenorphine via Telemedicine Encounter, 88 Fed. Reg. 12890 (Mar. 1, 2023).

[30] Mifeprex (mifepristone) Information, US Food & Drug Admin., www.fda.gov/drugs/postmarket-drug-safety-information-patients-and-providers/mifeprex-mifepristone-information; Am. Coll. of Obstetricians & Gynecologists v. U.S. Food & Drug Admin., 472 F.Supp.3d 183, 194 (D. Md. 2020).

[31] Food & Drug Admin. v. Am. Coll. of Obstetricians & Gynecologists, 141 S.Ct. 578 (2021).

[32] Alice Miranda Ollstein & Darius Tahir, FDA Lifts Curbs on Dispensing Abortion Pills During Pandemic, Politico (Apr. 12, 2021), www.politico.com/news/2021/04/12/abortion-pills-481092; Information about Mifepristone for Medical Termination of Pregnancy Through Ten Weeks Gestation, US Food & Drug Admin., www.fda.gov/drugs/postmarket-drug-safety-information-patients-and-providers/information-about-mifepristone-medical-termination-pregnancy-through-ten-weeks-gestation (last updated Mar. 23, 2023).

[33] Patricia J. Zettler, Eli Y. Adashi, & I. Glenn Cohen, *Alliance for Hippocratic Medicine v. FDA — Dobbs's* Collateral Consequences for Pharmaceutical Regulation, 388(10) *New Eng. J. Med.* e29 (1), e29(1–3) (2023).

[34] The Availability and Use of Medication Abortion, Kaiser Fam. Found. (June 1, 2023), www.kff.org/womens-health-policy/fact-sheet/the-availability-and-use-of-medication-abortion/.

F *Privacy*

The Health Insurance Portability and Accountability Act (HIPAA), which sets privacy and security requirements for health care providers and certain other entities handling health information, prohibits providers from communicating with patients or transmitting patient information over most commonly used platforms. In March 2020, HHS announced that during the pandemic it would "exercise enforcement discretion and ... waive potential penalties for HIPAA violations against health care providers" delivering telehealth services over common platforms, including FaceTime and Zoom, as long as they were not public-facing.[35] Many states also provided guidance on state health privacy laws for telehealth providers. HHS announced that the discretionary enforcement for HIPAA violations related to telehealth will conclude at the end of the public health emergency, with a 90-day transition period for entities to become compliant.[36]

IV DATA ON TELEHEALTH ADOPTION DURING THE PANDEMIC

These changes and reforms to telehealth regulation, and many others, permitted a massive surge in telehealth adoption during the COVID-19 pandemic. While the week before the pandemic saw only 13,000 Medicare telehealth visits, the last week in April 2020 saw 1.7 million.[37] By the end of 2020, there were 52.7 million Medicare fee-for-service telehealth visits, a sixty-three-fold increase compared to 2019.[38] Medicaid and Children's Health Insurance Program beneficiaries saw a twenty-fold increase in telehealth visits, from six telehealth visits per 1,000 beneficiaries in February 2020 to over 150 telehealth visits per 1,000 beneficiaries in April 2020.[39] From April 2019 to April 2020, private insurance claims for telehealth increased by more than 8,000 percent.[40]

Telehealth provided access to many health care services, making possible treatment that would have otherwise been delayed or prevented by the pandemic. Providers met virtually with patients, over the phone or by videoconference, to

---

[35] OCR Announces Notification of Enforcement Discretion for Telehealth Remote Communications During the COVID-19 Nationwide Public Health Emergency, US Dep't of Health & Human Servs. (Mar. 17, 2020), www.hhs.gov/about/news/2020/03/17/ocr-announces-notification-of-enforcement-discretion-for-telehealth-remote-communications-during-the-covid-19.html.

[36] HHS Office for Civil Rights Announces the Expiration of COVID-19 Public Health Emergency HIPAA Notifications of Enforcement Discretion, US Dep't of Health & Human Servs. (April 11, 2023) www.hhs.gov/about/news/2023/04/11/hhs-office-for-civil-rights-announces-expiration-covid-19-public-health-emergency-hipaa-notifications-enforcement-discretion.html.

[37] Seema Verma, Early Impact of CMS Expansion of Medicare Telehealth During COVID-19, Health Affs. Blog (July 15, 2020), www.healthaffairs.org/do/10.1377/hblog20200715.454789/full/.

[38] Samson et al., supra note 2, at 4.

[39] Chu et al., supra note 4, at 1.

[40] Robin Gelburd, Telehealth Growth in April Suggests Continuing Impact of COVID-19, Am. J. Managed Care (July 7, 2020), www.ajmc.com/view/telehealth-growth-in-april-suggests-continuing-impact-of-covid19.

provide non-urgent care visits or other routine consultations to manage medical and psychiatric conditions. Among medical specialties, gastroenterology, neurology, endocrinology, and psychiatry saw the greatest telehealth adoption during the pandemic, while obstetrics/gynecology, oncology, ophthalmology, physical therapy, and orthopedics saw the least.[41] More than half of endocrinologists, gastroenterologists, neurologists, pain management physicians, and psychiatrists used telehealth at least once during the COVID-19 pandemic between March and June 2020.[42] Telehealth in pediatrics varied by location and type of provider, with many visits for endocrine, nutritional, and metabolic diseases, and mental and neurodevelopmental disorders.[43]

Telehealth utilization rates varied widely across the country. One study found that between May 20, 2020 and June 16, 2020, 47.6 percent of visits in Massachusetts were via telehealth, compared to only 8.4 percent in South Dakota.[44] The Assistant Secretary for Planning and Evaluation similarly reported that between January and December 2020, the highest use of telehealth by Medicare beneficiaries was in Massachusetts, Vermont, Rhode Island, New Hampshire, and Connecticut, while the least use was in Tennessee, Nebraska, Kansas, North Dakota, and Wyoming.[45] There was also greater telehealth adoption in urban areas, counties with low poverty rates, and areas with a higher COVID-19 prevalence between March and June 2020.[46]

These explosive telehealth utilization rates decreased as the pandemic wore on, but stayed significantly above pre-pandemic levels. After quarantine ended for most people in early May 2020, telehealth use decreased, though it was still about thirty-eight times above the pre-pandemic level.[47] These telehealth rates leveled out during the summer of 2020, plateauing at about 17 percent of all outpatient visits. Some specialties saw significantly higher continued telehealth use, in particular psychiatry and substance use treatment, maintaining telehealth rates at about 50 percent and 30 percent, respectively. Neurology, family medicine, and internal medicine also

---

[41] NORC at the Univ. of Chi., Changes to Telehealth Policy, Delivery, and Outcomes in Response to COVID-19 11 (Dec. 2020), www.pcori.org/sites/default/files/PCORI-Landscape-Review-NORC-Changes-Telehealth-Policy-Delivery-Outcomes-Response-COVID-19-December-2020.pdf; Sadiq Y. Patel et al., Variation in Telemedicine Use and Outpatient Care During the COVID-19 Pandemic in the United States, 40 *Health Affs.* 349, 353–54 (2021).

[42] Patel et al., supra note 40, at 353.

[43] Alison Curfman et al., Pediatric Telehealth in the COVID-19 Pandemic Era and Beyond, 148 *Pediatrics* e2020047795v (2021); Stormee Williams et al., Pediatric Telehealth Expansion in Response to COVID-19, 9 *Front. Pediatr.* 642089 (2021).

[44] Sadiq Y. Patel et al., Trends in Outpatient Care Delivery and Telemedicine During the COVID-19 Pandemic in the US, 181 *J. Am. Med. Ass'n Intern. Med.* 388, 388–91 (2020).

[45] Samson et al., supra note 2, at 11.

[46] Jonathan P. Weiner et al., In-Person Telehealth Ambulatory Contacts and Costs in a Large US Insured Cohort Before and During the COVID-19 Pandemic, 4 *J. Am. Med. Ass'n Network Open* e212618 (2021).

[47] Oleg Bestsennyy et al., Telehealth: A Quarter-Trillion-Dollar Post-COVID-19 Reality, McKinsey & Co. (July 9, 2021), www.mckinsey.com/industries/healthcare-systems-and-services/our-insights/telehealth-a-quarter-trillion-dollar-post-covid-19-reality.

sustained higher rates of telehealth video visits through March 2021.[48] Other specialties, especially surgical specialties, largely returned to in-person visits.[49]

Despite the decrease in telehealth utilization, the changed landscape endured. Patients and providers alike indicated high satisfaction with telehealth and a desire to continue using telehealth after the pandemic. A May 2020 Press Ganey survey found that 96.3 percent of patients were likely to recommend a telehealth visit with their provider to others.[50] Providers have also reported positive experiences with telehealth. One survey of a large health care system found that clinicians "feel that they are able to not only provide equal quality of care in a video visit and an in-person visit, but also to establish rapport to the same extent via either type of visit."[51]

V TELEHEALTH RISKS AND LIMITATIONS

While the COVID-19 pandemic highlighted telehealth's potential, it also raised several risks and limitations associated with telehealth use, in addition to the challenges discussed above.

A *Disparities in Telehealth Access and Use*

Telehealth aims to improve access to health care, but the experience during the pandemic made it plain that access is not equitable. A major disparity related to telehealth is the "digital divide" – the gap in access to technology, access to Internet coverage, and digital literacy. Lack of access to technology prevents many populations from accessing telehealth. People without a smartphone, computer, or tablet may not be able to use telehealth or may only be able to use audio-only services, which providers largely view as inferior. Older adults, people of color, and low-income populations are less likely to have the technology at home needed for telehealth access.[52] The technology necessary for telehealth, and in some cases the website accessibility of the telehealth platform, pose further challenges for some populations, as many platforms are not accessible for people with disabilities, particularly visual, hearing,

---

[48] Inst. for Healthcare Pol'y & Innovation, Univ. of Mich., Telehealth Incubator Research Snapshots 8 (Dec. 2021), https://ihpi.umich.edu/sites/default/files/2021-08/Telehealth_Research_Snapshots_Databook_2021.pdf.

[49] Chartis Grp., Telehealth Adoption Tracker (Sept. 8, 2021), https://reports.chartis.com/telehealth_trends_and_implications-2021/.

[50] Press Ganey Special Report: The Rapid Transition to Telemedicine: Insights and Early Trends (2020).

[51] Inst. for Healthcare Pol'y & Innovation, Univ. of Mich., supra note 47, at 37.

[52] Lauren A. Eberly et al., Patient Characteristics Associated With Telemedicine Access for Primary and Specialty Ambulatory Care During the COVID-19 Pandemic, 3 *J. Am. Med. Ass'n Network Open* e2031640 (2020); Eric T. Roberts & Ateev Mehrotra, Assessment of Disparities in Digital Access Among Medicare Beneficiaries and Implications for Telemedicine, 180 *J. Am. Med. Ass'n Intern. Med.* 1386, 1386 (2020).

or speech impairments, or cognitive disabilities.[53] Many telehealth platforms are only in English, are primarily designed for English speakers, or have limited access to interpreters, preventing effective use for patients with limited English proficiency or who are non-English speaking.[54] The design of telehealth technologies is frequently not made with the specific needs of various populations in mind.[55] Access to Internet coverage is also necessary for telehealth. Half of low-income Americans and a third of rural Americans lack broadband access at home.[56] Digital literacy, or the ability of people to use technologies, also contributes to disparities in telehealth. Older adults in particular have less digital literacy, hindering their ability to use telehealth.[57] Without addressing the digital divide, telehealth may leave certain populations behind, including those already experiencing health disparities.

Consistent with these barriers, studies have shown that people in rural areas, older adults, people with Medicaid, and patients whose preferred language was not English had lower rates of telehealth adoption during the COVID-19 pandemic.[58] Relatedly, older age, Black race, Latinx ethnicity, Medicaid insurance, and lower income were associated with decreased use of telehealth with video and increased use of audio-only telehealth services. While telehealth seeks to promote access to health care, it may be exacerbating existing health disparities.

B *Telehealth Appropriateness and Effectiveness Across Health Care Contexts*

There are also concerns about telehealth's appropriateness and effectiveness in different health care contexts. Some benefits of telehealth are broadly accepted, including "refilling prescriptions, treating low-severity symptoms, and counseling for mental health."[59] Telestroke care has been used for decades and is an effective, life-saving tool.[60] A systematic review indicated that outcomes of telemental

---

[53] Rupa S. Valdez et al., Ensuring Full Participation of People with Disabilities in an Era of Telehealth, 28 *J. Am. Med. Informatics Ass'n* 389, 390 (2021); Carli Friedman & Laura VanPuymbrouck, Telehealth Use by People With Disabilities During the Pandemic, 13 *Int'l J. Telerehabilitation* (2021).

[54] Nicole Wetsman, Telehealth Wasn't Designed for Non-English Speakers, Verge (June 4, 2020), www.theverge.com/21277936/telehealth-english-systems-disparities-interpreters-online-doctor-appointments.

[55] Kimberly Noel & Brooke Ellison, Inclusive Innovation in Telehealth, 3 *npj Digital Med.* 89 (2020).

[56] Utsha Khatri et al., These Key Telehealth Policy Changes Would Improve Buprenorphine Access While Advancing Health Equity, Health Affs. Blog (Sept. 11, 2020), www.healthaffairs.org/do/10.1377/hblog20200910.498716/full/; Mark E. Dornauer & Robert Bryce, Too Many Rural Americans Are Living in the Digital Dark. The Problem Demands a New Deal Solution, Health Affs. Blog (Oct. 28, 2020), www.healthaffairs.org/do/10.1377/hblog20201026.515764/full/.

[57] Kenneth Lam et al., Assessing Telemedicine Unreadiness Among Older Adults in the United States During the COVID-19 Pandemic, 180 *J. Am. Med. Ass'n Intern. Med.* 1389, 1389–90 (2020).

[58] Patel et al., supra note 40, at 352, 357; Eberly et al., supra note 51; Loretta Hsueh et al., Disparities in Use of Video Telemedicine Among Patients With Limited English Proficiency During the COVID-19 Pandemic, 4 *J. Am. Med. Ass'n Network Open* e2133129 (2021).

[59] Kurt R. Herzer & Peter J. Pronovost, Ensuring Quality in the Era of Virtual Care, 325 *J. Am. Med. Ass'n* 429, 429 (2021).

[60] Mehrotra et al., supra note 1.

health relating to assessment and treatment of mental health conditions were not significantly different when compared with in-person care.[61] The same review found that care delivered by telerehabilitation was generally equivalent to or yielded better outcomes than in-person care. Telehealth has also been effective in detecting post-operative complications related to appendectomies and colorectal surgeries.[62] Additionally, a study also found that in the obstetric field, telehealth interventions improved outcomes related to smoking cessation and breastfeeding, and decreased the need for high-risk obstetric monitoring office visits while maintaining maternal and fetal outcomes.[63] Telehealth was also found likely to yield clinical improvements in nutrition management for older adults living at home when compared to usual care or no intervention.[64]

Alongside the benefits of telehealth, there also exist some drawbacks to using it as an delivery method. Naturally, there are limitations in which tests, assessments, and examinations can be accomplished during a telehealth visit without a patient having additional medical technologies at their disposal. For example, assessments of blood pressure and cholesterol during telehealth primary care visits decreased during the COVID-19 pandemic.[65] Further, many types of care, even if they can be initiated over telehealth, necessitate subsequent in-person visits. Between 10 and 20 percent of patients require an in-person biopsy after a telehealth dermatology visit and 38 percent of patients receiving a diabetic retinopathy screening via telehealth require an in-person follow-up.[66] Another study showed that patients using direct-to-consumer telemedicine for diagnosis of acute respiratory infections were more likely to have a repeat related visit within seven days than similar patients who visited their providers in person.[67] Patients may be seeking this follow-up care because they were directed to, due to a worsening of their symptoms, or due to concerns about the inability to conduct a physical examination or the quality of care provided by a telemedicine visit. These issues of proximity may also have impacts on the accuracy of diagnosis and consequently on the quality of treatment. For example, a study reported

[61] Erin Shigekawa et al., The Current State of Telehealth Evidence: A Rapid Review, 27 *Health Affs.* 1975, 1978 (2018).

[62] Asim Kichloo et al., Telemedicine, The Current COVID-19 Pandemic and the Future: A Narrative Review and Perspectives Moving Forward in the USA, *Fam. Med. Community Health* 8(3): e000539 (2020).

[63] Nathaniel DeNicola et al., Telehealth Interventions to Improve Obstetric and Gynecologic Health Outcomes, 135 Obstetric Gynecology 371 (2020).

[64] Shigekawa et al., supra note 60, at 1980.

[65] Herzer & Pronovost, supra note 58, at 429.

[66] Lori Uscher-Pines & Ateev Mehrotra, Telehealth Alone Will Not Increase Health Care Access for the Underserved, Health Affs. Blog (Dec. 15, 2016), www.healthaffairs.org/do/10.1377/hblog20161215.057859/full/.

[67] Kathleen Yinran Li et al., Direct-To-Consumer Telemedicine Visits for Acute Respiratory Infections Linked to More Downstream Visits, 40 *Health Affs.* 596 (2021).

that in-person dermatology performed better for diagnostic accuracy than tele-dermatology; within this, a higher diagnostic concordance was found between in-person dermatology and live video as compared to asynchronous communications (submitting data for review by a provider at a later time).[68] A 2018 study examining patients seeking care for a sore throat found that telemedicine exhibited poor agreement with the in-person physical examination on the primary outcome of tonsil size, but exhibited moderate agreement on coloration of the palate and cervical lymphadenopathy, and suggested that physical examination likely remained an important part of the diagnostic process.[69]

While telehealth has been seen to be successful during the pandemic overall, it is not effective or appropriate in all health care contexts. Further research is required to determine how the efficiency of telehealth can be maximized to discern those specialties and services for which telehealth is suited and those for which it is not ideal. Research comparing the impact of in-person visits and telehealth visits on health outcomes will also prove very valuable.

C Telehealth Utilization and Spending

Furthermore, there has been debate as to whether increased telehealth coverage in the long term will drive up health care utilization and, in turn, health care spending. The convenience of telehealth may promote excessive, unnecessary utilization; as such, some studies have indicated that telehealth coverage expansions would increase overall health spending.[70] There is conflicting evidence as to whether this has been the case in practice. One study of ambulatory visits between October 1, 2019 and April 30, 2021 at a large New England health care system found that adopting telehealth did not increase the overall volume of visits and that most telehealth visits were substitutive, not additive.[71] This evidence must be considered in light of the fact that such care was sought during an ongoing pandemic, and it is unclear where telehealth services will be substitutive or additive in the absence of these circumstances. For example, a study of Blue Cross Blue Shield of Michigan patients between 2011 and 2017 found telehealth visits for all conditions except mental health were associated with a higher rate of subsequent visits and increased health care utilization.[72]

---

[68] Shigekawa et al., supra note 60.

[69] Moneeb Akhtar et al., Telemedicine Physical Examination Utilizing a Consumer Device Demonstrates Poor Concordance with In-Person Physical Examination in Emergency Department Patients with Sore Throat: A Prospective Blinded Study, 24 *Telemed. J. e-Health* 790 (2018).

[70] Mehrotra et al., supra note 1.

[71] Kori S. Zachrison et al., Changes in Virtual and In-Person Health Care Utilization in a Large Health System During the COVID-19 Pandemic, 4 *J. Am. Med. Ass'n Network Open* e2129973 (2021).

[72] Xiang Liu et al., Comparison of Telemedicine Versus In-Person Visits on Impact of Downstream Utilization of Care, 27 *Telemed. J. e-Health* 1099, 1099 (2021).

D *Telehealth Fraud*

From the beginning of the pandemic, HHS recognized the potential for health care fraud in telehealth, especially as its use increased. To mitigate provider risk and incentivize telehealth adoption, HHS allowed providers to reduce or waive patient copayments for telehealth services during the COVID-19 pandemic, which typically would violate the Anti-Kickback Statute.[73] While this eased the quick transition to telehealth, it did not prevent fraud and abuse in the growing telehealth market. The relaxed regulatory environment increased the risk of upcoding (billing for more expensive services or more time than was spent with the patient), misrepresenting the services provided, and billing for services not rendered. Studying telehealth use during the first year of the pandemic, the HHS Office of the Inspector General found 1,714 providers – receiving $127.7 million in Medicare fee-for-service payments – that posed a high risk of fraud, waste, or abuse of telehealth services.[74] Some large telehealth fraud schemes have involved telehealth providers billing for consultations that did not occur and receiving bribes to order unnecessary testing, durable medical equipment, and pain medications, sometimes with no or limited patient interaction. Two such cases brought by the Department of Justice in 2020 and 2021 alleged $4.5 billion and $1.1 billion in losses to Medicare, respectively.[75]

VI THE FUTURE OF TELEHEALTH

Steps have already been taken to secure telehealth's future place in the US health care system. Some reforms have already been implemented, while many other proposals at the federal and state levels remain pending.

A *Federal and State Reforms and Proposals*

Many of the changes implemented during the pandemic have been made permanent. In 2021, CMS permanently added several telehealth services to its list of

---

[73] Medicare Telemedicine Health Care Provider Fact Sheet, supra note 6.

[74] Medicare Telehealth Services During the First Year of the Pandemic: Program Integrity Risks, US Dep't of Health & Human Servs. Office of the Inspector General (Sept. 2022), https://oig.hhs.gov/oei/reports/OEI-02-20-00720.pdf.

[75] National Health Care Fraud and Opioid Takedown Results in Charges Against 345 Defendants Responsible for More Than $6 Billion in Alleged Fraud Losses, US Dep't of Just. (Sept. 30, 2020), www.justice.gov/opa/pr/national-health-care-fraud-and-opioid-takedown-results-charges-against-345-defendants; National Health Care Fraud Enforcement Action Results in Charges Involving Over $1.4 Billion in Alleged Losses, US Dep't of Just. (Sept. 17, 2021), www.justice.gov/opa/pr/national-health-care-fraud-enforcement-action-results-charges-involving-over-14-billion.

Medicare-covered services, including group psychotherapy and psychological and neuropsychological testing.[76] In 2022, CMS authorized Medicare payments for telehealth services furnished "for purposes of diagnosis, evaluation or treatment of a mental health disorder" on a permanent basis. CMS also expanded the ability of Opioid Treatment Programs to provide counseling and therapy services using audio-only telehealth, while Substance Abuse Mental Health Services Administration extended the rules permitting telehealth prescribing of methadone by Opioid Treatment Programs.[77] The FDA permanently removed mifepristone's in-person dispensing requirements in January 2023.[78] Since March 2021, at least 25 states have passed laws expanding access to telehealth, including allowing telephone visits and requiring telehealth services be accessible for people with disabilities, older adults, and people with limited English proficiency.[79] Twenty-one states have adopted payment parity as of May 2023, with an additional seven states having conditional payment parity.[80] Arkansas passed legislation allowing providers to establish a relationship and treat patients in an audio-video or audio-only telehealth visit and to prescribe non-controlled substances.[81] At least nine states have permanently allowed for audio-only telehealth visits in Medicaid.[82] Five new states joined the Interstate Medical Licensure Compact, easing licensing barriers for telehealth providers in those states.[83]

Other changes have not yet been made permanent, although several telehealth policy proposals have been made at the federal and state levels. Multiple bills have been introduced in Congress to remove Medicare's geographic restrictions on

---

[76] Calendar Year (CY) 2021 Medicare Physician Fee Schedule Final Rule, Ctrs. for Medicare & Medicaid Servs. (Dec. 2, 2020), https://s3.amazonaws.com/public-inspection.federalregister.gov/2019-24086.pdf.

[77] Calendar Year (CY) 2022 Medicare Physician Fee Schedule Final Rule, Ctrs. for Medicare & Medicaid Servs. (Nov. 2, 2021), www.cms.gov/newsroom/fact-sheets/calendar-year-cy-2022-medicare-physician-fee-schedule-final-rule; Methadone Take-Home Flexibilities Extension Guidance, Substance Abuse Mental Health Servs. Admin., www.samhsa.gov/medication-assisted-treatment/statutes-regulations-guidelines/methadone-guidance (last updated Nov. 18, 2021).

[78] Information about Mifepristone for Medical Termination of Pregnancy Through Ten Weeks Gestation, supra note 31.

[79] JoAnn Volk, Madeline O'Brien, & Christina L. Goe, State Telemedicine Coverage Requirements Continue to Evolve, The Commonwealth Fund (Dec. 20, 2022), www.commonwealthfund.org/blog/2022/state-telemedicine-coverage-requirements-continue-evolve.

[80] Jared Augenstein & Jacqueline Marks Smith, Executive Summary: Tracking Telehealth Changes State-by-State in Response to COVID-19, Manatt (June 9, 2023), www.manatt.com/insights/newsletters/covid-19-update/executive-summary-tracking-telehealth-changes-stat.

[81] H.B. 1063, 93rd Gen. Assemb., Reg. Sess. (Ark. 2021).

[82] Jacquelyn Rudich et al., State Medicaid Telehealth Policies Before and During the COVID-19 Public Health Emergency: 2022 Update, U.S. Dep't of Health & Human Servs. Ass't Secretary for Planning & Evaluation (Nov. 22, 2022), https://aspe.hhs.gov/sites/default/files/documents/190b4b132f984db14924cbadood19cce/Medicaid-Telehealth-IB-Update-Final.pdf.

[83] Press Releases, Interstate Medical Licensure Compact, www.imlcc.org/news/press-releases-and-publications/ (last visited Jan. 24, 2021).

telehealth coverage.[84] Other bills have sought to expand access to telehealth for specific types of health care services. The Women's Health Protection Act of 2023 would protect providers' ability to deliver and patients' ability to access telehealth medication abortion services.[85] The Expanding Access to Mental Health Services Act would allow Medicare to permanently cover behavioral health counseling services provided via audio-only telehealth.[86] Many states have also proposed legislation to expand coverage of audio-only telehealth services, to require coverage parity and payment parity for telehealth services, and to provide the cross-border provision of telehealth services. Other states have let their temporary waivers expire or actively sought to reel back their telehealth expansions; for example, a New Hampshire bill was introduced seeking to end audio-only coverage and telehealth payment parity.[87]

Still other changes implemented during the pandemic have gone unaddressed. No reforms have been made to HIPAA to expand technologies that can be used for telehealth. Although there has been an increase in telehealth fraud enforcement, no changes have been made to the current regulatory scheme to prevent telehealth fraud in the first place.

B *Uniform Law Commission Draft Legislation*

The Uniform Law Commission, the largest state law-drafting organization in the country, approved the Uniform Telehealth Act in July 2022 to aid states in developing their own telehealth legislation.[88] The November 18, 2021 draft of the Telehealth Act explained that the Committee sought to capture two broad goals with the model legislation: to emphasize parallels between the delivery of telehealth services and in-person traditional services; and to establish a registration system for out-of-state practitioners to reduce existing licensing barriers. As approved, the Act sets forth the circumstances under which a practitioner may provide telehealth services in a state. It does not, however, engage with the critical questions of coverage parity or payment parity. Further, passed in the wake of *Dobbs v. Women's Whole Health Organization*, the Act poses potential obstacles for the telehealth consultation and prescribing across state lines on matters relating to reproductive choice. This has led some former supporters of the idea of uniform telehealth legislation to object to the finalized version without further amendment. The future of the Uniform Telehealth Act remains uncertain and thus far no states have enacted it.

---

[84] To amend title XVIII of the Social Security Act to remove geographic requirements and expand originating sites for telehealth services, H.R. 134, 118th Cong. (2023); Fair Care Act of 2022, H.R.8588, 117th Cong. (2022); Telehealth Modernization Act, S. 368, 117th Cong. (2022).

[85] Women's Health Protection Act of 2023, H.R. 12, 118th Cong. (2023).

[86] Expanding Access to Mental Health Services Act, H.R. 635, 118th Cong. (2023).

[87] H.B. 602, 2021 Leg., Exec. Sess. (N.H. 2021).

[88] Uniform Telehealth Act (Unif. Law Comm'n 2022).

VII CONCLUSION

The telehealth landscape has been permanently transformed by the COVID-19 pandemic. Providers are expanding their telehealth services. Companies and health systems are experimenting with new telehealth innovations, from using artificial intelligence to remotely adjust a patient's insulin dose to using drones with cameras to consult with patients in their home while delivering medications or medical supplies. The telehealth market is growing, with non-traditional companies such as Walmart entering the telehealth space.

But for telehealth's success to continue in the future, regulatory reforms are needed. The changes implemented to permit telehealth adoption are largely temporary, with some having already expired and others set to expire at the end of the declared COVID-19 public health emergency. Further, there are risks and limitations with telehealth, resulting in greater health disparities and potential fraud and abuse. Several telehealth policy proposals have already been made at the federal and state levels, considering issues from coverage and payment parity to cross-border provision of care to expanding the locations where Medicare and Medicaid patients can receive telehealth services. Additional reforms should take into account the challenges observed during the COVID-19 pandemic and seek to promote telehealth's future success, and continued research is needed to determine the proper role of telehealth in the US health care system.

Going forward, the lessons from the pandemic should inform future policymaking so telehealth can continue to thrive and promote access to health care for all.

19

Changes in Methadone Regulation During COVID-19

Zoe M. Adams, Taleed El-Sabawi, William H.
Coe, Hannah Batchelor, Janan Wyatt, Mona
Gandhi, Ida Santana, and Ayana Jordan*

I INTRODUCTION

The COVID-19 pandemic has created a natural experiment for the treatment of opioid use disorder (OUD) that decades of advocacy could not achieve. Evidence-based treatment for OUD currently exists in the form of medications for opioid use disorder (MOUD), including buprenorphine, naltrexone, and methadone. Methadone, a long-acting, synthetic opioid used to treat OUD that is approved by the Food and Drug Administration (FDA), is the oldest MOUD and has a significant body of evidence to demonstrate its safety and efficacy. Despite this, access to methadone is significantly limited in the United States due to federal regulations that place unique restrictions on its use to treat OUD. Unlike any other medication in the United States, patients must initially report to an opioid treatment program (OTP) *daily* to receive their methadone dose. It takes at least one year for a patient to receive a fourteen-day supply of take-home doses (THDs) and two years for a twenty-eight-day supply.[1] The justifications for these stringent regulations have included fears that the medication would be diverted for recreational use; however, as we demonstrate in this chapter, much of the motivation for such strict regulation also derived from racist sentiment by regulators.

Since the federal regulations governing methadone were introduced in 1972, advocates of methadone treatment for OUD have suggested that THD policies should be relaxed to increase access to it.[2] Until the COVID-19 pandemic,

---

* We would like to thank Melissa C. Funaro, Clinical Librarian, Harvey Cushing/John Hay Whitney Medical Library, Yale University, for her assistance with the literature review, and Gabriella Lopez, Elon University Law Class of 2021, for her assistance with citations and formatting.

[1] 42 C.F.R. § 8.12(i)-(j) (2021).

[2] Jerome H. Jaffe & Charles O'Keeffe, From Morphine Clinics to Buprenorphine: Regulating Opioid Agonist Treatment of Addiction in the United States, 70 Drug & Alcohol Dependence S3, S5, S7 (2003); Inst. of Med. et al., Federal Regulation of Methadone Treatment 12 (Richard A. Rettig & Adam Yarmolinksy eds., 1995).

however, methadone continued to be more strenuously regulated due to the lack of political power among those prescribed methadone (a higher proportion of Black, Indigenous, and People of Color);[3] competing financial incentives of OTPs, where THDs can minimize financial return;[4] and the lack of pharmaceutical lobbying efforts to support the deregulation of this generic medication.

During the pandemic, the Substance (Ab)use and Mental Health Services Administration (SAMHSA) relaxed regulations surrounding THDs, along with the Drug Enforcement Agency (DEA), which authorized OTP employees, law enforcement, and the National Guard to allow for methadone doorstep delivery to limit viral spread. Prior to the pandemic, people were required to attend OTPs in person to obtain their medication up to six times a week taking one to two years to be deemed eligible for fourteen- or twenty-eight-day THDs, respectively; this was widely viewed as a major barrier to methadone access.[5] We focus on the federal SAMHSA waiver, released in March 2020, which allowed "clinically stable" patients enrolled in OTPs to immediately receive either fourteen or twenty-eight days of THDs, regardless of time enrolled in treatment.[6] This chapter tells a larger story about methadone regulations in the United States and how COVID-19 prompted a historic change in the way the medication is dispensed. We begin with a history of the 1972 federal methadone regulations and the sociopolitical context that informed this legislation, paying specific attention to what motivated the initial restrictions on THDs. We next describe SAMHSA's March 2020 waiver and pertinent results from research studies conducted in the United States and internationally on how increases in THDs during COVID-19 affected overdose rates, diversion, and patient preferences. We then conclude with our preliminary survey data, contextualized within this growing body of scholarship, which assess patient experiences with increased THDs due to COVID-19 at a for-profit OTP located in Nashville, Tennessee.

II BACKGROUND

A *The Base of Evidence for Methadone*

Methadone has been shown to decrease opioid overdose deaths and all-cause mortality, while also increasing adherence to substance use disorder treatment and

---

[3] Anne Schneider & Helen Ingram, Social Construction of Target Populations: Implications for Politics and Policy, 87 *Am. Pol. Sci. Rev.* 334, 338 (1993).

[4] Giliane Joseph et al., Reimagining Patient-Centered Care in Opioid Treatment Programs: Lessons from the Bronx During COVID-19, 122 *J. Subst. Abuse Treat.* art. 108219, at 3 (2020).

[5] COVID-19 FAQ, US Dep't of Just. Drug Enf't Admin. Diversion Control Div., www.deadiversion .usdoj.gov/faq/coronavirus_faq.htm (last visited Oct. 6, 2021).

[6] Substance Abuse & Mental Health Serv. Admin., Opioid Treatment Program (OTP) Guidance (2020), www.samhsa.gov/sites/default/files/otp-guidance-20200316.pdf (hereinafter, Opioid Treatment Program).

decreasing the rates of infectious diseases associated with intravenous substance use.[7] It is correlated with improved health-related quality of life, physical, and mental health outcomes,[8] as well as with higher rates of employment and metrics of "social stability."[9] Methadone is more effective than readily available behavioral health treatment modalities that emphasize an abstinence-only approach.[10]

Notwithstanding these benefits, THDs of methadone have been stringently regulated. Accidental overdose or co-ingestion – particularly in patients who are unable to store their medication in a locked box – as well as non-prescribed and illicit use of opioids are ongoing fears that currently guide the strict regulation of methadone. However, while diversion exists, there is evidence to support the conclusion that increasing access to this medication reduces hospital admissions and otherwise promotes recovery.[11] Countries with more flexible THD guidelines do not report increased levels of overdose deaths,[12] and several randomized controlled trials have found no difference in treatment retention or diversion in patients receiving daily supervised dosing versus THDs with contingency management.[13] Thus, allowing for more flexible THDs would permit easier access to this lifesaving medication, yet such reforms are hindered by the sociopolitical history of methadone regulation.

B *The Sociopolitical History of Methadone Regulations*

The sociopolitical history of methadone regulation in the United States is rooted in racist theories of criminality and social deviance that motivated early regulation of narcotics, and these same racialized constructions continue to inform *where* and *how* methadone is dispensed.[14] During the mid-1960s, methadone maintenance treatment began to be accepted as effective medical treatment. Physician-researchers began framing methadone as a treatment geared toward criminals who

---

[7]   Luis Sordo et al., Mortality Risk During and After Opioid Substitution Treatment: Systematic Review and Meta-Analysis of Cohort Studies, BMJ, at 1, 4 (Apr. 26, 2017).

[8]   Icro Maremmani et al., Substance Use and Quality of Life Over 12 Months Among Buprenorphine Maintenance-Treated and Methadone Maintenance-Treated Heroin-Addicted Patients, 33 J. Subst. Abuse Treat. 91, 93 (2007).

[9]   Gavin Bart, Maintenance Medication for Opiate Addiction: The Foundation of Recovery, 31 J. Addict. Dis. 207, 217 (2012).

[10] Barbara Andraka-Christou, The Opioid Fix: America's Addiction Crisis and The Solution They Don't Want You to Have 10 (1st ed. 2020).

[11] Einat Peles et al., Earning "Take-Home" Privileges and Long-Term Outcome in a Methadone Maintenance Treatment Program, 5 J. Addict. Med. 92, 94–96 (2011); Alexander Y. Walley et al., Methadone Dose, Take Home Status and Hospital Admission Among Methadone Maintenance Patients, 6 J. Addict. Med. 186, 190 (2012).

[12] Open Soc'y Inst., Lowering the Threshold: Models of Accessible Methadone and Buprenorphine Treatment, 12, 27 (2010).

[13] Rosella Saulle et al., Supervised Dosing with a Long-Acting Opioid Medication in the Management of Opioid Dependence 2 (Cochrane Drugs & Alcohol Grp. eds., 2017).

[14] Mical Raz, Treating Addiction or Reducing Crime?: Methadone Maintenance and Drug Policy Under the Nixon Administration, 29 J. Pol'y Hist. 58, 60–61 (2017).

used drugs, namely young Black men.[15] Black people who used drugs in the early 1970s were depicted as threats to "community" safety, rather than people suffering from the sequelae of structural violence.[16] This fit squarely with President Nixon's desire to disrupt Black communities, by associating Black persons with heroin and then heavily criminalizing it. By expanding methadone, President Nixon could also make good on his campaign promise to be "tough on crime." By the early 1970s, he began a nationwide expansion of methadone maintenance treatment and created the Special Action Office of Drug Abuse and Prevention, which was instrumental in the establishment of the FDA's 1972 regulations.

Many private, for-profit methadone clinics closed because they no longer met the FDA's standards and were soon replaced by federal, state, and city-funded methadone clinics that served growing Black and Latinx populations who could now afford this treatment. Many rapidly gentrifying neighborhoods in urban cities did not want methadone maintenance treatment programs on their city blocks, which pushed methadone clinics into what physician-anthropologist Helena Hansen and historian Samuel Roberts have called "geographically marginalized" spaces where "local opposition is less organized, such as low income and Black or Latinx neighborhoods."[17] In line with the narrative that methadone was being used to treat criminals, the 1972 regulations required urine reports and mandated behavioral therapy, mimicking carceral procedures and solidifying methadone's place in a larger structure of racialized surveillance.[18] This history continues to fuel structural inequalities in opioid treatment access, where methadone is dispensed in OTPs and remains highly regulated.

In contrast, the pharmaceutical company that originally developed buprenorphine – Reckitt and Colman – played a significant role in paving the way for new legislation that would make that medication increasingly accessible and profitable. In the 1990s, company representatives used their lobbying power to convince members of Congress to allow physicians to prescribe "certain FDA[-]approved opioids without being subject to the current regulations," in other words, the regulations surrounding methadone.[19] Reckitt and Colman also founded a non-profit organization that launched advertising campaigns casting buprenorphine as a solution to the opioid addiction experienced by White suburban communities.[20] These lobbying efforts, coupled with Reckitt and Colman's racialized framing,[21] resulted in

---

[15] Id. at 65.
[16] Keturah James & Ayana Jordan, The Opioid Crisis in Black Communities, 46 J. L. Med. *Ethics* 404, 412 (2018).
[17] Helena Hansen & Samuel K. Roberts, Two Tiers of Biomedicalization: Methadone, Buprenorphine, and the Racial Politics of Addiction Treatment, 14 *Critical Persps. on Addiction* 79, 91 (2012).
[18] Federal Regulation of Methadone Treatment, supra note 2, at 6.
[19] Jaffe & O'Keeffe, supra note 2, at S9.
[20] Julie Netherland & Helena Hansen, White Opioids: Pharmaceutical Race and the War on Drugs that Wasn't, 12 *Biosocieties* 217, 232–33 (2017).
[21] Id. at 229.

the Drug Addiction Treatment Act of 2000, which allows buprenorphine to be prescribed in office-based settings by physicians who have undergone an eight-hour course,[22] and leaves the methadone regulations unchanged. Governmental agencies justified the continued and much more stringent regulation of methadone because they considered the medication, when compared to buprenorphine, to be a more potent opioid agonist with higher "abuse" potential. Access to buprenorphine is concentrated in predominantly White neighborhoods, and Black patients are less likely to receive this less regulated MOUD compared to White patients.[23] Rooted in racialized understandings of criminality, methadone has been regulated for the protection of "the public," rather than for the safety, efficacy, and treatment of people with OUD.

C *OTPs and Restrictions on Take-Home Methadone*

At present, methadone is regulated by three federal agencies – the FDA, DEA, and SAMHSA – making methadone the most regulated pharmaceutical medication in the United States.[24] The FDA monitors the safety and efficacy of methadone and has approved the medication for specific medical uses, including the treatment of chronic pain and OUD. Because methadone is considered a controlled substance, it is also regulated by the DEA. The 1971 Controlled Substances Act gives the DEA and the FDA joint authority over the scheduling of drugs that have potential for misuse. However, unlike other controlled prescription medications, methadone is subject to a *third* layer of regulatory control by SAMHSA if it is being prescribed to treat OUD. Only OTPs are permitted to dispense methadone for the treatment of OUD, and methadone is subjected to restriction on THDs.[25]

SAMHSA sets the accreditation standards for OTPs and promulgates guidelines that govern the frequency, dosage, and dispensing of methadone by OTPs.[26] If methadone is being prescribed for pain management, it can be prescribed by office-based practices, and offices need not comply with the SAMHSA regulations.[27] There is no base of evidence to justify this distinction.

Perhaps the defining features of methadone regulations are the location limitations, namely that patients are not allowed to take the medication home with them and that it must be dispensed in an OTP. Since 1972, federal regulations surrounding

---

[22] Andraka-Christou, supra note 10, at 46. As of April 28, 2021, medical providers are no longer required to take an eight-hour (for physicians) or twenty-four-hour (for advanced practice providers) course before prescribing buprenorphine to fewer than thirty patients.
[23] William C. Goedel et al., Association of Racial/Ethnic Segregation with Treatment Capacity for Opioid Use Disorder in Counties in the United States 2–3 (2020).
[24] Andraka-Christou, above note 10, at 125.
[25] Medication Assisted Treatment for Opioid Use Disorders, 42 C.F.R. § 8.1 (2001).
[26] Accreditation of Opioid Treatment Programs, 42 C.F.R. § 8.3 (2001).
[27] Andraka-Christou, supra note 10, at 125.

THDs have mandated that patients receiving methadone for the treatment of OUD must *travel* to OTPs *almost daily* to receive their medication under directly observed therapy for at least the first ninety days of treatment, and often for longer periods of time.[28] Directly observed therapy means that health care providers must, according to SAMHSA, watch patients "drink and speak after dosing" to ensure medication adherence and diversion control, treating patients as if they have "done something wrong" and are involved in the carceral system.[29]

Per SAMHSA guidelines, OTPs may gradually increase the number of THDs by one THD per week every ninety days until one year, when patients are eligible to receive a fourteen-day supply, or two years, when patients may receive a twenty-eight-day supply.[30] Even though the guidelines allow for a twenty-eight-day supply after two years of treatment, many OTPs across the country continue to require that patients come in more frequently. The laws of individual states also vary widely in terms of when patients are able to qualify for increased THDs. Some states do not even allow *any* THDs to be given to patients.[31]

SAMHSA's current regulatory scheme actively disincentivizes OTPs from issuing THDs based on varying types of reimbursement.[32] For instance, some private, for-profit OTPs can bill for the number of times patients physically present to the clinic – a major source of financial revenue. In some instances, even if a patient is "clinically stable," financial incentives are prioritized over maximizing quality of life and patient care for people with OUD.[33] Furthermore, patients who are allowed a twenty-eight-day supply continue to be scrutinized by OTPs. For instance, despite attaining the maximum number of THDs, many patients are still required to present to a clinic weekly for urine toxicology screens and random bottle counts, often traveling long distances with little notice.[34]

Under the SAMHSA guidelines, OTP leadership can evaluate a patient's eligibility for THD privileges based on "regularity of clinic attendance," absence of recent substance use and criminal activity, and the "stability of the patient's home environment."[35] Such subjective determinations invite bias, particularly against Black, Indigenous, and People of Color, and against persons living in rural or economically disadvantaged communities. Many OTPs also establish their own internal guidelines, including prohibiting patients from receiving increased THDs

[28] Id. at 126.
[29] Substance Abuse and Mental Health Serv. Admin., Federal Guidelines for Opioid Treatment Programs 18 (2015).
[30] 42 C.F.R. § 8.12 (2001).
[31] Jaffe & O'Keeffe, supra note 2, at S5.
[32] Corey S. Davis & Derek H. Carr, Legal and Policy Changes Urgently Needed to Increase Access to Opioid Agonist Therapy in the United States, 73 Int'l J. Drug Pol'y 42, 44 (2019).
[33] Joseph et al., supra note 4, at 1.
[34] Andraka-Christou, supra note 10, at 126.
[35] Federal Guidelines for Opioid Treatment Programs, supra note 29, at 53.

for cannabis-positive urine toxicology reports, even if they have been consistently adherent to methadone treatment.[36]

D *The Disruptive Nature of Daily Methadone Dosing*

Traveling to an OTP daily to receive methadone is extremely disruptive to the lives of people with OUD. The SAMHSA regulations about THDs prior to COVID-19 require patients to take time away from childcare, school, and work to access methadone. Employment security, which promotes treatment adherence, has also been shown to be compromised, given the need to accommodate the demand of daily medical appointments.[37] Moreover, the cost and time of travel to OTPs, particularly for rural populations, can be prohibitive.[38] Further, there are privacy and stigma concerns for patients at OTPs, which often require patients to line up outside to receive medication. This contrasts with buprenorphine, which can be prescribed inside providers' offices and does not require directly observed therapy. Many grassroots organizations, including the Drug Policy Alliance, medical societies such as the National Academy of Medicine and the American Society of Addiction Medicine, and directly-impacted groups, like the Urban Survivors Union, have called for sweeping changes in the regulations surrounding methadone and the provision of THDs.[39]

III A WAIVER FOR TAKE-HOME METHADONE DURING COVID-19

SAMHSA's federal waiver during COVID-19 addressed some of these barriers. In line with social distancing protocols put in place to reduce the spread of COVID-19, SAMHSA's March 2020 waiver granted exemptions to the regulations on THDs.[40] Under the waiver, which remained in effect in some states through 2021, patients deemed "clinically stable" by OTP leadership can receive a fourteen- or twenty-eight-day supply regardless of their time at the OTP. As a result, thousands of patients have received increased THDs, a historic shift in care for people with OUD.[41] However, OTPs are not uniformly funded (e.g., for-profit, city-funded, or state-funded). Coupled with variable clinical discretion about which patients

---

[36] Andraka-Christou, supra note 10, at 128.

[37] Lindsey Richardson et al., Addiction Treatment-Related Employment Barriers: The Impact of Methadone Maintenance, 43 *J. Subst. Abuse Treat.* 276, 281–82 (2012).

[38] Paul J. Joudrey et al., Drive Times to Opioid Treatment Programs in Urban and Rural Counties in 5 US States, 322 *JAMA* 1310, 1310 (2019).

[39] Jaffe & O'Keeffe, supra note 2, at S7; Corey S. Davis & Elizabeth A. Samuels, Opioid Policy Changes During the COVID-19 Pandemic – and Beyond, *J. Addict. Med.*, May 2020, at 1, 2; Brendan Saloner et al., A Public Health Strategy for the Opioid Crisis, 133 *Pub. Health Rep.* 24S, 29S (2018).

[40] Opioid Treatment Program, supra note 6.

[41] Editorial Bd., Post-Coronavirus Pandemic, Methadone Should be Just as Easy to Get, Bos. Globe (May 24, 2020), www.bostonglobe.com/2020/05/24/opinion/post-coronavirus-pandemic-keep-methadone-easy-obtain/.

receive increases in THDs, there has been immense heterogeneity in how OTPs enforced the SAMHSA waiver. Furthermore, there is no centralized data collection system that tracks how many OTPs across the United States adopted SAMHSA's waiver and how many patients received increases in THD after March 2020.

Since SAMHSA issued the waiver, research groups across the United States, Europe, and Asia have examined the effect of increased THDs during COVID-19 on patient preferences and experiences with treatment, diversion, and fatal and non-fatal overdose rates. To further substantiate our survey results in the context of other studies conducted during COVID-19, our team conducted a literature search. On September 9, 2021, a search on the following databases was conducted: MEDLINE, Embase, and APA PsycInfo on the Ovid platform and Web of Science Core Collection (Clarivate). Search terms included both controlled vocabulary terms and keywords for the concepts of "opioid treatment" and "take-home medication." The search was limited to articles published between March 2020 and September 9, 2021 on the effects of COVID-19 on take-home medication use for opioid treatment. The database search was supplemented by a focused Google search for unpublished literature.

Most studies had multiple outcomes related to changes in OTP services during COVID-19, but we only included measures related to methadone THDs. A summary of key findings is included in Table 19A.1, which can be found in the Appendix (published online).[42] Overall, these findings demonstrate three key points: (1) most OTPs in the United States and internationally significantly increased the number of THDs in response to COVID-19;[43] (2) diversion and overdose rates did not significantly increase as a result of increased THDs;[44] and (3) most OTP providers wanted increases in THDs to become a permanent fixture of methadone dispensing.[45]

A *Patients' Lived Experiences with Increased THD During COVID-19: Lessons from an OTP in Nashville, Tennessee*

Contextualized by findings from other studies in Table 19A.1, our survey data sought to understand how THDs during COVID-19 impacted patients' quality of life, perceived stigma, lived experience, and OUD treatment outcomes at a for-profit OTP in Nashville, Tennessee.

1 Methods

To understand the impact of these changes on patients with OUD, our research team obtained informed consent and conducted telephone surveys of eligible patients at

---

[42] For further explanation of the methodologies used in this chapter, please see the Appendix at https:// petrieflom.law.harvard.edu/assets/publications/Chapter_19_-_Adams_Appendix_-_Final_Version.pdf.

[43] See Appendix, notes 1–4, 6–9, 13.

[44] See Appendix, notes 2, 4, 6–9, 13.

[45] See Appendix, notes 5, 10–11, 13–14.

TABLE 19.1 *Demographics of research participants from Nashville OTP*
The second column indicates gender and race/ethnicity options read aloud to patients.
The third column indicates the number of participants with the corresponding percentages that chose each option.

Demographics (n = 22)*		
Gender	Woman	11 (50%)
	Man	11 (50%)
	Non-Binary	0
	Other	0
Race/ethnicity	American Indian or Alaska Native	1 (4.5%)
	Asian or Asian American	0
	Black, African, or African American	1 (4.5%)
	Caucasian	19 (86.4%)
	Hawaiian Native or Pacific Islander	0
	Non-Caucasian Hispanic or Latinx	0
	Other: Caucasian/American Indian	1 (4.5%)

* Demographic questions were incorporated into the survey at a later date and therefore represent 22 of the 34 total participants.

a for-profit OTP in Nashville about their experiences receiving increased THDs during COVID-19. The survey instrument consists of twenty-four questions, with free text boxes to capture patients' direct comments. The survey was administered from June to August 2020, with demographic questions (including race and gender) incorporated in July, after seven participants had already completed the survey. Due to the negative impact that THDs had on this for-profit OTP's financial status, this OTP decided to no longer provide twenty-eight-day supplies of THDs, thus ending our data collection prematurely. After collection, the open-ended responses were analyzed to identify common themes and narratives using qualitative methods. Because of the small sample size, this chapter presents the results of the qualitative analysis, with frequency statistics provided only for context. Note that this is one partner site in an ongoing multi-site (six nationwide OTP) trial.

Light gray points indicate the number of THDs per week given to an individual participant prior to the exemption, and the corresponding dark gray points represent the number of THDs per week given to the same participant after the exemption was issued.

2 Results

Demographic data are available for twenty-two of the thirty-four participants. Eleven identified as women and eleven identified as men (n = 22). One identified as American Indian or Alaska Native, one as Black, African, or African American, nineteen as Caucasian, and one as Other: Caucasian/American Indian (n = 22) (Table 19.1). Prior to COVID-19, more than half, eighteen of thirty-four participants

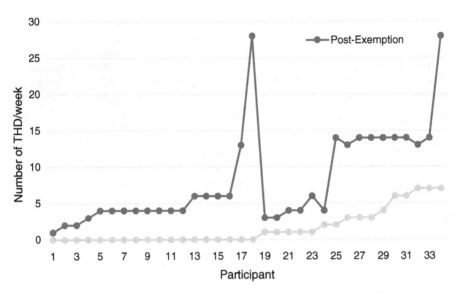

FIGURE 19.1 Number of THDs per participant pre- and post-COVID-19 exemption

(52.9 percent), were not receiving THDs, five were receiving one THD per week (14.7 percent), and two were receiving two THDs per week (5.9 percent). After the COVID-19 exemption, THDs ranged from one to twenty-eight THDs per week among this population (Figure 19.1). The following is a summary of the salient themes that emerged from the analysis.

Participants reported taking great care with storing their THDs to prevent diversion. All participants indicated their THDs were locked (n = 34), with thirty-one out of thirty-four participants (91.2 percent) storing THDs in a lockbox, two out of thirty-four participants (5.9 percent) storing THDs in a cupboard or cabinet, and one out of thirty-four participants (2.9 percent) storing THDs under the bed (Table 19.2). Furthermore, no participants stated that they had shared, given away, or sold their THDs or had any THDs stolen since the change in their THDs during COVID-19.

Three out of thirty-four participants (8.8 percent) took THDs in greater amounts than prescribed, citing under-dosing or the need to self-medicate to manage symptoms as motivating factors (Table 19.2). For example, one participant stated: "One time because my dosage wasn't enough, ... I needed to take more to make myself not be sick, and therefore I needed to take more. Now that I'm on the right dosage I do not need to." Another participant identified "stress" and "anxiety" specifically related to his health during the pandemic as his reason for taking more than prescribed. No participants reported they had overdosed on opioids since their recent increase. Barriers to treatment adherence prior to the COVID-19 regulation, which

TABLE 19.2 *Safety measure quantitative responses*
The first column represents an abbreviated description of the question asked to each
participant (see Section III.A.1 for full-length survey questions). The second column
indicates the options read aloud for participants. The third column indicates the
number of participants who chose each option.

Safety Measures (n = 34)		
Storage location of THD	Lockbox	31 (91.2%)
	Bookbag/purse	0
	Cupboard/cabinet	2 (5.9%)
	Other: under bed	1 (2.9%)
Locked	Yes	34 (100%)
	No	0
Missed THD	Yes	3 (8.8%)
	No	31 (91.2%)
Taken more THD than prescribed	Yes	3 (8.8%)
	No	31 (91.2%)
Overdosed from opioids	Yes	0
	No	34 (100%)
Shared, given away, or hold THD or had THD stolen	Yes	0
	No	34 (100%)

allowed for increased THDs, were related to transportation difficulties, causing
missed OTP appointments. For example, one participant said that "[it was] hard
getting back and forth," because he lived an hour away from the clinic. Similarly,
another participant said that he lived forty minutes away from the clinic and did not
have enough money for gas to make it to his appointment.

*Thirty-two out of thirty-four participants (94.1 percent) overwhelmingly pre-
ferred THDs to dosing at the OTP in part because the burden caused by frequent
commuting to an OTP to receive a dose was at least partially relieved* (Table 19.3).
Participants reported living 35 to 120 minutes away from their OTP and described
travel to the OTP as a "huge inconvenience" and "burden ... [as there is] no other
closer clinic." Some participants reported that, prior to the increase in THDs, the
frequent commute to the OTP *interfered with their work duties* and cited the *childcare difficulties* that commuting created. One woman stated, "it's better to have take
homes just because of work and I have a daughter and am starting to work again,
so it's inconvenient to come [to the clinic] multiple times a week." One participant
described her new dosing schedule as "a lot easier and less stressful" because previously she was often "running late to work." Another stated that they had "been able
to hold down a job" due to the increase in THDs. Other participants explained that
the *financial difficulties* of travel were barriers to treatment. For example, one participant stated "sometimes [I] would miss going to clinic due to financial reasons"
such as not having enough gas money or bus fare.

TABLE 19.3 *Patient preference quantitative responses*
The first column represents an abbreviated description of the question asked to
each participant (see methods for full-length survey questions). The second column
indicates the options read aloud for participants. The third column indicates the
number of participants who chose each option.

Patient Preferences (n = 34)		
Dosing preference	Taking it with me	32 (94.1%)
	Coming into clinic	0
	No preference	2 (5.9%)
	Positive	31 (91.2%)
Impact on quality of life	Negative	1 (2.9%)
	No Impact	2 (5.9%)

*Thirty-one out of thirty-four participants (91.2 percent) reported that THDs
contributed to improvements in their overall well-being.* "It's been life changing
to have my medicine with me," confided one participant. Another stated, "I wake
up … my first thought is that I don't have to wake up and worry about feeling bad. I
can wake up clear minded. I can live a full happy life, and not be stuck chasing dope
or feeling sick." One participant stated that due to the need to frequently report to
the OTP, he "wasn't able to travel for six years, missing family vacations and stuff. It
was a whole lot. Mentally." Some participants said that increased **THDs** *provided
more time for family obligations*. One woman stated, "I help take care of my in-laws
and not having to run to the clinic every day is quite helpful." Another reported,
"because I have 2 kids, and I have to get them ready for school, but [now] I don't
have to run out there every day to get my dose. Anything is better than every day."
Other participants reported *reduced stress and hassle of presenting to the clinic as
frequently.* "I mean it's less stressful, I live in [town] so it's far to drive all the way to
the clinic just to get a dose and come all the way back." Another participant said that
she doesn't "freak out if there is an accident and doesn't make it" to the clinic, resulting in a missed dose. Another reported, "It's [THDs] helping me tremendously …
and I'm not so stressed."

Participants stated that increased THDs contributed to a *greater sense of stability and accomplishment in treatment.* "[It] feels like you've accomplished a lot
more not having to go as often. Before it was so long to get increased take-homes,"
one participant explained. She further expressed feeling more "successful" with the
program now compared to before when she had to come in every day. Another
participant described his increase in THDs as: "Definitely a positive reinforcement
to stay clean."

Participants also reported that THDs *decreased the stigma* they felt from being in
methadone treatment. One participant described daily dosing as a "dehumanizing
process" as the strict guidelines often make patients feel as though they are being

"treated like criminals." Another participant commented that since an increase in THDs, he felt like he was "living a more normal life" and that he was "no longer concerned about how friends at work feel about [him] going to a methadone clinic every day."

Some participants reported that the increase in THDs provided a *sense of safety during the pandemic*. One stated, "I've got a two-year-old who is immunocompromised and an 88-year-old father who is at risk. [I] cannot afford to come in during COVID." No participants felt the increase in THDs had a negative impact on their quality of life. "I would definitely be on board with take-homes after this," one participant concluded. "It has been a definite improvement in my life, and I hope it continues."

IV DISCUSSION AND RECOMMENDATIONS FOR FUTURE POLICYMAKING

COVID-19 produced a natural experiment to study how increased THDs impact patient experiences, preferences, diversion, and overdose rates. As found in studies conducted during COVID-19 across the United States,[46] as well as internationally,[47] none of our participants reported diversion or overdoses since the increase in THDs, and approximately 94 percent of our participants stated they preferred increased THDs, saying that being able to take their medication home with them improved their quality of life. Our findings add to the growing body of evidence demonstrating that increased THDs can eliminate unnecessary barriers to methadone treatment, while simultaneously decreasing the burdens shouldered by patients in treatment. Our study and others provide the data needed to aid policymakers in creating more patient-centered, evidence-informed substance use disorder policies that counter unfounded narratives that have prevented access to more just methadone treatment.

Our study does have limitations that must be taken into consideration. First, we are presenting one site of a larger trial, thereby resulting in a smaller sample size, with a majority White cohort, and a lack of experimental design. These findings will need to be validated by a larger sample size, one more representative of the diverse population of people in methadone treatment. Nevertheless, the narratives that emerged from the data remain useful as a testament to how increased THDs had a positive impact on employment, family life, and feelings of self-worth, bolstering the case for regulatory reform. Moreover, because of institutional racism, which fueled the heavy regulation of methadone, such stringent methadone policies disproportionately affect Black and Latinx communities,

---

[46] See Appendix, notes 4, 7–9, 12.
[47] See Appendix, notes 2, 4.

who are also less likely to have access to less heavily regulated medications for OUD, such as buprenorphine.[48] Therefore, policies that decrease access to THDs are not only an issue of access to care, but also a racial justice issue that involves health equity. As such, methadone THD policy reform requires immediate action.

Given our results, in concert with other domestic and international studies (Table 19A.1) showing an overall positive trend with increased THDs, SAMHSA's COVID-19 waiver, should be extended indefinitely. However, there must be additional federal support and legislation, as individual states currently have the authority to not enforce the exemptions on THDs. For instance, even though increases in THDs have not been shown to increase overdoses or diversion, on September 30, 2021, OTPs in Pennsylvania were ordered to scale back their increases in THDs and reverted to the pre-COVID-19 restrictions.[49] With a record 93,000 overdose deaths in 2020, removing barriers to methadone access is paramount: increased THDs must be prioritized in order to prevent unnecessary deaths.[50]

Furthermore, as written, the relaxed guidelines give OTPs permission to increase THDs when certain treatment milestones are met, but OTPs are not incentivized financially to do so. Like other health care providers, some OTPs are financed through fee-for-service arrangements, which allow them to bill for daily medication provision and drug testing. If OTPs provide THDs, they can no longer bill for the daily clinic visit, thus resulting in decreases in financial revenue for the clinic. Therefore, the increase in THDs must be accompanied by payment reforms that incentivize THDs. Such reforms can take many forms, including bundled payments and quality-based payments. Second, the language in SAMHSA's waiver regarding "clinical stability" is problematic and invites OTP clinicians to make subjective determinations that are likely informed by bias, particularly against racial and ethnic minorities and persons living in rural and/or economically disadvantaged communities. As such, SAMHSA should commission a taskforce to assist it in defining "clinical stability" and issue guidelines based on their findings.

COVID-19 has demonstrated that federal regulatory agencies must be proactive about increasing access to methadone treatment. Participants in our study frequently reported that the distances they had to travel to reach an OTP were a major barrier to care. Increasing the number of THDs permitted helps address the barriers to showing up daily to the facility, but it does not address the number of OTPs, which

---

[48] Goedel et al., supra note 23, at 1.
[49] Governor Tom Wolf, Gov. Wolf Signs Bill Extending COVID-19 Emergency Regulation Suspensions, Expanding Family Caregiver Supports (June 11, 2021), www.abc27.com/news/health/coronavirus/gov-wolf-signs-bills-extending-covid-19-regulation-suspensions-and-to-support-family-caregivers/.
[50] Josh Katz & Margot Sanger-Katz, "It's Huge, It's Historic, It's Unheard-of": Drug Overdose Deaths Spike, NY Times (July 14, 2021), www.nytimes.com/interactive/2021/07/14/upshot/drug-overdose-deaths.html.

has remained largely stagnant over the past fifteen years.[51] Studies such as ours, and others in Table 19.A.1,[52] have demonstrated that there is little risk of diversion or overdose deaths due to increases in THDs, suggesting that fears of diversion are likely exaggerated. Thus, the United States should revisit new models of methadone dispensing, such as pharmacist-administered dosing or prescriptions by primary care providers, as in Canada, the United Kingdom, and Australia.[53] Integrating methadone treatment into our health care system would decrease the carceral overtones of addiction treatment, and patients would likely feel less stigma toward their OUD diagnosis.

---

[51] Nicholas Chadi & Paxton Bach, Methadone Matters, Pub. Health Post (Mar. 8, 2019), www.publichealthpost.org/viewpoints/methadone-matters/.

[52] See Appendix, notes 2, 4, 7–9, 12.

[53] Susan L. Calcaterra et al., Methadone Matters: What the United States Can Learn from the Global Effort to Treat Opioid Addiction, 34 *J. Gen. Intern. Med.* 1039, 1041 (2019).

20

Reproductive Justice after the Pandemic

How "Personal Responsibility" Entrenches Disparities and Limits Autonomy

Rachel L. Zacharias, Elizabeth A. Dietz, Kimberly Mutcherson, and Josephine Johnston[*]

I INTRODUCTION

COVID-19 laid bare the responsibility that American laws, policies, and society have long placed on individuals to ensure their own health and well-being. Policies guided by an ethic of "personal responsibility" particularly restrict reproductive justice (RJ),[1] a framework and set of objectives first defined by Black women as the human rights to have children, not have children, and parent children in safe, healthy, and sustainable communities.[2] RJ goes beyond an articulation of reproductive rights; it is an analytic and movement-building tool that describes how people are inseparable from the systems that they are in,[3] and how those systems make their choices possible (or not).[4] As we will make clear, the RJ framework is relevant not

[*] The authors thank I. Glenn Cohen, Abbe Gluck, Katherine Kraschel, and Carmen Shachar for the opportunity to highlight the necessity of reproductive justice amidst and beyond the COVID-19 pandemic. In particular, the authors sincerely thank Katherine Kraschel for her expert and thoughtful editing and guidance on this piece. Thank you as well to Laura Chong, Jessenia Khalyat, and the staff of the Solomon and Petrie Flom Centers for their fantastic work coordinating this symposium and special issue. Ms. Zacharias additionally wishes to sincerely thank Holly Fernandez Lynch for her mentorship and collaboration on questions of telehealth and family leave throughout the COVID-19 pandemic. Ms. Johnston additionally wishes to thank the Donaghue Impact Fund at the Hastings Center for their support for this work. Finally, the authors are sincerely grateful to the founding and continuing reproductive justice advocates, scholars, and health care providers for their resilient and assiduous work promoting reproductive justice.
[1] Ron Haskins, The Sequence of Personal Responsibility, Brookings (July 31, 2009), www.brookings .edu/articles/the-sequence-of-personal-responsibility.
[2] Reproductive Justice, SisterSong Women of Color Reprod. Just. Collective, www.sistersong.net/ reproductive-justice.
[3] RJ centers women but explicitly acknowledges gender non-conforming and trans people and how interlocking systems of power bear on people of all genders in reproduction. See Loretta J. Ross & Ricki Solinger, Reproductive Justice: An Introduction 6 (2017). We therefore use "people" rather than "women."
[4] What is Reproductive Justice?, If/When/How: Lawyering for Reproductive Justice, www.ifwhenhow .org/about/what-is-rj/.

only to issues of reproduction and family, but also to understanding the social conditions in which individuals create families with children.

American laws and policies obstruct RJ when they ascribe blame to Black and Brown people for not meeting societal standards of family, health, and flourishing. These polices presuppose that there are certain normatively correct family structures and ways to be in the world, which are largely defined by racist, classist, and sexist ideals.[5] Personal responsibility policies attribute harms – including reproductive and other health inequities, environmental exposures, poverty, and food and housing insecurity – to individuals' choices, rather than to the social, economic, historical, or political conditions that shape those choices. These policies additionally punish marginalized people who already experience structural forms of injustice, concentrating their force on Black people, other people of color, and trans people, instead of creating conditions to foster RJ.

Overall, COVID-19 policy under the Trump Administration relied heavily on an ethic of personal responsibility, as illustrated by those lawmakers who called for people to wear masks and socially distance without creating policy mechanisms that would require them to do so.[6] Yet certain responses to COVID-19 resulted in a small number of long-standing barriers to RJ falling away. For instance, some laws, policies, court orders, and procedures catalyzed by COVID-19 temporarily *increased* access to reproductive health care for some and allowed workers paid and protected time off from work to care for themselves and their family members.[7] These responses employed personal responsibility in a way that was empowering rather than controlling, facilitating recognition of reproductive autonomy by removing barriers to it and entrusting individuals to manage their own care needs.

Enacting RJ-enhancing policies should not require a pandemic. In this chapter, we call for more laws and policies that equitably enable personal power consistent with RJ. These laws and policies see people as worthy and capable of making decisions about their own and their family's health, and therefore remove barriers to, and provide the underlying support for, personal decisions. We begin by outlining how the ideology of personal responsibility has been woven into the fabric of US policy, consistently holding marginalized people accountable for maintaining prescribed standards of family, health, and well-being, while simultaneously neglecting structural conditions that impact many marginalized communities and exacting heavy tolls for non-compliance. Then, we identify three examples of RJ-enhancing policy changes enabled by the COVID-19 pandemic. While states and the federal government continued to invoke personal responsibility during the pandemic, certain policy changes recognized individuals' personal power and removed barriers to reproductive autonomy.

---

[5]   Elisa Minoff, The Racist Roots of Work Requirements (Ctr. for the Study of Social Pol'y ed., 2020).
[6]   Kimberlee Kruesi, Governors Stress "Personal Responsibility" Over Virus Orders, PBS News Hour (July 4, 2020), www.pbs.org/newshour/health/governors-stress-personal-responsibility-over-virus-orders.
[7]   See infra Section III.

Although these RJ-enhancing, COVID-19-based policies were in some cases time-limited and predominantly benefited people who already had means, they provide a kind of "proof-of-concept" for further RJ-enhancing changes to law and policy. To be truly consistent with RJ, future such measures must exist outside an ideology that conditions deservingness on blamelessness. Instead, conditions must exist which make such enhancements available to and possible for everyone. We conclude that RJ, as a goal and a framework, should undergird all US reproductive and social policy.

II RESPONSIBILITY IN US REPRODUCTIVE AND SOCIAL POLICY

COVID-19 did not inaugurate policies structured by personal responsibility. The ethics of personal responsibility and individual autonomy have been deeply engrained in US culture since the country's founding.[8] In the twentieth century, Republican and Democratic administrations alike promulgated policies demanding personal responsibility, particularly reproductive, health, family, welfare, and housing policies – some of the realms most critical to RJ.[9] Two national Democratic-administration initiatives – the Moynihan Report and Clinton-era welfare reforms – offer incomplete but instructive historical insight into the logic of personal responsibility and its opposition to RJ. These initiatives promoted the shifting of care for families from governments to individuals, while determining that individuals' worthiness of social assistance (needed for said family care) depended on their ability to care for themselves. They created a punitive regime that conditioned financial assistance on satisfying bureaucratic requirements of correct family structure, vastly reducing the aid available directly to individuals and families.

In the 1965 report *The Negro Family: The Case for National Action*, the assistant secretary of labor to the Johnson Administration, Daniel Patrick Moynihan, argued that Black families' matriarchal structures would slow the progress of Black men, and, in turn, that of Black women.[10] The report articulated the racial injustice that Black families experience in terms of individual failings that could be acted on through government policy.[11] It did so through a focus on what it called the "pathology" of "broken homes," which, it concluded, are too often headed by women dependent on welfare.[12] These supposed indictments helped to explain why,

---

[8] Elizabeth H. Bradley & Lauren A. Taylor, *The American Health Care Paradox: Why Spending More is Getting Us Less* 41 (2013).

[9] See, for example, Sandra Morgen, The Agency of Welfare Workers: Negotiating Devolution, Privatization, and the Meaning of Self-Sufficiency, 103 *Am. Anthropol.* 747, 747–61 (2001); Adam Gaffney, The Neoliberal Turn in American Health Care, 45 *Int'l J. Health Servs.* 33, 33–52 (2015); Nancy Tomes, *Remaking the American Patient: How Madison Avenue and Modern Medicine Turned Patients Into Consumers* 1–16 (2016).

[10] Daniel Patrick Moynihan, The Negro Family: The Case for National Action 29–45 (Mar. 1965), https://web.stanford.edu/~mrosenfe/Moynihan's%20The%20Negro%20Family.pdf.

[11] Id. at 47.

[12] Id. at 12.

in Moynihan's words, "the circumstances of the Negro American community in recent years has probably been getting worse, not better."[13] The report and its policy proposals are then framed as an act of care: attending to racial inequity and proposing interventions. But the mechanisms through which it understood that inequity, and therefore the interventions that it proposed, framed individuals and the ways that they behave and engage in family-making as the source of their own difficulties. In an analysis of the Moynihan Report, Professor Grace Hong notes that "[i]n the neoliberal moment, 'care' becomes the conduit for violence."[14] Government abrogates responsibility for injustice in favor of punishing Black people, and particularly Black women, for making what it sees as the "wrong" choices.

The Personal Responsibility and Work Opportunity Reconciliation Act of 1996 (PRWORA),[15] signed by President Clinton, formed part of the set of Congressional Republican-led "Contract with America" reforms that sought to streamline government and require work.[16] The Act is a defining moment in the history of personal responsibility-based US policy. Its advocates promised that PRWORA would reduce the number of people on welfare and create self-sufficiency through employment by imposing limits on the number of years that people could receive cash assistance and the work requirements for that assistance.[17] PRWORA also sought to use welfare eligibility rules to bring about "proper" families (i.e., those with two married parents);[18] it did this by imposing work requirements on people with past-due child support payments,[19] and by seeking to prevent teen pregnancy through abstinence-only sex education.[20] The law substantially reduced the number of people who received assistance, though it did so largely through cuts to benefits,[21] and through imposing sanctions (disproportionately for people of color) that made those in need ineligible for benefits – not by lifting people out of poverty.[22] White people were also able to

---

[13] Id. at ii.

[14] Grace K. Hong, *Death Beyond Disavowal: The Impossible Politics of Difference* 20 (2015).

[15] Personal Responsibility and Work Opportunity Reconciliation Act of 1996, Pub. L. No. 104-193, 110 Stat. 2105.

[16] Brendon O'Connor, The Protagonists and Ideas Behind the Personal Responsibility and Work Opportunity Reconciliation Act of 1996: The Enactment of a Conservative Welfare System, 28 *Soc. Just.* 4, 4 (2001).

[17] Presidential Statement on Signing the Personal Responsibility and Work Opportunity Reconciliation Act of 1996, 32 Weekly Comp. Pres. Doc 1487, 1488 (Aug. 22, 1996) (hereinafter, Presidential Signing Statement); see also Personal Responsibility and Work Opportunity Reconciliation Act of 1996 Conference Report Consideration, 142 Cong. Rec. S9387 (daily ed. Aug. 1, 1996) (statement of Rep. Howell Heflin).

[18] Notably, the Defense of Marriage Act, Pub. L. No. 104-199, 110 Stat. 2419 (1996), passed the same year, forbade federal programs from recognizing marriages between gay or lesbian couples.

[19] Personal Responsibility and Work Opportunity Reconciliation Act § 365; see also Presidential Signing Statement, supra note 17.

[20] Personal Responsibility and Work Opportunity Reconciliation Act § 912.

[21] Vann R. Newkirk, The Real Lessons from Bill Clinton's Welfare Reform, Atlantic (Feb. 5, 2018), www.theatlantic.com/politics/archive/2018/02/welfare-reform-tanf-medicaid-food-stamps/552299.

[22] Michael Bonds, The Continuing Significance of Race: A Case Study of the Impact of Welfare Reform, 9 J. Afr. Am. Studs. 18, 20 (2006).

leave welfare rolls for jobs (a key goal of the Act) in greater proportions than racial minorities, in part due to employer preferences for White employees.[23] In effect, the Act required personal responsibility, but did not create the conditions for equitably realizing and supporting it.[24]

Like other invocations of personal responsibility, PRWORA is inextricable from its racial context, including the erroneous and racist suppositions that Black people are lazy and need to be coerced into work.[25] PRWORA imagined a kind of undesirable Black family (headed by a poor single mother intent on gaming the system) that could be improved through legislation tethering work to notions of stronger and better families.[26] Sexist notions of White womanhood that praised stay-at-home parenting for women with young children did not extend to Black women, who were expected to find and pay for substitute care for their children while engaging in low-wage work.[27] Accordingly, some state welfare systems, afforded more discretion to administer cash assistance under the Act,[28] conditioned families' receipt of cash assistance on whether their family structure and practices were acceptable to the state. Some states enacted caps on cash assistance based on family size,[29] thereby casting family size as a privilege of the wealthy and as a sign of irresponsibility in the low-income community. Poor children were presumed to be both a drain on taxpayer dollars and an impediment to their mothers' transition from welfare to work. Welfare caps sought to both control Black and other low-income individuals' reproductive and familial choices and make Black women "available" to engage in more low-wage work.

Dangerous rhetoric about personal responsibility was also a hallmark of the Obama presidency. In the wake of the 2008 financial collapse, President Obama declared that "[w]hat is required of us now is a new era of responsibility – a recognition on the part of every American that we have duties to ourselves, our nation[,] and the world."[30] That speech, which did not talk meaningfully about race, asked

---

[23] Id.

[24] The Effects of the Personal Responsibility and Work Opportunity Reconciliation Act on Working Families: Hearing Before the H. Comm. on Educ. & Workforce, 107th Cong. (Sept. 20, 2001) (statement of Heather Boushey), www.epi.org/publication/webfeatures_viewpoints_tanf_testimony/.

[25] Minoff, supra note 5, at 9.

[26] Dorothy Roberts, *Killing the Black Body: Race, Reproduction, and the Meaning of Liberty* 17–19 (1997). This idea is not new: before PRWORA, state legislators proposed to mandate or incentivize sterilization or long-acting birth control for women receiving welfare benefits. Elizabeth Siegel Watkins, From Breakthrough to Bust: The Brief Life of Norplant, the Contraceptive Implant, 22 *J. Women's Hist.* 88, 93 (2010).

[27] Nina Banks, Black Women's Labor Market History Reveals Deep-Seated Race and Gender Discrimination, Econ. Pol'y Inst. (Feb. 19, 2019), www.epi.org/blog/black-womens-labor-market-history-reveals-deep-seated-race-and-gender-discrimination/.

[28] Pamela Loprest, Stefanie Schmidt & Ann Dryden Witte, Welfare Reform Under PRWORA: Aid to Children With Working Families?, in *Tax Policy and the Economy* 157, 161 (14th ed. 2000).

[29] Sojourner A. v. N.J. Dept. of Hum. Servs., 828 A.2d 306 (N.J. 2003); Roberts, supra note 26, at 70.

[30] President Barack Obama's Inaugural Address (Jan. 21, 2009), https://obamawhitehouse.archives.gov/blog/2009/01/21/president-barack-obamas-inaugural-address.

Americans to make then-unspecified hard choices, anchored by values of "honesty and hard work" – the bedrocks of personal responsibility. Yet even cursory scrutiny of the causes of the 2008 recession makes clear that catastrophic losses of housing, savings, and jobs were not a failure of hard work but the result of predatory lending and poor government oversight.[31] Solutions to the recession did not lie in individual people making better choices, but in better industry practices and stronger government policies.

The kind of personal responsibility in reproductive matters called for in the Moynihan Report, enacted into the Clinton welfare reforms, and invoked by President Obama demands that everyone take responsibility for their own actions and individually contribute toward a common goal, with both the goal and the means to effectuate it limited by racist notions of deservingness and what constitutes "good" families. This is manifest in the punitive regime PRWORA created: (1) a set of requirements to work, undergirded by notions of proper family structures, in order to receive assistance; (2) the lack of an attendant guarantee of jobs; and (3) a social system that makes job acquisition more difficult for those already marginalized and where much available work does not pay a living wage.

RJ stands in ideological opposition to this regime of personal responsibility. Where personal responsibility forecloses structural explanations for people's personal struggles (while creating the conditions for many of those struggles), the RJ framework is an explicit invitation to analyze structures and develop solutions that acknowledge interdependence. As our federal policy examples illustrate, when applied to reproduction and families, the ideology of personal responsibility generates policies that control individuals' choices about reproduction and family form. Myriad examples also exist in state and local policy; for instance, some states condition the receipt of public health insurance on individuals' perceived self-sufficiency and deservingness, choosing not to expand their Medicaid programs under the Affordable Care Act,[32] or to enact work requirements to access Medicaid.[33] RJ instead insists that people can and ought to be considered instead as autonomous, capable of acting in the best interests of themselves and their communities, and, perhaps most importantly, of making their own calculations about what it means to be responsible. To enhance RJ, reproductive and social policies must not merely recognize individuals' reproductive autonomy and personal power, but must also create the conditions to enable them.

---

[31] The Financial Crisis Inquiry Report: Final Report of the National Commission on the Causes of the Financial and Economic Crisis in the United States, at xvii–xxii (2011).

[32] Allison K. Hoffman & Mark A. Hall, The American Pathology of Inequitable Access to Medical Care, in *The Oxford Handbook of Comparative Health Law* (David Orenlicher & Tamara K. Hervey eds., 2020).

[33] Laura D. Hermer, Personal Responsibility: A Plausible Social Goal, but Not for Medicaid Reform, 38 *Hastings Ctr. Rep.* 16, 17 (2008); Minoff, supra note 5.

III THE DISPARATE IMPACTS OF PERSONAL RESPONSIBILITY IN COVID-19

Personal responsibility, long an ideological lodestar in US policy, was easy to adopt for the pandemic response, especially given the role that individual behavior has in public health efforts to prevent viral transmission.[34] In lieu of robust and uniform policy actions and social support, the United States, led by an Administration sorely lacking public health expertise or the basics of good government, left people to personally manage their COVID-19 prevention and care. The federal government issued no stay-at-home mandates and provided sparse funding for protective equipment, testing, treatment, and, initially, vaccines.[35] Aside from a $1,200 stimulus check in April 2020 and another $600 check in January 2021, as well as a temporary top-up to unemployment benefits, individuals have received very little financial assistance from the federal government, particularly when compared with other developed nations, many of which were less hard hit but provided more financial assistance to individuals, families, and small businesses.[36]

The federal government left vulnerable Americans to navigate their own financial solvency, including the cost of health care and other necessities, even while millions of jobs were lost and poverty rates rose.[37] States and localities varied widely in terms of whether or not they considered lack of federal pandemic support to be a problem. Some states considered individual choice – afforded by ideologies of personal responsibility – to be a moral necessity, while others saw relegations to individual choice as critically endangering their most vulnerable residents.

Once again, the individual was the wrong object of responsibility. COVID-19 does not merely infect and affect individuals: people live, work, travel, and commune with others – some because they want to, many others because their jobs or families require it.[38] Essential health care and other workers are disproportionately women and people of color.[39] They are most likely to be exposed to COVID-19 through their labor; their exposure risk is compounded by the improper mask

[34] Lindsay F. Wiley & Samuel R. Bagenstos, The Personal Responsibility Pandemic: Centering Solidarity in Public Health and Employment Law, 52 *Ariz. State L. J.* 1235, 1240–43 (2020).

[35] Lindsay F. Wiley, *Federalism in Pandemic Prevention and Response, in Assessing Legal Responses to COVID-19* 65, 66–67 (2020); Nancy J. Knauer, The COVID-19 Pandemic and Federalism: Who Decides?, 23 *N.Y.U. J. Leg. Pub. Pol'y* 1, 3–4 (2020).

[36] Tracey Lindeman, What Canada's COVID Response Can Teach the U.S. About Social Safety Nets, Fortune (Oct. 23, 2020), https://fortune.com/2020/10/23/canada-unemployment-cerb-economy-growth-coronavirus/.

[37] Zachary Parolin et al., Monthly Poverty Rates in the United States During the COVID-19 Pandemic 2, 4–5 (Ctr. on Poverty & Soc. Pol'y, Working Paper on Poverty and Social Policy, Oct. 2020).

[38] David Holtz et al., Interdependence and the Cost of Uncoordinated Responses to COVID-19, 117 *Proc. Nat'l Acad. Scis.* 19837 (2020).

[39] Francesca Donner, How Women are Getting Squeezed by the Pandemic, NY Times (May 20, 2020), www.nytimes.com/2020/05/20/us/women-economy-jobs-coronavirus-gender.html.

wearing, lack of vaccination, and other risky behaviors of those they encounter.[40] Research shows that racial and ethnic minorities across all ages, and particularly those aged between twenty-five and fifty-four years, have experienced significantly higher COVID-19 mortality than White people.[41] Once exposed, these same people were more vulnerable to morbidity and mortality from the virus.[42] Treating risk as an individual responsibility ignores the ways that an individual's risk is affected by the actions of others. Once again, personal responsibility fails by imagining that people will voluntarily do the work of accounting for one another without requiring them to do so.

Given this, it is surprising that the emergency conditions surrounding COVID-19 also catalyzed some long-needed reforms, which move toward RJ by reframing notions of responsibility. Here, we provide three examples of RJ-enhancing policy changes prompted by the pandemic: (1) telemedicine-supported abortion access; (2) remote access to judicial bypass hearings; and (3) paid family and medical leave. Their immediate justification was health, specifically the reduction of risk of viral spread due to in-person contact. But their impact was to remove the presumption that people are blameworthy for the social conditions in which they find themselves; that they are at fault for their own need. The fact that these changes were possible, but politically feasible only with the catalyst of a pandemic, makes manifest that often policies are conditioned on the idea that deserving help requires that a person be deemed blameless for their need.

A *Telemedicine-Supported Abortion Access*

Telemedicine allows physicians to supervise patients remotely accessing abortion care. Allowing individuals to remotely access medication abortions increases access to abortion care, especially for people of color, people with disabilities, people living in rural areas, and low-income people.[43]

At the beginning of the pandemic, policy changes by both public and private actors supported the near-instant adoption and implementation of telemedicine care, which included reproductive health care services, such as contraception prescriptions and

---

[40] William F. Marshall, Why Are People of Color More at Risk of Coronavirus Complications?, Mayo Clinic (2020), www.mayoclinic.org/diseases-conditions/coronavirus/expert-answers/coronavirus-infec tion-by-race/faq-20488802.

[41] Mary T. Bassett, Jarvis T. Chen & Nancy Krieger, The Unequal Toll of COVID-19 Mortality by Age in the United States: Quantifying Racial/Ethnic Disparities, 19 Harv. Ctr. for Population & Dev. Studs. Working Paper Series 2 (June 12, 2020).

[42] Samantha Artiga & Kendal Orgera, Changes in Health Coverage by Race and Ethnicity Since the ACA, 2010–2018, Kaiser Fam. Found. (Mar. 5, 2020), www.kff.org/racial-equity-and-health-policy/ issue-brief/changes-in-health-coverage-by-race-and-ethnicity-since-the-aca-2010-2018.

[43] Megan K. Donovan, Self-Managed Medication Abortion: Expanding the Available Options for U.S. Abortion Care, 21 *Guttmacher Pol'y Rev.* 41, 43 (2018); David S. Cohen & Carole Joffe, *Obstacle Course: The Everyday Struggle to Get an Abortion in America*, 13, 60–63 (2020).

some preventative, screening, and routine care.[44] Initially, telemedicine implementa-
tions could not include medication abortion due to a Food and Drug Administration
(FDA) "Risk Evaluation and Mitigation Strategy" (REMS) policy, which bars the distribution of mifepristone, the first of two medications used in medication abortion, at
pharmacies and limits it to registered providers at clinics and hospitals, on the pretextual
basis of safety.[45] But in 2020, litigation brought by the American College of Obstetrics
and Gynecology, with the RJ collective SisterSong as one of the co-plaintiffs, successfully enjoined the REMS policy nationwide for several months to enable medication
abortion by telemedicine during the COVID-19 pandemic.[46] The plaintiffs' American
Civil Liberties Union lawyers particularly framed the legal issue in terms of the disproportionate impact of the FDA policy on low-income people of color.[47]

Even with the FDA's policy enjoined, a number of state regulations continue
to forbid telemedicine exclusively for abortion care.[48] And, in January 2021, the
Supreme Court stayed the federal district court's injunction order, reinstating the
FDA REMS policy and again singling out abortion care for unnecessary and harmful burdens to treatment.[49] In her dissent, Justice Sonia Sotomayor reiterated the
particular RJ concerns, noting that the FDA allowed many other drugs, including
some controlled substances, to be dispensed without in-person visits, and questioning why a similar approach could not be taken to abortion medications, especially
given the disparities in prevalence, morbidity, and mortality from COVID-19 for
Black and Brown communities.[50]

Despite existing state bans and the Supreme Court's ruling on the REMS policy,
the conditions of the pandemic may yet catalyze lasting change for remote abortion access. At the time of writing, the Biden Administration's FDA is "exercising
enforcement discretion" of its REMS policy for mifepristone and reviewing the
policy more broadly.[51] If this review leads to policy change, it will be long overdue –
multiple administrations have failed to take on board RJ-centered advocacy and
lawyering highlighting the harmful effects of FDA's REMS policy, particularly on

[44] Carmel Shachar, Jaclyn Engel & Glyn Elwyn, Implications for Telehealth in a Post-Pandemic Future, 323 *JAMA* 2375, 2375–76 (2020).
[45] Compare Food & Drug Admin, Risk Evaluation and Mitigation Strategy (REMS) Single Shared System for Mifepristone 200MG 1-3 (Apr. 2019), with Ctr. for Drug Evaluation & Rsch., Risk Assessment and Risk Mitigation Review: 202107Origis000, at 2 (2012), and Nat'l Acads. of Sci., Eng'g & Med., The Safety and Quality of Abortion Care in the United States 55 (2018).
[46] Food & Drug Admin. v. Am. Coll. Obstetricians & Gynecologists, 472 F.Supp.3d 183, 233 (D. Md. 2020).
[47] Complaint at 33, 36–37, Food & Drug Admin. v. Am. Coll. Obstetricians & Gynecologists, 472 F.Supp.3d 183, 233 (D. Md. 2020) (No. 8:20-CV-01320).
[48] The Availability and Use of Medication Abortion, Kaiser Fam. Found. (June 16, 2021), www.kff.org/womens-health-policy/fact-sheet/the-availability-and-use-of-medication-abortion/.
[49] Food & Drug Admin. v. Am. Coll. Obstetricians & Gynecologists, 141 S.Ct. 578, 578 (2021).
[50] Id. at 590.
[51] Carrie N. Baker, Advocates Cheer FDA Review of Abortion Pill Restrictions, Ms. Mag. (May 11, 2021), https://msmagazine.com/2021/05/11/fda-review-abortion-pill-restrictions-mifepristone-biden/.

marginalized people.[52] However, the pandemic's conditions laid bare these harms for policymakers and made clear that RJ-centered abortion care is possible and necessary. What has been missing is the will of federal and state governments to adopt policies centering on the collective, rather than the individual.

B *Remote Access to Judicial Bypass Hearings*

Following the Supreme Court's affirmation of laws requiring parental consent for abortion on the basis of minors' safety in *Bellotti v. Baird* and *Planned Parenthood v. Casey*, more states have required that minor patients seeking abortion obtain parental consent.[53] In these jurisdictions, minors who are not able to get parental consent for any reason may receive an abortion *only if* they receive a "judicial bypass" order from a judge. It is well documented that judicial bypass requirements pose particular barriers to low-income and disabled young people, people who live in rural communities, and young people who became pregnant as the result of violence from accessing safe and legal abortion.[54] Accessing abortion through judicial bypass is further known to be a humiliating and traumatic experience for many young people.[55]

During COVID-19, court proceedings in some jurisdictions were moved to remote venues, a change that anecdotally increased young peoples' access to abortion by alleviating the logistical and emotional barriers of judicial bypass hearings.[56] With remote hearings, young people did not have to miss school, pay for or arrange travel to court, or experience acutely daunting or traumatic in-person hearings in courtrooms or judicial chambers discussing their reproductive decisions. Although we believe that the underlying laws should be fully repealed, we note that this small policy change inches toward RJ. If made permanent, it could be especially impactful to young people for whom travel, missed school, or the in-person hearing represent even greater hardships or trauma.

C *Paid Family and Medical Leave*

The pandemic has made obvious the interconnectedness of America's underpaid workforces. The pandemic catalyzed Congress to pass temporary paid family and

---

[52] Id.; see also Greer Donley, Medication Abortion Exceptionalism, 107 *Cornell L. Rev.* 627 (2021), https://scholarship.law.pitt.edu/cgi/viewcontent.cgi?article=1403&context=fac_articles.

[53] Bellotti v. Baird, 443 U.S. 662, 649 (1979); Planned Parenthood of Se. Pa. v. Casey, 505 U.S. 833, 899 (1992); Jon Wong, Young People Deserve Access to Abortion Care Swiftly, Without Shame or Stigma, If/When/How: Lawyering for Repro. Just. (July 16, 2018), accessible at www.ifwhenhow.org/resources/overview-young-peoples-access-to-abortion-care/.

[54] Wong, supra note 53.

[55] Kate Coleman-Minahan, Amanda Jean Stevenson, Emily Obront & Susan Hays, Young Women's Experiences Obtaining Judicial Bypass for Abortion in Texas, 64 *J. Adolescent Health* 20 (2019).

[56] This anecdote stems from one of the author's (RLZ) work supporting minors seeking judicial bypass in Pennsylvania.

medical leave,[57] for which Americans have advocated for decades. Paid medical, family, and sick leave is essential for people to have time, funds, and for many within America's current structure of health coverage, insurance to care for their own health needs as well as those of their dependents. Paid leave, as well as pay for family home care, are also critical to people's financial stability,[58] and is thus especially critical for marginalized people who are more likely to work in jobs that most expose them to the pandemic. Economic stability has lifesaving importance for many, including victims of domestic violence who are separating from and leaving abusive partners.[59]

Unfortunately, mandatory COVID-19 paid leave, already limited to employees at large companies, health care employers, and otherwise,[60] expired on December 31, 2020 and was only replaced by a voluntary tax credit for employers through March 2021.[61] However, like remote abortion care, the pandemic's conditions catalyzed long-requested conversations about the necessity for paid leave. At the time of writing, Congress is considering including some form of paid leave in its 2021 domestic social policy bill.[62]

These changes are particularly laudable because they model policy that is materially beneficial without conditioning access on blamelessness. But, as already noted, the three examples of long-overdue, RJ-enhancing policy changes described above are or were temporary and limited in scope. More problematically, even these temporary advances best serve those who already have means: people who have legal, financial, and logistical access to telehealth providers to manage abortion and people in employment positions from which paid leave can be taken.[63] Thus, while these COVID-19-stimulated policy changes were laudable, some were not only ineffectual for marginalized individuals (for whom they were most needed), but in practice further entrenched harms to them by requiring them alone to continue to work when they or their family members were sick and to overcome numerous barriers to seek reproductive care in person. Despite these limitations, the three examples provide proof-of-concept for more robust future changes.

Centering the RJ framework in future policies is critical to remedying inequity. Mainstream reproductive rights discourse, which has been largely controlled by

---

[57] Families First Coronavirus Response Act, Pub. L. No. 116-127 § 3102, 141 Stat. 178, 189 (2020).

[58] Mercer Gary & Nancy Berlinger, Interdependent Citizens: The Ethics of Care in Pandemic Recovery, 50 *Hastings Ctr. Rep.* 56, 1–2 (2020).

[59] Ralph Henry, Domestic Violence and the Failures of Welfare Reform: The Role for Work Leave Legislation, 20 *Wis. Women's L.J.* 67, 68–69 (2005).

[60] Paid Leave Under the Families First Coronavirus Response Act, 85 Fed. Reg. 19,326, 19,327 (Apr. 6, 2020).

[61] Consolidated Appropriations Act, 2021, Pub. L. No. 116-260 § 286, 134 Stat. 1182, 1989 (2020).

[62] Caitlyn Kim, House Democrats are Bringing Back Paid Leave in Their Spending Bill, NPR (Nov. 3, 2021), www.npr.org/2021/11/03/1052121244/pelosi-says-house-democrats-are-bringing-back-paid-leave-in-their-spending-bill.

[63] Families First Coronavirus Response Act, Pub. L. No. 116-127 § 3102, 141 Stat. 178, 189 (2020).

White middle and upper-class women and from which COVID-19 telemedicine abortion and paid leave changes stemmed, is rooted in the neoliberal conceptions of choice that "locate[] individual rights at [their] core, and treat[] the individual's control over her body as central to liberty and freedom."[64] While this conception of reproductive rights is distinct from the personal responsibility policies discussed that seek to *explicitly* punish individuals for non-compliance with social standards, any policy focused on individual choice "obscures the social context in which individuals make choices, and discounts the ways in which the state regulates populations, disciplines individual bodies, and exercises control over sexuality, gender, and reproduction."[65]

In contrast, as we have shown, an RJ approach rejects conceptions of blameworthiness and addresses the ways that economic and institutional constraints on women of color and other marginalized people can restrict their choices.

IV A CALL FOR RESPONSIBILITY COMPATIBLE WITH AND ENABLING RJ

In her dissent from the Court's decision to reinstate FDA's REMS program, Justice Sotomayor made plain the intersectional implications of requiring pregnant people to risk exposure to COVID-19 to receive a prescription for medication abortion. First, she explained that COVID-19 makes pregnant people more susceptible to bad outcomes.[66] Then, she noted that:

> [M]ore than half of women who have abortions are women of color, and COVID-19's mortality rate is three times higher for Black and Hispanic individuals than non-Hispanic White individuals. On top of that, three-quarters of abortion patients have low incomes, making them more likely to rely on public transportation to get to a clinic to pick up their medication. Such patients must bear further risk of exposure while they travel, sometimes for several hours each way, to clinics often located far from their homes. Finally, minority and low-income populations are more likely to live in intergenerational housing, so patients risk infecting not just themselves, but also elderly parents and grandparents. These risks alone are significant deterrents for women seeking a medication abortion that requires in-person pickup.[67]

Justice Sotomayor's dissent, which Justice Elena Kagan joined, focuses not on those who are most able to move forward with abortion care despite the in-person requirement, but on those for whom this rule creates an undue burden to accessing

---

[64] *Policing the National Body: Race, Gender and Criminalization in the United States*, at xi (Anannya Bhattacharjee & Jael Silliman eds., 2003).

[65] Id.

[66] Food & Drug Admin., 141 S.Ct. at 582.

[67] Id. at 585.

care. In true RJ fashion, Sotomayor centers those most vulnerable people who are affected by the outcome of this case – women of color and women who are low-income – and finds that the policy imposes an "unnecessary, unjustifiable, irra-tional, and undue burden" on the constitutionally protected right to abortion. Unfortunately, Sotomayor's RJ-informed approach did not convince the majority of Supreme Court justices, who saw no reason to interfere with the FDA's assessment that, even in a pandemic, in-person prescription of abortion medications should be required. As Justice Sotomayor points out, the majority maintained this view despite the failure of the FDA to provide any reasons "explaining why the Government believes women must continue to pick up mifepristone in person, even though it has exempted many other drugs from such a requirement given the health risks of COVID-19."[68] The majority's refusal to require reasons from the FDA and lack of interest in the real-world impact of the FDA's policy is consistent with an approach to personal responsibility that understands financial and logistical (and in this case, even health-related) barriers to accessing abortion care as the responsibility of the individual rather than as facts about American society that American regulators have a responsibility to consider when making policy. In this way, the majority upheld and affirmed an atomistic and hands-off conception of responsibility – and, through it, of individual autonomy – rather than an understanding that seeks to empower individuals so that they can choose how to care for themselves and their families. Though people seeking abortions received no relief from the Supreme Court, the FDA did finally relent under the continued weight of advocacy and evidence that its rule inhibited access to needed care without creating safety benefits to those seeking medication abortions. On December 16, 2021, the agency reversed course by announcing that it would jettison the unnecessary in-person dispensing require-ment for mifepristone – thus easing a burden that had persisted for far too long.[69]

This expression of personal responsibility has long structured reproductive policy in the United States, bolstered by a sense that it is an uncontroversial and bipartisan appeal to an individualism highly prized by Americans. But it rests on an impover-ished and often unrealistic notion of individual autonomy that foregrounds the idea of individual choice while failing to support the necessary conditions to enable all, or even most, individuals to actually make choices consistent with their own values and interests. The COVID-19 pandemic has further exposed the failure of this con-ceptualization of autonomy by making clear the profound ways in which individual flourishing is not an individual matter.

Recognizing a fuller understanding of autonomy has driven this move in repro-ductive ethics from a negative to a positive rights approach – an approach led by the RJ movement. In the RJ approach, responsibility is not eliminated. Rather, RJ calls

---

[68] Id. at 590.
[69] See Food & Drug Admin., Questions and Answers on Mifeprex (2021), www.fda.gov/drugs/postmarket-drug-safety-information-patients-and-providers/questions-and-answers-mifeprex.

for policies that enable and promote personal power, simultaneously recognizing interdependence and facilitating autonomy. Such policies are even more necessary in light of state laws, including those in Texas, Mississippi, and up to twenty other states, that imminently challenge the constitutional right to abortion.[70]

The pandemic catalyzed limited expressions of RJ-centered policymaking, in changes permitting remote management of reproductive care and remote judicial bypass of laws requiring parental consent for minors' abortions, as well as policies expanding access to paid family leave. These policies reflected the reality of our interconnected existence, if obliquely. They removed barriers to people making personal decisions, if temporarily. They illustrate that RJ-consistent policy is possible in the United States. Adopting an RJ approach in future policy allows us to recognize our society's interdependence. Doing so is necessary for all our health and flourishing.[71]

---

[70] Elyssa Spitzer & Nora Ellmann, State Abortion Legislation in 2021, Ctr. for Am. Progress (Sept. 21, 2021), www.americanprogress.org/issues/women/reports/2021/09/21/503999/state-abortion-legislation-2021/; Abortion Policy in the Absence of Roe, Guttmacher Inst. (Oct. 1, 2021), www.guttmacher.org/state-policy/explore/abortion-policy-absence-roe.

[71] Since the writing of this chapter, abortion rights and access have been fundamentally diminished following the Supreme Court's overturning of Roe v. Wade, Planned Parenthood of Pennsylvania v. Casey, and the acknowledgement of a constitutional right to abortion in Dobbs v. Jackson Women's Health Organization, 142 S. Ct. 2228 (2022), subsequently passed or triggered state laws significantly or completely limiting abortion rights and access, and pending litigation challenging the FDA's long-standing approval of mifepristone to be used as a first step in medication abortions. (In contrast with this chapter's call for the FDA to use its expertise and discretion to further increase access to mifepristone, this litigation seeks to entirely overturn the FDA's expert judgment and eliminate access to mifepristone for abortion.) These and further attacks on the legal right to access reproductive health care only make greater and more urgent the need for laws and policies rooted in reproductive justice and providing for conditions enabling personal power and autonomy.

21

Abortion At-Home and At-Law During a Pandemic

Joanna N. Erdman

I INTRODUCTION

Abortion law has long been preoccupied with place, that is, where an abortion happens. In the nineteenth century, growing commercial markets in so-called "ladies' remedies" justified stricter criminal laws, which confined legal abortion to the medical clinic.[1] Abortion law today continues to authorize certain places of care and to outlaw others, unfairly restricting supply and frustrating access. During the COVID-19 pandemic, clinic-based restrictions on abortion access became the targets of advocacy, leading to authorizations for the remote provision and local delivery of abortion pills. People could now access abortion without leaving their homes: abortion at-home.

Homes are built structures, but they are also inventions.[2] Abortion law creates the places that it regulates and thus shapes the experience of abortion within them.[3] Yet homes are also imbued with meaning by the people who live there. The law may thus anticipate abortion at-home, but its practice within the home will also come to shape the law that authorizes it. Rooted in this relationship of law and place, this chapter explores abortion at-home during the COVID-19 pandemic. After an introduction to abortion pills and abortion law in Section II, Section III examines features of COVID-19 authorizations for abortion at-home in Europe and the United States. Despite differences among them, all the authorizations reflect a crisis management discourse, designed to conserve access to care during the pandemic, but conserving much more in the continued clinical control of abortion and the social norms of abortion law. Against this conservative view, in an alternative legacy, Section IV speculates on how abortion at-home, normalized within the everyday tasks, products, and people of home life, may lead to a radical change in its practice, especially during a time when people have formed new relationships to their home

---

[1] John Keown, *Abortion, Doctors and the Law: Some Aspects of the Legal Regulation of Abortion in England from 1803 to 1982* (1988); James C. Mohr, *Abortion in America: The Origins and Evolution of National Policy, 1800–1900* (1978).

[2] Henri Lefebvre, *The Production of Space* (Donald Nicholson-Smith trans., Basil Blackwell 3d ed. 1992).

[3] Irus Braverman et al., *The Expanding Spaces of Law: A Timely Geography* (2015).

and invested new meaning in it. This chapter concludes by imagining a future for abortion law born of the pandemic but radicalized in the home.

II ABORTION PILLS AND ABORTION LAW

A common regimen of early abortion with pills involves a person swallowing one tablet of mifepristone to block the hormone progesterone needed to sustain a pregnancy, and twenty-four to forty-eight hours later, inserting four tablets of misoprostol between the gums and cheeks to induce contractions.[4] The abortion takes place over a period of days with cramping and bleeding stronger than a usual menstrual period and similar to an early miscarriage.

The science behind abortion pills was revolutionary, but their effect in the world was not. In 1988, after French authorities approved mifepristone, the company that developed the drug Roussel-Uclaf abandoned distribution because of a social backlash.[5] The minister of health intervened, declared mifepristone the "moral property of women," and returned it to market, but Hoescht Marion Roussel proceeded cautiously thereafter. Global registration was slow, and regulatory agencies adopted strict prescription and dispensing controls on the drug.[6]

In 2000, when mifepristone was approved in the United States, the cover of *Time* magazine heralded, "The Little White Bombshell: This Pill Will Change Everything."[7] It did not. The Food and Drug Administration (FDA) imposed strict distribution controls, including a ban on retail pharmacy access,[8] and later subjected mifepristone to a Risk Evaluation and Mitigation Strategy (REMS), requiring that people both access and take the drug in-clinic.[9] Many countries imposed similar controls on misoprostol, especially after a campaign by its manufacturer to dissuade its off-label use for abortion, but misoprostol has not been similarly restricted in Europe or the United States.[10] Many of the controls on mifepristone remain to this day, including unique prescriber registration, restricted in-clinic distribution, and/or the supervised taking of the pill.

Rather than any revolution, abortion pills were folded into abortion law and made subject to its norms and conceits. Abortion law, even the most liberal variant, follows

[4] World Health Org., Medical Management of Abortion (2018).
[5] Alan Riding, Abortion Politics Are Said to Hinder Use of French Pill, NY Times, July 29, 1990, at 1, www.nytimes.com/1990/07/29/world/abortion-politics-are-said-to-hinder-use-of-french-pill.html.
[6] Beverly Winikoff & Carolyn Westhoff, *Fifteen Years: Looking Back and Looking Forward*, 92 Contraception 177 (2015).
[7] Margot Talbot, *The Pill that Still Hasn't Changed the Politics of Abortion*, New Yorker (Apr. 4, 2016), www.newyorker.com/news/news-desk/the-pill-that-still-hasnt-changed-the-politics-of-abortion.
[8] Lars Noah, A Miscarriage in the Drug Approval Process?: Mifepristone Embroils the FDA in Abortion Politics, 36 *Wake Forest L. Rev.* 571 (2001).
[9] Mifeprex REMS Study Grp., Sixteen Years of Overregulation: Time to Unburden Mifeprex, 376 *New Eng. J. Med.* 790 (2017).
[10] Yap-Seng Chong, Lin-Lin Su & Sabaratnam Arulkumaran, Misoprostol: A Quarter Century of Use, Abuse, and Creative Misuse, 59 *Obstetrical & Gynecological Surv.* 128 (2004).

a logic of control. Abortion is lawful within the provisions of the law, and any act taken outside of them with the intent to end a pregnancy – including to prescribe, administer, or supply any drug – is prohibited.[11] Legal abortion is a place-bound practice, figuratively and literally. Abortion must be practiced within the provisions of the law, which often authorizes the physical places of care.

Place-based control of abortion can be tracked to the mid-nineteenth century in Europe and the United States, when the medical profession campaigned for stricter criminalization.[12] These campaigns were premised on the moral wrong of abortion and its unsafe practice, although abortion early in pregnancy was relatively safe. Rather, historians identify professional self-interest and social control as the primary motivations. The medical establishment was concerned with a growing and profitable market in home-use abortifacients, which reflected the frequency of abortion in White, middle-class homes. The professional self-interest in quashing this market coincided with a patriarchal and nativist fear that women within these homes were abandoning their familial duties, leading to declining birth rates among this social class. To stem this threat, criminalization, as an act of medical and social control, took abortion from the home and confined it to the clinic.

The clinic is therefore not only a physical place but an institution of control, and by raising the prospect of a "post-clinic abortion," abortion with pills thus threatens the control of the law.[13] For this reason, even in relatively liberal contexts and despite decades of advocacy, abortion at-home remained but an idea prior to COVID-19. In the United Kingdom, the home use of misoprostol was allowed by executive orders, but a criminal statute, the Abortion Act 1967, mandated in-clinic prescription and administration of mifepristone.[14] French law similarly did not allow telemedical abortion, requiring that mifepristone be administered in-clinic in the presence of a physician or midwife.[15] In the United States, despite a relaxation of the REMS that allowed the pills to be taken at home, federal law still required that mifepristone be dispensed in a clinical setting, and so prohibited its distribution by mail, pharmacy, or online.[16] Moreover, some state laws prohibited abortion at-home by bans on telemedical abortion or remote provision regardless of federal drug regulation.[17]

---

[11] Antonella F. Lavelanet, Brooke Ronald Johnson & Bela Ganatra, Global Abortion Policies Database: A Descriptive Analysis of the Regulatory and Policy Environment Related to Abortion, 62 *Best Prac. Rsch. Clin. Obstet. Gynaecol.* 25 (2020).

[12] Keown, supra note 1; Mohr, supra note 1.

[13] Emily Bazelon, The Dawn of the Post-Clinic Abortion, NY Times Mag. (Aug. 28, 2014), www.nytimes .com/2014/08/31/magazine/the-dawn-of-the-post-clinic-abortion.html.

[14] Abortion Act 1967, c. 87, § 3 (Eng.); Jordan A. Parsons, COVID-19 Governmental Decisions to Allow Home Use of Misoprostol for Early Medical Abortion in the UK, 124 *Health Pol'y* 679 (2020).

[15] French Public Health Code, arts. R2212-9–R2212-19, R2212-1–R2222-3.

[16] FDA, Mifeprex (Mifepristone) Information (Dec. 16, 2021), www.fda.gov/drugs/postmarket-drug-safety-information-patients-and-providers/mifeprex-mifepristone-information.

[17] Guttmacher Inst., State Law and Policies: Medication Abortion (2020), www.guttmacher.org/state-policy/explore/medication-abortion.

Abortion law before COVID-19 required some "touch" to a clinical setting, however formal or perfunctory. The fact that people already consumed abortion pills at home and ended their pregnancies at home proved of little persuasion in changing the law. This is because the in-clinic requirements of abortion law have always been as much discursive as real. They maintain the social control of the law. During COVID-19, when clinics shuttered and hospitals overfilled, and any safety pretense for these restrictions strained the most common of sense, abortion with pills found its revolutionary context – or perhaps not.

III ABORTION AT-HOME AS CRISIS MANAGEMENT

There is a popular notion that crises create an opportunity to reform the status quo by threatening the structures that underlie it.[18] Yet, in the thick of crisis, reform is often not a priority. In conventional crisis management, the imperative is to "bring things back to normal." Reform comes only from the desire to change something so that everything else can stay the same. COVID-19 authorizations for abortion at-home in Europe and the United States reflect this idea.

In 2020, five European countries (Ireland, England, Wales, Scotland, and France) introduced executive orders or other measures that authorized abortion at-home by allowing for patient consultations by video or phone (remote provision), designating the home as a site of abortion care, and/or permitting the online purchase, home delivery, or local pharmacy pick-up of abortion pills.[19] In the same year, authorization in the United States came via litigation. The FDA refused to suspend the in-clinic distribution requirement for mifepristone despite doing so for other drugs. The American Civil Liberties Union filed a lawsuit challenging this requirement for mifepristone and found early success when a federal district court judge ordered the FDA to suspend its enforcement during the pandemic.[20]

These authorizations were all designed to ensure access to abortion during the pandemic, limit exposure to the virus, and conserve health system resources.[21] They achieved these aims, but they also conserved certain social norms of abortion law. This section explores these conservative features of the COVID-19 authorizations.

First, the authorizations often framed abortion at-home as a mere practice innovation under the law to ensure continued access to care – that is, doing the same thing a different way. The Irish minister of health explicitly introduced remote provision as a revised model of abortion care to emphasize that it required no reform

---

[18] Arjen Boin & Paul 't Hart, Public Leadership in Times of Crisis: Mission Impossible? 63 *Pub. Admin. Rev.* 544 (2003).

[19] Caroline Moreau et al., Abortion Regulation in Europe in the Era of COVID-19: A Spectrum of Policy Responses, BMJ Sexual & Reprod. Health (2020), http://dx.doi.org/10.1136/bmjsrh-2020-200724.

[20] Am. Coll. of Obstetricians & Gynecologists v. U.S. Food & Drug Admin., 506 F.Supp.3d 328 (D. Md. 2020).

[21] Michelle J. Bayefsky, Deborah Bartz & Katie L. Watson, Abortion during the COVID-19 Pandemic – Ensuring Access to an Essential Health Service, 382 *New Eng. J. Med.* e47 (2020).

of abortion law.[22] In Ireland, the Health (Regulation of Termination of Pregnancy) Act 2018 requires that a medical practitioner "examine the pregnant woman" to stay within the law and avoid criminal sanction.[23] According to the minister, this requirement did not preclude clinical examination by phone or video.

Continued clinical control was the most emphasized feature of the authorizations. "No touch protocols" promised that medical practitioners could and would do everything they ever did to administer abortions at-home.[24] The English order promised that the "medical practitioner" would carry out the "treatment" (abortion) as authorized by law, which restricts provision to "nine weeks and six days" on the day "mifepristone is taken."[25] The Scottish order required practitioners to continue to file the green approval and yellow reporting forms under the law.[26] When the Christian Legal Centre challenged the UK authorization as ultra vires of the Abortion Act 1967 because abortion at-home would not be "carried out" by practitioners, but by patients, the Court of Appeal denied the review by emphasizing the control of the doctor, who "remains in charge [of the abortion] ... even if they do not perform every part of it."[27] Medical organizations led the charge for abortion at-home in every country.[28] In April 2021, after the US elections, when the FDA announced that it would not enforce the in-clinic distribution requirement for mifepristone, it did so by letter to the American College of Obstetrics and Gynecologists, the lead plaintiff in the American Civil Liberties Union lawsuit.[29] Even after the FDA permanently removed the in-person requirement, the REMS still required that a certified provider pledge they can date pregnancies accurately and will remain in control of the abortion throughout.[30]

---

[22] Valerie Ryan, Telemedicine Abortion Consultations Permitted – Health Minister, Irish Med. Times. (Mar. 27, 2020), www.imt.ie/uncategorised/telemedicine-abortion-consultations-permitted-health-minister-27-03-2020/.

[23] Health (Regulation of Termination of Pregnancy) Act 2018 § 12 (Act No. 31/2018) (Ir.).

[24] Elizabeth G. Raymond et al., Commentary: No-Test Abortion: A Sample Protocol for Increasing Access During a Pandemic and Beyond, 1010 *Contraception* 361 (2020).

[25] Dep't of Health & Soc. Care, The Abortion Act 1967 – Approval of a Class of Places (Mar. 30, 2020), https://assets.publishing.service.gov.uk/government/uploads/system/uploads/attachment_data/file/876740/30032020_The_Abortion_Act_1967_-_Approval_of_a_Class_of_Places.pdf.

[26] Scottish Gov., Abortion – COVID-19 – Approval for Mifepristone to be Taken at Home and Other Contingency Measures (Mar. 31, 2021), www.sehd.scot.nhs.uk/cmo/CMO(2020)09.pdf.

[27] R (Christian Concern) v. Sec'y of State for Health & Soc. Care, [2020] EWCA (Civ) 1239.

[28] Brit. Pregnancy Advisory Serv., Open Letter to: Rt. Hon. Matt Hancock MP, Secretary of State for Health (Mar. 28, 2020), https://drive.google.com/file/d/1TujbubXHjaN7H6FD2U5CvZvtFTmqj CXD/view; Statement by Am. Coll. of Obstetricians et al., Abortion Access During the COVID-19 Outbreak (Mar. 18, 2020), www.acog.org/news/news-releases/2020/03/joint-statement-on-abortion-access-during-the-covid-19-outbreak.

[29] Letter from US Food & Drug Admin. to Am. Coll. of Obstetricians & Gynecologists (Apr. 12, 2021), https://twitter.com/ACOGAction/status/1381781110980501512.

[30] US Food & Drug Admin., Questions and Answers on Mifepristone for Medical Termination of Pregnancy Through Ten Weeks Gestation (Dec. 16, 2021), www.fda.gov/drugs/postmarket-drug-safety-information-patients-and-providers/questions-and-answers-mifeprex.

Rather than disrupt the status quo – abortion as a clinically controlled practice – abortion at-home conserved it. Virtual examinations are still medical examinations, telemedicine is still medicine, and the home is no different, and, most importantly, not inferior to the clinic. This conception of non-inferiority reflects a convention of abortion research and was central to all the authorizations, which cited evidence showing that abortion at-home was not unacceptably less safe or resulted in substantially worse outcomes than the status quo.[31] The routine citation of this research softened any radical edge to abortion at-home, specifically because research is always revisable with new evidence, and thus so too, the authorizations premised upon it. With the UK orders set to expire within a month, the government continued to consider "all the evidence" before deciding whether to make abortion at-home a permanent feature of the law.[32]

This is a second conservative feature of the authorizations, their temporary status, born and time-bound to a historic state of emergency. Sunset clauses were attached to the orders in Ireland and Wales, which meant they were to be automatically revoked with the end of emergency COVID-19 legislation.[33] In England, the secretary of state for health and social care reissued its order because this clause was mistakenly left out.[34] In Scotland, an accompanying letter explained the order's temporary status with the stated intention to return to the status quo when abortion at-home was "no longer necessary in relation to the pandemic response," that is, when "there was no longer a serious and imminent threat to public health posed by the … coronavirus in Scotland."[35]

This temporary status reflected an effort to allow abortion at-home with as little change to existing law as possible. This is a third conservative feature of the authorizations. In the United Kingdom, the Abortion Act 1967 authorizes a medical practitioner to carry out an abortion in a hospital or other approved place.[36] Abortion in any other place is a criminal offense. The English and Welsh orders both temporarily approved the "home" as a "class of place" for abortion under the Act.

[31] Katherine Gambir et al., Effectiveness, Safety and Acceptability of Medical Abortion at Home Versus in the Clinic: A Systematic Review and Meta-Analysis in Response to COVID-19, 5 *BMJ Glob. Health* e003934 (2020).

[32] Polly Toynbee, Will Easy, Early Abortions Become Another Casualty of the Tories' Culture War?, Guardian (Feb. 10, 2022), www.theguardian.com/commentisfree/2022/feb/10/abortions-tories-culture-war-doctors-covid-women.

[33] Health Serv. Exec. & Dep't of Health, Revised Model of Care for Termination in Early Pregnancy (Apr. 7, 2020) (Ireland); Welsh Minister for Health, The Abortion Act 1967 – Approval of a Class of Place for Treatment for the Termination of Pregnancy (Wales) (Mar. 31, 2020), https://gov.wales/sites/default/files/publications/2020-04/approval-of-a-class-of-place-for-treatment-for-the-termination-of-pregnancy-wales-2020.pdf.

[34] Paul Waugh, Home Abortions Made Easier As Law Relaxed During Coronavirus Outbreak, Huffington Post (Mar. 30, 2020), www.huffingtonpost.co.uk/entry/hancock-home-abortions-easier-coronavirus-lockdown_uk_5e8213e5c5b66149226ba985.

[35] Scottish Gov., supra note 26.

[36] Abortion Act 1967, c. 87, § 12 (Eng.).

The Scottish order was more restrictive, approving the home only where a medical practitioner "considers that it is not advisable or not possible for the [patient] ... to attend a clinic."[37] The approval of abortion at-home, in other words, was entirely consistent with the aims of a criminal statute, and more so, with the nineteenth-century physician-led campaign for its enactment, given that telemedical abortion was justified as necessary to protect against a growing online market in abortion pills.[38] Indeed, before COVID-19, the FDA in the United States acted similarly to shut down this online supply for breach of the REMS.[39] The intended effect of approving abortion at-home was to channel all abortion into a single controlled system. The UK orders thus did not challenge the control logic of abortion law but traded on it.

In France and the United States, authorizations for abortion at-home were also anchored in existing abortion law, albeit constitutional rather than criminal. When French authorities justified the legality of the order authorizing teleconsultation and direct pharmacy pick-up of abortion pills, they referenced the constitutional status of abortion rights, declaring that the "[COVID-19] health crisis must not call into question our most fundamental values: those of the emancipation of women and their right to their bodies."[40] Constitutional abortion rights doctrine also anchored the US authorization and then undid it. In 2020, the US federal district judge who suspended the in-clinic requirement reasoned that it posed an undue burden on the right to abortion, namely by increasing the risk of COVID-19 infection for oneself or family.[41] When the Supreme Court later reinstated the requirement on an emergency motion, it reasoned from the same constitutional doctrine and against a strong dissent that emphasized the undue burden of the requirement, especially for people of color and from low-income communities, who faced greater risk.[42] For those outside the United States, its constitutional doctrine on abortion rights is indeed "strangely disorienting ... a sort of fascistic madness,"[43] especially when it proves futile to keep people safe during a pandemic. Moreover, abortion at-home challenges basic ideas

---

[37] Scottish Gov., *supra* note 26.

[38] Sonia Elks, Millions of Women Feared at Risk of Backstreet Abortions During Pandemic, Thomson Reuters Found. (Apr. 3, 2020), https://news.trust.org/item/20200403144228-3cop8; Abigail R. A. Aiken et al., Demand for Self-Managed Online Telemedicine Abortion in the United States During the Coronavirus Disease 2019 (COVID-19) Pandemic, 136 *Obstetrics & Gynecology* 835 (2020); Abigail R. A. Aiken et al., Demand for Self-Managed Online Telemedicine Abortion in Eight European Countries During the COVID-19 Pandemic: A Regression Discontinuity Analysis, *BMJ Sex. Reprod. Health* 150 (2021).

[39] US Food & Drug Admin., Warning Letter to Aidaccess.org re: Causing the Introduction of a Misbranded and Unapproved New Drug into Interstate Commerce (Mar. 8, 2019).

[40] Le Conseil d'Etat, IVG Médicamenteuse à Domicile durant l'état d'urgence Sanitaire – Décision en Référé du 22 mai (May 22, 2020); Gouvernement de France, Communique de Press, Face à l'épidémie, le Gouvernement se Paris, le 3 Avril 2020 Mobilise pour Maintenir les droits des Femmes en Matière d'IVG, (Apr. 3, 2020).

[41] Am. Coll. of Obstetricians & Gynecologists, 427 F.Supp.3d at 216.

[42] Am. Coll. of Obstetricians & Gynecologists v. U.S. Food & Drug Admin., 141 S. Ct. 578 (2021).

[43] Robin West, Reconsidering Legalism, 88 *Minn. L. Rev.* 703 (2003).

in US abortion law, for example, altering the path to an abortion and so too the opportunity for substantial obstacle, yet any radical implications of the post-clinic abortion were held off in constitutional argument, which proceeded by established doctrine.[44] When the FDA eventually changed course to allow abortion at-home, it cited no constitutional right but rather the evidence of the safety of the practice.

Together these conservative features of the COVID-19 authorizations reflect the paradox of a crisis management discourse. Crisis creates an opportunity to reform the status quo, as much as it supports the status quo as solace in a risk-filled world. In these authorizations, abortion at-home conserved the clinical control and social norms of abortion law. The home was merely a temporary place to weather the storm.

IV ABORTION AT-HOME IN RADICAL SPECULATION

In the COVID-19 authorizations, whether court judgments or administrative orders, the home itself received little attention. In the English order, for example, the home was described simply as a permanent address or usual residence.[45] Yet the home is so much more. Indeed, there is a long tradition in creating meaning from the empty abstractions of law. This part speculates on the ways abortion at-home, as authorized by law, but normalized in the home, may lead to a radical change in its practice. In challenge to a conservative view of these authorizations, this part asks: What if everything does not stay the same? What if abortion at-home does more than remove access barriers and otherwise leave everything else the same?

When nineteenth-century criminal statutes took abortion from the home and the market, and relocated care to the clinical setting, it not only restricted access to abortion, but also changed the people and practices of abortion, the experiences, and even the nature of it. In the United States, criminalization outlawed domestic practice by midwives, many Black and Indigenous women, suppressing the knowledge and norms of their practice.[46] These included beliefs about abortion rooted in people's perceptions and experiences of their bodies, including beliefs in their acts as no abortion at all but as the bringing back of the menses and health.[47] By giving the medical profession authority over abortion, the law displaced these ways of knowing and doing abortion.[48]

---

[44] Yvonne Lindgren, When Patients Are Their Own Doctors: Roe v. Wade in an Era of Self-Managed Care, 107 *Cornell L. Rev.* (2021).

[45] Dep't of Health & Soc. Care, The Abortion Act 1967 – Approval of a Class of Places (Mar. 30, 2020), https://assets.publishing.service.gov.uk/government/uploads/system/uploads/attachment_data/file/876740/30032020_The_Abortion_Act_1967_-_Approval_of_a_Class_of_Places.pdf (last visited Apr. 12, 2021).

[46] Melissa Murray, Race-ing Roe: Reproductive Justice, Racial Justice, and the Battle for Roe v. Wade, 134 *Harv. L. Rev.* 2025 (2021).

[47] Laurie A. Wilkie, Expelling Frogs and Binding Babies: Conception, Gestation and Birth in Nineteenth-Century African-American Midwifery, 45 *World Archaeology* 272 (2013).

[48] Stephen Turner, What's the Problem with Experts?, 31 *Soc. Stud. of Sci.* 123 (2001).

With abortion at-home, this history may reverse as the medical practitioner is invited into the home, a place of experience that reflects the person who lives there and over which they have greater control. In many ways, the practice innovations of abortion at-home reflect this shift of control.[49] Ultrasounds to date pregnancy are replaced by "LMP," an acronym for last menstrual period, something medical practitioners know from their patients. Routine clinic follow-ups are replaced by self-administered pregnancy tests to assess the success of an abortion. Most importantly, step-by-step instructions are shared on dosage and routes of administration, how many pills to take and how to take them, and how to care for the patient (yourself) throughout the process. There is a know-how quality to this information, which reflects not simple instruction, but a belief and trust in people and their bodily experiences of abortion. Medical practitioners may instruct, but the purpose of their instruction is to support people to have abortions on their own and ultimately to let go of control.[50]

At home, people know things and do things that a medical practitioner cannot. At home, people may improvise or improve on standard practice – or create new practices. The off-label use of misoprostol for abortion came from such tinkering.[51] In-clinic restrictions, even requirements that abortion pills be picked up from a clinic rather than a local pharmacy or mailed by post, affect the experience of them. When people must face the world outside in leaving their home, or the comforts of home life, there is a sense of the observation of others, the clinic staff and other patients, and an attention to some external environment, the path to the clinic, the world around it, and the clinic itself.[52] Being in these places imprints on the experience of abortion, by marking the pills as controlled objects and the abortion itself as clinical care. Abortion at-home originates in a different place, within the material cultures and social relations of the home.[53]

The home is also a place of multiple influences, which makes it difficult for the law to keep its promise of control. Today, an ever-growing suite of social media platforms, such as YouTube, Reddit, and Facebook, as well as abortion apps (one affectionately nicknamed, the *abortion siri*) and popular magazines (e.g., *Teen Vogue, Self*), promise everything anyone ever needed or wanted to know about managing abortion at-home.[54]

[49] Kathryn Fay, Jennifer Kaiser & David Turok. The No-Test Abortion is a Patient-Centered Abortion, 102 *Contraception* 142 (2020).

[50] Wendy Simonds et al., Providers, Pills and Power: The US Mifepristone Abortion Trials and Caregivers' Interpretations of Clinical Power Dynamics, 5 *Health* 207 (2001).

[51] Helena Lutéscia Coêlho et al., Misoprostol: The Experience of Women in Fortaleza, Brazil, 49 *Contraception* 101 (1994).

[52] Lori A. Brown, *Contested Spaces: Abortion Clinics, Women's Shelters and Hospitals: Politicizing the Female Body* (2013).

[53] Christina Buse, Daryl Martin & Sarah Nettleton, Conceptualising 'Materialities of Care': Making Visible Mundane Material Culture in Health and Social Care Contexts, 40 *Sociol. Health Illn.* 243 (2018).

[54] Steph Herold, Need an Abortion? There's an App for That (Jan. 22, 2020), www.bitchmedia.org/article/abortion-apps-spreading-misinformation; DIY Abortion: How to Have an Abortion When the Abortion Clinics Shut Down, Reddit, www.reddit.com/r/preppers/comments/6j1a1t/diy_abortion_how_to_have_an_abortion_when_the/.

In contrast to a (tele)medical consultation, within these information networks, people speak in their own voice and narrate their own experiences apart from the scripts of the law. Moreover, people not only share information on abortion, but also produce new knowledge about abortion based on the practice of it.[55] Such information gains authority by its usefulness, not its legal authorization.

The association of abortion at-home with a commodity (pills), rather than a service, may also change the social relations around it, including by patients reidentifying as consumers in the navigation of abortion markets.[56] The very term "abortion pills" signals this change, a deliberate denotation that questions the status of mifepristone and misoprostol as medicines, and thus the prescription and other controls on their distribution. When abortion pills are mail-ordered, home-delivered, and picked up in local retail pharmacies, they circulate in ways more common to other household products of need and leisure. Home abortion paraphernalia, such as pregnancy tests, ibuprofen, and soothing teas, can already be added to an Amazon cart. This materiality of abortion at-home may augment other features of it. The telemedical consultation may start to resemble more of a checkout counter than a doctor's visit, leading people to question the need for a prescription at all, but also the more general belief that only regulated systems of medical control can guarantee abortion safety.[57]

Abortion services in Europe and the United States have always functioned as a market, even if highly regulated, but abortion is rarely seen or talked about as such.[58] These markets have been dominated by a small set of organizations, strongly aligned with the medical establishment, and at least in Europe, with state provision. The markets in abortion pills, however, are much more diverse, involving more people and connections between them. Authorizations for abortion at-home were motivated in part by a desire to extinguish these markets or protect people from them, and while they may have had this effect in the short term, over time this effect may diminish, especially as the abortion markets themselves, the regulated versus unregulated, become harder to distinguish. In the United States, for example, many start-up abortion clinics began to advertise services during the pandemic and online pharmacies began shipping pills directly to patients.[59] People themselves may also come to feel differently about these markets. As abortion at-home becomes a more

---

[55] Bushra Alama, Amy Kaler & Zubia Mumtaza, Women's Voices and Medical Abortions: A Review of the Literature, 249 *Eur. J. Obstet. Gynecol. Reprod. Biol.* 21 (2020).

[56] Arjun Appadurai, *The Social Life of Things: Commodities in Cultural Perspective* (1986); Ruth Fletcher, Reproductive Consumption, 7 *Feminist Theory* 27 (2006).

[57] Steph Black, What I Learned from Buying Abortion Pills Online (Feb. 8, 2021), https://rewirenewsgroup.com/article/2021/02/08/what-i-learned-from-buying-abortion-pills-online/.

[58] Jody Lynee Madeira, Conceiving of Products and the Products of Conception: Reflections on Commodification, Consumption, ART and Abortion, 43 *J. L. Med. Ethics.* 293 (2015).

[59] Carrie N. Baker, How Telemedicine Startups Are Revolutionizing Abortion Health Care in the U.S., Ms. Mag. (Nov. 16, 2020), https://msmagazine.com/2020/11/16/just-the-pill-choix-carafem-honeybee-health-how-telemedicine-startups-are-revolutionizing-abortion-health-care-in-the-u-s/.

mundane affair, the medical controls of regulated access may also become more burden than protection. People may become comfortable with forms of consumer protection familiar to small-scale community distribution and online commerce in securing a safe supply of abortion pills.[60] Despite the expiry dates on its authorization, abortion at-home, once a habitual practice, may thus prove a more permanent feature of home life.

Speculating on abortion at-home as commodity and consumption also invites reflection on the social and cultural norms around it, including the inequalities of relying on private markets to fulfill constitutional rights. This lesson came early for abortion with pills when mifepristone was pulled from the French market for fear of commercial boycott and lost profits. As against the commercial context of abortion pills, however, the normalizing of abortion within the intimate and interior spaces of the home may also change the sociality of it. Abortion may become less a solitary act of the body than an act of home life, taken to support the social and economic well-being of a household. Support for abortion at-home during the pandemic, for example, centered on the home and life within it: loss of household incomes or housing itself, the care burdens of young children in the home, and violence that makes it difficult for people to leave their homes.[61] In the end, these contradictions of the home as a place of care and consumption, protection and risk, freedom and control may prove the most radical element of abortion at-home and confound the control of the law.

V CONCLUSION

In 1990, when the UK Abortion Act 1967 was reformed to allow the health secretary to designate a "class of place," the amendment was criticized as a backdoor to abortion at-home, or worse yet, do-it-yourself (DIY) abortion.[62] Thirty years later, during the COVID-19 pandemic, "DIY abortion" remains a pejorative term used by critics to denounce abortion at-home as a dangerous practice, one set outside the law and showing contempt for its social norms.[63] This critique might explain why the authorizations for abortion at-home reflected a crisis management discourse, one designed to conserve access to abortion care during the pandemic, but conserving much more in the continued clinical control of abortion and the social norms of

[60] Chloe Murtagh et al., Exploring the Feasibility of Obtaining Mifepristone and Misoprostol from the Internet, 97 *Contraception* 287 (2018).

[61] Patrick Butler, Two-Child Benefit Cap Influencing Women's Decisions on Abortion, Says BPAS, Guardian (Dec. 2, 2020), www.theguardian.com/society/2020/dec/03/two-child-limit-on-benefits-a-key-factor-in-many-abortion-decisions-says-charity.

[62] UK Parliament, Debate on Human Fertilisation and Embryology Bill (June 21, 1990), https://publications.parliament.uk/pa/cm199890/cmhansrd/1990-06-21/Debate-17.html.

[63] Natalie Clarke, What Is the Truth about Abortions by Post?, Daily Mail (May 28, 2020), www.dailymail.co.uk/femail/article-8367467/Abortions-post-got-rushed-approval-lockdown-troubling-stories-emerging.html.

abortion law. Since their advent, abortion pills have been folded into abortion law and made subject to its control, namely by restrictions requiring some touch to a clinical setting. While place-based abortion law has long been justified as a measure of safety, social control was always a primary motivation. The clinic was never only a physical place, and always an institution of control. On a conservative view, the COVID-19 authorizations brought clinical control into the home during a historic but time-bound state of emergency to conserve the social norms and thus the status quo of abortion law. On an alternative view, by returning abortion to the home, the authorizations may have a radical legacy. The home, after all, is an inhabited space shaped by the people who live there. At home, within the material cultures and social relations of home life, people will learn and create new ways of knowing and doing abortion. Abortion at-home will change what it means to have an abortion, but then again, the law has always known this truth. Every revolution starts at home.

Global Responses to COVID-19

Introduction

Michelle M. Mello

Several themes unite the wide-ranging chapters in Part VI as the authors explore what lessons can be learned from the disparate ways in which governments around the globe responded to the COVID-19 pandemic. First, there is a complicated relationship between democratic institutions and a nation's ability to respond to serious disease outbreaks. Reasonable people might hypothesize that democracy is a handicap during public health emergencies. Authoritarian governments can get even draconian things done quickly, quashing public resistance. Further, the more the law dilutes power in order to impose checks and balances and prevent abuse, the more it hobbles a swift response. But, on the other hand, democratic institutions make it harder for government to deny or downplay public health threats without detection, and federalism and other forms of power decentralization make it possible for some units of government to mount a vigorous pandemic response, even if others refuse.

In Chapter 22, "COVID-19 and National Public Health Regimes: Whither the Post-Washington Consensus in Public Health?," Tess Wise, Gali Katznelson, Carmel Shachar, and Andrea Louise Campbell empirically investigate how effectively countries with different political, legal, social, cultural, economic, and organizational structures stemmed the early spread of COVID-19. The authors report the surprising finding that the countries whose systems appeared best prepared for a public health emergency enjoyed no clear advantage. Neither development nor democracy significantly predicted governmental effectiveness in fighting disease spread.

In Chapter 23, "A Functionalist Approach to Analyzing Legal Responses to COVID-19 Across Countries: Comparative Insights from Two Global Symposia," Joelle Grogan and Alicia Ely Yamin also consider the connections between democratic institutions and governmental performance during health emergencies – specifically, a nation's performance in protecting human rights. Drawing on findings from two multi-country symposia, they conclude that formal legal regimes (for example, whether a country uses emergency-powers laws or ordinary legal powers) may be less important to whether a country avoids abuses of power during a pandemic than the social and political environment in which these regimes function.

Grogan and Yamin voice greater suspicion about undemocratic regimes than Wise and her coauthors, perhaps because their conception of an effective government response includes consideration of human rights concerns.

In Chapter 24, "A Tale of Two Crises: COVID-19, Climate Change, and Crisis Response," Daniel Farber worries about democratic nations' ability to solve global crises when their governments are fractured and polarized. He considers the connections between the two seminal global crises of our age: COVID-19 and climate change. Farber's analysis finds that although the pandemic induced short-term reductions in carbon emissions, its longer-term impacts on how societies obtain and use energy are more uncertain. He notes opportunities to pursue a "green recovery," using economic stimulus funds to invest in clean energy, but also the prospect of long-term damage to public transportation infrastructure. Farber trenchantly observes that while both crises have generated fervent hopes for technological rescues, making technology effective in combating the crises requires complex social investments.

In Chapter 25, "Vaccine Tourism, Federalism, Nationalism," Glenn Cohen highlights the complexities that federalism layers on already thorny problems such as vaccine allocation. Democratic institutions, he underscores, can be both friend and foe during health emergencies. Cohen asks who, among several different groups of community outsiders, may have a morally legitimate claim to a community's vaccine doses, and why. Fixing on communitarian principles as a lodestar, he offers a helpful definition of who belongs to a community for the purpose of vaccines.

A second theme connecting the chapters pertains to measurement. Answering questions about the optimal form of governance during pandemics begs the question: Optimal for what? Which outcomes are most relevant to assess? For instance, should we focus on COVID-19 cases and deaths, as Wise and colleagues do, or a more holistic assessment of how countries balance disease response with individual rights protections and equity considerations, per Cohen and Grogan and Yamin? Further, how can we rigorously conduct cross-national comparisons when countries differ in so many ways?

The ambitious empirical analysis undertaken by Wise and her coauthors illustrates the challenges. Countries have different levels of baseline vulnerability to infectious disease spread due to features unrelated to their legal, political, and social structures – for example, different levels of rurality and population mobility, and entry into the pandemic at different times, when different levels of knowledge had accumulated about how SARS-CoV-2 spreads. Figuring out how to rigorously isolate effects and control for confounding factors will occupy analysts of COVID-19 governance for some time.

For now, we can reach only tentative conclusions about how much political, legal, and public health systems matter to effective pandemic response. It is valuable to make the point, as Wise and her coauthors do, that prepositioning is not destiny when it comes to fighting novel pathogens. But some caution is warranted before concluding that redressing historical underinvestment in public health and health care systems will not help next time. On the contrary, Grogan and Yamin argue, it is reasonable to continue to operate on the assumption that having a well-functioning health care system and a public health system that assures equitable access to preventive and therapeutic measures will help avoid loss of life. Similarly, Cohen's chapter gives rise to the inference that investing in advance planning for pandemic countermeasure allocation will yield dividends.

A final thread uniting the chapters is the notion of community. For many reasons and in many respects, COVID-19 led to the rapid drawing of lines around communities throughout the world. From the allocation of vaccine doses to the imposition of community mitigation orders, national, state, and local communities asserted themselves in defining their own individual pandemic responses. While this patchwork created interesting natural experiments to study, as the chapter by Wise and her coauthors shows, it likely undermined an effective global response to the virus. Whereas other global crises – most notably, World War II – cultivated social solidarity and a widening of the concepts of community and belonging, COVID-19 drove social fragmentation. Not only did this complicate disease response (for example, by prompting vaccine tourism and perpetuating inequities in COVID-19 outcomes among population subgroups), it may also have enervated the prospects for global cooperation to solve other problems, such as climate change. Our joint future may depend on redefining community. To the searching questions that Grogan and Yamin ask at their chapter's end – "who should exercise power, of what sort, and over whom?" – might be added, "who should exercise *care*, of what sort, and for whom?"

Collectively, these chapters shed much light on the critical question of what constitutes good governance during a pandemic and how it can be secured for populations around the world.

22

COVID-19 and National Public Health Regimes

Whither the Post-Washington Consensus in Public Health?[1]

Tess Wise, Gali Katznelson, Carmel Shachar, and Andrea Louise Campbell

I INTRODUCTION

On June 2, 2016, the Center for Strategic and International Studies Global Health Policy Center in Washington, DC hosted a conversation with Jim Yong Kim, then president of the World Bank Group. Kim's talk was entitled "Preventing the Next Pandemic." Framed by the Ebola crisis that was just winding down in West Africa, pandemics in 2016 were presented as primarily a problem for developing countries. In his introductory remarks, the Center for Strategic and International Studies moderator, J. Stephen Morrison, even felt it necessary to remind the audience that understanding pandemics "mattered" for "US national interests."[2] The primary pandemic-prevention mechanism proposed by the World Bank was emergency pandemic financing and insurance. In his remarks, however, Jim Yong Kim also argued that health was central to more than just national well-being: it was a key driver of economic growth and development. He cited findings from the Lancet Commission Report that, between 2000 and 2011, about 24 percent of income growth in developing countries resulted from improvements in health.[3]

Kim's position reflected what is sometimes called the "Post-Washington Consensus," or the conclusion that development strategies should emphasize a broad array of social policies beyond what had been originally emphasized by the "Washington Consensus" of the 1980s and 1990s. The originator of the Washington Consensus, John Williamson, suggested that public expenditure priorities be

1   For further explanation of the methodologies used in this chapter, please see the Methodological Appendix at https://petrieflom.law.harvard.edu/assets/publications/Chapter_22_-_Wise_-_Final_Version_-_appendix.pdf.
2   Ctr. for Strategic & Int'l Stud., Preventing the Next Pandemic: A Conversation with the World Bank President (June 2, 2016), www.youtube.com/watch?v=tXWJWHkgl8k&t=1825s.
3   Id.; Dean T. Jamison et al., Global Health 2035: A World Converging Within a Generation, 382 Lancet 1898, 1944 (2013).

redirected toward "neglected fields" such as "primary health and education, and infrastructure."[4] Nevertheless, scholars generally agree that the Washington Consensus was characterized by a dominant orthodoxy that countries should "stabilize, privatize, and liberalize."[5] When the Post-Washington Consensus was proposed in the mid-2000s, health again emerged as an area scholars saw as key for development,[6] though, as evidenced by Kim's suggestions regarding pandemic insurance and financing, market-forward solutions are still seen as central, reflecting an international trend toward leveraging financial markets for development that some have dubbed the "Wall Street Consensus."[7]

Health will undoubtedly be central to any emerging global development consensus, but as the COVID-19 pandemic has made clear, a broader global consensus on public health, including the vision of society informing the concept of "the public," is needed. In this chapter, we use data from the World Bank and other (Post-) Washington Consensus institutions to create a snapshot of global public health on the eve of the COVID-19 pandemic. We find that (Post-)Washington Consensus institutions saw the world as having varying levels of public-health-related development and social priorities. We then examine how countries from different clusters in this space fared in the early stages of the COVID-19 pandemic (in other words, before vaccinations became available in at least a few countries). We find that the countries supposedly best prepared for a public health emergency had no systematic advantage and even lagged behind countries that were supposedly not as well prepared in the early stages of the pandemic. Similarly, other classifications of public health preparedness from the pre-COVID-19 period, such as the World Health Organization's Joint External Evaluation Tool or the Global Health Security Index, which did not adequately predict detection time and mortality in the early months of the COVID-19 pandemic, also fell short.[8] From our data and case studies, we are concerned that a tradeoff between democracy and government effectiveness may

---

[4] John Williamson, Democracy and the "Washington Consensus," 21 *World Dev.* 1329, 1332 (1993).

[5] Dani Rodrik, Goodbye Washington Consensus, Hello Washington Confusion? A Review of the World Bank's Economic Growth in the 1990s: Learning From a Decade of Reform, 44 *J. Econ. Literature* 973, 973 (2006); Ali Burak Güven, Whither the Post-Washington Consensus? International Financial Institutions and Development Policy Before and After the Crisis, 25 *Rev. Int'l. Pol. Econ.* 392 (2018).

[6] John Williamson, A Short History of the Washington Consensus, in *The Washington Consensus Reconsidered: Towards a New Global Governance* 28 (Narcís Serra & Joseph E. Stiglitz eds., 2008).

[7] Rick Rowden, *From the Washington Consensus to the Wall Street Consensus* 17 (2019). On the increased use of financial markets for development, see Peter Volberding, *Leveraging Financial Markets for Development: How KfW Revolutionized Development Finance* (2021).

[8] Najmul Haider et al., The Global Health Security Index and Joint External Evaluation Score for Health Preparedness Are Not Correlated with Countries' COVID-19 Detection Response Time and Mortality Outcome, 148 *Epidemiology & Infection* e210 (2020). On the Joint External Evaluation Tool, see World Health Organization, Joint External Evaluation, Zoonotic Diseases Action Package Conference (2017). On the Global Health Security Index, see Nuclear Threat Initiative & Johns Hopkins University Centre for Health Security, Global Health Security Index (2019).

be a lesson taken from experiences in the early stages of the COVID-19 pandemic and suggest instead that a social democratic perspective on public health that links justice and efficacy is needed.

II CREATING A TYPOLOGY OF PUBLIC HEALTH REGIMES

To create a typology of public health regimes that characterizes the variation in national public health on the eve of the COVID-19 pandemic from the perspective of institutions such as the World Bank, we group countries by similarity in "political, legal, social, cultural, economic, and organizational structures" related to public health.[9] While Asthana and Halliday emphasize that scholars can tailor public health regimes to study particular areas, such as nutritional inequalities or anti-smoking campaigns, we look broadly to see whether grouping countries by general indicators of public health can help us understand performance in response to the early stages of the COVID-19 pandemic. Our indicators of public health-related factors come primarily from World Bank and United Nations data, with two additional indicators of democracy, using the 2018 POLITY5 scores,[10] and ethnic and linguistic fractionalization, from measures developed by Alesina et al. in 2003.[11] Table 22.1 below shows the full set of indicators.

When conducting a global analysis, choices of indicators are limited to what is widely available and reliably measured. This limits what we can choose to explore and has theoretical implications because existing data do not come into existence by chance. Our analysis relies primarily on World Bank data, which, we argue, are indicators of a weak "Post-Washington Consensus" in public health.

These indicators arise from a contested paradigm. The Washington Consensus of the 1980s and 1990s on effective development strategies was associated with Washington-based policy institutions with strong international influence – such as the International Monetary Fund, the World Bank, and the US Treasury – which were proponents of neoliberal development policy.[12] Before the mid-2000s, when a spate of studies called its effectiveness into question, the Washington Consensus represented the dominant ideology in the area of development.[13] Though there have been numerous efforts to move beyond the Washington Consensus, such as the Post-Washington Consensus, no new dominant ideology has taken hold.[14] As Joseph

---

[9] Sheena Asthana & Joyce Halliday, Developing an Evidence Base for Policies and Interventions to Address Health Inequalities: The Analysis of "Public Health Regimes," 84 *Milbank Q.* 577 (2006).

[10] Center for Systemic Peace, www.systemicpeace.org/.

[11] Alberto Alesina et al., Fractionalization, 8 *J. Econ. Growth* 155, 158 (2003).

[12] See supra note 4.

[13] Narcís Serra, Shari Spiegel & Joseph E. Stiglitz, Introduction: From the Washington Consensus Towards a New Global Governance, in *The Washington Consensus Reconsidered: Towards a New Global Governance* 3 (Narcís Serra & Joseph E. Stiglitz eds., 2008).

[14] Id.; Güven, supra note 5, at 392 (2018).

TABLE 22.1 *Global indicators of public health*

All from World Bank (except where indicated)				
Political	Legal	Social and Cultural	Economic	Organizational Structures
Corruption control; regulatory quality; government effectiveness (average percentile rank last ten years); legislative and executive indices of political competitiveness; and Polity scores assessing autocracy vs. democracy (from Center for Systemic Peace)	Rule of law, and voice and accountability (average percentile rank last ten years)	Status of women (female labor force participation, percentage of women in legislature, gender discrimination law in employment); heterogeneity (ethnic, religious, and linguistic fractionalization measures from Alesina et al. 2003); and demographics (total population; life expectancy; percent aged sixty-five+; fertility rate; population growth rate; percent rural)	Spending capacity and priorities (gross national income per capita; and health spending and military spending as percentage of GDP); and inequality (Gini index)	Capacity (hospital beds and physicians per 1,000 population); cost (out-of-pocket spending per capita); conditions (percent of population using at least basic sanitation services; percent overweight); and presence of autonomous regions

E. Stiglitz put it in 2008, "If there is a consensus today about what strategies are most likely to promote the development of the poorest countries in the world, it is this: there is no consensus except that the Washington Consensus did not provide the answer."[15] Despite being a contested consensus, the (Post-)Washington Consensus still looms large in contemporary indicators such as those we draw upon in this chapter, understandings of concepts such as "governance," and global targets such as the Sustainable Development Goals.[16]

---

[15] Joseph E. Stiglitz, Is there a Post-Washington Consensus Consensus?, in *The Washington Consensus Reconsidered: Towards a New Global Governance* 41 (Narcís Serra & Joseph E. Stiglitz eds., 2008).

[16] Christiane Arndt, The Politics of Governance Ratings, 11 *Int'l. Pub. Mgmt.* 275, 275 (2008).

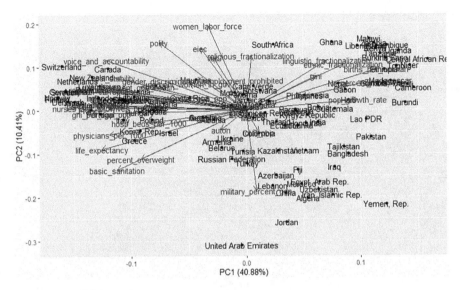

FIGURE 22.1 PCA results

A *Principal Component Analysis*

Principal Component Analysis (PCA) is a statistical method used to project high-dimensional data into a lower-dimensional space while preserving as much variation as possible. The "principal components" uncovered by PCA are linear combinations of the indicators that define orthogonal axes of variation. Running PCA on our 116-country dataset reveals two main components (see the Methodological Appendix in this chapter for the methodological details). Figure 22.1 shows how countries map onto them.

1 A Primary Component of "Development"

Countries' scores on the primary component, accounting for 40.9 percent of the overall variance, are graphed along the x-axis in Figure 22.1. We interpret these scores as broad indicators of public health-related development in the context of a weak Post-Washington Consensus.

The primary component distinguishes between, on the one hand, nations with good governance, high levels of health infrastructure, a more elderly and urban population, higher income levels, and longer life expectancy, and, on the other hand, nations with lower indicators of good governance, lower levels of health infrastructure, a younger and more rural population, lower income levels, and shorter life expectancy. We describe this component in more detail in the Methodological Appendix.

2 A Secondary Component of "Social Priorities"

The second component, explaining 10.4 percent of the variation in the data, is characterized by political distinctions that, in linear combination, explain variation

Cluster plot

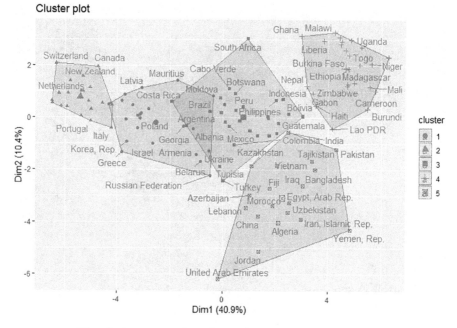

FIGURE 22.2 Five clusters – our selected grouping

orthogonal to (independent of) the first component. Countries' scores on the second component are graphed on the y-axis of Figure 22.1. We describe the secondary
component as a measure of "social priorities" related to public health. The social
priorities component is characterized by women's position in society, military spending, and democracy. Countries that score low on social priorities, and cluster at the
center bottom of Figure 22.1, have lower levels of women in the workforce, higher
military spending, and lower levels of democracy compared to countries with higher
scores. Again, we describe this component in more detail in the Methodological
Appendix.

B K-Means Clustering to Identify Public Health Regimes

We apply a second statistical method, k-means clustering, to group the countries
based on their similarities within our statistical space to define groups that we call
public health regimes.

Theoretical motivation, certain statistical indicators, and face validity suggest
that five clusters are optimal (see the Methodological Appendix). Figure 22.2 shows
our clusters graphed over the first two components from the PCA. Table 22.2 sum-
marizes the public health regimes that we find using five-cluster k-means.

TABLE 22.2 *Public health regimes and key characteristics*

Cluster	1	2	3	4	5
Public Health Regime	Medium-High Development Democracies	High-Development Democracies	Medium-Development Democracies	Low-Development Semi-Democracies	Medium-Low Development Semi-Autocracies
Countries	Albania, Armenia, Belarus, Bulgaria, Chile, Croatia, Cyprus, Czech Republic, Estonia, Georgia, Greece, Hungary, Israel, South Korea, Latvia, Lithuania, Mauritius, Moldova, Poland, Russian Federation, Slovak Republic, Ukraine, Uruguay	Australia, Austria, Belgium, Canada, Denmark, Finland, France, Germany, Ireland, Italy, Japan, Luxembourg, Netherlands, New Zealand, Norway, Portugal, Slovenia, Spain, Sweden, Switzerland, United Kingdom, United States	Argentina, Bolivia, Botswana, Brazil, Cabo Verde, Colombia, Costa Rica, Dominican Republic, Ecuador, El Salvador, Guatemala, Honduras, Indonesia, Jamaica, Kyrgyz Republic, Malaysia, Mexico, Mongolia, Nicaragua, Panama, Paraguay, Peru, Philippines, South Africa, Sri Lanka, Thailand, Tunisia, Turkey	Benin, Burkina Faso, Burundi, Cameroon, Central African Republic, Ethiopia, Gabon, The Gambia, Ghana, Haiti, Kenya, Lao People's Democratic Republic, Liberia, Madagascar, Malawi, Mali, Mozambique, Nepal, Niger, Tanzania, Togo, Uganda, Zambia, Zimbabwe	Algeria, Azerbaijan, Bangladesh, China, Egypt, Arab Republic, Fiji, India, Iran, Islamic Republic, Iraq, Jordan, Kazakhstan, Lebanon, Morocco, Pakistan, Tajikistan, United Arab Emirates, Uzbekistan, Vietnam, Yemen

(continued)

TABLE 22.2 *(continued)*

Cluster	1	2	3	4	5
Public Health Regime	Medium-High Development Democracies	High-Development Democracies	Medium-Development Democracies	Low-Development Semi-Democracies	Medium-Low Development Semi-Autocracies
"Development Component" Variables (top six variables)					
Percent Sixty-Five+ (Cluster Avg.)	15.0	17.9	6.6	3.0	5.1
Government Effectiveness (Percentile Rank, Cluster Avg.)	66.9	91.4	49.0	22.8	39.0
Regulatory Quality (Percentile Rank, Cluster Avg.)	70.1	90.6	50.9	27.5	32.0
Rule of Law (Percentile Rank, Cluster Avg.)	63.0	91.8	40.9	27.6	32.0
Life Expectancy (Years, Cluster Avg.)	76.1	81.5	73.3	60.8	72.1
Gross National Income (Per Capita, International $, PPP, Cluster Avg.)	$23,050	$47,324	$12,144	$2,735	$12,741

"Social Priorities Component" Variables (top six variables)

Female Labor Force Participation (Rate, Ages Fifteen+, Cluster Avg.)	45.7	46.2	40.0	47.6	28.2
Military Spending (% GDP, Cluster Avg.)	2.0	1.4	1.3	1.2	3.1
Polity Score (−10 to +10, Cluster Avg.)	7.9	9.7	7.2	3.7	−2.1
Exec. Index of Electoral Competition (1 to 7, Cluster Avg.)	7	7	7	6.3	4.8
Basic Sanitation (% pop. using, Cluster Avg.)	94.9	98.9	81.3	28.1	82.5
Religious Fractionaliz'n (0–1 index, Cluster Avg.)	0.48	0.44	0.31	0.57	0.33

III HOW HAVE DIFFERENT PUBLIC HEALTH REGIMES
FARED IN THE CONTEXT OF COVID-19

We now examine how different public health regimes fared in the COVID-19 pandemic. We draw on data from the University of Oxford's COVID-19 Government Response Tracker (OxCGRT),[17] for government response outcomes, and from Johns Hopkins University, for cases and deaths.[18] These datasets, while the most comprehensive data available at the time of writing, are not infallible. For example, in low- and middle-income countries, even during non-pandemic times, most deaths occur outside of the hospital system and are unlikely to have a cause-of-death certified by a physician.[19] Noh and Danuser find that in half of the fifty countries they explored, actual cumulative COVID-19 cases were estimated to be five to twenty times greater than the confirmed cases.[20]

The first set of outcomes we examine is how fast COVID-19 spread and how comprehensive the government response was. We might expect a comprehensive response to slow the spread and variation in response and speed to vary across public health regimes we established in the previous section. Interestingly, neither pattern is borne out in the data.

In Figure 22.3, the x-axis indicates the number of days between the first and the 10,000th reported case in each country. The y-axis displays the maximum government containment score (0 to 100) over the period from January 1, 2020, and April 10, 2021, the maximum data window allowed at the time of analysis.[21] Maximum government containment comes from OxCGRT and includes the sum of fourteen indices from the areas of containment and closure policies (e.g., closing schools) and health system policies (e.g., public information campaigns) scaled to vary

---

[17]   Thomas Hale et al., Oxford COVID-19 Government Response Tracker, Blavatnik Sch. of Gov't (2020).

[18]   Ensheng Dong, Hongru Du & Lauren Gardner, An Interactive Web-Based Dashboard to Track COVID-19 in Real Time, 20 *Lancet Infect. Dis.* 533, 533 (2020).

[19]   Lene Mikkelsen et al., A Global Assessment of Civil Registration and Vital Statistics Systems: Monitoring Data Quality and Progress, 386 *Lancet* 1395, 1395 (2015).

[20]   Jungsik Noh & Gaudenz Danuser, Estimation of the Fraction of COVID-19 Infected People in US States and Countries Worldwide, 16 *PloS one* e0246772 (2021).

[21]   The government containment score comes from the OxCGRT data and contains measures of school closures (0 = no measures to 3 = require closing all levels), workplace closures (0 = no measures to 3 = require closing all but essential workplaces), canceling of public events (0 = no measures to 2 = required cancelling), restrictions on gatherings (0 = no restrictions to 4 = restrictions on gatherings of fewer than ten people), public transport closings (0 = no measures to 2 = required closings), public information campaigns (0 = no public information campaigns to 2 = coordinated public information campaign), stay-at-home measures (0 = no measures to 3 = required not leaving the house with minimal exceptions), restrictions on internal movement (0 = no measures to 2 = restricted movement), international travel controls (0 = no measures to 4 = total border closure), testing policy (0 = no testing policy to 3 = open public testing), contact tracing (0 = no contact tracing to 2 = comprehensive contact tracing), face covering policies (0 = no policy to 4 = required outside the home at all times), and vaccination policy (0 = no vaccine availability to 5 = universal vaccine availability). These indicators were combined and scaled to create an index varying between 1 and 100.

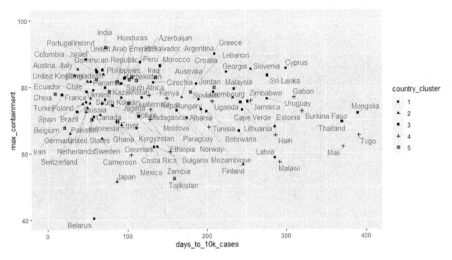

FIGURE 22.3 Max government containment vs. speed of spread

between 0 and 100. Taking a government's maximum score on this metric produces a somewhat blunt measure of the initial COVID-19 response, but one that reflects the broad contours of important variation in government responses. In the Methodological Appendix, we show an alternative measure using the average government containment, which does not change the substantive results. The shape of the marker indicates the country's cluster (public health regime).

Figure 22.3 and Table 22.3 indicate that none of the public health regimes we identified had a distinct advantage against COVID-19 in slowing the spread during the early phases of the pandemic. The **High-Development Democracies** (Cluster 2), which we would expect to be the best prepared, actually had the fastest spread, with only 95 days on average to reach 10,000 cases and 77 days on average to reach 1,000 deaths. While we might attribute the seemingly outstanding performance of the **Low-Development Semi-Democracies** (Cluster 4) to poor data quality, the fact that the **High-Development Democracies** did worse than **Medium-** and **Medium-High-Development Democracies** (Clusters 1 and 3), and even worse than **Medium-Low-Development Semi-Autocracies** (Cluster 5), is harder to attribute to data quality issues. This pattern persists even after accounting for population and examining the number of days to reach 100, then 500, deaths per million. Levels of containment were similar across all public health regimes, except for **Low-Development Semi-Democracies** (Cluster 4), which had somewhat lower average and maximum containment than other public health regimes.

In sum, the **High-Development Democracies** of Cluster 2, those we expect would be best prepared, were likely to see a faster spread than countries with any other public health regime.

TABLE 22.3 *Public health regimes, speed of spread, government response*

Cluster	1	2	3	4	5
Public Health Regime	Medium-High Development Democracies	High-Development Democracies	Medium-Development Democracies	Low-Development Semi-Democracies	Medium-Low Development Semi-Autocracies
Days to 10k cases (Cluster Avg.)	158	95	146	220	99
Days to 1k deaths (Cluster Avg.)	216	77	118	250	151
Days to 100 deaths per million (Cluster Avg.)	188	78	138	244	196
Days to 500 deaths per million (Cluster Avg.)	216	194	201	Not reached	269
Avg. Containment (Jan 2020–Apr 2021, Cluster Avg., 0–100)	49.3	51.0	53.1	40.2	51.4
Max Containment (Jan 2020–Apr 2021, Cluster Avg., 0–100)	76.0	74.2	74.7	65.5	75.3

346

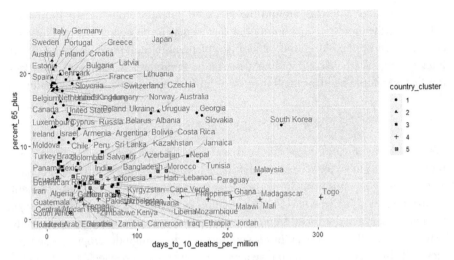

FIGURE 22.4 Percent sixty-five plus vs. days to reach 10 COVID-19 deaths per million population

We might attribute some of this rapid spread to location, data quality, and demographics. However, examples from across the world highlight that these factors alone were not enough to determine a country's destiny. For example, in Figure 22.3, **Thailand** stands out as a country that managed to slow the spread significantly despite geographical proximity to, and a close trade relationship with, China.

Figure 22.4 examines another factor that may have increased the challenge of containing COVID-19: the percentage of a country's population aged sixty-five and older. For this analysis, we examine the number of days it took to reach the threshold of ten deaths per million. We see a negative relationship – countries with younger populations took somewhat longer to reach ten deaths per million – but there are some notable outliers, particularly **South Korea**, which has an older population, but was one of the slowest to reach the ten deaths per million threshold (260 days).

In general, there is no strong correlation between what we identify as a country's prior public health regime and its performance in the early stages of the COVID-19 pandemic. If anything, countries we might have expected to perform the best, those with the most consolidated democracies and higher levels of governance, income, and state capacity (the high-development democracies of Cluster 2), did worse in slowing the spread and lowering the death rate than countries in other clusters. In the face of the COVID-19 pandemic, the weak (Post-)Washington Consensus in public health is not indicative of less devastation even among its best students, just as the (Post-)Washington Consensus did little to stop the Great Recession of 2007–2009 from affecting wealthy countries around the globe.[22] Explaining this underperformance will take further analysis, but contributing factors may be demographics (as Cluster 2 countries tend to be older) and difficulty implementing non-pharmaceutical social interventions. We now conduct brief case studies to produce suggestions for key factors that we should be incorporating into our understanding of good public health.

IV CASE STUDIES

We chose to investigate China, Thailand, and Israel through brief case studies. China is unique on a global scale because of its large population and experience of coping with an emerging virus first. China is a Cluster 5 country (medium-low development semi-autocracy). Thailand is a Cluster 3 country (medium-development democracy), though it bucks the dominant trend of its group by being an autocracy with a Polity score of -3. Finally, Israel is a Cluster 1 country (medium-high-development democracy).[23] Table 22.4 shows comparative pandemic outcomes and selected background characteristics for each country relative to its cluster. The performances of these countries stand out in comparison to the poor performance of the United States and the other high-development countries of Cluster 2.

A *China*

China, where the novel coronavirus originated, experienced rapid spread to 10,000 cases, but quickly controlled the disease, ultimately performing better than the rich democracies of Cluster 2. The effective Chinese response was facilitated by public health and industrial capacity, and by governmental and cultural factors.

After the first cases were reported in Wuhan in December 2019, lockdowns, school closures, and transport suspensions quickly followed. Coordination among government offices, extensive testing, and a national system of contact tracing facilitated the response, as did the early use of Fangcang hospitals to isolate mild-to-moderate cases from both homes and conventional hospitals. Although China has a large elderly population, only 3 percent live in nursing homes, minimizing one major source of infection experienced in some Western countries. Testing and quarantine measures for travelers aimed at preventing imported cases. China's status as the world's largest manufacturer of personal protective equipment also facilitated its reaction.[24]

---

[22] Justin Yifu Lin, *Against the Consensus: Reflections on the Great Recession* 99 (2013).

[23] With more space, we would have liked to include a Cluster 4 (low-development semi democracy) country, but these countries are the most hampered by low rates of data collection on COVID-19, especially in the early stages of the pandemic. See Kevyah Cardoso, Measuring Africa's Data Gap: The Cost of Not Counting the Dead, BBC News (Feb. 22, 2021), www.bbc.com/news/world-africa-55674139.

[24] Talha Burki, China's Successful Control of COVID-19, 20 *Lancet Infect. Dis.* 1240, 1240 (2020).

TABLE 22.4 *China, Thailand, Israel, and United States pandemic outcomes*

	China (Cluster 5)	Cluster 5 Average	Thailand (Cluster 3)	Cluster 3 Average	Israel (Cluster 1)	Cluster 1 Average	United States (Cluster 2)	Cluster 2 Average	Global Average
Days to Reach 10k Cases	10	99	370	146	49	158	57	95	134
Days to Reach Ten Deaths per Million People	Not reached	61	Not reached	63	14	51	9	21	61
Max Government Response (0–100)	78	75	69	75	88	76	70	74	73
Percent Pop. Sixty-five+ (%)	9.4	5.1	10.5	6.6	11.2	15	14.5	17.9	9.4
Percent Pop. Overweight (%)	30	48	29.6	49.8	63.3	55.2	66.4	56.7	47.1
Hospital Beds per 1,000	3.4	2.3	2.1	2.0	3.1	5.7	2.9	4.5	3.1
Basic Sanitation (%)	79	82.5	97.3	81.3	100	94.9	100	98.9	76.5
Polity (−10 to +10)	−7	−2.1	−3	7.2	6	7.9	8	9.7	5.6
Government Effectiveness (Percentile Rank 1–100)	64	39	64	49	87	67	91	91	54

Among the public, "fresh memories" of the SARS-CoV outbreak hastened the response, as did ready compliance with mask wearing.[25] In general, the pandemic countermeasures were less fettered by concerns with civil liberties. "In China, you have a population that takes respiratory infections seriously and is willing to adopt non-pharmaceutical interventions, with a government that can put bigger constraints on individual freedoms than would be considered acceptable in most Western countries," noted Gregory Poland, director of the Vaccine Research Group at the Mayo Clinic, adding that the response in the United States has been hampered by "hyper-individualism" and a "raucous anti-vaccine, anti-science movement that is trying to derail the fight against COVID-19."[26] At the same time, the pace of vaccination was relatively slow because the country's inactive-virus-based vaccine candidates took longer to manufacture, because millions of doses were donated to other nations to bolster foreign relations, and because, ironically, the effective response undercut urgency among the population, in contrast to the United States and United Kingdom, where raging infection rates spurred desperation over getting vaccinated.[27]

B *Thailand*

Thailand illustrates the phenomenon of good governance without democracy, and its success in containing the pandemic is likely to reinforce calls for an emphasis on governance over democracy in the emerging public health consensus.[28]

In March 2019, Thailand held elections for the first time since 2014, when a military coup overthrew its democratically elected government. Unfortunately, the 2019 election was widely considered to have been designed to prolong and legitimize the military's dominant role in Thailand's governance.[29] Between 1996 and 2018, Thailand's ranking on the World Bank's Worldwide Governance Indicators fell. Between 2002 and 2018, Thailand's global rank decreased from the 65th percentile to below the 20th percentile for political stability, and from the 60th percentile to the 20th percentile for voice and accountability. However, government effectiveness remained relatively stable (around the 65th percentile). Kantamaturapoj et al. report that public services remain functioning with adequate quality, "reflecting a degree of independence from political pressure and a capacity to formulate and implement policies among bureaucrats."[30]

[25] Id. at 1240.

[26] Id. at 1241.

[27] China's Vaccine Campaign Hits a Few Bumps, Nat'l Pub. Radio (Feb. 3, 2021).

[28] See, for example, Responding to COVID-19: The Rules of Good Governance Apply Now More Than Ever!, OECD, www.oecd.org/governance/public-governance-responses-to-covid19.

[29] Freedom House, Freedom in the World 2020: Thailand, Freedomhouse (2020), https://freedomhouse.org/country/thailand/freedom-world/2020.

[30] Kanang Kantamaturapoj et al., Legislating for Public Accountability in Universal Health Coverage, Thailand, 98 *Bull. World Health Organ* 117, 117 (2020).

Since 2002, Thailand has provided comprehensive health benefits to its entire population through a universal coverage scheme with a high level of financial risk protection, as well as voice and accountability provided through legislative provisions and a deliberative process.[31] This health system was put to the test when, on January 13, 2020, Thailand was the first country to detect a case of COVID-19 outside of China.[32] After an initial spike in cases, Thailand went 102 days between May and September without any reported local transmission of COVID-19.[33]

Thailand's public health response to COVID-19 was swift and comprehensive. The Thai government quickly recommended the use of face masks and this was met with 95 percent compliance from the Thai population.[34] Tracing and quarantining were set up by rapid response teams, who isolated cases in facilities rather than in homes. When demand for N95 face masks spiked amid a global shortage, a new factory was constructed in a month, supplying free N95 masks to health facilities.[35] By the end of July 2020, a laboratory network for diagnosing COVID-19 using PCR (polymerase chain reaction) tests was active in 78 percent of Thailand's seventy-seven provinces.[36]

Although Thailand was successful in the initial stages of its response to the COVID-19 pandemic, Marome and Shaw raise concerns over the Thai government's handling of the social and economic fallout from declining tourism revenue.[37]

C *Israel*

Israel is one of the medium-high-development democracies that showed moderate success at COVID-19 containment during the initial months of the pandemic by utilizing centralized leadership. Inspired in part by a shortage of surge intensive care unit capacity, the Israeli Ministry of Health took control of hospital referrals and admissions and pioneered a containment strategy that included significant early travel restrictions and quarantine of travelers.[38] The Ministry of Health also took advantage of Israel's strong digital health and surveillance capabilities to implement

---

[31] Id.

[32] World Health Org., COVID-19: WHO's Action in Countries—Thailand (Sept. 2020), www.who.int/docs/default-source/coronavirus/country-case-studies/thailand-c19-case-study-20-september.pdf?sfvrsn=d5534183_2&download=true

[33] Id.

[34] Viroi Tangcharoensathien et al., Are Overwhelmed Health Systems an Inevitable Consequence of COVID-19? Experiences from China, Thailand, and New York State, 372 *Brit Med. J.* 1, 2 (2021).

[35] Id.

[36] See supra note 30.

[37] Wijitbusaba Marome & Rajib Shaw, COVID-19 Response in Thailand and Its Implications on Future Preparedness, 18 *Int'l J. Env't Res. Pub. Health.* 1089, 1095 (2021).

[38] Eyal Leshem, Arnon Afek & Yitshak Kreiss, Buying Time with COVID-19 Outbreak Response, Israel, 26 *Emerg. Infect. Dis.* 2251, 2251 (2020).

digital tracking, although this initiative was eventually struck down by the Israeli High Court of Justice as requiring legislative authorization rather than executive action.[39]

There were also favorable demographic factors at play. Israel tends to be younger than other industrialized countries, such as those in Cluster 2, due to relatively high fertility rates.[40] Ethnic segregation may have also served as a protective factor for some communities, such as the Israeli Arab population, in the first wave of infection.[41]

Interestingly, Israel's strong centralized response to the pandemic and its emphasis on technology, including digital health, may ultimately allow it to be a COVID-19 "success story." Then-Prime Minister Benjamin Netanyahu was able to secure a significant number of COVID-19 vaccine doses by, in part, promising a significant amount of data to manufacturers.[42] This promise was feasible because Israel had already created a national database that included the health information of 98 percent of its citizens. As a result, Israel may be the first country to immunize virtually all of its citizens over the age of sixteen and, therefore, potentially the first to control the pandemic via vaccination. Therefore, Israel may serve as a good reminder that this analysis considers the initial response and first wave of the pandemic, rather than the full life cycle of COVID-19.

V DISCUSSION

The relative failure of the United States to slow the spread of COVID-19, along with the mediocre performance of high-development democracies in general, is continued evidence of the failure of the (Post-)Washington consensus in public health. As we look forward toward a still-hazy emerging public health paradigm, countries such as Thailand, South Korea, and Israel will likely become models that others will hope to emulate. For Israel and other similar success stories, we see a noteworthy pattern of above-average government effectiveness combined with below-average levels of democracy relative to their cluster peers.

The assumption that development and democracy are the sole predictors of pandemic preparedness and responsiveness has been challenged as agreement is emerging that Western countries have fared poorly. In an essay in the *Intelligencer*, "How the West Lost COVID-19," David Wallace-Wells identifies slowness of response in

---

[39] Glenn I. Cohen, Lawrence Gostin & Daniel Weitzner, Digital Smartphone Tracking for COVID-19: Public Health and Civil Liberties in Tension, 323 *JAMA* 2371, 2371 (2020).

[40] Daphna Birenbaum-Carmeli & Judith Chassida, COVID-19 in Israel: Socio-Demographic Characteristics of First Wave Morbidity in Jewish and Arab Communities, 19 *Int'l J. for Equity in Health* 1 (2020).

[41] Id.

[42] Shelly Simana, Is Israel Trading Medicine Information for Vaccines? Ethical and Legal Considerations, The Bill of Health (Jan. 25, 2021), https://blog.petrieflom.law.harvard.edu/2021/01/25/israel-covid-vaccine-health-data/.

the early stages of the pandemic amidst fear of how citizens might perceive rapid shutdowns as one major factor.[43] In the United States, for example, the first instinct of governments was to downplay the severity of the virus, while in East Asia, countries acted quickly and decisively despite incomplete information about the nature of the virus. This may in part be due to an arrogance that Western countries' perceived development would shield them from the consequences of a pandemic. However, identifying precisely "how the West lost COVID-19" has been difficult. Multiple factors, including chance, contact with Italy, climate, and air conditioners, may all be at play. This is consistent with our analysis – no one set of indicators emerged as a reliable explanation for successes or failures in the early stages of the pandemic.

In noticing a tension between government effectiveness and democracy, we see a need for the future global consensus in public health to transition from a neoliberal vision of society to a social democratic one, in which the risks and costs associated with sickness are shared by the whole society, not only sick individuals, emphasizing that justice and efficiency must be linked together.[44] This linkage is desirable to avoid a world in which government effectiveness and democracy appear as tradeoffs, as they seem to be in our data, which arise from the neoliberal tradition embodied in the (Post-)Washington Consensus. In imagining the evolution of the Post-Washington Consensus in public health following COVID-19, we should cast off the centering on Washington and the neoliberal tradition that, in our analysis, fails to predict success in early pandemic responses. Instead, to prepare for the next global pandemic, we should focus more strongly on the connection between public health and democratic institutions, rather than government effectiveness in the abstract.

---

[43] David Wallace-Wells, How the West Lost COVID-19, Intelligencer, NY Magazine (Mar. 15, 2021), https://nymag.com/intelligencer/2021/03/how-the-west-lost-covid-19.html.

[44] Sylvia Walby, The COVID Pandemic and Social Theory: Social Democracy and Public Health in the Crisis, 24 Eur. J. Soc. Theory 22, 24 (2021).

23

Mapping COVID-19 Legal Responses:
A Functionalist Analysis

Joelle Grogan and Alicia Ely Yamin

I INTRODUCTION

The global COVID-19 pandemic caused by the novel coronavirus SARS-CoV-2 has focused the world's attention on the central importance of population health to the economic and social well-being of societies and to the multilateral order that depends upon a globalized, interconnected world. It has also highlighted the challenges to the democratic rule of law posed by the widely varying actions adopted by governments in response. The notion that health and democratic rights are intimately connected is not new. For example, Robin West asserts that the sovereign is given a monopoly on coercion in exchange for security against a life that is "nasty, brutish and short" and that the baseline condition of the sovereign's legitimacy lies in the protection of human health and well-being.[1] Therefore, according to West, health protection is foundational, not peripheral, to the liberal philosophical tradition.[2] Similarly, public health and health promotion is a precondition to substantive democracy – as those hobbled by infirmity will be unable to meaningfully engage in democratic self-governance. Historically, movements for universal health care, including the adoption of the National Health Service in the United Kingdom,[3] were democratic struggles to enlarge democratic inclusion.[4] Further, as laid bare during the pandemic, health systems have a role to play in sustaining and reproducing core democratic commitments to formal and substantive equality.

Drawing both on our respective scholarship in these fields as well as on insights from two global symposia on governmental responses held during the early phase of the pandemic, this chapter links analyses of democratic institutions and their capacity to maintain fundamental rights protections with the functioning of health systems

---

[1] Robin West, Reconsidering Legalism, 88 *Minn. L. Rev.* 119, 130–35 (2003).
[2] Id.
[3] Donald W. Light, Universal Health Care: Lessons from the British Experience, 93 *Am. J. Pub. Health* 25, 26 (2003).
[4] Vicente Navarro, Production and the Welfare State: The Political Context of Reforms, 21 *Int'l J. Health Servs.* 585, 614 (1991).

and protections for the health rights of diverse people in practice. From April 6 to May 26, 2020, the "COVID-19 and States of Emergency" symposium, co-hosted by the *Verfassungsblog* and Democracy Reporting International, published eighty-two reports and commentaries on states of emergency and the use of power in response to the pandemic.[5] From May 12 to June 12, 2020, the "Global Responses to COVID-19: Rights, Democracy and the Law" symposium, hosted by the Petrie-Flom Center, produced thirty Bill of Health entries, each of which responded to three questions regarding: (1) the legal vehicles used in response to the pandemic; (2) the effects of these on marginalized populations; and (3) the roles of legislative and judicial oversight.[6] The analytical reports on the early months of the pandemic were authored by over 120 contributors worldwide, including academics drawn from the fields of international and constitutional law and health and social policy, as well as judges and lawyers specializing in public, administrative, and international law. These comparative approaches contrasted with efforts in those early days to produce repositories of laws and policies enacted with no contextualization.[7] As both symposia sought a diversity of perspectives about the preexisting legal architectures, as well as complex social and political impacts of governmental responses, they are not susceptible to a simplistic tabulation. Thus, the conclusions presented in this chapter should be read as reflecting the authors' joint interpretations of reported findings across the separate symposia.

This chapter proceeds as follows. First, it considers whether the use of emergency powers (e.g., the declaration of a constitutional state of exception or the use of legislative emergency frameworks which allow for the exceptional use of executive power outside normal constraints) is preferable to using ordinary legislation in managing the impacts on civil liberties of a health and social crisis. This chapter argues that whether countries are successful in limiting the potential for abuse of power in emergencies is dependent on the social and political environment in which the legal rules operate, as much as whether formal limitations and checks on the use of power are present. Second, the pandemic raises questions regarding the role of health policymaking and health systems as democratic institutions, which have been inexorably affected by decades of privatization and reduced social spending on health. This chapter suggests that the background rules that structure health systems (public health and care) and decision-making regarding priorities are as critical to understanding governmental responses as the legal recognition of health-related rights.

---

[5] For all country reports, see Joelle Grogan, Introduction and List of Country Reports, VerfBlog (Apr. 6, 2020), https://verfassungsblog.de/introduction-list-of-country-reports/.

[6] For all country reports, see Bill of Health, Global Responses to COVID-19: Rights, Democracy, and the Law, https://blog.petrieflom.law.harvard.edu/category/blog-symposia/global-responses-covid19/.

[7] See, for example, COVID-19 Government Response Tracker, Oxford, www.bsg.ox.ac.uk/research/research-projects/covid-19-government-response-tracker; COVID-19 Law Lab, https://covidlawlab.org. Subsequently, other researchers, including the Lex-Atlas project and the CompCoRe projects, developed a more extensive and detailed compendium of comparative legal analyses. See Lex-Atlas: COVID-19, UCL, https://lexatlas-c19.org/; CompCoRe, https://compcore.cornell.edu/.

II STATES OF EXCEPTION AND EMERGENCY

States of exception or emergency enable the exceptional use of powers, typically by the executive outside ordinary legislative processes or scrutiny, justified on the basis of the necessity of an urgent response to an emergency. By their nature and the strength of justifying urgency which calls for their use, emergency powers are at heightened risk of misuse or abuse where significant action can be taken with limited capacity for oversight, and where subsequent judicial review of executive discretion can be "so light a touch as to be non-existent."[8] The extended duration of the COVID-19 pandemic, in addition to concerns that the virus will become endemic, have extended the duration of executive dominance of decision-making,[9] leading to concerns that this will further global trends towards the autocratization and "decay" of democracies which were in motion prior to the pandemic.[10] Even as some countries have lifted many of the most restrictive measures on liberties at the time of writing, most provisions enacted have remained in place on statute books or in practice, leading to concerns that the modes of governance employed during the pandemic have normalized the exceptional in relation to public health emergencies.

Emergencies should not function as opportunities to permanently shift the balance of power toward the executive, resulting in decision-making that is all but unaccountable. Both symposia also underlined the importance of ensuring not only the limited nature of states of exception but, critically, the necessary limitations on the use of power during the emergency. For this, international human rights instruments, including the International Covenant on Civil and Political Rights, the American Convention on Human Rights, and the European Convention on Human Rights, have provided guidelines for safeguards on the use of exceptional power, which are typically premised on: (1) identifying certain non-derogable rights (e.g., the prohibition on torture and the right to a fair trial); and (2) requiring the use of emergency powers to be proportionate, necessary, non-discriminatory, and temporary in nature.[11] Health emergencies, including the current pandemic,[12] have been interpreted to come within these provisions.[13]

---

[8] David Dyzenhaus, The Constitution of Law: Legality in a Time of Emergency 41–43 (2006).

[9] Tom Ginsburg & Mila Versteeg, Binding the Unbound Executive: Checks and Balances in Times of Pandemic, Int'l J. of Const. L. (June 24, 2021), www.law.virginia.edu/scholarship/publication/mila-versteeg/1334721.

[10] Tom Daly, Democratic Decay: Conceptualising an Emerging Research Field, 11 *Hague J. Rule L.* 9, 9–11 (2019).

[11] See Cassandra Emmons, International Human Rights Law and COVID-19 States of Emergency, VerfBlog (Apr. 25, 2020), https://verfassungsblog.de/international-human-rights-law-and-covid-19-states-of-emergency.

[12] See, for example, Eur. Convention on Hum. Rts., Fact Sheet, Derogation in Time of Emergency (updated Sept. 2020), www.echr.coe.int/Documents/FS_Derogation_ENG.pdf.

[13] See, for example, UN HRC, General Comment No. 29, Article 4 (States of Emergency): International Covenant on Civil and Political Rights (2001); ECHR, Guide, Article 15 (Derogation in Time of Emergency): European Convention on Human Rights (updated Apr. 30, 2021), www.echr.coe.int/documents/Guide_Art_15_ENG.pdf.

A majority of countries in the symposia declared a "state of emergency" (or the domestic equivalent: e.g., a "state of exception" or "state of catastrophe") or relied upon some form of emergency powers in response to the pandemic. The symposia demonstrated a broad range and form of domestic design of both states of emergency regimes and on constitutional and legal safeguards on their use. Examples of constitutional states of exception ranged from highly prescriptive, tiered, and differential states of exception requiring legislative approval depending on the perceived severity of the emergency (e.g., Estonia and Peru) to open-ended and discretionary provisions providing for an exclusively executive decision on what constituted a "threat" (e.g., Cameroon, Malaysia, and Thailand). A number of states alternatively introduced new legislative (rather than constitutional) states of emergency (e.g., France and Bulgaria) or introduced new powers which were designated as "emergency." The latter legislative forms of emergency powers would have been expected to be subject to ordinary democratic checks and balances, including parliamentary scrutiny and judicial review, though often were not, either by legislative design or the degree of deference displayed by parliaments and courts.[14]

In the use of emergency power, a central question is the safeguarding of civil liberties through the permissible degree to which rights can be limited or states may derogate from rights protections. The "limitation" of rights, often as part of a domestic balancing exercise between competing rights or overriding public interest (e.g., the requirement to wear masks in public), is distinguishable from derogation, which is envisioned as a temporary suspension of certain (not all) rights during an emergency subject to a range of justificatory conditions (e.g., proportionality and temporariness) and the oversight of external human rights bodies, in the case of international instruments, or domestic courts, in the case of protections on constitutional rights. What is notable is that while nearly all states acted to place highly restrictive limitations on the exercise of rights, including movement, assembly, and worship, only a minority of these states in the initial phase of the pandemic made official notifications of derogations from international human rights instruments.[15]

There is no common reason why some states did, or did not, declare a state of emergency and it should not be assumed that it was to avoid ostensibly higher levels of scrutiny which may be expected under ordinary legislative processes. For example, a number of populous states, including Brazil, Bangladesh, Indonesia, and India, eschewed a declaration, likely for political reasons to either avoid negative historical associations of abuse of emergency powers or in the underestimation or downplaying of the severity of the pandemic threat. States which did not rely on emergency provisions instead relied on ordinary health legislation. Restricting power within ordinary democratic and legal constraints is in line

---

[14] Joelle Grogan, States of Emergency, VerfBlog (May 26, 2020), https://verfassungsblog.de/states-of-emergency.

[15] See Niall Coghlan, Dissecting COVID-19 Derogations, VerfBlog (May 5, 2020), https://verfassungsblog.de/dissecting-covid-19-derogations/; Emmons, supra note 11.

with what Martin Scheinin advocates as the principle of normalcy: addressing the health emergency through "normally applicable powers and procedures and insist[ing] on full compliance with human rights, even if introducing new necessary and proportionate restrictions upon human rights on the basis of a pressing social need created by the pandemic."[16] However, in some more concerning cases, any form of parliamentary legislative procedure was abandoned in favor of executive decrees and presidential or ministerial circulars (e.g., Cameroon, India, Turkey, and Vietnam). These measures were emergency powers in effect, though were not considered so in form. The effect in practice of reliance on ersatz "ordinary" powers was the avoidance of safeguards which otherwise were designed to control power under emergency. The commonality exposed is that without a requisite degree of democratic oversight and input, the negative consequences which can arise both under a state of emergency and upon reliance on ordinary legislation are indistinguishable.

Evident from analysis of both symposia is that whether a state has declared a state of emergency is not a reliable indicator of potentially abusive executive practices. Such practices include the targeting of populations in vulnerable circumstances: for example, the Romani in Slovakia (state of emergency), prisoners in Peru (state of emergency), and religious minorities in India (no state of emergency) and Bangladesh (no state of emergency). The wider sociopolitical context is a stronger factor in gauging the likelihood of abusive practices. The autocratizing states of Hungary (declared a state of emergency) and Poland (no declared state of emergency) have both taken advantage of the pandemic to further consolidate executive power, to the detriment of the separation of powers and democratic checks and balances, with the former taking the opportunity to adopt emergency legislation empowering the executive to amend any law of any value in a way which is all but immune from any legislative scrutiny,[17] and the latter adopting questionable restrictions on human rights via executive decrees rather than through parliamentary statute, as required by the constitution for such a limitation of fundamental rights.[18] Paired with the temporary closure of courts, or the restriction of access to only a limited type of cases, and compounded by a pre-pandemic trend toward the demolition of judicial independence in both states, any effective judicial remedy is all but moot.[19]

---

[16] See Martin Scheinin, 'To Derogate or Not to Derogate,' OpinioJuris (Apr. 6, 2020), http://opiniojuris .org/2020/04/06/covid-19-symposium-to-derogate-or-not-to-derogate/.

[17] Kriszta Kovács, Hungary's Orbánistan: A Complete Arsenal of Emergency Powers, VerfBlog (Apr. 6, 2020), https://verfassungsblog.de/hungarys-orbanistan-a-complete-arsenal-of-emergency-powers/.

[18] Jakub Jaraczewski, An Emergency By Any Other Name? Measures Against the COVID-19 Pandemic in Poland, VerfBlog (Apr. 24, 2020), https://verfassungsblog.de/an-emergency-by-any-other-name-measures-against-the-covid-19-pandemic-in-poland/.

[19] See Laurent Pech, Patryk Wachowiec & Dariusz Mazur, Poland's Rule of Law Breakdown: A Five-Year Assessment of EU's (In)Action, 13 *Hague J. Rule L.* 1, 1–43 (2021); Laurent Pech & Kim Lane Scheppele, Illiberalism Within: Rule of Law Backsliding in the EU, 19 Camb. Yearb. Eur. Leg. *Stud.* 3, 19–26 (2017).

The essential focus, therefore, should be the use and not the form of power, and whether safeguards in the form of legislative oversight and/or judicial review have been effectively utilized – not whether they exist at all. However, this appears all the more challenging in times of crisis if both legislatures and the courts tend to be deferential to the actions of the executive and unwilling to exercise robust forms of oversight or review.[20] Such experience also lends support to the argument of Mexican Supreme Court Justice Alfredo Gutiérrez Ortiz Mena that while courts should be more deferential in cases where formally declared exceptions have been declared, they should exercise heightened review ("strict scrutiny") of the arrogation of ordinary powers by the executive even in times of crisis.[21]

However, there is also emerging evidence of good practices which are not dependent on an emergency/ordinary powers dichotomy, and instead reveals good governance practices inculcated within the wider sociopolitical ecosystem. Those states which aligned law and policy with principles of legality and legal certainty, as well as clarity in public communication, scrutiny, transparency in decision-making, and publication of underlying rationale for (in)action, and engagement with external expertise, civil society, and criticism to reform law and policy have, more often, correlated with higher levels of both public trust and compliance.[22] These practices are essential to effective strategies to combat the virus and the preservation of democratic legitimacy. By correlating infection and mortality rates with levels of restriction adopted, and the impact on ordinary life and governance, we can highlight countries from among the symposia which have epitomized this approach. For example, New Zealand's strategy of early response and engaging a combination of ordinary powers aided by some emergency provisions, and framed by recommendations and social nudges, along with robust parliamentary oversight and government accountability, have correlated not only with lower infection rates but also high levels of public trust. Such practices are evident among the responses of the "best responders" to COVID-19:[23] Finland, Iceland, Singapore, South Korea, and Taiwan. However, such "political

---

[20] Joelle Grogan & Alice Donald, Lessons for a "Post-Pandemic" Future, in Joelle Grogan & Alice Donald, *Routledge Handbook of Law and the COVID-19 Pandemic* (2022).

[21] Comments of Justice Alfredo Gutiérrez Ortiz Mena, Constitutional Democracy and the Role of High Courts in Times of Crisis: The Case of Mexico (Oct. 23, 2020), https://petrieflom .law.harvard.edu/events/details/constitutional-democracy-and-the-role-of-high-courts-in-times- of-crisis.

[22] See Sheila Jasanoff & Stephen Hilgartner, A Stress Test for Politics: A Comparative Perspective on Policy Responses to COVID-19, in Joelle Grogan & Alice Donald, *Routledge Handbook of Law and the COVID-19 Pandemic*, 294–98 (2022); Grogan & Donald, supra note 20, at 483–84.

[23] See, for example, Ian Bremmer Best Responses to COVID-19, Time (June 12, 2020), https://time .com/5851633/best-global-responses-covid-19/; Tom Frieden, Which Countries Have Responded Best to COVID-19?, Wall St. J. (Jan. 1, 2021), www.wsj.com/articles/which-countries-have-responded- best-to-covid-19-11609516800.

trust needs to be continually earned, and traditions of transparency are deeply ingrained; they do not begin during pandemics."[24]

In sum, the symposia have revealed that the use of power within the wider socio-political context, not the form of legal authority, should be the starting point for reimagining democratic controls to contain abuses of civil liberties. First, conditionality within either constitutional provisions or domestic legal frameworks, or even under obligations to international standards on the use of emergency powers, cannot alone limit abuse. Second, neither the declaration of a state of exception nor the exclusive reliance on ordinary legislative powers is a reliable indicator of the likelihood of abuse of power during the pandemic. A stronger indicator, albeit one often more difficult to identify than legal text, is the sociopolitical ecosystem in which legal measures are operating: autocratizing states have capitalized on the emergency to further consolidate power, despite formal legal or constitutional safeguards, while states inculcating democratic values of trust and accountability prior to the pandemic, by contrast, have embodied these values in response. Thus, efforts to reform in order to mitigate the dangers of excessive restriction, arbitrary discrimination, and hypertrophied executive action through formal legal rules alone are largely ineffective, and must instead focus on building a robust democratic system of an independent judiciary and on encouraging active government engagement with parliamentary processes, including debate, review, and scrutiny.

III HEALTH, HEALTH SYSTEMS, AND DEMOCRATIC DECISION-MAKING

The pandemic has brought far greater attention to connections between population health and health systems, on the one hand, and democratic legitimacy of government actions, on the other. The pandemic revealed clearly that inequalities in access to care, as well as in outcomes, reflect larger patterns of discrimination and marginalization within societies, and that normative commitments to the equal dignity of diverse members of the society is encoded in health systems, just as it is in justice systems, for example.[25] Reflections on these symposia suggest that it is insufficient to examine whether health-related rights (including the right to life with dignity when interpreted to include aspects of health care, e.g., India) are enshrined directly in constitutional norms or incorporated from international human rights law through constitutional blocs. It is just as critical to understand the structural conditions that enable health-related rights to be exercised in practice, including the formal and informal practices of subjecting health policies to democratic justification.

---

[24] See Alicia Ely Yamin, Global Responses to COVID-19: An Inflection Point for Democracy, Rights, and Law, Bill of Health (June 12, 2020), https://blog.petrieflom.law.harvard.edu/2020/06/12/global-responses-covid19-reflections/.

[25] Alicia Ely Yamin & Tara Boghosian, Democracy and Health: Situating Health Rights within a Republic of Reasons, 19 *Yale J. Health Pol'y, L. Ethics* 87, 87–123 (2020).

COVID-19 struck a world already reeling from multiple waves of austerity. Even in countries where universal health care is guaranteed under law (e.g., the Netherlands and the United Kingdom), the symposia underscored that governments' role in financing and provision of public health and care has shrunk dramatically over the last few decades. Indeed, just as socioeconomic rights, such as health, were being formulated and incorporated into constitutions across much of the world, including in most states represented in the symposia, neoliberal economic governance has driven reductions in budgets for public health and increased privatization of health care sectors. International financial institutions have played no small part in driving these trends in the Global South. From the late 1980s to today, loan conditions attached to structural adjustment, fiscal consolidation, and the like have prompted steep cuts in public health spending, the flexibilization of labor in health sectors, increasingly stringent intellectual property restrictions on access to medicines imposed through trade agreements, and the privatization of services and supply chains, together with sweeping disruptions in social determinants of health.[26] At the same time, the political capacity to resolve social demands for health has been constrained by loan agreements that convert these fiscal issues or trade-related aspects of intellectual property into questions for technocratic expert panels to resolve.[27]

Therefore, it is unsurprising that despite health rights being enshrined in constitutional law in each case, contributions to the symposia suggest that countries with well-functioning health care systems, particularly those considered "sacrosanct" in the political culture (e.g., Canada), are inevitably better placed to tackle a major health crisis than those with weak or dysfunctional health systems (e.g., South Africa, Argentina, and Colombia) or those whose systems were already in a state of total collapse prior to the crisis (e.g., Ecuador). Nor is it surprising that chronic shortages are often further compounded by widescale corruption when a sudden influx of emergency funds incentivizes opportunism (e.g., Nepal). However, this insight points to the need for international and comparative legal analysis to pay closer attention not just to the grafting or importing of human rights into domestic law,[28] but also to the structural changes needed, to ensure the infrastructure for fair provision, locally and globally, that legal frameworks based on neoliberal imperatives have made impossible.

The symposia further highlight the importance of decision-making processes in relation to health to the meaningfulness of health rights in practice, as well as the preservation of democratic legitimacy. At one level, at least since Rudolf Virchow's work on the social origins of disease and the need to address epidemics through

---

[26] Alicia Ely Yamin, When Misfortune Becomes Injustice: Evolving Human Rights Struggles for Health and Social Equality 94–98, 128–30 (2020).

[27] Id. at 94–99.

[28] Roberto Gargarella, The Engine Room of the Constitution: Latin American Constitutionalism, 1810–2010, at viii (2013).

political, not merely medical, means, there has there been an awareness of public health policies and health systems as sites of democratic contestation.[29] As already noted, movements for universal health coverage were often struggles for democratic inclusion. The more recent technocratic conceptualization of health is a contingent historical response to increasingly neoliberal socioeconomic transformations, coupled with technological innovations based on accelerating medicalization after World War II, and biomedicalization in the twenty-first century.[30]

Nonetheless, by the time COVID-19 emerged, decision-making processes regarding health, within health systems and beyond, had largely been exiled from democratic deliberation to insulated islands of professional expertise. As a result, during the pandemic, we have witnessed the widespread adoption of an overly simplistic dichotomy of "objective scientific truth versus political power," coupled with considerable partisan politicization across a number of the countries included in one or both of the symposia (e.g., Brazil under President Bolsonaro and the United States under President Trump). In both symposia, this dichotomy has become encapsulated in the tension of who is (and should be) the decisionmaker, marking often a radical reformulation of roles – for example, "doctor as politician" in Croatia,[31] and "public opinion as epidemiologists" in the Netherlands.[32] Devi Sridhar, a leading public health academic, deploys an analogy to express the need for deference to infectious disease experts in setting policy: "It's like being on a plane and the engine does not work. Everyone gives their opinion on what should happen instead of trusting the people who have engineering experience and have done that for years."[33]

However, there is a difference between politicized dismissal or cherry-picking of empirical scientific evidence and accepting that the forms of knowledge needed to respond to COVID-19 in a democracy have inherently political dimensions that go beyond the expertise of infectious disease specialists and epidemiologists. As Sheila Jasanoff wrote before the pandemic, in relation to science more broadly than health, "risk":

> is not a matter of simple probabilities, to be rationally calculated by experts and avoided in accordance with the cold arithmetic of cost-benefit analysis …. Critically important questions of risk management cannot be addressed by technical experts

---

[29] Rudolf Virchow, Disease, Life, and Man (1958).

[30] See, generally, Adele E. Clarke et al., Biomedicalization: Technoscience, Health, and Illness in the US (2010); Viviane Quirke & Jean-Paul Gaudillière, The Era of Biomedicine: Science, Medicine, and Public Health in Britain and France after the Second World War, 52 Med. Hist. 441 (2008).

[31] Nika Bačić Selanec, Croatia's Response to COVID-19: On Legal Form and Constitutional Safeguards in Times of Pandemic, VerfBlog (May 9, 2020), https://verfassungsblog.de/croatias-response-to-covid-19-on-legal-form-and-constitutional-safeguards-in-times-of-pandemic/.

[32] Antoine Buyse & Roel de Lange, The Netherlands: Of Rollercoasters and Elephants, VerfBlog (May 8, 2020), https://verfassungsblog.de/the-netherlands-of-rollercoasters-and-elephants/; Brigit Toebes, COVID-19, the Netherlands, and Human Rights: A Balancing Act, Bill of Health (May 26, 2020), https://blog.petrieflom.law.harvard.edu/2020/05/26/netherlands-global-responses-covid19/.

[33] Devi Sridhar, Good Morning Britain (Nov. 5, 2020), https://twitter.com/gmb/status/1324272948820267008.

with conventional tools of prediction. Such questions determine not only whether we will get sick or die, and under what conditions, but also who will be affected and how we should live with uncertainty and ignorance.[34]

In the reflections from both symposia, and throughout this pandemic, measures implemented to prevent or slow the spread of the virus have had a disproportionately negative impact on vulnerable populations, including the elderly, prisoners, persons with physical or mental disabilities, migrants, racial and ethnic minorities, and refugees and migrant workers. Analyses across countries of different income levels (e.g., Spain, Ireland, Chile, Colombia, Kenya) noted that the sudden onset of mass unemployment among part-time and informal workers, the shutdown of childcare and schools, and stay-at-home orders that led to spikes in domestic violence, had devastating impacts on women. For the millions living with poverty, malnutrition, or with high rates of potential comorbidities, including tuberculosis and HIV, in cramped conditions and with limited access to water (e.g., Argentina, Guatemala, Nepal, Nigeria, and South Africa), the most prevalent political and medical messaging of "stay home and wash your hands" ignored endemic socioeconomic disparity and the underlying structural inequalities which have enabled and embedded it.

There is no reason to believe that public health expertise offers a privileged domain of knowledge in weighing containment of transmission against losing access to other socioeconomic rights and basic needs, such as food, housing, and education. Indeed, Dr. Jonathan Mann, a founder of the "health and human rights movement," argued based on his experience with HIV/AIDS that all "health policies and programs should be considered discriminatory and burdensome on human rights until proven otherwise."[35] In the different dynamics of the COVID-19 pandemic, policies dictated by utilitarian calculations of public health experts have shown themselves to be particularly apt to be rife with blind spots. Cloaked in an aura of objective, apolitical "scientificity," and justified under the idea of safeguarding an unchallengeable good, which is made to appear of heightened necessity when coupled with a generalized fear, these prescriptions are insulated from normal democratic deliberation.

Further, the fallaciously denominated "health versus wealth" tradeoff – public health restrictions versus opening the economy – has in many countries involved dueling fields of expertise and cost-benefit calculations between economists and public health experts, as opposed to enlarging our imagination of how decisions regarding health can be brought into the realm of public reason. As Jasanoff and Hilgartner assert, as both national and international authorities consider the lessons of COVID-19:

> they should revisit their established institutional processes for integrating scientific and political consensus-building. If free citizens are unable to see how expertise

---

[34] Sheila Jasanoff, Science and Public Reason 168 (2012).
[35] See Jonathan Mann et al., Health and Human Rights, 1 *Health Hum. Rts.* 7, 16 (1994).

is serving the collective good, at all levels of governance, they will sooner rebel against expert authority than give up their independence. Just as a sound mind is said to require a sound body, so COVID-19 has shown that the credibility and legitimacy of public health expertise depends on the health of the entire body politic.[36]

As reflected in the symposia, the pandemic has only heightened the urgency of grappling with the lack of public accountability and democracy in current health governance across most of the world, and imagining new institutions, processes, and methods for restoring normative questions to addressing health policy in pandemic and "normal" times. The critical role of reasoned justification for how health systems function has often been evidenced by its absence during COVID-19. For example, decisions regarding what services are deemed "essential" have often disproportionately affected sexual and reproductive health and rights.

Insights provided by both symposia indicate that decisions on whom to prioritize and where to allocate testing and treatment have also been questioned (e.g., Croatia, Slovakia, Nepal, and the Netherlands). Across societies, evidence suggests that the social legitimacy of health decisions, just as in others, is based on both sociohistorical context and in the case of local health systems the slow building of trust, which does not happen overnight when a pandemic breaks out. The reflections in these symposia confirm lessons from previous epidemics (e.g., HIV/AIDS and Ebola) in that the best way to implement public health policies, as well as preserve the legitimacy of the health system and government more broadly, is to engage a wider number of constituencies in a meaningful and equitable manner on an ongoing basis, as opposed to undertaking ad hoc consultations during times of crisis.

Whether allocating vaccines or scarce equipment, supplies, and treatments, which follow different logics, there is growing agreement among health ethicists that decision-making processes regarding health require the same principles suggested earlier for the promulgation of COVID-19 measures more broadly – as well as for expectations of democratic decision-making in general. These include: (1) explicit justification and transparency of rationales; (2) transparency about empirical and normative uncertainty; (3) openness to address and include diverse perspectives on competing criteria for decisions, ranking of criteria, and why they matter; (4) inclusion of the perspectives of marginalized and disadvantaged populations as to the formulation of choice criteria, as well as disparate impacts; (5) willingness to revise policy decisions in light of populations' negative experiences with implemented decisions and critical feedback on the rationales for the decisions; and (6) regulation and enforcement of (1) to (5).[37] In addition to including distinct constituencies in

---

[36] Jasanoff & Hilgartner, supra note 22, at 297–98.

[37] Example, P.M. Maarten et al., Stakeholder Participation for Legitimate Priority Setting: A Checklist, 7 *Int'l J. of Health Pol'y & Mgmt.* 973, 976 (2018); WHO Consultative Group on Equity and Universal Health Coverage, Making Fair Choices on the Path to Universal Health Coverage (2014); see also Alicia Ely Yamin & Tara Boghosian, Democracy and Health: Situating Health Rights within a Republic of Reasons, 19 *Yale J. of Health Pol'y, L. Ethics* 87, 110–21 (2020).

specific allocation decisions or the tradeoffs between containment and other health concerns, such as mental health, reflections on the first phase of pandemic response in the symposia, together with other studies,[38] suggest that democratizing health policy requires making visible how the issues are framed in legal and policy analysis, including structural forms of subordination and exclusion that invariably affect distributions of health and ill-health.

In sum, the effectiveness, as well as legitimacy, of governmental responses to COVID-19 call for thinking more deeply about the role of health systems as democratic social institutions and the ways in which they formally and informally enshrine normative values from macro to micro levels in both pandemics and normal times. As Scott Burris argues, health law is not a matter of "just the formal rules, but how these rules are enacted every day" by the health care program implementers and providers, as well as users of the system.[39] The meaning of health rights, and health laws more broadly, invariably depends upon how multiple actors understand how they relate to other sets of rules and norms beyond the health system. Neither constitutionalization nor legislation enshrining health rights in formal law is an adequate indicator of the normative and social legitimacy of specific health policymaking and priority-setting in practice. Structural conditions underpinning meaningful access, together with the nature of processes for making health-related decisions and setting priorities, are equally critical.

Bringing health policy under the purview of public reason, as is taken for granted with respect to other rights, will likely call for a paradigm shift that enables diverse persons to see public health and access to care in normal times, as well as pandemics, not as the domain of technocratic experts alone, but as assets of (social) citizenship.

IV CONCLUSION

The global but differentiated impacts of the sweeping COVID-19 pandemic present an opportunity, and an imperative, for reflection on the legal, social, and institutional changes required for advancing public health, as well as for strengthening the rule of law moving forward. Joint reflections on the contributions to the symposia, together with other scholarship, suggest at least three insights for building stronger democratic institutional structures to withstand the pressures both of pandemic and autocratizing forces. First, the use of power within the wider sociopolitical context, not the form of legal authority, should be the starting point for reimagining democratic controls to contain abuses of civil liberties. Second, the institutional arrangements and structural conditions necessary to ensure access to public health, as well

---

[38] See CompCoRe, https://compcore.cornell.edu/.

[39] Scott Burris, From Health Care to the Social Determinants of Health: A Public Health Law Research Perspective, 159 *U. Pa. L. Rev.* 1649, 1655 (2011).

as to medical care, are as important as formal legislative regimes enshrining health-related rights. Third, democratic decision-making processes that include participation by a wide array of experts, as well as by constituencies affected, afford space to critique government (in)action, and are linked to responsive reforms are more effective both in producing equitable health outcomes and in preserving confidence in the rule of law. In short, the COVID-19 pandemic has illustrated starkly that health, perhaps more dramatically than any other area of law and policy, involves what Britton-Purdy et al. refer to as "the need for political judgments about the gravest questions: who should exercise power, of what sort, and over whom? What should count as a human need, and what claims should politically recognized needs give us against the state and thus against one another? Whose dreams come true, and who is enlisted in the realization of others' schemes?"[40]

---

[40] Jedediah Britton-Purdy et al., Building a Law-and-Political-Economy Framework: Beyond the Twentieth-Century Synthesis, 129 *Yale L. J.* 1784, 1827 (2020).

24

A Tale of Two Crises

COVID-19, Climate Change, and Crisis Response

Daniel Farber

I INTRODUCTION

A viral pandemic and a change in global climate are utterly dissimilar in a physical sense. The pandemic is an abrupt emergency, while climate change is a long-term problem, though one requiring an urgent response. In a sense, both can be considered crises. Despite their differences, the pandemic and the climate crisis have many linkages. The response to the pandemic can impact the carbon emissions that drive climate change, while the pandemic's economic effect may prompt government responses which impact such emissions. In the meantime, efforts to respond to this public health crisis and to the climate crisis must both contend with the frailties of human nature and of existing political institutions.

Section I of this chapter investigates the effect of COVID-19 on carbon emissions. There was a sharp initial reduction in emissions, with the question being how much of this reduction, if any, will persist. Section II turns to the possible impact of economic recovery measures on climate change. Some jurisdictions planned green recoveries, which may succeed in accelerating the transition to a low-carbon economy. Part III discusses the governance issues that have arisen regarding climate change and the pandemic; these governance issues have proved remarkably similar. Part IV then offers some concluding thoughts about the relationship between these two global crises.

II THE IMPACT OF THE PANDEMIC ON CARBON EMISSIONS

The linkages between COVID-19 and climate change are complex. One connection involves fossil fuel consumption, which declined during lockdowns. Fossil fuel use is the primary cause of climate change, but may also indirectly increase susceptibility to COVID-19. Fossil fuels are also prime sources for ultra-fine particulates (known technically as PM2.5) due to emissions by power plants and vehicles. Several studies connect past air pollution levels with COVID-19 mortality rates, which is not surprising given the general association between air pollution and susceptibility to respiratory diseases. A 2019 study linked PM2.5 to 200,000 US deaths per year, mostly due to respiratory and cardiovascular issues.[1] A Harvard study found that an increase of one microgram per cubic meter in PM2.5 causes an 8 percent increase in the COVID-19 death rate.[2] Thus, jurisdictions that had taken steps to reduce carbon emissions may also have indirectly helped themselves in terms of the pandemic by reducing vulnerability due to PM2.5.

Another indirect connection between COVID-19 and climate change relates to extreme weather events, which climate change has amplified. Certain disaster response efforts, including evacuations and mass sheltering, provide opportunities for viral contagion, helping exacerbate the pandemic.[3]

The most direct linkage, however, ties COVID-19 to economic dislocation and then to carbon emissions. It was initially expected that the economic shutdown associated with the virus would at least have the beneficial side effect of reducing carbon emissions. That direct effect on emissions seems to have been transitory. As we will see, however, some of the economic changes caused by the pandemic may have longer-lasting impacts on emissions.

Initially in China and then across the globe, the pandemic slashed economic activity and shut down transportation. By April 2020, emissions had fallen by about 17 percent globally and 25 percent in the United States.[4] But by mid-June, global emissions had begun to recover, leading to a roughly 9 percent decline below 2019 levels in the first half of 2020. In the United States, the Energy Information Agency estimated a 10 percent drop in carbon emissions for 2020 as a whole, with a 6 percent rebound in 2021 as the economy recovered.[5] Even if the 2020 emission cuts had

---

[1] Benjamin Bowe et al., Burden of Cause-Specific Mortality Associated with PM2.5 Air Pollution in the United States, JAMA Network Open (Nov. 20, 2019), https://jamanetwork.com/journals/jamanetworkopen/fullarticle/2755672.

[2] Xiao Wu, Rachel C. Nethery, M. Benjamin Sabath, Danielle Braun & Francesca Dominici, Air Pollution and COVID-19 Mortality in the United States: Strengths and Limitations of an Ecological Regression Analysis, Sci. Advances (2020), https://advances.sciencemag.org/content/6/45/eabd4049. This result was consistent with the findings of other researchers. Id. For a survey of the literature, including studies from countries other than the United States, see Thomas Bourdrel, Isabella Annesi-Maesano, Barrak Alahmad, Cara N. Maesano & Marie-Abèle Bind, The Impact of Outdoor Air Pollution on COVID-19: A Review of Evidence from In Vitro, Animal, and Human Studies, 30 *Eur. Respir. Rev.* 200242 (2021).

[3] Renee N. Salas, James Shultz & Caren G. Solomon, The Climate Crisis and Covid-19 – A Major Threat to the Pandemic Response, *New Eng. J. Med.* (July 15, 2020), www.nejm.org/doi/full/10.1056/NEJMp2022011.

[4] Corinne Le Quéré et al., Temporary Reduction in Daily Global CO2 Emissions during the COVID-19 Forced Confinement, 10 *Nature Climate Change* 647 (2020).

[5] US Energy Info. Agency, Short-Term Outlook (Nov. 10, 2020), www.eia.gov/outlooks/steo/. These estimates are based on data regarding fuel consumption and energy output. It is more difficult to detect the emission changes from measurements of atmospheric concentrations, partly because of the large seasonal variation in concentration levels. See also Zhu Liu et al., Near-Real-Time Monitoring of Global CO2 Emissions Reveals the Effects of the COVID-19 Pandemic, Nature Commc'ns (Oct. 14, 2020), www.nature.com/articles/s41467-020-18922-7.

been permanent, they would have been far less than what is required to meet global emissions targets.[6]

In China, the world's largest carbon emitter, emissions dropped 20 percent in early 2020, but then rebounded by April 2020 to 2019 levels, or slightly above.[7] The planning, permitting, and construction of new coal-fired power plants leaped in the first half of 2020.[8] Yet the central government also announced efforts to prioritize clean energy, cross-province transmission, and flexibility measures.[9] Thus, it is not clear how the pandemic will impact longer-term emissions growth.

The impact of the pandemic on the global oil industry was especially severe. Because of COVID-19-related restrictions on travel and the general economic downturn, oil prices crashed by almost 50 percent between December 2019 and March 2020.[10] In some cases, prices went negative, with well owners having to pay to have oil taken off their hands.[11] At one point, some oil futures dropped momentarily to a price of negative $37 as producers anticipated having to pay firms to take charge of their oil.[12] The price collapse seems to have accelerated trends in the industry due to the long-term prospects for oil usage. By June 2020, major oil companies such as Shell and BP were writing down the values of their oil and gas assets by tens of billions of dollars.[13] In September 2020, BP announced a radical shift in its strategic planning, away from petroleum and toward renewable energy.[14] The decline of the industry is mixed news in terms of emissions. The direct effect of a shift away from oil would clearly be beneficial. Yet there is also a risk connected with the economic decline of the industry. As demand declines, wells go out of use, and less solvent or

---

[6] Alexander Kaufman, COVID-Related Emissions Drop "Just a Tiny Blip" in Long-term Climate Trends, Yale360, (Nov. 25, 2020), https://e360.yale.edu/digest/covid-related-emissions-drop-just-a-tiny-blip-in-long-term-climate-trends.

[7] Liu et al., supra note 5, at fig. 2b.

[8] Energy Monitor, A New Coal Boom in China: Country Accelerates New Coal Plant Permitting and Proposals (June 2020), https://globalenergymonitor.org/wp-content/uploads/2021/01/China-coal-plant-brief-June-2020Eng.pdf.

[9] Id.

[10] Frank Schneider & Allie Schwartz, The New World of COVID-19: Paradigm Shifts in the Oil and Gas Industry, Nat'l L. Rev. (Sept. 30, 2020), www.natlawreview.com/article/new-world-covid-19-paradigm-shifts-oil-and-gas-industry.

[11] Id.

[12] Id.

[13] Danica Kirka, Shell Takes $22 Billion Hit on Lower Oil, Gas Prices, Associated Press (June 30, 2020), https://apnews.com/article/0d7addddga596eba2f34b736fce1f030.

[14] According to the *Washington Post*:

> Led by a new chief executive, BP is trying to reinvent itself as an energy company in the age of climate change. The company is shrinking its oil and gas business, revving up offshore wind power and developing solar and battery storage. It is even considering installing electric car charging kiosks at its U.S. gas stations, part of a drive to eliminate or offset its carbon emissions to a net zero level by 2050.

Steven Mufson, Big Oil's Green Makeover, Wash. Post (Sept. 15, 2020), www.washingtonpost.com/climate-solutions/2020/09/15/bp-climate-change-transition/.

responsible operators may simply abandon marginal wells without properly capping them. Those abandoned wells may result in significant environmental problems, including leakage of methane, a potent greenhouse gas.[15] Further uncertainties and additional strategic shifts took place in the aftermath of the Russian invasion of Ukraine, which abruptly raised global oil and gas prices.

The longer-term impacts of the pandemic on transportation remain uncertain. Telecommuting increased dramatically in some countries in the early days of the pandemic, with nearly all workers who were allowed to do so engaging in the practice.[16] By September 2020, about 12 percent of those workers had returned to the workplace in the United States, although trends were quite different in various occupations. To the extent that telecommuting remains common after the pandemic, the result should be a decline in the carbon emissions associated with commuting. It also remains to be seen how much business and educational travel may be replaced by the use of electronic media even after the pandemic ends.

A more ominous possibility is a permanent decline in public transportation. During the pandemic, use of public transit declined precipitously, leaving public transportation systems in a perilous financial condition. Experts warn of the possibility that service cuts could send public transportation into a "death spiral" in which financial woes lead to service cuts, which decrease ridership and thereby lead to deeper financial distress.[17] The end result could be to throw more riders back into cars, resulting in far greater emissions.

Forecasting the long-term impacts of COVID-19 on the economy or society more generally is difficult. It could result in permanent shifts in some economic sectors or in broader societal trends, such as increasing appreciation of the governmental role in controlling risk, the need for investment in public health, and deference to experts. Alternatively, it could turn out to be merely a blip in terms of longer-term trends, with little or no long-term impact. We have little precedent to draw upon in making predictions. The last pandemic of similar severity took place under very different circumstances over a century ago in the form of the 1918 influenza. As Robert Schiller, a Nobel-Prize winning economist, has pointed out: "Big events like

---

[15] Emily Pontecorvo, Abandonment Issues, Grist (Dec. 1, 2020), https://grist.org/energy/plugging-abandoned-oil-wells-carbon-offsets/.

[16] RAND Corp., Telecommuting and Work in the COVID-19 Pandemic: Are Workers Returning to the Workplace or Staying in Their Home Offices? (2020), www.rand.org/pubs/research_reports/RRA308-11.html. Internationally, the degree of telecommuting varied between countries, although complete global data does not seem to be available. In the European Union, telecommuting increased everywhere, but with substantial versions in the extent of the increase between countries. See Eur. Comm'n, Telework in the EU Before and After the COVID-19: Where We Were, Where We Head To (2020), https://ec.europa.eu/jrc/sites/default/files/jrc120945_policy_brief_-_covid_and_telework_final.pdf.

[17] Christina Goldbaum & Will Wright, 'Existential Peril': Mass Transit Faces Huge Service Cuts Across U.S., NY Times (Dec. 6, 2020), www.nytimes.com/2020/12/06/nyregion/mass-transit-service-cuts-covid.html.

a pandemic have the potential to leave behind a trail of disruption. They can create social discord, reduce people's willingness to spend and take risks, destroy business momentum and shake confidence in the value of investments."[18] Prediction is fraught even for experts. As Schiller explains, "[e]pisodes as far-reaching as this one are scarce, widely spaced in time, and so different in circumstances that statisticians cannot easily compare them systematically."[19]

III A PATH FORWARD

It is possible that the most important long-term climate effect of the pandemic, at least in some jurisdictions, will involve the economic recovery rather than the pandemic itself. Economic stimulus proved necessary to deal with the economic downturn. The biggest question was whether the economic recovery could be used to promote sustainability. Economic stimulus measures offer the opportunity for major investments in low-carbon technologies, which could accelerate the energy transition. Experience has shown permanent beneficial effects from stimulus spending on green infrastructure and energy-related research and development.

International institutions strongly advocated using the recovery to accelerate the energy transition away from fossil fuels. In a speech making the case for a green recovery, the deputy managing director of the International Monetary Fund said: "Let me end by emphasizing that the time to act, especially with lower oil prices, is now. The decisions we take now will shape economies and the global system for decades. Europe must, and is, setting a high bar that should galvanize action elsewhere."[20] Along the same lines, the International Energy Agency produced an ambitious green recovery plan requiring investment of $3 trillion over three years.[21] The agency estimated that its plan would increase global gross domestic product by 1.1 percent every year it was in effect, create nine million jobs per year, and result in a $4.5 billion ton decrease in annual emissions by 2023.[22]

One ambitious green stimulus to date has been adopted by the European Union.[23] Out of €1.8 trillion euro ($2 trillion) in funding, almost a third of the spending targets climate action. The stimulus targets €91 billion euros per year for EU grants and loan guarantees for building improvements, such as rooftop solar panels and insulation, at least €20 billion for developing hydrogen as an energy source, another

---

[18] Robert J. Shiller, *Why We Can't Foresee the Pandemic's Long-Term Effects*, NY Times, (May 29, 2020, updated Aug. 4, 2020).

[19] Id.

[20] Tao Zhang, *Opening Remarks – COVID-19: Opportunities for a Green Recovery* (May 22, 2020), www.imf.org/en/News/Articles/2020/05/22/sp052220-opening-remark-zhang.

[21] Int'l Energy Agency, *World Energy Outlook Special Report: Sustainable Recovery* (June 2020), www.iea.org/reports/sustainable-recovery.

[22] Id.

[23] See Rhodium Grp., *It's Not Easy Being Green: Stimulus Spending in the World's Major Economies* 5 (Sept. 2, 2020), https://rhg.com/research/green-stimulus-spending/.

€20 billion for adding 15 gigawatts of renewable generation, €20 billion more for zero-emissions vehicles, and €40–60 billion for zero-emission trains.[24] The spending deal was greeted enthusiastically by the German environmental minister. She commented that: "[n]ever before, has so much of an EU budget been allocated to combating climate change. The commitments to climate action and environmental protection are important and necessary, but the distribution of funds must reflect that."[25]

Some individual European countries also invested heavily in a green recovery. About a third of Germany's $145 billion stimulus plan was directed to public transportation, electric vehicles, and renewable energy.[26] Meanwhile, France invested $8.8 billion in a plan to become the main producer of electric vehicles in Europe.[27] In November 2020, the United Kingdom announced a plan for a "green industrial revolution," with an investment of £12 billion, building on £5 billion committed to a green recovery.[28] Some countries have also imposed conditions on funding. Sweden required Scandinavian Airlines to accelerate its goal of a 25 percent reduction in emissions by five years, whereas the French required a 50 percent emission cut for Air France as a funding condition.[29]

East Asia has seen significant green recovery efforts.[30] China is investing $1.4 billion in charging infrastructure,[31] and possibly much more in other green stimulus funding.[32] Like China, Korea and Singapore are also emphasizing spending on

[24] Kate Abnett, Factbox: Key Climate Spending in EU's 'Green Recovery' Plan, Reuters (May 27, 2020), www.bloomberg.com/news/articles/2020-07-21/eu-approves-biggest-green-stimulus-in-history-with-572-billion-plan. A key part of the plan is the €672 billion Recovery and Resilience Facility, which countries can tap to finance their recovery plans. Thirty-seven percent of the funds must be devoted to climate-related initiatives. Eur. Comm'n, The Recovery and Resilience Facility, https://ec.europa.eu/info/business-economy-euro/recovery-coronavirus/recovery-and-resilience-facility_en. The recovery plan builds on previous EU planning for a "Green Deal." See Sebastiano Sabato & Boris Fronteddu, A Socially Just Transition Through the European Green Deal? (Aug. 2020), www.etui.org/publications/socially-just-transition-through-european-green-deal.

[25] Ewa Krukowska & Laura Millan Lombrana, EU Approves Biggest Green Stimulus in History With $572 Billion Plan, Bloomberg Green (July 21, 2020), www.bloomberg.com/news/articles/2020-07-21/eu-approves-biggest-green-stimulus-in-history-with-572-billion-plan.

[26] Renee Cho, COVID-19's Long-Term Effects on Climate Change – For Better or Worse (June 25, 2020), https://news.climate.columbia.edu/2020/06/25/covid-19-impacts-climate-change/.

[27] Id.

[28] Her Majesty's Gov't, The Ten Point Plan for a Green Industrial Revolution (Nov. 2020), www.gov.uk/government/publications/the-ten-point-plan-for-a-green-industrial-revolution. Given that spending will extend until 2030, it is not clear how much of the funding should be considered "green stimulus," though it is probably no coincidence that the plan was announced during the pandemic.

[29] Yamide Dagnet & Joel Jaeger, Not Enough Climate Action in Stimulus Plans (Sept. 15, 2020), www.wri.org/blog/2020/09/coronavirus-green-economic-recovery/.

[30] Alex Dewar, Raad Alkadiri, Rebecca Fitz & Jamie Webster, How COVID-19 is Changing the Pace of Energy Transitions 2 (Sept. 2020), https://web-assets.bcg.com/4d/1b/1fab91c1439bad272a22a8596952/bcg-how-covid-19-is-changing-the-pace-of-energy-transitions-sep-2020.pdf.

[31] Rhodium Grp., supra note 23, at 7. It can be difficult to separate recovery-related spending from background funding plans, given the general lack of transparency in China. Id.

[32] See Dewar et al., supra note 30, at 5 (estimating $200 billion in Chinese green stimulus measures).

electric vehicles.[33] Climate action also figured in recovery plans elsewhere. Nigeria's stimulus included $620 million for rooftop solar, while Colombia's plan includes $4 billion for zero-carbon energy and transmission.[34] It is possible, however, that the after-effects of the economic recession due to COVID-19, along with the economic dislocations caused by the Ukraine invasion, might impair the financial ability of some countries to address climate change going forward.

In terms of COVID-related spending, $26 billion of the massive US COVID-19 spending program has been devoted to rail transit and mass transit, the only "green" components of the spending plan.[35] Subsequently, Congress passed major legislation with massive spending for infrastructure and climate-related incentives.[36] It is unclear how closely related these projects are to the COVID pandemic, since they are not framed in terms of pandemic response. The precedent of large scale spending set during the pandemic may, however, eased the way politically for this additional legislation.

Even if the direct effects of COVID-19 on emissions turn out to be transitory, a green stimulus may be more durable. Experience from the Great Recession provides at least suggestive evidence of long-term impacts from stimulus funding. On the heels of the 2008 financial crisis, the US Congress enacted a stimulus plan providing $90 billion for renewable energy and energy efficiency.[37] By many accounts, that 10 percent chunk of the stimulus bill changed the trajectory of renewables in America. By 2011, the United States had reached the Energy Information Agency's forecast of US renewable capacity for 2030.[38] Due to the stimulus and other policy initiatives, "U.S. solar electricity generation increased over 30 times from 2008 to 2015, and wind generation has increased over three times."[39] Moreover, the "share of wind turbine equipment manufactured domestically rose from 25 percent in 2006–07 to 72 percent in 2012."[40]

---

[33] Id. at 7–8. For a detailed description of Korea's ambitious plan, see Jae-Hyup Lee & Jisuk Woo, Green New Deal Policy of South Korea: Policy Innovation for a Sustainability Transition, 12 *Sustainability* 10191 (2020), www.mdpi.com/2071-1050/12/23/10191/pdf.

[34] Dagnet & Jaeger, supra note 29.

[35] Rhodium Grp., supra note 23, at 6.

[36] On the new legislation and its effects, see The Rapid Policy Evaluation and Analysis Tool Kit project (REPEAT) at Princeton REPEAT, Preliminary Report: The Climate and Energy Impacts of the Inflation Reduction Act of 2022, at 7 (August 2022); Megan Mahajan, Olivia Ashmoore, Jeffrey Rissman, Robbie Orvis, and Anand Gopal, Modeling The Inflation Reduction Act Using The Energy Policy Simulator (Aug. 2022), https://energyinnovation.org/wp-content/uploads/2022/08/Modeling-the-Inflation-Reduction-Act-with-the-US-Energy-Policy-Simulator_August.pdf.

[37] Shannon Osaka, Obama's Recovery Act Breathed Life into Renewables. Now They Need Rescuing., Grist (June 1, 2020), https://grist.org/energy/obamas-recovery-act-breathed-life-into-renewables-now-they-need-rescuing/.

[38] Id.

[39] Joel Jaeger, Michael Westphal & Corey Park, Lessons Learned on Green Stimulus: Case Studies from the Global Financial Crisis 15 (Nov. 20, 2020), https://wriorg.s3.amazonaws.com/s3fs-public/lessons-learned-on-green-stimulus-case-studies-from-the-global-financial-crisis.pdf.

[40] Id. at 3.

Globally, there is also reason to believe that the green stimulus programs of the Great Recession strengthened national efforts significantly. According to researchers at the World Resource Institute, "[t]he United States, China, and Germany became renewable energy leaders in part because of programs coming out of the Great Recession."[41] Meanwhile, "China's solar PV [photovoltaic] manufacturing capacity increased by a factor of 20 between 2007 and 2011."[42] Proof of causation is difficult given the difficulty of establishing the pathway that these countries would have taken absent the Great Recession. Nevertheless, the evidence is certainly suggestive of a causal link.

The EU and countries such as Korea are leveraging their pandemic recovery efforts to reduce their emissions and strengthen sectors of their economy relating to clean energy. Other countries may have allowed the opportunity to slip by. Still others lacked the resources to undertake green recovery efforts of their own. These heterogeneous responses may widen the gap between the laggards and the leaders in clean technologies and climate action.

Like public health responses to the pandemic, economic recovery efforts implicate national governance systems, as does climate policy. The next section discusses the lessons of the pandemic response for future efforts to control emissions. As it turns out, despite their very different natures, there are strong resemblances between the governance issues exposed by the pandemic and the governance challenges facing climate action.

IV THE PANDEMIC RESPONSE AND CLIMATE GOVERNANCE

What can we learn from COVID-19 about what works and does not work in governance? How will COVID-19 impact future international cooperation?

While the COVID-19 crisis could end up advancing climate action, it has mixed lessons for climate governance. Like the response to climate change, the response to COVID-19 has been loosely coordinated at the international level and often featured bottom-up action by local jurisdictions. As the public health response to COVID-19 demonstrates, policies that require costly behavioral changes are difficult to implement, particularly over longer time periods.

Moreover, populist movements and leaders pose a challenge to global (and sometimes even national) cooperation. To be successful, climate governance will have to learn from the successes and failures of the coronavirus responses.

---

[41] Id.

[42] Id; see also Dewar et al., supra note 30, at 2. For a survey of the available information about green stimulus during the Great Recession and discussion of methodological problems, see Shardul Agrawala, Damien Dussaux & Norbert Monti, What Policies for Greening the Crisis Response and Economic Recovery? Lessons Learned from Past Green Stimulus Measures and Implications for the COVID-19 Crisis 25–28 (May 2020), https://doi.org/10.1787/c50f186f-en. The economic benefits of green stimulus programs seem clear. Id. at 31.

Globally, the direct response to the pandemic has largely taken place at the national or regional level, with international institutions largely playing a supportive role.[43] Some nations responded vigorously to the crisis. In the United States, the Trump Administration did not press for aggressive public health measures in order to avoid burdening the US economy through public health measures.[44] President Trump also withdrew the United States from the World Health Organization (WHO).[45] State governments, to varying extents, implemented their own public health measures.[46] As with climate change, partisan and ideological affiliations are the main determinants of public attitudes toward public health responses to the pandemic.[47]

The picture for climate policy is quite similar. Just as he withdrew the United States from the WHO, President Trump withdrew the country from the Paris Agreement.[48] As in the case of COVID-19, the Trump Administration prioritized the economy over addressing environmental problems.[49] The Trump Administration has also systematically eliminated prior federal efforts to reduce carbon emissions.[50] The lack of any sustained federal effort to address climate change created a policy vacuum.

---

[43] Mary Dobbs, National Governance of Public Health Response in a Pandemic?, 11 *Eur. J. Risk Reg.* 240 (June 2020). Apart from the WHO, international financial institutions such as the International Monetary Fund or regional development banks have also played significant roles. See David Klenert, Franziska Funke, Linus Mattauch & Brian O'Callaghan, Five Lessons from COVID-19 for Advancing Climate Change Mitigation 13 (Aug. 2020), https://pubmed.ncbi.nlm.nih.gov/32836842/.

[44] See Philip Bump, Scott Atlas Will Forever be the Face of Surrender to the Coronavirus, Wash. Post. (Dec. 1, 2020), www.washingtonpost.com/politics/2020/12/01/scott-atlas-will-forever-be-face-surrender-coronavirus/. Atlas is a retired physician who moved from being a health policy analyst at a conservative think tank to being President Trump's closest adviser on the pandemic.

[45] Katie Rogers & Apoorva Mandavilli, Trump Administration Signals Formal Withdrawal From W.H.O., NY Times (Oct. 22, 2020), www.nytimes.com/2020/07/07/us/politics/coronavirus-trump-who.html. For an overview of the role of the WHO and other international institutions in the pandemic context, see Armin von Bogdandy & Pedro Villarreal, International Law on Pandemic Response: A First Stocktaking in Light of the Coronavirus Crisis (Mar. 26, 2020), https://ssrn.com/abstract=3561650.

[46] Kirsten Engel, Climate Federalism in the Time of COVID-19: Can the States "Save" American Climate Policy?, 47 *N. Ky. L. Rev.* 115, 127 (2020). In Brazil, a similar dynamic took place, with individual states taking strong public health measures, despite the opposing view of the populist Bolsonaro regime. See Terrence McCoy, Should a Coronavirus Vaccine Be Mandatory? In Brazil's Most Populous State, It Will Be., Wash. Post (Dec. 7, 2020), www.washingtonpost.com/world/the_americas/virus-mandatory-vaccine-brazil-bolsonaro/2020/12/06/31767b4a-33e5-11eb-8d38-6aea1adb3839_story.html.

[47] Shana Kushner Gadarian, Sara Wallace Goodman & Thomas Pepinsky, Partisanship, Health Behavior, and Policy Attitudes in the Early Stages of the COVID-19 Pandemic (Mar. 27, 2020), https://ssrn.com/abstract=3562796.

[48] Lisa Friedman, U.S. Quits Paris Climate Agreement: Questions and Answers, NY Times (Nov. 4, 2020), www.nytimes.com/2020/11/04/climate/paris-climate-agreement-trump.html. For further discussion of the Paris Agreement, see Daniel A. Farber & Cinnamon P. Carlarne, Climate Change L. 67–72 (2018).

[49] Engel, supra note 45, at 116.

[50] Id. at 119.

As with the pandemic response, climate action in the United States was largely bottom up, with the initiative coming from state and local governments.[51] Unlike public health, where states have historically taken the lead (partly for constitutional reasons), environmental protection has generally been dominated by federal regulation. In a deviation from that pattern, states have addressed climate change on many fronts.[52] They have also been active in promoting renewable energy, sometimes under the climate umbrella and sometimes independently. Many states have adopted renewable portfolio standards mandating that utilities obtain a certain percentage of electricity of the electricity they sell in the state from renewable sources. By forcing utilities to buy renewable energy, these mandates promote the development of more solar and wind energy.[53] There are significant variations in these standards from state to state.[54]

Some states have gone further to reduce the use of fossil fuels by adopting cap and trade schemes. In 2006, Governor Arnold Schwarzenegger signed the California Global Warming Solutions Act, usually referred to as AB 32,[55] which required California to reduce emissions to the 1990 level by 2020. As another important example of state-level action to address climate change, nine eastern states combined to form the Regional Greenhouse Gas Initiative (RGGI, pronounced "Reggie").[56] RGGI created a multistate emissions trading system for power plant emissions with the goal of cutting emissions. This "polycentric" response has been characteristic of climate policy.[57]

Both the efforts to combat climate change and the response to the pandemic have been hindered by the resurgence of populism in many parts of the world. Populist nationalism undermines international cooperation, which is essential for dealing with global threats such as pandemics and climate change. Populism also undermines faith in experts, leading to a willingness to disregard expert views in favor of misinformation. President Trump embodied both aspects of populism, but he was not alone. In Brazil, President Jair Bolsonaro followed a similar path for the coronavirus,[58] as well for climate change.[59] Though neither remain in office, the risks posed by populism continue.

---

[51] Id. at 116–17.

[52] For more about state climate-related policies, see Farber & Carlarne, supra note 47, at 185–89.

[53] Nat'l Renewable Energy Lab., Renewable Portfolio Standards (Mar. 21, 2020), www.nrel.gov/state-local-tribal/basics-portfolio-standards.html.

[54] SB 350 (de León), Chapter 8.5, Statutes of 2015, codified at Cal. Health & Safety Code § 44258.5 *et seq.*

[55] AB 32 (Nuñez), Chapter 488, California Statutes of 2006, codified at Cal. Health & Safety Code § 38500 *et seq.*

[56] See www.rggi.org/.

[57] Klenert et al., supra note 42, at 14.

[58] See Antonia Noori Farzan & Miriam Berger, Bolsonaro Says Brazilians Must not be 'Sissies' about Coronavirus, as 'All of Us Are Going to Die One Day,' Wash. Post. (Nov. 11, 2020), www.washingtonpost.com/world/2020/11/11/bolsonaro-coronavirus-brazil-quotes/.

[59] According to the *Guardian*, "Brazil's foreign minister, Ernesto Araújo, has warned that climate change was a plot by 'cultural Marxists[,]' and President Jair Bolsonaro made a

Underlying the shared governance issues for climate change and the pandemic are psychological and sociopolitical commonalities. Humans can be taken unaware in situations where change is not linear but instead shows dramatic or exponential growth.[60] They can also do poorly with respect to anticipating that their own actions can unintentionally cause great harm.[61] These psychological issues have been amplified by political divisions. Just as they are often more skeptical of vigorous political action to address climate change, those on the political right tended toward delayed responses to the disease, resisted stringent control measures, and were receptive to early termination of control measures.[62] Conservative media have played a significant role in fostering these attitudes, even controlling for the ideology of the audience members.[63] This political divide has been most obvious in the United States, but is echoed elsewhere in the world.[64] Political preferences plus psychological barriers have combined to provide fertile ground for conspiracy theories stoked by Internet misinformation efforts.[65]

Both crises also share a common hope that technological advances may be crucial to long-term solutions, meaning vaccines in the case of COVID-19 and advanced energy technologies in the case of climate change. But technology is not a *deus ex machina* that will save the day on its own. People must be educated about the value of vaccines, and hundreds of millions (ultimately billions) of doses must be distributed and administered. The emergence of variants may require continued advances in vaccine design and renewed efforts by governments to ensure the manufacture and broad distribution of subsequent booster shots. With regards to climate change, coordinated changes must be made in electricity systems along with incentives to abandon existing assets in favor of massive new investments. Thus, government policy will retain a critical role in both crises.

V CONCLUSION

The COVID-19 outbreak has several links with the issue of climate change. The restrictions adopted in many places in response to the coronavirus caused an immediate decline in carbon emissions, although the impact on emissions faded over time. The effect on the transportation system may prove longer lasting, perhaps for

campaign promise to pull Brazil out of the Paris climate accord before reluctantly backing off." Dom Phillips, Resistance to the 'Environmental Sect' is a Cornerstone of Bolsonaro's Rule, Guardian (July 27, 2020), www.theguardian.com/global-development/2020/jul/27/resistance-to-the-environmental-sect-is-a-cornerstone-of-bolsonaro-rule-brazil.

[60] See Klenert et al., supra note 42, at 7.

[61] Id. at 9.

[62] Id. at 14.

[63] See Christopher Avery et al., An Economist's Guide to Epidemiology Models of Infectious Disease, 35 J. Econ. Persp. 79, 99–100 (2020).

[64] Klenert et al., supra note 42, at 14.

[65] Id. at 15–16.

good (in substituting virtual meetings for physical ones) and for bad (in undermining public transit). In some places, green recovery programs may provide a route to accelerating the energy transition, with long-term economic and environmental effects. Thus, the longer-term effects of the pandemic on emissions remain uncertain but are likely to be mixed on balance.

Despite their obvious differences, the pandemic and the climate crisis have encountered similar governance institutions and political trends, and with similar effects. Bottom-up governance has featured heavily in both responses, with nations and subnational jurisdictions playing the leading roles. Efforts to respond to both crises have run into headwinds due to the global upsurges in nationalism and populism, which have frustrated efforts at global cooperation and undermined support for the measures recommended by experts. Unfortunately, there is no solution in sight to the weaknesses in governance systems, which will continue to be a source of frustration. At the same time, we can take some satisfaction from the partial successes which we have been able to achieve, despite the frailties of human nature and the flaws in human governance.

25

Vaccine Tourism, Federalism, Nationalism

I. Glenn Cohen*

I INTRODUCTION

In early January 2021, the news stories started rolling out focused on so-called "vaccine tourism" to the sunny state of Florida. Non-Floridians were getting the coveted Pfizer and Moderna vaccines that were severely limited in supply. There were reports of a "celebrity lawyer from Argentina [who] got the vaccine while she was visiting Florida," and an Argentine television personality whose mother was vaccinated in Miami.[1] Two "India travel agencies ... reportedly market[ed] vaccine travel packages," including roundtrip airfare and "a shot upon arrival" for two thousand dollars.[2] And, closer to home, a travel insurance broker in Canada reported that many of his clients who typically flew south for the winter but had decided to stay put were changing their minds once friends told them they could travel to Miami and get vaccinated, rather than waiting months or longer in Canada.[3]

Government officials in Florida were none too pleased. The mayor of Miami chafed, "[i]t's sort of a slap in the face to this community that is desperately trying to get vaccinated."[4] Florida's governor initially tried to distinguish different kinds of non-Floridians seeking vaccines:

> [I]t is difficult to block non-residents from getting vaccinated because Florida attracts so many snowbirds.
>
> "We're a transient state," DeSantis said Monday during a news conference in Miami. "You'll have people that will be here and it's not like they're just on vacation for two weeks."

---

* I thank Prue Brady for excellent research assistance with this chapter.

[1] Florida Officials Cracking Down on COVID-19 "Vaccine Tourism," CBS (Jan. 21, 2021), www.cbsnews.com/news/florida-covid-vaccine-tourism/?ftag=CNM-00-10aab7e&linkId=109654223.

[2] Id.

[3] Id.

[4] Id.

Still, while it would be difficult to turn away snowbirds, tourists who are "flying by night" are a different matter, DeSantis said. "We're discouraging people who come to Florida just to get a vaccine," he said.[5]

By late January, the state sought to do more than "discourag[e]" those from out of state or out of country from vaccination in Florida; amidst some confusion, the state sought to restrict vaccine access to "those who can prove state residency using a state driver's license or other official documents, such as a deed, rental agreement or utility bill."[6]

Was it right to do so? This chapter analyses the phenomenon of vaccine tourism and seeks to answer that question. Section I situates vaccine tourism in the larger phenomenon of medical tourism and describes what is undesirable about it. Section II seeks to answer the question of when a state should try to prevent international vaccine tourism head-on, arguing that states should adopt a communitarian conception of who qualifies that is tied to the purpose of the good in question. For vaccines, such a conception makes it appropriate for states to prohibit "tourists" from coming to a state such as Florida from abroad for the purpose of getting vaccinated. At the same time, this rationale does not justify excluding undocumented persons or even those who are not permanent residents but who have substantial ties to the community, such as part-time residents. Section III considers objections to the argument and briefly highlights some adjacent issues, such as whether interstate vaccine tourism is different from international vaccine tourism in the ethical analysis. Throughout this chapter, I use the state of Florida in the United States as my "home state" and the United States as my "home country" for ease of exposition, but I mean the arguments I offer to be more generally applicable. One editorial note as I review the proofs in April 2023: this chapter was written during the height of the COVID-19 pandemic. It reflects the facts on the ground as they then stood and captures my thinking while being "in the thick of it." I have resisted the impulse to "Monday morning quarterback," that is, to go back and change parts of it to reflect what actually transpired after I wrote it.

---

[5] Jane Musgrave & John Pacenti, COVID-19 Vaccine Tourism? Florida Could Be Hot Spot as Governor Discourages Outsiders, USA Today (Jan. 12, 2021), www.usatoday.com/story/travel/news/2021/01/12/covid-vaccine-tourism-florida-discourages-outsiders-seeking-shot/6626445002/.

[6] Megan Reeves & Allison Ross, Florida Limits Coronavirus Vaccines to Permanent, Seasonal Residents, Tampa Bay Times (Jan. 21, 2021), www.tampabay.com/news/health/2021/01/21/is-florida-vaccinating-non-residents-or-not-its-hard-to-get-an-answer/. For its part, the Centers for Disease Control and Prevention (CDC) COVID-19 Vaccine Task Force took different positions as supply changed. As it describes its position, "when there were limited supplies of COVID-19 vaccine available, [the] CDC allowed states to limit COVID-19 vaccination to residents and others temporarily living in the state to assure that all such individuals would have the opportunity for timely vaccination." CDC, COVID-19 Vaccine Task Force Position on Citizenship and Residency, www.cdc.gov/vaccines/covid-19/citizenship-residency-position.html (last updated Oct. 21, 2021). By contrast, its later position was: "Now that COVID-19 vaccine supply availability has increased, there is no longer a public health rationale for excluding individuals who are not residents of a state or locality from being vaccinated in another state or locality. Therefore, residents and others who live in any state or locality should be allowed to get vaccinated in any state." Id.

II WHAT IS WORRISOME ABOUT VACCINE TOURISM?

"Vaccine tourism" might be thought of as a subspecies of "medical tourism" or "medical travel." As defined in my prior work, it involves patients traveling from one country (the home country) to another country (the destination country) for treatment.[7] Vaccine tourism resembles most forms of medical tourism that involve "queue jumping," such as a Canadian patient in need of a hip replacement traveling to a US state and paying for it out of pocket, rather than waiting for her turn on her home province's wait list.[8]

Vaccine tourism shares three ethically worrisome aspects with that queue jumping example. First, there is a concern that only those who are sophisticated, able-bodied, and wealthy enough to travel can take advantage of this opportunity. In the case of COVID-19, there is no reason to think that the "vaccine tourism eligible" population matches the populations that we might be most inclined to prioritize for vaccination – those who are at higher risk by virtue of health status, community spread, or workplace exposure. There is an additional wrinkle in that there is considerable moral luck in the question of what the ordinary visa regime means for the ability of an individual of a particular country to travel to the United States or another country.

This complication is further highlighted in the early period of the COVID-19 pandemic given the additional extraordinary restrictions on travel between certain countries.

Second, depending on the availability of the COVID-19 vaccine in the destination country, non-citizens and non-residents who queue jump may displace (and thus delay) access for citizens and residents. Importantly, even when COVID-19 vaccine access at some point becomes plentiful in a country such as the United States, vaccine tourism may still foster a problematic displacement of priority: in this case, the doses that are taken by vaccine tourists are ones that might otherwise be donated to the hardest-hit countries, either directly or through programs such as the COVID-19 Vaccines Global Access Facility.[9]

Finally, as with other forms of medical tourism, there is a risk to the patient of being infected with COVID-19 as part of the travel process and a corresponding worry that that patient will infect others. The documented cases of multi-drug

---

[7] I. Glenn Cohen, Patients with Passports (2014).

[8] Id. This is in contrast to "circumvention tourism" involving travel for a service illegal in a patient's home country (e.g., abortion, aid in dying) or travel for services illegal in both the patient's home and destination country (e.g., travel to purchase a kidney for transplant). Id.

[9] Of course, there is no guarantee that a country such as the United States will donate such "excess" doses. Many high-income countries, such as the United States and Canada, have made plans to stockpile more doses than they will use. If the choice is between a particular dose adding to a stockpile versus being used for a vaccine tourist, the latter seems less objectionable, even if less ethically good than the alternative of donation to a low-income country.

resistant bacterial infection spreading via medical travel serve as a precursor to some of what we face in COVID-19 air travel.[10]

All that said, in policy design one always wants to make sure that the cure is not worse than the disease. In thinking about how to discourage or prohibit vaccine tourism for any of the categories discussed in the following section, we want to make sure that the techniques employed do not end up shutting out vulnerable communities. In particular, one might be concerned that overly rigorous requirements for residency documentation might intimidate undocumented persons or those who already feel profiled by the state, preventing them from seeking out vaccination. This is a hard thing to measure, especially ex ante, but one should treat this as a background consideration in policy design related to administrability above and beyond questions of entitlement, to which I turn next.

III WHO IS ENTITLED TO A HOME COUNTRY'S VACCINE DOSES?

Given all this, is a state such as Florida (or a country as a whole) justified in adopting legal means to deny vaccine access to vaccine tourists?

My answer is a qualified yes. It is qualified because we need to be careful to distinguish a spectrum of potential vaccine tourists. As to international vaccine tourism, one might conceptualize a spectrum that includes:

Non-citizen/non-resident on a temporary stay: This would include, for example, an Argentine citizen/resident who travels to Florida for the purpose of getting vaccinated and leaves shortly thereafter.

Non-citizen/part-time resident: This would include, for example, the Canadian "snowbird" who travels to Florida under established immigration channels every year for part of the year and resides in that community.

Non-citizen/full-time resident: This category itself contains a spectrum of kinds of relationships with the United States. At one end are permanent aliens who have not (or not yet) applied for US citizenship: for example, a Brazilian citizen with a US green card residing in Florida. Somewhere in the middle of the spectrum is someone with an immigration status which allows them to live in the United States but explicitly does not permit them to transition to citizenship, a temporary status such as a Canadian citizen working in the United States on a TN visa. Then there are individuals who are undocumented workers, non-citizens who as a legal matter have no entitlement to work or live in the country but may have built long-standing ties (indeed, familial connections in some cases) in the country: for example, a Haitian worker in Florida without lawful citizenship or residency in the United States who works and lives with her family in the state.

Citizen/non-resident: This would include, for example, a US citizen who has lived in Bolivia for the last ten years and flies to Florida for a vaccination.

---

[10] Cohen, supra note 7, at 48–50.

Citizen/resident: This would include, for example, a US citizen who resides in Florida.

Who in this spectrum has an entitlement to be vaccinated in the United States?

When laid out in this way, one can see three possible principles as to who should be entitled to vaccines distributed by a home country government (in this instance, I will continue to use the United States as my example).[11] First, *territoriality*: anyone who finds themselves in the United States territory, as a geographical matter, is entitled to a vaccine. Second, *citizenship*: anyone who is a citizen of the United States is entitled to a vaccine. Third, *communitarian*: anyone who is a member of the community in the relevant sense is entitled to a vaccine.

These principles could be individually sufficient (e.g., if citizenship is individually sufficient then both the citizen/resident and the citizen/non-resident are entitled to vaccination), or individually necessary (e.g., if citizenship is a necessary condition then all non-citizens must be excluded, even those who reside in the country). Multiple conditions could also be jointly sufficient or jointly necessary. To make things more complicated, while I have framed it as a matter of "entitlement" – an on/off switch – one could have a more nuanced account of priority setting where one who, for example, satisfies all three conditions has priority over someone who satisfies only a particular two, and so on.

All this shows how complex the picture of moral claims to vaccination is. I do not aim to offer a full theory in these few pages, but I do want to use this theorizing to explain why I think citizen/residents, non-citizen/full-time residents, and most (if not all) non-citizen/part-time residents, but not non-citizen/non-residents on a temporary stay, are entitled to vaccines supplied by the US government.

One way of putting this in terms of the theories developed so far is that I would reject a strong version of the territoriality principle in favor of a communitarian principle. Although it is not my focus, I also think there is a strong argument in favor of the citizenship principle, which would also justify vaccine access to US citizens living abroad, in addition to whomever the communitarian principle picks out as entitled to vaccine doses from the United States.

Before I delve into the communitarian approach, I want to raise one assumption of the argument I offer – that the United States is entitled to the doses it has purchased through advance purchase agreements, that these "belong" to the United States to distribute in a way that achieves its goals. While I think most people have assumed that this premise is true, it is not self-evidently true. One could, for example, think that all vaccine doses should be viewed as common global property and allocated by need or some other framework of distribution. For the purposes of this chapter, I am going to just assume that the United States has a claim over the doses it has purchased, if only because I think any other arrangement would be politically

---

[11] More accurately, perhaps three "intuitive" or "plausible" principles – one could certainly imagine many more.

impossible to imagine in our current moment. Readers who think this arrangement is unjust can take what follows as an argument operating in the sphere of "non-ideal justice," or a second (or fifteenth!) best solution.[12]

A Developing the Communitarian Approach Based on the Nature of the Good

The communitarian principle is that anyone who is a member of the community in the relevant sense is entitled to a vaccine. Now we have to unpack what it means to be a member of the community "in the relevant sense" for generating a claim to a US vaccine. Here it might be useful to start with an argument I offered in a 2014 article in which I analyzed a question somewhat similar to vaccine entitlement: Should non-resident/non-citizens (i.e., a French citizen who lives in Paris) be morally entitled to be waitlisted for US organs?[13] One of the difficult parts of that argument required justifying why a non-citizen/non-resident was not entitled to be waitlisted but an undocumented person living in the United States did have such an entitlement. I justified that on a particular communitarian conception relating to reciprocity:

> [T]he key reciprocity is *not* between organ donation and receiving … but instead is between investment in the infrastructure of organ procurement and allocation and shared decision-making as organs *vel non*. It is this reciprocity that US citizen-residents share but that foreigners ordinarily lack, and thus this form of reciprocity justifies US citizen-residents' priority, at least in the case of equally matched foreigners and US citizen-residents.
>
> One interesting implication of this approach is that the strength of the argument varies with the amount that the home country's citizen-residents (as against foreigners) have invested in or contributed to their country's organ procurement and allocation system. Undocumented immigrants frequently pay into the US system through social security and other tax resources from which they do not draw, such that we can say that they in fact meet the investment prerequisites. Further, the OPTN [the Organ Procurement and Transplantation Network, the main organization setting policy for organ procurement and distribution in the U.S.] suggests that they frequently "pay in" more directly through organ donation. Second, the continued presence of undocumented aliens as residents in the United States, both with families and as part of communities, complicates our moral relation to them in a way that is not true in the case of true foreigner.[14]

But, as with most approaches to just distribution, our analysis of what is just must be closely tailored to the good in question. Human organs eligible for transplant,

---

[12] Example, John Rawls, A Theory Of Justice § 39, at 244–46 (1971).
[13] I. Glenn Cohen, Organs Without Borders? Allocating Transplant Organs, Foreigners, and the Importance of the Nation-State (?), 77 *Law Contemp. Probs.* 175 (2014).
[14] Id. at 197–205.

say a kidney, are *not* collectively owned – most people do not think you have a rights claim to my kidney by virtue of being a fellow citizen or fellow resident of the same country.[15] The kidney belongs to me, not the United States. That is the reason why the argument for a preference for US residents for organs procured in the United States requires a more roundabout argument about common investment in the system of procurement and distribution by members of the community.

In the case of vaccine doses that are in the possession of the US government, by contrast, these doses really do, in some sense, belong to the United States *qua* national government. They were purchased by the US government,[16] purchases that were funded by US taxpayers. Those taxpayers include citizen/residents and many non-citizen/full-time residents. They do not include non-citizen/non-residents.[17] Whether or not part-time residents qualify as taxpayers may depend on their immigration status, tax treaties between the United States and their country of citizenship, and the amount of time they spend in the United States.

---

[15] But see Cécile Fabre, Whose Body Is It Anyway? 72–123 (2006) (offering some provocative arguments to the contrary).

[16] What should we make of the fact that the vaccine doses were also the result of US investment in their development? It would be tempting to tether the argument to the multi-billion dollar investment by the United States in COVID-19 vaccine clinical trials, production scale-up, procurement, and delivery as part of Operation Warp Speed. But this might generate some unusual implications. First, while it would offer a hook for Moderna and Johnson & Johnson vaccines, Pfizer did not accept funding from the program. Example, Assistant Secretary for Public Affairs, Health & Hum. Servs., Fact Sheet: Explaining Operation Warp Speed (Jan. 21, 2021), www.hhs.gov/coronavirus/explaining-operation-warp-speed/index.html [https://perma.cc/U5DF-FF9R]. That would seem to suggest one set of entitlements and priorities for one vaccine but not the others. Second, it would seem to suggest that to determine if a particular non-US citizen/non-US resident had an entitlement claim to a particular vaccine, we would need to determine what investment his or her home country had made to its development such that we might draw distinctions between different home countries in terms of who could justifiably travel to the United States for vaccine tourism. Neither of these implications doom the argument, but they do make it less appealing.

One might also worry that the argument would generate obvious distributional effects between wealthier countries who invested in development and poorer ones who did not. But, of course, similar distributional effects follow from allowing the United States to prefer its own citizens for vaccinations because it was able to make advance purchasing agreements at prices that Liberia, for example, was not. Thus, this seems to me a strong argument against allowing claim rights for investment-to-innovate only if one was also prepared to make the stronger argument that the United States is not justified in prioritizing its citizen-residents for the doses it actually purchased. This relates back to the assumption I introduced earlier.

[17] Indeed, undocumented immigrants frequently pay into the US tax system through Social Security and other tax resources from which they do not draw. Example, Henry Ordower, Taxing Others in the Age of Trump: Foreigners (and the Politically Weak) as Tax Subjects, 62 *St. Louis U. L.J.* 157, 171 (2017). Is it possible that there are some undocumented persons who do not pay taxes? Perhaps, though if we broaden the scope to include things such as sales tax, it becomes increasingly unlikely. Moreover, there are also citizens who do not pay taxes – lawfully or otherwise – but we do not, for example, restrict them from sending their children to public schools or other taxpayer-funded benefits. This seems no different. In any event, even if this communitarian principle was understood to exclude them, the second one I discuss will bring them back in.

There is a second communitarian pathway worth exploring. This goes more directly to the nature of the good and is, if anything, more straightforward. Why is vaccination sought? To protect oneself and to protect the community in one which lives – be it very small (one's family), larger (one's workplace), or larger still (everyone one encounters within a few feet indoors). If this is the "purpose of the good," to sound somewhat Aristotelian, then the criterion for distribution should follow from it. Those who live in a particular community have a reciprocal relationship of a sort – the capacity to put others at risk of COVID-19 infection and the capacity to be put at risk by the COVID-19 infections of others. This remains just as true whether one is a citizen/resident or an undocumented person.

B *How to Treat Part-Time Residents?*

How does this criterion of distribution apply to the non-citizen/part-time resident? It seems to me that their entitlement claim scales up in proportion to their comparative risk of infecting or being infected by others in the community. Someone who lives in Florida for six months of the pandemic but then goes home is at substantial risk of being infected or infecting others in Florida during those six months. It would make sense from a public health/purpose of the good perspective to give them an entitlement to the vaccine during their period of Florida residency.

Now, perhaps one might agree that the part-time resident has an entitlement to the vaccine (or, to put this perhaps better, it would not be unjust to provide them a dose) but suggest that they ought to be of lower priority than the citizen/full-time resident, or even the non-citizen/full-time resident. To put this practically, a state such as Florida might roll out its vaccine in waves that put the part-time resident behind similarly situated full-time residents. One way of thinking about this is through a kind of "expected value" analysis tied to the purpose of the good. If the purpose of vaccinating Floridians is to prevent people in Florida from being infected or infecting others and allow the reopening in Florida, then vaccinating a four-month, part-time resident might generate a reduced advance toward that goal in contrast to vaccinating a full-time resident.[18]

As a back-of-the-envelope metric, that may sound plausible, but as we delve deeper into modeling this, I suspect it would show that things are actually considerably more complicated. For example, if we look back at the COVID-19 data, we would likely find that the difference in "expected value" for vaccinating the part-time versus the full-time resident depends on when in the various waves of the virus

---

[18] If part of the goal of COVID-19 vaccination is to enable the return of the workforce, one might make a similar point that part-time residents are much less likely to be full-time workers in the state. Moreover, one might suggest that for full-time residents the benefit of the vaccination is carried forward for an indefinite time since residency in the state is for an indefinite time, whereas the part-time visitor may never come back. This might be used to develop more subtle forms of prioritization, but I suspect that adding the extra complexity may not be worth it.

we were discussing, where the part-time versus full-time residents lived (including where they fall on the social vulnerability index compared to full-time residents), their ages and health statuses, as compared to full-time residents, etc. I suspect we would find as much within-group variability amongst part-time residents as one would between part- and full-time residents, if not more. At the very least, as a matter of principled policy-setting, we ought to demand consistency. That is, if a state favored reduced priority for the part-time resident *for this reason*, then it should also apply the same reasoning *within* its full-time resident population and give more priority based on a similar expected value analysis. Perhaps we can characterize some of the decisions that states made regarding priority for the elderly and health care workers in this way.

At some point, though, I think we will reach a place familiar to the law of asking about what has been called "administrability" or "formal realizability" concerns, where the difficulty of administering a rule might matter as much as its fairness.[19] That is, even if sub-rules that parse the part-time resident community would be more ethically justifiable, at some point the benefits are outweighed by the complexity of the undertaking and the game is no longer worth a candle. Perhaps this point is particularly salient in the COVID-19 vaccine context when we remember how huge an undertaking it was to begin rolling out the vaccine and the goal of doing so as quickly as possible.

Where has all this landed? I have argued that when a state such as Florida decides to whom it should make COVID-19 vaccines available, it certainly should make them available to full-time US citizens who are residents of Florida, as well as full-time non-citizen residents of Florida. I think there is a strong argument for also extending it to part-time residents of Florida so long as they substantially meet the communitarian principle for which I have argued: having the reciprocal capacity to put others at risk of COVID-19 infection and the capacity to be put at risk by the COVID-19 infections of others.[20]

By the same token, a state such as Florida should reject providing the vaccine to those who visit for a temporary stay, the true vaccine tourists. Why? First, providing them vaccines incentivizes this kind of travel, which is problematic for all the reasons with which I began.

Second, non-citizen/non-residents who are temporary visitors have no strong claims on the communitarian or citizenship theories of entitlement I have sketched out; all they can offer is territoriality as a basis for their claim. But the nature of this good is such that mere temporary presence in the territory does not generate a strong claim to the good. To be fair, it is true that even on that temporary visit one might

---

[19] Example, Duncan Kennedy, Form and Substance in Private Law Adjudication, 89 *Harv. L. Rev.* 1685, 1688 (1976); J. M. Balkin, The Crystalline Structure of Legal Thought, 39 *Rutgers L. Rev.* 1, 43 (1986).

[20] But, as I suggested earlier, it may be justifiable to give such individuals less priority in proportion to how much they are a part of the community in a relevant sense. This strikes me as a place where things are less clear.

put others at risk of infection or be put at risk of infection, but the surest way to guard against that risk is not to encourage travel for the purpose of getting vaccines. Further, while in some sense non-citizen/non-residents who are temporary visitors are extremely temporary members of the community, lines must be drawn and this one does not seem that hard as an exclusionary one.[21]

IV SOME OBJECTIONS AND LAST THOUGHTS

Having now set up the basic structure of the argument, I want to consider a few objections. The first objection is one I addressed earlier – that the starting assumption that any vaccine doses belong to a home country is problematic from a global justice perspective.

A second objection is that vaccine tourism plays an important role in bringing money back to hard-hit communities. That is, attracting vaccine tourists from abroad will fill hotel rooms, restaurants, and planes in a way that helps hard-hit communities. I have several responses. First, it is far from clear to me that the descriptive claim is correct: It may depend on how many places are offering doses to outsiders and how they compete. For example, many vaccine tourists might flock to flight hubs such as New York or Los Angeles, rather than Fairbanks, Alaska, such that the expected gain to the Fairbanks community never arises. Second, even if the gain were real, I think some might argue from the "purpose of the good" that this justification – bringing in money for hard-hit communities – is nevertheless not permissible. Vaccine doses are not, the argument goes, general purpose goods to make people's lives go better but instead have a particular function – preventing infection – that guides their distribution. This can be connected to a bioethics literature on "indirect" versus "direct" benefits and "separate spheres": Some argue that in decisions about allocation, the further away one gets from the purpose of the good in how it provides benefits, the less justified we are in counting that benefit in deciding allocation priority.[22]

The easiest way to illustrate this would be to imagine another allocation scheme that the state of Alaska could adopt which might be even better at creating income to be given to the poorest people in the state: auctioning off doses to the highest

---

[21] One might find an echo of this question in, of all places, the constitutional law of personal jurisdiction in US civil procedure. In Burnham v. Superior Court, 495 US 604 (1990), Justice Brennan and Justice Scalia famously dueled on whether mere presence in a state with service of process was enough as a basis for personal jurisdiction (Scalia's view) versus the idea that even in such a brief visit, the individual had formed enough connection with the state to have purposefully availed himself enough of its protection, thereby justifying personal jurisdiction (Brennan's view).

[22] See, for example, Dan W. Brock, Separate Spheres and Indirect Benefits, Cost Effectiveness & Res. Allocation [pincite] (2003), https://resource-allocation.biomedcentral.com/track/pdf/10.1186/1478-7547-1-4.pdf; Frances M. Kamm, Morality, Mortality: Death and Whom to Save from It 107–15 (1993). For my own thoughts on this debate, see I. Glenn Cohen, Rationing Legal Services, 5 J. L. Anal. 221, 275–82 (2013).

bidders from outside the states. If that would be impermissible, the argument goes, why is deliberately attracting vaccine tourists to bring in money for hard-hit communities any better? When to count indirect benefits requires swimming in choppy philosophical waters, but the easiest lifesaver one can throw is to say whether it is all-things-considered *ethically* permissible. When the allocator (the US government) shares vaccine doses, surely enabling the state to make money is not the allocators' criteria for distribution – it distributes doses based on population size, not the degree to which a state is economically depressed. There may be other forms of allocation of federal funds that are meant for this latter problem, but vaccine doses are not such an allocation. It would be as though a friend lent you his or her car to take your mother to the hospital and you instead used it to make money off Uber rides. That would be impermissible because the car (or vaccine doses) was given for one purpose but you are using it for something very different. This is all the more so when, as with vaccine doses, there are multiple rival claimants, instead of a car that is merely sitting idle.

One final point before I close: Does the argument look different when we are discussing interstate medical tourism within a country (say travelers from New York to Florida) as opposed to people coming from abroad? A little. The communitarian arguments for excluding temporary visitors to the state persist in the interstate case, but are admittedly a bit weaker. Why weaker?

The New Yorker's tax dollars have gone to support the purchase of the vaccine doses just as much as the Floridian's, so that is not distinguishing. And while it is true that only the Floridian has the reciprocal relationship of putting others at risk and being put at risk of infection *in Florida*, we might go up a level of generality and say both have the same reciprocal relationship as to infection *in the United States* as a whole, which begs the question of why Florida and not the United States is the right level of analysis.

There is an answer but it is a little less satisfying – that is, that the United States decided to allocate doses to individual states initially based on population per capita above the age of eighteen.[23] It follows from that decision that any time New Yorkers take doses in Florida, that is one less dose of the share Florida was allocated for Floridians. At the extreme, imagine if the entire population of New York City were to arrive in Miami and claim doses. That would mean that New Yorkers had received more than they were entitled to and Floridians less. That would frustrate the logic of allocation the federal government settled on, as well as bring with it the risk of infection spread discussed earlier. It might also stymie attempts to key the reopening of a state to vaccination metrics. If that feels a little less satisfying as a reason, it is because the initial choice to distribute by state by population feels like

---

[23] Example, Lisa Simunaci, US Dep't of Def., *Pro Rata Vaccine Distribution is Fair, Equitable* (Dec. 11, 2020), www.defense.gov/News/News-Stories/Article/Article/2441698/pro-rata-vaccine-distribution-is-fair-equitable/.

more of an artifact of the need to quickly administer these vaccines rather than the result of a deeper moral reason connected to entitlement. One could have imagined rolling out the vaccine across the United States by population age, for example, irrespective of state.

This points to a bigger truth: The opportunity for interstate medical tourism is itself the result of vaccine federalism, or, more accurately, federalism in the way in which allocation criteria were set. Individual states got to decide whether and for how long to prioritize certain age bands, essential workers, and so on. Those differences inevitably provided incentives for interstate medical travel. This could have been avoided – the federal government could have done more to set uniform allocation policy (compare, for example, the allocation of organs to transplant where there are national rules rather than individual states setting their own policies). Perhaps in future planning, the decision to allocate doses to individual states initially based on population per capita above the age of eighteen is worth revisiting.

Epilogue: COVID-19 in the Courts

Abbe R. Gluck and Jacob Hutt[*]

I INTRODUCTION

Most accounts of the law's intersection with a major public policy issue have litigation at least in the background. COVID-19 is no exception. Many chapters in this book detail policy areas – from prison health, to access to reproductive care, to worker safety, and more – in which litigation over aspects of the pandemic response played a major role. Other areas that were prominent in courthouses, although not as detailed in the foregoing pages, include election law, free exercise of religion, and the defining of services, including gun shops, as essential or not for purposes of preventing or ensuring access during the emergency. For many of these fields, the litigation shined a salutary light on systemic problems that preexisted COVID-19 but that COVID-19 made impossible to continue to ignore.

Yet the legacy of the COVID-19 litigation transcends its already significant impact on the many specific areas that COVID-19 touched. Most broadly, the arc of COVID-19 litigation is a story about the relationship among individual rights, courts, and governments. COVID-19 brought with it an initial period of judicial deference to expert leaders who curtailed individual liberties to deal with an unprecedented emergency. But later, the pandemic litigation ushered in a decline in deference that not only reversed many government actions, but also has outlasted and ties into mounting conversative opposition to the modern regulatory state. Courts grappled with deference both to state governments, and the temporary restrictions they imposed on individual liberty, and to major federal executive actions, taken under broad – but sometimes antiquated – statutory authorities.

The individual rights story begins with *Jacobson v. Massachusetts*,[1] a century-old Supreme Court precedent counseling deference to the state and its expertise in the name of public health. It continues, at least thus far, with religious liberty as

---

[*] In 2021, Abbe Gluck served as Special Counsel to the President, as the lead lawyer for the White House COVID-19 Response Team. This chapter was written after her government service concluded, and all views here are her own.
[1] 197 U.S. 11 (1905).

a particularly ascendent right coming out of the pandemic litigation, with other rights, such as those of the incarcerated, receiving new and needed attention, but ultimately not prevailing.

As Lindsay Wiley details in her chapter, courts engaged intensely with the interplay of the *Jacobson* precedent and our modern civil rights jurisprudence, including with certain individual rights that have received special protection in recent decades, such as reproductive rights, Second Amendment rights concerning guns, and free exercise of religion. In the face of challenges involving religious gatherings in particular, *Jacobson* appeared to be teetering on the brink of extinction, a development that rang alarm bells for public health experts, who chronicled the risk to more than a century's worth of judicial deference to the judgment of scientific experts on matters ranging from sanitation to compulsory vaccination.

But just as the *Jacobson* wars were coming to a climax, the overarching litigation narrative of the pandemic shifted. The Biden Administration followed through on its promise to take more direct control over the pandemic than had its predecessor, and its executive actions offered bigger litigation targets. Suddenly, the fight was no longer about *Jacobson*. Instead, it became a struggle between an increasingly textualist, anti-deferential judiciary and long-standing regulatory authorities such as the Centers for Disease Control and Prevention (CDC) statute and the Occupational Safety and Health (OSH) Act – enacted in 1944 and 1970, respectively. As the litigation wore on, many courts gave unduly cramped readings to these public health acts, seeking specificity from laws that were instead broadly drafted to be nimble in unforeseeable circumstances.

If anything, the pandemic has illustrated the unpredictability of public health emergencies and the need for broad statutory authorities that are flexible enough to address the next crisis.

The OSH Act, for example, provides the Occupational Safety and Health Administration (OSHA) with exceedingly broad authority; yet the courts became dissatisfied with broad authorities and instead sought specific and detailed delegations. It is historically significant that President Biden's pandemic orders coincided with a conservative movement already underway to curtail the reach of federal executive power. Fueled largely by Justice Neil Gorsuch's discomfort with congressional delegations to administrative agencies, the Supreme Court used the COVID-19 cases as an opportunity to entrench a mostly-dormant legal doctrine that curtails deference to administrative actions on questions of major economic, policy, or political significance without a clear statutory authorization for that precise action from Congress.

This doctrine, called "the major questions doctrine," had been utilized only a handful of times before COVID-19 since it was first introduced by Justice Antonin Scalia in 1994.[2] In 2021, however, the Court used it to vacate a stay of a ruling

---

[2]　MCI Telecomms. Corp. v. Am. Tel. & Tel. Co., 512 U.S. 218, 231 (1994).

invalidating a CDC COVID-19 order delaying evictions and then returned to the doctrine much more provocatively to stay President Biden's "vaccine or test" rule, which was promulgated under the generous authorities of the OSH Act. Other similar COVID-19 cases followed. Later the same term, the Court applied the doctrine in an important environmental case, making clear it was here to stay and was not just for COVID-19.[3] The ascendance of the major questions doctrine may be one of COVID-19's most important legal legacies and the one with the biggest implications for the future of the modern administrative state.

From a jurisprudential standpoint, what is interesting is that the Court made these significant doctrinal moves largely through statutory, rather than constitutional, law. The big displacements were not opinions holding that Congress did not have the authority to impose an immunization requirement (and the Court in fact upheld some more limited requirements, as detailed later), but rather that the President and his agencies did not have that authority in some areas because Congress had not specifically enumerated it. Some view these judicial efforts as just a first step toward what might be a more seismic shift in the constitutional law of delegation. But, at the moment, and thus in contrast to the early, *Jacobson*-heavy cases of the pandemic, the focus has been on congressional authorization and administrative authorities, and not on individual rights.

As such, the litigation arc went from individual to governmental; from constitutional to regulatory; from deferential to restraining. Perhaps that arc was inevitable given the unprecedented duration of the emergency; perhaps that arc was also especially likely given that government responses to the pandemic morphed over time as governments moved from early tools such as individual lockdowns to later tools such as population immunization.

The final point to make about this litigation arc is that it was unusually *fast*. Almost none of the Court's major COVID-19 cases arrived on the ordinary procedural path, in which cases typically take years to be fully litigated in the lower courts before they arrive for Supreme Court review. Instead, the COVID-19 era also marked the ascendance of the so-called "shadow docket," through which the Court gives expedited review to an issue that is presented not on the merits, but as an application for emergency relief (often after an injunction is issued by a lower court). Unlike a typical Supreme Court case, cases presented via the shadow docket usually do not have full merits briefing, oral arguments, or a final decision from the courts below. Decisions are often issued without a signed opinion.

During the 2020 term, the Supreme Court considered sixty-six cases on the shadow docket, more than half of which concerned disputes in which COVID-19 played a central role,[4] compared to seventy-nine cases decided with full briefing

---

3 West Virginia v. EPA, 142 S. Ct. 2587 (2022).

4 This count includes cases that began as applications for emergency relief that after referral to the full Court were treated as petitions for writ of certiorari, granted, and vacated.

and on the merits that term, just two of which substantially related to COVID-19.[5] For so many momentous legal decisions to come through this procedural shortcut, rather than with the benefit of full deliberation, was – like so many other aspects of COVID-19 – unprecedented.

II LOCKDOWNS, ACCESS TO ESSENTIAL SERVICES, AND INDIVIDUAL RIGHTS

Individual rights cases involving lockdowns and the suspension of gatherings and business operations were the paradigm cases that dominated court dockets from March 2020 until the middle of 2021. Legal claims were largely constitutional or state-law based, meaning they typically involved alleged infringements on individual liberties, such as the First Amendment or the right to bear arms, by state or local action taken in the name of the public health emergency. Governments were largely victorious in the first six months or so. Courts deferred to emergency authorities under the century-old Supreme Court precedent *Jacobson v. Massachusetts*, as discussed in Wiley's chapter, or sometimes under statutes passed by state legislatures.

As the months passed, however, some courts grew less deferential to emergency measures, despite the fact that the *Jacobson* case itself, which concerned a small-pox vaccination requirement, was grounded in long-term public health concerns, not any temporally limited state of emergency. Some of that judicial frustration produced opinions that articulated individual liberties in new ways or at least reconciled *Jacobson* with modern liberties jurisprudence in ways less accommodating of government authority than they had before.

In the context of reproductive care, for example, early cases challenged the categorization of abortion as an elective surgical procedure that hospitals could suspend along with other procedures. Brought before the Supreme Court's 2022 ruling striking down *Roe v. Wade*, cases saw states invoking *Jacobson* as a trump card to *Roe* and its progeny. But courts generally ruled instead for plaintiffs during this early period, recognizing the importance of *Jacobson* deference but holding that, even under *Jacobson*'s own framework, deference likely could not permanently displace access to a fundamental right when the public health benefit was relatively limited.[6]

Litigation also ensued to compel the Food and Drug Administration (FDA) to lift in-person dispensing requirements for mifepristone, one of two pills required

---

[5] October Term 2020, SCOTUSblog, www.scotusblog.com/case-files/terms/ot2020; Kalvis Golde, In Barrett's First Term, Conservative Majority is Dominant but Divided, SCOTUSblog (July 2, 2021), www.scotusblog.com/2021/07/in-barretts-first-term-conservative-majority-is-dominant-but-divided; Stephen I. Vladeck, The Shadow Docket: How the Supreme Court Uses Stealth Rulings to Amass Power and Undermine the Republic (2023). Our count lists consolidated challenges as separate unconsolidated cases to present a more relevant comparison to the shadow docket.

[6] See, for example, Adams & Boyle, P.C. v. Slatery, 956 F.3d 913 (6th Cir. 2020); Robinson v. Att'y Gen., 957 F.3d 1171 (11th Cir. 2020).

for a medication abortion. A federal court granted a preliminary injunction, halting the in-person requirements, but the Supreme Court in early 2021 stayed the injunction by a 6–3 vote.[7] Later that year, the FDA eventually lifted those requirements itself, citing in part, as evidence of mifepristone's safety, data from the period the injunction was in effect. Litigation over mifepristone and its dispensing requirements remains ongoing as this book goes to press.

The cross-pressure between modern rights-based claims and *Jacobson* escalated with guns. Early in the pandemic, firearms retailers generally lost cases challenging their closures as non-essential businesses. In cases from New York and California, for example, the courts held that *Jacobson* was still controlling and focused on the temporary nature of the closures, their neutrality across all kinds of businesses, and the relationship of closures to the public health goals the state governments were trying to achieve.[8] But later the tone started to change. In one California case, the district court early in the pandemic had upheld, under *Jacobson*, a challenged restriction on all gun and ammunition shops and firing ranges. Two years later, however, the Ninth Circuit found *Jacobson* "inapplicable" to rights to which the Supreme Court in "the intervening century since *Jacobson*, … [has] determined that some level of heightened scrutiny applies."[9] The notion that *Jacobson* might not apply *at all* when a right entitled to heightened scrutiny is implicated was novel; it also appeared in the religion cases, as detailed later in this section.

One area that has not seen significant modern heightened rights development is the prison context, specifically the Eighth Amendment and the statutory rights of the incarcerated to be protected from "deliberate indifference" to their health or safety. As such, perhaps it is no surprise that governments were more successful in deflecting lawsuits demanding social distancing, dedensification, and other health measures in prisons. Courts tended to defer to prison officials when there was any evidence that officials had taken some actions to address the pandemic, even where those actions were not the kinds of measures that incarcerated individuals and health experts demanded.

For example, in *Valentine v. Collier*,[10] the federal appellate court in Texas, the Fifth Circuit, halted an injunction imposed by a lower federal court that required prisons to take certain public health measures to curb the spread of COVID-19. The appeals court found that the prison officials' actions had been reasonable because they had instituted a policy requiring masks and social distancing and had some

---

[7] FDA v. Am. Coll. of Obstetricians & Gynecologists, 141 S. Ct. 578 (2021).

[8] See Dark Storm Indus. LLC v. Cuomo, 471 F.Supp.3d 482 (N.D.N.Y. 2020), appeal dismissed, cause remanded sub nom., No. 20-2725-CV, 2021 WL 4538640 (2d Cir. Oct. 5, 2021); Altman v. Cnty. of Santa Clara, 464 F.Supp.3d 1106 (N.D. Cal. 2020).

[9] McDougall v. Cnty. of Ventura, 23 F.4th 1095, 1108-09 (9th Cir. 2022), reversing and remanding, 495 F.Supp.3d 881 (C.D. Cal. 2020); see also 38 F.4th 1162 (9th Cir. 2022) (vacating and remanding in light of N.Y. State Rifle & Pistol Ass'n, Inc. v. Bruen, 142 S. Ct. 2111 (2022)).

[10] 140 S. Ct. 1598 (2020); 141 S. Ct. 57 (2020).

testing available. The Supreme Court denied emergency relief twice, the second time over the dissent of Justice Sonia Sotomayor, joined by Justice Elena Kagan, who would have deferred to the on-the-ground factual judgments of the district court, which included evidence that masking and distancing requirements were not followed; test results came back too late to control the spread; and the prison continued to house infected inmates with uninfected ones. Justice Sotomayor found that, "far from 'dispell[ing]' an inference of deliberate indifference, the prison's actions highlighted by the Fifth Circuit only confirm it." Other cases involving incarcerated individuals challenged judges to evaluate their powers over sentence reduction and temporary release.[11]

In the education context, another instance in which there is generally not a heightened standard of review, courts largely rejected challenges to school-based vaccination. Different kinds of conflicts arose when some localities sought to impose more protective public health measures, specifically mask mandates, in states where the governor had lifted or even prohibited such restrictions. Those cases implicated state-level constitutional and statutory claims about the state-local government relationships,[12] although in some cases, individuals and advocacy groups brought claims under federal statutes, including the Americans with Disabilities Act and the Rehabilitation Act, on behalf of disabled students seeking additional protective measures.[13] These cases were supported by federal investigations conducted by the Department of Education's Office of Civil Rights.

Election law cases were also prevalent, especially running up to the November 2020 presidential election, and the challenges to COVID-19 measures were more successful – likely because certain election law doctrines provided special protections that sidelined *Jacobson*-type deference. For example, one major case involving the use of absentee ballots related to the presidential primary in Wisconsin, a critical swing state in the 2020 election.[14] Because of COVID-19, about one million more voters than in 2016 signed up to receive an absentee ballot and vote by mail. With the system overwhelmed, interested parties sued to extend the postmark date for absentee ballots in the state for reasons that included the fact that many voters had not received their ballots on time. The case made its way up to the Supreme Court,

[11] See, for example, United States v. Haney, 454 F.Supp.3d 316 (S.D.N.Y. 2020); United States v. Roberts, 612 F.Supp.3d 351 (S.D.N.Y. 2020); United States v. Perez, 451 F.Supp.3d 288 (S.D.N.Y. 2020); United States v. Hernandez, No. 18 CR. 834 (PAE), 2020 WL 1445851 (S.D.N.Y. Mar. 25, 2020).

[12] See, for example, Abbott v. City of San Antonio, 648 S.W.3d 498 (Tex. App. 2021); Abbott v. Jenkins, 665 S.W.3d 675 (Tex. App. 2021); Alexandra Cnty. Sch. Bd. v. Youngkin, No. CL22000224-00 (Va. Cir. Ct. Feb. 4, 2022).

[13] See, for example, Arc of Iowa v. Reynolds, 24 F.4th 1162 (8th Cir. 2022), reh'g granted and opinion vacated, No. 21-3268, 2022 WL 898781 (8th Cir. Mar. 28, 2022), and vacated, 33 F.4th 1042 (8th Cir. 2022) (remanded to 4:21-cv-00264, 2022 WL 16627483 (S.D. Iowa Nov. 1, 2022)); E.T. v. Paxton, 41 F.4th 709 (5th Cir. 2022); Hayes v. DeSantis, 561 F.Supp.3d 1187 (S.D. Fla. 2021); Seaman v. Virginia, 593 F.Supp.3d 293 (W.D. Va. 2022).

[14] Republican Nat'l Comm. v. Democratic Nat'l Comm., 140 S. Ct. 1205 (2020).

where the Court stayed a preliminary injunction issued by the district court on the basis of the so-called *"Purcell* principle": the idea that a federal court should not intervene in a state's election rules close to an election. The dissenters, led by Justice Ruth Bader Ginsburg, argued that the majority's decision would lead to "massive disenfranchisement."

Also related to the subject of absentee ballots, in October 2020, the Supreme Court partially stayed a preliminary injunction that would have lifted a witness requirement for absentee ballots in South Carolina in an effort to make absentee ballots more accessible during the pandemic.[15] The Court also stayed an injunction that would have required curbside voting in Alabama, sought by advocates for disabled individuals who did not want to vote inside.[16] In another high-profile case, Democratic officials in Pennsylvania successfully sued all the way up to the state supreme court to secure declarations on a number of election-related issues, including extending absentee ballot deadlines.[17] Republican petitioners, backed by President Trump, unsuccessfully sought review in the U.S. Supreme Court. Justices Samuel Alito and Clarence Thomas each wrote opinions suggesting the Pennsylvania Supreme Court may not have the authority to alter the absentee ballot deadline.[18] In doing so, they relied on a controversial constitutional theory with roots in *Bush v. Gore* called the independent state legislature doctrine, which argues that only state legislatures, not state executives or courts, can regulate the procedures of elections under the US Constitution. The theory was also referenced in other COVID-19/election-related shadow docket opinions.[19] In one of its final decisions of the 2022 term, the Supreme Court ultimately repudiated this theory.[20]

But the most successful refutations of *Jacobson* came from those raising free exercise of religion claims in the face of generally applicable pandemic mitigation efforts. The initial wave of these cases came in the context of city and statewide orders to avoid large indoor gatherings. The first major case to reach the Supreme Court was *South Bay United Pentecostal Church v. Newsom*,[21] in which religious institutions challenged California's order capping the number of people allowed in indoor gatherings, including to 25-percent capacity in indoor religious services. Siding with California, a 5–4 Court embraced *Jacobson* and public health authorities. Although the case was decided on the shadow docket without a signed decision, Chief Justice John Roberts wrote a concurring opinion, in which he quoted

---

[15] Andino v. Middleton, 141 S. Ct. 9 (2020).

[16] Merrill v. People First, 141 S. Ct. 25 (2020).

[17] Pa. Democratic Party v. Boockvar, 238 A.3d 345 (Pa. 2020).

[18] Republican Party v. Degraffenreid, 141 S. Ct. 732 (2021) (Thomas, J., dissenting & Alito, J., dissenting); Republican Party v. Boockvar, 141 S. Ct. 1 (2020) (statement of Alito, J.).

[19] Democratic Nat'l Comm. v. Wis. State Legislature, 141 S. Ct. 28, 29, 34 n.1 (2020) (Gorsuch, J., concurring & Kavanaugh, J., concurring); Moore v. Circosta, 141 S. Ct. 46, 47 (2020) (Gorsuch, J., dissenting).

[20] Moore v. Harper, No. 21-1271, 2023 WL 4187750 (June 27, 2023).

[21] 140 S. Ct. 1613 (2020). This case is often referred to as South Bay I.

Jacobson for the principle that "our Constitution principally entrusts '[t]he safety and the health of the people' to the politically accountable officials of the States 'to guard and protect.'" He noted that comparable secular activities, such as "lectures, concerts, movie showings, spectator sports, and theatrical performances," had the same restrictions.

But six months after *South Bay*, the Court – with Justice Amy Coney Barrett now on the bench instead of Justice Ginsburg – reversed course in two cases, *Roman Catholic Diocese v. Cuomo*,[22] and its companion, *Agudath Israel v. Cuomo*.[23] The cases were brought by Catholic and Orthodox Jewish religious organizations, which challenged restrictions on their indoor worship by the New York state government. The Court concluded that the restrictions likely were not neutrally applicable because comparable secular activities were less restricted than religious worship. Rather than analogizing worship to lectures or concerts, the Court drew connections to "acupuncture facilities, camp grounds, garages … and all transportation facilities." Significantly, Justice Gorsuch's concurrence chastised the Chief Justice's *South Bay* opinion for "reach[ing] back 100 years" to invoke *Jacobson*.

One of the Supreme Court's most expansive decisions on religious accommodations following the New York cases came in April 2021, when religious plaintiffs challenged California's restrictions on the number of households (three) that could gather indoors together for violating their free exercise rights to host prayer groups. In an unsigned opinion, a 5–4 Court held that California violated the Free Exercise Clause because it treated "comparable secular activities more favorably than at-home religious exercise, permitting hair salons, retail stores, personal care services, movie theaters, private suites at sporting events and concerts, and indoor restaurants to bring together more than three households at a time."[24] Over objections by the dissenters that the Court should have deferred to the views of experts, the Court subjected the regulation not to *Jacobson* deference but rather to the most demanding constitutional standard of "strict scrutiny," holding that the government must "narrowly tailor" its regulation in furtherance of "interests of the highest order" and "show that the religious exercise at issue is more dangerous than those [other permitted secular activities] even when the same precautions are applied."

To a large extent, the local nature of the early cases reflected the absence of dramatic federal actions. The federal government did not issue many major COVID-19 executive orders or regulations before President Biden took office on January 21, 2021. While both President Trump and his Secretary of Health and Human Services (HHS) had issued various important emergency declarations, the powers triggered by those declarations – powers such as loosening restrictions on telehealth, enabling use of the Defense Production Act to ease supply shortages, or expanding

---

[22] 141 S. Ct. 63 (2020).
[23] 141 S. Ct. 889 (2020).
[24] Tandon v. Newsom, 141 S. Ct. 1294, 1297 (2021).

the categories of medical personnel who could immunize patients – did not prompt any major litigation in 2020. Nor did some of the other agency-specific regulatory actions taken during that time, such as the mortgage foreclosure relief programs issued by several agencies, including the Departments of Housing and Urban Development, Agriculture, and Veterans Affairs, and the CDC's initial orders placing a moratorium on evictions.

Congress also took action of its own in the form of relief packages. In the first month of the pandemic, Congress passed three major pieces of legislation, detailed in earlier chapters by Huberfeld and Hammond et. al.,: the Coronavirus Preparedness and Response Supplemental Appropriations Act, the Families First Coronavirus Response Act, and the Coronavirus Aid, Relief, and Economic Security (CARES) Act. Major litigation did not ensue over any of this legislation, apart from a pair of successful challenges by Alaskan Indian tribes, which went all the way to the Supreme Court, seeking eligibility for monetary relief under the CARES Act.[25] Nor did major litigation stem from later relief bills or the American Rescue Plan Act (ARPA) of 2021. One exception was a series of challenges to the race- and sex-based allocation of relief programs under the ARPA.[26]

III THE FEDERAL PHASE OF THE RESPONSE AND THE DECLINE OF DEFERENCE

But just as the individual liberties litigation reached a fever pitch, the story shifted. The Biden Administration took more direct control over the pandemic – issuing a dozen executive orders immediately upon taking office, including extending the CDC eviction moratorium and orders restricting cruise-ship sailing, imposing public health restrictions on travel and on federal lands, and eventually taking executive actions to incentivize or compel vaccination in various settings. Some employers, school systems, and universities followed suit.

Lawsuits followed. But interestingly, the most important showdowns over the major federal actions were not constitutional law showdowns, as they had largely been in the first phase of pandemic litigation. Rather, they were regulatory – and ultimately produced precedents curtailing administrative authority that will have great significance far beyond COVID-19.

The first noteworthy decision, *Alabama Association of Realtors v. Department of Health and Human Services*,[27] concerned the CDC's renewal of its order imposing an eviction moratorium, which was issued under the CDC's statutory authorities to control the transmission of communicable diseases. The CDC under the Trump

---

[25] Yellen v. Confederated Tribes of Chehalis Rsrv., 141 S. Ct. 2434 (2021).

[26] Example, Vitolo v. Guzman, 999 F.3d 353 (6th Cir. 2021); Wynn v. Vilsack, 545 F.Supp.3d 1271 (M.D. Fla. 2021); Miller v. Vilsack, No. 21-11271, 2022 WL 851782 (5th Cir. Mar. 22, 2022).

[27] 141 S. Ct. 2320 (2021); 141 S. Ct. 2485 (2021).

Administration had initially issued the order in September 2020; Congress legislatively extended the moratorium until January 31, 2021, after which the CDC under the Biden Administration issued a series of extensions into the summer. Numerous suits were filed challenging the different iterations of the order and, by June 2021, a challenge had reached the Supreme Court on the shadow docket. After a brief reprieve, occasioned by a concurrence by Justice Brett Kavanaugh assuming the order would soon expire, the CDC extended the moratorium again, and the case returned to the Court. This time, the Court ruled against the CDC, in an opinion that rejected the CDC's interpretation of its long-standing public health authorities on the basis of a highly textualist reading. Under 42 USC § 264(a), the CDC has authority to:

> make and enforce such regulations as … are necessary to prevent the introduction, transmission, or spread of communicable diseases from foreign countries into the States or possessions, or from one State or possession into any other State or possession. For purposes of carrying out and enforcing such regulations, the [CDC] may provide for such inspection, fumigation, disinfection, sanitation, pest extermination, destruction of animals or articles found to be so infected or contaminated as to be sources of dangerous infection to human beings, and other measures, as in [its] judgment may be necessary.

The Court's cramped reading of the statute was the product of a pre-COVID-19 and long- running debate among the justices over how to interpret laws; the more conservative faction of the Court generally prefers a more literal, rather than purpose-based, approach. As such, the Court refused to allow the first sentence of this section of the CDC authorization statute (from the Public Health Service Act), which conveys extensive authority, to inform the second, exemplary sentence. Instead, six justices applied a textualist rule of statutory construction, the so-called *"ejusdem generis"* rule, which counsels that terms in a list be construed to be like one another. Because the CDC's moratorium on evictions – which the agency contended would prevent the interstate spread of disease by reducing new interstate travel, homelessness, and cohabitation – was not like "fumigation" and the like, the Court read the statute to cabin what until that point had been understood as very broad statutory authority.

But the Court went further than that. Its decision also invoked the then-largely moribund "major questions doctrine." Specifically, the Court held that even if the breadth of the CDC's authorities was ambiguous, "the sheer scope of the CDC's claimed authority … would counsel against the Government's interpretation. We expect Congress to speak clearly when authorizing an agency to exercise powers of 'vast economic and political significance.'"

While at the time it was not clear that the sentences quoted here would usher in a series of follow-on decisions in the same vein, they did. *Alabama Association of Realtors* marked the beginning of the Court's wholehearted embrace of the major questions doctrine – one of the most important legal developments of the 2021 term.

The doctrine had been introduced by Justice Scalia in the 1990s, and since then, the Court had only occasionally invoked it in sporadic decisions.[28] But following the CDC case, the Court again relied on the major questions doctrine to stay the Biden Administration's OSHA "vaccine or test" rule.

In November 2021, OSHA had issued an emergency temporary standard under its authority to issue emergency standards "necessary to protect employees" from "grave danger from exposure to substances or agents determined to be toxic or physically harmful or from new hazards."[29] The Biden standard required employers with 100 or more employees require their workers to be vaccinated or else to be masked and tested weekly. After twenty-seven states and several private businesses challenged its validity, the case ultimately came before the justices on the shadow docket.

The case, *National Federation of Independent Business v. Department of Labor*,[30] was the Supreme Court's most full-throated embrace yet of the major questions doctrine. Despite the clear statutory authority to OSHA to issue an emergency temporary standard, the Court expressed concern with "expand[ing] OSHA's regulatory authority without clear congressional authorization." The Court concluded that allowing OSHA to have such authority, "simply because most Americans have jobs and face those same risks while on the clock," constituted a major question, and Congress would have to authorize OSHA more directly to do so. Justice Stephen Breyer in dissent, joined by Justices Sotomayor and Kagan, noted that the Court did not even dispute that COVID-19 was a "new hazard" or "physically harmful agent" when "read in the ordinary way," but the majority nevertheless concluded that even with Congress' expansive language, the statute did not authorize OSHA's action.

Justice Gorsuch, joined by Justices Thomas and Alito, would have gone even further. His concurrence emphasized the relationship of the major questions doctrine to constitutional doctrines limiting excessive delegation. Significantly, the concurrence implied that even had Congress been clearer in giving OSHA the power to issue such a "vaccine or test" rule, "that law would likely constitute an unconstitutional delegation of legislative authority." In other words, Congress might not even be able to give OSHA such authority to protect the public.

Interestingly, the fact that the capacious statutory authorization at issue in the OSHA case was enacted fifty-two years prior was a minus, not a plus, for Justice Gorsuch. The section, he wrote, "was not adopted in response to the pandemic, but some [fifty] years ago at the time of OSHA's creation" – a position similar to the one the Court took in the CDC case, that even a broadly drafted congressional authorization designed to stand the test of time could not be adapted to meet new crises.

---

[28] See MCI Telecomms. Corp. v. Am. Tel. & Tel. Co., 512 U.S. 218, 231 (1994); FDA v. Brown & Williamson Tobacco Corp., 529 U.S. 120, 160 (2000); Utility Air Regulatory Grp. v. EPA, 573 U. S. 302, 324 (2014); King v. Burwell, 576 U.S. 473, 485–86 (2015).

[29] 29 U.S.C. § 655(c)(1).

[30] 142 S. Ct. 661 (2022).

The key point is that these cases have set an exceedingly high bar for Congress. In the process, they are part of the larger effort by several justices to curtail the scope of the administrative state. With the specificity requirements of the major questions doctrine, Congress either must draft laws with perfect foresight of the precise emergent issues that agencies entrusted with the public health will face or be able to react in real time with in-the-moment statutory authorizations. Neither is realistic, which is precisely the reason that Congress has previously drafted these public health authorities in more capacious terms.

Similar challenges were brought against other federally imposed vaccination requirements. In September 2021, the Biden Administration instituted a mandate requiring that all federal contractors become vaccinated pursuant to its authority under the Federal Property and Administrative Services Act to make its "system" of contracting more "economical and efficient." More than two dozen states successfully challenged the order, both under the major questions doctrine and under federalism principles that health and safety, including mandatory vaccination requirements, are typically the domain of the states.[31] The Fifth Circuit also affirmed a nationwide injunction against a different vaccination mandate for federal employees, based on the President's statutory authorities to "prescribe regulations for the conduct of employees in the executive branch."[32] That decision built on cases involving the federal contractor mandate and *National Federation of Independent Business*.

Fast forward to April 2022. A lower federal court used the same rationale to vacate the CDC's mask mandate on transportation – a critical pandemic public health initiative that President Biden announced on his second day in office and that had been in effect for fifteen months.[33] The CDC had issued the order pursuant to its core authorities to prevent the transmission of disease. The lower federal court rejected the CDC's reading of its own statute and, as in the eviction order case, applied textualist methods of statutory construction to conclude that the statute's broad authorization did not control and that the statute's list of exemplary authorities, such as "sanitation," could not include masking. The court also relied on another modern tool of conservative statutory construction, known as "corpus linguistics," to search a database of American English to determine the primary

---

[31] Georgia v. President of U.S., 46 F.4th 1283 (11th Cir. 2022); Kentucky v. Biden, 57 F.4th 545 (6th Cir. 2023); Kentucky v. Biden, 23 F.4th 585 (6th Cir. 2022); Louisiana v. Biden, 55 F.4th 1017 (5th Cir. 2022); Missouri v. Biden, 576 F.Supp.3d 622 (E.D. Mo. 2021) (motion to voluntarily dismiss appeal granted in No. 22-1104, 2023 WL 3862561 (8th Cir. June 7, 2023)); Brnovich v. Biden, 562 F.Supp.3d 123 (D. Ariz. 2022); Florida v. Nelson, 576 F.Supp.3d 1017 (M.D. Fla. 2021) (motion to voluntarily dismiss appeal granted in Florida v. Adm'r, NASA, No. 22-10165-AA, 2022 WL 18282863 (11th Cir. Oct. 26, 2022)). The Ninth Circuit ultimately reversed Arizona's successful challenge in Brnovich. Mayes v. Biden, 67 F.4th 921 (9th Cir. 2023).

[32] Feds for Med. Freedom v. Biden, 63 F.4th 366 (5th Cir. 2023), aff'g 581 F.Supp.3d 826 (S.D. Tex. 2022). In May 2023, the Biden Administration rescinded both the contractors and employees mandates. Exec. Order No. 14099, 88 Fed. Reg. 30891 (May 9, 2023).

[33] Health Freedom Def. Fund, Inc. v. Biden, 599 F.Supp.3d 1144 (M.D. Fla. 2022).

linguistic sense of "sanitation" in 1944 when the CDC statute was enacted. The approach the court took was decidedly undynamic and inflexible. On appeal, this decision was vacated as moot.[34]

The court, like many other courts that had ruled against pandemic measures, also expressed particular discomfort with the fact that this particular public health measure had never been deployed before. This novelty objection was another new development that came out of the COVID-19 major questions cases. In the end, these cases significantly hamper the ability of federal agencies to try new things even when those new things fall within the letter of the governing statute. This is a major impediment for health agencies combating new threats.

This new hurdle to innovative policy solutions has been extended beyond traditional public health authorities. In June 2022, the Supreme Court invoked the major questions doctrine to block the EPA from using its longstanding statutory authority under the Clean Air Act Amendments of 1970 to require coal-fired power plants reduce their electricity output or increase energy production from cleaner sources than coal, specifically natural gas, wind, or solar power.[35] One year later, the Supreme Court again invoked the major questions doctrine to hold unlawful the Biden Administration's student-debt relief program under the HEROES Act of 2003.[36]

At the same time, it would be an overstatement to say that deference on questions of public health vanished during the pandemic. The courts have been much more sympathetic to vaccination requirements in more traditional contexts, such as education and areas involving health and safety.

For example, on the same day that the Supreme Court stayed OSHA's "vaccine or test" rule, it stayed two injunctions that would have halted a similar vaccination requirement for health care workers imposed by HHS, in *Biden v. Missouri*.[37] HHS had relied on provisions allowing it to issue rules "necessary in the interest of the health and safety of individuals who are furnished [health care] services." Unlike in *National Federation of Independent Business*, the Court was comfortable with this vaccination mandate, holding that it was consistent with health care workers' mission to "protect their patients' health and safety." Chief Justice Roberts and Justice Kavanaugh, the two justices to switch their votes between *National Federation of Independent Business* and *Biden v. Missouri*, did not write to explain their position, but one relevant difference from the OSHA mandate might have been that HHS has traditionally regulated the "qualifications and duties" of health care workers.

---

[34] Health Freedom Def. Fund v. President of U.S., No. 22-11287, 2023 WL 4115990 (11th Cir. June 22, 2023).

[35] West Virginia v. EPA, 142 S. Ct. 2587 (2022).

[36] Biden v. Nebraska, No. 22-506, 2023 WL 4277210 (June 30, 2023).

[37] 142 S. Ct. 647 (2022).

The majority stressed that "vaccination requirements are a common feature of the provision of health care in America." Compare that to *National Federation of Independent Business*, where the Court contended that OSHA "ha[d] never before adopted a broad public health regulation of this kind."

Under these dueling rationales, federal courts split over a vaccine and masking requirement for schools that participated in the federal Head Start program, in which the federal government has broad powers to regulate safety for young children. Refusing to grant a preliminary injunction against the rule, the Sixth Circuit Court of Appeals relied on *Biden v. Missouri*, noting that "similar statutory language" supported the health care worker mandate, and that both actions were consistent with the "long-standing practice of [HHS]."[38] However, two lower federal courts in the Fifth Circuit halted enforcement of the same requirement in half of the states, relying in part on major questions and the danger of giving HHS "unlimited power" over the program.[39] Later, in March 2023, one of those two courts vacated this rule nationwide.[40] Fewer than two months later, HHS announced it would remove the challenged requirements.[41]

Deference was also granted in the education sphere. Interestingly, the Court, via Justice Barrett, did not accept review of a Seventh Circuit petition denying injunctive relief from the University of Indiana's vaccination requirement. The appeals court opinion, written by noted conservative Judge Frank Easterbrook, relied on *Jacobson* and highlighted that "[h]ealth exams and vaccinations against other diseases … are common requirements of higher education."[42] Judge Easterbrook elaborated that universities often require their students to waive all sorts of rights as conditions of enrollment, such as their First Amendment right to decide what to read and write. Over the course of the pandemic, the Supreme Court would also signal deference in the education sphere by refusing to give relief to public school teachers in New York City and San Diego from vaccination requirements imposed on them by the cities.[43]

Similar deference was also granted to the military's vaccination mandate. In 2021, Secretary of Defense Lloyd Austin issued a directive requiring all members of the armed forces to become vaccinated for COVID-19, and each branch of the military issued vaccination requirements for its members. In one instructive case, the Department of Defense's general order, explicitly extended to National Guard

---

[38] Livingston Educ. Serv. Agency v. Becerra, 35 F.4th 489 (6th Cir. 2022).

[39] Louisiana v. Becerra, 577 F.Supp.3d 483 (W.D. La. 2022); Texas v. Becerra, 577 F.Supp.3d 527 (N.D. Tex. 2021).

[40] Texas v. Becerra, No. 5:21-CV-300-H, 2023 WL 2754350 (N.D. Tex. Mar. 31, 2023).

[41] Press Release, Early Childhood Learning & Knowledge Ctr., Head Start Vaccine and Testing Announcement (last updated May 2, 2023), https://eclkc.ohs.acf.hhs.gov/about-us/press-release/head-start-vaccine-testing-announcement.

[42] Klaassen v. Trustees of Ind. Univ., 7 F.4th 592, 593 (7th Cir. 2021).

[43] Doe v. San Diego Unified Sch. Dist., 142 S. Ct. 1099 (2022); Keil v. City of New York, 142 S. Ct. 1226 (2022); Maniscalco v. N.Y.C. Dep't of Educ., 142 S. Ct. 1668 (2022).

personnel, survived a challenge led by the Governor of Oklahoma under the major questions doctrine since "there is nothing 'transformative' about a force protection measure first conceived and enforced by General George Washington when he required members of the Continental Army to be inoculated against smallpox."[44] Navy SEALs and Air Force Officers also brought challenges for exemptions to vaccination mandates under the Religious Freedom Restoration Act and the Free Exercise Clause. One such case reached the Court on the shadow docket and, in a 6–3 decision, the Court partially stayed a preliminary injunction against the Navy mandate.[45] The Court held that the Navy could consider SEALs' vaccination status when "making deployment, assignment, and other operational decisions." Justice Kavanaugh concurred, stressing that "courts traditionally have been reluctant to intrude upon the authority of the Executive in military and national security affairs." The Court would go on to deny relief from the Air Force's vaccination mandate.[46]

The same 6–3 Court also denied emergency relief on the shadow docket in free exercise, equal protection, and Title VII challenges to both the State of Maine and the State of New York's vaccination mandates for health care workers.[47] In October 2022, the Court also declined to hear a challenge to New York City's municipal worker vaccination mandate.[48]

* * *

The pandemic laid bare overlapping crises of equity, safety, and accessibility. The litigation across virtually every sector of our society reflected those crises and, in many instances, helped advance progress. But, as a matter of legal doctrine, where we go from here remains to be seen. *Jacobson*, while wounded, survives. The outcome for the federal government seems more mixed. Sector-specific vaccination requirements generally fared better than broader ones, even ones issued by public health authorities endowed by Congress with generous powers to use their expertise and react.

Had the Biden Administration not pushed the CDC eviction moratorium before the Court a second time after the Court warned of its concerns – via Justice Kavanaugh's swing-vote concurrence – the first major questions decision

---

44 Oklahoma v. Biden, 577 F.Supp.3d 1245 (W.D. Okla. 2021).
45 Austin v. U.S. Navy Seals 1-26, 142 S. Ct. 1301 (2022).
46 Dunn v. Austin, 142 S. Ct. 1707 (2022). In the National Defense Authorization Act of 2023, Congress ultimately required the rescission of the vaccination mandate for the armed services, and Secretary Austin complied accordingly. Memorandum from the Secretary of Defense to Senior Pentagon Leadership, Commanders of the Combatant Commands Defense Agency, and DOD Field Activities Directors, Rescission of Aug. 24, 2021 and Nov. 30, 2021 Coronavirus Disease 2019 Vaccination Requirements for Members of the Armed Forces (Jan. 10, 2023).
47 Does 1-3 v. Mills, 142 S. Ct. 17 (2021); Dr. A. v. Hochul, 142 S. Ct. 552 (2021).
48 Marciano v. Adams, 143 S. Ct. 298 (2022).

would not have been issued. Would that have made a difference for the OSHA case and the successful entrenchment of the doctrine in the ensuing litigation that swirled around vaccination requirements and later in the EPA context? One can never know.

But what we do know is that health authorities need space to act quickly and effectively to address public health crises. If we have learned anything from COVID-19, we have learned that. The Court's OSHA decision was a damaging step back in that regard. Going forward, attempts to cabin the major questions doctrine – for example, only to cases with true statutory ambiguity – and to dislodge the new notion that regulatory novelty is fatal, would be helpful doctrinal advancements. No less importantly, on the legislative side, Congress must try to strengthen public health laws with broad, nimble, and modern authorities that will better equip agencies to address the next crisis, while still satisfying the Court's new demand for more specific delegations. This is no short order. But as the pandemic recedes, we cannot forget the critical role that government played, and must continue to play, in the face of public health crises.

Printed in the USA
CPSIA information can be obtained
at www.ICGtesting.com
LVHW051532291123
765132LV00006B/306